PSYCHOLOGICAL COMMENTARIES

On the Teaching of

G. I. GURDJIEFF

AND

P. D. OUSPENSKY

by

Maurice Nicoll

LONDON
VINCENT STUART
1957

FIRST PUBLISHED IN THIS EDITION 1952
BY VINCENT STUART (PUBLISHERS) LTD
55 WELBECK STREET LONDON WI
SECOND IMPRESSION 1953
THIRD IMPRESSION 1957
ALL RIGHTS RESERVED
PRINTED IN GREAT BRITAIN
AT THE PITMAN PRESS
BATH

CONTENTS

Great Amwell House, 1946

Great Amwell House, 1947

Great Amwell House, 1948

Quaremead, Ugley, September 22, 1945

THE SECOND LINE OF WORK

There are three lines of Work. The first line of Work is work on yourself in connection with what the Work teaches. The second line of Work is work in conjunction with other people who are in this Work. The third line of Work is work in relationship to what the Work is aiming at.

Let us take the second line of Work, work in connection with other people who are in the Work. Let me say to begin with that if you are in a group of people who are studying this Work and you make no endeavour to get to know them or to understand them, you are not doing the second line of Work. No man can work on the first line only. To work only for yourself would only increase your self-love, your self-vanity. As regards this working in conjunction with other people there are many things said in the Work that are very useful to remember. It is sometimes a matter of astonishment to me that people who have been in the Work —or who imagine they have been in the Work—for many years never make the slightest attempt to connect themselves with other people except through their prejudices and buffers—that is, they only wish to know people of whom they approve, people who have the same buffers as they have. Such people make no progress in the Work—that is, they do not change. There is a saying in the Work that people whom you meet in groups and dislike at first are often those people whom you like later on, but this change only takes place through work on oneself and through evaluation of the Work, which always leads to work on the third line of Work. When a number of people meet together they eventually tend to quarrel. Unless the force of the Work is behind a number of people who meet often together, they will break up into different forms of antagonism. As mechanical people, they are bound to quarrel. This is why it is said that life as a Neutralizing Force always disunites people and makes them split up into antagonistic cliques. But the Third Force that comes down from a different channel altogether is a uniting force that can hold people together if those people value the Work. And this discipline, carried out through feeling the value of the Work, brings people together in unusual ways and enlarges their life, and they begin to form what is called an accumulator—that is, a group of people who forego some of their mechanical reactions and begin to a certain extent to obey the Work and thus transmit its influences. This is a wonderful thing. And it is exactly in this wonder of the Work that people begin to change and become healed internally. You must understand that the Work is a healing force and that in many ways it is contradictory to life and its influences—in fact, it is actually said in the Work that the Work is against life—and you must understand by this that the influence of the Work, the understanding of what

B   779

it means, goes against influences and values that come from life. You have only to look round to-day, in this so-called time of peace, to see how life disunites people and forms fresh quarrels, fresh antagonisms in every direction. Then you will understand why it is said that life is a disruptive force and that the Work is a uniting force.

In regard to the second line of Work which can be called making relationships with other people, we have to remember that the Work teaches us that we are mechanical. This is a deep saying, far more deep in its meaning than any of us has realized. What does it mean that a person is mechanical? It means that he or she always acts in the only way in which he or she can act at any given moment. We think that people do things intentionally but cannot see that people do things mechanically. A person, for example, who tells a lie under certain given circumstances, is not doing it deliberately but mechanically —namely, his or her machine always at such a moment acts in this way—that is, tells a lie. Naturally we hate to think that we are machines in this sense. We have the illusion that we are always doing things consciously, deliberately, intentionally. This is not the case. Whatever we do, whatever we say, however we behave, whatever we think, whatever we feel, is mechanical. G. once said: "You are all different kinds of machines—some are typewriters, some are sewing-machines, some are mincing-machines, and so on." This view of human nature is unpleasant and yet it is true. There are many scientific theories about Man being a machine. You pour in petrol and get certain results. What interested me very much in the teaching of this Work was the idea that from *one* point of view Man is a machine—that is, as long as he does not try to wake up and work on himself. He need not be a machine if he seeks to awaken from sleep and sleeping humanity. This interested me because it was a reconciliation of scientific and spiritual ideas about Man. Man is a machine, but he can become something that is no longer a question of machinery, if he follows teaching coming from those who are not machines—that is, teaching coming from the Conscious Circle of Humanity. The apparent paradox is thus reconciled and becomes a harmonious thought instead of a contradictory thought on the opposites. If you say: "Is so-and-so a machine?" I will answer you: "To which man do you refer?" He may be a mechanical man, or a man beginning to awaken, or even a Conscious Man. If he is a mechanical man he is a machine. If he is a Conscious Man he is not a machine because he has risen above his mechanicalness and is on a higher level. As you know, the Work divides mankind into seven categories. Three are mechanical—Nos. 1, 2 and 3 Man—No. 4 Man is transitional, and Nos. 5, 6 and 7 Man belong to the Conscious Circle of Humanity and can no longer be called machines. But the vast majority are mechanical, governed by external impressions.

Now in relating yourself to other people—that is, beginning to think what the second line of Work means and to apply it—it is sometimes said that you must begin with the idea that other people are machines.

But this is quite wrong and should never be said. What you have to begin from is the idea that you yourself are a machine. Only through self-observation carried out rightly can you begin to see your own machine, your own mechanicalness. However, as we are we take ourselves and other people as being fully conscious, as capable of independent action, as not being ruled by past associations—in short, as not being machines. So in consequence we blame people very much for not behaving to us as we think they ought to behave and through this we start trains of inner talking and negative emotions. Probably you all know how we are always very disappointed in other people. We expect our husbands and our wives, our sisters and cousins and aunts, and our friends, to be quite different from what they are, and all this lays down a kind of secret grievance in us, a form of Internal Considering, which cannot be cured unless we understand about mechanicalness. It is like a typewriter finding fault with a mincing-machine. It is like complaining that a pair of gloves of a different size from your own does not fit you. We have to start by seeing our own mechanicalness. As you know, we all take ourselves for granted. And what does this mean? It means that we take ourselves as being fully conscious, capable of making every right adaptation to circumstances—in short, of having no machine laid down in us at all. We are quite certain that we have no fixed attitudes, ways of talking, no fixed tendencies, or even no habits. We may admit to a few physical habits but I do not think that anyone easily admits to having any emotional or mental habits. But the Work teaches that we have habits in Intellectual and Emotional Centres that are far more important than physical habits and far more significant. People grow up as Anglicans, as Roman Catholics, as Presbyterians, as Quakers, as Methodists, as Atheists, as Agnostics, or even as scientists, and they are perfectly certain that their minds and their emotions are quite free from mechanicalness—that is, that they are open-minded. All this has eventually to be made conscious and overcome so that a man begins to be universal in outlook and in his feelings. But it cannot be overcome unless your self-observation is keen and full of integrity, otherwise you will not shift from where you are and you will remain a mechanical man or woman in life—that is, you will not change—and so will not understand what the second education means, the real University that you have to attend to become healed, through External Considering.

So one of the first great ideas in this teaching in regard to our relationship to other people is to realize first of all that we are mechanical and that what we do and what they do is inevitable, being mechanically determined. Many people think that they have reached this point of view and take up a kind of resigned attitude to other people. This is a pure fiction. It means that they have not seen their own mechanicalness, and so they get caught up in the great wheel of mechanical life, thinking that they are conscious and yet being more and more mechanical even than others. Now to regard yourself as mechanical is extremely difficult and extremely painful but it will change your whole relationship to other people. When you have realized that you cannot help doing something, you will realize that other people cannot help doing something and you will no longer feel this fatal criticism, this contempt, that underlies so many people's psychology. This will give you a right basis to begin to have relationship in the Work-sense to other people. Do you remember this sketched-out first octave of the Work which started from the note *Do* which was called 'evaluation of the Work'? It is of course an ascending octave, so the next note is *Re*, which was called 'application of the Work practically to yourself.' The third note *Mi* was called 'realization of your own difficulties'. Now a man who begins to realize his own difficulties in the Work will no longer blame other people as he used to mechanically, because everything you realize in yourself frees you from other people. I mean that if you realize your own difficulties you will realize other people's difficulties in proportion. The more you see in yourself the more you see in other people. If you are blind to yourself you will never understand other people, and, as you know, one of the things we are seeking in this Work is understanding which is said to be the most powerful force that we can create in ourselves. The word 'create' is used in regard to understanding. If you behave mechanically you will create nothing because mechanicalness creates nothing. It is only if you begin to be more conscious that you begin to understand this difficult word *'creation'*. And for full understanding, we must practise all three lines of this Work and we must get to know ourselves far more deeply than we used to. But unless there is the third line of Work as well, the first two lines of Work will peter out after a time. This is natural enough because how can you expect this Work to continue to maintain its force unless you attend to the third line, to the aim of the Work, to what the Work itself is trying to do at the moment. You must remember that the third line of Work is getting into contact with the Third Force, the Neutralizing Force, of the Work, and it is exactly this that prevents the Third Force of life from interfering with it and bringing it down to zero in the Emotional Centre so that the Work loses all its force for you.

Now when you seek to make relationship with someone else, you have to create the person by seeing him or her distinctly. Most people have fixed ideas, not only about the kind of persons they like, but about what people are like. These ideas are practically always wrong and are seen to be so eventually in the Work. They are probably based on what we have been taught or have read about in novels. You cannot take a person simply as your opinion of him or her. Nor can you take a person merely as what he is in life or is reputed to be. To make relationship with a person you have to see the person differently from the way you would see him or her in life. If you have never undermined yourself and your own opinion of yourself you will never be able to do this. You will simply accept people at their face value and you will only wish to know people who have the same buffers and the same attitudes as you have, as I said before. So you will never move, you will never shift, from where you are—that is, you will never change. But the Work is about self-change.

The second point that I would like to speak about to-night in regard to relationships towards others is that not only are other people machines as you are yourself, but they are not one person. Another person is many different persons, nice and unpleasant, intelligent and stupid. To take another person as one unvarying 'I' does him or her great harm. But again the real question is: Have you yet seen that you are many different persons, and that you are not one permanent person, but a mixture of different 'I's who act through you at different moments? You may be able to see changes in people, you may be able to see that he or she is in a good mood to-day, but have you seen the same thing in yourself and not taken it as one person changing, but as changing persons in you? How strange is this form of egotism that seems to dominate us, that makes us think that we ourselves are always one and the same person. You will notice that both the realization of our mechanicalness and the realization that we are not one but many different 'I's strikes at our egotism and self-love. Through self-love we attribute everything to ourselves. That is why we are taught in esotericism, especially in the Gospels, that the only cure for self-love is love of God. This means that we gradually come to the conclusion that we do nothing ourselves and that everything in us comes from some other source. Sometimes I say to you: How do you move your body? How do you think? You cannot give an answer. And yet everything you do you ascribe to yourself. You even ascribe love to yourself, perhaps one of the worst sins. The point is that the Work teaches that we are recipient organisms, that we receive everything and that we can do nothing ourselves, neither think, love, nor anything else. In attributing to ourselves the existence of a real permanent 'I' we not only do enormous harm to ourselves but we do enormous harm to other people in taking them to be one permanent 'I', one permanent person.

The third point in relating ourselves to others depends on the science of external impressions. We do not notice how we behave and so often give a quite wrong impression to other people. We may have difficulty in expressing ourselves, we may have some feature that refuses to give to others, or that makes us not say quite enough for the other person to understand what we mean, we may be jealous and not notice that we express it the whole time, we may be negative and shew it in intonation, and so on, and yet we may be surprised that other people do not seem to care for us. The science of external impressions is a subject that we have only talked about once or twice before and that we will talk about later on. It means acting towards another person in such a way that the other person can understand you. It requires a conscious attitude towards the other person which we are at present scarcely capable of having. As a rule we are extremely clumsy with one another. I think you will all admit this. We make a wrong impression on someone

783

without knowing it. That is because we do not know ourselves enough through self-observation and therefore do not know about the other person internally. We do not know how to get to a person and think that a frontal attack, so to speak, is good enough. Of course, that will only increase second force and here comes in that part of the Work that deals with four categories of behaviour: foolish sincerity, foolish insincerity, clever sincerity, and clever insincerity. In our relationship with one another these four categories of behaviour are important to study in connection with the science of external impressions. Foolish sincerity is the most mechanical and stupid thing as regards relationships with one another. People call it telling the truth. It is better to use foolish insincerity. This may surprise you. But in our relationships with others we must above all things avoid foolish sincerity where a person blurts out something that may poison another person's soul and do infinite harm. Relationship with one another demands a great deal of attention, as, for example, stopping negative emotions at once. As we are, we cannot talk about behaving consciously to one another because we are not conscious men or women yet, but we can try to practise what conscious behaviour means and live more consciously every day. I say, live more consciously every day, on purpose. You can live more consciously every day if you understand what the Work teaches you to avoid. If you will follow the Work in your behaviour you will feel something happening to you because the Work is a lever to lift you up to another level and immediately you apply it to yourself—that is, sound the second note *Re* in the Work-octave—you will feel yourself lifted up.

Quaremead, Ugley, September 29, 1945

COMMENTARY ON MAKING DECISIONS
IN THE WORK

In making decisions in the Work the mind must be free from its bondage to mechanical attitudes. Otherwise you will make decisions always from your Personality, from what you have been taught as being right and wrong. This freeing of the mind only begins when you let the Work enter into your mind and so change your mind. It is the Will that must make decisions, not the will of your mechanical mind. Will belongs to every centre and every part of a centre and, in fact, to every 'I'. If the Work and its ideas have not begun to change your mind you will always make decisions in terms of your own mind which judges things in a mechanical way according to what you have been brought up to think right and wrong. In other words, you are not making right decisions in the Work-sense from this laid-down, already-formed mind that you are using and have always used in life. It is exactly this so-called mind that the Work begins to attack in order to lead to change of mind—that is, in order to change the way you think about everything. On one occasion G. was talking about decisions. At that time I happened to make a note about what he said which I will now give you in the exact words that I have recorded. He said: "You cannot make a decision from one 'I'. For example, you make a small decision not to smoke, while you are sitting quietly. The next moment you get up and light a cigarette. When you are not in Moving Centre—that is, not moving about—you may make a decision that instantly is forgotten when you begin to move. This is making a decision from a small 'I', let us say, in the Intellectual Centre." G. said that these decisions made in small 'I's when, as it were, you are in a certain passing state of mind, are quite useless. He added: "They are not quite useless because they shew you how difficult it is to make a real decision. Such decisions shew us how we cannot control our machines—namely, all our centres." He was of course speaking about how decisions in the Work-sense must come from a much deeper level than that on which such small 'I's exist. Now, as you all know, we make decisions of this small kind continually, as when we have eaten too much we make a decision not to eat so much again and all these decisions are made on the superficial level of the opposites and are practically always, if you notice, formed in words. Real decisions are not formed in words because they come from a much deeper source.

G. went on to speak about decisions in the following terms that I will give you just as he said them: "The ordinary decisions we make are mechanical and these are quite different from conscious decisions. A man tries to alter one thing without seeing how it is connected with other things. This means that he is not properly conscious and so he makes a mechanical decision." Then G. began talking about what he called *binaries* (the word *binary* comes from the Latin *binarius*=consisting of two). He gave us an example of a binary: necessary and unnecessary —these are opposites. He said that a decision in the Work-sense does not lie in the binaries but in the Neutralizing Force or Third Force that turns a binary into a *ternary* (meaning 'threefold' or a 'triad'— from Latin *ternarius*). He said that our life is led in binaries—that is, opposites. This is called the Law of the Pendulum under which we are mechanical. He said: "You have a dispute with yourself between Yes or No. This binary situation in yourself must be transformed by Third Force and turned into a ternary or triad. In general Man, since he does not remember himself and so has not got Third Force in his life, is always swinging between the opposites—that is, his life is always in binaries which are irreconcilable. This struggle between Yes or No is not solved by going either with Yes or with No. A third factor has to be found which turns these binaries into a triad or ternary which no longer resembles the situation that was produced by the state of being in binaries or opposites. Yes or No becomes something quite different which we can only describe as Yes and No. You will remember Third Force unites the opposites and contains something of them both and yet is neither of them. When the mind finds something between Yes and No a decision can be made." In G.'s words, the binary becomes ternary—that is to say, the opposites become included in the triad and from this a result can take place which leads to what he called a *quaternary* (which comes from the Latin *quaternarius* = consisting of four). This quaternary is active. It consists in first of all a union of the binaries or opposites through the Third Force, so making a ternary and leading to a result which makes it a quaternary. Through this result, which in a sense can be called active, as was said, a further development can take place. G. said: "Every dispute with oneself should eventually lead to a new state of oneself. It should not give rise to a habitual or accustomed side. It leads to a new state *via* a ternary, which leads on to a quaternary. As long as the binary state remains, the old state, the former state, will remain, and the person will simply swing back to the old position. The path leading to the knowledge of unity consists first of all in a struggle of Yes or No—that is, a binary state, to begin with —but it should lead to decision—that is, to a ternary state which is neither Yes nor No—and this gives a real result—i.e. it leads to a quaternary. A struggle of Yes-No is not in itself soluble. A third factor must be found whereby Yes and No become combined by a Third Force into something quite different from Yes or No. This forms a ternary and this forms the result called a quaternary."

G. said that the whole secret lies in a man's remembering himself —that is, giving himself the First Conscious Shock. He said that an ordinary man is incapable of growing or of doing in any real sense because he lacks this Third Force which is produced by this First Conscious Shock of Self-Remembering. "There is," he said, "a kind of gap in Man which he should fill himself and which unless he fills it leads to continuing in binaries—that is, he continues in the opposites."

On another occasion G. said: "At this point comes in the individual as distinct from mechanical man. What is the most important thing?" he once asked us. He said: "The most important thing is to realize that we do not remember ourselves, and that for this reason we do not actually exist as individuals in our experience."

Now you will see from all that G. said that he was talking about something that it takes a great many years to understand although the Work is constantly teaching us this very point. You will notice that he says that decisions cannot be made from the opposites but from some other force which is neither Yes nor No and that he connects with the state of Self-Remembering. "This state of Self-Remembering," he said many times, "is a state that Man was born to possess but he has lost it. A man is born with the power to remember himself but as he is brought up amongst sleeping people—that is, amongst people who do not remember themselves—he soon loses this power. He falls asleep himself through the hypnotism of other sleeping people amongst whom he grows up, and for this reason this Work must start with talking about the state that Man must reach which is his birthright. That is why I say to you all that you must practise Self-Remembering." G. used often to talk about this and I will give you in so many words what he said. He said that esoteric teaching at one time used to be only necessary in regard to the Second Conscious Shock, for Man is not born with the possibility of giving himself this shock and cannot give it to himself unless he is taught how to do it, but that now owing to the fact that Man has fallen so much asleep he has to be taught how to give himself the shock of Self-Remembering before anything can be done to trans-form him. G. used to talk a great deal about how Man has lost this state given to him at birth and he used to point to the modern world and say in many different ways that if we want to study how Man has lost this state of Self-Remembering and what consequences have arisen from this loss of Consciousness we have only to look round and see what is happening in this world, this world in which millions of people are behaving in a way that can lead to no solution and can only get worse and worse. "No one," he said, "now remembers himself or even thinks it is necessary, and for this reason there has been a drop in the level of Consciousness, and this level is descending more and more every day and as a consequence people are becoming more and more governed by external circumstances and more and more helpless to remedy their troubles."

Now let us return to the subject of making a decision in the Work. First of all we are taught to make decisions, but we are taught this, as it were, in order to shew us how we cannot keep them, to see, in short, how we are really mechanical. But, as you know, this realization of our mechanicalness is one of the forms of Self-Remembering. We no longer place reliance on our machines although we observe them at work. We try this and we try that but we find that it leads nowhere. For example, we do this, and then we find we do not move, and so on. We make effort in this direction and find that as a consequence we make less effort in some other direction. Through self-observation and not becoming depressed and negative by our failure we can approach a point in which we can realize that decisions cannot be made in this way that we have been trying to make them hitherto. We find the ground of decisions to lie much deeper than we thought and so we learn to have this patience towards ourselves which is so necessary. We begin to see what we want to happen to us to change us, and yet in a way we know that we cannot do it ourselves exactly, and that this change that we internally wish for will not come about by making any sudden decisions through small 'I's on the opposites, and at the same time we wish for this change to take place however we may feel in regard to it. Then the decision is becoming emotional—i.e. it is penetrating much more deeply than the level of small sudden 'I's, sudden forms of self-torture.

Now, speaking from another point of view, and yet about the same thing really, it is the Third Force of the Work that can change us. The first thing the Work says we can do is to remember ourselves and in connection with that it teaches many other things that we can do, such as inner separation from negative thoughts and feelings, and so on, but all these secondary things that it teaches are connected with Self-Remembering. Take, for example, the teaching of the Work about identifying with ourselves or with external events. All this is connected with Self-Remembering. All this is studying how we cannot remember ourselves because, as you know, if you are very identified with your negative emotions or with the behaviour of someone towards you, you are not in a state of Self-Remembering but the very reverse. If you are indulging in inner talking and internal considering and self-justifying, etc., you are not remembering yourself, you are not in the third state of Consciousness, which is defined as a state of Self-Remembering. The teaching of the Work is to lift us up to this state which we should have and which we were born to have. In this third state of Consciousness, at this level, influences can reach us which can help. It is as if we put our heads above the water and felt the air and the sunlight. If any of you are trying to remember yourselves at any moment of the day and if you do it at whatever moment you can and quite sincerely, you will always notice a sudden brightness round you. Now if we were in a state of Self-Remembering we should know how to make decisions, but when we are asleep in ourselves, when we are identified and worried about ourselves, we make decisions from binaries, as G. called them—from the opposites. G. said: "The struggle between Yes and No is not solved by Yes or No—i.e. the opposites or binaries." If we were always in a state of Self-Remembering, always in the third state of Consciousness, our decisions would be real ones that would lead to a real result which G. called leading to a quaternary.

There is a story about a blind girl whose five brothers go out into the world in turn, thinking they can do, but they all fail and become lost in the world. Then the blind girl goes into the world. She does not think she can do, but she holds on to a thread that she has woven, one end of which is bound fast to the Sun. She never lets go of this thread and as a result she can do—she is able to help her brothers and other people in the world simply because she does not trust in herself to find the way but looks to the thread to guide her. Why is this girl shewn as being blind? She is blind to the external world. She does not act through her senses but she holds on to something internal. Now if a person could remember himself all the time and notice everything that caused him to identify—that is, to cease to self-remember—he would be holding on to this thread that comes from the Sun, from a higher level. And if such a person's decision were always to remember himself, whatever was happening to him, he would be in the third state of Consciousness, and his decision would be a real decision which has nothing to do with opposites or binaries. Yet to ordinary people it would not seem like a decision, this decision that one should remember oneself, this decision to fight for Self-Remembering every day in spite of everything.

Quaremead, Ugley, October 6, 1945

COMMENTARY ON THE APPLICATION OF THE
WORK-IDEAS TO ONESELF

It has often been said that this Work is to make us think. Mr. Ouspensky used to emphasize that people do not think. They read the newspapers instead or ask their friends what they ought to think or they follow the general consensus of opinion. This lack of individual thinking leads to mass-thinking. Mass-thinking is directed by someone who tells people how to think by broadcasting, by propaganda. On one occasion, when I was talking to Mr. Ouspensky about this, he said that in the past century people used to think for themselves far more than they do nowadays. "People," he said, "used to think more individually. To-day it could be said that people have given up thinking and simply wish to be told what to think. The Work," he added, "is to make us think for ourselves." On another occasion he said that the only way for a man to be awakened nowadays is through his thinking part. "Look at the increasing sleep of humanity," he added. "It is extraordinary that people give up the one thing that is left to them—namely, the power of thinking for themselves. All these books, papers, radios, and so on, prevent people from thinking, but they are supposed to increase thought."

Now *to think* is quite different from *to remember* and it is again quite different from having fixed opinions. If people take the Work as a cut-and-dried subject that they simply store in their memory then they do not think about the ideas of the Work for themselves. When people cease to think for themselves they surrender the one part of them that can still lead to awakening. We tend to wish everything to be duly explained for us without the effort of finding our own solution—i.e. without the effort of thinking for ourselves. If a person puts to himself these questions: "Who am I? What am I?" he or she will tend either to find out from someone some answer to these questions or regard them as morbid. The Work says a great deal about: "Who am I?" and "What am I?" but what it says is in general terms so as to give a guide to the individual thinking. The Work, for example, says that we are all asleep in life and that we live in a world of sleeping people in which everything goes in the only way it can go. If I ask the Work: "What am I?" the answer is that I am a man asleep. Now it is quite possible simply to accept the idea that we are all asleep and that we live in a world of sleeping humanity, without ever thinking about it individually. In that case the Work becomes similar to propaganda and people will say: "Oh, yes, we are all asleep and we live in a world of sleeping people," and perhaps they will add: "Well, that is what the Work teaches us." This is memory without thought. This is not applying the Work to oneself through thought. In fact, you can accept the ideas of the Work simply because you do not wish to think. All this means that the Work is merely in your memory, as something learned by heart and not as yet engaged with your individual thinking and so combining with yourself. It has not yet caught fire. Through self-observation you may see that you are asleep and begin to think about your own state of sleep for yourself. This is intelligent effort. This is applying the Work to yourself intelligently. You may then begin to think: Is it true that humanity is sleeping and that everything happens in the only way it can happen as long as people are asleep? If you meditate and observe you will then begin to catch sight of the truth of one of the great ideas of the Work. You will do this for yourself. This idea of sleep will then be no longer a matter of the memory but an actual experience that you have begun to undergo and which will change you. Learning things by heart is not the Work save in a limited sense. When you learn a thing by heart it lies merely in the formatory memory. Why it is called learning by heart I do not know, because the heart is emotional. Now it is said in the Work that the ideas that it teaches must become emotional. It is necessary to *feel* them. It is necessary actually to feel, for example, that you yourself are asleep and that you yourself are going without any real inner direction. Just to be told that you are asleep and that humanity is asleep and to repeat it like a parrot is to miss what the Work is about and so is a sin against the Work. It means that you have never observed yourself in the light of the Work. But the Work is light and it is you yourself who have to realize that you are asleep in the light and truth of the Work and that you live in a world of sleeping humanity in which everything happens. Then these ideas will no longer be a mere matter of the memory, a mere matter of looking up in your notes, but will become a continual living experience. When this starts the Work is no longer formatory memory like trying to remember a scientific book or an article that you have read but a process taking place in you and changing you—changing your whole way of thinking.

I want to emphasize further this matter of the Work lying in your memory and the Work lying in your individual understanding. You may easily remember the idea that you are asleep and you may accept this idea without any individual thought of what it means. I mean, you may take it as true. But nothing is true for you unless you have seen its truth for yourself. You may remember all the ideas of this Work and accept them in that way and simply call upon your memory to answer questions. The Work then lies only in your outer superficial memory and has not yet combined with you through emotional perception of its truth. You may indeed possess beautiful notes in black and red ink of everything that has been said in the Work and think that you know about the Work. But you will know nothing about the Work. It has made no contact with you yourself and the subject of the Work is you yourself and the ideas of this Work are actually to change this thing called you yourself. You may, for example, have the most exact notes about everything that has been said about negative emotion or about levels of Being and what you have to do in order to make your Being grow. And yet it may simply lie in your memory without your having done a single thing to apply the Work to your own Being through self-observation. Now one of the greatest dangers of this Work is that it becomes purely formatory, purely a matter of memory. People have sometimes said to me: "Why don't you make a full draft of all the ideas of this Work and everything that is said in it so that we could read it over and over again for ourselves?" Why? Because it would simply then lie in the outer memory and in such a case you may be quite sure that the whole level of the Work would drop to zero. It would be something outside you and not inside you. It would not be emotional. It would not touch you. A system of esoteric teaching that always takes itself as final—i.e. living more and more externally—may be mere memory. It is always possible to answer questions in this Work from mere memory but that will give no force. You will then understand nothing. You will then not see what any of the ideas mean. You will simply be a parrot repeating from your memory phrases that you have heard without understanding their significance. It is in this way that real teaching becomes eventually useless and for this reason all esoteric teaching has to be re-cast and given afresh so as to keep it living. There are very many dead systems that formerly had life in them. The reason why they died is that people no longer try to understand the ideas that they taught. Let us repeat that memory and thinking are two different things. You can think about what you remember or you can simply remember and use your memory in a kind of automatic way. If you have ever been an examiner of candidates you will always know when the candidate is speaking only from memory or whether he is speaking from what he has thought about. I am told that nowadays examinations are merely a matter of memory but in my earlier days this was not the case. In examining candidates one might see that they had a good memory of the subject, chapter and page, but they had never thought about the meaning of what they remembered and often one would find that a person who did not shew a very good memory for the data of the subject shewed individual thinking about it and this was regarded as of a much higher order than mere memory.

Let us take, for example, the Ray of Creation, which may be in a person's memory. I am here answering a question that was recently asked me. The question took this form more or less: Could you explain what the Ray of Creation is? Now here you have an idea which requires individual thinking. The Ray of Creation can become emotional in its meaning to a person who begins to think about it. It shews, for example, where we are and indirectly what we are and who we are and what we have to do and where help can come from. But if you take the Ray of Creation simply as something that has to be remembered the whole point of this great diagram is lost. What does the Ray of Creation shew us emotionally—that is, through emotional perception of its meaning? It shews us a terrific Universe ordered in scale from above downwards and it shews us that we are at a place in this vast machinery that is very low down. It shews our earth as a very tiny point. Now what is the difference between merely register-ing all this in the memory and thinking about its significance? There is all the difference. If you think individually about the Ray of Creation and put yourself on the earth in your mind, it will become emotional. It will then give you emotions you do not have ordinarily. For what reason? For the reason that it lessens our barbarian egotism and self-sufficiency. It hits at our prestige, at our self-esteem. From the standpoint of the Ray of Creation, emotionally perceived, we are practically nothing, practically of no importance whatsoever and yet given a chance. The Work says that we are so small in the totality of the Universe that if the existence of the human race ceased we should scarcely be missed. And yet we are given a chance as the Side-Octave shews.

Now there is memory and knowing based on memory—i.e. simply knowing what you remember, which is not really knowing but merely remembering—and then comes this distinction between knowing and acknowledging. You may remember a great many things about yourself and you say then that you know yourself. Do you acknowledge what you know from that memory? Now there are many kinds of memory. All the memory that is acquired in the Work through self-observation is stored up in a different place in centres because it has an emotional quality connected with the memory you have gained through self-observation. Emotion changes us. Self-emotions keep us as we are. Superficial memory will never change you because it is in a sense external to you. But what becomes deeper and more interior in you can change you. But this cannot begin to happen unless the mind changes first of all—i.e. unless you begin to have from the Work different ideas about yourself and about life. This is new truth. This new kind of thinking gradually becomes emotional and affects Being. It begins to awaken the Emotional Centre which is the supreme object of the Work—not the Emotional Centre that you have at present which is filled with self-feelings, but a different Emotional Centre. It is this which changes you. But if the memory of the Work remains a purely formal memory, a note-book memory, nothing of this kind can happen. Indeed, you have not yet begun the octave of the Work which starts from evaluation of a teaching of this kind in the midst of the world as it is now. The second note of the Work-octave is the application of the ideas of the Work, and the third note is the realization of your own difficulties in regard to the Work—what is standing in your way. But merely to hear the Work and repeat it from memory and write it down in note-books cannot change you. You could learn Chinese or French in exactly the same way and that belongs to the external memory and will not change you—that is, make you into a different kind of man or a different kind of woman. But at first it is necessary to record and to register the ideas of the Work in the external memory—that is, the formatory or moving part of the Intellectual Centre. This is inevitably the first step. One must get to know about the ideas of the Work and register them. What I am talking about is the next state—i.e. when these ideas must become emotionally perceived through application of them to yourself, first of all to your thinking and then to your Being. When it is said that this Work is to make you think in a new way it means that the ideas of the Work must begin to change your way of thinking, and you cannot expect this to happen until you have registered the ideas by hearing them many times so that you will know them in your memory. The next stage is that you must apply these ideas to yourself through self-observation. Self-observation connects the ideas of the Work to yourself. If you do not practise self-observation the ideas of this Work will remain outside you as mere matters of memory. But all the ideas of this Work are spermatic —that is, they are very potent and can generate in you not only a new way of looking at things but a new way of feeling about things.

In other words, the Work can give you understanding which is very closely connected with intelligence. It is through understanding or intelligence that we escape from the continual repetition of the same thing in our lives. If you use this Work through intelligence you will begin to change but this can only happen when you take the Work into yourself and begin to live it. As regards the development of intelligence the ideas of this Work are inexhaustible. The Work is to make you think and if you begin to think real thoughts about the Work you will find your thinking is nourished from a source that never fails.

Quaremead, Ugley, October 13, 1945

COMMENTARY ON THE OBSERVATION OF ONE'S PSYCHOLOGY

At a recent meeting here we were speaking about Man's having a body and also a psychology. A short note was written about this which I wish now to be read:

"Everyone is fastened to a particular kind of body by birth and then is fastened later on to a particular kind of psychology by upbringing. The Work starts not with the body but with the kind of acquired

793

psychology to which we are fastened by upbringing. You can spend your time in trying to make the body better or the psychology better. The Work is first about studying one's own acquired psychology and, so to speak, seeing it, seeing through it. It says that this is not *you* and as long as you take *you* as yourself you are asleep. If you, Mr Smith, take *you* as Mr. Smith, and Mr. Smith as you—as 'I'—you are asleep. In the same way, if you, Mrs. Smith, take yourself as you, you are asleep. The Work begins by uncritical observation of this Mr. Smith or Mrs. Smith which you take as you—as yourself. The object of the Work at first is to see this Mr. Smith, or Mrs. Smith, and separate from them. The reason for this is that everyone has a real self—a real 'I'—which is never attained by being Mr. Smith or Mrs. Smith. The life belonging to Mr. Smith or Mrs. Smith is not his or her real destiny, for both of them are invented people and not yet real people and so attract quite wrong things. But as often as not, or more often than not, people prefer to lead the life of this Mr. Smith or Mrs. Smith, especially if they are in easy circumstances. And even if they are continually in difficult or tragic circumstances they cling to being Mr. Smith or Mrs. Smith all the time—that is, to the acquired psychology which is called both Personality and False Personality. But it is this clinging to Mr. Smith or Mrs. Smith that is False Personality —that is, their invention of themselves. Whether we have been brought up at Eton or in the Navy or the Army or in any school or profession, it is exactly this acquired psychology that we have to overcome—that is, this tedious invention of ourselves. How tedious after a time it is to see people brought up in these different spheres completely identified with themselves and their acquired psychologies with which their vanity is connected. You remember that the Work says that you have to realize your own nothingness eventually before you can receive the full baptism of the Work. There are many ancient esoteric symbols for what a man has to become to undergo regeneration, and re-birth. Certainly this is impossible as long as he is identified with his acquired psychology, with his circumstances or birth. The symbol is of a cup or a wine-glass that is upside down in him. This cup has to be turned up the other way and, being empty, it can receive quite new ideas—i.e. the ideas that regenerate a man or a woman and change them into different beings altogether.

Now the point is that every one of you has a body given to you by life and a psychology that has been acquired by upbringing. A beautiful woman marries a handsome man but what about their respective psychologies? As often as not they find that their psychologies are completely incompatible. A person's face, unless you are very subtle, does not give you that person's psychology. But the chief idea here is that each one of you has a different psychology that has been acquired through upbringing and about which you know absolutely nothing."

We were talking on another occasion about this question of each person's having a psychology and I said that it was extraordinary that it takes us so long in the Work to realize that we have each of us a particular kind of psychology quite apart from our physical body. As you know, the Work starts with your psychology, with the kind of person you are psychologically. We agreed that this recognition that one has a particular kind of psychology with various attitudes and buffers and opinions, and so on, is not experienced by people in general, and that people, since they do not see their psychology, always imagine that they are open-minded, unbiassed and, as it were, quite free in their psychological make-up. People start from this idea. They may be aware of their bodies but not of their psychologies. They do not see, for example, that they may be psychologically extremely narrow, extremely difficult, extremely biassed. Quite the contrary, they feel that they are without any psychology, as it were. And so they get to the illusion, amongst many others, that they can always help everyone, comfort them, mother them and father them, and so on. Now the Work starts with self-observation, and self-observation does not start with the body which after all you can observe in the mirror every day, but with what kind of person you are psychologically. It is only through self-observation that you can begin to see what you are like psychologically. You may be very beautiful or handsome as regards your body but what are you like psychologically? Now to imagine that a beautiful woman has a beautiful psychology or that a handsome man has a handsome psychology is pure nonsense. I said in connection with this discussion how extraordinarily difficult it is for people to separate from the sensory impressions of one another. This seems as if we still cannot get beyond physical appearance and take physical excellence of one kind or another as meaning at the same time similar psychological development. It is like thinking that because a peacock has a marvellous display of beauty in its feathers it has therefore an equally beautiful psychological development. You will agree with me that when you hear a peacock speak you will not think that it has a most beautiful mind or a most beautiful emotional development. I think that it is worth while speaking about this great difficulty that people have in regard to self-observation. Self-observation does not consist in looking in the mirror and making yourself up to look more beautiful or handsome. This is merely observation of the body and leading the life of the body and feeling your sense of 'I' from your physical appearance. Self-observation is not done through looking at yourself in a mirror except under certain conditions. Self-observation is looking at your own psychology—i.e. at the kind of man, the kind of woman you are, psychologically. This seems to be very difficult for a great many people to understand—namely, that they are a physical body and also that they all have a particular form of psychology or mental make-up. It is to this psychology or mental make-up that the Work directs its attention through self-observation. But it is quite true to say that many people after hearing this Work for many

795

years never really observe what they are like psychologically. They take their psychology for granted. They take all their prejudices, all their ways of taking daily things, all their psychological reactions, for granted. In other words, they do not see themselves, and you can only see what you are like psychologically through self-observation. The trouble is that people never practise self-observation and so never bring themselves to account, always feeling that they have no psychology. They feel that all that they do and say is quite right. This second education that the Work consists in is about observing this psychology that everyone so easily takes for granted not noticing that it is a definite thing, a definite make-up, from which they can gradually become free if they practise to begin with the first line of Work—that is, self-observation in the light of this teaching. This requires a considerable effort. Sometimes people make this effort for a time and begin to catch a slight glimpse of themselves and what they are like psychologically and then go to sleep again perhaps for many months and perhaps for ever. To feel that one's opinions are all wrong, actually to see that one has behaved wrongly all one's life, psychologically speaking, is a very difficult thing to accept.

Now the development of Consciousness which this Work is all about is first of all to see what you are like psychologically and as a result to begin to distrust very much your psychological behaviour. This may be impossible for the majority of people. I mean by that that it would be just as well that they do not see what they are like psychologically. And it would be much better for such people to carry on just as they are with all their acquired psychology, all their buffers, with their attitudes, their opinions, and so on. But anyone who has in himself Magnetic Centre is capable of changing, psychologically speaking. And it is with these people that I wish to deal in the Work—that is, with people who are not identified completely with themselves, because otherwise there is no chance to change. A man or a woman who has never doubted himself or herself but who is always convinced of being right from his or her acquired psychology—i.e. from what they have been taught—is not suitable for this Work. Sooner or later such people will come up against the possibility of realizing that they cannot take themselves for granted as they have done hitherto but must alter their whole way of taking things, their whole way of judging things. Now if they cannot stand this, if, in short, they are completely fixed in their own acquired psychology, remember that nothing can be done with such people except to avoid any frontal attack on them.

Now this is a very short paper but it is about this subject which is the most important thing to understand early in the Work as far as I know at present. A man or a woman coming into this Work must be able to realize after a time that their psychology may be wrong from the Work point of view. They must realize that what they have to do in this Work is to change their psychology to which they are fixed and which they take as the only psychology they can have. How many of you can say: "I may be all wrong, all my viewpoints may have been wrong. I may have a quite wrong idea of everything, including myself. All my judgments in the past may have been wrong." Such thoughts change one provided one has something else to hold on to that teaches one what is right. But if you start off this Work with the deep conviction that you are all right psychologically as you are and merely wish to hear out of a kind of curiosity what the Work teaches you will never get anywhere at all. The subject of this Work is you yourself. How can you change if you remain the same? How can you change psychologically if you always remain the same psychologically? How can you change if you accept your present psychology and take it as final, as the last word, as it were, in psychological development?

Now you all know perhaps how difficult it is to shew a person that he or she is taking things in the wrong way. Instantly you give offence. But supposing that this person has some power of self-observation, supposing that he or she can begin to see what is meant by uncritical self-observation and through it see what they are like and have been like hitherto? Then the Work can come down on that person as a force that leads to inner change, inner development. It is exactly through self-observation that the Work can grow and can become not merely a source of mutual recrimination or judgment. This ancient phrase: "Know thyself" means exactly this. If through uncritical self-observation you have seen the kind of woman, the kind of man, you are, you will be able to stand all shocks in this Work and be able to go with it and receive its force. But if you have never noticed the kind of person you are and how you behave towards others mechanically—i.e. every day—and if you have never observed your own imaginations of yourself and seen through them, how can you expect your psychology to change or how can you expect to understand what the Work is about?

Now what is it we have to observe in ourselves to change our psychology? This Work teaches that we have to observe ourselves psychologically from a certain definite angle. All the practical side of the Work that is taught over and over again is about how one has to observe oneself—i.e. one's psychology. Do you wish me to enumerate again all the things that the Work teaches about practical self-observation? I think it is always necessary that we should be reminded of what we have to observe in ourselves. Take one thing only: Are you making internal accounts all the time? Are you feeling that you are unhappy or badly treated or not given your right position? Are you always self-justifying when in a sense you know you are at fault? Are you indulging in long trains of negative emotion? Notice when you take offence and then think about False Personality. This is especially important for some of you. Try to see False Personality in yourself through self-observation. Try to see how it complicates your ordinary life in such a way that when you might with a little more consciousness have taken a situation calmly you prefer to make an uproar. Try to

797

observe your opinions and when you are speaking from your opinions
without any real thought. Pull yourself up sometimes and say to yourself: "What are you thinking about? What are you feeling?" Observe
it. Observe how much of the time you are fast asleep and reacting
mechanically the whole time, not giving that conscious shock to yourself
called Self-Remembering. Observe how you never make any real
effort but always avoid real effort. Observe all your forms of internal
considering and try to observe your fantasies about yourself and don't
believe them. Observe what you are caught by, what you are always
held down by, and what turns you sour, and work against these things
by inner separation. All these, and many other things, as the Work
teaches, have to do with changing your psychology. For example,
observe whether you are negative at this moment. Are you going with
it? Are you going to identify with this negative emotion at this moment?
Or are you going to separate from it and not go with it? This is work on
oneself. Do you all understand that you have fixed and habitual attitudes
such as that you expect a meal at a certain fixed hour and so on? Can
you change your attitude to such fixed things in yourself? Can you
change the way when you read the newpapers you feel instantly negative
—i.e. mechanically negative towards one person or another? This is
mechanical reaction due to your acquired psychology so try to notice
how you psychologically react to everything that you are confronted
with and try to change it, in the light of what the Work teaches. Above
all, notice when you get negative. Notice this especially before it has
gone too far and do everything you can to separate from this negative
reaction. This is real work on yourself and it will give you very much
if you do it. But as long as you take yourself for granted nothing can
happen to you at all. In this Work we have to learn that we are all
wrong in everything that we do and say and feel and think, from the
standpoint of Higher Man—i.e. Conscious Man.

Quaremead, Ugley, October 10, 1945

A NOTE ON THE LAW OF FATE

When we struggle against identification many unnecessary
emotions disappear. What does it mean to struggle against identification? This question brings us to ask ourselves: "What is it in
myself that makes me identify with this or that event, with this or
that situation?" The answer is that it is one's own level of psychology.
We were speaking last time about this so important point—namely,
that we all have a certain psychology that causes us to react and behave
as we do. In my own case, if I can begin to see this psychology that I
take for granted in myself which has been acquired from innumerable

influences on me from childhood and which in the Work would be called in my case Nicoll, and if I begin to try to separate from some of these habitual mechanical reactions to Nicoll, I will then have a chance to change my level of Being. But if I cannot see Nicoll I shall not be able to change in my Being.

Now Nicoll in my case is called Personality, and Personality is under the Law of Accident. But there is a certain part of this acquired psychological machinery (which in my case is Nicoll) that is called False Personality. And this is under even more laws than Nicoll is under. What are the characteristics of False Personality? They consist in ascribing everything to oneself through vanity or pride. The acquired Personality itself may contain both good and bad things, good and bad habits, but what keeps them active is really the power of the False Personality which holds everything together just as it is and makes change of Being so very difficult and such a process of being wounded and hurt and upset.

Let us speak again about the Law of Accident and the Law of Fate. But I must warn you to begin with that it is not at all an easy idea to understand. In other words, it is something that you have to understand rather than something that is explained in so many words to you. The first thing that we must grasp is that we have different levels in us. Man is a small cosmos, a microcosmos, reflecting to a certain extent the great Cosmos or Macrocosmos. The Macrocosmos is given to us in the form of the Ray of Creation that you can all see is based on different levels. A high level, such as, let us say, the level of the Sun, is under 12 orders of laws, and the lower level under which we live is under 48 orders of laws. The Work says as a general formulation that the Essence in us is under 24 orders of laws and the Personality taken as a whole is under 48 orders of laws. Now supposing that a man is very identified with his Personality through his False Personality which latter is under an even greater number of laws—the Work says that such a man is under the Law of Accident. He may be killed when he should not be killed—that is, he may be killed through the Law of Accident because he is identified with his Personality. All this Work consists from one side in not identifying with the Personality, particularly with the False Personality, and in separating from the Personality. If you are completely identified with yourself as you are and take yourself for granted and do not see that you have anything called a psychology or a Personality, if you always act mechanically from your acquired Personality and take it as yourself, you are not under the Law of your Fate which belongs to Essence or the more internal side of you. Everything you do is in a sense unreal because *you* are not really doing it from yourself. As understanding grows in a man or a woman in the Work they see more and more that lots of things they have been thinking and saying are not real and do not really belong to them at all but have been acquired by imitation. Now you know that the Work says that understanding is the strongest force that we can create in ourselves and

799

the more understanding that we have in our personal Work the more results we shall get. When a man does something from his understanding he is not acting mechanically from his False Personality—he is acting from something more internal, something deeper, and when this is the case, he is more likely to be under the Law of his Fate. But when he acts from the purely external side of himself, from some excited dutiful side, he is more likely to be under the law of Accident. A man who does everything because he wants to be just the same as other people is of course a man who is not acting from anything internal. He is acting from the outer side of himself, from the Personality, speaking in general. He does not really think what he is doing or even feel what he is doing, save that he is doing his duty, as he was taught. He is going with the mechanical stream of things, and he has no trace of individual thinking, of individual feeling, in regard to any situations that arise, but always acts mechanically according to the formation of his own Personality. In other words, there is no real man there, no real individual, but a kind of mass-produced man. Such a person is under the Law of Accident more or less and such a man has very rarely any sincere moments with himself. He goes with his psychological machinery that has been laid down in him and simply is his machinery —that is, he is completely identified with his Personality and takes his Personality as himself. He never questions what he does, he never thinks about what he does. Such a man belongs to the mechanical circle of humanity and is a long way from the Conscious Circle of Humanity. His views are stereotyped, his buffers are fixed, his attitudes are acquired, and so there he is—quite an excellent kind of man, but quite asleep to himself. Such a man is not under the Law of his Fate.

Now supposing such a man begins to observe himself in the light of the teaching of this Work and begins to notice what he says and how he behaves and occasionally begins to wonder why he says these things and always behaves like that—such a man is beginning to observe himself and through self-observation begins not to identify with himself. This man, this woman, has begun to pass into a more internal person— himself—herself. They are beginning to separate from the Personality, and especially from the False Personality which governs external life. They are beginning to pass into themselves, into a deeper level of themselves. In other words, they are beginning to pass into what is really in them, what is essential. And, through this struggling against being identified with themselves as they mechanically are, they inevitably find that many emotions that they have hitherto taken as necessary become unnecessary. They find that many unnecessary emotions disappear from their lives and this also applies to many thoughts, many ways of thinking, which they formerly thought were so important. All this means a movement inwards, towards the essential part of oneself, which is the real part. And this movement begins to make a man, a woman pass more and more under the Law of their essential Fate, to be what they are and should be essentially. Eventually they may come actually under the Law of their own Fate. Notice that the Law of Fate that belongs to the Essence is composed of fewer laws than the laws governing the Personality, this corresponding to rising in the Ray of Creation, or the Macrocosm, to that level called the planetary level, which is under 24 laws. Notice also that this is called in the Work development. You might think that development means increase of laws but if we take the level of the Moon in the Ray of Creation it is under 96 orders of laws and this is no development. On the contrary, it is a descent into increasing and useless perplexity. All development consists in becoming more internal in your understanding through seeing what you are like and separating from it and at the same time it signifies a raising of the whole level of your being in terms of the Ray of Creation to a level where fewer laws exist. The Work teaches that it is possible for a man to reach the level of the Sun in himself. As you know, in the Ray of Creation, the Sun, as it is called, is under 12 orders of laws, and such a man has Real 'I' or Master at work in him —i.e. he obeys these highest principles concealed in Man's psychology. But this is very far from us at present. At present we are all concerned with separating from the Personality and seeing what the Personality in ourselves is like, and one way of seeing ourselves is, as was said, seeing unnecessary emotions. Do you imagine that worrying is an unnecessary emotion? Do you think that feeling rather tragical about everything is an unnecessary emotion? Do you think that being very concerned about the way that someone is going or that the world itself is going may possibly belong to the category of unnecessary emotions? The Work says that all negative emotions are unnecessary, whether they are anxious or worrying or what you might call dutiful emotions. Some people, very anxious to do this Work, often say something like this: "I believe in this Work, I believe it will help me. I would like so much to know what it is I have to give up." They ask this question anxiously or even tragically. As it were, they clasp their hands and say: "What have I to give up?" Well, the answer is that it is exactly this clasping of the hands, this tragic attitude, that they have to give up. They have to see that they are identified with being anxious and this is the very thing that they have to sacrifice. But do you expect a person who is very identified with himself to understand what is meant? This is the great difficulty in teaching this Work. When people say they will give up, for example, their will, they make a great mistake. They speak as if they had will, as if they could give it up as a final act, as something finished for ever. All this is illusion. Of what use is it to give up what one has not got? And what is it that these people have to see first of all, before they even begin to understand what the Work is about? They have to see, through long observation of themselves, that they have not got Will, but many different wills. Each 'I' in turn has a different Will, so how can they give up Will? The Work says there is only one thing that we can give up—our own suffering. But do you imagine that people see this quite easily? Do you imagine that it is something quite simple to give up your mechanical suffering? And yet it is the only thing that we can give up at our present level. Give up your suffering. Cease to suffer uselessly. Does that connect with your negative emotions, with your self-pity, with your private ideas about your undetected significance? Yes, it is all this that is connected with your suffering. When you have done some act of this kind on yourself for one moment you will feel a lightness and happiness that will shew you that the Work is quite right in what it says. You will see for yourself the truth of what the Work teaches. And no one can do this Work unless he begins to see the truth of what this Work teaches through his own experience. Now to give up one's suffering demands that one does not identify with all that one is at present. It demands that one begins to see that one has an acquired psychology that reacts in a certain way mechanically from which one is beginning to separate by personal and sincere work on oneself. And this is a movement towards the real side of oneself, the internal side, the essential side, which is under 24 laws of Fate. Fate is what we should be. Everyone is created to be something through Fate and the more he or she becomes this essential individual that they were created to be, the more do they pass under fewer laws. Fate really means that which is primarily ordained, one's own real destiny. When a man begins to will this Work into his own life he will inevitably pass towards his inner growth, his inner destiny. Certainly he may become something quite different from what he was in life. Many accidental things, that belong to his Personality and especially to his False Personality, may fall away from him. But such a man will be doing this Work and reach a point that it is possible for certain people to reach, a point which gives him his true centre of gravity and his true Being. He will then no longer be an artificial man, an invented man, on the surface, but he will become a Real Man. The object of this Work is to make us real men and real women, not invented people, governed by False Personality, for, as such, nothing that happens to us, or let us say, very little, really belongs to us at all. If you remember the principles of this Work, and if you try to put your will, such as you have, from 'I's that wish to work, into following these principles, into following certain rules that you were taught, especially about wrong talking, inner and outer, if you begin to obey the central idea that you must, for example, remember yourself, it may be said that you are giving up your ordinary will, such as it is. By following the Work, by meditating on it, by thinking about it and bringing it into your life every day, in a fresh way, you will begin to pass towards the real side of you, and so out of the Law of Accident. From one point of view you do not have to give up anything, nor do you have to be told to do something. So much of this Work consists in not doing something that you always did. But here lies a long struggle to understand how very gentle the influences of this Work are. You have, for example, to give up your negative emotions. What does it mean to give up your negative emotions? It means in the first place to follow what the Work says. But how can you give them up? First of all, you have to observe them, and then try not to identify with them. Most people, about five minutes after they get up in the morning, begin to identify with negative emotions—i.e. they identify with their habitual personal reactions to life. They do not observe what happens to them simply because they have no self-observation in the Work-sense. They let themselves go. They do not remember themselves. They do not hold themselves together internally. In other words, they instantly fall asleep on rising. They pass the day in attracting to themselves situations and things that would not come to them if they remembered themselves. Half an hour's work in the morning can make a great difference all day long. You can all see for yourselves what it means to be under the Law of Accident and the Law of Destiny or Fate. But people have to find this out for themselves. People often open letters the moment they get up. I wonder why. Is it necessary to be plunged immediately into the accidents of life without having formed in youself a certain resistance to life, without having a certain sacred moment with yourself of Self-Remembering, so that life and all its accidents do not instantly rush in and occupy the whole psychology?

Quaremead, Ugley, October 27, 1945

THE OBSERVATION OF 'I's AND STATES

Every 'I' produces its own state. Everyone is in a certain state at a certain moment owing to an 'I' that produces this state in him or her. If you find it difficult to study different 'I's in you there are two things that help. Different 'I's are grouped in personalities within the Personality—for example, a man has a certain personality connected with his college and a quite different personality connected with his domestic life. These sub-divisions of the Personality as a whole are themselves composed of many different 'I's. On one occasion Mr. Ouspensky was talking about the difficulty of seeing different 'I's and said we should try to see groups of 'I's which might be called sub-personalities. A man goes to his club and he has a certain personality; he then goes to his office where he has a different personality; and then he goes home where he is in a different personality. The other way of studying 'I's is to notice one's state. As I said, each 'I' produces its own atmosphere, its own state in oneself. In viewing any matter, if we have any power of successive observation, we soon recognize that we take it in different ways at different times. This is because of the shifting kaleidoscope of 'I's. When a particular 'I' is predominant we view things through this 'I' and the next moment when a different 'I' comes up we view the matter in a quite different way. Now one can easily become negative or depressed when one begins to notice this in oneself. But this is quite wrong from everything that the Work teaches us. We have no Real 'I', no permanent 'I', and have to realize it. We have to see the truth for ourselves. This continual change of different 'I's in us is exactly what we are told to observe. Sometimes people say: "Cannot you make up your mind definitely as to what you think about Mr. X? Do you like him or not?". But this question is foolish because it all depends which 'I' you are in when you happen to meet him. Each 'I' will induce a different state in you and in each different state you will view him differently.

Now if you have begun to have Work-memory through self-observation you will begin to know this already. This means that you no longer believe in your momentary different states—i.e. in your different 'I's which keep coming up in turn. 'I's cannot be overcome save by self-observation and non-identifying. A person may have the idea that he should really make up his mind definitely, let us say, about Mr. X. I will ask you this question: "What is going to make up your mind?" Each 'I' will make up your mind quite differently—that is, each 'I' will give you a quite different outlook towards him. If you begin to observe your 'I's and not identify with him you will finally get a picture of Mr. X. composed of all the different angles that each 'I' in you sees. You will therefore get a composite picture of Mr. X.—not a picture based on the opposites but a full picture of him. I will add here that this is quite impossible unless you can see different 'I's in yourself. If you have no memory arising from moments of self-observation and Self-Remembering you will never be able to get a full picture of Mr. X. And what is the reason? The reason is that you have no composite picture of yourself yet and therefore are still in Imaginary 'I' whose power over us makes us say 'I' to every 'I'. As you know, you have to get rid of the idea that you are one unvarying person. This hits Vanity and Pride, perhaps even more especially at Pride. You know how difficult it is for a person to admit that he has changed his mind. I think this is Pride. You surely all know people, if you don't know yourself already, who think they are always the same. Such people are living under a delusion. They do not see that at every moment they change owing to a succession of different 'I's that come into their conscious sphere and take charge of it for the moment and induce a certain state. Do you remember what was said about 'I's, how each 'I' is Caliph for a moment? After a time it is quite possible to reach that stage in the Work in which you do not believe so much in yourself as a real person. This is part of the loosening process of the Work and gives a form of consciousness that life rarely grants us—i.e. the new consciousness that comes through self-observation in the light of esoteric teaching. This consciousness gradually begins to approach the Third Level of Consciousness, or the Level of Self-Awareness, or the State of Self-Remembering, or Self-Consciousness. I can think of no better definition of what Self-Awareness means than that you begin to be aware of typical 'I's in you and do not allow them to become Caliphs and do not identify with the states they induce.

Now do you recognize your states and do you recognize that at every moment you are in a particular state and in each state you see things differently just as in walking round a house you see it from quite different angles at every moment? You may not be able to see an 'I', because I think sometimes people think of an 'I' as something written on the blackboard and do not see that an 'I' can only be detected by the state it produces in you. An 'I' cannot be recognized as an 'I' just like that. It can only be recognized by observing the intellectual and emotional state that it induces. For example, you find yourself having certain thoughts and feelings. Or you are in a mood. Perhaps you do not yet realize clearly enough that this is due to an 'I' in you that is predominant at the moment. You are identified with this 'I' and see everything through this 'I'. You are thinking through it, you are having its thoughts, you are feeling through it, you are feeling its emotions. Now if you are observing your thoughts and your emotions and after a time begin to recognize that you have had the same thoughts and emotions previously, you will begin to recognize that this is an 'I' in you, and if you have any memory through self-observation you will know quite well that these thoughts, these emotions, become quite different later on—i.e. when a different 'I' is predominant in you. In fact, you may laugh at these thoughts, these emotions, and wonder why you took everything in that way. This is exactly what an 'I' is. You cannot see an 'I' itself as you can see a human being or a butterfly or a piece of coal: it is not an object outside you. You can only observe an 'I' through its effects on you, through what it is suggesting to you, through what it is saying to you and trying to make you think and trying to make you feel. It is a very good thing to ask oneself sometimes: "In what state am I?" After a time in the Work you will find that this is a difficult question to answer because you have so many memories of different states, apart from the one you are in, that you do not accept the particular state that has come in through the 'I' that is trying to induce it and to make you believe in it at the moment. In other words, you begin to shift and sway away from your successive states—that is, from the power of successive 'I's that seek to hypnotize you and make you obey them. This is movement towards Real 'I'. Real 'I' of course obeys nothing but itself and controls all other 'I's. But in order to approach this psychological state where Real 'I' lives—and it is a long journey—you must first of all not submit to your changing 'I's which are not you, not Real 'I', but which are always trying to persuade you that they are you. Every 'I' says to you something like this: "Look now, this is what you really are. I am you and this is how you feel, this is how you really think." And I assure you that these 'I's are very clever hypnotists and in the vast majority of people their action is extremely successful. The vast majority of people believe in every successive 'I' that flits into their minds at a particular moment.

So try to notice 'I's through observing your states. We begin this Work by noticing our states and the quality of our thoughts and the quality of our feelings. Let me give you one more example. Someone came to me the other day and said: "I feel rather hopeless about my progress in the Work." I said: "Why do you not observe this 'I' in you?"

Quaremead, Ugley, November 3, 1945

A NOTE ON RELAXATION

It is a long time since we spoke about relaxing. On several occasions in the past we were told that we had to relax and to practise relaxation every day. Of course this has become a familiar word having no meaning nowadays in ordinary parlance, but when the Work speaks about relaxing it is speaking about something quite different that we should all practise. Let me remind you what the Works says about relaxing. It says that all relaxation must begin with the small muscles, such as the small muscles of the face, the fingers and the toes. We were taught to begin with the face and to put internal attention into the small muscles of the face and to relax them—the muscles round the mouth, the muscles round the eyes, and even the eye-muscles themselves.

Now if we speak about relaxing we have to speak about internal attention. We have two kinds of attention, one external and one internal. For example, when one observes oneself, one's moods, thoughts, and so on, one is using internal attention—i.e. attention not directed towards any external object, visible, tangible, or audible, through the senses. Self-observation is not about anything that the senses can see, hear, etc. but about what only the internal sense can observe. This is internal attention. In regard to placing consciousness through attention into different parts of your body, you must begin this gradually. For instance, can you become conscious through internal attention in a particular part of your body, let us say, your left foot, and then switch it over to your right foot, and so on? It is quite useless to try to relax unless you have some idea of what internal attention directed towards a particular part of the body means. As I said, the Work teaches that relaxation begins with relaxing the small muscles of the face. It would be no good trying to relax if your eyes were screwed up and your mouth pursed and your jaws clenched. For this reason it is necessary to become internally conscious of the state of the muscles in your face, to begin with. And this act of internal attention will produce in you the right condition for relaxing the whole body. The point however is that you have to do it. As you know, most people have no time to do anything like that. They are always carried on in the life-stream of useless thoughts, anxieties and worries. And people even think that to interrupt this purely mechanical stream of things that occupy them the whole time is something that they should not do, that is quite wrong, and so on. But this is not the case. If you can interrupt this mechanical stream that governs you, the stream of life, this cinema-film, that is always running through you, even for a moment, you will begin to get force. So try to begin with putting your internal attention into the muscles of your face and notice how much attention is lying there.

Mr. O. once said that modern life is always producing tensions in our muscles, anxious expressions, hurried movements, and all this wastes an enormous amount of energy. But, for Heaven's sake, do not try to relax the small muscles of your face when you are crossing Piccadilly Circus. This would be a great mistake. In fact, it might be called making right effort at the wrong time, and if you make right effort at the wrong time, or wrong effort at the right time, you will get into difficulties. There is a time for everything—that is, a right time at which to do things. For this reason I wish to-night to have the following passage from Ecclesiastes read about the right time to do things, for if you make an effort at the wrong time, even although the effort may be right, it will have no result.

> "To every thing there is a season, and a time to every purpose under the heaven: a time to be born, and a time to die; a time to plant, and a time to pluck up that which is planted; a time to kill, and a time to heal; a time to break down, and a time to build up; a time to weep, and a time to laugh; a time to mourn, and a time to dance; a time to cast away stones, and a time to gather stones together; a time to embrace, and a time to refrain from embracing; a time to seek and a time to lose; a time to keep and a time to cast away; a time to rend, and a time to sew; a time to keep silence and a time to speak; a time to love and a time to hate; a time for war and a time for peace." (*Ecclesiastes* III 1-8)

Imagine standing still amid the traffic and trying to relax the small muscles of your face and then if you are run over complaining that you were told to do it. This is merely foolishness comparable with the foolishness of people in the early Work who were told to go against mechanicalness and thought it would be a good thing to eat coal, or to stand upright in empty buses, or to eat with the knife in the left hand and the fork in the right hand. All these efforts are useless because they are not intelligent. This Work is about intelligent effort.

We asked a question the other day at one of the meetings here: "Have you studied your Being yet at all and have you noticed what in your Being you should change in the light of the Work?" Supposing you have never observed your Being at all and keep on trying to do this Work just as you are told, will it do you any good? Will it connect itself with yourself? Supposing, for example, you never notice your negative emotions, your envy, your jealousy, and so on, and yet you always try to work on the Emotional Centre in a theoretical way, will it do you any good?

Now we have to speak to-night about posture, about muscles—in short, about Moving Centre. I suppose you know that each centre hypnotizes the other centres. Supposing a man in his Moving Centre invariably adopts a depressed muscular posture and the small muscles of the face express gloom of some kind—do you think that such a man will be able to have pleasant emotions or interesting thoughts? Certainly not. He is chained by his muscular posture. You all know that depressed states make us look depressed in posture. If one is intelligent enough in the Work one will alter one's posture if one is trying to separate from the negative emotion that has got hold of one, because each negative emotion will produce its own muscular posture. A man comes into the room, bent, drooping, gloomy-faced, and you know at once that he is in a negative state, which may be habitual, unless he alters his muscular posture. In the same way, to return to the question of the small muscles of the face alone, if a person always has a drooped mouth, a weary or troubled or anxious look, you know quite well that this person is in a bad state and that unless you can make this person smile or stand more upright he may remain hypnotized by his posture. Understand please that posture is not merely a question of the big muscles of the body but of the small muscles as well. I mean that it is no good standing upright with a gloomy face because the face—that is, the hundred and one small muscles that control the expression of the face—is most directly governed by the Emotional Centre, for the face reflects the emotions more than anything else does. You would not like a man speaking between his teeth to tell you that he loves you. One would know at once that he was lying and merely using words without any real meaning, which unfortunately is our condition most of the time. Now, since the Moving Centre can hypnotize the Emotional and Intellectual Centres, it is a good thing to notice your posture and your facial expression, your face-posture, at times, and to study through internal attention how to alter these postures. The reason is that if you relax the muscles, especially the small muscles, you will get into a different state of emotion and of thought. Have you ever noticed that they begin to assume certain postures, certain facial expressions? Now supposing that just at that moment either this man or this woman observes himself (or herself) and starts by relaxing the muscles, both large and small, would it be possible for the state of rage to continue and grow? Certainly not. Unfortunately we never work on ourselves just at the moment when we should, because we much prefer to fall into typical mechanical reactions to the ordinary affairs of life rather than to take them more consciously with some degree of Self-Remembering. In fact, a man flying into a rage, if he could observe the tensions in his muscles, would really be a man who could remember himself at the critical moment and this would entirely change his behaviour.

Try therefore to study relaxation when you can. Notice how your face-muscles are contracted and try by putting your internal attention into the face-muscles to relax them. I advise you to begin with the muscles round about your eyes and then the muscles round about your nose (those muscles which sneer so easily) and then the small muscles all round your mouth and your cheeks; and then put your internal attention into those muscles which are just under the chin and in the front of the neck and then go round the back of your head and relax those muscles that make you stiff-necked, and then into the bigger muscles round your shoulders and gradually descend through internal attention right down to your toes. Of course this takes a long time but it is a very good thing to try to do. I have left out the muscles of the hands. I should have said: Pass from the shoulders down the arms to the hands and begin with the wrist-muscles. Put your internal attention into your wrist-muscles so that your wrists are quite flexible, quite dropped down, and then try to go into the small muscles of the fingers and relax them. Everyone in going through the muscular tensions in their bodies in this way will get to know for themselves certain groups of muscles which are not ordinarily relaxed properly. Remember above all that you cannot relax just by saying to yourself: "Relax". It is an actual exercise of internal attention. It is a directed effort that has to be made comparatively consciously and even if you do it only once a week you will get results. Often people are kept awake at night because of a certain group of muscles being in a tense state. They may observe their Emotional Centre and their Intellectual Centre and try to relax—i.e. not identify with these two centres—but they do not observe through internal attention the muscular contractions that exist in their body. Now this paper is about muscular relaxation. It is about relaxing the Moving Centre. I will remind you again that the Work says that every centre can hypnotize another centre. In the case of Moving Centre this means that certain typical postures and typical expressions induce in you typical emotions and typical thoughts. For example, a hurried person, who cannot stop rushing about, is a person who has a Moving Centre that assumes certain positions or postures, or rather, in this case, certain movements, which belong to the same idea, and therefore is always hypnotized by Moving Centre assuming these postures and movements. These hurried movements would induce hurried and anxious emotions and hurried and anxious thoughts. This is where illness sometimes is so good. I can only say that I have noticed it in myself very often. Illness quietens Moving Centre and so often does a great deal of good by relaxing us. Perhaps some of you have noticed the same thing. I may not be emotionally anxious or have any reason to be, but if I am accustomed to make hurried movements and apparently never have time for anything, my Moving Centre will hypnotize my Emotional Centre into feeling anxiety and being harassed. Of course we must not think for a moment that we are all going to begin to walk about majestically and slowly just to shew off how we are relaxed. One has to be really relaxed through internal attention when one wishes to be and when one feels one needs to be relaxed. If you will start with the small muscles of your face and do this exercise quite sincerely you will be very surprised to find out how very often rather difficult and worrying thoughts completely cease. For example, stop frowning for a short time. I mean, don't just stop frowning because you are told not to frown but through internal attention really go into the muscles that are frowning, and lo and behold, all your frowning thoughts will disappear. This means that they are kept going by the posture of your face. Again, people who stick out their jaws and clench their fists find that it is quite remarkable if they can cease to do this—they feel quite alien from themselves. But, since we all wish to remain mechanical and do not wish to change at all, I fancy that these people will very soon stick out their jaws and clench their fists and make chests as before.

Now in discussing this paper please remember that we start in the Work with relaxing the muscles of the face and this takes a lot of practice in putting the consciousness into these muscles and relaxing them one by one, and remember especially the small skin-muscles just underneath the chin and the muscles at the back of the neck. In my personal experience I have found that relaxing the wrist-muscles when I have no time to do anything else is extremely useful. Let your hands drop because the hands so easily express violence.

Quaremead, Ugley, November 17, 1945

WORK ON THE EMOTIONAL CENTRE

At the last meeting here a question was asked about how to work on the Emotional Centre. The great trouble with the Emotional Centre is that we are always identified with it—that is, with the emotions that we are under at any particular moment. We have the greatest difficulty in separating ourselves from the emotional state of the moment. We take our emotional state for granted. For example, we feel emotionally jealous, which is a different thing from feeling instinctively jealous, and we are completely identified with this emotion. Or again, we are emotionally depressed, and once more we take this as our state, as something we do not challenge. As you know, the Work teaches that the Emotional Centre is the most difficult centre to deal with. You have heard that it is called the mad elephant, and it is also said that we must try to bring up two tame elephants on either side of it, one of which is the Intellectual Centre and the other the Moving Centre. The whole question lies in the difficulty of observing Emotional Centre in a non-identified way. The reason is that we identify with our emotions more than with anything else and so I repeat, we take our emotional state always for granted—not as something that we have to observe and separate from. Everyone has a typical series of constantly recurring emotional states which vary from the greatest excitement and enthusiasms to the most depressed and morbid feelings. But because the force of the emotions is so blinding people remain fixed on the turning wheel of their emotions. In other words, people do not distrust their emotions but take them as if they were genuine and quite real states. They accept their emotions as right at any particular moment. And because emotions are so difficult to observe, owing to our tendency to identify with them, they do not observe them as something to observe and not go with. The starting-point always lies in self-observation and in this case observation of the emotional state. Now can any of you do this yet? Can you observe your emotional state without taking it for granted as being your real state? Have any of you yet got in your Work-memory the knowledge of some of your typical recurrent emotional states? Do any of you yet question your particular emotional state? In other words, as I said, do you challenge your emotional state and say to yourself: "Why am I in this emotional state? What is it due to? And in connection with what has it arisen?" The effort of internal attention will then begin to separate you from the emotional state and you may be able thereby to disarm it—i.e. not go with it, not believe in it, not take it for granted.

There are two sources of our emotional states at any moment. One source is some external stimulus, such as a person not behaving rightly to you, or saying something rather unpleasant to you, and the other is the typical habitual emotion coming from a pathetic feeling about your past. The overcoming of the past is one great line of personal work on yourself. Most people have such a great register of unhappy moments which they have nourished so much that often it is very difficult for them to escape from these pathetic states which of course only give rise to continual negative emotions which only create useless suffering. This personal work is of a very special type and everyone must be able to face it, after a time. The whole of the past must be cancelled eventually. In other words, you must have nothing against anyone. You must forgive all debts. And, as has been often said recently, you can only do this by completely changing your opinion of yourself through self-observation. The other source is how people behave to you externally each day. You become negative with someone for acting in a certain way to you which you think is wrong. And you must all see that these two sources, inner and outer, of negative emotion, are very closely connected. On one occasion when Mr. Ouspensky was talking about this subject and how we identify with every emotional state, he gave as a supreme formula: *To non-identify take nothing seriously except the Work.*

Now in regard to being negative and having an unpleasant emotional state towards a particular person—supposing you have got to the point of being able to observe that you are in an unpleasant emotional state, and this of course means that you do not quite identify with it, so let us suppose that you are slightly conscious of being in a negative state towards a particular person—how are you going to deal with it? Here all the work that you have done personally comes in. Try to formulate what it is that makes you negative as regards this person and then look into the book of your own self-observation, into your own records of yourself—that is, into your Work-memory—and try to see whether what you find so difficult to bear in this other person is not something that you also have in yourself. Realizing that you are just as difficult in yourself as the person that you criticize produces instantly the magical feeling of surrender, of cancelling, of freedom. But in order to do this, you must use the Intellectual Centre. In other words, you must think: Here comes in a very good example of what thinking in the Work-sense means, and I can assure you that whenever you think in this way it will give you the greatest feeling of freedom that you have ever experienced.

Again, suppose that you are negative because someone says something unpleasant to you. This is really the same thing as I have been speaking about. It is extremely difficult to meet and you may not be able to meet it at the moment. Now every event that happens to you, such as someone saying something unpleasant to you, should be capable of being transformed. All this Work is about transforming ourselves, both in relationship to our past and in relationship to what is happening to us now. I can only say: Have you ever said anything unpleasant to other people and can you later on bring the memory up of having said something equally unpleasant? Once again I can assure you that if you can do this you will find that this little event of someone saying something unpleasant to you will become completely cancelled, completely neutral, although, as I said, you may not be able to do all this just at the moment when someone is unpleasant to you. So much of our personal work is done after the event. It is quite useless to forgive: you have to cancel. And this is always done by finding the same thing in yourself, and you will always find it if you are sincere. No one can behave to you otherwise than you behave to other people because your Being attracts your life. Do you understand that this must be so if it is possible to believe in psycho-transformism? The trouble with us is that we will take ourselves for granted as being nice and sweet people, and you must remember here that you may not have said something unpleasant externally yourself but you have thought something and consented to it. In the Work you must understand that what you think psychologically in yourself, in your own privacy, counts just as much as what you say. I am speaking of those thoughts to which you have consented, those cheques to which you have signed your name. They count just as much as what is said openly. The Gospels often speak of this. But the case is quite different with a person in the Work into whose mind come many unpleasant thoughts about other people but who does not consent to these thoughts. He sees quite easily how he could combine chemically with them but he will not allow these combinations really to take place, and after a time his temptation is over. This is real temptation, because all real temptation is about the Work. When you do not go with unpleasant thoughts and feelings about other people but are quite aware of them, you are really working on yourself. This is personal work. If you are so foolish as to say: Why do I have these thoughts and feelings about other people? you are quite wrong. You are only praying to end strife in yourself, but all strife gives the possibility of development and I suppose it is almost right to say that all development consists in not identifying with what one is taught by the Work not to identify with. If you consent to negative, bitter, or suspicious thoughts, do you not see that you have been tempted successfully and that the small vessel of the Work that you are trying to make, the small retort, has already got a leak in it which may take you weeks to repair and often it is a very small thing, apparently trivial, that completely exhausts your force, because it makes a leak in you. Thoughts of self-pity of course make holes in you. You become, instead of a retort, a cullender, full of holes, in which everything poured into you, everything you have done for yourself, leaks out. Take *envy*. Envy seems a slight thing but it makes a very big hole. Take *malice*. Take the sting in your tongue or in your letter. That makes a very big hole. Or take hatred arising from being offended. All these states are states of identifying.

All psychology, all real psychological teaching, is about how to make a man grow, and it has a very definite object, the idea being that if a man retains his force in a certain way he can create in himself a new man, a different person. The metaphors used to convey this teaching have varied in different ages. In the alchemical teaching, which dealt apparently with turning lead into gold, but which really dealt with changing Man himself into a new being, there is always this idea of a retort, something that cannot be penetrated by wrong influences, something that brings together all the essential parts of the man, through a certain friction transforming them into a new body.

We seek to reach a higher level of Being. What is one sign of a higher level of Being? Let me turn the question in this way: Do you think a person who is full of self-pity, of envies, jealousies, complaints, malices, depressions, and negative states of all kinds, can enter the Kingdom of Heaven? What is the Kingdom of Heaven? Why, nothing but what the practice of real psychology leads to—which in this Work it is called "Higher Being". So we have something definite to do. It is not a theory nor an invention: it is permanent teaching. Everything in this Work teaches us about something quite real and definite. It is a *way* leading to something definite and possible for those who can hear. It is about Man and his permanent meaning —not his local meaning. And there is therefore something that will necessarily respond to Man if he makes the right requests and efforts —for Man has meaning and the Universe has meaning.

Now let us return to the original question of how to deal with the Emotional Centre. This is a difficult thing and no one can expect to deal with it for many, many years. But people who wish to do this Work must begin to deal on their own scale with their unpleasant emotions because the Work teaches that practically all the emotions that we know are unpleasant. For instance, triumphing over a rival is a very unpleasant emotion although at our level we take it as a pleasant emotion. And even the pleasant emotions that we ordinarily experience turn into the most unpleasant emotions in a flash once our pride or vanity is touched. The reason is because all our emotions are based on self-love which is touching them and if there is plenty of flattery we feel very fine, but if there is not flattery we feel very depressed. For this reason it is a very good thing to distrust one's emotions whether pleasant or unpleasant, and especially one should distrust enthusiasms.

Now the Work teaches that there are emotions that do not change —it calls them positive emotions. It does not call our ordinary emotions positive—it merely calls them pleasant or unpleasant. The Work teaches that we do not have real emotions yet. I think from my own experience that occasionally we do have real emotions for a very short time and they are always completely free from all self-love. But I also think that they are very rare and easily invented. Now the Work says that we cannot create positive emotions for ourselves. It says that positive emotions do come to us sometimes if we have worked genuinely and they come as rewards. It also says that the characteristic of a positive emotion, which comes from Higher Emotional Centre, is such that it never turns into an opposite. Our ordinary so-called love turns very easily into hate. A positive emotion has no opposite because it belongs to the Third Force which is between the opposites. As you all know, the purification of the Emotional Centre is one of our great objects. We can reach it only through the purification of the Intellectual Centre through new ideas both about ourselves and about other people and about the meaning of all life on Earth. When the mind begins to see new Truth, then the Emotional Centre can begin to give up these false emotions. The ultimate object is to awaken the Emotional Centre so that it can receive positive emotions. And while this is very far from us at present we all know surely how much work we have to do on our present Emotional Centre and our present emotional states that result from it. We have, for example, to give up having our own way all the time. Do not think that this can be done in a moment. It takes such a long time for us to realize what it means, this having our own way in everything. But when we begin to dissolve our ordinary mechanical feeling of ourselves—and I would say here: how many of you are sure that you are perfectly all right in yourselves? —then we shall begin to break up the very sources of this self-love and these self-emotions that at present govern everyone. It is only the things that you most despise in yourself that are probably some good. Christ was not born in a manger without significance as to what can grow in Man.

Quaremead, Ugley, November 24, 1945

WORK ON ATTITUDES

In this short paper let us return once more to the idea of attitudes. The Work teaches that we must observe our attitudes. You can call attitudes merely points of view that you always mechanically take, but this definition is merely introductory to the idea of attitudes. You can only observe attitudes to begin with by their results. An attitude is something formed through long habitual taking-for-granted thinking. The first thing is that we have to allow the truth of the idea that we have attitudes, typical points of view, typical ways of taking things, and that this of course belongs to our mechanical and therefore dead psychology —that is, that side of our psychology that cannot change. You can have an attitude to the weather, an attitude to religion, or to science, an attitude to other people, an attitude to politics, and so on. What people do not see is that their undiscovered attitudes create a great deal of misery for them and prevent them from understanding. No one, of course, admits that he or she has typical attitudes.

Let me quote indirectly a recent observation that was sent to me. The observation was as follows: "I had been trying to keep myself awake a little, more than once during the day, by observing myself uncritically. I noticed that it was just as if a bit of me was separated from the rest of me and was watching the rest of me. One side of myself was observing the other side but observing it quite uncritically. This other side of myself which I was observing was taking an often-recurring life-situation in its own way. Quite suddenly I had a sense of remembering the future. The result was that the whole situation changed. It was not only the future but it seemed that I observed the past and the future together in regard to this same situation that I was faced by and that I saw my attitude to it and seemed to become free from it."

Let me make some comments from the Work point of view on this observation, which is a good one. There is a certain side of the Work connected with the idea of Karma-Yoga. This has nothing to do with acting or playing a rôle in life consciously which probably none of us can do except for a brief time, as we are at present. Karma-Yoga has to do with work on the actual situation that we are in karmically, and finding the right way to behave towards it. It is quite impossible to practise Karma-Yoga unless one has self-observation —that is, unless one can divide oneself into an observing side and an observed side. At every moment each of us is taking some event, some situation in life, in a mechanical typical way through attitude chiefly. The practice of this aspect of the Work connected with Karma-Yoga has nothing to do with changing the situation itself but with changing the way you take it. If anyone has practised self-observation sincerely and really reached that stage in which he is not satisfied with himself and does not think that everything he says or does is always right, then it is possible to practise this side of the Work connected with that particular form of Yogi teaching called Karma-Yoga. Now you must all understand that to be able to take this step means that you have really got somewhere in the Work and are willing to work on yourself and no longer completely identify with yourself as you are, which as you know is usually a very unsuccessful self. I will make only one or two points here. The first is: How many of you know or have realized that you can take a typical situation, a typical event, in a different way from what you have ordinarily done? The second point is: Can you yet observe yourself uncritically. Everything recurs in your personal lives, the same situations arise, the same events, and the same mechanical psychology meets them and reacts in the same mechanical way, day by day and week by week. In all the attempts of esoteric teaching to try to make us awaken and become different from what life has made us, the practice of Karma-Yoga is something that we can undertake intelligently and one which will give us immediate results. You will notice that in the above example when this uncritical self-observation took place there was a sense of the future and also a sense of the past. The typical attitude, the characteristic reaction towards the situation, became conscious and at once there was a sense of the future—that is, that this thing has taken place over and over again. And suddenly there was a feeling of liberation from this hitherto unrecognized self-imprisonment, self-bondage, due to one's mechanical psychology, one's mechanical make-up. Here you have a very good example of what the Work means practically on this side, but usually we are so immersed in sleep or so identified with every typical mechanical reaction, so much so that we always behave in exactly the same way towards ever-recurring situations, continually lose force and remain in our state of deep sleep, because you must remember that if you wish to awaken you must find in what way you can save force and store it up and no one can awaken unless he begins to accumulate force and to store it up. And it is often dull and dead moments which take force in everyone's life every day, these customary ways of taking daily things through customary attitudes towards them that cause a constant leakage of force.

Now it is a very good thing to think as an exercise that you are taking to-day in an entirely new way. I say it is a good exercise in the morning to try to take everything that happens, all the usual discords and unpleasant tasks and so on, in an entirely new way, if you can, for a short time. It gives you a glimpse of what work means and what transformation means—that is, transforming your ordinary daily life and taking it in a quite new way.

In connection with this example given above I was asked: Is this a question of Self-Remembering or self-observation? Whenever you have a double sense of the future and past meeting together in the present moment it always has a quality of Self-Remembering. In this case it was reached by uncritical self-observation which lifted the consciousness to a higher level—i.e. that of Self-Remembering or the third level of consciousness. Now if you observe yourself critically you never reach this level through self-observation. Why? Because you will always be self-justifying, complaining, negative, and all the rest of it, which belong to the second level of consciousness, the so-called waking state. But if you can really observe yourself uncritically you will pass from this complaining, unpleasant level to a quite new state of consciousness and you will see yourself standing in Time. Now suppose that you can be sufficiently awake to observe at a particular moment how you are taking some situation, some event, and suppose that you can observe yourself uncritically, that means that you can observe that part of yourself that is taking things in this mechanical, ever-recurring way. If the observing 'I' is really uncritical it begins to move towards Real 'I' which is never critical. But if you are observing yourself with an 'I' that belongs to a lower level—i.e. a critical 'I'—then you will not reach the level of Self-Remembering. In other words, the *quality* of your observation is not fine enough, and you will simply be at that level at which you have to argue with other 'I's. Your best 'I's are uncritical 'I's, 'I's that never judge either you or other people. Your worst 'I's are your fault-finders, your jealous, envious, malicious, complaining 'I's. Through them how can you observe yourself uncritically? But through the pure feeling of the Work you can observe yourself uncritically as a mere nobody—not as a ridiculous and absurd creature, as of course we all are, without exception, because this would be critical—but simply as a nobody, as nothing. And I remind you here that unless we can realize our own nothingness we can get nowhere.

WHERE WE LIVE PSYCHOLOGICALLY

Man is defined in the Work first of all by what he eats and what he breathes and where he lives. Every living animal is defined in the same way—namely, by what it eats, what it breathes, and where it lives. A fish, for example, is different from a man in this respect because a fish lives in the water and breathes in a quite different way from a man and eats different food. The Work also teaches that in this great machine of Organic Life everything eats everything else. The Work, in fact, says that the whole Universe is based on the idea of eating and being eaten. Just think for a moment, can any one of you live without eating something else? Let us take simply Organic Life itself—namely, this sensitive film which surrounds this small planet called the Earth. This sensitive film is fed by the great energy of the Sun, to begin with, but everything in Organic Life on this Earth exists only by eating something else. Some of you have heard this idea before into which I am not going further to-night. I will return to the opening phrase: Man is defined in this Work by what he eats, what he breathes and where he lives. Now let us take this idea psychologically and not literally. Let me ask you: What do you eat psychologically? What do you breathe psychologically? And where do you live psychologically? Supposing you are very fond of eating negative emotions? Supposing you love long, unhappy thoughts? Or supposing that you love hearing negative stories, unpleasant rumours about other people? Psychologically some people eat nothing but unpleasant impressions, unpleasant remarks. They are attracted to unhappy, uneasy situations. They like unpleasant things, they like to talk negatively. This is their food. Again, they breathe in, psychologically speaking, not Truth, but false things, lies, unpleasant things.

But what I want to speak to you about to-night is *where* you live. In what part of yourself do you live? In what part of your psychological country do you usually live? Let us once more try to understand what one's psychology means as distinct from the external world of space, for we should continually make this effort. Everyone has a much greater psychological space or country in themselves than they know in the physical sense. They may not have travelled round the world, they may even know only their own little village, and yet psychologically they inhabit a particular place which is exactly correspondent with physical space and physical place. When you have begun to observe yourself you begin to see that you have psychological space in you as distinct from physical space. You begin to understand what it means that you may be in a very bad place in yourself at any particular moment, just as you might be in a dark, evil street full of robbers, gun-men and so on, in the external physical sense. It takes a long time for us to understand that we can be in a dangerous and evil place in ourselves and to realize this requires a great deal of objective strength towards oneself. After a long time I began to have a more objective relationship to myself in the sense that I began to realize that at some moment or other I was in a very bad place in myself and surrounded by very bad 'I's—in fact, evil 'I's—and that I must be very careful how to behave, just exactly as if I were in a very bad slum surrounded by extremely evil-looking people. What is so extraordinary is that people do not notice that they have a much bigger psychological country that they are living in than the external world that they know. I was speaking the other day to someone about this and this person said: "I do not understand what you mean by psychological country. Where is it? How do we find it?" It was impossible for me to explain anything further in this particular case because the person to whom I was speaking was extremely externally-minded and saw only things outside and not things inside. That is, the world for him was only what is registered by the senses and not what is registered by self-observation. Now every devil and angel is already in you in this psychological country to which you gain access through your own self-observation. This enormous country, full of cities and deserts and forests, peopled by all these devils and angels, is the country that we have to learn about through self-observation. For we must move about in it as intelligently and carefully as we move about in the external world that we see revealed by our senses. If a man is attacked in some slum people say: "Why do you go there? Why do you continue to walk down these dangerous streets and meet these dangerous people?" But we are so asleep, so dead to our own inner state, so unrecognisant of what the Work is teaching us about this inner country in which we are always in a certain place, that we only dimly understand the parallel. After a time a man in the Work begins to know where he is in his own psychological country, amongst what 'I's he is, and through the light that comes with self-observation he begins to know when he must shift his position.

Now the most useful forms of Self-Remembering are about this inner psychological country of which we gradually become more aware through personal work on ourselves. We learn to remember ourselves in this inner country when, for example, we find ourselves for one reason or another in a bad place in it. And so we learn what silence means and what tact to ourselves means. Exactly the same things apply to a psychological place as to a physical place—I mean, it is just as if we are in a pretty tough spot in external space and know quite well we must use silence and tact to escape. The great danger is that we do not realize that we have a continual shifting of position in regard to where we are living psychologically in ourselves and that as a consequence a thing which was harmless yesterday is not necessarily so to-day. If you do not understand about psychological space you can understand about different 'I's in you. Which 'I's are nearest to you at present? What are these 'I's like? You could ask yourself exactly the same questions in regard to physical space, could you not—namely, looking round you could say: "What kind of people am I amongst at this moment? Do I care for them? Do I wish to be with them?" When your relationship to your inner life, to your inner psychological space, becomes as vivid and real as is your relationship to external space, to visibly-seen things, then you may be quite sure that you begin to understand the meaning of this Work. To which 'I's in you are you going to consent and to which 'I's are you going to be extremely tactful and to which 'I's are you going to play the part of avoiding them at all costs? When the Psalmist said: "We have walked in unpleasant places", I have thought that this defines so well the stage of a man understanding that he has spent a long time in walking in unpleasant places, in his own inner world.

So to return to this phrase that Man is defined by where he lives, taking the whole definition as given at the beginning of this paper, if we take it psychologically and not merely literally, it is a very good question to ask yourself sometimes: "Where am I living in myself at this moment?" Now, suppose you have never worked on yourself for a week? Suppose you have swelled your internal accounts, or suppose you are full of the idea of "if only". Now let me ask you: "In what kind of a place are you living in your slums?" I suppose that a person living in the slums of himself, in the lowest interpretation of everything, must make effort to get out just as a person actually living in physical slums who has the idea that he might better himself knows quite well that he must make effort to escape from his physical position. It seems to me to be exactly the same thing. Do you know your slums? Do you agree with me that many people live very much in their slums—i.e. in slums of their psychological country, of their psychological world? Take all the envies and jealousies and poor, mean, negative things that go on in each of us. Do you think they are, in short, slums? I would say from my observation of myself that they are exactly the slums. Everything can be taken in the heaviest, most negative way without the slightest trace of transformation. But this Work is about transforming one's life. It is about efforts that lift you above the level in which it is so easy to live all one's life although one is dressed up outside in the very reverse of slum-clothing. Yes, the Work begins with the slums. Something valuable is there.

Now you will find, if you have reached a certain stage of self-observation, that in the turning wheel of inner experience you will return again to your slums inevitably and here at this moment you have to be most awake and make most inner effort. At another point you find you do not have to make so much effort because you are not living in a bad place in yourself. But there is always a certain point in the turning wheel of your own psychology where you must be exceptionally careful and most silent, most tactful, and most clever with yourself to get out of this place as best you can without having been robbed of everything. We have all got to realize this turning wheel of our own psychology. I said something above about "if only". Now suppose you eat—and let me remind you that Man literally is defined as what he eats, what he breathes, and where he is—let us take this phrase "if only". Is that good food to eat, psychologically speaking? Suppose that I am eating all impressions on the basis of "if only"? This faded food, this dead, negative food, will not make it possible for me to transform anything in my Being. The attitude represented by "if only" prevents work. But we can always work. We can always go into another part of our psychological country if we observe and separate from some typical habitual 'I's.

Quaremead, Ugley, December 8, 1945

ON OBEYING THE WORK

When you begin to obey this Work you cannot do as you like. However, it takes us a very long time before this begins to become clear. It is not something that can be learnt by heart or told you by someone else but it is actually a growth of one's own experience. It is of course connected with keeping one's aim. To act from one's aim is to act without being identified, but, again, it takes us a long time before we know what aim means. At first it is something that we think about in words without seeing what these words mean. Aim gradually becomes clearer to us as always having to do with self-change. Now no self-change is possible if we always do what we like. Let us put the matter a little differently. If we always do what is pleasing to us and easy to do, no self-change is possible. The central idea of the Work is self-change, and the central teaching of the Work is that Man is an unfinished creation, a self-developing organism, one whose only real task is to complete itself. If we do not grasp this significance of the Work we shall never be able either to make a right aim or to keep it in the right way. The force of the Work will not help us. The Work cannot help us unless we are doing what the Work is teaching. How, for instance, can the Work help us if we never remember ourselves? Many people make aim that has nothing to do with the Work or is not done in connection with any feeling of the Work. Let us suppose my aim is to climb the highest mountain in the world. Could this possibly be called a Work-aim? But suppose you say that no one would have an aim of that kind now. Well, let us say that a person makes a small aim to cook an excellent dinner. There are so many ways in which that excellent dinner can be cooked —I mean, psychological ways, not ordinary ways. Now suppose you have made a big and real aim that you are going to try to remember to act in life without identifying and that you are going to try to practise this great Work-exercise at least several times a day. Then, of course, in taking this small aim of cooking an excellent dinner in conjunction with this general and real aim, it would really be one example and you would have to cook it without being identified and if anything went wrong or someone put in something wrong, you would have to separate from those 'I's that will start to become negative. But it is very difficult not to do everything personally and there is always that form of internal considering which the Work stresses which consists in thinking that even the weather itself is bad on purpose.

You can always tell when you are working by a curious feeling which in a way can be compared with the feeling one used to have on returning to school. You cannot quite have your own way and when you are having your own way you are quite aware of it and not very happy. A school in the Work-sense first of all gives you this feeling externally, so to speak—although you are free to leave—but later on this feeling must be in you without any surrounding school. Then you will not do things personally in the same way as you formerly did. There will, of course, always be two divisions of 'I's, two people, in you—one who wishes the Work and one who does not—and the struggle between these two will always continue because there must be strife at the bottom of work. Work begins when a man starts to struggle with himself. I said above that when you begin to obey this Work you cannot do as you like. The Work is really Conscience; at first it is outside you; you hear it speaking in the Work-teaching. Man has Conscience but it is buried. This Conscience that the Work speaks about is the same in everyone. When I first heard this it seemed to me extraordinary that this was the case. How could Conscience be the same in everyone? But when I reflected that the Work also teaches that Higher Centres exist in everyone, only unheard, the idea did not seem so extraordinary. Man having gone so deeply asleep has to be taught now from outside. This Work is esoteric teaching from outside at first. If a man feels it emotionally, if something in him responds to it, and finally if he persists for a long time, he finds that the Work is in him as well as outside him. Then he must obey the Work. He may not know for a long time how to. But the intention must be there in him. And after a time he will be shewn the way or the Work will find a way for him—often quite the contrary to what he supposed.

All this depends on obeying the Work first of all through the mind and the emotional thinking and finally with the Will as a whole—namely, with the whole mass of the man. But this latter stage is far from us at present. When the Work is in you in the above sense you begin to know how to act in life with non-identifying. Some people might call it acting impersonally but I do not agree with the use of this word. You can act very personally without identifying. You remember that we are all blinded with identifying, that we are all rendered deaf and dumb by it, and that identifying is our most terrible enemy. Only the Work has the strength to overcome this terrible power.

Quaremead, Ugley, December 22, 1945

THE PARABLE OF THE HORSE, CARRIAGE AND DRIVER

PAPER I

In speaking of the inner state of a mechanical man, G. made many analogies. On some occasions he compared the inner state of a man to a Carriage, Horse and Driver—and he emphasized that it was very important for us to think about what these three distinct things in Man mean. The point of the analogy is that these three distinct things are not in right relationship to one another. The Driver is not on the box of the Carriage; the Horse is not properly fed, nor rightly harnessed to the Carriage; and the Carriage itself is in a bad condition. "What," G. asked once, "is the reason of all this? The reason is that the Driver is sitting in the public house spending his money on drink and giving no food to the Horse and no proper care to the Carriage. In order to change this state of affairs," G. said, "it is necessary that the Driver receives a shock, to awaken him."

Now the interpretation of this analogy or parable can be approached from many different sides, some of which have already been explained. To-night I will take up more especially the point that the Driver after realizing his state must eventually climb up on to the box of the Carriage —that is, he must rise in his level to reach a place of control. But first we must understand that it is possible to take the rousing of the Driver in many steps. He must be shaken out of his drunken slumber, and then he must stand up, and then move himself out of the sphere of the public house, and then observe the Horse, and then the Carriage, and so on. After attending to the Horse and Carriage he must climb on to the box and finally take hold of the reins and start driving as best he can. As you know, the parable goes on to say that if he does all this a fourth factor *may* appear on the scene—i.e. the Master may be found sitting in the Carriage and giving directions to the Driver as to where he must go. But, it is added, the Master will never seat himself in the Carriage unless the Driver is on the box and has begun to take hold of the reins and has done what he could for both the Horse and the Carriage. This parable is really about the whole object of the Work. The object of the Work is to reach Real 'I' in oneself—through the long inner path through oneself, through Self-Remembering and work on oneself. Real 'I' is the Master in the parable. We are taught that as we are we have no Real 'I' and have no inner stability and never know what we really have to do. In our present state first one 'I' takes charge and then another 'I'. Our state is comparable to that represented in the parable of the Tower of Babel. From that parable, apparently we once had inner unity but something went wrong and multiplicity appeared— namely, from being one we became many. In general, our Being is

823

defined in the Work as being characterized by multiplicity as distinct from the Being of a Conscious Man. We are a crowd of different 'I's pulling in different directions, all with their own forms of self-will, and what we rather grandly call our will is nothing but the resultant of all these different wills. So our task is to attain unity, and no single 'I' that we know or can observe at present has the strength to give us this unity and arrange and subordinate all the 'I's into a whole. We can however form substitutes for Real 'I' which, beginning with Observing 'I', are called in ascending sequence of importance and power Deputy-Steward and Steward. We are fortunate if we have a Deputy-Steward to look after our household affairs and still far more so if we ever attain to that level where we have Steward controlling affairs. But beyond Steward lies Master or Real 'I', the reaching of which is the chief aim of all. You will see in the parable of the Horse, Carriage and Driver that there is no chance of our attaining to the level where Master or Real 'I' exists or of hearing his voice and receiving his instructions as to what we have really to do with our lives unless we first of all waken out of the sleep, out of the stupor that we exist in, which is represented by the Driver sitting in a drunken sleep in the public house. The first task then is to awaken the Driver for unless this has taken place the Horse cannot be attended to, nor the Carriage. The Carriage can be said to represent the body and people may think that they can start only with the body but this is wrong—in fact, it may put the Driver into a deeper sleep. What is the method of this Work in regard to the awakening of the Driver and the nature of the shock? If the Driver realizes that he is in a drunken sleep this may be sufficient to make him try to wake up. With what is he drunk? One thing is imagination. We are drunk with imagination. I have heard it said in the Work that at one time humanity on Earth was going forward too quickly in proportion to the rate of development of the Moon and the Earth and had to be held back. The Overseer called the Chief Engineer and explained to him the difficulty. The result was that Man was given imagination. Then from that time everything went on without difficulty. The imaginary began to replace the real. As you know, the Work speaks about Imaginary 'I'. Man believes that he has Real 'I' as he is, just as he imagines he is fully conscious. He believes that he is a real individual, unchanging, permanent, with full will and full consciousness. He has no Real 'I' but his imagination creates Imaginary 'I' in him. He hides from himself his extreme inner weakness by means of imagination. Now if a man realizes that he has no Real 'I', no Real Will, that all he has felt and thought about himself in this respect can simply be called Imaginary 'I', then he is beginning to awaken from the drunken sleep in the public house where he spends his money in imagining. This is one side of the position of Man from the esoteric point of view. We remind ourselves here that the problem of esotericism is always the same—namely, how to awaken Man from his state of sleep and make him realize he is asleep. Esoteric teaching takes Man not only as not yet conscious, but drunken with imagination and wasting his force in falsity and violence. You will then see the necessity for beginning with self-observation—the observation of one's sleep. All forms of teaching are quite useless unless the Driver awakens. You can see the reason why. A man may be given some teaching while he is drinking in the public house and this teaching will go into his imagination and increase his state of sleep. If he is told that he is an angel in Heaven he will believe that he is and drink more than ever. Certainly this will increase his state of sleep, his state of imagination. Many good people indulge in this form of drink. Unfortunately there are many sorts of teaching that have this effect as their object—i.e. pseudo-teachings that only increase imagination. In the Work, however, we are given nothing to feed our imagination about ourselves but quite the contrary. I have found nothing flattering in this teaching. There is nothing flattering, for example, in being told that we are machines that have no Real 'I', that we are nothing but pictures of ourselves, that what we call 'I' is nothing but imagination, that we have no Real Will, that we are a mass of contradictions which we do not notice owing to having so many buffers and different forms of padding, that we are not conscious yet, and so on. It is not pleasant to be told that we are mechanical, just machines, and that we do nothing consciously. But teaching of this kind will not tend to prolong our sleep in the public house if we value and apply it to ourselves. When we realize, even to a small degree, that we are mechanical, and that this machine, in which hovers Imaginary 'I', does everything—we experience a shock. This shock may be nothing more at first than an uneasy feeling that we are not quite what we supposed hitherto. Yet even this feeling is the beginning of awakening and it will increase if nourished because it is truth. All awakening has a sour taste—like going back to school. Now when you begin to awaken from your sleep to a small extent you are beginning to remember yourself—not your Imaginary 'I', but something deeper, which eventually leads to Real 'I', which is our truth. The power of imagination however is so great that people do not wish to wake up and experience even momentarily the harsh taste that comes with a moment of greater consciousness. They try to drown it, even though their suffering and unhappiness in ordinary life-affairs are very great. You can see people who are plagued by one thing or another, from which they could escape if they woke up, deliberately preferring to be plagued rather than face awakening and standing up and leaving the public house and taking their place eventually on the box of their own carriage.

You know that it is said about sacrifice in this Work that, as we are, we have nothing to sacrifice, nothing worth sacrificing, save one thing —namely, our negative states, our negative suffering, our depressions and songs of misery. We can only sacrifice what we love. Our pictures of ourselves cause us to ascribe to ourselves much that does not exist, except in imagination. One cannot sacrifice something that exists only in imagination. But we so love our suffering, our sadness, and disappointments, our negative states, that here we have something to sacrifice so that the direction of our love can change. When I first heard this I thought it a very strange viewpoint and one that did not apply to me until I began to observe myself and then I began to see it was true. You notice how people intoxicate themselves with their own suffering and cannot listen to anyone else's and are always dwelling on their suffering, either openly or secretly, commiserating with themselves. This dwelling on suffering is a form of imaginative drunkenness. It is a fascinating form of drunkenness on which the Driver can spend a great deal of money. Do you know your own typical public house song of misery—often actually sung in an actual public house?

In order to awaken, the Driver must begin to think. The ideas of this Work fall on us at first as from a great distance. We hear a voice saying things over and over again. We do not notice much of what is said. We are dreaming of other things or waiting for our little accumulators to fill up again, so that we can run around once more as before. After a time something falls on the ear of the sleeping Driver. He hears something and stirs and perhaps looks up for a moment. "Yes," he thinks, "that is quite true." He has begun to think. If things go well with him his hearing improves and instead of drinking all the time, he sometimes thinks and sometimes merely drinks. He is still in the public house. His Horse is still starving. The harness is in bits and pieces and the Carriage unrepaired and unpainted. But he is not yet aware of all this. His thinking is not yet strong enough to become emotional and get him on his feet and make him go to the door and look for himself at his inner state.

Now I will skip several steps in the parable and come to the idea that the Driver must climb on to the box. To drive he must ascend above the level of the ground. But before this can happen he must say: "I will drive." That is a decision and it is followed by having to go *up*. Now here is something very strange, because actually he has to go down. He cannot drive from Imaginary 'I', from False Personality, from anything in him that thinks *it can do*. He will never be able to drive from pride or vanity, but only from what is lowest in him in this respect— from what is most simple and humble and genuine and sincere. So to go up he must go down. When he says: "I will drive", if he thinks he can do it himself and for himself, he will break reins, smash wheels and fall off. This decision "I will drive" must be said with a delicacy of understanding that implies the existence of something else being necessary. For where are you going to drive? You will have to be told and then obey and so you are not the Driver in the imperious sense of the man who imagines he *can do* and merely does what he pleases. *To do* in the Work-sense ultimately means to obey the Master who may *suddenly* appear in the Carriage.

826

THE PARABLE OF THE HORSE, CARRIAGE AND DRIVER

PAPER II

We spoke last time about the parable of the Horse, Carriage and Driver, which is one of the parables of the Work dealing with Man's inner situation. You will remember that the Driver in this parable is sitting in the public house and the Horse and Carriage are outside and both in a bad state. The first thing that must happen is that the Driver must awaken from his drunken sleep and attend to the Horse and the Carriage and eventually climb on to the box and take hold of the reins. Then it is said that he may find the Master sitting in the Carriage behind him directing him in which direction to drive. In our last conversation about this parable I dwelt more especially on the point that the Driver has to climb up to the box and indicated that he cannot drive the Horse and Carriage from the level of the ground. From this level he cannot control anything. At the same time I said that a man might come to the point where he says: "I will drive." This happens when through long observation of himself he begins to see that he must do something with himself and can be no longer carried along in the idea of his mechanical life. But although he makes this decision: "I will drive", yet he is far from the possibility of driving. Further stages are necessary and further experiences with himself. His attention will be drawn to certain sides of himself. In that internal communion with oneself that comes from the growing need of the Work and the growing new knowledge of oneself gained from self-observation, he will perceive in many ways that he must climb up in himself before he can drive—that is, reach another level—otherwise he is bound to fail continually and probably simply give up trying to do anything with himself in the way of self-change. In other words, he has to climb up to the level of Self-Remembering because no one can drive his Horse and Carriage unless he has something of that intensity of Consciousness and Self-Awareness that belongs to the Third State of Consciousness to which the Work points. What is it that the Work says is the most important thing for us to practise? It says that we must become more conscious and, in fact, begin to reach the level of Self-Remembering, Self-Awareness and Self-Consciousness. Some people, not understanding the Work, although in contact with it, see that life goes anyhow, that it is a tragedy, a complete muddle, a veritable Babel. And having got to this point they perhaps become negative, without comprehending that this is exactly what the Work teaches about life. They simply stick, not seeing the Work, but only the chaos of life. The Work teaches that a man must see that everything does happen in life and realize that it is because Man is not properly conscious. The Work constantly emphasizes that life is mechanical and that this is due to Man himself being asleep, not properly conscious. Yes, but the Work adds that the practice of this teaching is to make an individual man more conscious when he has realized all this and it gives him instructions as to how to become more conscious and so reach another level of himself. When a man observes himself over a long period sincerely he becomes startled and through this a little more conscious of himself. If he does this with a continual renewal of the meaning of the ideas taught in this Work he will become still more conscious even though it is painful, and begin to reach a level in himself where he can begin in the right way to control lower sides in himself, smaller 'I's in mechanical parts of centres that have hitherto controlled him. It is this rising up in oneself from mechanical death, which one mistook for life, that is the object of the Work. Ordinarily speaking, we live at a low level of ourselves. For example, we live far too much in small unpleasant 'I's, in dull, stupid, mechanical parts of centres, in silly dreams, and so we too contribute to the general sleep of humanity. Yes, we then help to keep the world-sleep. It is exactly wakening out of the sleep of humanity in which one is sharing that is referred to in the parable of the Driver in the public house asleep in dreams and illusions about himself. For a man to wake up he must begin to cease to have illusions and false imagination, and so here comes in the acute work done from self-observation that separates a man from himself and makes it possible to leave the public house.

Let us continue to talk about the stage where the Driver must climb on to the box. Understand that this is not a sharply divided stage, but a gradual process is meant of trial and error. Everything is done by order in the Work—by the Law of Seven. For example, he makes a definite aim and keeps on failing. He learns gradually, but in order, that he cannot keep his aim because he goes to sleep continually and this is because he gets down amongst small 'I's that know nothing about his aim or the Work. He does not *think* enough. I use this word deliberately—i.e. that he does not *think* enough. Here thinking is both remembering and thinking. Thinking and remembering interlock. You have to defend your aim by pumping truth into it as you have seen it. You have to call together in your understanding all truths concerning your aim—I mean, Work-ideas and insights—otherwise your aim will deviate. It will then only become a vague memory instead of being a constantly renewed source of truth to you. All truths of this Work will fight for you when you have got into a more or less central position in yourself in regard to your aim. But you must continually re-visit, re-stimulate yourself in regard to these truths and insights. The Work fights for you only when you engage with it mentally through emotional acknowledgement. I said recently that if the ideas or truths of this Work stood round you and transmitted their force you would be able *to do*. Owing to our limited consciousness and our level of mind which only holds one thing at a time, this is not possible. It is possible at a higher level, however—that is, light increases as our level is raised. With regard to everything bad and wrong in you which you may have noticed in action as well as in thought, the ideas of this Work, if perceived as true, will fight for you. Only in that way can what is wrong and bad and unnecessary in you be changed. You cannot do it yourself. You go to war. Work-'I's will fight with mechanical 'I's if you go on giving them the force of the ideas of this Work and renewing it always. It is they that fight for you, these Work-'I's, contacting the Work-ideas. For example, when you are negative a Work-idea suddenly comes into your mind, and you find it possible to fight with that negative state—or it simply vanishes. This is an example of the Work fighting in you and for you. That is why valuation of the Work is so important. It is useless to think you can do all this yourself and by yourself. This thing that you call yourself is useless and as often as not it is your worst self, your most mechanical, habitual self, which cannot possibly lead you any-where and will never withstand any temptation to sleep. Everyone who has felt this Work deeply and over a sufficient length of time has already other selves that can fight. But we try to fight ourselves with ourselves—our habitual selves—and not with our new selves. When we are negative we try to fight our negative state with this thing "ourself". And often we make aims when we are negative—that is, when we are at an even lower level than our ordinary "ourself" is.

Now when a man is in a negative state he mechanically thinks lies. The truth of the ideas of the Work does not reach him. But it is this that can fight for you. So when you are negative it is important to try to think the truth, by an effort. A negative state, allowed by inner slackness to persist, drives away the Work and all its possible influence on you. When a man is in a negative state the negative part of his Emotional Centre induces a current of lies that flows through his Intellectual Centre. Negative states are only supported by lies in the Intellectual Centre. You cannot think a lie if you are in a good state. It is usually the same lies that are brought up, if you observe yourself closely. When a negative state in the Emotional Centre induces lies in the Intellectual Centre it means that wrong connections in thought and memory are made, often traceable very far into the past, so that in consequence they have become habits of thinking which have never been challenged by yourself. This is a bad state to be in. People begin to die from such lies. In these lies that are excited by negative states in the Intellectual Centre important things are left out and unimportant things are over-emphasized, or what is pure imagination is mingled with what is real, especially with the aid of pride and vanity and suspicion which have never been corrected, and many other self-injurious distortions are made, due to blaming and to internal account-making in general. All this remains incredible to one, unless one catches oneself through self-observation in the act of enjoying these lies. In this inner tangle many live most of their lives without making any attempt to deal strongly with all this dirt and mess laid down in their psychic life. Now there can be no question of its being possible to climb up on to the box as long as one is full of all this dirt and mess of lies or evasions or distortions of the truth which form a kind of midden within us. You will try to climb up on to the box full of this mess of lies and, since you always feel yourself as the leading person in yourself, you will always feel these habitual lies in yourself which can only be annihilated by a new revelation of yourself coming from the fuller light of consciousness, belonging to the Third State of Consciousness—that is, to Self-Awareness. This is where the light will cure you. The light of consciousness will make it impossible for these habitual lies to cling so closely and to form so large a part of the customary feeling of yourself whereby you have hitherto recognized yourself.

So mounting the box is obviously a long process and, as I said, there is an order in it. The question is of course this: "What mounts the box?" If a mass of habitual, ingrained lies mounts the box nothing will happen. You can in no wise say that the Driver has mounted the box, because the Driver must be purified by the Work. When he is about to mount he comes to a definite test. Is he really sufficiently awakened yet? Is he really prepared to drive although perhaps he may have said: "I will drive." He may get up to the box in imagination but in this case he is still asleep and he will fail. Then he may persuade himself that he has done his very best and feel self-pity and give up for the time being. But he has as yet done nothing really. He has not faced himself with himself and with the difficulties in his Being. So the whole thing remains purely imagination. He is making effort in imagination but he is not making real effort. People can take the whole of this Work in their imagination and never make any real effort whatsoever. Now when you make a real effort or a relatively real effort, you never become negative when you fail. This is a sign. Your failure makes you think more and remember more. But when you make an effort in imagination, an imaginary effort, not a real effort, you become negative very quickly and pass into your gallery of self-pity with all its ancestral portraits. Now the outer is like the inner. If you go to a carpenter's shop and pretend to saw a piece of wood you are making an imaginary effort. You may handle lots of tools and make a noise as if you were working but you are really doing nothing and you will get no result. It is exactly the same thing in the inner psychological world. You have got really to make an effort, as far as is in your power, in your psychological world. Take as it were your self-satisfaction which is the bane of some in this Work—that is, the worst thing in them. No one who is filled with self-satisfaction can possibly do this Work and any idea of their climbing up on to the box is quite out of the question. Why? Because a self-satisfied man or woman feels that he or she is already on the box. Actually they are still fast asleep in the public house spending all their money in generous forms of imagination about themselves. However, when we begin to realize practically and by direct insight and by mental perception that we are nothing and cannot do, we are very close to being able to get on the box. So one goes down to go up. But no one will ever realize his own nothingness—I mean, genuinely and not theoretically, save through the power of this Work. And for a very good reason. To realize one's own nothingness in a real way without having this Work to hold on to might easily destroy a man or turn him into a mass of negative emotion. But to realize increasingly, and in order of experiences, one's own nothingness has nothing to do with negative emotion. Quite the contrary, it can begin to transmit the Work. Yet one does not climb up to the box simply by realizing one's own nothingness but by a double and paradoxical process in which one has to make effort on the one side and yet know on the other side that one can do nothing without help.

Quaremead, Ugley, January 12, 1946

THE UNOBSERVED SIDE OF OURSELVES

Recently we had a conversation once more about this dark side of ourselves. I explained before that this means the side of ourselves that we do not know or do not accept and that the object of self-knowledge by the method of self-observation was to bring this not yet known side of ourselves into the light of consciousness. The whole object of self-knowledge is to make more conscious our knowledge of ourselves. The idea is that when you have many things in you that you do not know and do not accept—i.e. things that are not conscious to you yourself—then these things complicate your life very much and cause all sorts of situations which would be avoided through self-knowledge. In general it can be said that we put this unknown or unconscious side of ourselves into other people or, to use a term in modern psychology, we project this side of ourselves and see it in other people. For example, we see them as liars, or unfaithful, or mean, or untrustworthy, and so on, in relation to our own qualities in this respect. The Work says, in regard to this, that we live in a very small part of ourselves. This means that our consciousness extends to a very small part of ourselves. Such a situation makes us very badly related to other people, to life and to ourselves. The idea of this Work is to enlarge consciousness. We have, we are told, to become far more conscious to ourselves through direct self-observation, so that all sorts of narrow pictures that we have of ourselves are destroyed and we begin to live in a larger edition of ourselves. We can take it as a general rule in the Work that when we are up against someone else we may be sure that that is the very thing we have to work on in ourselves. This gives us an entirely different orientation and in my opinion it is the beginning of real work. The thing you criticize so much in other people is something lying in the dark side of yourself that you do not know or acknowledge. You only see this dark side, this unconscious, unknown side of yourself, reflected into other people so that it is always their fault and never your fault. Everyone lives in a very small consciousness, a very petty world of self-reactions, of personal reactions, and this small space that they live in is full of all sorts of sensitivenesses. As you will admit, some people live in this small part of themselves in which consciousness is confined to a small area of the totality of their psyche. What keeps us all in this small consciousness is the action of buffers, of pictures of ourselves, of fixed opinions, of negative attitudes. When we are in such a condition the dark side of ourselves is very great, but when the light of self-observation is thrown into this dark side, consciousness of ourselves increases through self-knowledge, and after a time we begin to feel differently from what we used to feel. The centre of gravity of 'I' in us begins to change. In other words, Imaginary 'I', this 'I' that we are always serving and keep going, which is not ourselves at all, begins to be dissolved. We find that we are nothing like what we imagined and as this takes place so do our relations to other people expand. Instead of living in a narrow world of prejudices, of violent likes and dislikes, owing to the expansion of consciousness in ourselves we find a larger relationship with other people. This is due to a growth of consciousness by the method of uncritical observation which is the basis of the whole Work on its practical side. The result is that this sensitive bundle of personal reactions, this continually being upset and hurt, this inability to meet any criticism from others, begins to disappear, and we enter a larger world. We become more universal. We no longer feed our pictures of ourselves as we did. We no longer think of ourselves in the same exclusive way, but begin to realize our own helplessness, so we can endure the helplessness of other people. Now the Work says we must endure one another's unpleasant manifestations. But it is impossible to endure one another's unpleasant manifestations in the right sense of the meaning of the word unless we see our own unpleasant manifestations and know them and accept them. This destroys illusions about ourselves. Unless you accept your fault-finding side you will always be negative because this sensitive bundle of personal reactions surrounded by the darkness of yourself that you do not know or acknowledge will be the chief thing that you meet life with. And it will be something that is completely unadapted to life, something incomplete, inadequate, that will cause you misery all through your life unless you correct it by conscious work on yourself. Your little personal ego-world will be upset at every moment and you will have no strength for life and no endurance unless you meet this dark side by conscious recognition and realize that everything that you are so critical of in others is expressing itself in you all the time but is not yet included in your consciousness of yourself. So you can see why the Work lays such stress on this Imaginary 'I' that people live in. Suppose you criticize a man who has made conscious to himself a considerable part of this dark side. That is to say, this man has brought up into his consciousness by his own work many sides of himself that he never realized existed in him, and has accepted them. Will such a man bear criticism more easily than a person who is still living in pictures of himself and has never really faced himself by direct observation? I am quite sure that if a man through the power of this Work really observes himself, really notices when he criticizes and blames others, and always brings it down to something in himself that he had not recognized, such a man will be far more balanced and therefore far more capable of enduring the next step in inner development. So many anxieties would go, so many illnesses would disappear, so many emotional crises would vanish, so many storms in tea-cups would cease to exist. You are accused, for example, of being a liar. You furiously defend yourself, you practise all the arts of self-justifying—which, I may remind you, is one of the specific things we have to work on—and an immense uproar results. Of course you are a liar. But if you are always going to keep your lying out of your conscious sphere and refuse to know it and refuse to acknowledge it, how can you accept it? You are always defending yourself against yourself, in order to keep your Imaginary 'I' going, your imagination of what you are. But suppose you have made this dark side far more conscious and you are accused of being a liar, you will not then react from your bundle of sensitive personal reactions, or from a picture of yourself, because you know quite well that you also are a liar and that you often lie. So you will accept criticism without changing colour. Many things are said in the Work about realizing our own nothingness. It was said at some time or other that a man or a woman in the Work must come to the point at which they realize their own nothingness before they can take a step further. What does it mean to be *something*? I will try to explain to you what I understand by this. You feel, for example, that you are broadminded and tolerant. I think a little real self-observation and remembering yourself will shew you that you are not and that under some circumstances you are very intolerant and extremely narrow-minded. Now this recognition that you are sometimes intolerant and narrow-minded will neutralize the picture that you have of yourself that you are always tolerant and broad-minded. The result will be that you will feel that you are *nothing* in this respect. You then cease to have in yourself aims about being something. You will no longer go about saying: "Thank God, I am broad-minded and tolerant," because you will remember, through the memory that Observing 'I' has laid down in you, so many occasions on which you were the reverse, so instead of being something artificial through buffers, you will become *nothing* in regard to this special quality on which you prided yourself. You will learn, in other words, not to trust this idea that you have of yourself. It is not a moral issue that we are concerned with here but a broadening of consciousness. Self-observation is like a ray of light that penetrates the darkness inside us.

The result of this ray of light is to bring into consciousness the unknown and unaccepted sides of ourselves. This softens everything in us and takes away a great deal of our violence. We all have to overcome in ourselves the violent man and the violent woman because all violence is due to lack of consciousness. If you can see another as you see yourself you will never be violent towards him or her. You will notice that you are only violent when you think you are not like the other person, that you are not such a brute or a beast or a liar and so on. This one-sidedness makes violence.

At a recent conversation one person said: "When you feel violent towards a person and make an effort not to feel violent the next time you see the person, you find that he or she seems to have changed. Can this be that *you* have changed—not the other person?" Yes, this is quite right. By becoming more conscious in the act of violence you have not reacted mechanically and so you yourself have changed a little. But the supreme change comes when you can see that what you are violent about is something in yourself that you do not accept. Then if you can keep that conscious you will never be violent to the other person, which, in the real sense of the word, is sympathy. The real meaning of sympathy is feeling *with* the other person. But you cannot feel *with* another person unless your own feelings are conscious to you. Sometimes in private Work-talks people discover that they both have been through the same experience. This is *sympathy*. But sympathy in the sentimental sense is useless and it always contains a grain of conceit and patronage. If you want to help anyone in this Work you must feel at a lower level than they are through your own self-knowledge.

Now another person said in a recent conversation: "I found it difficult to find the same thing in myself that makes me violent towards other people, until I began to see that it might take a different form." Yes, this is a very good observation, especially when you rather pride yourself on something that you have a picture of yourself as being or doing and you find that someone else does not satisfy you in this respect and get violent with them as a result. In that case your violence comes from unrecognized, unacknowledged sides of yourself which are very close to what you pride yourself on. Let me try to explain this more fully. If you are a very careful person and pride yourself on it you may get violent with a person whom you do not think careful according to your standards, but you will always find that you are not careful in the way that you imagine you are and that there are many gaps in your so-called carefulness which you project into other people and blame them for. You may be sure that you are acting from a picture here and not from self-knowledge and that your picture may have had a justification from your point of view, but yet it does not correspond to the truth because no picture ever does. You may be careful but you also imagine that you are careful and your imagination prevents you from seeing how careless you are often about very important matters. A man, for instance, may pride himself on being reliable and blame people for not being reliable, and even blame them violently, without seeing that he is not reliable in many other ways and that the reliability is a picture reinforced by imagination based on a fact. As soon as you think you are good at something and your pride and vanity enter this idea that you are good at something, you will always find that you are most sensitive here and most liable to become violent. In other words, you are being *something*. If you could see all the mistakes and blunders that you make yourself, if you could see your contradictions, if you could become conscious of your failures, in regard to what you think you are good at, you would no longer be sensitive or violent but tolerant and at the same time would have more understanding. Sometimes people cannot allow that they are not good at things because of a certain inner weakness in them. What is this inner weakness due to? It is due to this unacknowledged side, the dark side, which, as it were, contains, amongst other things, all that they are not willing to accept. You may be good at a thing, but you must also acknowledge gradually, especially as you get older and need a wider consciousness, that you are not good at it at the same time and realize, in short, that you are not what you thought. Then you no longer identify in the way you did and you become simpler inside. This letting in of the other side, of the dark or not observed side, does not weaken you, but really strengthens you. Someone asked: "Is it bad, the dark side?" You must understand that everything you do not acknowledge appears at first sight bad. It is the devil because the devil is always what is unknown, unacknowledged or not understood. If someone had invented the radio a few centuries ago he would have been burned as an agent of the devil. The dark side does not mean anything evil in itself. It means simply that it is evil to you, with your present estimation of yourself. It is evil to you, because when you admit it into your consciousness your present estimation of yourself will change. The result will be that you will be much better than you were before. You will be much better because your present estimation of yourself kept up by imagination, and by buffers, and by pictures, and by continual lying, has been weakened, and you have entered a larger world of consciousness. You should not think of the dark side as evil except to your Imaginary 'I' which is one's worst evil. If your Imaginary 'I' is full of imagination about what you are, and if this imagination becomes destroyed by admitting what is antagonistic to you, you will begin to lose this wrong, sensitive Imaginary 'I', and your consciousness will broaden out and you will cease to be what you imagine yourself to be and move a step towards Real 'I'. All the Work is against Imaginary 'I' with which each one of us faces life so inadequately. The teaching of the Work sets out to destroy the power of Imaginary 'I' but at first everything that threatens Imaginary 'I' seems to be very evil—in fact, the devil. That is why I think it was once said in the Work: "The devil is also necessary." So many people identify themselves with God without any justification and even imagine that they have intercourse with God continually. All this belongs to Imaginary 'I' and in such cases God has indeed to take the aspect of the devil and destroy this imagination, these pictures, these phantasies, this self-merit, and all this nonsense that the Work attacks so strongly in each of us.

Now for practical work I would suggest once more that you really observe yourself when you are critical or violent towards another person in the Work and turn the whole thing round the opposite way and try to find in yourself what it is that you are critical and violent about in the other person. This will make your dark, unobserved side more conscious to you because you may be certain that if you are very critical and violent about someone else it is simply a projection of what is in you, in this dark—i.e. unconscious—side of yourself, the side that you do not know about yet, the side you have not yet observed, the side that is to become the object of your self-knowledge. Let me remind you here that self-observation is a very clean dry light and that it will brook no falsehood and will give you no self-satisfaction at first. Let me remind you also that if you are negative towards someone else, no matter what is the external cause, the fact that you are negative is your own fault from the Work point of view. We have to squeeze negative emotion out of ourselves like wringing out washing. It is you yourself who have to deal with this negative state, quite apart from the external exciting causes, and here the whole object and meaning of the Work comes in. If you have the strength of the Work, little can touch you from without except when you are asleep for too long. It is a sign. But you can always right the state by work and understanding. Everyone has difficulties in this Work with everyone else. Do not think that my mission is necessarily to decrease these difficulties. Everyone is work for someone else. Just imagine what would happen if we were to be all sweet outside and hissing like snakes inside. No, we have got to work in regard to one another and not expect ideal people or surroundings. This is the second line of the Work—work in connection with other people. It is always my fault if I am negative, whatever the external situation. Does this give a different centre of gravity at once from the life centre of gravity? *I* have to work. And I *can* work if I *will*. And I have to take my life as work and work on my life. So there must be no "if only". I remember some people saying in the early Work: "If only we had much nicer people in the Group." But the Group, whatever it may be, is simply a general sample of life and that is exactly the sphere in which we all have to do our work in connection with others. It is well to realize this deeply because it lightens the Work through acceptance.

ON PUTTING FEELING OF 'I' INTO THE WORK

We spoke recently about the Driver mounting the box of the Carriage. It has often been said in the Work that unless a man believes in Greater Mind it is impossible to do this Work. The Work teaches that there is a Conscious Circle of Humanity. The Conscious Circle of Humanity always through the ages has tried to awaken the Mechanical Circle of Humanity. But it cannot do this by compulsion. You may remember the idea of Man, one of the great sign-posts in the Work. The Work says that Man is created a self-developing organism, but to develop he must believe in Greater Mind. As you have probably already noticed, Nature, the external world, does not tell you anything. It is neutral. You can come to one conclusion or another about Nature. You can say God exists or you can equally well say that God does not exist. Why is there not clear evidence of Greater Mind? It was once said that suppose God were floating overhead on a cloud it would destroy the whole idea of God, who is invisible, and a spirit that only Truth finds within us. People would have to believe in God. People would be compelled by the evidence of their outer senses to acknowledge the existence of the Higher. But since Man is created a *self*-developing organism, this would destroy his meaning. In other words, we have to come to our own conclusions through our own individual thinking. A man can only develop in the esoteric sense through his own individual understanding by work on his knowledge and Being. Otherwise he could not be self-developing. I have often thought how disappointing it would be to draw your bedroom curtains in the morning and see God hovering overhead on some brazen cloud staring at you. And you would feel far more unbelief than ever before. We are left in a kind of freedom to choose for ourselves and find our way to the meaning of our own existence. The realization that Greater Mind exists is an internal process—a way. As you know, a sign of Being is the possession of Magnetic Centre. A man who has Magnetic Centre has the feeling that there is something else apart from external values, but the idea of Greater Mind will not thereby exist in him. For example, such a man may become aware that there are two great streams of literature in life, one the ordinary stream, including the newpapers, Financial Times, Sporting News, murders, politics, and so on, and another that is remote from all this and apparently speaks about something quite different—as the Gospels, for instance. But he will not thereby understand about Greater Mind or Conscious Humanity. Now we understand that the Conscious Circle of Humanity cannot compel Man to believe, owing to the nature of the case, and the conditions under which Man is born. You cannot force a self-developing organism. If you study the Ray of Creation—and people should think about it more—you will understand that the Will of the Absolute only reaches this Earth through a number of increasing laws and influences—through an increasing machinery. We in our position in the Ray of Creation are immensely far from the Absolute. We are under 48 orders of laws with their conflicting influences and meanings. It was once said that if the Absolute were to manifest itself directly the whole of the Ray of Creation would be destroyed and that it would be like playing a game of cards in which suddenly all the rules of the game were destroyed. As a result the whole game would vanish. When we speak of Greater Mind we mean at least that there exist Intelligences greater than ours comparable, in comparison with ours, to Divine Intelligence. The Ray of Creation is full of this meaning. There is higher and higher meaning, a ladder of Intelligence. If a man is blind to this—to the Ray—his higher parts of Centres, the emotional and intellectual parts which conduct his meaning, will never awaken. His eyes will be on the ground. On the other hand, if he has a right Magnetic Centre and has, say, already distinguished between the two classes of literature of which we have spoken, and especially if he feels that this life cannot be explained in terms of itself but must have some other interpretation on some other level of meaning, then he is on the way to perceive for himself, by inner perception, the existence of Greater Mind. And in consequence of this perception that Greater Mind exists he is capable himself of receiving with right valuation the teachings that eventually originate in Greater Mind.

As you know, we live in a very small part of our centres—we live in the basement of the house in which we psychologically exist. It is said in the Work that Man is the wrong way up. It is also said in regard to the bodies of Man, that he works the wrong way round. If we turn our eyes down to the ground like animals and look only downwards to the external world and interpret everything only according to our sense-evidence, we are thinking the wrong way round. We are taking the view that Nature creates herself. How could that be? We then think that matter makes mind. This is Plato's definition of a materialist. He is upside down. The Ray of Creation shews us that the Mind of the Absolute creates the successive condensations of matter. It teaches us that we live in a created Universe. This belief turns a man the right way up.

I will make a brief comment about the feeling of 'I' in this Work—that is, of 'I' being in the Work. Eventually Work can become stronger than life—Work-'I' stronger than life-'I'. What the Work gradually lays down in one can become stronger eventually than what life has laid down and can control it. Then one is the right way round—that is, one is not driven from the wrong end. You remember that this idea is clearly represented in the diagram of the four possible bodies of Man, called first, second, third and fourth.

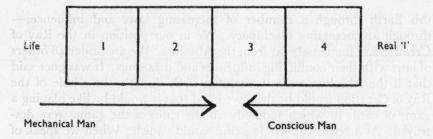

| Life | 1 | 2 | 3 | 4 | Real 'I' |

Mechanical Man → ← Conscious Man

Let us suppose a man attains to this level of development and that Real 'I' or Master directs him. Then he works in the direction 4, 3, 2, 1. An ordinary man is worked from the other end and in place of organized bodies 2, 3 and 4 there is nothing formed in him and he is not in touch with Real 'I'—in fact, he is in the position of the man in the public house. The question I will put is: Do you think a man who does not feel the existence of Greater Mind can ever attain to Real 'I' in himself? Can he reach a higher level of himself if he believes there is nothing higher? There is one thing quite definite that can be experienced in the Work—that is, a change in the feeling of 'I'. No one can change themselves without change in the feeling of themselves. This means a change in the feeling of 'I'—of what they feel as 'I' and say 'I' to. But do you think any change possible without believing in Greater Mind?

I want you all to think for a practical exercise about all the Diagrams that indicate something higher, to go over them in your minds.

Quaremead, Ugley, January 26, 1946

NOTE ON THE EFFECT OF EARLY IMPRESSIONS

Our earlier impressions tend to have a stronger effect than later ones. This can produce in us a feeling of unreality as we get older. In earlier life the impressions laid down on rolls in our centres entering *via* the senses, and also those from inside originating from the imagination, are more vivid and intimate and real. So when we return to scenes of earlier life and find everything altered by new buildings and shops, and trees cut down, lanes vanished and so on, it seems unreal and we cannot believe it, as it were—cannot believe the evidence of our senses—because the strength of our earlier impressions on rolls contradicts the impressions entering us at the moment. A sense of unreality results.

It is the same with earlier imaginings. In youth a person may identify with many intimate imaginings of what he or she is going to grow into, what position, what palace, they will possess, and how many servants and what chorus of praise and sympathy will surround them. These and similar imaginings can form very strong impressions on rolls in centres. The result will be that in growing up a sense of discontent or of disappointment, or a sadness, pervades the outlook, the cause being unknown to the person although it is still evident in the imagination. The tendency will be to look backwards because life as it is experienced will seem in some way unreal, the reason being that in view of the forms of expectancy laid down by the early imaginings the life is not what was expected. The cure for both of these sources of unreality is the idea of recurrence and the thoughts that come from it when we realize that the life will return as before and if we want it different we must work on ourselves now. As we know, work on imagination is one of the things that we have to do.

It is some time since imagination has been spoken about. Among the many things that uselessly consume force, one is undirected imagination—where we lie passive to our imagination and bathe ourselves in it. This gives a distaste for life. Try to observe at least one form in yourself. Then try to observe something laid down in rolls by imagination that causes you to expect in a way that does not correspond with what you get. This makes you unable to appreciate what you have.

In this connection another Work-thought that cures is that one's Being attracts one's life and that therefore it is no good blaming life.

Quaremead, Ugley, February 2, 1946

ON KEEPING THE WORK ALIVE IN ONESELF

In this Work the Will-part of us must be affected with love of what the intellectual part knows and believes. We realize through self-observation that we do not will what we know. The Emotional Centre is the seat of the Will, the Intellectual Centre is the seat of what we know, and according to the diagrams of the Work the intellectual part of us is the seat of consciousness. We have, in this diagram to which I am referring, Consciousness put in the top compartment, Will put in the second, and Attention in this third or lowest compartment. On one occasion it was said that no one can keep his aim in the Work unless Consciousness, Will and Attention co-operate. When a man makes an aim he usually makes it from a small side of himself, his knowledge, and very soon forgets it—that is, ceases to be conscious of it. He makes his aim from knowledge. But he is not sufficiently conscious of his aim to maintain it. In the meantime his will—i.e. his several wills—go in different and opposite directions and his attention is scattered in endless ways. The combination of Consciousness, Will and Attention is not achieved.

We spoke recently of what it means to put the feeling of 'I' into the Work. In what sense can any of you say that you have a feeling of 'I' in this Work? What do you mean by it? And how often are you during the day aware of this feeling of 'I' as something quite distinct from the ordinary changing feelings of 'I' that we have in our general affairs of life? We are given the task of remembering ourselves at least once or twice a day. Do you find this is possible or is it merely a matter of memory without anything real resulting? To remember oneself means to get into a quite different state in oneself. A different feeling of 'I' belongs to this state because it is a lifting up of consciousness to a higher level—that is, out of the so-called waking state or second state of consciousness that we have in ordinary affairs which is peopled by small 'I's. To remember oneself something of Will must be contributed to the action. It is not a thought nor can it be a matter of mere memory. Now I may remember that I have to remember myself but not actually remember myself—that is, it remains a question of memory and nothing more. This is a common state to be in. All the same I may attribute merit to myself in having remembered that I should remember myself. It is like remembering that you must write that letter and feeling meritorious at remembering and not writing the letter. You must *need* to remember yourself in order to do so and when need comes in Will comes in —that is: *I* desire to remember myself, *I* wish to remember myself. There is a sentence that used to be given to us to say in the earlier Work: "I *wish* to remember myself". This is nothing to do with "I think I should remember myself." A great deal of one's personal work is spent in thinking and not doing what we think. The Will-part of us is not involved and so we go back to the opening phrase: "The Will-part of us must be affected with love of what the intellectual part knows and believes."

This marriage between the intellect and the Will so often spoken of in esoteric literature of the past is indicated in this Work by the teaching that there must be a union between new Knowledge and Being before any new understanding is born in a man. From Knowledge alone we can and do make many intellectual decisions—in fact, we constantly make them—but all this takes place in only one centre, the Intellectual Centre, and the Emotional Centre is not involved. We have all heard how this Work must be received first by the intellect and how first of all it must be registered in the most mechanical side of the Intellectual Centre—i.e. the formatory part. Unless the Work is well registered here it remains weak, like imperfect French. But it will remain inoperative unless a person thinks about the ideas and applies them to his own Being. Now our Will belongs to the Being-side of us because it is our level of Being that eventually decides what we do—our vanity perhaps or our pride. I may intellectually decide to act in a certain way but my level of Being causes me to act in a quite different way. I therefore increasingly perceive something in me that acts independently and ignores my fleeting decisions. On many occasions it was said in the earlier days that the object of this Work is to awaken the Emotional Centre which is the seat of the Will but that this is not possible unless the intellectual part of us awakens first. What does it mean that the Intellectual Centre must awaken in this Work? It means to begin with that we no longer take the Work as something on the blackboard that we have to memorize. The next stage is that the mind begins to see the truth of the ideas of the Work. When a man begins to see the truth of this Work after years of personal work he passes into a difficult stage of it because the state of his Being does not yet become affected by the truth of the knowledge taught him by the Work that he sees now through Intellectual Centre. It might be said that this is really the first stage of the Work because then his Being becomes a real problem and the observation of his Being becomes a matter of real practical concern to him. When a man begins to see the truth of this Work for himself, without the help of others, he begins to have his own source of work in himself. It grows on him. He is, to a small extent, awake—that is, awake in some small part of his mind—but if he imagines that this is enough he is greatly mistaken. In fact, he is only beginning to understand what the Work means in regard to himself and what he has to work on and why.

At a recent meeting someone said: "When you really see your position in the Ray of Creation, see how low down *you* are, and what possibilities there are, everything begins then." This is a good observation because it is an example of how the Work can become for a moment emotional. Some pay little attention to the great cosmological diagrams, not understanding that they are a source of making the Work really emotional and so connecting the Emotional Centre and the Intellectual Centre. The Ray of Creation can prove the most emotional diagram of all. Now when the Work becomes emotional it begins to affect the Will-part of us. It begins to affect our Being. A thought does not affect our Being in the same way as an emotion does. You have all noticed that some emotional crisis affects you far more deeply than any thoughts and may indeed alter you for the moment. Alter what? Alter your ordinary forms of Will, your desires. It no doubt sounds strange to some that the diagrams of the Work really can awaken the emotions. But is it so strange when you think that all these diagrams tell us of the existence of Greater Mind, of what is above us, of what is greater than ourselves? You know that at present, as we are, the Emotional Centre is governed by self-emotions. Emotions of self-liking, of vanity, of self-love, dominate the Emotional Centre and so make it so susceptible to negative emotions, as when, for example, our vanity is hurt. It is only in the presence of something far greater that the Emotional Centre awakens to its true work and begins to lead towards Higher Emotional Centre. It can be said that we do not bring the ideas of the Work into our minds sufficiently every day to keep the Work alive in us. Every idea, every teaching, every diagram, in this Work, belongs to one organic whole, and no side of it can be left cold for too long. We do not, for example, think nearly enough about esoteric teaching itself throughout the ages and what its object was and from whom it came. We do not see enough difference between this teaching and life. Nor do we realize that this Work can only be kept alive in us and active through conscious efforts to think about it and to keep on re-arranging it in our minds and giving it a value greater than the business of daily life. The Work must be above our life-'I's however much we have to use our life-'I's in our ordinary tasks. Otherwise the Work falls down into mechanical parts of centres and is there assailed by endless doubts and, in short, torn to bits or, indeed, crucified. One significance of Christ being crucified lies in the fact that in life esoteric teaching and psychological understanding are always dragged down and crucified by literal sensual minds. This idea is shewn in the Work by the fact that C influences sown into the world by Conscious Humanity always turn into B influences and indeed sometimes into A influences.

I now wish to speak shortly about the subject of keeping the Work alive in oneself once it has been formed to a certain extent. It has to be protected. That is the main point. It has to be regarded as something in us that is forming itself and that we have to be careful about. This is a curious relationship and perhaps some of you have not realized it. You, the ordinary you in life, have to keep the Work alive in you although this 'you' is not in the Work. What the Work is forming is in you but you are not it and so you have to keep it alive. It is like this: If you think that you can work all the time you will have things in the wrong order. You are mistaking yourself for something forming in you to which you have to attend a great deal at intervals. No one can work all through the day and night but you can be aware of the Work in you and retain the feeling of 'I', that the Work is in you—i.e. a continual awareness of it. This does not mean always thinking of the Work while you are doing your daily tasks because then you are in mechanical 'I's and your thoughts tend to run on mechanically and create an inner confusion. On one occasion it was said in answer to some question that I have forgotten: "It will be work for you not to work." I understood this to mean, at least in one sense, that always dimly thinking of the Work in the midst of life-affairs and worrying about it is quite useless. Either work or do not work. And remember that all work is always a relatively conscious action. But I see no reason why a person trying to thread a needle should think it necessary to meditate on the Ray of Creation. I am sure that the only result will be to connect negative feelings with the Ray of Creation. If you get constant wrong associations with Work-ideas the laying down of the Work in your mind will be in a tangle. The transforming instrument will be wrongly connected. It is just like those people who are very fond of explaining how sadly they failed to remember themselves. They connect Self-Remembering with negative associations so that every time they try to remember themselves there are dragged in automatically these negative associations. You usually find that people like this enjoy being failures.

To return to this early formation of the Work in oneself—it can be compared, as it were, with a small new Being gradually being organized in oneself whose will is scarcely enough to be felt as yet. If we felt it, we should feel a new Will in us. When we take some life-situation as Work our reaction to it is different from our mechanical reaction and the results are different. In such a case we behave towards the life-situation more consciously, according to our level of understanding. The whole power of the Work in our understanding would transform every life-situation—but we have no such understanding at present and, if we are sincere and do not pretend, we know this and acknowledge our knowledge. Now we can establish in ourselves with certainty that to take a life-situation in a Work-way rather than in a mechanical way changes our relation to the life-situation. This is one of the things that we can see for ourselves *is so*. That is, we can be certain about it. In the earlier days of this teaching, this point was often insisted on— namely, "What can you be certain about in the Work so far?" Start from that. When we have no certainties in the Work, we have no centre of gravity, no *point* in the Work, as it is called. We have not started, or rather, this new thing has not started. It used often to be said that for some years we can only work through borrowed force, but that the time will come when this borrowed force, coming from another, is gradually withdrawn, until one has to find one's own force to continue. It is at this stage that it is so necessary to establish certainties in oneself concerning the Work. This demands a fresh reviewing *at intervals* of all the ideas of the Work and gaining another crop of meaning from them. It is only from the living ideas of the Work that has life in itself that one's own Work-'I's can be kept alive. This new thing, this new Being, has to be nourished until it is strong enough to maintain its own existence. For this reason we have to act in such a way as to protect this Being in ourselves and nourish it. All new insights, observations and experiences that we can establish for ourselves as certainties nourish it. It is particularly the inner perception of the truth of one or another of the Work-ideas that nourishes it. For through this the side of the Will is drawn into this new thing. When you will to do this Work your Will passes through the knowledge you have of it and the two increase.

When the Work in us becomes stronger than life, the whole machine reverses, is driven from the opposite end. Then the Work is stronger than life. For us, however, the question is how to keep this small, weak Being alive until it can become active. So we are like guardians to ourselves and it is here that often our cleverest life-'I's can help in protecting this new thing from life 'I's. There are many 'I's that hate the Work and seek to ridicule it because they are threatened with death. It is indeed just by the struggle with these 'I's that seek to destroy the Work in us that this new thing sown by the Work can grow and, as I said, in this clever 'I's can help. One must not let doubting, slanderous, sneering 'I's attack this new thing that is forming but meet

844

them cleverly. So one must wage war with them *outside* the place where the Work is forming this new Being in us and not let them enter that place. They enter *us*—yes—but must not penetrate to that inner place we are guarding. Bad talking opens the way to this place directly and destroys anything forming there. That is why so much emphasis is laid on the danger of bad talking about the Work itself.

Quaremead, Ugley, February 9, 1946

COMMENTARY ON ONE'S LEVEL OF BEING

One person writes to me as follows: "*I realize that I can do and experience nothing beyond my level of Being.*"

My reply is that this observation, which is an intelligent one, divides itself into two parts—i.e. "I can do nothing beyond my level of Being" and "I can experience nothing beyond my level of Being." In regard to the first part: "I can do nothing beyond my level of Being"—this is correct. A man cannot do beyond his level of Being because his level of Being will always make him do what he has always done. This, in the Work-sense, is not doing. It is not doing in the Work-sense because it is mechanical. What we do mechanically according to our level of Being is not doing. We may think we are doing—in fact, we think we are doing at every moment—but IT is doing. Our mechanical Being is doing. To do, in the Work-sense, is to go against mechanical doing, and mechanical man cannot do in the Work-sense. Whatever he does, in the ordinary sense, is due to his mechanical Being. The observation is quite correct in so far as it says: "I realize that I cannot do beyond my level of Being."

Now the second part of the observation: "I cannot experience beyond my level of Being," is not correct. If it were correct, no one could shift from where he is. Everyone would be tied down to his level of Being and would be incapable of growing—that is, would be incapable of any growth of Being. A man, a woman, can experience beyond their level of Being momentarily. They can have flashes of something that belongs beyond their level of Being. This is what can carry us on. Otherwise our situation would be hopeless. If we did not know a little what a thing was like we would not seek it.

Another question was asked: "*How is it that we can experience beyond our level of Being?*"

The answer is that our level of Being is not one thing but is composed on a small scale of slightly different levels of Being. This was recently compared with telegraph wires on one of the ordinary telegraph posts some of which are higher and some of which are lower. Put differently, it means that we have 'I's on different levels in our Being —that is, better and worse 'I's. We have, for example, 'I's connected

845

with Magnetic Centre, and 'I's that are simply immersed in life. We can speak about our general level of Being as a level characterized by sleep and mechanicalness, but if we take our Being on a different scale —i.e. on a much smaller scale—our Being, although it is mechanical in the general sense, has within it gradations or degrees of less mechanical and more mechanical. For this reason it is possible for us to experience something beyond our general or average level of Being. As I said before, unless it were so we would be fixed down permanently in our present level of Being. This means that our receptive side is greater than our doing side. We therefore find ourselves in the position in this Work of being able to *see* better than we can *do*. In certain situations we have flashes of understanding in which perhaps we see quite clearly what we should do and yet we find it impossible to do what we have seen. We are dragged down by our average level of Being which is that which does. We see, for example, quite clearly in a moment of insight that we should behave in a certain way but when the practical moment comes we behave in the former way. This discrepancy is inevitable and must be endured with the very greatest patience.

A question was then asked: "*What then should I do?*"

This question always arises in everyone's mind. The Work-answer is about what you should not do. The question should be: "What then should we not do?" It is just here that the Work comes in. The Work teaches a great many things that we should not do, for example, that we should not identify with our negative emotions, and so on. But such is our impatient nature that we want to have a definite answer as to what we should do. In fact, our whole psychology is based on this idea —i.e. "Tell me exactly what I should do." This urgent illusory doing-impulse has to be overcome in the Work completely. It is a life-impulse, it is a life-thought, a life-feeling, and the paradox is that in life we always have a feeling that we can do and yet from the Work-point of view we are really doing nothing because all the time our level of Being is making us act mechanically in every situation and this we call doing. For this reason the Work speaks about realizing our mechanical-ness as one of the first steps towards greater Being. If you will always attribute to everything you do in life the idea that *you* are doing it of course you will never quite understand where the Work comes in. By observation one has to come to that point at which one realizes that when one thinks one is doing one is not doing in any way whatso-ever but IT is doing, the machine in us is doing, one is doing mechanically what one has always done before. Here no question of *doing* in the Work-sense enters. IT is doing. In my case Nicoll is doing; in your case Smith, Robinson, Brown is doing.

There was a question: "*Well, how can I do in the Work-sense?*"

The answer is that you cannot do as you are in a Work-sense.

"*Then, what am I to do?*"

"Realize that you cannot do. Realize the mechanicalness of your Being."

"*Then do you mean that I cannot do anything at all and that I have to think so?*"

"No, you have to *realize* that you cannot do things, not think so."

"*How can I realize this?*"

"You can only realize it by observing yourself. If you observe yourself sincerely over a sufficient period you will begin to realize that you cannot do—i.e. that you always do as you always did and that you cannot change yourself. You know how you always think you can change yourself and how you are quite certain that you could be different if you wanted to and you know that you always think this about other people. But you have to realize that you cannot be different from what you are and from that to be able to realize that other people cannot be different from what they are. I remember on one occasion when someone asked: 'What then shall we do?' the answer was: 'Enjoy yourselves.' Now this person said: 'It would be the easiest thing in the world for me to enjoy myself, but I am a serious man—I have difficulties to face—and I have no time to enjoy myself.' You will see that this person had the idea that he could enjoy himself quite easily if he wished—that is, he had an ingrained conviction that he could enjoy himself, that he was doing his duty instead. Of course the answer is that he could not enjoy himself as he thought he could, he could not step out of his mechanicalness which made him do what he was doing. It is like a typewriter shouting at a bicycle and saying: 'Why do you go round and round?' and the bicycle shouting: 'Why do you go up and down, clack, clack?' Neither can alter its machinery. And so it is with us. We are mechanical and our first step is to realize we are machines, and that everything we do in all our relationships, in all the thoughts and feelings we go with, we identify with. But the Work teaches that we are not machines if we begin to wake up. A machine cannot change itself, a machine cannot remember itself, a machine cannot awaken. But, the Work teaches, we can awaken, we can remember ourselves, we can change ourselves."

"*How then is all this possible?*"

"It is only possible by following what the Work teaches. The Work begins with self-observation whereby gradually we may realize how we are machines and how we react mechanically to everything. When we begin to realize that we react mechanically to everything and have always been taking these mechanical reactions as 'I' and thinking that *we* are doing, then we begin to realize that we are really mechanical and that that gift we are given as distinct from animals and pure machines is that we can increase consciousness through observing that we are machines and that all our lives up to now have been mechanical —a series of petty, personal, sensitive, mechanical reactions to everything. Just at this point comes in the whole idea that Man can cease to be a machine. This entry of another consciousness of himself is the beginning of the Work. Such a man no longer takes himself for granted. Now the Work teaches that you have to do certain things

847

which takes the form of not doing certain things as, for example, in general, not identifying—that is, not putting your feeling of 'I' into all your mechanical reactions. So the Work consists for a long time in not doing things, according to the instructions laid down so clearly in this Work on its practical side."

"*Then do you mean that we can do nothing at all?*"

"Yes, you can do one thing. You can remember yourselves. That is the only thing said on the positive side of doing in this Work. Everything else is a process of not doing, not behaving mechanically."

"*How can I remember myself?*"

"By realizing that you never remember yourself."

"*But I am sure that I always remember myself.*"

"You may be sure that you always remember yourself but just notice whether you do."

"*But I always do what I do consciously.*"

"Do you always speak quite consciously, knowing exactly what you are going to say?"

"*Yes, I am sure that I do everything consciously and I am quite aware of what I am saying and doing all the time.*"

"In that case you must observe sincerely and see whether it is quite true. If you are sincere with yourself you will find that you do and think and feel mechanically and that for the greater part of the day you are not aware of yourself at all."

"*I do not agree with you.*"

"Well, in that case you must practise self-observation. It is only through self-observation done sincerely and uncritically that you can come into the standpoint of this Work in regard to yourself. If you take yourself for granted as being a conscious person who does everything consciously and deliberately you are not able to connect yourself with this Work. This Work will fall on deaf ears."

"*What is the object of self-observation?*"

"The object of self-observation is to make you aware of the fact that you are not in any way what you think you are. The object of self-observation is to shew you by direct self-experience that you are really a mechanical person who cannot help doing what you do at every moment and that if you want to change yourself, which is the object of this Work, you have to realize this."

"*Is not this an extremely depressing point of view?*"

"Yes."

"*Then why should I take up this Work?*"

"I see no reason why you should if you are quite satisfied with yourself as you are."

"*I always think that introspection is a very morbid thing.*"

"I agree with you but the Work does not teach introspection but conscious uncritical self-observation. Introspection is mechanical: observation is conscious."

"*Don't you think this Work makes one very self-centred.*"

"Exactly the opposite. It shifts you from this self-satisfied, self-centred view of yourself. It makes you really think you are nothing like what you thought. In short, this Work done rightly is very painful to you and will smash up all your self-centredness. As regards the remark that this Work is selfish, you must all understand that this Work is going against your selfishness at every moment, against your self-complacency. This Work is to wake us up and if applied rightly it is a very powerful and painful thing. It is something that destroys your self-complacency, your selfishness, your self-esteem, your phantasies about yourself, your pictures of yourself and, in short, your False Personality. It makes you see yourself naked—makes you see what you are really like. It destroys the Pharisee in you. It makes you see that you have to do something about yourself before you try to help other people."

"*But surely helping other people comes first.*"

"How can you help other people unless you have become more conscious of yourself? How can the blind lead the blind? Before you start off helping other people for heaven's sake look at yourself and see whether you can really help yourself to begin with. Do you call this self-satisfied imposing your self-will on other people helping them? The Work can help you to change and when the Work has begun to change you then you can help other people according to the degree that the Work has changed you in yourself and then your help will be valuable. But to start as you are, thinking you can help other people as you are, means simply that you impose your ideas of what other people should be on them without realizing what you are like yourself. The more you change in yourself through pain and self-realization, the more you see what you are like yourself without self-justifying, the more can you help others. The less blind you are to yourself the more you can help people who are still blind to themselves, but to become less blind to oneself takes many years of hard work and much pain and much overcoming of self-will, self-love, and much overcoming of prejudices, of thinking that you know everything, thinking that you are a starting-point in yourself. This Work teaches us to start from a quite different point from what we imagine we are. This Work does not begin with False Personality—i.e. with what we imagine we are. The whole world is full of False Personalities and each False Personality thinks he or she knows best. The Work is a very big thing that gradually drains away from us all these imaginings and falsities about ourselves. Then perhaps we can begin to help other people, but in a quite different way from what we would have started from before we met the Work and before it began to act on us internally through its simplicity and sincerity. The Work is a very wonderful thing if you begin to apply it to yourself, something very quiet and gentle and absolutely genuine at every point where it really begins to penetrate through layers of falsity and imagination that lie in us uppermost . If you begin to have Work-'I's in you—that is, 'I's that begin to catch some of the meaning of the

Work, then you may have insights beyond your average level of Being, and these insights, if affirmed in the best part of your mind as truth, will gradually change you and begin to work on your level of Being and alter Being. Then gradually what you know on your best side will be able to be done and carried out by your Being. The Work says that this transformation is possible in everyone if they will only work on themselves. So begin by thinking what non-identifying means, with yourself, with your thoughts and your feelings. It is not doing, and gradually this process of not doing will enable you on a very small scale to do."

Quaremead, Ugley, February 16, 1946

COMMENTARY ON GIVING UP ONE'S SUFFERING

You have often heard before that the only thing that we can sacrifice in the Work is our suffering. The Work teaches that we have to have a new kind of suffering not based on our ordinary mechanical suffering. All change in oneself can only take place by giving up what one was and becoming something different. To change oneself means to become different. I cannot change myself if I remain the same person that I am mechanically. Therefore in order to change I must give up something, sacrifice something. The idea of sacrifice runs through all esotericism. It is quite obvious why. The reason is that you cannot change yourself unless you give up or sacrifice something that you are at present. It has often been repeated in this teaching that change of Being means that you must alter something in yourself, in your Being. You cannot be what you are and at the same time change. Change of Being always involves giving up something and so sacrificing something in your Being. And the Work says that the first thing that you have to sacrifice—and here I may say emphatically the *first* thing—is your ordinary mechanical suffering. Now unless you see what is meant here you will not start the Work aright in yourself. You will begin from your own ideas of what you have to sacrifice or give up and that will be no good and will lead to no results. A man, a woman, must give up their suffering and sacrifice that first of all, because this can lead to a change of Being. For this to happen one must be able to see through self-observation what one suffers from.

I remember that Mr. Ouspensky spoke very early about this question. He said first of all that everyone without knowing it has fallen into typical forms of suffering from which they derive self-justification—namely, they justify their suffering and so take it for granted as part and parcel of themselves. He called it a kind of thing that you drag behind you all the time or push in front of you. He

850

described very clearly in words that I have not remembered enough how people are chained to this suffering that they have accumulated according to their own ideas of life and how it has treated them. He said: "All this suffering belongs to the side of Personality." He said: "People suffer uselessly but cling to their suffering. People have not found life to be what they supposed it would be and instead of seeing their forms of imagination and their acquired attitudes to life they only think they have real, genuine suffering and so feel in consequence that no one really understands all that they have been through, and so on. Everyone," he said, "is dragged down by this acquired suffering from which come all internal considering and account-making. All your internal considering and account-making," he said, "is based on this acquired suffering which people value very much." He spoke about the impossibility of escaping from the Personality with its acquired attitudes and buffers save through a force entirely new that can destroy all this litter, this useless mess in ourselves. He said: "We have to begin to think in a new way both about life and about ourselves and this is only possible when we feel a new force entering us carrying with it new ideas, new ways of taking in things. The redemption from suffering is difficult but possible, whereas in life it is impossible. When you begin to understand this Work and all that it teaches and compare it with what you are you will understand what I mean. You will see how what you are is quite different from what this Work teaches that you should be." Mr. Ouspensky used here a phrase that I always remember. He said: "When you begin to be alongside this Work and become conscious of what you are like through self-observation you will see how you are not like this Work, how your Being does not correspond with it." People asked: "Then what should we do?" The answer always was: "You must remember yourselves and the first thing you must give up is your suffering." I think he meant, as regards the latter part of what he said, that as long as you carry your suffering with you you cannot do the Work. You have to give it up—that is, you have to sacrifice this strange thing in you that is the basis of all internal considering and account-making. On another occasion Mr. Ouspensky said: "No one can reach a higher level of Being unless he gives up his present forms of suffering." At that time he was talking about our idea of justice and was emphasizing how what we call justice has nothing to do with justice. He said: "Justifying yourself is always from your own idea of justice. For example, everyone justifies their negative states." He meant that everyone has a sense of what is justice *for them* and finding that life does not correspond to it they cling to this sense of what they think should be justice for them. Consequently we justify our negative states, our internal considering, and our account-making, and if we view the whole thing from the Work point of view we begin to realize that we cannot justify ourselves on our own ideas of justice. We have to act from another sense of justice. Suppose you talk wrongly in this Work and you are brought to the point of having to confess that you have talked wrongly, you will find that you always justify yourself on the basis of your own ideas of justice—personal justification of yourself. And behind that will lie your suffering which springs from the idea of justice that you have acquired and imitated. This has to be broken by something higher, by some higher form of what is justice. You may say to yourself: "Towards life I am quite right in feeling injustice but towards the Work and its ideas I cannot say the same thing." In the Work we are under a new discipline, a new sense of justice—namely, of what is right, of what is just, from a higher level. So we have to learn to serve another set of ideas quite different from those we have acquired from life. Mr. Ouspensky said: "We are like monkeys. A monkey can justify himself in terms of being a monkey, but we are trying to become human beings and can no longer justify ourselves in terms of being monkeys." He constantly emphasized that we are being taught in this Work ideas and self-discipline which were not necessary in life. He said: "We are trying to obey higher laws—i.e. we are trying to become conscious people so that we can live amongst conscious people and learn how to behave amongst this higher level of Beings. This Work comes from conscious people."

Now to return to this question of the first thing that we have to sacrifice—namely, our mechanical suffering—it is quite clear that first of all we all have to become aware of what forms our mechanical suffering takes. Unless we are conscious of a thing we cannot sacrifice it. You cannot start from something that you are unconscious of. The Work is to increase our consciousness of ourselves, of our state of Being. No one can work on his Being unless he is beginning to observe what his Being is like. The Work says that everyone as regards Being has his or her own form of suffering, of negative emotions, of grievances, of sad thoughts and feelings, and so on. This applies to everyone. There are no exceptions. And this thing in ourselves we are told to sacrifice at the very outset of this teaching. Therefore it is very necessary to try to observe one's form of suffering.

You may ask: "What are these forms of suffering that we have to sacrifice?" There is the suffering of man towards woman, of woman towards man. For example, a man may feel that he has never met the woman who really understands him. Or he may feel simply that he has never been properly appreciated or given a chance, and so on. Or a woman may feel that she has never been married—or that she has never had any children—or that she is always having children—and this is her suffering. Then take all the mechanical forms of suffering that arise from feeling that you have never been understood by your parents, your husband, your wife, or your children. I think it would be impossible to enumerate all the forms of suffering that people form in themselves and cling to as the most valuable things in their lives. And it is exactly this suffering derived from life and all its awkwardness that has to be sacrificed. And here I would remind you of what was said recently about 'if only': 'if only I had been given a better chance,' 'if only I had had a child,' 'if only I had met the right kind of person,' 'if only the war had not broken out when it did,' 'if only I had not invested my money in German marks,' 'if only I had been taller,' 'if only I had not got the face I have,' 'if only I had more money,' 'if only I could meet better kinds of people,' 'if only I had had more sympathy in all my troubles'—this 'if only' is connected with all your mechanical suffering that has to be sacrificed. Another form of suffering is a sense of failure. The strange thing is that this can be enjoyed. A person having made no real effort in life may fail and in a curious way enjoy his failure, or a person may think he has done his best to make relationship with someone who is difficult for him and having failed to do so may enjoy his failure. This curious form of suffering cannot be gone into in this paper. As I say, this is a very curious form of suffering whereby some people adapt themselves to life by being failures and liking to talk about it. But in such cases you will always find that they have some form of pride or vanity that makes it possible for them to pretend that their failures are genuine, falling back on the feeling that they are or could have been successes at something else, especially if they have pride in their social position, birth, or something of the same kind—i.e. in something purely negative, not really themselves. I have sometimes thought that this is the most difficult form to deal with when people admit failure, holding always secretly on to something else. This is a spurious kind of suffering. At the same time, it must be seen through and sacrificed. Behind it lies the sacrifice of pride and vanity. But this example only shews how extraordinarily insincere people are with themselves and how self-deception makes it possible for them to carry on their lives. We do not see the other side of the whole matter, the dark, unaccepted, unacknowledged side, but that is why the Work says that uncritical self-observation lets in a ray of light into this dark side which stands in the way of all individual development in everyone. We are all frauds, but we do not see through our fraudulence and in the Work we must begin with this. All our mechanical suffering is fraudulent only we will not admit it. Fraudulent suffering is the keynote to what we have to sacrifice. Real suffering is utterly different and always opens us to a higher level: fraudulent suffering closes us. It is extraordinary how a moment of real suffering makes everything false fall away from you and at such moments you understand quite plainly what this Work is about, but fraudulent, self-invented suffering comes between us and Higher Centres—that is, between us and the voice of the Work that is always speaking to us, and which we have to learn at first from outside, from a teacher, and after a time can begin to hear speaking to us inside.

The extraordinary thing is that you meet people very often who deny that they have any kind of mechanical suffering. They are usually very self-complacent people and quite dead in themselves, and yet if you are clever with them you will soon find out that they have their private forms of suffering derived from life. Now it is a very good idea to try to observe your typical forms of mechanical suffering and here it is a good thing to try to observe your phantasies —i.e. the passive work of the imagination in you. I remember once being very much struck with the idea that at least a million people die every week and probably far more and that many of them think that they are going to a better place. They are all full of their own personal problems, their own grievances, their own suffering on this Earth. How many of these people do you think—suppose that you were some kind of Being on a higher level who had to direct them to different places in the spiritual world—how many of these people would strike you as not being of the ordinary type? Would not each one of them come to you complaining—i.e. bringing to you all their mechanical sufferings, grievances, all these questions about how someone did not say Good-morning to them, and how many would come to you quite clean, without any grievances, without any sufferings from the Earth, and when asked what they wanted, would answer, not that they wanted justice, but that they wanted to know more and *be* more and *understand* more. This vision impressed me very much and made me think very deeply about what I might be under these circumstances. We have often spoken about forgiving debts and about how it means cancelling complaints against others. All our Earth-problems are of no value at all at a higher level of Being, and our work is to cancel our Earth-problems, our Earth-suffering, our internal accounting, our negative states towards others, our grievances towards others, our dislike of others and our hate of others. Otherwise we aie earthbound and so like those monkeys of which we have spoken. Do you think this is a very harsh idea? I fancy we can gain some idea of what all this means, even from life. If you want to reach a higher position in life, can you bring your grievances in all the time, your personal, petty problems, in view of the position that you wish to reach?

Mr. Ouspensky once said to me: "People do not understand that this Work is about going somewhere and that it lays down definite instructions as to how you can go there, provided you work on yourself, and that therefore, as a person advances, the Work changes for him." He was talking to me at the time about something in myself that was holding me up and he said: "Don't you see that it is nothing to do with me, this, but that it is in yourself, and that as long as you do not work on it and try not to identify with it, it will always hold you back?" He said: "You object to these people, but they are you and you are them." Naturally at that time I did not see that this was part of my suffering. I did not realize that this was one of the meanings of giving up one's suffering. On another occasion he said to me, looking at me sideways: "Why do you enjoy your negative emotions so much?" And I always remember not exactly what he said but this look he gave me sideways. It was, in fact, through this look that he gave me that I began to observe that I did enjoy my negative emotions—that is, my mechanical suffering. I suppose that by now many of you begin to understand how much you enjoy your negative emotions. The Work says that to reach a higher level of Being there must be no negative emotions and that the negative part of the Emotional Centre must be destroyed in us. Otherwise, if with our present forms of suffering Higher Centres came they would simply intensify everything a thousand times. On one occasion I heard G. say: "We must destroy our Emotional Centre." Being still very young in the Work I thought what a terrible thing this would be and how harsh and cruel everything would be if one's Emotional Centre were destroyed. When I became older in the Work I realized so very clearly what was meant. Our Emotional Centre, as it is, is nothing but self-emotions with the resultant negative emotions arising from them. The purification of the Emotional Centre must, practically speaking, destroy the Emotional Centre in us as it is now, with all our little personal, sensitive, difficult reactions, our little personal feelings about everyone, our bundle of sensitive likes and dislikes—in short, our very small petty emotions, that we have as long as self-emotions govern us. When you begin to serve this Work really you have to lose these petty, daily, small self-emotions and you can only do so by realizing that the Work is much bigger than you. We spoke about this recently in connection with the realization of Greater Mind. You have to serve the Work and not yourself. The Work must not be a function of yourself but you must become a function of the Work.

What does serving the Work mean? It means obeying what the Work teaches you. It was said recently at a meeting that you must understand that serving the Work means serving it psychologically, to begin with. Suppose that you were about to pass on some unpleasant scandal and you suddenly remembered yourself in connection with what the Work teaches and did not pass on this scandal, knowing that to do so is mechanical and that it would only do harm —then you would begin to serve the Work. Or suppose that you wish to be negative because someone has not treated you in what you think the right way according to your own form of justice and you remember yourself and do not react mechanically, then you will be serving the Work. To serve the Work means to obey what it teaches you to practise on yourself. You want to be gloomy and moody, to object, and so on, and you observe your state and begin to separate from it—then you are serving the Work. And in so doing you are giving up some of your mechanical suffering. Or suppose you are about to pass into one of your typical force-losing states of worry, of complaining, of being upset about everything, of disliking everything—suppose that you observe this and cease to identify with it because of the feeling of the Work in you—then you are serving the Work psychologically. You are beginning to work on yourself, you are beginning to see what the Work means in yourself. You are beginning to obey something that is not yourself. All this belongs to giving up your suffering. But to work on

855

your typical forms of suffering, close and sincere observation of your Being is necessary, and directing the Work on to those places in your Being through the light of self-observation, and trying not to go with these reactions, not to identify with them, not to put feeling of 'I' into them, and the more you value the Work in which higher meaning is something above the meaning of life, the more will the Work help you to overcome your mechanical suffering.

Quaremead, Ugley, February 22, 1946

THE PSYCHOLOGICAL MEANING OF FOOT

On one occasion it was said by Mr. Ouspensky that he had leather to sell for those who wish to make shoes for themselves. There are two kinds of shoes. The first shoes are made by life in us. We learn to behave in certain ways, to think that these people are right and those people are wrong, we imbibe ingrained attitudes through imitation according to our social position, and all the rest of it. Some of these shoes are made more by the mother and some more by the father. When you see a person walking in his father's shoes or perhaps in his mother's shoes, you understand that that person is not awake yet. All this has reference to the *feet* and we have to think to-night about the meaning of the feet esoterically. Life-shoes wear out sometimes and on the other hand sometimes they remain permanent. A person who has never questioned his acquired life-attitudes, his buffers, his prejudices, and so on, will perhaps have permanent shoes, made by the action of life on him. At the same time it is possible for a person to come to the point in which his or her shoes get worn out. Now the shoes are that with which we walk on the Earth. Esoterically speaking, our feet are where we touch external life and the shoes that cover our feet represent the attitudes and prejudices and opinions that we meet life with. When the Work says it has leather to sell to make shoes it means of course to make new shoes so that we can walk in life in a different way. The foot, psychologically speaking, is the most external part of us, the part of us that meets with life. You have heard about the First Conscious Shock which takes place at the point where external impressions enter us. Ordinarily there is no shock here. External life enters us and we behave towards it always in much the same way. We take every thing as we have always taken it. We behave in the same way. We relate ourselves to external circumstances, to people, to all that belongs to external life in the way we always have done. The First Conscious Shock consists in the transformation of impressions. If you take everything coming in through the senses from external life in the same way as you have always done you will not transform life.

856

Every time you see A. or B., who exist in external life, whom you see and hear through your external senses, you react to them in the same way as you always have done. You are not working on yourself, you are not giving yourself the First Conscious Shock, which consists in receiving external impressions *in a new way*. A man, a woman, heavily prejudiced, orthodox, and opinionated, will naturally find it very difficult to take in impressions in a new way. Where their psychological feet touch life they will always walk in the same manner.

Now if we turn this into Work-terms we can say that in such a case we behave mechanically. So the mechanical side of us is our *feet*. As long as we behave mechanically towards every situation we will always walk in the same places, psychologically speaking—that is to say, we will not be giving ourselves the First Conscious Shock or transforming incoming impressions. Remember that all you see and hear, all the people you know, all that you read, is incoming impressions, because we are only in contact with external life through incoming impressions from our senses. It is just at this point of incoming impressions that the Work teaches something quite definite. If these incoming impressions always fall in the same place in you and excite the same reactions, the same dislikes, the same likes, the same judgments, the same criticisms, the same thoughts, the same feelings, then nothing can shift you from where you are. You will not be doing this Work. In such a case one is a pure machine, a pure example of mechanical behaviour. Your feet, which are this mechanicalness through which you touch life, will always walk in the same way.

We were speaking recently here about how the Work from the very beginning teaches us that we have to go against our mechanical-ness and also how this is impossible unless by long observation we can see our mechanicalness. This is the introduction to the Work. A man, a woman, who cannot observe themselves and their mechanical behaviour cannot work on themselves. They take their mechanical be-haviour for granted, being certain that their automatic condemnations, their criticisms, their prejudices, their contempts, and so on, are absolutely right. In short, they take life in the only way they can as long as they do not observe how they take it. I think the main point lies here—namely, that, accepting these mechanical reactions to other people, to external life, they feel that they are not only absolutely right but that no other way of taking people and the events of life could be possible. This is a mistake. Sometimes quite genuinely a person may say to me: "How can I take this or that person differently because I feel sure that this or that person is wrong and not the kind of person that I would ordinarily know if I could help it?" This means that there is no act of transformation taking place in them. The external impressions come in and, like the automatic telephone exchange, ring up the same reactions in them and they feel that this is the only way to react. Speaking recently about this, I said it was a good thing to read the Sermon on the Mount and to realize that it is all about reacting in a new way. To react as a Pharisee is one thing—a Pharisee means one who reacts in a fixed and prejudiced way—but the Sermon on the Mount has nothing to do with praise of the Pharisee in us. It has to do with destroying the Pharisee—with taking things in a quite different way. So it belongs to the teaching about the First Conscious Shock—that is, the transformation of incoming impressions. But we always take incoming impressions of other people, of life-situations, in the same way. We are not creating this First Conscious Shock. We are still wearing our life-made shoes. Certainly we are not shod with the leather of the Work.

From what has been said you can understand that the foot represents the purely mechanical side, or Personality governed by False Personality. In this Work we are told that we have to make Personality, speaking in general, more and more passive. That is to change one's mechanical reaction. Personality is something acquired in us, chiefly through imitation. You have a mother-personality, a father-personality, a mixed personality, a school-personality, a college-personality, and so on. As long as this personality, however acquired, is active in you, you will always take every person in the external world, everything said, everything read, everything seen, in exactly the same way as you have always done, and you will feel that you are quite right in taking things in that way. Why? Because you have never challenged your Personality, you have never begun to observe this thing called Personality in you, but have accepted it as Truth. You stand on your Personality, just as you stand on your feet, because, psychologically, your most inveterate and habitual psychology is your feet. The psychological man, the psychological woman, rests on the feet of the most mechanical 'I's in the moving parts of centres. It is the basis of your reactions, the source of how you behave.

Now the Work has leather to sell, to make new shoes, new feet, new ways of behaving towards life and all its incidents. It is a marvellous thing to realize that you can behave differently towards any single thing in life, that you need not take it as you are taking it, and that, in short, you can behave differently and feel differently *provided you begin to think differently*—that is, change the mind. As you know, this Work is to make us think differently and from that gradually to feel differently, and eventually to see ourselves with new eyes. Do not you ever get tired of the way you behave? It would indeed be wonderful not to think, not to feel and not to behave in the way we always mechanically do. When Smith realizes Smith and wishes to separate from Smith, he begins to understand what this Work is about. He begins to see what mechanicalness means and through self-observation to realize the mechanical figure in him, the pure machinery, to which hitherto he has been a complete slave. It is said in the Work that the realization of our mechanicalness is the first step towards Self-Remembering. The quality of the First Conscious Shock is sometimes denoted by the term Self-Remembering. It is said that if a man will give himself this Conscious Shock in the midst of his cares and anxieties he will create in himself new force. In fact, he will actually make new hydrogens, new energies in himself. It is in this sense that it is meant that the realization of mechanicalness is one of the first forms of Self-Remembering. It is a form of transformation of impressions, of the transformation of our whole relationship to ourselves and so to outer life. It is a step towards not being a pure mechanical function of the Personality. If you can understand something about this First Conscious Shock that takes place just where incoming impressions enter you from outer life, you will begin to feel the magical experience that you need not take this typical situation in the typical way you have always taken it, that you need not feel this dislike that you always feel, this hatred, this disgust, this boredom, this sadness. You begin to learn what it means that you need not identify with everything. So you begin to see where, in what direction, new life *can begin*. All this belongs to the understanding of the First Conscious Shock which is transformation, to the realization that one need not react to impressions as one has always done.

As I said, this mechanical, habitual side of us is called, esoterically, *foot*, the psychological basis of yourself, what you stand on at present. There is a very interesting passage in Isaiah, which begins with the strange remark that you must turn away your foot from the Sabbath. Isaiah is an esoteric book. It is full of esoteric teaching. That means at once that it cannot be taken literally just as any parable in the Gospels cannot be taken literally. It has inner meaning behind its literal meaning. Let us take this first phrase: "If thou turn away thy foot from the Sabbath"—If you take that literally, what can it mean? If you take the Sabbath as going to Church it seems to mean that if you turn your foot away from Church it would be a good thing. But of course it does not mean this. You have to understand the passage psychologically. The foot is your most mechanical 'I's situated in the most external part of centres, the parts where you touch the ground—i.e. external life—and react to this external life mechanically. If you turn yourself away from your mechanical reaction in connection with the Sabbath, then you may get something worthwhile. Let us quote the whole passage :

"If thou turn away thy foot from the sabbath, from doing thy pleasure on my holy day; and call the sabbath a delight, and the holy of the Lord honourable; and shalt honour it, not doing thine own ways, nor finding thine own pleasure, nor speaking thine own words: then shalt thou delight thyself in the Lord; and I will make thee to ride upon the high places of the earth; and I will feed thee with the heritage of Jacob thy father: for the mouth of the Lord hath spoken it." (*Is.* LVIII 13, 14)

If you look at these strange verses psychologically, you see that they are full of meaning and they tell you exactly what this Work tells us now. This Work tells you that if you go against your mechanicalness even for a short time you will get some result. The meaning of Sabbath

in its original sense is *cessation*. The meaning of the Sabbath is to cease
from your mechanical self, to cease from having your own way, from
speaking as you do ordinarily, and so on. You can have your Sabbath,
your cessation from your mechanicalness, whenever you like. For
example, you can have a cessation from your mechanical self for half
an hour and even for five minutes. What does it mean to cease from
doing your will? It means to do the will of the Work. For example, at
this particular moment, to do the will of the Work instead of serving
your self-will may mean not to identify with your present suffering.
Or it may mean not to justify yourself as you are doing. Or it may mean
to externally consider that person. All this the Work teaches us. Or
it may mean for you at this moment to stop making internal accounts,
to stop internal considering : this is what the Work teaches us. It may
mean not to go with negative emotions or believe in them, but to
separate from them: this the Work teaches us. It means, in short, all
that the Work teaches us. And when we try to do this for a short time
we have our own Sabbath, our own cessation from ourselves. So we
turn our foot away. Most people think that Sabbath is rest from life-
work, but esoterically the Sabbath means work on yourself by ceasing
from yourself. It is a good thing to work on yourself sincerely for a
short Sabbath and try to bring the whole of the ideas of the Work into
your mind so that they lift you up from mechanical life. The Work is
a higher power acting on us but we must bring the whole of the Work
into our minds and the whole meaning of it to lift us up from too petty
talking, too many life-anxieties, too easily-indulged jealousies, to this
higher power, and if we do this Work we will always find results.
But do not start with turning away only from your physical appetites.
Rather begin to turn away from things in your emotional and
thinking centres. Turn away from being negative, from feeling that
other people should do what you find you have to do. Turn away from
your identified states, from your ordinary judgments of other people.
Turn away from your depression. Turn away from the feeling that
you are right. Turn away from all the Work teaches us to turn away
from. For then one can get new force which Isaiah, in the same chapter,
describes in these words:

> "And the Lord shall guide thee continually, and satisfy thy
> soul in dry places, and make strong thy bones; and thou shalt be
> like a watered garden, and like a spring of water, whose waters
> fail not." (*Is.* LVIII 11)

This is a description of the results of giving the First Conscious
Shock.

COMMENTARY ON BEING SEALED AGAINST LIFE

Eventually we must become channels for this teaching. If we can pass on this teaching as it is taught we get something for ourselves. In order to do this something must be sealed in us, sealed tight against the effect of things happening outside us. The Work must be given a place in us where eventually nothing from the external world can affect it. We spoke some time ago about the Work being like a new being forming in oneself and how one has to protect this being and fight for it often against the logic of the external senses. We spoke last time of the meaning of the foot. Your foot is your external side which touches life. I will speak some time more fully about what the eyes mean in contrast with the foot. But, briefly, the eyes mean esoterically one's inner psychological understanding as distinct from the under-standing that one gains from the senses or one's foot. It used often to be said in the Work that we have to go against life. For example, you read the papers and see how everyone in the world seems to be angry and violent and you may have the thought: "What is the good of the Work if everything is going in this way?" Now does not such a thought mean that you have not sealed off the Work from the influences of life? One is letting one's attitude to the Work get mixed with things belonging to the great machinery of life, just as if one expected external life to correspond with or conform to the Work. This sealing of oneself off from life so that one can guard and keep separate the Work-ideas is necessary. It has to be done sooner or later. The Work is under other laws than life is. Its source is from another direction. If you judge the Work by what happens in life you will not understand it. Here in this Work we are studying something different from life. We seek to come under influences different from the in-fluences of life. We try to form something in ourselves that life cannot shake, whatever happens in life, whether war or peace, poverty or wealth, bad weather or good weather, failure or success. The idea is that we have to form in ourselves a place where the Work exists and have to guard this place. As you know, the Work teaches that every-thing that happens in life happens in the only way it can happen. It says that life is a great machine. It teaches that Organic Life on Earth serves a cosmic purpose. This sensitive living film surrounding the Earth is used for a deliberate purpose. Yet there is a chance for Man, an individual man, to disconnect himself from some of the mechanical laws of life and begin to grow through more conscious laws. When you take this standpoint the non-correspondence of life with what you expect becomes no longer a source of negativeness. And if you feed sufficiently on the ideas of the Work you are able to guard this inner place that we spoke of and then events that formerly dragged you down into negativeness no longer have that power because you begin to have the power of the Work, as I have often told you. Do not try to find the Will of God in life. The Lord's Prayer begins with the idea that God's Will is not done on this Earth but may be done for you.

We spoke last time about making shoes and how the Work had leather to sell to make new shoes. We also spoke about how our life-shoes wear out—at least, in certain cases, because some people seem satisfied with their life-shoes. One ancient teaching of esotericism was given under the name of Hermes. From this arose the term "hermetically sealed" which was used in esoteric alchemy. Esoteric alchemy was based on the idea that Man as base metal could be transformed into gold—i.e. that Man regarded as some metal, say lead, as he is at his present stage, could become by some knowledge and the practice of it turned into gold. This was esoteric alchemy. Exoteric alchemy was based on the idea that actual lead could be turned into gold, which is a possibility. A hermit was a person who followed the teaching of Hermes and sought to seal himself off from the effects of life by going into a cave or desert. This is not the idea of the Work. It would be getting rid of life artificially. We have to seal ourselves from the effects of external life when they are actually happening to us. Here comes in the idea of practising non-identifying. With what, by the way, are you identified at this moment? Of course, without self-observation you have no idea. Without it one is simply identified. The state remains in darkness. It is not brought into consciousness. In general, when such is the case, at most moments one is not making an effort to separate oneself from the effects of external life, and so there is nothing sealed. Such a person is not living consciously. How can we say that such a person is working? But he will not recognize that he is behaving in this way unless he lets light into his inner darkness—i.e. observes his state. When you do not know how you behave, all this is dark to you. Yes, you are doing it all the time, but you do not know that you are doing it. This is the strange thing. You are not conscious. You are asleep to yourself. It is correct in this case to say the person is a machine, a mechanical person. Now in a machine nothing is sealed, nothing is made tight against the impact of external things. It is turned by life, as a machine is turned by a belt.

Let us return to what was said at the beginning of this paper that each one of us must become a channel for the teaching of this Work. To become a channel in this sense the Work must be sealed off from life—otherwise life will keep changing it. So one must never put the hand on the mud of one's feet and bring it up to one's eyes. The understanding of life is one thing and the understanding of this Work is another thing. Life must not prevail over or stand higher than the Work. A man in this Work is a man who in spite of external circumstances, whether they are helpful or not, continues to work. Life does not shake his understanding of the Work. His eyesight, which in this case means insight, maintains him. Esoterically there are two kinds of blindness. There are the blind people whom Christ healed—people who are blind internally. And there are the blind who have had their inner sight awakened and now are blind to external life. We know that we can take a thing from a life point of view and from a Work point of view. When one takes something as work the result is different. There is a higher level of understanding above that on which one's feet rest. On this level one realizes that everything that happens to one in life is the best thing that could happen to one, if one takes it as work —as a means of development. You realize in a practical way how you are created a self-developing organism. You no longer take life as an end in itself or expect it to be as you wished, but you take it as a means to an end. I bring in here once more the phrase that to an intelligent person neither life nor one's own life can be understood in terms of itself. An additional idea is necessary. Have you ever meditated on this when you were in life-difficulties? Have you glimpsed that they may be just what you need?

In ancient myths many esoteric ideas were introduced in the form of allegories which if taken literally seem nonsense, but if taken psychologically have meaning. You remember when Odysseus landed on the island of Circe he was given by Hermes a magic herb which protected him against her enchantment although his companions were turned into swine by her spells. Do you think this was an actual herb? Maybe—perhaps aconite. But I fancy that this Work, if it were really taken into oneself, would begin to have the same effect —namely, to protect you from the enchantments of life, from its illusions, from its mirrors. You remember the Work-myth that we are all in a hall of mirrors? In it everyone is rushing, as they think, straight ahead, to progress, but owing to the mirrors constantly changing their angle everyone is only going round and round in a repeating circle. A man may already feel something of this. I mean, that we may think that we are tricked by life and not merely blame people or things. Yet without the ideas of the Work we have no way of understanding this right suspicion. I was turning over some notes the other day written long ago and came across this passage which I will quote. It was concerned with a man who had recently joined the Work. He said he had the impression when he returned from any entertainment or social function that he had been tricked, not by the entertainment or by his hostess, but by something he only felt dimly but it was always present with him, some power that made him feel rather a fool and seemed to use him for purposes of its own and yet not malevolent so much as business-like and practical—acting for its own purposes amongst people who are foolish enough to let themselves be hypnotized by it. I quote this because it seems to me that here you have a man who is beginning to have traces of Magnetic Centre. He feels in some way that he is being used by some power which he cannot resist and which is tricking him. I would say that if a man begins to feel that life is tricking him, if he begins to feel this Hall of Mirrors, he is already beginning to reach a stage in which this Work and its ideas could become useful to him. I mean, that he might understand that life and his own life cannot be understood in terms of themselves but need another interpretation. So the Work might be of use to such a person.

Quaremead, Ugley, March 9, 1946

A NOTE ON THE DIFFICULTIES OF GIVING OUT AND RECEIVING ESOTERIC TEACHING

To-night I will speak about the difficulties of esotericism, both from the point of view of its being given and of its being received. We might imagine human life on Earth as comparable to some vast hotel into which air has to be blown to keep people alive. This ventilating-system can be compared with the Conscious Circle of Humanity trying to introduce air or spirit into the people in this enormous hotel—otherwise the people in this hotel would gradually die. Such a danger exists now. If this air were cut off people would actually die—that is, if mankind were cut off from higher levels.

In the Gospels it is said that a man must be born of air. The word in the Greek for air or spirit is the same. In some of the ancient Gnostic writings Man is divided into different classes from the standpoint of esotericism—that is, into more or less mechanical. There is, for example, the hylic man, the lowest type of Man, which we would call No. 1 Man. The word 'hylic' comes from a Greek word meaning matter or wood. Such a man is a wooden man—a fairly good definition, if you come to think of it. The next class was the pneumatic man—the air-man. In the Greek the word πνεῦμα means air or spirit. A pneumatic man is thus a man who has spiritual understanding as distinct from literal, material or wooden understanding. Such a man may perhaps see life spiritually as a combat between Good and Evil rather than only as a means of gaining his own advantage. Perhaps he sees life as the Will of Man fighting against the Spirit of Evil in a Universe of mystery. In any case, he sees life in a different way from the hylic or wooden man. We can understand Christ's words, that a man must be born of spirit or air, in the sense that he must come into an entirely new understanding. The Work gives us a different view of life. In seeking to make us take ourselves and life in a new way it is spiritual in that it seeks to transform us from the purely material standpoint. I will add here in parenthesis that the Gnostic Schools preceded the advent of Christ by one or more centuries and anticipated his coming, and that in the Gospels there are one or two purely Gnostic parables such as that of the Unjust Steward. 'Gnostic' comes from γνῶσις which means simply 'knowledge'—that is, it was a term that referred

864

to certain schools of knowledge that were not purely material—i.e. not business schools. In this Commentary I will use the term 'spiritual man' in the Gnostic sense as distinct from a materially-minded sense-based or wooden man. The trouble in using this term is that it has been so over-used. As I said, through the Work one can have a spiritual understanding about the meaning of life quite different from the literal, wooden interpretation of life. Things have another meaning. In other words, we get to that point in which we realize that life as transmitted through our ears and sight is the outer appearance, not the reality, of things. We spoke last time about the Hall of Turning Mirrors. Humanity rushes, as it thinks, forward. Actually the mirrors turn and Humanity goes round and round. This especially. applies to the hylic man who, so to speak, sees his future always in front and pursues this phantasy. He is immersed in life : he is identified with everything that happens in life and so he takes life as it appears and so as an end in itself. But nothing in life is what it appears to be.

Now the Work teaches that the Conscious Circle of Humanity are sowing into life spiritual ideas—namely, ideas that separate us from the power of external life as seen, as read of every day in the papers, as experienced in our ordinary domestic situations. It has to make and keep going a connection through which higher influences can reach Man asleep. There is another interpretation and through it another feeling of life and of one's own life which can begin through understanding this Work, and this comes from the Conscious Circle of Humanity who give out influences different from life. Where there is no vision the people die. To-day, when vision is ceasing, the power of external life, of machines and war, increases. Man must serve one or the other. Without vision, without the influences from Conscious Man, Humanity is enslaved by outer life. Because it has no inner life, having given up the idea of religion, it has nothing with which to resist outer life. When there is no inner life one passes into the power of outer life completely. Man becomes helpless—a creature of mass-movements, mass-politics, of gigantic mass-organizations. Certainly we can suppose that ants must have no inner life. Some people say: If there be such a thing as the Conscious Circle of Humanity, why do they not appear openly and tell everyone exactly what to do? As a matter of fact, they have always been telling people what to do in different teachings and religions all through the ages, and some have appeared. But they cannot compel Man, they cannot have police-systems, they cannot force people to awaken, by torture, because Man is created a self-developing organism. Any religious system of force is at once a dead system. You cannot make a man awaken by external force or compulsion. A man can only begin to awaken from his own understanding and his own will to awaken—which begins when he sees his state. For that reason the Conscious Circle of Humanity is limited by higher laws than those on this Earth. It has therefore to work indirectly. The forces of life can work directly and violently on people by means of police-systems and guns and all the savagery that we have seen in this century and indeed throughout history on a smaller scale, but such compulsion does not wake a man internally, it does not lead to self-development, it does not make Essence grow. I am saying all this in connection with what was said recently that we have to keep the Work in a separate place in ourselves and guard it from the influences and appearances of life. This is impossible unless people understand eventually as much as they can of what this Work teaches—otherwise they will fall into various deep pits of thinking derived from life and not from the Work. They will say: "Why does not God or this so-called Conscious Circle help Humanity?" They will say: "Why is not something done straight-forwardly and plainly? Why are not people told exactly what to do and made to do it?" But a man can only grow through his own choice and his own understanding and from inside, because it is the individual man in himself, the essential man, that the Work and all other esoteric systems seek to awaken. It is the internal, not the external man, that must grow. For this reason the Work must be kept separate and guarded in our minds. I spoke recently about the foot and the eyes and what they mean psychologically—that is, esoterically. I said you must not let your hand touch your foot or shoes and carry mud up to your eyes, because this is sin. Sin meant originally in the Greek to miss the mark. The mud on your foot—the mud of life—must not be mixed up with your understanding of the Work. We all lie mechanically and so we do not accept it. This is mud on the feet. We all justify ourselves and think we do not. It remains dark to us—this is mud. Above all, we identify, and never see it. We identify with our suffering. We feel undersized at one moment and oversized at the next. We take our lives as they have turned out as our basis—what we rest upon in thinking or feeling what we are. This is mud. The wrong feeling of 'I' is mud. We all take our self-merit as valuable : it is mud. We have many ideas of superiority: this is mud. Everything from False Personality is mud. Every interpretation of life, as appearance, as seen, without any transforming ideas, is mud. Mud, therefore, is a long study. But I find it too difficult to give you a handbook on mud—simply because mud is our way of taking life and its results on one's imagination of oneself, and the Work is something quite different. If we could see internally the meaning of our lives and the kind of people we are in the light, the consciousness, of the Work, if we could lift our level, if we could see what it means that *we cannot do*—then indeed we would see no longer merit on our feet but mud. The worst kind of mud is formed by various ways of thinking we can do—i.e. that we are right—and by feeling merit for it. We spoke recently about suffering and how the Work teaches us that we have nothing real to sacrifice save our suffering and indignation. That suffering, that negativeness, that long, unchecked, making of inner accounts of the results of internal considering, of not being rightly appreciated—all that is indeed mud in the light of the

Work. It is an Augean Stable of filth through which a river of water must flow to cleanse it. River is water : water is esoteric truth. It is still a curious matter how people take filth in the wrong way. I mean, they do not see the filth of their False Personality, of merit, of superior feelings, of self-complacency. When a man feels the power of the Work-ideas, he begins to *see* internally. His inner sight opens and he then makes contact with the Conscious Circle of Humanity. He receives influences different from those entering his senses from life. But he must keep his feet washed. When Christ washed the feet of his disciples, it meant that his teaching, if understood and followed, cleansed the external man, the external woman, from the mud of False Personality. Try to bring the Work into your minds when you feel negative and see what it means for yourselves to "wash the feet".

When a man feels the Work and senses its meaning, the sight that he now has psychologically is different from the sight that he has had from the foot. He now sees Smith as his foot, so to speak. He sees the mud of his foot, but he must not lift that mud up to his eyes which are viewing a different order of meaning, a different world; a different level of consciousness. There are many phrases in the Old Testament about this. I quote one passage:

> "And it came to pass, when Joshua was by Jericho, that he lifted up his eyes and looked, and, behold, there stood a man over against him with his sword drawn in his hand: and Joshua went unto him, and said unto him, Art thou for us or for our adversaries? And he said, Nay, but as captain of the host of the Lord am I now come. And Joshua fell on his face to the earth, and did worship, and said unto him, What saith my Lord unto his servant? And the captain of the Lord's host said unto Joshua, Put off thy shoe from off thy foot for the place where on thou standest is holy. And Joshua did so." *(Joshua* V 13-15)

This means that he lifted up his spiritual eyes and saw that he was confronted with a sword—i.e. that he was confronted with spiritual truth which was contrary to the way he was trying to go. Sometimes we may have such an experience ourselves when we lift up our eyes in this sense. We may see that we are going quite contrary to the truth of this Work—that we are going with our foot when we should go with our eyes. The very fact that he is told to look up (he lifted up his eyes) means that he no longer looks down at his feet. He becomes aware of another path to follow, quite different from that which he would have followed if he had been looking downwards at his feet. Self-Remembering is lifting up the eyes. David said: "I will lift up mine eyes unto the hills whence cometh my help." *(Psalm* 121).

To lift your eyes up in this Work is to remember yourself—i.e. to have insight into its meaning—because the spiritual eyes are inside, not outside. We speak in this Work of the inner senses. When a man remembers himself he gathers about him all the Work that lies in him and all his understanding of it. This is his most supreme form of

Self-Remembering. He then sees the issue with new eyes and all that the foot was muddy with—namely, all that he was identified with and taking personally, all his life-resentments and internal accounts and useless suffering, and all the rest of it. All this vanishes as if it were nothing when seen through the spiritual eyes, the spiritual insight. From the standpoint of esotericism we are all blind, looking down at our feet. When Christ healed the blind it meant not merely something literal but something psychological. "Whereas I was blind, now I see." Paul had to be struck blind before he could see. This Work is to make us see. One has first to see one's foot, so it begins with self-observation. Through Smith observing Smith, which is his foot, and separating, he enters possibly another range of influences and perhaps begins to make contact with the influences of this Work. This is practical work. But it must be kept separate from the feet, and the mud of the feet must never be brought up by the hands to the eyes.

Quaremead, Ugley, March 16, 1946

FURTHER NOTE ON SEALING ONESELF FROM LIFE

At a recent meeting here we spoke further about the question of sealing ourselves from the effects of life. I spoke last week about *inner stop*. This is a Work-phrase and it means that there are certain situations in which we must stop impressions from taking a negative form. We must stop this internally as an act of the Work. I said that supposing you see someone in this Work whom you do not like, and every time you see this person you allow negative impressions to fall on you, and accept them and so identify with them, the result will be that sooner or later you will discharge these negative impressions in words and deeds on someone else or on the person whom you dislike. Your dislike is nourished by what it feeds on and what it feeds on is your continual reception of unpleasant ideas about this person. So, if you take in unpleasant impressions, eventually you will have to give them out. Inner stop means that you do not allow the impressions to have an effect on you. You do not argue about them but you simply stop them inside. The other point that was mentioned was that we have to make ourselves passive to life. Things do not go the way that we expect them to go and as a result we are continually upset. To make oneself passive to life is of course a very great matter. We have to begin to try to make ourselves more passive to what happens and this requires great inner activity. It requires a very conscious relationship to oneself. In my case it means to make Nicoll passive to what happens so that what he experiences is something that *I* do not accept necessarily. You will see at once that unless I can make a distinction between 'I' and

Nicoll I cannot make myself passive to life. If I take Nicoll as 'I' and 'I' as Nicoll, then I will be always under the domination of life and its changing events. I will be simply a mechanical man.

Now it has been said very often that this Work must be protected from life just as small children must be protected. How will you protect the Work from life so that it can grow and develop? If your name is Smith, you must protect the Work from Smith. This means that you can only protect the Work in yourself if you can separate from your mechanical Personality. You cannot add the Work to Smith. You have to start with Smith and begin to see Smith and to become different from Smith. Then you can make a place in yourself for the Work, because otherwise Smith, who will never understand the Work, will always pull it to pieces and destroy it. The Work starts with inner separation from your Personality. Your Personality has been acquired through the Third Force of life and the Third Force of life will keep it active—that is, life will keep, in my case, Nicoll, in its power. I have to separate from Nicoll: I cannot straightway overcome Nicoll because Nicoll is very powerful in comparison with 'I' for a long time. But the very act of beginning to see Nicoll, in my case, makes something else in me which is not Nicoll. This *new* thing which is separated from Nicoll is a part of me that can grow and receive and understand the Work, but for a long time this small, detached part of me must endure Nicoll and Nicoll will constantly take charge. Self-observation, in my case, is the seeing of Nicoll. All this occurs to every one of you—or at least it can if you observe yourselves. Observing 'I' does not identify with what it observes. I observe myself but that does not mean that I can change what I observe. Something in me begins to observe me. This 'something', which is Observing 'I', is the starting-point of a new place, which leads to Deputy-Steward, Steward, and Real 'I' or Master. But if nothing in me has ever observed me, and if, simply, I am always myself, the Work cannot start in me. I will be unable to make any inner stop in myself except from outside social reasons such as fear of loss of reputation in which case it is not 'inner stop'. I will never understand where the Work begins. Certainly, I will never be able to make Nicoll passive. I will be Nicoll all the time.

When a man begins to observe himself genuinely, when he begins to distinguish between this outer and inner, between his feet and the mud on them and his eyes, his insight, he then begins to enter the Work genuinely. He may have thought he was in the Work years before. He begins to see what his task is. Whereas he was blind, he now begins to see. He has insight into himself. He begins to see his feet which have carried him anywhere.

Whenever you take every psychological event in you as 'I', such as an unpleasant train of thought, or an unpleasant mood, you put the feeling of 'I' into it. You take it as yourself, as 'I', not as IT. Some people identify with all their thoughts and moods and feelings and sensations. They say 'I' to them all. They do not understand the Work.

By an act of Self-Remembering you draw the feeling of 'I' out of these inner states. But even self-observation can partly do this, because, if I observe a state in myself, I am no longer completely that state of mind. If I observe an unpleasant train of thought in myself I no longer identify completely with that unpleasant train of thought. Now identification is putting the feeling of 'I' into whatever happens. You can identify with your negative states—that is, you can take them as 'I'. If your name is Smith, instead of saying Smith is negative, you say: "*I* am negative."

You can reach a stage in this Work in which you begin to have a feeling of freedom from your moods, your emotions, and your thoughts. You observe them starting off, but you do not go with them, because you do not feel that they are you—that is, they are not 'I'. You may not be able to stop them. The Work does not say that you can stop your moods and thoughts just like that. It says that you can separate from them or observe them. It is quite true to say that you may get tired of your thoughts or your moods or your feelings. This may be simply that they wear out and will repeat themselves or it may mean that you have reached a stage in your consciousness of yourself in which you have something else in you that gets tired of them. Some negative emotions are certainly so difficult to deal with that it is a good thing that they wear themselves out. Yet if this happens *unconsciously* without any attempt at self-observation they will renew themselves after a short time. But if you have practised self-observation you will remember about them next time they come round. This is called Work-memory —that memory that comes from self-observation, which is a special form of consciousness. Self-observation is a conscious act. You will know that you have been through this or that before and that these states lead nowhere and so you will not identify with them so fully as you did formerly. This means that you begin to become sealed to a very small extent from their power, and later on in the Work you may become almost completely sealed from the power of certain old trains of thought, certain old moods, certain old feelings. You will not consent to them, you will not believe them. You will say: "I have been here before," and remember what happened and quickly depart. You will know better some evil places in your psychological country. A state is a place. Psychological places can be re-visited, but we are told what places to avoid—that is, what states to separate from—to seal ourselves from. But self-observation is the first necessity. What is self-observation? Let us imagine a play going on and a large audience looking at it, absorbed by it. This is yourself and your many 'I's and the stage is life. When you observe yourself you turn round and look at the audience.

THE IMPORTANCE OF OBSERVING MECHANICAL
DISLIKING

In the recent Commentaries the main subject has been the sealing of oneself from life. The Work cannot be formed in a person if he puts it right on the wayside of his life. The seed of the Work will not grow if it is scattered on the wayside, as is clearly shewn in the parable given by Christ of the Sower and the Seed in which it is said that "the sower went forth to sow, and as he sowed, some fell by the wayside, and the devil came and devoured them." The devil, of course, is ordinary life and the world of the senses, and so the outer mechanical side of us which is occupied with all the cares and anxieties of life. We understand so far that the Work must be protected in us from outside effects and must gradually penetrate more interiorly until finally it leads to contact with Higher Centres and Real 'I'. In this connection at a recent meeting we spoke about things that help to isolate us from the outer influences of life. All that the Work teaches comes in here. First we spoke about how knowledge of our Being helps because we no longer trust ourselves or take ourselves for granted or live on the surface of ourselves but begin to realize how we are many and how there are very dangerous 'I's in us from which we must separate. The next point was how we must practise non-identifying. Then we spoke about the importance of remembering oneself in the midst of life and through that feeling the difference between life and oneself. Self-Remembering is, of course, the supreme thing to use. And finally we spoke about how necessary it was to stop internal considering, which always arises from life-situations and which keeps us down in mechanical 'I's which cannot possibly understand the Work and will only destroy it. It is obvious then that we have to create a special place for the reception of the ideas of this Work. To-night I will add one or two other comments on this question of how we must begin to seal a place in ourselves from life. I will mention first mechanical liking and disliking. If a person has very strong disliking he will only reinforce his Personality. When you reinforce your Personality you do not seal yourself from life but increase your vulnerability to life. Some people admire their strong dislikes and prejudices but that is a mistake.

Let us reflect for a moment on what is the ultimate object that we have to attain. Before a man can be re-born, the Work teaches, he must realize his own nothingness. A person who has very strong dislikes and justifies them certainly does not realize his own nothingness. He feels himself very much to be something. It is a good thing to work on one's mechanical dislikes. But first of all it is necessary to be able to observe them. This is always the starting-point. If a man could really begin to feel his own nothingness he would be moving inwardly towards Real 'I' and certainly he could not be so full of mechanical dislikes. A strong feeling of dislike simply strengthens our mechanical Personality. We are told, in fact, to like what we now dislike, for this is acceptance, and all acceptance means the giving up of useless suffering. If you persist in dislike and justify it and make a mass of internal accounts in connection with it, you are simply adding to your mechanical suffering and wasting your force and stopping the development of understanding. One of the ways towards feeling one's own nothingness genuinely is to begin to try to like what we dislike. To live in mechanical disliking is to live mechanically and in that case your Being will remain exactly the same and you will therefore attract exactly the same events. Or it is a good thing to say to yourself: "What is my Being like in regard to disliking?" This is a practical way of beginning partly to see one's quality of Being. You get a man, for example, who objects to most things, who dislikes most people. This arises from his level of Being. He may find life very difficult but he does not connect it with his state of Being. He does not see that, as long as all these dislikes and prejudices and narrow attitudes exist in him, his Being cannot change, and certainly such a man will never be able to get near that point called in the Work the realization of one's own nothingness. Such a man will probably think that everyone dislikes him and that if he could only go to a new environment and start over again things would be different, but actually his Being would at once attract the same situations and after a short time in which he felt enthusiastic at meeting new people he would find the same difficulties. For this reason it is important to work on one's dislikes, especially on one's strong dislikes, which only increase the power of the Personality and through that the power that life has over us. There will then be the question of sealing oneself from the effects of life, because strong dislikes will connect oneself with life continually, at every moment. There will be not even a breakwater and certainly not a sea-wall in such a man. In observing your disliking, start with your strong dislikes and try to make a list of them and write them down. Then say to yourself: "How is it that I dislike this person or that nation?" Now I will tell you a way of beginning to deal with your strong dislikes, once you have observed them. There are such things as irony and humour. I will only add that it is a good thing to begin to be ironical about yourself and amused by your prejudices.

Now you will remember that we have to live more consciously in life. All this 4th Way is based not on faith, or hope, or love, but on increase of consciousness. Faith, hope and love, which have been in the past the basis of three major religions, are not excluded, but the emphasis in the 4th Way is laid upon increase of consciousness, and that is why the 4th Way begins with self-observation, the object of which is to make us conscious of ourselves, of what we are like—namely, to make us have real impersonal knowledge of our Being. If a man has strong mechanical dislikes and is controlled by them he is not living consciously. On the contrary, he is living mechanically. But if a man observes himself and becomes aware of his strong mechanical dislikes and the prejudices and attitudes that lie behind them, and begins to struggle with himself and refuse to go with them in a completely identified state, he is then breaking new ground in his own Being, and attempting to live more consciously. A moment or two of conscious behaviour in the midst of life each day can give one increase of force and alter things a little. We can all work for a few moments every day in a real way. As I have told you repeatedly, we cannot work continuously because we have not sufficient force of consciousness. But every moment in which you behave more consciously and see clearly how you might have behaved mechanically gradually increases the force of consciousness in yourself. You may not see any particular result for the time being, but you will gradually see the result—that is, you will gradually notice that some mechanical reactions, mechanical thoughts, by which you had been chained down hitherto, have less and less mastery over you and with that will come a change in the feeling of what you are. You may imagine that you used to be a stronger kind of person but you are wrong, because your strength lay in mechanical reactions. You thought your violence was your strength. Violence in the Work is always weakness. And so you begin to see a little what it means to realize your own nothingness. It is this realization of nothingness that can attract new Being. But this feeling cannot be invented. It is no good *saying* that you are merely nothing for such phrases conceal a great picture and so belong to False Personality. One feels it but does not say it. No one speaks of real feelings. When you begin to have traces of feeling your nothingness and dislike of your hitherto-ness, you find yourself flexible and so more capable—in fact, you feel released. Released from what? In my case, I feel released from Nicoll. As I said, strong Personality is always a sign of weakness in the Work-sense. When a man cannot separate himself from himself owing to his strong mechanical system of likes and dislikes, of thinking he is right and others are wrong, he is a weak man in the Work-sense. Such a man cannot change—he cannot seal himself from life—i.e. from himself—and so the Work can never find its right soil. The seed of the Work will be sown by the wayside and so his mechanical centres, the devil, will come and snatch it up. In general, it is the Personality that is the devil. Good soil is that which stands behind Personality, that more interior understanding which is not influenced at every moment by the flickering events of life and by the mechanical responses of the Personality to these events.

Let me remind you what self-observation is, because without self-observation no sealing can take place. A man is composed of many 'I's amongst which sits Observing 'I'. These 'I's are all looking at a play on the stage: the play represents life. This is the situation of Man asleep. When a man begins to observe himself, Observing 'I' turns round from the stage and looks at the audience and notices how each one is reacting. Some of these 'I's are perhaps jumping up and down and shaking their fists at the play, others are absorbed in it, others snoring, and so on. Observing 'I' begins to notice all these different reactions in the audience. This is self-observation.

Quaremead, Ugley, March 3, 1946

COMMENTARY ON ACCEPTANCE OF ONESELF

Someone asked recently: "Is self-observation a moment of accepting oneself or does that come afterwards?" Self-observation is different from accepting oneself. The point about self-observation is that it must be uncritical. It is through the work of Observing 'I' that we begin to awaken to what we really are and see our contradictions. Owing to the fact that we are many and that our level of Being is characterized by multiplicity of 'I's and so by lack of unity—lack of Real 'I'—we live in fragments which are not joined together and never clearly see that this is the case. So we are, without seeing it, all very difficult and contradictory.

To-night I wish to speak about acceptance. Acceptance comes after the work of uncritical Observing 'I'. Self-observation is not acceptance but what self-observation does is to present you with a fuller consciousness of yourself and, through the new material that it has collected in its special memory, you have to come to the question of acceptance that all these things are true of you. There is however a *curious state* in us all owing to which we do not accept ourselves. It is a curious state because we may know something about ourselves but will not admit it to ourselves. It does not belong to our general estimate of ourselves, to what we accept about ourselves, and one reason for this is that the action of False Personality with its picture of what we pretend we are like prevents this clear insighted acceptance from taking place. This is part of our hypnotic sleep. Here comes in the activity of self-justifying. But at the root of the whole problem lies this question of the hypnotic sleep of Man, which is kept up by buffers. Buffers prevent us from seeing contradictions and so prevent us from awakening from sleep. Buffers replace Real Conscience. If we had Real Conscience we would see and feel all sides of ourselves together. Such a state would completely destroy False Personality and all forms of imagination that contribute to its strength. We would become simpler, nicer. We all have buffers in every part of a centre but do not see them. Buffers take the place of Conscience, of Consciousness. As long as we are well-buffered we get through life fairly easily and have a good sense of our worth. Yet if buffers were suddenly destroyed in us we would go mad. Now it is only through the new memory that forms itself around Observing 'I' that we can begin gradually to see contradictions and become simpler. I spoke

874

some time ago about the dark side of us, the side that we do not properly admit into our consciousness and both know about and do not. Mr. O. once said: "We see only one half of things." We have to accept this dark side. It does not seem to correspond to our estimate of ourselves. Self-observation is compared, as we all know, with a ray of light let in to our inner darkness. So we gradually find that we are not what we thought or imagined. This is the beginning of self-change. We gradually find that Imaginary 'I' does not fit us properly. We are trying to be something that we are not and this produces a psychological inner strain. We do not correspond to ourselves. Here the idea of False Personality comes in. You say, for example: "Thank God, I am not like that publican." You may remember the parable. If you say this you are lying to yourself through the action of False Personality which always lies to you and always seeks to be superior to others. You *are* like that publican. You are no better and no worse than that publican. How can a person gain any peace, any inner balance, if all the time he is saying in so many words: "God, I thank thee, that I am not as the rest of men, extortioners, unjust, adulterers, or even as this publican. I fast twice in the week; I give tithes of all that I get"? And imagine calling in God who is defined as "living and active, and sharper than any two-edged sword, and piercing even to the dividing of soul and spirit, of both joints and marrow, and quick to discern the thoughts and intents of the heart." (*Heb.* IV 12.) Whatever we may understand by God, we may be quite sure that we can hide nothing from this supreme force of consciousness and that all our buffers, all our pictures, our pretences, all our inner lies, and everything to do with False Personality, all this is nothing but so much dirt. As we are, we live on one side of a circle. We live in the front or the back. So we cannot walk round the full circle of Being. We only admit part of our Being at a time. Mr. O. said we must see both sides together. Because we live in a half-circle of ourselves, and the other half is buffered off and not accepted in consciousness, we are easily upset. Do you think there is anything that we can be accused of that is not to some extent true? I cannot believe that a man who has become conscious of the full circle of himself would lose anything save the valueless things of False Personality. Would not this give such a man a greater inner stability? Such a man would no longer have buffers—and let me remind you here that once a buffer is destroyed it can never re-form itself. I fancy that such a man would never be rendered useless by anything that was said to him, that might in another man offend his self-love, his vanity, his pride, and produce endless hatreds and recriminations and jealousies.

When people talk to me about their private difficulties and their hidden life I do not find anything astonishing because I have learned through this Work that all these things are also in me and that it is useless pretending they are not. Do you remember that the other person who prayed said: "God be merciful to me a sinner," and it was said: "This man went down to his house justified rather than the other."

Notice, not self-justified, but justified of God. No one can feel his own nothingness unless he accepts this other half of the circle. Then he will feel no illusions about himself and in a quite strange way he will feel at peace. He will feel stronger, not weaker, and it is then that he will be shewn what he has really to work at and transform because he is then no longer building on the sand of False Personality.

Quaremead, Ugley, April 6, 1946

FURTHER NOTE ON ACCEPTANCE OF ONESELF

PRELIMINARY NOTE ON SILENCE

The Work says much about the practice of Inner Silence. One must practise the sealing of oneself from oneself, as regards mechanical talking—the sealing of oneself from one's mechanical self, from mechanical talking, from scandal, bad talking, which makes it so difficult to seal oneself from oneself. The Work can only grow from what is sealed in oneself and protected from life. We can know many things about one another, but never speak of them. One rule of the Work is that when we meet each other, accompanied by strangers, we do not recognize each other. This is an example of silence. I will speak further of this, and what the intention of it means, at a later meeting. Ordinarily—that is, mechanically—everyone blurts out how he or she saw so-and-so with so-and-so. This is mechanical and usually scandalous talking. This is what is meant by the verse in the Book of Proverbs: "The wicked man speaketh with his feet." (*Prov.* VI 13.)

*   *   *

At a recent meeting it was said that one must not work against one's Being until one has accepted it. It must be understood that this means something on a very big scale. We have, of course, as we are, to try to work on our Being according to what the Work teaches us to do in that respect. I find this very difficult to explain. Let me try to give some approximate example. Let us take mechanical talking about which the Work speaks so much. If I do not accept the fact that I talk mechanically I will not be able to change it. I will say that I work against mechanical talking in myself, that I always do my best not to talk mechanically, yet at the same time, if you can see what I mean, I am not necessarily accepting that I talk mechanically. I am still working from False Personality—therefore my work will be unreal. Some people, Mr. Ouspensky once said, work all the time in a kind of dream. They do not really see, he added, what they are working on. For this reason he emphasized so much that we have to see this other side which we keep in darkness and do not properly accept. As was

876

explained, this is due to the curious action of buffers in us which prevents us from seeing what we are really like and what we have in ourselves. Things have to be driven home into us before we can find the strength really to see and change ourselves. That is why sometimes it is very useful to be told by your teacher that, for example, you talk mechanically. It becomes a shock, although in a sense you have admitted that you do, but you do not do anything about it. When a person tells you that he knows quite well that he is a liar and admits it quite easily, you may be quite certain that he has not accepted the fact that he is a liar. If he really understood emotionally that he is a liar he would never mention it just like that. As I said, the action of buffers is very curious because it keeps us in a sort of half state. We both know and we do not know. But the actual fact has not yet been driven home into our consciousness that we are liars and lie practically every time we open our mouths. Just in the same way a man can acknowledge that he has many different 'I's in him, he may talk glibly about it all, but he does not yet accept it. He does not see emotionally that it is quite true that he is not one but many different people. In such a case the Work rests on the surface of such a person and has not yet penetrated and become real to him. He may say that he observes himself every day but he is not really observing himself. He imagines he observes himself and so he lives in Imaginary 'I'. The Work has to penetrate into all centres eventually. The great problem of the Work is how to awaken the Emotional Centre. When the Emotional Centre is awakened your whole theme of yourself changes. You see that you do not remember yourself; you see emotionally that you do lie, that you do speak mechanically; you see emotionally that you do not work on yourself but all the time pretend that you do. It is the awakening of the Emotional Centre that drives things home so that we realize these strange words: "Thou art the man." David, after he had taken Bathsheba for his wife, having caused her husband Uriah to be slain in the forefront of the battle, was visited by the prophet Nathan, who told him a parable. The parable was about a rich man with many flocks and a poor man who had only one ewe-lamb. Although the rich man had many sheep he took the poor man's one ewe-lamb and killed it when he needed a meal for a guest. On hearing this David said in anger: "The man that hath done this is worthy to die." Whereupon the prophet said to him: "Thou art the man." (*II Sam.* XII 7.)

You know how difficult it is when an accusation is brought home to you, how you turn and twist and justify yourself and find excuses. In other words, you cannot accept it. This Work becomes very real and grim as people advance in it and that is why acceptance is so necessary. Acceptance destroys Personality and all imagination about oneself and brings one to a new basis from which the Work can start. But for this to happen, real self-observation must take the place of imaginary self-observation. Something must be broken in us before we become sane—before we can begin to awaken.

Let us review briefly what this Work teaches us about Man on this Earth. The Work says that Man on this Earth is asleep and that the whole world is full of sleeping people and for this reason nothing can go right with the world. The Work says that this sleep is a strange form of sleep and calls it hypnotic sleep and here the Work-parable comes in, in which it is said that there were two farmers who had a great many sheep. Being very lazy and mean, when they found that some of the sheep were escaping, they decided to hypnotize the sheep and to tell them that everything was very beautiful and wonderful and to teach them to sing hymns and to make them believe that they were all going to Heaven. Actually all that they wanted was the wool on the sheeps' backs for their own purposes. This state of hypnotic sleep which humanity lies in is not outside you but inside you. This is why the Work says that everyone lives in False Personality and in Imaginary 'I'. If this hypnotic state is to be broken we have to wake up to ourselves and as long as we are governed by False Personality and Imaginary 'I' we shall remain asleep. It is for this reason that the Work teaches us so much about what we have to do, what we have to observe, and what we have to work against and separate from in ourselves.

Let us speak for a moment about negative emotions. You know the Work teaches that the Emotional Centre is dominated by negative emotions and that this beautiful and wonderful instrument, which if purified can give us even clairvoyance, is rendered useless by all the self-emotions arising from False Personality. When people identify with the infinite variety of their negative emotions they remain in a state of hypnotic sleep and are used by these two farmers who simply want their wool and their flesh, and so it is a good thing to study how to awaken.

All awakening begins with self-observation through which you gradually realize that you are not the person you thought you were—that is, if you accept what your Observing 'I' gradually teaches you about yourself. All this is called making Personality passive so that Essence can grow. When you can accept every accusation and insult without reacting violently you are beginning to understand the place from which this Work can grow and produce another being in you, so notice what upsets you most violently, what makes you indignant, what makes you say that you cannot stand it any longer, for this is a very good guide to self-observation and to what you have to observe. When you begin to feel your own nothingness you begin to receive the help of the Work to replace that nothingness by something. So you have to go down a long way before you begin to go up.

THE PARABLE OF WALKING ON THE WATERS

In a short time we will start the teaching of this Work from the beginning. At present we will continue to speak of this question of sealing oneself. I remind you that the Work cannot fall on our ordinary selves and grow and produce results. A person must feel the Work as something utterly different from life and all he has learned from life. You can say it is spiritual, not physical, not material, not *outside* you, as life is. For that reason it was said that the Kingdom of Heaven is *within* you. We spoke about the meaning of "within" or "inner". As a practical example it was said that Observing 'I' and the practice of self-observation move the centre of gravity of consciousness inward. You begin to see *yourself* as something outer, acquired, *you do not just be yourself*. You begin to see a new you. This is a movement inwards.

To-night I wish to refer to the parable of Christ walking on the waters in connection with the idea that we must seal ourselves. We must seal ourselves sometimes from life and from the way we take life. They are really the same, but not quite. The man, the woman, easily upset, must seal themselves from life—that is, from what upsets them. But this depends whether they can separate from that side which is upset. So it is a sealing of oneself from life and from one's mechanical Personality which latter determines for one how one reacts to life, takes life, judges life, and feels one is right or wrong. In my case I may be able to seal myself from Dr. Nicoll and the way he takes everything. That does not mean that I overcome Dr. Nicoll. It means simply that I have a place, a locked room, a private room, where Dr. Nicoll cannot enter. Here the Work can grow. After a time, this inner place, gained through self-observation, when it is strong enough, can no doubt overcome Dr. Nicoll. But at first this is impossible. Yet if I ever get as far as this a distinction is made—a separation inwardly. I am now *two* —not one. No one, the Work says, can shift himself from where he is unless he divides himself into two—becomes an observing and an observed side. If you have Magnetic Centre you are in a sense two, but not yet actually. You have the possibility of the Work. All growth is by division. One cell divides into two. Man as a self-developing organism, a cell, must become two first of all. In my case I and Nicoll must become a very real experience of inner separation. I observe Nicoll doing things yet am not Nicoll. This is not easy. It is easy to hear—not easy to do. To do what the Work teaches is one thing: to hear what it says is another. The second note in the Work-Octave of personal development is, we are told, to apply what the Work teaches to ourselves. This is not understood save after long contact with the ideas and a real struggle about the whole matter. The Work begins to fight with life in you. People say, for instance: "Oh, the meeting was all about self-observation and we have heard all that so often." No doubt you have. But have you ever really observed yourself consciously and uncritically and looked at yourself from this absolutely neutral angle where no self-justifying or excuses count? Or are you all the time taking yourself as yourself and thinking it is the only way to take life?

In the parable about walking on the waters we have an idea that exists in different form in the Work. Suppose we could always remember ourselves. Then we should be at the third level of consciousness and all that took place lower down at the second level, where in my case Nicoll exists, the so-called waking state of consciousness, would have no power over me. That is, you would be sealed from your mechanical ways of thinking and feeling and acting and taking life and judging it and so on. So you would, as it were, *walk on yourself*. Now imagine that you suddenly identify. Then you would sink. Where would you sink? You sink down to the ordinary level of yourself—in my case to Nicoll—to how you take life, view life, think of life, judge life, as you were taught—that is, as your Personality was laid down in you—to what you acquired.

Let us quote the parable:

"Jesus therefore perceiving that they were about to come and take him by force, to make him king, withdrew again into the mountain himself alone. And when evening came, his disciples went down unto the sea; and they entered into a boat, and were going over the sea unto Capernaum. And it was now dark, and Jesus had not yet come to them. And the sea was rising by reason of a great wind that blew. When therefore they had rowed about five and twenty or thirty furlongs, they behold Jesus walking on the sea, and drawing nigh unto the boat; and they were afraid. But he saith unto them, It is I; be not afraid. They were willing therefore to receive him into the boat: and straightway the boat was at the land whither they were going." (*John* VI 15-21)

Every parable in the Gospels is about something in this Work. Suppose that you have to make some parable about Self-Remembering or about False Personality and so on, you would find yourself writing parables just as they are in the Gospels. Let us think what this parable means about Christ walking on the waters. It is more fully explained in one of my chapters on the Gospels but we can understand to a certain extent what it means now. Notice that Christ was tempted to become a king on Earth and then he went up into a high mountain. What do you think this means? Always understand that Christ was tempted as we are. It would be a great temptation to be made King of the Earth. But he went up into a high mountain. Surely that means that he remembered himself, remembered what he had to do, what his task was. Exactly the same idea in different images comes into the next part of the parable. The storm arising at sea represents the storm that arises in us all, let us say, when we get negative, when we identify. Christ walking on the waters represents a state of being in which he could walk on all these stormy waters of himself and not sink. The two ideas, going up into the mountain (after he was tempted to be King of the Earth) and again, how he walks on the stormy waters of himself, are similar. They represent the state of Self-Remembering. And the interesting thing is that when Christ says: "It is I", the Greek constructionis very emphatic. Literally it means: "I am I" (ἐγώ εἰμι), which, as you know, is the definition of Jehovah who said once: "*I am that I am*". The third state of consciousness which none of us has attained except in flashes is that state in which one remembers oneself, one becomes 'I' above all the other little 'I's in oneself. So you can see that these illustrations in these parables are about Self-Remembering shewing how Christ had the complete power of remembering himself, of finding Real 'I' in himself, which gave him power over all his life-'I's. And this of course means that he could seal himself from himself and the effects of life on his human self.

Two sides of Self-Remembering are spoken about in this parable. When Jesus withdrew himself into the mountain he remembered himself in what we can call a passive way—that is, he withdrew himself from himself and reached a higher state of consciousness in which no further contact existed with his lower 'I's. Then we find that the other side of Self-Remembering is also mentioned. He went down into the stormy sea and walked on it. One of the greatest teachings of this Work is that we are not properly conscious and that we cannot do anything with ourselves in a real way until we begin to reach the higher level of consciousness called Self-Remembering, Self-Consciousness, Self-Awareness. You will remember that I spoke to you all about this recently when I said that the Driver has to climb up to a higher level —otherwise he cannot drive his horse and carriage. The practice of Self-Remembering is possibly not so difficult as you think. It is a rising above one's stormy seas, above one's Personality, jealousies, envies, anxieties, cares, and all the rest. Many times it has been said to you that unless you believe that there is a higher level both in yourself and in the categories of mankind—i.e. a conscious circle of men—you will not be able to remember yourself. If you have Magnetic Centre in you you have always known in a strange way that there is something higher; but Magnetic Centre by itself can only lead you to the Work and cannot keep you in it. If you hear the Work with your mind and not with your external ears, you begin to see what it is about, you begin to find in yourself endless verifications. Through the power of the Work taking the place of Magnetic Centre you can begin to remember yourself, but if you take life as itself you will sink—i.e. once a difficulty arises in life and you feel yourself badly treated you will identify with all the small 'I's in yourself that have been formed in you by your upbringing. So you will fall down, you will sink into the waters of your own Personality, and then you will forget yourself and become just an ordinary mechanical man serving Nature. Merely to try to remember oneself by withdrawal, by going up into the mountain, is not enough. This will certainly give you an idea of what you have to do, what your real aim is, but then, having heard with your inner mind what you have to do, you will have to go out into life and walk on the waters and not sink. But let me repeat, as long as you take yourself as yourself, you will never get anywhere in this Work. If you cannot observe yourself, you cannot shift from where you are.

Quaremead, Ugley, April 20, 1946

A NOTE ON FALSE PERSONALITY AND IMAGINARY 'I'

Let us once more think about the *Three Lines of Work*. We are taught that a person must do the three lines of Work sooner or later, otherwise nothing can ensue. The first line of Work is work on yourself through self-observation, and applying the ideas of the Work practically to yourself—that is, not identifying with your negative states, and so on. The second line of Work is work with other people in the Work and externally considering them. This line is very important for many of you at present. The second line of Work depends on seeing a person as yourself. "I am them and they are me." In the second line of Work it is necessary eventually that people you are working with in the Work begin to exist in you and become Work 'I's. "Thou shalt do no murder" means on the psychological level, as distinct from the literal level, that you give existence to another in yourself and do not murder that existence by temporary acts of self-will, This gives a field of force and is the beginning of forming a Work-accumulator. In the Work this is possible. In life it is not possible because life divides people through hatreds, scandals, etc. If you have followed the first line of Work sincerely you will begin to see that you are not what you imagine. Then, and then only, can you do the second line of Work rightly. You see that what you criticize in others exists also in yourself. If you try to do the second line of Work in a charitable way without having followed the strict discipline of the first line of Work, if you have not seen that in yourself exists so much that you criticize in others—you cannot do the second line of Work rightly. You will do it sentimentally, piously— that is, in an entirely false way. You will then be awfully kind to a person whom you really hate, which is a horrible thing. The third line of Work is about my work and what I am aiming at. It has to do with how this Work can be carried on, how each of you can help me to carry on this Work. Some people can do the first line of Work to a certain extent and also touch the third line of Work, but all three lines are equally important.

To-night I wish to speak to you about the first line of Work and to a certain extent about the second line. Recently it was said that False

Personality and Imaginary 'I' are two different conceptions in the Work, although sometimes we have spoken of them almost together as if they were the same thing. Let us take the conception of False Personality in us all. No one can do the second line of Work if False Personality is predominant in him or her. False Personality is the unreal thing in us. Personality is not really in the same category. All of us have to have strong Personality in ourselves. For example, we all have to learn our jobs in life and be able to do something more or less in life. Personality is the acquired side and the Work says you should have a good acquired Personality before you can really do this Work, but False Personality is quite different. I may as a result of my training have acquired from my Personality a certain knowledge of medicine. This is quite right. A person who has never learnt anything from life and cannot do anything in life is not a suitable person for this Work. People who try to enter this Work, who have done nothing in life, who know nothing in the ordinary sense, who have never had the patience to learn anything, who are no good at any jobs in life, are quite un-suitable for this Work. They have not in the faintest degree touched this level which the Work calls Good Householder. That is why I often ask, when someone suggests bringing in a new person into the Work: "What has he or she done?" If I hear that this person has done nothing at all, has taken up this or that and dropped it and is incapable of adapting to life in any way, then I am reluctant to accept this person. We were once upon a time all of us asked in the early days of the Work, when we tried to introduce a new person: "What is he? What has he done?" On one occasion that I remember very well I thought that someone would be suitable and I was cross-examined very severely about what this person had done, what he was, what he knew. I remember that I answered that he was a very nice person but had not done anything at all and I was told that it was quite impossible to have such a person in the Work. O. said to me on one occasion: "You are trying to bring in a person, however nice he may be, who has not gone through the ordinary life-training. Such a person", he added, "will enter this Work, having failed in life, thinking that here in this Work he will have an easy time." So you must all understand that in bringing new people into this Work you must be intelligent and not bring in a lot of tramps who are no good in life.

Let us continue with the attempt to understand what False Person-ality means. Every one of us, whether we are good at life or not, has very strong False Personality. Let us begin by saying that False Personality is an invention of yourself—a pretence. It is something unreal in you, which only self-observation, uncritical and sincere, can modify, and finally make passive. We have been speaking for a long time about how we are not what we imagine we are. Sometimes I deliberately work on someone in this connection—i.e. the undermining of False Personality. When I see it is quite impossible to do anything in this direction I stop. Sometimes I wait and if nothing happens I know at once that this person cannot be touched yet as regards False Personality—that is, the imaginary feeling that the person has of himself or herself. In short, there is something of which such people cannot let go and certainly should not until they have come to that point in the Work where some other place in them is sufficiently furnished to allow them to let go of their imaginary ideas about themselves. One interesting thing about a person who is very strongly in False Personality is this: such people are always on the opposites. They are always comparing themselves with other people in the sense of feeling better than they are, or, more rarely, worse. They are always making discriminations from the False Personality about other people. They are, as it were, dividing people into two classes: "People I approve of and people I disapprove of."

There was a teaching in mediaeval times based on the word κένωσις —i.e., emptying yourself of yourself. All the Sermon on the Mount is about it. Perhaps some of you have read that rather interesting esoteric book that comes from Sufi literature—The Conference of the Birds. Here it is related that the Birds set off on a journey, corresponding to the path of the Work, and when they reach their goal they have lost all their feathers. If you see what this Work is, you realize that it is a journey, a path, that you have to follow. We have to lose our feathers. By doing so we make room for something else to enter us. Something we were full of becomes emptied and then something else can come in, and that which comes in is just what will change us. It is impossible for any of us to add a cubit to our stature by ourselves, but the False Personality thinks it can and it will fight to maintain itself. I remember one occasion, when Mr. Ouspensky was talking about the False Personality and how it can only give us unreal things and only attract unreal things, unreal people and unreal position, he said: "I had come to the conclusion a long time ago that there was no escape from the labyrinth of the opposites, of the contradictions, in which we ordinarily live, except by an entirely new road, unlike anything we have hitherto known, but where this road began I was unable to say. I could only say that I knew already as an undoubted fact that beyond the thin film of false reality there existed another reality from which for some reason we were separated and it seemed to me that the way to this unknown path might be found in the East, in some teaching that I knew nothing about."

So you will understand that False Personality gives us false reality and makes us do things which if we have a deeper understanding we may hate to do and of which we may feel the futility and yet be unable to change the course of our lives. When we are in False Personality—in life—in externals, and so in rivalry—we cannot place ourselves in internal reality. We are glued to the outer sense of things. A person then is an outward thing, an appearance of flesh. So one does not see where or what that person is psychologically—internally—that is, the Being of the Person escapes one. This is the giddy round of outward appearance. I mean, it is false reality, and so unhappy. To place oneself *inside* reality, which is always in motion, to adapt to its changing direction, and to try to grasp it apart from time and change—that certainly is a movement inwards and a new vision of what is real. A stiff person with stiff frozen values cannot possibly reach this fluid state of truth. To such a person truth is *stone*—inflexible. But to a person who begins to separate from False Personality and Imaginary 'I' truth becomes water—that is, *relative* or *flexible*—not "either-or", not Yes *or* No—but both Yes *and* No. This redemption from that frozen psychological death that grips so many so early is possible for anyone who takes the following of the ideas of the Work as more important than his fixed opinions and psychological habits. I would add here that to anyone who grasps the Ray of Creation and its tremendous meaning even a little it will be difficult to sit in his small vanity and pride. Apparently, from that great diagram, we are curiously unimportant people—in view of many higher levels of Beings. This emotion weakens vanity and pride—and so weakens False Personality. So the Work says: "Unless a man can believe in *Greater Mind* he is useless in this Work."

Now we come to the conception of Imaginary 'I'. Imaginary 'I' is the imagination that we have a real permanent 'I' that always answers consciously, behaves consciously and consistently. We imagine that we are always one permanent person and always the same. Imaginary 'I' is what gives us a false, unreal sense of unity. The reality that False Personality and Imaginary 'I' manufacture is that through which we try to live our lives. On one occasion G. said: "It is the greatest mistake to think that Man is always one and the same. A man is never the same for long. He is continually changing and yet he imagines himself to be the same 'I' all the time. It is difficult for him to accept that from one moment to another the 'I' in him changes. He is convinced that he is a unity, a real person. But he seldom remains the same even for five minutes. We think that if a man is called Ivan, he is always Ivan. Nothing of the kind. Now he is Ivan, in another minute he is Peter, and a minute later he is Nicholas or Sergius. And all of you think he is Ivan the whole time and perhaps you know that Ivan cannot do a certain thing—i.e. he cannot tell a lie—and then you find that he has told a lie and you are surprised that he, Ivan, could have done so. In fact, you will say, perhaps quite rightly, that Ivan cannot tell a lie. It was Nicholas who lied and when an opportunity presents itself for this 'I' called Nicholas to be upper-most Nicholas cannot help lying. You will be astonished when you realize what a multitude of these 'I's, Nicholas, Peter, and so on, live in one man. If you learn to observe them there is no need to go to a cinema."

These words of G. make us think again of the definition of the Being of Man in this Work. The Work says that Man's Being, in this state of sleep in which he is, is characterized by multiplicity—that is, by lack of unity. Instead of having a real unity we have this Imaginary 'I', this imaginary unity, which is entirely false, and so two people meet together and hope to be happy, not understanding that they are many, in each case about a thousand different women and about a thousand different men. A woman thinks, let us say, that she is marrying Ivan, but she is also marrying Nicholas, and all the others, and vice versa.

We will end this paper simply by saying that False Personality is one thing and Imaginary 'I' is another thing, but they both give us a false reality. That is why the Work teaches us so much that we must observe False Personality and observe Imaginary 'I' and try to get behind this imaginary reality to a deeper reality where things are quite different.

Quaremead, Ugley, April 27, 1946

COMMENTARY ON ATTITUDES

We have not spoken for some time about attitudes. In the last paper we spoke about False Personality and Imaginary 'I'. It was said that these two Work-conceptions are different. Yet sometimes they come close together. I will review briefly in a slightly different way the difference between False Personality and Imaginary 'I'. False Personality is that which gives you an entirely unreal existence and only attracts to you unreal things. It makes you identify with what is not yourself. On one occasion I was talking to Mr. Ouspensky about this and he said: "It is a great handicap to have a long line of descent." I asked him why this was and he said that people identify with their ancestors and yet they themselves are born into the world completely free from ancestors—that is, their real Essence comes into the world quite apart from the conditions into which it is born. In so many words he added: "If you feel pride in your origin in Time and Space you will never get to your real self." I remember that he repeated to me twice that we have to understand that we are not born through our parents but that our Essence comes down from the stars as something quite independent of our origin. In other words, what we have to understand is that in Self-Remembering we do not remember our ancestry or even our parents. We came down from an entirely different source. If you want to see what False Personality is like listen to two charwomen talking together. One of them says that her grandpapa had a house of his own and lived in style. The other one will perhaps say that her grandmother had ten years penal servitude and was in the papers. This curious thing called False Personality can actually make us feel that we are somebody because we had at one time or another a very distinguished, very notorious ancestor who committed several crimes and gave the police a great deal of trouble. False Personality is a very extraordinary thing to study both in yourself and in other people.

Now as regards Imaginary 'I', it was said that Imaginary 'I' is the imagination that you are always one and the same person and that you speak consciously on every occasion, that you know what you are doing, and, in fact, that you can do.

Now we pass to the question of attitudes. All this Work consists in separating oneself from one's unreal 'I's. False Personality is one unreal side of us and only attracts unreal things: Imaginary 'I' also attracts unreal things. But in this work of separating oneself from what is unreal the Work teaches many accessory ideas to which we have to apply self-observation. Attitudes are unreal things in us. Each one of you has certain ingrained attitudes or points of view, from which you regard everyone else and also regard yourself. They are chiefly connected with False Personality. Let me give you an example of an attitude. A man has acquired an attitude which makes him think himself in some way superior to certain people. When he meets these people his attitude operates mechanically in him. He does not like these people. Yes, but he does not like them from attitude, from mechanicalness. Suppose that I try to make this particular man see the value of some people towards whom he has this mechanical attitude. I introduce him to them, I begin to talk about them, what they have done, what they have been through, and so on. After a time he unbends. He is very surprised to find that these people are not at all what he thought they were. He will find they are quite interesting people. What is happening to such a man? What is happening is that one has got round his mechanical attitude through which he cannot take in new impressions, and one has, so to speak, undermined him. Undermined him in what? Undermined his False Personality, his negative and restricting attitude, and freed him therefore from part of his mechanical, acquired side. This man will now feel freer. The very expression of his face will begin to change, his way of talking will change, and instead of feeling any loss he will feel a sense of gain.

On one occasion Mr. Ouspensky was talking to me about attitudes. He said that attitudes are very difficult things to observe in oneself. He said: "They are laid down very early in us through our acquired psychology—i.e., through what we have been taught—and they are, practically speaking, always negative attitudes. He said that what people call a good education is what gives a person typical negative attitudes and when these negative attitudes have been properly implanted this young person is said to be properly educated. He said that in English education as far as he knew great emphasis was laid on boys and girls in growing up getting good negative attitudes and that as far as he could see that was the only education that was given. On one occasion I suggested that some of us should sing him some English sea-shanties. I was standing near him at the time and he smiled at me and looked at me and said: "Most of these people have been brought up with typical negative attitudes. How could they possibly sing sea-shanties? I could not bear sea-shanties sung with an Oxford accent." Now negative attitudes become gradually fixed in us and then become buffers. A typical negative attitude, unless one escapes from it, gradually settles down, as it were, and becomes crystallized out as a buffer. Once it has become a buffer it is very difficult to see. A buffer, I will remind you, is that which prevents us from seeing contradictions in ourselves. That is why a well-buffered man is often such a success in life. He appears to have a strong will. His buffers prevent him from seeing anything wrong with him and yet such a man from the Work point of view is a very weak man. He is very low down in the Scale of Being. Sometimes people have brought to me people for this Work and I have seen that they have very strong buffers. Then I know that it will be practically impossible to teach this Work to them because they are too weak inside. That is, they have nothing behind their façade of buffers which keep them in good humour with themselves, and if one should try to destroy a buffer in such people they might literally go mad because they have nothing internal, nothing behind them, nothing real.

In this Work, we begin with the idea of impersonal self-study—that is, we begin with the idea that we have to obtain knowledge of our Being. This can only begin obviously by means of turning round and looking into ourselves consciously, noticing how we speak and behave and so on. This is a movement inwards. Only in this way can a man begin to separate himself from himself. One part of this practice of conscious self-study is to observe our attitudes. When we reach the point of being able to observe attitudes to a small extent this actually starts something going in us which may lead to something strange, to new thoughts and feelings. So it is said that this Work begins with self-observation. We none of us know that we have attitudes. In general, we all take ourselves for granted just as we are and so never see that this is what we are—that is, that our state of Being attracts what happens to us the whole time. How many of you have ever realized that things are your fault? This is quite an easy thought if you take it sentimentally and pathetically. We surely all know this spurious form of self-blame, but what I mean is: how many of you have ever seen in a stark naked way without any self-justifying that something was entirely your fault and that in so many words: "Thou art the man."? Because we have this peculiar illusion about ourselves which is called hypnotic sleep in the Work we do not imagine that we have any particular attitudes. Now, as was said, our attitudes are practically always negative attitudes by means of which we distinguish ourselves from other people and so stimulate this false conception of ourselves called False Personality. Mr. Ouspensky once said: "We must get to observe and know all our negative attitudes. We may in a sense observe our negative attitudes but we take them as being perfectly right. But," he added, "the point here is that we really do not see that they are attitudes implanted in us by our education and by imitation and that they are not really ourselves at all." He said: "We must not only observe but know well in our memory what our attitudes are definitely and permanently." And he added: "Negative attitudes never pay—they simply make you empty. And when we once realize this we have no right and no excuse for identifying with them." On another occasion he said: "Attitudes never think. They work automatically. They are like hard places in the Intellectual Centre, like crystallized thoughts, and since they are practically always negative they finally become buffers." He once asked me: "How do you know when a person is speaking from fixed attitudes?" I said I did not know and he said: "You should know it at once. You become bored, you begin to yawn, when a man is speaking from fixed opinion. He is not thinking. Now attitudes are laid down in the Intellectual Centre and they take the place of real, individual thinking. They affect the Emotional Centre, but their starting-point is in the Intellectual Centre. If you see a person full of acquired attitudes and nothing else, you will feel at once that it is impossible to speak to this person. That is, you cannot free his thinking from these acquired attitudes."

On another occasion Mr. Ouspensky said: "If you are full of negative attitudes you will never be able to get in touch with any of the higher parts of centres in yourself and so not with any higher level of Being." He gave an illustration. He said: "When you have a great many negative attitudes of which you are quite unaware and which you have accepted as being you, it is just as if you have an enormous number of overcoats and you keep on wearing all these overcoats all the time and so it is impossible to reach you. In such a case," he added, "a man cannot pass through the narrow way of this Work, which is a question of inner sincerity. He will not be able to get through the doors and narrow passages unless he begins to discard all these overcoats that he knows nothing about and takes as himself."

I would add that you may be able to observe attitudes in other people fairly well and we know when a person is speaking from a typical attitude. It is certainly tiresome. It is far more difficult to observe typical attitudes in oneself and yet this has to be done. You can notice it partly by watching your intonation. This is one way out of many. When you are speaking from attitude you will notice that you are speaking in a flat dead voice. You will notice this in other people so try to see it in yourself. Then you may begin to see how ordinarily your life is made perhaps so unhappy, because of these attitudes which you have acquired and never seen through.

THE STUDY OF MECHANICAL ASSOCIATIONS

Change of Being depends on inner work on oneself. No one can change their Being without inner Work because unless they can separate themselves from their level of Being they cannot change and all separation depends on the observation of one's own Being. For example, science cannot change the level of Being of Humanity or the level of Being of yourself. Science is something external connected with the study of the outer world but self-observation is a question of inner study, the study of yourself. Recently we have been speaking about the study of False Personality in oneself, the study of Imaginary 'I', and last time we spoke about the study of attitudes and buffers in oneself. To-night, amongst other things, I will speak about the study of associations in oneself.

We all of us have in us a great number of purely mechanical associations which connect up centres in different wrong ways. These associations belong to our acquired psychology and so to our Personality. We can imagine these associations to be composed of a network lying over the centres and connecting them up in different ways. Then whenever a chain of associations is touched at one point the stimulus will cause the whole chain of associations to become active. In the study of associations it is best to begin with the Intellectual Centre. If you admit a certain thought into your mind it will ring up, so to speak, the Emotional Centre and all the other centres and so produce automatically certain feelings, certain movements, and certain appetites. All this belongs to our mechanicalness. One of the main objects of self-study through self-observation is to observe our machinery. It takes a long time for people to realize that what they take themselves as is really a machine. The Work consists in separation from this machinery. Habitual chains of association form a very strong part of this machinery. If you have attained some degree of self-observation, which means at the same time that you have a certain power of seeing your machinery, you will be able then to study associative paths between centres—that is, how one thing rings up another quite automatically. Centres in us are wrongly connected together by these associations. I said just now that you should begin to study by observation how associations automatically work, how a thought can ring up the whole chain of associations and lead to certain results. It is also possible to study associations from the side of Moving Centre—for example, you begin to walk quickly, impatiently, and instantly a whole series of emotions and thoughts automatically present themselves. The associative machinery can be studied from the intellectual side or from the moving side. For example, sitting in a certain posture will automatically arouse certain associations which will affect the Emotional Centre and the Intellectual Centre—namely, your feelings, your moods and your trains of thought. If you bear in mind that your centres are not free and do not work in the right way owing in part to all these mechanical associations that you have acquired, and if you have some degree of self-observation you will often be secretly amused with yourself in noticing how some accidentally aroused chain of associations wishes to grip you and make you identified. If you can notice this you will find after a time that these automatic chains of associations lose their power over you and this means that you are really becoming less of a machine than you were before you began to work on yourself.

As was said, associations make a network round centres. This network is gradually acquired from one's earliest childhood. As a result centres cannot work properly—i.e. they cannot do their own work. Consequently impressions from the external world cannot fall on the right place. They connect with things where there should be no connections. When you begin to realize to a certain extent that you are mechanical and that you are chained to a machine which is not really yourself at all, you will be able' to see how your life has, amongst other things, been governed by its automatic associations. You are already separated to a small extent from yourself as you thought you were. This already is a great step forward in inner work on yourself. It is also a step towards Self-Remembering because, as you know, one of the first experiences of the great meaning of Self-Remembering lies in the realization of one's mechanicalness. You are not your machine but something else. You need not take everything in the way you have always taken it, because you are something else. But this realization that one is not one's mechanicalness, not one's False Personality, not one's Imaginary 'I', not one's negative attitudes, not one's laid down associations, is always accompanied by a feeling of pain, or, as Mr. Ouspensky once said, a sour feeling, and he said on one occasion that very few people could bear this pain or sour feeling about themselves and so preferred to fall back into what they had always been. At the same time I would add that this painful or sour feeling is also accompanied by a feeling of freedom, a feeling of wonder that one has always been a slave to all this machinery which one has imagined to be one's real self.

When you have new thoughts in your mind, new ways of thinking laid down by the Work, you begin to escape from mechanical associations starting from the Intellectual Centre. These new thoughts, these new ideas that the Work teaches us, begin to give us a new way of thinking, a new mind. And this new mind can eventually make right connections between centres if it is given time enough. I do not see how it is possible to break mechanical associations without a complete new set of thoughts, ideas and eventually a new understanding. Life connects the machinery up all wrongly. It makes people take political sides, religious sides, and so on, but the influences of the Work produce in a person quite new associations, quite new connections. This Work is to make us think in a new way and that means at once that we cannot think in old ways. If we cannot think in the old ways then a host of mechanical chains of associations will be broken. At the moment it is very interesting to make some observations about mechanical chains of associations and I would be glad if any of you would be able to give some actual observations of purely mechanical associations that you have noticed in yourselves.

Quaremead, Ugley, May 11, 1946

FURTHER NOTE ON FALSE PERSONALITY

In a discussion on the paper about the difference between False Personality and Imaginary 'I', I noticed one serious mistake. It was said that Imaginary 'I' is an illusion from birth. A small child has no Imaginary 'I'. Surely you all know that a small child never says 'I'. He uses his name—he speaks of himself in the third person. He says, for example, "Bobby wants this", or "Baby wants this". Surely there is no question of Imaginary 'I' in the innocent state of a small child. The beginning of Imaginary 'I' comes when the growing child says, instead of "Baby wants this", "*I* want this". This is the beginning of Imaginary 'I'. A small child does not feel himself as Imaginary 'I'. The formation of Imaginary 'I' comes later. We have to learn to speak of ourselves in the third person. For example, in my case, I have to come to the point in my internal development of consciousness, through the work of separation, of saying: "Nicoll wants this", not "*I* want it". The formation of Imaginary 'I' belongs to a development which is acquired. You know the Work says that we are all born amongst sleeping people, also in a small sense we are all awake at birth. We are born into a world of sleeping people who say 'I' all the time without having the slightest realization of what they mean, so a small developing creature begins after a time to imitate the sleeping people round him, and at a certain moment says: "I wish this". Before that point, it is, as it were, innocent, but once it begins to say: "I wish this," it has become infected by the sleeping people by whom it is surrounded and begins to think that it exists as 'I'. You must remember that the development of Personality is that which is acquired by contact with life in early days, so both False Personality and Imaginary 'I' begin to take charge and from that point the growing person begins to have an entirely false relationship to himself. Amongst all these things that are acquired by imitation and example—in short, by the environment—are first of all and most important of all Imaginary 'I' and False Personality. The child begins to think that it has an 'I', a real permanent 'I'. Have you ever noticed when a child begins to say 'I' for the first time? And have you also noticed in what way it says 'I'? As far as I have observed it is always imitative. The child begins to imitate one or the other

892

parent or the nurse or anyone who stands closely to him. But, as you know, this is necessary because Personality with all its sins and faults and wrong connections has to be made in an ordinary growing person because this formation of Personality in general constitutes eventually what we as adults in this Work have to work against and separate from gradually.

As regards False Personality, it gives rise to very many wrong emotional reactions. False Personality is based on pretence, especially on imagining that you know something. The realization of our ignorance of even what we know can begin to undermine the tremendous power of the False Personality. It is unnecessary for me to say that False Personality always wishes rewards, medals, reputation, and all the rest of it. It strives to get the better of other people. It is ambitious. It tries to keep itself going at all costs—and all this is pretence. And behind this pretence lies an enormous ignorance and helplessness which I call the dark side of a person—i.e., the side he will not accept and will not admit into consciousness. To be amongst people with very strong False Personality is real torture for a man or a woman who has separated to some extent from the domination of his or her False Personality. When the False Personality is dominant it arouses all sorts of self-emotions in the Emotional Centre which can never lead to anything real. Two giants, the Work says, walk in front of us, called Vanity and Pride, and arrange everything for us in advance. This is the action of the False Personality on us so that we cannot, while we are under that domination, help leading false lives.

G. once said that the whole of the external world, all that is going on now, all that you read in the papers, is maintenance of False Personality—i.e., it is all a maintenance of what is unreal, invented. False Personality dominates our emotional reactions more than anything else does. O. once said: "If you can manage to turn all emotions arising from the False Personality against yourself, it will have a very different effect." He added: "Find in yourself what you hate in others and turn it round and begin to object to yourself and to hate yourself if you can. You can only see yourself through turning your emotional reactions round about and directing them towards yourself." Later on he said: "Real work is on the Emotional Centre. All that this Work teaches which must enter the Intellectual Centre first of all and be registered there finally becomes concentrated on the state of your Emotional Centre and its mechanical reactions."

When you do things from False Personality you are doing them externally. In such a case there is nothing internal in you that corresponds to what your False Personality is saying or doing. You are, in other words, pretending, inventing, keeping up something which is not you. Real Personality is different from False Personality because a man may have acquired a perfectly good knowledge of how to make something in which case he is more sincere. He has something real. He may, for example, be able to paint very well. He has acquired this.

But he may pretend to paint much better than he does or, in other words, he may pretend to a knowledge that he has not really got. All Personality, whether false or real, belongs to the acquired side and this acquired side must be built up as strongly as possible. That is why the Work says you must have a good Personality and that is why G. once said: "I can always talk to a man who knows something, such as a man who can make good coffee."

Next let us speak about behaviour from False Personality. A typical situation, constantly stressed in esoteric psychology, is always about doing a thing externally, without any internal side in yourself corresponding to what you are doing. For example, you may affect outwardly a belief that inwardly you are contemptuous of and despise. You pretend to a belief in which you do not believe. This means that nothing can grow in such a person's inner world. If the internal side—that is, the more essential and real side—is negative to this external side that manifests itself outwardly in life, if what he privately thinks wholly contradicts what he publicly professes, and if at the same time he cannot give up his external outward behaviour, a man is esoterically dead. He is governed by his False Personality and its ambitions and cannot give up this side and will never face himself internally, and in that case he is incapable of any inner development. Psychologically, esoterically or spiritually, this man is a living lie and he will never face the lie that he is. There are so many parables and sayings about this in the Gospels in connection with the Pharisees that it is unnecessary to say anything further except that the Work teaches that personal work on oneself depends entirely on inner sincerity with oneself. If False Personality is very strong there cannot be any sincerity with oneself, and one's life, although it may be a great success outwardly, is from the higher standpoint of esotericism a complete failure because there is nothing real there, nothing genuine. For that reason we have in the practice of this Work, which is based on self-study, through self-observation, to begin to notice the action of False Personality which always creates for us unreal life and takes away from Essence or our real side all possibilities of growth and causes us to have a thousand and one cares and anxieties which are quite unnecessary, which only make us more and more unhappy and constantly involve us in situations and problems that have no real existence. To be amongst people in whom the False Personality is to some extent in abeyance is to be in an entirely new world. This experience, which is possible for you all, while you are in it causes you to wonder what on earth you have been doing all this time. And certainly, to use the expression "what on earth you have been doing" is correct because what you have been doing is in or on the "earth" of yourself, the most outward, external side of you turned towards the world.

Now the inner part of a man is his will and his understanding. If the ideas of this Work no longer rest on the surface of yourself but begin to penetrate, if you begin to see for yourself the truth that they conduct, you move inwards towards the more internal side and so move away from the False Personality with all its inventions, pretences and forms of internal considering. When you realize that there is nothing that you can condemn in another person that is not in yourself as well—in fact, when you realize the meaning of the phrase: "Thou art the man"—you move inwards, to a more real existence, and begin to see everything in terms of a deeper meaning. Suppose we take moral arrogance or the temptation of power. Have you ever observed these two factors in yourself in connection with False Personality? You may think that you have no moral arrogance, for example. That impression of truth which leads, not to moral arrogance, but to the realization of the kind of person you really are, will give rise to mercy and to a much wider range of affection and quite possibly to a better state of bodily health. It is the same as regards the increasing temptation of power which encourages False Personality, but this is not the truth, esoterically speaking, although thousands have mistaken it for such and followed this path which leads to so much deliberate and also unconscious cruelty, and I mean by cruelty not only to others but to yourself, to the sides of you which can grow. Do you think that following moral arrogance and the love of petty domestic power will lead you to realization of your own nothingness? Can you conceive that such a path will make Personality more passive and enable all these unnourished, unwatered, real sides of you that belong to the Essence to grow and so change your level of Being? One of the teachings of this Work is to make Personality passive. In order to do that you have to see and observe what keeps Personality active in such a way that you always feel you are right. As long as False Personality dominates Real Personality the latter will be under the wrong leader and go in the wrong direction. False Personality ascribes everything to itself. It is certain that it can do. It is just here that moral arrogance and the temptation of power enter. But if the more internal part of you begins to become conscious, begins to become awakened through genuine self-observation sincerely done, you will begin to avoid these very ordinary temptations and instead of feeling a loss you will feel a gain. How difficult it is to talk to a person who, without knowing it, is full of moral arrogance, who, without knowing it, thanks God that he or she is not like other people. I have told you often that the simplest psychological mechanism in us is to see evil or short-comings in others and never to see them in ourselves. Here belongs the great idea of the Work that we have to become far more conscious of ourselves. The only path that leads in that direction is that of self-observation which changes our whole idea of ourselves and so destroys False Personality.

COMMENTARY ON SELF-REMEMBERING

We are taught in this Work that we are not conscious and that we do not remember ourselves. The Work says that the chief difficulty confronting any higher stage of humanity or of oneself is due to the absence of consciousness. We imagine we are fully conscious and that everything we do and feel and think is a conscious process. However the Work says that Man is asleep and that sleeping people can never bring about a better state of affairs. Our level of Being is characterized by this state of sleep which we are told first of all to study in ourselves. This state of sleep which defines from one angle our level of Being inevitably attracts the life belonging to that level of Being, the result of which we can see in the world to-day. Were people even a little more conscious the whole state of outer life would alter and what everyone thinks should be done in the name of common sense could be done. As you know, the emphasis in this Work is laid on this factor called consciousness. This Work is not based on faith or hope or love directly but on consciousness. Consciousness in the Work is called light. For example, if I remain in my ordinary state of consciousness which is really a state of sleep, my level of Being will attract what belongs to it. On a small scale some people are a little more conscious and others a little less. A man of low Being, a man without any trace of self-observation, if he is in power, will attract all that belongs to his level of Being.

To-night I wish to speak once more about Self-Remembering and what the Work teaches in regard to how we can change our own level of Being. You know that this Work teaches us to become more conscious of ourselves and that this begins with a certain form of self-observation. We are told to observe ourselves along certain lines which are quite definite and which everyone should know. Now Self-Remembering is an act which can be directed towards anything you like. A person may, for example, always remember his or her own misery and keep it in the forefront of themselves. The Work calls this negative Self-Remembering. This is not really a conscious act, as Self-Remembering must become eventually, but it is a mechanical Self-Remembering. Take, for instance, your different forms of internal accounts that you have made in the past—that is, what you think other people owe you—all the incidents in which you feel that you have not been given a proper chance. If you keep all this in the forefront of yourself it is exactly an example of negative Self-Remembering. Which self are you remembering in such a case—or which selves? You are remembering negative selves or 'I's. That is, you do not really in the Work-sense remember yourself, but you remember certain selves in you quite easily and these selves are in the negative sides of centres. People feel that they are no good. This is negative Self-Remembering and it leads nowhere. Real

Self-Remembering is to try to remember something that you are not, if you will allow this paradox for the moment to pass without argument. All real Self-Remembering begins with something to do with this Work. For example, it is said that when you remember yourself, you must try to remember your aim. Your aim must always be connected with something that concerns the ideas of this Work and to form such an aim you must already have had some considerable experience of self-observation from different angles of the Work. When you make an aim which is the definite result of self-observation, say, that you are always negative in connection with something or other in the past or in the present or both, then you can make a real Work-aim not to express this negative emotion outwardly and eventually not to identify with it internally in your Intellectual and Emotional Centres. This begins to form what is called Deputy-Steward in yourself—i.e. you put some 'I's that begin to understand what this Work is about in charge of you so that although you may constantly forget yourself—fall asleep—you are reminded that something is wrong in regard to your inner state. Eventually Steward will begin to appear. Steward is a much higher level than Deputy-Steward and comes down from above as help for you. Above Steward lies Real 'I'. If we could get in touch with Real 'I' directly without having to pay all that is necessary for this inner development, then we should be able to remember ourselves in the Work-sense of that term. But we have to start from where we are and gradually by a process of inner separation and selection learn not to go with certain 'I's and give the preference to other different 'I's which stand on a slightly higher level of our average being. But negative Self-Remembering is one of our very great difficulties and will stand in the way of any further inner growth. It is very easy to feel that one is no good, that one understands nothing, that one is not making any progress. It is very easy to yield to these 'I's that say "if only this", "if only that". All this is negative Self-Remembering and has to be separated from eventually. In fact, it is sometimes very astonishing to realize that what we thought was our genuine humility is nothing of the kind and that it is nothing but an artifice arising from our False Personality—i.e., that it is a form of vanity or self-pride.

You have heard that the only thing that we can sacrifice is our suffering. What does sacrifice mean? Sacrifice means originally *to make holy*. Does it mean that we have to make our suffering holy? No, its meaning is far deeper. As long as I identify with my suffering, as long as I ascribe it to myself, I will remain identified with it. Now whatever was made holy originally meant that with which all personal connection had been given up. It belonged then to God. If you like you can substitute for the word "holy" the word "conscious". You cannot become conscious of anything in yourself as long as you identify with it. To become really conscious of anything in yourself is to be no longer identified with it, no longer it. If I become conscious of my mechanical

897

forms of suffering and internal account-making and my negative states, they are no longer me. I detach myself from them, I let them go, as it were, I no longer feel myself by means of them. As a result, my feeling of myself will change. This act allows transformation to work and whatever is real in your suffering you will meet on a higher level completely transformed into something else, but as long as you tie yourself down to your suffering and really feel yourself through your suffering—in fact, feel your own importance in this way—you cannot expect any transformation. As I once said long ago, it is like standing on a plank and trying to lift the plank. You have to step aside, and then it is quite easy to lift it.

Whenever we remember ourselves in the mechanical sense by remembering our miseries and suffering, we are like Lot's wife. Our heads are turned round the wrong way and we look back into the past and then we are nourished by all sorts of unhappy memories which are engraved on rolls in negative parts of centres. We have to remember that we are now in this Work. This at once is a real form of Self-Remembering. A negative person must learn through personal self-observation not to remember his accounts and not to go with typical small negative 'I's that lie around like sharp points in the ground which only open old wounds. "We have," said G. on one occasion, "to learn how to walk. In order to walk it is necessary to have good shoes." And he added that he had leather to sell from which it was possible to make good shoes but that everyone had to make his own shoes out of this leather that G. had for sale. We must understand, of course, that he was talking about walking in oneself and avoiding dangerous places. Then we can walk in life without being upset and hurt by all the changing events that come to us from every quarter.

Enough has been said to shew that Self-Remembering does not mean always to remember your negative self. In this connection I will give you one definition of external considering and its meaning. It was said on one occasion at the early Groups that external considering means to forget oneself and to think what the other wants, and it was added that in this way two results will follow. The first is that one can help, and the second is that one gets help. But if you really come to think about the whole question you will see that all real Self-Remembering is simply forgetting yourself, your ordinary self, your ordinary negative 'I's, your ordinary forms of internal considering, and all the rest of it, and feeling certain that some further state of yourself exists above all this personal uproar that takes place all day long in each one of you, with which you keep on identifying, and when the Work says that we have Real 'I' above us you must understand that this act, so to speak, of separating from False Personality, deliberately at some moment every day, is designed to make it possible for us to come in contact with the first traces of Real 'I' which is already there and which is our real goal.

898

COMMENTARY ON IDENTIFYING

We are told in this Work that one of the things that we have to observe in ourselves is identifying. It is said that identifying is the most terrible force acting on this planet that keeps people asleep and so prevents them from awakening. As we are—that is, as mechanical people, who do everything mechanically and have not got any proper consciousness—we identify at every moment. We identify with our thoughts, with our feelings, and we identify with what happens in outer life. In this way we are kept in prison without realizing it—and only through the development of consciousness can we get out of this prison. Only a few people wish to do so—namely, those people who have what is called Magnetic Centre and therefore feel that there must be something different and seek to try to find it. All of us have what are called unnecessary emotions, the source of which is identification. Our Emotional Centre, which is the most important centre in us and is capable eventually of connecting us with Higher Emotional Centre, is in a very bad state. In the first place it is full of acquired negative emotions which we have imitated from others. By birth our Emotional Centre is free from negative emotions and by birth we are born in a very small way awake. There is a kind of innocence in small children which they lose very soon through identifying. This innocence, if we can call it so, belongs to Essence, but soon it becomes surrounded by Personality and False Personality, and we lose our original centre of gravity which passes from Essence into Personality. We then become, so to speak, invented people carrying on a fictitious life. You have only to look back at some of the older magazines, say, of forty or fifty years ago, to notice how artificial everyone looks in the illustrations or photographs and how unreal the romances and stories are. One wonders how people could behave like that, dress like that, do things like that, and yet we are in exactly the same state of hypnotism at every moment. Now when you look at these older prints, these older stories, and wonder how people could do things like that, you are really looking at the power of identifying and the power that identification has over humanity. And yet you think that you yourself are not identified at all. As you know, humanity is kept asleep for certain reasons but it is always possible for a certain number of people to awaken from this sleep which comes partly through identifying. Each one of you is identified at this moment. Each one of you has a hundred and one unnecessary emotions. Each one of you is identified with a hundred and one unnecessary thoughts. When a man is totally asleep he is identified with every thought that comes to him automatically and every mood that arises in him automatically, and every feeling. He takes all this as his life and, in fact, more than this, he takes it as his necessary life. In the work of self-observation we are told in what direction to observe ourselves

899

and the reason for this is to be able to separate ourselves very gradually from all these unnecessary forms of identifying with transient thoughts, moods and feelings. We then begin to have something that stands behind us. We then begin to see ourselves, as it were, on the stage in front of us. We begin to see all sorts of different 'I's in us, saying this and thinking that, and behaving like that and holding forth like that, as something unreal, something that is not oneself, something that has nothing to do with Real 'I'. In other words, we begin to see our mechanicalness. All this is a very great step to take and once a person has taken it he or she can never be the same person again. But the power of identifying is so tremendous that even although we may reach a state when for a moment we are separated from our Personality, at the next moment we fall down right into it—that is, when we have reached the stage of having been able to "walk on the waters" for a moment, at the next moment we sink. We are then once more in the small theatre of our mechanical selves with its self-dramas.

The Work says that we must struggle every day with identifying and that this struggle takes very many forms and directions. For example, a man may, through self-observation, realize that he identifies with someone or with some forms of thought or emotion, and may for a time separate himself from that particular kind of identifying, but he will find that he begins to identify with something else far more. At first he accepts this and is quite certain that in this respect he is not identified. Then he realizes what has happened. So the struggle must continue all his life. Sometimes people say: "Surely we should identify, because then we feel real, we feel real emotions, and so on." This is not correct. You can feel no real emotions if you identify—in fact, the Work says that as we are we know only one emotion or one taste—the taste of being identified. As you know, we identify particularly with our negative states, with our negative moods, and with our negative thoughts. The Work speaks very little about positive emotions. At the same time, it says that positive emotions are possible, but that they have no trace of identifying, no taste of identification. They are not self-emotions, forms of self-liking. All self-emotions are forms of identifying. Positive emotions have no such taste and are not self-emotions. We cannot create them at present unless we try to do this Work sincerely, unless especially we try to follow the three lines of the Work. The first line is work on oneself, which begins with sincere and uncritical self-observation according to what we are taught by the Work to observe. The second line is work in connection with one another, to understand one another and not to react mechanically to the unpleasant manifestations of others in the Work, to learn a common language and so externally consider them. The third line is to help those teaching the Work and to assist in the transmission of it. If these lines are followed, especially the first and second, we may have as a reward flashes of positive emotion whose taste, whose instantaneous quality, is utterly different from the ordinary heavy emotions amongst which we live. What we might call our positive emotions are not really positive emotions because they turn very easily into their opposites—namely, into negative emotions. For example, you are feeling very pleased with yourself, you are feeling fine, feeling good, and all the rest of it, and someone says something to you of an unpleasant nature, and the next moment you are plunged into negative emotion. Now the point about real positive emotions is that they never have an opposite in them—that is, they can never turn into negative emotions. They may come in a flash and then disappear, but they cannot turn into any opposite thing, into a negative state. And also they always make you see things that you never saw before, like a sudden vision—that is to say, their cognitive value is very great. The next moment you have dropped down to an ordinary level and you forget what you saw and cannot record it and yet you know that you saw something that you had never seen before, some aspect of truth, of meaning.

Now if anybody has had in the past or does have in the future such traces of positive emotion, he or she must register them as being of very high value even although one cannot remember what exactly happens. The most hopeless thing is to regard them as mere nonsense. Positive emotions cannot reach us in the second state of consciousness, but they can reach us in the third state of consciousness—i.e. Self-Remembering or Self-Awareness. When a man is absorbed in his private interests, in his self-emotions, in his vanity, in his self-complacency, in his moral arrogance, in his feeling that he is always right, in his complaints, and all the rest of it—that is, when a man is completely identified with himself—he can never receive a trace of positive emotion. That is why it is so necessary to begin to work on oneself and to separate oneself from oneself. When a man remembers himself, he is not identified—that is, when a man reaches the third level of consciousness that exists in all humanity and is really their birthright—he is in a state of consciousness that can receive help from Higher Centres—namely, from Conscious Humanity—but when a man is in the second state of consciousness he is always in a constant state of identifying, identifying with money, identifying with people, and identifying with ambition and identifying with himself, and so he is asleep and under the Law of Accident. In the second state of consciousness, the so-called waking state, nothing from a higher level of being can reach us. So everything will go in the only possible way it can go because everyone is then a machine and no one can do.

COMMENTARY ON MEMORY

People so often not only try to explain themselves by their past, but feel themselves only by it. What do we mean by our past? What we call our past may be only one explanation of our present and a very inadequate one. What we call our past is our memory of it. But what we call *our* memory does not explain either the past or the present. Our memory is according to our level of Being. Our personal memory is so often a false, distorted thing. The point is that we remember very little —let us say, one hundred-millionth part of all that happened. I often doubt if we ever can remember anything as it actually was. Our memory depends on our powers of reception and is by no means objective. Do you remember, for instance, all that happened outside and inside you in the external world and in your mind even yesterday? Or last week? Or last year? Of course you do not. You remember scarcely anything of the sum-total. Please do not pretend you do. But some pride themselves on having a very good faultless memory and even say so. Another person remembers differently. So there is a quarrel —a very tedious kind of quarrel. Now what memory we have connects things in its own subjective way. But do you suppose that this thin, subjective memory really connects things aright? Can you really see your life through your memory? It is true to say that the past must exist for the present moment to exist. But what is your present moment that your past so often creates for you? Is it a real one, or an invention of the past? What is the thing you cling to called "memory of the past"? I do not think it is reliable. Can you remember what *you* did as well as the other person? You remember what *he* or *she* did. Is your so-called memory anything you can really trust? From my own experience in this Work I would say at once that it is the most unreliable guide to follow and that one has practically to cancel it. Our memories are private liars, that we carry about carefully. Do not think that to remember yourself is to remember your past. To proceed into the future with this false memory is not any solution to one's life. I would say, rather, forget—overcome—your past. It is all so much nonsense to imagine we have infallible memory. Oh, this memory that folk cling to and hug in an ecstasy of unhappiness! The realization that what *we* call our past—that is, what we believe that we remember as our past— is not something to base our present moment on, is a step in awakening —otherwise we continue to sit in a darkness of our own making, a darkness made by our subjective ideas of our past, which we say is real memory. We have no real, unchallengeable memory. Yet the Work says we have a real memory, only it is not accessible to us at the ordinary levels of consciousness. Everything is recorded. Everything we saw, everything we did and said, everything we felt and thought, is there— on rolls in centres and in their sub-divisions. But our access to this real memory is, mercifully for us as we are, concealed from us. The action of uncritical Observing 'I' begins to restore in a small part real memory —but only to the extent that a person can stand it without going completely mad. We have a system of buffers, to mention one factor, that prevents us from being conscious in real interior memory. Real interior memory is opened at death—it is called a "book" in the New Testament. If your imagination of yourself, your false notions of yourself, your False Personality with its invented notions of what you are— if all this has, in this life, been to some extent separated from, not identified with, and so seen through, then perhaps one might bear a little this opening of the "book" which is described in Revelation in the following words:

"And I saw the dead, the great and the small, standing before the throne; and books were opened: and another book was opened, which is the Book of Life: and the dead were judged out of the things which were written in the books, according to their works."

(*Revelation* XX 12)

This means that at death we become conscious in the 4th Dimension —that is, all the life becomes conscious to us—and then we see what really happened. Why two books? Ah, that is indeed a question to think about.

In that interesting Persian esoteric story called "The Conference of the Birds" the same idea appears. The birds had at last, after losing all their feathers, reached the presence of the Sovereign. "But", it is said, "first of all a register was placed before them, in which every detail of the deeds that each one of them had done or omitted to do, from the beginning to the end, was carefully entered."

*　　*　　*

Let us speak about memory from what the Work teaches. Every centre has its own memory and every part of a centre has its own memory. The qualities of these memories are different. We have not, in short, one memory, but first of all three memories, then nine memories, and then twenty-seven memories. This is because, taking three centres, Intellectual, Emotional and Instinct-Moving Centre, each has its own memory. Then, dividing each of these three centres into three parts, we have nine smaller memories. Again, each of these sub-divisions is again divided into three—so that we have $3 + 9 + 27$ memories—that is, thirty-nine different sorts of memory on different scales. On these thirty-nine memories everything we have seen, said, thought, felt, and sensed, is recorded. But our access to these thirty-nine memories is very slight. We live as a rule in one or two very small sub-divisions of centres. Let me add that even this category of memories is incomplete. The negative divisions of centres have been left out. If we divide the Intellectual and Emotional Centres each by a cross-line into two parts, the lower part being the negative side, then you can calculate for yourselves that we have another twenty-four memories.

Now in speaking about different memories in us, let us take something that we can easily grasp. Intellectual memory is different from emotional memory and again the memory of Moving Centre is different from intellectual memory and emotional memory. We must conceive very large things here, up which we crawl as small insects. A man may have learnt to ride a bicycle. That is, his Moving Centre remembers. But he cannot remember what he once knew of Chemistry. When he gets on a bicycle he finds soon that he can ride it. Something remembers. What remembers? His Intellectual Centre? Certainly not. He taps another memory, more easily accessible to him. But he cannot remember some chemical formula. So he will have to look it up. Yet he finds he takes it all in more quickly than a man who has never learnt Chemistry. After a time "things come back to him" and his intellectual memory revives—but only by some effort.

Now let us take Emotional Centre. A person remembers, as a rule, unpleasant negative emotions. They revive themselves, by mechanical associations, very easily. This kind of memory is not the same as the memory of Intellectual Centre or Moving Centre. The Emotional Centre is not under our control—that is, we cannot feel happy when we are unhappy. There are certain efforts possible here—but I speak of ourselves as ordinary people. An effort in connection with Intellectual Centre *can* change the direction of thought and one *can* recall something by concentration or by looking it up. But the memory of Emotional Centre, which means so often the memory of the negative part of Emotional Centre, is not altered so easily. One reason is because we have such long strings of unpleasant memories harboured there, that we take as real, as actual, and, in fact, *as* our past. When you think a thing is real, is actual, naturally you cannot alter it. So it is difficult to alter the memories belonging to the negative part of Emotional Centre. But once we begin to doubt their truthfulness, once we begin to suspect they are not wholly correct, then of course it is possible to separate from them. This is a fortunate moment. One, so to speak, discards the past as one imagined it to be, and steps right into the present with a certain delight, freedom, an "I need not be like this." One has always this feeling of delight when one gets free from one of the many chains anchoring us to what we have hitherto insisted is *ourselves*, and defended so uselessly with a useless expenditure of energy that could go toward a new edition of oneself, a new view of oneself, a new person. These chains, however, are very powerful. Only the intake of the Work—only the breathing in of another set of influences —can begin to dissolve them. For no one can free himself from what he is unless he feels the existence of what is higher than he is and begins to obey it. But people easily object to this idea—namely, that there is anything higher than themselves. We are set very hard and tight *in ourselves*. We cannot see that there is something higher *in ourselves* than we are ourselves—namely, higher levels of consciousness, higher levels of Being and Knowledge, higher levels of understanding and so of mercy. This awareness of something higher is a critical point in a person's movement towards internal awakening, and at this point everyone who has got as far as this has to undergo a long, difficult, and yet quite simple and straightforward struggle to tilt the balance which eventually makes the unforgiving Personality passive and merciful Essence active.

What connection has all this with memory? It has a very real connection, because unless a person begins to have a Work-memory and can see himself over a period he can never approach this point. Unless he has ceased to believe that he knows himself and is what he imagines he is and behaves as he thinks, he cannot change. Why? Because he is satisfied with his Imaginary 'I'. So he remains asleep, even if life knocks him very hard. It is never his fault, of course. He does not see that his level of Being—what he is—attracts his life. And he has no real memory —no Work-memory gained by self-observation. He takes himself for granted. The memory he has is not real memory but memory edited by vanity and prejudice. I repeat that of all we have done and said, of all we have seen and heard or of all that others have done to us or said to us—of all we have thought or felt or intended or wished—of all *our* behaviour and of all the behaviour of others to us—of all this we remember a hundred-millionth part and even so it is all wrongly connected. But we have a deeper memory accessible only to a higher level of consciousness, where it is all recorded as it actually was. The formation of Work-memory through Observing 'I' begins to lift memory to another level. Then perhaps, we will not eventually experience too disastrously the shock of being confronted with what we did or said or thought and what we imagined we did or said or thought.

Quaremead, Ugley, June 8, 1946

ON THINKING IN A NEW WAY

It is often said that this Work is to make us think in a new way but this is impossible unless people exert themselves mentally—namely, make mental efforts in connection with the ideas. Unless a person thinks of the Work and ponders it and connects it with himself or herself, the mind cannot be changed—that is, the person will continue to think in exactly the same way as formerly. Unless we think about the ideas of the Work and think about our behaviour and reflect as to whether we think about ourselves in the way the Work teaches, we will remain the same—that is, there will be no change of mind—no μετάνοια. That is to say, the Work will not influence us—nothing gets home to us. Then the Work lies, as it were, like so many unopened parcels in the Intellectual Centre. Now we have to seek and find for ourselves by what means we can be influenced by the Work. As you know, ordinarily people are influenced by life. The Work, as a system of ideas which actually form an organic whole, is so constructed that if it is taken in, if it is really united with, the whole mind begins to change, and as a result everything can be changed in us. One of the ideas that struck me emotionally from early in this Work was the idea that we are all asleep and that all that one reads in the papers is about people behaving in sleep and thinking that they can do in this state, but a still more powerful idea began to influence me later—the idea that I myself was asleep. Now ideas are more real than facts. You remember what O. said about ideas? He said that modern psychology does not realize the immense power of certain kinds of ideas and their realness. "Even in primitive philosophy", he wrote, "when men divided ideas into divine and human, they understood better the existence of different orders of ideas. Modern thought does not recognize this at all. Existing psychology and the theory of knowledge do not teach people to discriminate between different orders of ideas, nor point out that some ideas are very dangerous and cannot be approached without long and careful preparation. This occurs because modern psychology does not take into consideration the reality of ideas, does not understand this reality. . . . Ancient and mediaeval psychology understood better the position of the human mind in relation to ideas. It understood that the mind could not deal with ideas in a right way so long as the reality of them was not clear to it. And further the old psychology understood that the mind was incapable of receiving ideas of different kinds simultaneously or out of the right order—that is, it could not pass without preparation from ideas of one order to ideas of another order." O. compares esoteric ideas with complicated machines which it is impossible to use rightly unless one is prepared beforehand.

Now in this Work we have certain ideas taught us whose object is to transform our whole way of thinking. These ideas are given in small quantities, so to speak, at a time. Let us take once more the idea that Man is asleep. Now this idea is very dangerous unless it is taught rightly. What is the preparation that begins to make it possible to understand this idea rightly? The preparation consists in realizing through self-observation that one is oneself asleep. This takes many years of self-observation and mental exertion, many years of private thought and private reflection and inner dialogue. When this preparation has reached a certain point, the vision of Man asleep—of the world asleep—comes to a person in the right way. It no longer comes in a negative form, or with a feeling of superiority, but as an actual perception without any negative emotion or personal identification connected with it. In such a case we can say that one of the ideas of the Work has begun to influence a person and change that person's whole mode of thinking. But unless the Work has been pondered continually in the most intimate part of one's own private thinking, this really cannot be expected to take place. The person will only say in a parrot-like way that Man is asleep, or even that he himself is asleep, without realizing what it means. All the ideas of the Work convey great density of meaning but without personal thought and application they are merely so many signposts. A superficial knowledge of the Work helps no one, yet at the same time a superficial formatory knowledge of the Work is necessary as a first step. To understand an idea of the Work is quite different from knowing about it. The difference between knowing and understanding is incommensurable. It is quite possible to say to ourselves that in the affairs of ordinary life we are very rarely influenced by the Work. We know something about it and occasionally perhaps think about it for a very brief time, but the influences of life are far more powerful, therefore it is necessary to find and seek by what means the influences of the Work begin really to affect our lives and the way we behave and think and feel and so on. That is why we have to try to understand the Work and not merely to know it.

Now unless we have some kind of aim the Work cannot influence our lives for then we are not surrounded by the Work, but remain open to all the influences of life. We can compare aim in the Work with something inside which we stand for the time being. If we remember our aim in the midst of life we feel at once that two quite different things are acting on us—namely, life, which will always make us behave mechanically and this aim in which we are standing for the moment, which prevents us from behaving entirely mechanically. This is giving acknowledgement and so power to the Work. It may be only a transient experience but yet it is a very genuine one, and although it may eventually fail we at least get the taste for a moment of what it might mean to stand within the influences of the Work, and so have a certain power over the influences of life acting on our mechanical Personality. This is why the Work emphasizes so much the necessity of having some kind of aim. It may be even a short aim for a few moments, a few hours, but that is better than nothing. Aim is on many scales.

Now to nourish one's aim one must ponder the Work and here mental exertion is necessary. Aim can never become mechanical. Aim must be something that is consciously kept going through new supplies of thought and insight. It is just like building up a barrier near the sea. The sea keeps coming in and washing away parts of this barrier which have to be constantly renewed. It is quite true to say that as we are we may not be able to do this for long, but yet I repeat that if we have done it for a time sincerely we get a taste of what it might mean to reach a stage where the influences of the Work are more powerful than those of life. Let us take once more negative emotions. Here it is really quite possible to do something. But you cannot do anything, even for a short time, if you try to do it as a given task, as something that you were told to do. You have to do it from some degree of individual understanding why negative emotions are useless and harmful both to you and to other people. You have to realize, as deeply as you can, your slavery to negative emotions, and how much is said in the Work about getting rid of this slavery and all the reasons why. For these purposes you must collect in your mind many of the sayings of the Work and behind all that you must have some general conception of all that the Work teaches about inner development, about inner freedom. If you do this simply as a task, as something you have been told, without any intimate private understanding of the reason, you will not be able to resist life. The influences of the Work acting on you will be too feeble. In other words, you will not have any real point in the Work. Now if you make a temporary aim not to be negative towards a particular person, not to consent to the mechanically-induced negative thoughts and feelings, not to go with them, not to listen to them (and above all if you find the same irritating things in yourself) then you will be standing in the Work—standing in the influences of the Work—which then can reach you and begin to change you. This is standing within your Work-aim. The influences of the Work, which are different from the influences of life, can reach you. It is really quite simple. Make a clear-cut definite Work-aim of this kind and try to keep consciousness in it for a time. You will then see for yourself the result. But as a rule people never will make a simple clear-cut Work-aim of this kind. They merely worry or vaguely wonder what to do, not yet having heard with the mind what the Work teaches so distinctly about personal work on oneself and about what they must practise. I am fairly certain that some will ask: "What does the Work teach us to do as regards work on ourselves?" You have heard it with your ears over and over again. Yes, but who has really heard it with the mind and pondered it and exerted their minds over it, privately and intimately, and realized in which direction the path goes and what it means to begin to follow it? For the Work is a Way, a path—inner, quiet, stage by stage, and psychological—that leads to a definite goal. Others who gave us this Work have followed this 4th Way and seen for themselves where it leads.

Quaremead, Ugley, June 15, 1946

A NOTE ON RELAXATION

A man fully awake has no False Personality. For us who are studying how to awaken this means that the more awake we are the less are we in False Personality. Or, to put it the other way round, the more a person is in False Personality the more is that person asleep. Now a person who is asleep in False Personality has no real existence. There is no real person. A man must become quite open to himself without deception. This is true relaxation. He must cease to hold himself in certain beliefs about himself, poses, pictures, ideas of himself.

Anxiety and fear, which prevent us relaxing, subtly arise when a man endeavours to maintain what is not really himself. He lives on one side of himself at a time, and the rest is dark to him. He is not open to himself. The False Personality, always pre-occupied with different forms of internal considering, with questions of whether a good impression is being made and appearances kept up, causes a strain in Being. It is as if a man kept on standing on his toes and did not understand why he felt exhausted. All the time he is keeping something up which is not himself—something imaginary—something which does not fit him. And this happens with everyone. If we had no False Personality all this anxiety and nervousness which all secretly feel about themselves, whether they admit it or not, would vanish. Not only would our relationship to others change, but our relationship to ourselves. We then would understand what it is to relax. One reason is that the False Personality can only love itself. Self-love, which attributes everything to itself, keeps us in anxiety for it is afraid of loss of esteem and position. Now False Personality never admits anything. It is always right. If it pretends to confess its sins, it does so out of vanity, as a pose, to shew off, to gain merit and applause. This absurd thing composed of self-evident lies and false imagination you might think easily seen and destroyed. On the contrary its existence is most difficult to see and its strength is extraordinary. It will neither allow itself to be found out nor allow ourselves to find ourselves out—that is, what we really are. If it did, its power would be destroyed, and we should be free from our greatest enemy—that is, the person we imagine ourselves to be, whom we serve as slaves from the moment we wake up in the morning to the moment we fall asleep at night. So we cannot deeply relax when we serve in this way, for False Personality will keep on making us correspond to what it imagines itself to be. It will not allow a person to be at rest, but must prod him to act in the way he is supposed to act, to keep up his reputation, his character-rôle. So if a man has a picture of himself as being a hard worker the False Personality will drive him to work hard even at the point of death. It makes each of you keep up your pictures of yourself.

Now the strength of the False Personality depends upon buffers. Its strength is not in its self-evident lies and false imagination but in the buffers that lie like walls in centres and prevent us from seeing more than one side at a time. So we do not see inner contradictions. They prevent us from bringing two things together, both of which we know separately. Because they have this curious action, lies and imagination have the power to control us. The time comes when the Work finds us out for ourselves. One way in which it does this is to make a contradiction in us conscious to us—that is, to make us simultaneously more and more conscious of what lies on each side of a buffer. Ordinarily we would be conscious only of what lies on one side and after a lapse of time of what lies on the other, and so see no contradiction. So the False Personality, through the action of buffers, prevents us from meeting ourselves. It prevents a man from becoming quite open to himself without deception. So it is necessary to practise self-observation over a long period until its memory, which records both sides of a buffer, is strong enough to influence us. This makes it quieter. There is such a noise going on inside us due to False Personality—so many 'I's shouting. So we cannot relax.

Quaremead, Ugley, June 22, 1946

WORK ON THE EMOTIONAL CENTRE

At the London Meeting this week at which all Groups were present the teaching of the Work was begun afresh and one of the main ideas stressed at the beginning was that this system of teaching is based on the idea that Man was created specially as an experiment in self-evolution. The Work says that Man was created a self-developing organism as distinct from the animals. From this point of view Man is incomplete like a building not yet finished and it is left to him to finish his own building, to complete himself. For this reason certain teachings have always existed in the world which can be called "esoteric teachings". For example, this teaching that we are studying is sometimes called esoteric Christianity. This has nothing to do with exoteric Christianity.

At this Meeting the three centres of Man were touched upon and it was said that the Emotional Centre in Man is in a very bad state. Let us make some brief commentaries on this point that this teaching emphasizes so much. The Work says that we must work on our Emotional Centre and purify it, clean it out, get rid of unnecessary emotions that keep us asleep and keep us slaves to external life. Let us take a person who is always cross, always frowning, always bothered, always difficult, in fact, always a nuisance. In such a person the Emotional Centre is not working aright and it is necessary for such a person, through long trained technical observation, to become aware that this wrong working of the Emotional Centre exists in him or her. Now a person who is always cross, cantankerous, difficult, quarrelsome, and even venomous, has in this Work to realize that such a state of the Emotional Centre is quite incompatible with any self-development—that is, this person, whether a man or a woman, has to realize that to complete themselves in the sense of this teaching, to evolve, to develop, is quite impossible as long as the Emotional Centre in him or her remains in this mechanical state. The point is that such persons are quite unaware of the state of the Emotional Centre in themselves. They do not see that they are cross, difficult, fault-finding, unpleasant, angry, and so on. On the contrary, they have a picture of themselves as being very sweet and charming. Therefore a gap exists in them, a gap in their consciousness of themselves. This gap can only be filled in by sincere and conscious self-

910

observation carried out according to the instructions given in this teaching for self-observation. People all think they know themselves, but no one does. This is an illusion. Usually other people know more about ourselves than we do, but they, on the other hand, do not know themselves. So it is a very good thing to begin to observe the state of your Emotional Centre and the unpleasant manifestations that come from it mechanically. The Work teaches that the Emotional Centre is the most wonderful centre in us but that at present, in the state of sleep in which we all exist, it is inundated with negative emotions, with self-pity, with self-emotions, with self-esteem, and a hundred and one other similar forms of emotion that prevent us from really making contact with one another and so prevent us from understanding one another's difficulties.

Work on the Intellectual Centre is different from work on the Emotional Centre, but the Work begins with observation of the three main centres in us and we have to come to the point in which we realize through self-observation the state of two centres—i.e., what goes on all the time in the Intellectual Centre and what goes on all the time in the Emotional Centre. Here you have a man who always dislikes everyone, who jeers at people, who finds fault with people, and so on. Such a man does not know that this is the state of his Emotional Centre. Or a man feels himself always through superiority to other people but yet does not realize it. The emotional feeling of superiority is always based on self-esteem, on self-love, on self-feeling. In such a case the Emotional Centre does not work as it should, nor can it fill a person with the right feelings that give him inner meaning and so peace. So it is a good thing to observe the state of one's Emotional Centre, to observe it in action—i.e. to observe how it mechanically reacts to external events and particularly other people. Here lies a great task, which is really a life-task. This Work is for all one's life and through applying it we gradually undergo a transformation internally owing to the fact that we become more and more conscious of our real sides, and what we really are. This destroys illusions about ourselves.

When a man begins really to work on himself, when he has begun to see the depth of this teaching, he can no longer remain the same kind of man, a woman cannot remain the same kind of woman. He or she then begins to understand what it means that people are born on this Earth as self-developing organisms, and that there is a special task for everyone that has to be followed and worked out in order to attain this completion, this final development that is their real meaning for being on this very imperfect planet. Each one's task is different, but once the Work is understood in its broad outlines and once the truth of it is acknowledged internally, each one is shewn what it is necessary to work at. You must remember that the Work teaches that negative emotions are unnecessary, that they complicate life continually, that they produce all the unhappiness that exists in people's relationships to one another, and that it also teaches that it is possible gradually to free oneself from these unnecessary negative emotions. Once a person knows this and understands it and sees this inner truth he has already in his mind a secret of incalculable value. He need never be at a loss, whatever his circumstances, for he will always know what he has to do in any situation—that is, not to express negative emotions, and then, to separate from them, and finally not to have them at all. This Work does not teach that we have no right to have negative emotions, because that would be too difficult. It teaches that we have a right not to have negative emotions. All our troubles, domestic tragedies and so on, are mainly due to nourishing negative emotions, to feeling that we are *owed* something. I ask you—what do you think you are owed? Examine it —and then look at yourself. When you *see* what you are like, can you really think you are owed anything? I would say, No, I realize that, on the contrary, I *owe* to others. A phrase in the Lord's Prayer says: "Cancel what we owe to God, as we cancel what we think others owe us". That is, as long as your life is based on imagining that others owe to you, you will get nowhere. But as more and more you see that no one owes you anything and that it is always your own fault—then your accounts, spiritually, are cancelled. This gives the possibility of hearing higher centres and what they will tell you. But if you are a mass of internal considering, of self-pity, of feeling you have never had a chance, of feeling that your typical life-situation is exceptional, and that no one understands your peculiar difficulties—then you will continue to inundate the Emotional Centre with negative emotions. In that case it cannot perform its true functions and so cannot give you inner meaning and peace.

Quaremead, Ugley, June 29, 1946

NOTE ON SELF-REMEMBERING

The Work teaches that Self-Remembering immediately means better food for all the cells in the body. On the contrary, identifying in all one's life troubles, being negative, heavy, jealous, unhappy, and so on, which signifies an absence of Self-Remembering, means bad food for all the cells in the body. An act of Self-Remembering, in the midst of the uproar of life, gives new force. The whole body feels lighter, because then the cells composing the body receive new food—a class of food above vitamins. The body needs right food from the psychology. The relationship of the body to the state of oneself, that is, one's psychological state, is very intimate. A depressing negative state, a worrying state, an anxious state, produces bad food for the body. The Work teaches that the relation between the body and the mind is very fine, subtle and definite. Bad states of the mind, and especially bad emotions—such as small petty self-emotions, disliking, boredom, etc.—retard the right work of cells in the body. So the Work teaches that this effort to work on oneself, to pick up one's behaviour at any moment and transform it by an act of Self-Remembering changes the chemistry of the cells in the body. Man can be asleep in life although very busy. Man can be awake in life although very busy. The results are quite different. If a man begins to study what Self-Remembering means from realizing he does not remember himself but is simply a machine reacting to outside conditions always in the same way, he begins to see what the Work is about. If he flatters himself as being all right as he is, the Work remains shut to him. This means, internally, the active higher parts of ordinary centres in him remain shut to him. So he lives, on the whole, in the basement of himself, of his house. A man, a woman, should learn after a time what it means to work on themselves and not to remain just a function of external conditions—that is, upset, bored, unhappy, when external conditions are not agreeable to them, and excited and en- thusiastic when external conditions are favourable. This is to live in the opposites. Then one is certainly a helpless machine changing from misery to happiness and from happiness to misery. One does nothing to create one's own life, to create, in short, oneself. Life then drives us as a great belt drives hundreds of little machines. This is not a desirable state, for then there is *nobody*—one is really *nobody*, with no power of transforming any situation. One spends all one's money and then has nothing, so to speak. There is no reserve of force. Nothing is created in oneself. In this case one is identified with all that happens. In other words, one does not remember oneself. If a man, a woman, in some typical unhappy event of which there are many typical stereotyped ones *already made*—if they identify fully with them they lose force. They are machines, mechanically reacting to these typical stereotyped events, all prepared for them like the jumps on a racecourse. Yes, it is really like that. You come to a typical jump and fall. But if you remember your- self you need not—especially if you can say to yourself: "This is a typical situation that millions of others are in at this moment". That deprives it of its unique taste.

Now to repeat—"The Work teaches that Self-Remembering im- mediately means better food for all the cells of the body". But let me remind you that Self-Remembering depends finally on the sense of some- thing higher in yourself. When a man begins to apply the teaching of this Work practically to himself he begins, as it were, to fly a little above the surface of the earth. What he used to stumble at he no longer stumbles at. In other words, he is living on a higher telegraph wire—on a slightly higher level. What would have been a catastrophe is now perhaps only a momentary incident. I ask you all to think and reflect upon what it can possibly mean "to remember oneself" in the midst of troubles and anxieties and, in short, in the midst of the uproar of life's stereotyped daily incidents, daily events. In that way, to vary the image, one begins to see what it might mean to "walk on the sea" of oneself—in my case to walk on, and so above, Nicoll.

COMMENTARY ON FALSE PERSONALITY
AND SELF-LOVE

Questions are asked at different times in which the term "self-love" is used. I have explained that this term "self-love" is not used in this system of teaching and when I use it myself I have usually added that it is not a technical Work expression. In the early days of the Work in London we often discussed among ourselves why this word was not used and I remember someone saying that perhaps it was because it was either a worn out word or it did not contain any clear meaning. On one occasion, at a private talk among a few of us, Mr. Ouspensky said that if we could find another term for it, it might be of some use to describe False Personality. Various words were suggested such as "self-esteem", "self-admiration", "self-importance", and others, but when the term "self-liking" was suggested, he said that perhaps it came nearest to what he had in mind. He added that the whole question lay in the emotional reactions of False Personality in a man or woman. He said man, or woman, must be shaken to their depths to get rid of False Personality. We are easily offended and upset because False Personality is our feeling of ourselves and it is an imaginary thing, an acquired artificial mask, a pretended person that we like to imagine ourselves to be and are not. This False Personality takes itself as a unity and this is how Imaginary 'I' arises; it borrows, so to speak, the idea that it is a real person and so says 'I'. The keeping up of the False Personality takes a great deal of force. It makes us internally consider: it exhausts us. Mr. Ouspensky said that the False Personality always justifies itself in order to maintain its existence. This wastes force. In regard to the False Personality, which in my case is called Nicoll, he said that one has to be able to see that it is not really 'I'. He said it was composed of a certain grouping of rolls in centres and groups of 'I's which may shift from time to time in regard to their composition according to the environment in which one happens to be, and yet at the same time it always has the same quality of falseness, of something kept up—some invention. A man, for example, may amongst lower class people assume a certain pretence of himself and amongst higher class people assume another pretence of himself, and yet at the same time it is all the same thing—that is, it is False Personality. He said that we have to come to the point of being able to say to ourselves internally "this is not really I". He said that this inner separation—in my case from Nicoll—was the most important point in the Work, and was connected with making the Personality as a whole passive. He said that the study of False Personality was almost a life task and eventually could only be understood through the development of inner taste which led into Real Conscience. He said that Real Conscience apart from Acquired Conscience was one of our greatest internal senses, and that unless it had been given us, no one could awaken. Acquired Conscience is, of course, merely a matter of how we have been brought up and what we have been taught is right or wrong. He said that Acquired Conscience is different in every nation. It could be anything. It was a matter of imitation. Some people are taught by imitation and education that it is right to have many wives and others are taught that it is right to have one wife, and so on, in a thousand different ways, but Real Conscience is the same in all people, but it is buried beneath the surface of the False Personality. He said further that no one of course could ever act without some admixture of self—that is, in the sense of self-interest—but that usually it was *all* self-interest. People did not externally consider. He said that we are told to love our neighbours as ourselves and that one meaning is that we could not do things completely without self-interest or self-liking, but that half of it should be self and half love of neighbour.

I asked him to speak about the stages of emotional development—that is, the development of the Emotional Centre to its highest receptive powers—as it was formulated in the Gospels—namely, "love of oneself, love of one's neighbour, and love of God". It is recorded that Christ, when he was asked by one of the Pharisees which was the great commandment replied: "Thou shalt love thy neighbour as thyself". (*Matt.* XXII 37.) It is only possible to attempt to give a summary of what Mr. O.'s answer was. He began by saying: "False Personality loves itself only and all that flatters it or agrees with it. Unless a man can find something to love greater than himself he can never modify this inner state. Nowadays," he said, "people have got a very strange view of the Universe and take it all for granted as if it created itself and see nothing marvellous in it. How can a thing create itself? Scientists ascribe every discovery to themselves, not understanding that they are studying a Universe already given them which existed long before they were born. They even call stars by their own names. It is absurd. But False Personality ascribes everything to itself. In more ancient times when a man had sense of the miraculous and worshipped God as the Creator, both of himself and of the Universe, he was emotionally in a far better state than exists nowadays in the average human outlook. His understanding was better. He could stand *under* himself. In regard to what is said in the Gospels about love, you must realize that this is said in a very big sense, on a very big scale, and has meaning within meaning in it. These meanings destroy False Personality because when they begin to be understood by a man or a woman then the sense of the smallness of themselves in comparison with the great mystery of Creation begins to affect them emotionally. All greater emotions destroy the small self-emotions which arise from the narrow contracted sphere of the False Personality and its own minute self-liking and self-importance". He said, in so many words: "You know already that all sayings and parables in the Gospels contain immense density of meaning which reveals itself as we change in level of Being. To argue about whether

F*
915

Christ existed or not as an historical fact has little sense. In fact He did, and carried out his rôle deliberately. The point is that any man with any kind of discrimination and understanding who reads the Gospels for the first time knows at once that these brief records, these words, are completely different from anything that has ever been written since that time. But people read the Gospels mechanically; they do not understand what they read. They read about the Pharisees and Christ's continual condemnation of them, but they do not see that it applies to themselves—to their own False Personality. The Pharisee in you is your False Personality; it is always pretending to be what it is not. It is the Pharisee living in you. People even think sometimes that it is easy to understand that one must love God with all one's heart, with all one's soul, and with all one's mind, and imagine they do. They do not understand that this means first making Personality passive—a long task. They must give up completely the idea that they are their own creators, realize practically, by blow after blow, that something infinitely greater than themselves exists and that they are nothing. The trouble is that they think they understand what Christ said, and even quite religious people profess that they love God and do not observe that they insist on their own opinions and are a mass of False Personality so that really in the long run they love themselves". He added: "For example, they are liable to judge and condemn everyone who behaves in a way they do not like. That is, they hate in secret. Now what does "love of neighbour" mean? Who is one's neighbour? Some people perhaps think it means the person wno happens to live next door. Psychologically it has to do with those nearest you in Being, those near you in understanding, in what they seek, or who are going along the same road. That is why we must make a conscious relation to those in the Work—the second line of work. And then what does love of self mean? *Which self*? We have many selves. And finally, how can we understand what "love of God" means? It is something tremendous, something we may imagine we know about, but cannot know yet. Yes, people say they love God and then go and kill one another or hate each other, or talk evilly. How can that be love of God? Perhaps No. 7 man knows what "love of God" means—that is, a man belonging to the highest development possible to Man—certainly ordinary mechanical Man cannot know what it means. He may love his *own opinion* of God, the God he supposes he worships, but that is subjective, and if someone disagrees with him, he will be angry and even persecute him and wish to kill him. A state of *objective consciousness* (i.e., the fourth state of consciousness) would have to be reached before the meaning of Christ's words became fully understandable. All we can say of ourselves is that we do not know how to love others or God. That is the first thing. We must see that it is so. What we call love can turn to dislike, suspicion, jealousy or hate in a moment. Love means positive emotion and we do not know positive emotions. Their characteristic is that they never turn into opposites because they include all opposites. We only know emotions that turn readily into their opposites, and do so often in a flash. We call it love but it is not love. It is self-love. The term *love* is used in the Gospels in a special way. It is conscious love, conscious relation, not mechanical love, that is meant. That is clear enough. When a man begins to realize he cannot love as he is, then at least he is nearer truth. He is no longer a fool. He has at least got rid of some imagination, some part of False Personality, got rid of some make-up, and so is nearer the possibility of conscious love. What passes as love in mechanical life is chiefly imagination. What people call love is usually satisfied self-love. To love is to work. Love is work."

Some people, of course, disagreed with these words and were sure they knew what love was even though they were unhappy or sad in appearance, I noticed. At another time Mr. O. said that we could not form any conception of a "development of love" without a development of consciousness. He said: "This Work speaks mainly of a possible development of consciousness in Man; as Man is he is not yet properly conscious. Love must become conscious, not passion. Man is asleep. Everything in him is mixed with dreams, with imagination, and with negative emotions, to which he clings most of all. Most of his life takes place in his imagination. He is subjective and especially governed by False Personality—this false person he has to obey which is not himself. He cannot see anything as it is. But a man who reaches the highest state of consciousness is in a quite different state. While in that state he sees what everything really is. He is no longer in personal subjective meanings. He is objective and so universal. He can include all things in himself. This happens when a man becomes conscious in the highest or most real part of him—that is, in "Real I" in him. Such a man would understand what love of God is. But a man living in False Personality in which only small one-sided self-emotions occur, cannot do so. How could such a man, so prejudiced, so small-souled, so selfish, so negative, understand what love of God is—a man who even looks down on others if they do not belong to the same club, and utterly rejects a man of a different religion or nation?"

INNER SEPARATION

The technique of inner separation must be developed by practice. At first it can be said that a person has no power of inner separation simply because he has no idea that it is possible and says 'I' to everything. Nor has he an inkling that only along this path—this path of inner separation—can he reach a higher level of himself—a new sense of 'I'. An ordinary person is in a state of sleep. This is emphasized by the Work over and over again. People hear this said, but cannot see in what way it affects them. When the Work says an ordinary person is asleep it means that such a person takes himself not only as a conscious person, as a person who behaves consciously and knows what he is saying or doing, but also takes himself as *one*—that is, as a full-grown person, a solid 'I'. He uses 'I' in all he says or does as if *he* were doing it. In other words, he ascribes everything to himself. He ascribes his feelings, moods, thoughts, sensations, and his speech, behaviour and actions to himself, and even his digestion. This is what the Work means when it says that such a person is asleep. He is asleep because he ascribes everything to himself, and has no sense of anything higher than himself or higher in himself.

The first step in redemption from sleep is to begin to realize through uncritical self-observation that thoughts *come* to a man, feelings and moods *come* to him, sensations *come* to him with all their resulting actions and that in this respect he is a *machine*—a machine in whose complex machinery he participates wrongly at every moment, saying '*I*', '*I*', '*I*'. By saying 'I' in this way, he ascribes everything to himself. *The realization that one is a machine* is underlined in this teaching as the first step towards inner freedom and individual evolution. As long as a man or woman—that is, this man-machine or woman-machine that everyone, man or woman, ordinarily is—ascribes every psychic process, every thought, mood, action, and so on, to himself, he cannot advance *one single step*. He is fixed in his illusions. He then serves Nature—that is, the cosmic influences that use mankind for their own reasons, without pity, as we see so clearly to-day. The sin of Man is, so to speak, to miss the mark, to identify with himself. In the allegory in Genesis, Man ate of the Tree of Knowledge and thenceforward thought *he* knew what was right and wrong. That is, he began to ascribe everything to himself. (I will add here how extraordinary it is that the early chapters of Genesis are regarded as literal and not psychological. The attack of Science on Religion in the last century was based on the early chapters of Genesis, which were taken as literal—that is, there was an actual Tree, an actual seven days of creation, etc.)

Now this ascribing of everything to oneself, which is identification in its deepest form, leads a person to the idea that everything is due to him or her. Inner separation leads to an entirely different state—a new idea of oneself. As we are all so heavily engaged in ascribing everything to ourselves and so identify with every mood, thought, feeling and so on, that happens in us, we must continually be reminded by this Work that this ordinary everyday state of ourselves is utterly wrong. It is totally wrong from top to bottom. It is a state of *total* sleep —and from this state of total. sleep, through self-identifying, the Work endeavours to rouse us. This arousing is the beginning of awakening. *You* have no thoughts of your own—although you ascribe them to yourself. Your thoughts come to you. *You* have no feelings of your own. Your feelings arise mechanically according to circumstances and your typical machinery of reaction. For example, you sob and sigh *mechanically*. It is not *you* sobbing and sighing—*it* sobs and sighs. It is the particular sort of machine that you have acquired that causes these sobs and sighs. You identify with this *acquired machinery* and weep and wail just because this is how *your* particular machine reacts. But you think it is *you*—that is, '*I*'—sobbing and sighing. This is not the case. It is your machinery sobbing and sighing to which you say 'I'. Another kind of machine acquired under quite different conditions in another country would not sob and sigh when you do, but sob and sigh under quite different circumstances that you might marvel at and consider a joke. But if there is no conception, no insight into oneself, then of course you will continue to take your mechanical reactions as *you*—as '*I*'—and so ascribe them to yourself. How, then, can you ever awaken to a new edition, a new form, of yourself? It is obviously impossible. You will remain at the level of Being that you are at. But this Work is to raise Being. Have any of you thought enough yet as to what a step in level of Being might be? What do you see in yourselves by self-observation that is weak, lazy, self-pitiful, mean, narrow, prejudiced, ignorant, stupid, foolish, insincere, negative, jealous, revengeful, hurtful, suspicious, crooked, deceitful, inadequate, and a hundred and one other similar things that belong to lower levels of Being? Now suppose uncritical and sincere self-observation carried out with a sufficient and gradual passion begins to awaken an increasing dislike of what one is at present—I say, supposing that you begin to see that some of these things are in you and that "Thou art the Man"—how can one deal with them? Only by inner separation—that is, by not ascribing them to oneself. This sounds very strange and yet here lies one of the mysteries of the Work. As long as you ascribe *anything* to yourself you are identified with it and therefore say 'I' to it. Now 'I' in this sense cannot fight with 'I'. They are identical. For this reason, if a person begins to observe what is weak or lazy or self-pitiful and so on, and to realize that such things exist in him and *ascribes them to himself*, he will not be able to change. What you say 'I' to can never change. Only by inner separation can anything change in a man. If he observes meanness in himself or self-pity and can say rightly: "This is not I", then will that man, that woman, not be under the power of meanness or self-pity. . For a moment he is free.

919

In regard to all this, an increasingly delicate inner perception is required. At first everything is rough and violent. The formatory part which says: "Either this is true or it is not" is useless. In-between-the-opposites-thinking has to be slowly heard by the mind—that is, relative thinking. Sometimes a thing is wrong, sometimes it is right. People want a definite answer and so they are given stony commandments. They are written on tablets of stone: "Thou shalt not", etc. This form of truth is external and not yet flexible—not yet "water". But people who pride themselves on their downright common sense cling to the mental activity of the Formatory Centre—that is, the mechanical side of the Intellectual Centre which can only think in terms of the opposites—that is, the pendulum—and has no Third Force. They wish to know always: "Is this right or is it wrong? All I ask is a plain, definite answer." But truth as "water" is not like this.

Now I return to this mystery of not ascribing our thoughts, moods, etc., to ourselves and therefore saying always 'I' to them. One has to be able to say: "This is not 'I'." Take thoughts. A thought comes to you. You say 'I' to it. So you enter it and then it has power over you. But you need not do so. When Christ said that what enters a man does not defile him, this was meant. For example, negative thoughts enter us continually. If you have no enclosure, nothing sealed off in yourself, they simply invade you and you are helpless in their power and so you will act from them and express them in gesture, behaviour or speech or action. This comes out of you. Then you are to be blamed. This is a fault in you, arising from lack of inner separation. Then you are a machine, chiefly driven by negative thoughts and feelings. But if you have a Work-place in yourself, and sacred to yourself, and stand in it at least three times a day, you separate from these unpleasant or evil thoughts or moods—which are not *you* and nothing of them comes out from you. This is the beginning of creating something new in yourself —namely, the Work.

From what has been said it is now possible to disentangle and understand the *psychological* meaning of Christ's words, which referred apparently to literal food, ritually prohibited, but which really meant psychological food—thoughts, moods, and so on. A man may have evil thoughts that enter him but separates from them. He is guiltless. He cannot stop evil thoughts entering him. But they do not defile him. He can separate from them and not consent, not say 'I' to them. Christ said:

"Hear me all of you, and understand: there is nothing from without the man, that going into him can defile him: but the things which proceed out of the man are those that defile the man. And when he was entered into the house from the multitude, his disciples asked of him the parable. And he saith unto them, Are ye so without understanding also? Perceive ye not, that whatsoever from without goeth into the man, it cannot defile him; because it goeth not into his heart, but into his belly, and goeth out into the draught? This he said, making all meats clean. And he said, That which proceedeth out of the man that defileth the man. For from within, out of the heart of men, evil thoughts proceed, fornications, thefts, murders, adulteries, covetings, an evil eye, railing, pride, foolishness: all these evil things proceed from within, and defile the man." (*Mark* VII. 14-23.)

When you identify with an evil thought, you act from it. It enters you—and then comes out of you. The entry does not defile—but the act coming from it does. People are often disturbed by their thoughts. Their thoughts enter them from without. They think they are their thoughts—that they made them. This is wrong. The thoughts come to them. No one can think from himself. But people say they do. This is wrong. Thoughts come. Any kind of thought can enter you. Some thoughts are useful and need not be separated from. Thoughts fly into us from every quarter, as countless birds into a wide-open cage, and pass on. But they are not *our* thoughts. But you can make them all your own by saying 'I'—if you ascribe them to yourself. You think "I thought this." When you think *you* think from yourself, will *from* yourself, and imagine *you* did all you have done from yourself and do not realize it is all mechanical—that is, when you ascribe everything of your life to yourself—*you are asleep*. You are asleep in life and asleep in yourself. When you perceive your thoughts come to you and that you can identify or not with them, and when you also perceive you have no real Will, but only the resultant of desires of many shifting 'I's in conflict—then you begin to waken from sleep. You lose the life-idea of yourself. This picture of yourself falls away like a skin and something else begins to emerge, different from what you thought you were. You become aware of a whole set of new meanings. This is the beginning of psycho-transformism.

Quaremead, Ugley, July 27, 1946

ON LIVING MORE CONSCIOUSLY

It was once said that the fundamental cause of almost all the misunderstandings arising in the inner world of Man, as well as in the common life of people, is chiefly due to a psychological factor found in Man's Being at an early age and due to a wrong education, the stimulation of which gives birth in him to impulses of "Vanity" and "Self-Conceit". In this connection it was emphasized in the most solemn way that the happiness of Man, which depends on his reaching the 3rd State of consciousness—that is, the State of Self-Remembering or Self-Consciousness—which should be in the real man and the real woman—depends in the great majority of cases exclusively on the absence in us of the feelings of Vanity and Self-Conceit. We can recognize at once that the False Personality was being spoken of and we see also that the activity of the False Personality ceases in the 3rd State of Consciousness towards which we all strive to awaken by our work on ourselves and our work in connection with one another. Sometimes we attain states in which the False Personality is entirely shut out and we have a kind of illumination and happiness that is entirely unknown to us in the ordinary states of Consciousness in which we pass most of our existence. All sense of worry disappears as well as all the usual feelings of 'I'. All forms of jealousy, all forms of internal considering vanish. One is alone with oneself and tastes a new kind of Consciousness which is little short of a state of bliss. From time to time it is necessary for us to review what we are doing and what is the great idea lying behind the Work itself. We are taught that the 3rd State of Consciousness is our right by birth but we lose it and fall down into the 2nd State of Consciousness or so-called waking state which is very much like falling down from heaven to hell. In this 2nd State we are attacked on all sides by evil 'I's, by evil moods, by every variety of unhappy inner states from which only a sincere act of Self-Remembering can separate us. Instead of doing it we identify with everything that can assail us in the 2nd State of Consciousness—that is, the state of sleep in which all humanity lives and which, as if in sarcasm, is called full consciousness. When we view the Work in this light we see it has a supreme and clear aim and that everything said in the Work refers to attaining, to realizing, this aim. But how many of us in the daytime practise inner separation in a practical way in the recurring daily situations of life? Is it not true that most of us spend our time in states governed by the False Personality, to which we cling? So it is a good thing to remind ourselves that in the 3rd State of Consciousness the False Personality loses all its power over us and that we pass into an entirely new field of inner and outer experiences. As a rule we live in the wrong parts of centres but we have to realize as a personal fact that this is the case. Small 'I's take hold of us. We identify with them and exaggerate their importance and so we are kept in a state of sleep. Now you will find, if you observe yourself, that a great many of these small 'I's are linked closely with the False Personality—namely, with Vanity and Self-Conceit. Therefore we do not get a right feeling of 'I' and how can a man live rightly if all the time he is governed by a wrong feeling of 'I' —namely, by Imaginary 'I', which is born out of Vanity and Self-Conceit? Have you noticed how it goes in your own case? Have you ever noticed in other people how much they are impelled to do to keep up their Vanity and Self-Conceit and how useless and unreal or often simply silly it all is? Suppose at one stroke a magician could remove from all humanity Vanity and Self-Conceit—that is, False Personality —can you conceive the transformation that would take place all the world over? Can you imagine how many lies would cease to be told and lived and how many useless activities would straightway end? I think it is not too much to say that a major part of life as we know it would cease to exist. Nor is it too much to say that most people would not know what to do when they were thus purified and freed from Personality. But to be suddenly awakened in this way would rob most people of their very lives. They would not know what to do or who they were. For this reason all awakening must be a gradual process. There cannot be a rude shock but a gradual inner development of understanding through which a man gradually discards certain states of himself and begins to prefer better states of himself through inner choice. This leads gradually to awakening and when this path is followed it is characterized by the fact that people may have apparently quite by chance real moments in which they are close to the 3rd State of Consciousness and they recognize that they are in some quite new state which is accessible to them and which in ordinary life, when they are completely identified both with themselves and with external events, they do not know.

The first great stage of this Work is to awaken out of sleep. When that is strongly enough established a man knows what he has to sacrifice, what he has to die to, and he becomes able to sacrifice it, to die to it, and then his re-birth begins—that is, real transformation. But for a long time he is between two issues and then he must have great patience with himself and not expect to attain what he has not yet sufficiently paid for. We spoke once about patience as a very conscious thing which has nothing to do with resignation. When we cannot break through our bad states we must be patient with ourselves knowing the situation but being unable for the time being to do anything about it. We quoted the words of Christ which he spoke to his disciples when he was telling them what they would have to endure. He said: "In your patience ye shall win your souls," (*Luke* XXI 19), which means your relationship to Real 'I'.

Now in this connection I wish to say a few words about the right use of centres and parts of centres. We have to think about wasting force. Mr. Ouspensky once said that one of the worst things to do was to use higher parts of centres where only lower parts should be used. Lower parts of centres are not necessarily wrong because they deal to a large extent with our relationship to ordinary outside tasks. Without them we would not get on in life. The whole thing, he said, depends on gaining more light, more insight, through self-observation. Everyone should know by inner sensitiveness the difference when right parts of centres are working and when wrong parts are working. A man can spend his time in doing some small unimportant thing with full attention when it is quite unnecessary and simply results in a waste of force. On the other hand, he might do something that was important with zero attention—that is, with small parts of centres. For example, he might make an important decision with his formatory mind, simply by association. He then uses the registering part of the Intellectual Centre to make a decision whereas he should use the whole of the centre, both the emotional and intellectual parts, before he makes a decision. To

923

make a decision about Aim, for instance, from this part of Intellectual Centre, from such little 'I's, is to start from an active *Do*—i.e. a wrong triad is formed. Aim should always start from understanding—that is, from a passive *Do*. Only passive *Do* can lead to an ascending octave. If a man thinks he can do in regard to his aim, he will inevitably be unable to keep it. He will start from active *Do*. Many aims are made in this way by little 'I's without a man's realizing what he is doing and what second force he will be up against if he tries to follow his decision. Of course he fails almost at once to keep his aim. He then gets depressed and feels he cannot work and becomes negative because he cannot work, and so on. He then begins to absorb negative thoughts and feelings towards the Work, which is an extremely dangerous thing to do. Once O. said: "Try to make important things important and unimportant things unimportant." While speaking of this he mentioned parts of centres working with the wrong energy. I asked him this question: "What is an example of parts of centres working with the wrong energy?" He said: "One example is thinking in an excited way. This is not necessarily emotional part working as well, because when the Emotional Centre and the Intellectual Centre work rightly in unison, thinking is not excited but very quiet and clear. What I mean," he said, "is the wrong kind of energy working the thinking part —i.e. the energy may belong to some other centre such as the Instinct-Moving Centre or the Sex Centre. In such a case an effort must be made to prevent excited thinking by trying to get into the thinking centre and thinking clearly what it is that one is saying or wants to say." In this connection O. spoke about formulation. He said that just ordinary conversation is one thing and thinking is another thing and if one is going to think clearly while one is talking one should make an effort of inner attention and try to see what it is that one wants to express in words and find the right words. He added that often by using some mechanical phrase, or a slang expression or a cliché, the thought was interrupted and passed towards mechanical 'I's. "A machine", he said, "works far better with more light. In other words, we must use our machine more consciously at the right moment and even when we are talking casually we should be a little aware of ourselves and notice rather than observe what we are saying. We must try", he said, "to live more consciously, both internally and outwardly." Now this means we must try to have a more *conscious* relationship to our thoughts and feelings and a more *conscious* relationship to the effects of other people on us. All this leads to the attainment of the 3rd State of Consciousness, the State of Self-Remembering, or Self-Awareness, or Self-Consciousness. In connection with living more consciously both in our relationship to ourselves and to other people, we have to study to their very depths the many concealed actions of the False Personality which spring from Vanity and Self-Conceit. We seek, in doing the 2nd line of the Work, to live with one another in such a way that False Personality plays a very small part in our relationships.

A SHORT NOTE ON DIFFERENT WAYS OF
SELF-REMEMBERING

It has been said that Self-Remembering gives a shock to the whole Being and actually provides better food for the cells of the body. But we do not give this shock to ourselves ordinarily and for that reason it is called the First Conscious Shock, because it has to be done deliberately. It is not done in nature. The natural shock that is given to the body is the act of breathing. The act of breathing gives a shock to the Food Octave starting at *768* and transforming itself successively until it reaches *Si 12*. This is a mechanical shock. Now the First Conscious Shock is what was always emphasized in the earlier part of the teaching as the most important and the most practical thing that we can do. We must learn what it means to remember ourselves and practise it every day at least more than once. Since it is so important it is always a good thing to remind ourselves about it and once more to study it.

There are many different ways of remembering oneself but in every case it means not identifying with something and so separating from something by feeling one is different from it. There is no mechanical way of Self-Remembering. It is, speaking on a lower scale, like saying there is no mechanical way of self-observation. Both acts require intelligence and consciousness and vision. A monk may mutter prayers all day long and miss the mark completely. It might indeed be very much better for him if he took in impressions at a particular moment and did not mutter mechanical prayers. On one occasion, when Mr. O. was asked: "What is this pill that Sly Man makes and swallows?" he said that one meaning was that a Sly Man remembers himself in different ways under different conditions. I will quote his words. He was asked the question: "What is it that the fakir suffers years to get and the monk weeks and the yogi days?" He answered: "Understanding." He was then asked: "What is the pill that Sly Man takes?" He said: "It is composed of many things. One must self-remember to be able to take the pill." He was then asked in some connection that I have forgotten bearing on the same subject: "What is the difference between desire and will?" He answered: "We can do what we desire but if we do what we do not desire this shews Will." He then added that all Self-Remembering must have an element of Will-control. It is an act of doing—the only one we can make.

Now we know that this Work teaches that the only place where we can interfere with our machine in a right way is to give it the First Conscious Shock, or the shock of Self-Remembering. That is why aim must connect with Self-Remembering. To try to carry out aim without any state of Self-Remembering accompanying it is to try to do from the wrong place, from the machine itself. I once emphasized to you that the Driver must climb up on to the box—that is, he must be on a higher level before he can control the horse and carriage. Remember yourself and then remember your aim.

O. said more definitely about Sly Man's pill that it was different kinds of Self-Remembering. He said: "You must find it out for yourselves gradually. It has to do with different influences, one kind for one person, one kind for another person, and so different for each person. At different hours of the day it is different for each person." This means that we must learn to remember ourselves in different ways. It is one and the same thing only in the sense that it means that you separate from and cease to identify with something that is getting hold of you. Only in that respect it is always the same. It is always the same because it is a lifting of oneself above the level of ordinary 'I's, above the stream of thoughts, pre-occupations and moods, but the direction that it takes will be different. Self-Remembering always means a fuller state of consciousness, but you do not get a fuller state of consciousness by always looking at things in the same way, because that will either miss the mark or lead to mechanicalness. If one always looks through an eastern window, one will not see the sun all day. If you are in a bad state you remember yourself in one way, and when in a good state you have to remember yourself in another way and it is often more difficult. But in every case you do not give full belief to your state but to something you could be and indeed once were—something you have forgotten. In the act of Self-Remembering you distinguish yourself from the person you have become in life. And you distinguish yourself from your present thought and mood. Slowly it is given you to see that all this is not 'I'. Otherwise one simply remains one's random foolish thoughts and useless states—a kaleidoscope—and this is being asleep in mechanical states, in typical faults. Then we are at the mercy of every set of negative 'I's that seek to destroy us—and of these we have enough. Do you realize that everyone is being *eaten* all the time by bad states, bad 'I's, by useless identification, and so feeds the Moon? In a state of Self-Remembering this is impossible. The influences of the Moon do not penetrate to the 3rd State of Consciousness. When we understand this we know we must fight to remember ourselves. We simply must remember ourselves and stop considering. Struggle not to believe your states—only the state of Self-Remembering.

G. once said: "A man should be able to turn round in himself." Now this means that he is stuck to nothing in himself. When we identify we stick to things and so cannot get free and cannot turn round. It is true things matter. But non-identifying matters most. Things both matter and do not matter. It is a double feeling. Things are serious and not serious. People pestered Mr. O. to explain exactly what the pill of the Sly Man is. They were not content with having to study it for themselves and with the hint that it was different forms of Self-Remembering at different times. He answered: "If you would not identify with the idea of slyness, then you might understand better what is meant." He sometimes said: "A man may pass into a relative state of Self-Remembering without any direct effort. All that he notices is that he is in an unusual state and that he is not identified with anything. The whole of life and its cares is dropped away and yet he sees everything very clearly."

Now when we practise Self-Remembering we can have what we want. We can have what we want as long as we do not identify with it, because to identify is to cease to remember. "What have I to do?" was the constant cry in the early years of this Work. And the answer was always the same: "All you have to do is to remember yourself." Now if you think that this is a giving up of yourself you are quite wrong. It is finding yourself and losing what you took as yourself—all this mess one is. If we can get as far in this Work as to know Self-Remembering and to realize when we are not remembering ourselves we have gone a long way and reached a goal. For in this state of Self-Remembering, in the 3rd State of Consciousness, influences can reach us which cannot reach us otherwise—in fact, help can reach us. We are taught internally. Once we know or witness this help as a personal experience we understand the Work because its knowledge has led us to this point of perceiving truth. We see what the Work means, without words, because it shews itself. So I remind you again: "Try to remember yourself, do not merely think about it or discuss it, but try to do it privately, intimately; and if you can as yet do nothing better, try to stop your thoughts, try to separate from your inner state as it is at this moment and regard it as being of no consequence and not you. This may open something, may lift something up to the level of the 3rd State of Consciousness. Something at a higher level will then recognize you, become aware of you, as if you have stepped through a door."

Quaremead, Ugley, August 10, 1946

A NOTE ON SECOND BODY

To be happy apart from outer circumstances is a goal well worth striving for. Our happiness, such as we are, depends on outer conditions. The man who has reached a stage in which he has something independent of outer conditions, something which is independent of failure or success, cold or heat, discomfort or comfort, starvation or plenty, such a man has Second Body. What does it mean, Second Body? As we are, we only have one formed body—namely, the physical body— but it is possible for a man to form another body within himself. This is one of the teachings of the Work. This Second Body does not depend on the first body but in fact can control it. Whatever the circumstances affecting the first body, whether it is in prison or not, whether it is in discomfort or comfort, whether it is surrounded by evidences of wealth and power or by poverty, this Second Body remains uninfluenced. In the practice of non-identifying we begin to make this Second Body and, in fact, everything the Work teaches is connected with this goal. It is said that a person who is always making requirements is always unhappy. What does it mean, making requirements? It means that your happiness depends on certain outer things being right according to how you think they should be right. You don't like these people, you don't like these circumstances, you object to this or that, and so on. In such a case, you are making requirements and your happiness will depend on outer things which, if they are not what you consider right, will plunge you into depression and negativeness. Such a person has no inner state sufficiently developed—that is, no Second Body—to make it possible for him or her to be independent of the ever-changing conditions of life. It may surprise you to be told that you can often find happiness, when everything is going wrong, by practising the Work. You know that it has been said that everything that happens in life is a means and not an end. But have you thought what this signifies? Whatever the circumstances you are in, they can be taken from the Work point of view *as a means for non-identifying*. Do you see what is meant? People take life as an end and they do things in life from this point of view. They always seek results. They work for results. If they encounter failure they are rendered miserable. But in this Work we are told not to work for results, but whatever we do to practise non-identifying and Self-Remembering. Now if your happiness depends on the praise of other persons you are a machine. If your happiness depends on making money, again you are a machine, because you may lose money and destroy yourself. If your happiness depends on people treating you rightly according to your picture of yourself, surely something is wrong. To be always making accounts which arise out of making requirements cannot possibly be a source of inner peace of mind. To be always thinking that things are not as you wish them can only make you continually unhappy and negative. It is you yourself who have to awaken and have to hold in yourself the secret of being happy. And this holding means sealing yourself from the effects that outside events, outside conditions, have hitherto mechanically had on you. All of us have acquired absurdly typical ways of behaving towards people and outer conditions. It is just here that one can separate oneself by noticing through self-observation how one is reacting to the moment. Yes, it is well worth just noticing this—and often during each day.

Now in connection with all this, which you have already heard very often, I would like to-night to speak briefly once more about pictures, rôles and attitudes. When a man or a woman has a strong picture of themselves they are liable to be vexed by life. A picture of oneself is a fixed form of imagination about oneself. I used to think myself a good boy. (I need not say that it was a long time ago). It was quite definitely a picture of myself. Naturally, being a good boy, I could never tell a lie, and naturally, of course, I told a good many lies. I could not see the dark side of myself, what I actually was, but was kept on one side through the influence of the picture. You will be able to see that by having this picture of myself I told more lies than I needed. Everything false arouses its opposite. Now you know that we have to accept the opposite side of ourselves, or the dark side, which simply means the side that we are not properly conscious of and do not accept. Consciousness is light. What we are not properly conscious of is dark to us—i.e. in obscurity. A great deal of work has to be done for many years just exactly on this point. This is a very useful place to work on because it brings into the light of consciousness, through self-observation, knowledge of yourself that contradicts the pictures of yourself that have hitherto had power over you. It would be marvellous if our pictures fell away. A picture of oneself shuts out any reality. It is a picture and not what we really are. This picture prevents us from accepting sides of ourselves that do not agree with our pictures of ourselves. In consequence we get divided into a light and a dark side, and this creates great disharmony. One can see people living all the time in a picture of themselves and being constantly vexed or surprised.

The next point is rôles. Everyone has typical rôles that he plays. A person probably has five or six rôles that he uses for ordinary life. Now it is wrong to say that people use these rôles. The right way of putting it is that these rôles use people. Let us say an innkeeper once entertained royalty. This forms a rôle and he can never stop talking from this rôle which is like a gramophone record. I remember once that a question was asked in one of the earlier meetings in London as to how it is that people who in ordinary life seem to be at ease and talk a great deal become silent in the atmosphere of the Work. One reason is because they cannot use their ordinary life-rôles. They can, so to speak, turn nothing on and therefore do not know where they are. Now this means we live in some kind of artificial state. When you talk to a man with a lot of rôles you get an impression that he is not there just as you do when you talk to people who have very strong pictures of themselves.

The third point is attitudes. Pictures, rôles and attitudes prevent us from any real understanding of ourselves or of our lives and they all make us dependent on outer conditions. A man or a woman full of pictures, rôles or attitudes cannot form Second Body. He cannot get behind himself—cannot separate himself. How then is this to be remedied? It is only remedied by gradually seeing pictures, by becoming aware of rôles, by becoming conscious of attitudes. So it is necessary to observe oneself. Attitudes are very easily formed by upbringing. You are taught that this point of view is right and thereby you have an attitude laid down from an early age. You may, for instance, have been brought up amongst anarchists and think they are right. How easily our psychology can be seized hold of and spoilt by outer things! Now how can a man be happy in himself when he is full of unconscious rôles, of pictures and acquired attitudes that act on him all day.

Realizing this, it is well worth while in the great discipline of self-observation to notice very carefully what vexes you, what destroys such happiness as you are capable of experiencing. When you have made a good observation, try to find out whether it is due to a picture of yourself that was not satisfied by the behaviour of someone, or a rôle that you turned on that met with no praise, or an attitude that was completely useless. How often I have heard it said, in the earlier Work, to myself and to other people: "You have a wrong attitude—you are taking things in the wrong way owing to your attitude." As you know, attitudes are probably always negative attitudes from which we judge things and people. To be free, to begin to see things a little more as they really are, to begin to see other people a little more as they really are, how is this possible if we are full of pictures and attitudes that make us blind? How can we possibly imagine we can make simple relationships if we turn on our typical rôles and boast? It was once said: "Try to notice when you are talking from attitudes and try to notice when you are talking from rôles." If you cannot do this, try to notice it in other people who are doing the same. All these things belong to the external psychology, to the acquired Personality, which we have to make passive through self-observation and the insight and understanding that results from it.

The outer psychology must be eventually controlled by the inner psychology. This is reversal. This is the formation of a second organized body—an organized psychological body—composed of finer matters than the physical body. The beginning is self-observation and the memory and insight that arise from it. Through this we begin to form a new inner psychology that looks at the outer psychology—*Second Body*. Through this we begin to be more and more independent of the outer psychology and what is happening to it. So we begin to understand what happiness depends on.

Quaremead, Ugley, August 17, 1946

ON AWAKENING FROM SLEEP

We are studying a system of ideas sometimes called esoteric Christianity and which amongst ourselves we call the Work. This system of ideas shews us quite definite lines upon which we have to work on ourselves and all this work on ourselves depends on observing ourselves far more consciously than we ever do in life and observing ourselves in certain definite directions laid down by the Work. This Work is based on the idea that we are not properly conscious as we are now, but that a quite definite increase of consciousness is possible through which we begin to evolve. Mankind at present, this Work teaches, is not properly conscious and only by an evolution of consciousness can it reach any desirable state. It also teaches that because Man is not properly conscious everything that happens in the world, all disasters, wars, and other evils, necessarily take place, simply because Man is not properly conscious and does not know what he is doing or saying. Now we are taught in this Work that consciousness cannot develop unconsciously but by effort. Mankind at present is used by nature and so everything happens in the only way it can happen, but if Man became more conscious things would happen differently. In this Work we are told that a certain number of people can always become conscious at certain periods if they are willing to work on themselves and study how they are not conscious yet and how they can increase consciousness in themselves, and for this reason the Work begins with self-observation. A man must observe himself, he must notice himself, and gradually he must distinguish himself from this mechanical figure that he has hitherto been. By this personal work he can attain a higher level of consciousness called in this system the level of Self-Consciousness, Self-Remembering or Self-Awareness. These levels of consciousness are indicated by the following diagram:

Levels of Consciousness

4. Objective Consciousness

---

3. State of Self-Remembering, Self-Consciousness or Self-Awareness

---

2. So-called Waking State

---

1. State of physical Sleep with Dreams

As Man is, he lives in this second so-called waking state in which everything happens in the only way it can happen by innumerable chains of Cause and Effect. An evolution of mankind is impossible in a general sense. One man can evolve and become more conscious but humanity cannot do so unless each person works for an increase of consciousness, and such a thing is very unlikely—in fact, totally impossible for many reasons.

The state of Consciousness we seek to reach is the 3rd State—the State of Self-Remembering. So it is said so often in this Work that we must remember ourselves and that if we sincerely begin to try to remember ourselves we will gradually be shewn how to practise Self-Remembering at different moments and the different efforts needed. The first step however is to realize through the effort of long, uncritical

931

self-observation that we do not remember ourselves and that, in fact, all the time we are in a state of sleep. In this state of sleep we carry on our lives, we speak thousands of words a day, we make love, we write books, we kill one another. All is done in sleep.

This is one of the first things we are told—the first mystery, so to speak, that the Work teaches, the truth of which we have to realize for ourselves. Mankind is asleep. Yes—but you are asleep too. That is the point you have to see through your own uncritical self-observation. It is only when we begin to realize that we are asleep and that we are mechanical and not conscious beings, that we begin to awaken. Very much is said in the New Testament about Man being asleep and about the necessity of awakening. The word for "awaken" is unfortunately translated as "watch". It should be "awaken". Many words in the Gospels are wrongly translated, as μετάνοια, which does not mean "repentance" but "change of mind", change of the whole way of thought—such as a man undergoes when he realizes that the Conscious Circle of Humanity exists and that the idea of the Kingdom of Heaven is true. Another word that is wrongly translated is ἁμαρτάνω, which is rendered as "sin", when it means "missing the mark". The mark a man must aim at is the Kingdom of Heaven and for this he must first reach a state of Self-Remembering—that is, the 3rd State of Consciousness. He must aim at awakening, at becoming more conscious, at remembering himself, at being aware of himself. In my case, for example, I must be continually aware of Dr. Nicoll and feel more and more something in me that is distinct from him and that lies more interiorly behind him. In this way Personality becomes passive and Essence is activated. Essence lies behind Personality. The Personality that life has formed in you is not you. It is not I—but it calls itself I. It says I to you and you say I to it. This is sleep.

In order to remember himself more and more deeply, a man must believe in the existence of Greater Mind and he must begin to think psychologically apart from thinking literally. He must feel another reality of himself than that derived from life or parents. The Lord's Prayer begins with the raising of the whole meaning of oneself to another level of Consciousness, "Our Father which art in Heaven" . . . We must remember that this Work teaches that Essence comes down from a very high level in the descending Ray of Creation—that level in inner, invisible space that is represented in outer visible space by the Starry Galaxy. As was indicated above, the teaching of a higher level of Consciousness is not possible as long as the external world is taken as the sole reality. The first step is psychological understanding as distinct from literal understanding. In the parables that we have discussed so far we have seen that they cannot be understood literally but have a psychological meaning apart from their literal sense. And just as art is not a physical fact but an interpretation that is psychological and transmitted by the artist, so is all development to a higher level psychologically something apart from physical fact with which the

932

senses deal. In other words, psychological or spiritual development, psychological or spiritual understanding, is something abstracted from the literal facts of the senses. The inner development of Man is not through the physical sciences and can never be unless the ultimate findings of physical science pass into spiritual meaning. It is psychological understanding that raises a man above the sensual level of the mind. In speaking of the meaning of what he taught, Christ said: "It is the spirit that causeth to live: the flesh profiteth nothing. The words I speak unto you are spirit and will live." (*John* VI 63.) A man governed by his senses and believing only in the realities shewn by his five senses and refusing to believe that he is anything else, anything above physical reality, a man who believes nature created itself accidentally—that the atom somehow or other naturally came into existence with its terrible chained forces—such a man is dead in himself. He is dead psychologically, spiritually. Christ said that it was necessary for a man to "enter into life." That means to enter into a form of understanding which is not based on the senses—into a spiritual understanding of himself and others.

The power of the evident external world united to the power of science makes everyone think that the direction of Man's development lies outside him in the investigation and control of matter. But if we study esoteric ideas in both the Old and the New Testaments we find a quite contrary teaching. In the Old Testament the passage of the Children of Israel from Egypt is used as a "type" or image. St. Paul says: "These things happened to them for types." (*I. Cor.* X 11). It represents the passage of Man from a literal, sensual understanding to a psychological or spiritual understanding of his meaning. It is said in Isaiah (XXXI 3): "Egypt is flesh, not spirit." Egypt is Man, not God, and his horses are flesh, not spirit. The horse is an ancient symbol for the intellect. Horses of flesh mean the intellect chained to the senses and believing only the evidence of the senses. We also find that a sensual man who follows only what he sees and is without any ideas which can develop psychological understanding is called a man who dies or is dead. This does not refer to physical death. It refers to the soul, to the psychological side of Man—for a man can be psychologically dead and physically alive. It is said in Ezekiel: "The soul that misseth the mark, it shall die," but the prophet adds that if a man turn from his mechanical way of behaving and tries to live according to what he has been taught, then "he shall surely live, he shall not die." By going against himself—that is, against his soul—he shall find a new life in himself, a new meaning. Such a man will begin to live differently in the midst of life because he is no longer living just from himself, from his self-will, but living from a series of ideas that he has been taught and that have nothing to do with external life but refer to the inner development of his own psychology to a higher level. So it is said that if a man who has been living anyhow and following his undeveloped soul, which, nearly an animal, is the chief seat of his desire and self-love

933

—if such a man will *turn*, then "all his transgressions that he hath committed, they shall not be mentioned unto him: in his righteousness that he hath done he shall live." (*Ezekiel* XVIII 22.) God is made by the prophet to ask: "Have I any pleasure at all, if the wicked should die" (i.e. die spiritually) "and not that he should return from his way and live?" (*Ezekiel* XVIII 23.) All this is about awakening from sleep, by going against one's mechanical behaviour, mechanical thoughts and opinions, mechanical feelings.

In the New Testament the two kinds of men are mentioned. One is called "the psychic man"—that is, the man who follows his soul. This is the mechanical man, for the soul, unless opposed, does not grow, and remains the point of the most intense desire and self-love. The second kind of man is the spiritual or pneumatic man (πνεύμα-spirit). Christ speaks often about the necessity of being born of the spirit and becoming the spiritual or pneumatic man—a second man within the man of flesh. For this reason Christ says: "Greater love hath no man than this, that a man goes against his soul for his friends." (*John* XV 13.) This is rendered "lay down his life" which does not include the full meaning. To go against one's soul is exactly what we have to do in this Work. If you understand that this undeveloped soul is the seat of every mechanical desire, of vanity, pride, jealousy, and all the rest, you will then understand why the Work opens, on its practical side, with the teaching that one must begin to go against mechanicalness in oneself. But it begins actually with self-observation, with observing what is mechanical in you. And if you do this sincerely you will very soon realize that you are mechanical in the Intellectual Centre, in the Emotional Centre, and in the Moving Centre and in the Instinctive Centre. We are, in short, a mass of habits. That is, we are simply machines. We say the same things over and over again, we react to events in the same way, we get angry in the same way, we become negative in the same way. All this keeps us in a state of sleep—i.e. at the 2nd level of consciousness.

Quaremead, Ugley, August 8, 1946

FURTHER NOTE ON SECOND BODY

If a man follows the Work and practises it from his understanding and wills it from his understanding he begins to make Second Body in himself. Actually he is working in other rooms—that is, in the rooms of Third and Fourth Bodies. To work is to obey. To obey is to will. To act from the Work is to remember oneself. To remember oneself is to begin to make something new—i.e. Second Body. In this paper I am going to talk simply about "Second Body", although at the same

934

time this includes the formation of further bodies. If you will this Work and what it teaches and do it you will form something in yourself different from your mechanical psychology. You will form a new body. All this Work is so arranged in every detail that if you understand and practise it and more and more feel its daily presence, and try to will it and so to obey it, you will form a *new psychology in yourself* distinct from the multiple chaotic psychology of many 'I's that people possess ordinarily and believe to be a real 'I'. The difficulty is that people do not see that they have to obey and will this Work in their daily life—in daily incidents. People hear this Work time and again and still behave in daily life as if they have never heard what it teaches. Then, for example, they begin to argue as to whether one must become Balanced Man before one can form Second Body. The point is simply that if you hear, understand and will and so obey this Work you will reach a new stage of yourself. The Work will do the rest for you. A man, a woman, must *live* this Work.

Now let us try to understand in the simplest possible way what it means to hear, understand, will and so do this Work. Take the single point that you have to observe Personality in yourself through self-observation. This is connected with the supreme teaching that Personality must eventually be made passive in us before all the inner changes possible to Man can take place. Your Personality at present is in chaos, in disorder. It has no organization, although through the agency of *Imaginary 'I'* it pretends to have and deludes you. Your Personality is nothing but a mass of acquired contradictory 'I's and each 'I' at any particular moment can take complete charge of you. Now if you could hear, understand and obey the Work this would be impossible, for then your Work-'I's would take charge of you. At present a man who simply goes with his changing 'I's—that is, an ordinary mechanical man—has, in G.'s words, no real psychology and is nothing but a machine. If we follow Personality and its multiplicity of changing 'I's we are machines and we live under the hypnotism of Imaginary 'I'— that is, we imagine that we have a real permanent 'I'. Now through long self-observation this false idea of ourselves is gradually done away with. This happens when the Work begins to make Personality passive. As we are, we are victimized by the most stupid and silly little 'I's that take charge of us and which we imagine really know what is good and bad.

Now if we hear, understand and begin to obey the Work, we shall be gradually shewn what is really good and bad. For example, all negative emotions are bad, and must be worked against to our utmost capacity in daily life. Again, all forms of internal considering, of making accounts against others, are bad, and must be worked against. Again, all forms of self-justifying are bad. Again, and supremely, identifying is bad and must be struggled with in every possible way for the rest of our lives.

Let us take in the last connection a man who has a great deal of

935

self-pride. He is of course convinced that he understands what is good and what is bad, what is right and what is wrong, and he acts accordingly, even though it is quite contrary to what the Work would teach him. In this case, he neither hears nor understands nor obeys the Work. He will probably only add the idea of the Work to his self-pride and use the Work in this way. He will feel himself greater than the Work and so his Personality will be kept active. In other words, the Work will not reach him in his internal depths and start something growing there —namely, the growth of his Essence or real part. As you know, we are taught that in looking for Chief Feature we have to observe what belongs to our self-love and self-pride as one clue. In that case, the only approach to further inner development is through humility, through the real experience, constantly renewed, that one *does not know*—in fact, that one knows nothing but is always pretending to know. I often talk to you about the feeling of self-merit, the feeling that one is a special case, as it were, different from other people, the feeling of self-complacency, mild or arrogant superiority, and so on. All this arises from self-pride and self-love. A man must come eventually to the point in which he realizes clearly that he is nothing. Then he can become something. Then the Work takes the place of what he imagined. A man's self-pride can stand in the way of the Work acting on him and, in fact, it does, for many years, and he has, so to speak, fits of tremendous self-pride followed by fits of inner humiliation and for a long time he does not feel humility as his most real, interesting side and self-pride as his tiresome artificial side, and so does not catch the many forms of cognition and internal perception that are associated with the momentary absence of self-pride. This is the same as what happens in ordinary life amongst religious people. They profess to believe in God, but internally they do not. They believe in themselves. One can profess to believe in this Work, but internally one does not. However a few 'I's may, and then a long struggle has to take place inevitably between the 'I's that believe in this Work—that is, in something higher—and the 'I's that do not. When a man is in his Work-'I's he is quite different, but any accidental outer circumstance may suddenly shift him into his life-'I's which do not believe in the Work—that is, that do not believe there is anything higher than sensual external life. In this sense a man has to struggle between sense and spirit. All esotericism teaches the same thing and you will find it on every page in the Gospels. Now remember that there is no reason why you should do this Work. Always remember this. Always face yourself with this point—namely, that there is no reason why you should do this Work. There is no external proof of it. You can go on with life just as you do go on with it always. No one is asked to do this Work. It is simply a matter of your own choice. You are under no vows. But if you begin to hear it and if what you hear penetrates to a deeper level and you begin to understand something of it and begin to try to obey it in your daily life, then the internal thing that holds you to this Work will be your *understanding*. A man can easily go against his understanding, but in this case he will then find himself back in life just as he was. And if he finds this more satisfactory he should go back and forget as soon as possible any understanding of this Work that he possessed. In fact, he need not forget, because the Work will vanish from him by itself. In such a case a man will remain in the same state of his psychology as formerly. He will remain a mass of contradictory 'I's that take charge of him and compel him to do things at different times and to think that 'I' is acting. Such a man will of course never form *a new psychological body in himself*: he will live and die in multiplicity of being. He will have no self-knowledge and, in short, he will have done nothing for himself during his life-time except serve mechanical life. I wonder if some of you still think you should serve mechanical life as it is now. I ask you: have you faced yourselves with this question? Look at life now. Do you think it leads anywhere?

Now let us talk further about the question of Chief Feature being in some cases connected with self-pride, which we cannot separate from self-love. Such a man will always want to have his own way. Therefore he will not be able to obey the Work because the Work asks him to go against his self-will. It will not be something bigger than he is himself. You cannot obey something that you feel is smaller than yourself. This man will often feel that he is doing what ought to be done, what he thinks is right, but he will be having his own way—i.e. he will be acting from his self-love or his self-will. Self-pride, self-love and self-will cannot be separated. The self-pride is a manifestation of the self-love and the self-will is a manifestation of both. As I have often told you, when some of us were in France we were told that Personality had scarcely any right to exist. The will of Personality had to be sacrificed. A person may have objections to this and objections to that or he may make these requirements or *those* requirements before he agrees to anything. All these will be manifestations of the Personality under the aspect of self-pride, self-love and self-will—that is, the Work will not come first, but the self-will, the self-love, will come first. The mechanical, acquired Personality will direct one's life. The difficulty is that a person, whether man or woman, does not see for a long time that this may be the case. People, I notice, either pride themselves on being proud or say they have no pride. Self-pride is in everyone but in some the Chief Feature is very directly connected with it and in others only indirectly. Pride is a very latent quality in us all which is not easy to observe, but it can form a very strong barrier to a further step in development. We justify our pride very easily but when we begin by inner perception to taste this cold, hard, unforgiving quality we realize how important it is to soften it and put ourselves in the position of those we condemn through it or feel better than. You know the disciples were not accused of vanity. I often think that one of the distinctions between pride and vanity is as follows: vanity wants to be first, like those two disciples who wanted to sit one on the right hand and one on the left hand of Christ in Heaven, but pride is rather in what Peter said when he exclaimed:

"If I must die with thee, I will not deny thee." But he did. Through fear he denied Christ. Now suppose you begin to see pride as a personal daily experience through self-observation. Then you see one of these two giants that walk in front of us and decide our lives. If you understand something of the Work and have begun to wish to hold on to it so that it may change you in the indescribable and unfathomable way in which it does, once you value it enough, then you will see that you must obey the Work and put it higher than yourself by struggling against this pride, against the forms in which it expresses itself in your life. Remember we are now speaking of pride as a source of Chief Feature. Then you will be hearing, understanding and obeying the Work and this will begin to make in you *a new psychology*, a new person, which we can call Second Body. Do not begin to argue about something that does not concern us at present, as to whether such efforts will make Second, Third or Fourth Bodies. Such efforts will make a *new body* in you, a new person, a new psychology, because you will begin to follow, to practise, the Work itself. The Work itself is an organized whole which can create in you a new organism, a second and new person.

Remember that the Work is not by *addition* to what you are, but by transformation of what you are. The Work is to *change you*, not to add something to you as you are, but to change completely what you are *now*. You cannot do this Work and remain the same. You cannot add the new wine to the old bottle of yourself. Ask yourselves, some of you, have you really changed at all, and do you really wish to change *yourself*? Or are you full of self-merit? And if you wish to change, what is it you have to change, from what you understand of the teaching of the Work? Let me remind you of these words: "To act from the Work is to remember yourself." Then you will *will* the Work against your self-will. Even Christ himself said that He did not do His own will but the Will of Him that had sent Him. Do you see what esotericism means? The Work and all its careful and lovely teachings gives an opportunity of *willing* what it teaches and not acting from self-will. Self-will gets us nowhere. But meditate on what the Work teaches and notice whether you have ever, in your life, really acted from the Work—that is, if you have heard, understood and obeyed it at any moment.

RECAPITULATION ON ESSENCE AND PERSONALITY

Essence comes down to Earth and there is formed for it a physical body out of substances derived from both parents. Out of these substances, which make separate and distinct sets of the necessary materials for the formation of a body, some are selected from one parent and some from the other parent, the rest being discarded. The Essence is prior to the body through which it makes contact with the world. In this respect the Work corrects our customary sense-based view that the parents make the child. They supply certain materials which are made in them, and everything else is done. The only thing that can be said to be done by the parents is to bring the two sets of materials together. Then, if there is an individual Essence seeking manifestation, a child results. Now the death of several million beings, in the form of sperms, is involved in this first contact of Essence with the Earth. The presence of and the death of these vast quantities of living cells seems necessary for one of them to pass from the cosmos of cells to the cosmos of Man and so attain its goal by full development. We understand that the object of Essence in coming down to this Earth and seeking a body is to enable it to reach full development. But we are told that Essence can only grow to a certain limited extent under ordinary circumstances and that it requires a special food to develop any further. We may be sure that this special food will involve the death of something else. In this case it involves the death of Personality. First there is Essence, which can only grow to a limited extent. Understand here that the body is not the Essence itself. The body becomes full grown of itself if provided with physical food. But this is not the case with the Essence, which needs psychological food. The history of the development of the Essence is not the history of the development of the body. A fully developed body does not mean a fully developed Essence. A savage may have the strength of three ordinary men and the mind of a child of two. That is the tragedy. First, then, there is Essence and body only. Then Essence is active. Next there is formed gradually around Essence a covering called Personality and this surrounds the Essence. In the meantime the body continues to grow. As a rule a man does not reach any further stage. His body grows. His Essence remains undeveloped beyond a short growth, and Personality is formed. The man's centre of gravity of consciousness shifts more and more into the outer covering called Personality that life is forming in him, chiefly by imitation. The man, as it were, passes outwards into what is not him. In this way the Personality becomes active and the Essence becomes passive.

Few having passed in this outward direction under the hypnotic action of life ever return. But a great deal is said in esoteric literature, as, for instance, in the Gospels, about *turning*. A man who lives and dies in this state, in which Personality is active and Essence passive, is incomplete, unfinished. Such a man is sometimes called a seed, an acorn, an ear of wheat, or sometimes an unfinished house. In a general sense he is called Man asleep. The food that Essence needs for its further development is the Personality that has been formed round it. But it depends on the understanding of the man whether the Essence will get this food. Mechanically this will not happen. He must begin to *awaken* before this is possible and for this he must get *knowledge*. Through awakening he feels himself less and less through his Personality. In this sense Personality begins to die. Many 'I's must die for the man to be born. So here we see some analogy. These 'I's which form the population of the Personality have to be set in the right order—namely, the 'I's that can awaken must be set over those that cannot. An evil 'I', a negative 'I', must die. That is, it must be relegated to the furthest-away place and given no nourishment. Psychologically, we *are* most what we nourish most: and we nourish most what we love most. If we love negative 'I's most we nourish them most. By ceasing to love many 'I's whose quality we see in the light of the Work, we cease to feed them with our force and they begin to shrink. But they will soon recover and begin to speak, if you give them your blood to drink. When we draw force, through non-identifying, from an 'I', and if we understand why we are doing it, the force is taken from Personality in the direction of Essence. So we have to attack Personality in order to weaken it. All we learn in the Work has this for its object. Self-observation is to make Personality conscious to us, with all its 'I's, its attitudes, buffers, pictures, rôles, etc. If we do not work on Personality it will use all our force for itself and give nothing to Essence. Essence, which is really ourself, will be starved. If we do nothing with Personality we remain therefore seeds—unfinished houses—people asleep in ourselves—and as such, since we were created self-developing organisms, we are useless experiments, failures, whatever position we hold in the world. The Essence has been connected with a body, the body has grown up. The Essence has grown a little and Personality has surrounded it. Everything is now ready for the work of self-development through the death of Personality. It is at this stage that self-development can begin. But as a rule nothing further takes place. Man lives and dies a seed—asleep in a world of people asleep. But he does not guess that this is the actual case, although he may have heard it often.

FURTHER NOTE ON SELF-REMEMBERING

In a recent paper reference was made to the Sly Man in the 4th Way who knows how to make a pill and swallow it, instead of making all kinds of painful, prolonged efforts such as the Fakir or Monk makes. People can make all sorts of useless and unintelligent efforts to attain a higher level of Being, by asceticism, by torturing their bodies, keeping vows of silence, starving themselves, denying themselves all pleasure, elaborate rituals, repeating prayers mechanically, constantly doing unpleasant or unreasonable things, and so on. All this is not intelligent. The Sly Man sees what is wrong with him at the moment by self-observation and acknowledges it—that is, swallows it—and thereafter remembers himself in connection with it. He works personally on himself. Making the pill is only possible through seeing oneself by direct self-observation—that is, by personal work and formulating what one sees. In this way, one sees what effort is needed for oneself at a particular time in order to keep awake. What is needed by one person at a given time may be quite different from what is needed by another. For example, the Lord's Prayer can be seen as the Prayer of "Sly Man". Notice it is said first that it is useless to pray by vain repetitions: "In praying use not vain repetitions as the Gentiles do: for they think they shall be heard for their much speaking." (*Matt.* VI 7.) What is meant is not directly said—namely, that prayer must be conscious and not mechanical. It must be conceived by the mind and its meaning seen internally in relation to one's state of Being. Every word must be said consciously with full meaning. In this prayer (which we gabble in Church uselessly) we ask for *daily bread*: "Give us this day our daily bread." But in the Greek it does not mean *daily* but "what is needful." It also has the meaning of "trans-substantial bread" or "what is beyond ourselves." Bread does not mean literal bread, but "bread from heaven"—that is, psychological bread, psychological insight, mental nourishment, coming from a higher level, and so shewing us what is wrong and violent in our level of ourselves. To paraphrase the section: "Give us this day our daily bread" means "May we be given vision and insight and new meaning to-day so that we know what to do and how to work on ourselves to-day." So in one sense the pill is this "heavenly painful bread" that we have to swallow. It is the same as the manna in the desert. It is just as if we prayed to be able directly and sincerely to observe ourselves in the light of the Work and so through its mental illumination see what it is necessary to work on, and what has to be not identified with, etc.—and accept this flash of given insight or light —take it inwards and not argue about it or self-justify, but accept, acknowledge its truth. But most people argue about any true internal or external criticism of themselves and so do not swallow it—that is, accept it, and see it as truth about themselves.

When we are shewn something about our state of Being, whether by inner perception or by an outward suggestion or hint, we do not make a pill of it—that is, formulate it—nor swallow it—that is, accept it—as truth. But if we did, this would lead to direct and intelligent effort based on understanding. This is the way of Sly Man—that is, intelligent Man—and it is incommensurably superior to breathing exercises, ritual, starvings, torturings of the body, following mechanical disciplines, and so on. The 4th Way is based on *understanding*. The Work is the 4th Way—that is, it is not the Way of Fakir or the Way of Monk, or the Way of Yogi. In this Work *understanding* is the most powerful thing you can develop. Therefore it is necessary to begin to to try to *understand* what this Work teaches and *see for oneself* why it teaches it. What does that mean? It means in brief that you must *understand for yourself* why negative emotions must go, *understand* why self-justifying must go, why lying and deceit must go, why internal considering and grievances and making internal accounts must go. (Notice the Lord's Prayer says: "Forgive us as we forgive others.") You must understand for yourself why egotistical phantasies must go, why self-pity and sad regrets must go, why hating must go, why the state of inner sleep must go, why ignorance must go, why buffers and attitudes and pictures of yourself must go, why False Personality, with its two giants walking in front of you, Pride and Vanity, must go, why ignorance of oneself must be replaced by real uncritical self-knowledge through observation, why external considering is always necessary, and finally you must understand and see why Self-Remembering is utterly and totally necessary for you at all times if you want to awaken from the great sleep-inducing power of nature and the increasing mass-hypnotism of external life. All this is the Work and what it teaches —namely, what it is we have to do in order to awaken from the state of sleep in which we live.

Now if you see by uncritical self-observation something, let us say, arising solely out of False Personality, out of vanity and self-love, and so out of wrong self-memory, controlling you and speaking out of you and directing all your emotions and thoughts and facial expressions and movements, and if you see it clearly and formulate it—then you make a pill. Yes, but can you roll it between your fingers? Is it so clear, so definite, so objective yet? No, but it can become so, as under-standing of what the Work is about becomes stronger and as you become more responsible for it. You have then to swallow the pill— accept it—that is, see it is something *in you* and that *you are wholly to blame* because you have been identifying and saying 'I' to this thing in you up to now, which has been probably making you miserable and everyone connected with you even more miserable. I will not say that the swallowing of the pill is easy.

Now a person has no power of right self-observation save through the force of the Work. So in the case of a person who is secretly insincere in attitude to the Work you always find a curious inability to self-

, to see themselves. There can be no
of swallowing it in such cases. Consider
. You cannot understand the Work unless
it. To *understand* in the Work-sense requires
ration of *two* centres—the Intellectual Centre
tre.

Amwell House, September 28, 1946

TIME-BODY

In connection with a remark that the feeling of Eternity enters into
Self-Remembering, and does not enter into self-observation, we can
remind ourselves of some of the ideas on Time which are accessory to
this teaching. There are three visible accessible dimensions and three
invisible and ordinarily inaccessible dimensions. From this point of
view the real world is six-dimensional. Owing to our limited senses
we know only a three-dimensional world moving in Time and this we
take as the real world—that is, as reality, as all that is or can be. We
base our thoughts on this visible three-dimensional world moving in
Time. That is, our way of thinking is moulded on this reality which is
evident to our limited senses. It is, however, necessary to change our
way of thinking if any development in the level of Being or any increase
of consciousness is the aim. This teaching, as it is so often emphasized,
is to make us *think in a new way*. Let me here ask you: have you begun
yet through contact with the ideas of this Work to think in a new way?
For this to become possible the mind must be changed by new ideas,
by means of which new, hitherto unused connections are opened. In
this way new and wider realities of the mind appear beyond the given
narrow realities of the senses, with a corresponding increase of consciousness. Briefly put, one is aware of more than one was, and this
in many unusual directions. Not only is the general range and grasp
of the mind increased, but the awareness of oneself. For instance, to
be told that one is asleep and mechanical and that one does not know
oneself are new ideas. When applied practically, through self-observation, these ideas open up many new connections in the mind—in fact,
so much so that the whole conception and feeling of oneself begins to
alter and a new self may become perceptible, hidden at some distance
behind what we have up to now thought to be ourselves and the only
possible form of ourselves. Let us take this point in connection with
dimensions. The 4th dimension is that of Time. We do not see
Time or ourselves in Time. We do not see the Time-Bodies of ourselves
or of things. We think the past is dead. Our lives are living lines in
living Time. Owing to our relation to Time, however, we see only a

943

point in Time and then another and so on, and we call them present moments. Notice well that our five senses only work in the present moment, only register the present moment—not the past or the future. To see this clearly is the starting-point, in my opinion, of being able to understand something about dimensions beyond the senses. *Do you realize clearly that* you can only see or handle or taste an apple in the present moment? You cannot do so a moment ago or a moment hence —that is, in the past or in the future. So you are limited to this doubtful thing called the present moment, and all else we call past or future and regard as having no real existence. So we limit all possible existence to the present moment and imagine God exists only in it. This is called in this teaching, however, a cross-section of Time. Yet we are never in contact with this fleeting present moment to which we confine all existence. It is actual—yet it is doubtful—not to the senses but to consciousness. Our senses relate us to a present moment but our consciousness does not. We are not conscious in this present moment of the senses. It is too small and too quick to be properly conscious in. Our consciousness, working above sense, is a mingled confused thing, composed of past, present and anticipated future. By memory and by imagination we tend to live behind or in front of the present moment and cannot crowd ourselves into it. So we are never really in the external world as registered by the senses. They render things as it were like a succession of photographs made to follow in moving rapid succession, like a film. Yet, strange to say, each present moment is eternal. The present moment is both in Time and in Eternity. It is the meeting-place of Time and Eternity. Eternity enters every present moment in moving Time, at right angles to it. That is why, sometimes, in a state of Self-Remembering—that is, in the 3rd State of Consciousness—we feel Eternity. That is also why some things in the past stand straight out of Time—often trivial things. This is because at any moment, into any quiet unremarkable ordinary moment, the dimension of Eternity enters and we may happen to become conscious of it.

The relation of Time to Eternity is first represented by this diagram:

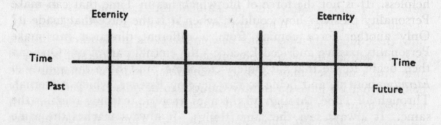

The horizontal line represents Time—the 4th dimension. The vertical lines represent the 5th dimension entering every moment every part of Time at right angles. Or, more simply, Time and Eternity can be represented as the Cross.

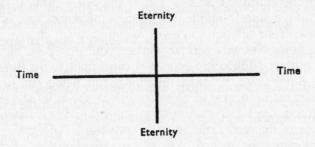

Man is both in Time and in Eternity. Eternity is vertical to Time —and this is the direction of Self-Remembering—the feeling of oneself *now*. Every *now* is eternal. To remember oneself the feeling of now must enter—*I here now*—*I myself now*—I distinct from past or future— *the nowness of myself*—*I now*. And if the act is successful you will know for yourself that Eternity is always in *now* and can be experienced as a different taste from Time. Notice that I do not speak any longer of the present moment registered by the senses, but of *now*, of this internal experience that Self-Remembering can actually give. Real 'I' is in Eternity—not in Time. Self-Remembering is out of Time and Personality. It is not surprising that Self-Remembering can give a feeling utterly different from that given by our relation to hurrying, anxious Time. Essence, being eternal, has not the feelings of Personality which are of Time only. To think from Time gives no real feeling of oneself, or rather it gives a wrong feeling—our usual feeling of ourselves. This is our usual sense of ourselves. We can notice how incomplete it is. Why do people act as they do? Because they do not feel themselves rightly. We know already that the Work teaches that we were created as an experiment—as self-developing organisms—and therefore we can understand why we feel incomplete and why a man, moulded only by life—that is, having only his acquired Personality active—must always feel incomplete, unfinished, and so internally helpless. It is not the force of life which lies in Time that can make Personality passive—how could it, when it is the force that made it? Only another force coming from a different direction can make Personality passive and feed Essence—the eternal part of us. One can then begin to see that all esoteric teaching must have the quality of *Eternity* about it, and being so can develop Essence, which is eternal. Through all Time, through all the ages, esoteric teaching remains the same. It always says the same things. It always teaches the same things. It is above Time and change. It is Eternity in Time—and so it speaks always of eternal life.

To return: the 4th dimension of Time contains all one's life. We

945

experience it moment by moment. It runs very fast and is only halted by the feeling of *now*. Our life lying extended in this dimension, inaccessible to our senses, is all there—in this invisible dimension. For this reason everything we do now affects the *past* as well as the future of our life. One act of non-identifying now influences *your past as well as your future*. Your relation to people in the past will change, by work on yourself now. Not only will you change your own past, but possibly theirs. This is very difficult to grasp so I come back to the beginning of this paper where it was said that to change our Being and to increase consciousness we need new ideas beyond those given by the senses. It was said in so many words that as long as our thinking is based only on the evidence of the senses, the mind cannot think differently and new connections cannot be opened. You will say that the past is dead, over, finished—just because your senses do not register it. If they did, you would think differently, but as they do not, you will say that the idea of the past life actually existing is nonsense. That is what it is. It is "nonsense", for the external senses do not register it, since they can only register the moment of Time called the present. The higher dimensions are not realities of the external senses, but of the internal senses. For instance, my whole life can be internally seen in a certain state of consciousness. Why? Because it is there. Where? In Time. And my future? It is also there, in the dimension that we experience as Time through which we are moving. Then I am pre-destined? Yes and No, because there are many parallel lines of Time like telegraph wires and one can be on one or another according to one's inner state. If you enjoy your negative emotions you will follow one line, and the lowest. To rise in a vertical movement one rises and follows another parallel line by non-identifying and by Self-Remembering—in short, by the Work, which enters Time at right angles and so is always vertically above you, whatever line you follow, and never in the future, for the future is in horizontal Time. One might speak of one's vertical future, however, as distinct from one's horizontal future. If Being develops, the direction is vertical. One will see one's life differently. Higher Being is *above* lower Being. At this moment you can go with 'I's below you or above you. You can spoil something silently in yourself or not. You can say something to yourself or not. It will all remain in the Time-Body, but on different levels, according to its quality. All the life is there—in the Time-Body. But by work now, things can be changed in the past and the Time-Body connected in a different way—as one might loop up bits of a long, flexible string and lengthen others. When we feel that all the past is there and living in the dimension of living Time, our sense of ourselves alters. Indeed, it alters very much, by our realizing first that passing Time cancels nothing and secondly that one can change things in the past now—not by useless sad regret, but by active work on ourselves. We are not connected with a dead past but with a living past. Every act of work vibrates through the whole Time-Body and alters things in it. I can act now on my past. I can change now my behaviour thirty years ago. Later on, we will speak of recurrence, of re-entering our lives once more and finding perhaps that some things have been changed, so that we begin to awaken earlier.

Great Amwell House, October 5, 1946

FURTHER NOTE ON TIME-BODY

In the previous paper it was said that the feeling of Eternity enters into Self-Remembering but not into self-observation. We observe ourselves in passing Time. We observe Personality which has been formed in passing Time by the action of life. We observe the different 'I's in it which have appeared at different periods of Time, chiefly through imitation. Essence is not of passing Time. It is not a temporal thing. In remembering oneself one does not remember the Personality but something prior to it that lies in the direction of Essence and can only be reached through it. To remember oneself in the Personality would be to strengthen it—to say "This is I" to it instead of "This is not I". If you say 'I' to the wrong thing you increase its power over you. You do not then separate from it. Life makes us identify with the Personality. It naturally makes us identify with what it has itself created in us. The Work is to make us cease to identify with what life has created in us and is now doing to us. To remember oneself, to summon up the purest, subtlest feeling of 'I' in connection with some prominent side of Personality would be to identify still more with what life has formed round Essence. It would be like washing paint off with paint. The purest, subtlest, most luminous and total feeling of 'I' lies behind the multiple feeling of Personality and its uproar of ambitions, anxiety, violence and negativeness. Into this feeling of 'I' of which I speak the feeling of Eternity enters every moment of Time, but in a direction we can never find as long as we are identified wholly with the Personality. While the Personality is wholly active, the direction is closed. Personality directs us to Time—to passing Time—that is, Life. Diagrammatically, the dimension of Eternity enters the dimension of Time at right angles. As the feeling of Time increases by self-observation and we begin to take time-photographs of ourselves—that is, studies of 'I's over long periods—the hypnotism of the present moment registered by the senses becomes lessened. The "present" is no longer confined to the instant—but broadens gradually into all one's life, as consciousness expands. We begin, in fact, to understand living Time—that is, we begin to understand that our lives lie in the invisible dimension of Time and are not confined to the snapshots of Time that our senses register. The past is living in its own present—and is changing. How can it be

G*   947

changing? Through reaching our consciousness. Consciousness is light: light changes everything. Shut in the prison of the senses we disbelieve in dimensions other than those of space which the senses shew us. How, if we believe only in what we can see, can we ever develop? How can we touch centres that are supra-sensible? How can we undergo change of mind—the first step in the development that esotericism teaches as being a man's meaning? If you believe there is nothing behind the scenes of visible life and that Nature created itself, how can you remember yourself? If you believe *you* are your visible body and that you cease with it, how can you remember yourself? When this Work says Essence comes down from the Stars it says something that can alter your life. The source of Essence is vertical to Time. Our origin is not in Time—in the past. This is a strange idea. But it is an idea that is necessary. It changes the mind and this is the first thing necessary. We begin to think in a new way—and how much there is to think about in a new way—and reach back to, in one's life, and change. One can see one's life quite differently—but not if one does not understand that it is living and is affected by all we do now and understand now. New understanding is the most powerful force we can create in the Work. It comes from new ideas. This force of new understanding not only alters the future but it alters the past. The whole Time-Body of a person is connected, just as one end of a stick is connected with the other. Tap it anywhere and it vibrates through its length. But the Time-Body is not straight. It is a circle, not quite closed.

This brings us to recurrence. The teaching is that if we do not "work" on ourselves the life recurs *just as before*. Nothing is altered. Why? Because we have not altered anything in ourselves. What does it mean to alter something in oneself? It means a growth of Essence. If Essence grows it will not attract the same life in recurrence. In the Work by the term "development" is meant a new growth of Essence. This can only take place by some manifestation of Personality ceasing to be active through the power of the Work. A man sees, through the light of the Work and his understanding of it, some negative manifestations of himself, let us say. By further observation he sees it more and more fully, extending through his life. Wishing to work on himself —that is, valuing the Work practically and not sentimentally—he begins to separate from it, in, so to speak, cold blood—deliberately. When he feels himself near the 'I's that lead into it, into this bad psychological place in himself, he does not identify with these negative 'I's in this place that always exists. If he finds that he is tending to get too close to them he remembers himself and when he feels the Work —that is, when he is in the presence of the Work-'I's—he recalls the observations he has made hitherto on this negative state and the moments of insight into it that he has had and what he has understood of the meaning of the Work and why he himself is working. In this way he strengthens his aim. He has given himself the First Conscious Shock and so created new hydrogens, new force. With this new force which he has created his power of not identifying is increased.

Now work of this kind, which is against one or other manifestation of the Personality, produces the right conditions for the growth of Essence. A struggle must *necessarily* take place at every stage of this growth. If Personality wins then there is no growth. Personality and self-will absorb the force and remain active and Essence gets nothing and so remains passive. *So we must be tempted.* One prays not to be led into temptation but delivered from evil, from Personality. Here we must think individually. The struggle is between what is unreal and what is real. But in this struggle it is only the light of the Work—that is, the force and illumination coming from Conscious Man in the form of esoteric teaching, as is the Work we study—that can separate you from Personality. This force is counter to the force of life. It sets up war in the man. But otherwise Essence cannot become active. Life made and keeps Personality active. The Work is to make Personality passive by the methods of the 4th Way so that Essence can grow and eventually become stronger than Personality, so that a man is no longer worked from outside—from life. This means the emergence of a new man, a new woman. This is the development meant—not an increase of what you are but the emergence of another new person, by making what you *are now* passive, along those lines taught so clearly by the Work. If Essence grows *after* Personality has been formed, it will not attract the same life in recurrence. But unless a man has another light than that of the visible Sun he will not be able to make Personality passive. He will not understand what it means. If he meets some pseudo-teaching his efforts will only increase Personality and he will remain on the wheel of mechanical recurrence.

You will understand therefore why it is said that a man with right Magnetic Centre is already at a far higher level of Being than others, however prominent, or scientific, and so on, who are without it and can only believe in their senses. The point of entry into esoteric teaching is the Magnetic Centre which can distinguish between things of life—that is, *A* influences—and things of Conscious Humanity—that is, *B* influences. Without this point of entry a man cannot separate himself from Personality because the force of life will hold him to it. The development of Essence will then be impossible. The man lives and dies a seed, an acorn, and the Work says he can be eaten by pigs, a painful business. He forms a source of food for what is beneath the Earth. A man into whom knowledge from Higher Man has entered, who begins to understand and to realize what he is, and eventually sees his own nothingness, who begins to work, this man can make Personality passive. That is, the Work makes it passive if he is of use. In that man there will be a growth of Essence. He will not go round in the same circle of life. If the development of Essence becomes full, if the essential man grows to his full stature—he will no longer experience life at the level of this Earth. It is that level called the Sun that demands the life of Man as well as the Earth and Moon. The Sun demands the developed

949

organism—Conscious Man. So Man was created a self-developing organism and given an Essence that came from the level of the Starry Galaxy.

Great Amwell House, October 13, 1946

THE RELATION OF MEMORY TO THE
FOURTH DIMENSION

Our memory is stored in rolls in centres. Impressions fall on rolls in centres. These are set turning by associations. When we are reminded of something it means that a roll has started turning in some part of a centre. Sometimes a roll just starts and stops again and we almost remember—a curious but common state. Sometimes more than one roll turns. When this happens the memory is much richer. When rolls are set turning simultaneously in three centres—let us say, in the Intellectual, the Emotional and the Instinctive Centres—the recollection has something of the quality of reality. But smell can almost turn the past into the present. The fine matters of smell touch the Fourth Dimension, of which we have recently been speaking.

Now my memory, say, of Paris is stored in rolls in centres. The memory of it is different in each centre, for each centre has a separate kind of memory. The impressions stored in the Instinctive Centre recall, say, its food and wine or its comfortable beds. The impressions stored in the Emotional Centre recall, say, its beauty in early sunlight. The impressions stored in the Moving Centre recall, say, athletic feats in crossing Paris streets. The impressions stored in the Intellectual Centre recall, say, the bookstalls by the river or thoughts about Notre Dame, and so on. All these impressions and a million and one others stored in rolls in different centres form my memory of Paris. Sometimes a Paris roll is set going by some accidental association and a bit of Paris appears in consciousness for a moment and perhaps some other rolls turn a little and I have a dim sense of other bits of Paris. This machinery of rolls lies in the brain. The brain is a machine enclosed in a box. If we knew enough and could look into the box and into the machine within it with much finer senses, that we possess but do not use, we could see these rolls turning. If another knew how to connect his machine with my machine he could know Paris through me and see what I saw. It would also be possible for him to observe an idea entering into my brain in one way and into another person's brain in a different way and he would then understand why we never agreed about anything and always remembered differently and were continually quarrelling. The brain is a small machine with a very high storage capacity and millions of wires connecting different parts of it. It is much the same in everyone, but the connections used are different in different people. When you judge another person it is certain connections you judge used by him, that do not correspond with the connections used by you. So one realizes that one's past also lies not only in rolls in centres but in the connections acquired by upbringing between these millions of wires that are now habitually used—that is, the paths in the brain that we always walk along. Among millions of other possible paths, our past, then, is one form, one possibility, one pattern, and one set of streets in a vast town. Now you see what is meant when it is said in this teaching that Time for us is the fulfilment of one line of possibilities but that at every moment there are lines branching out in every direction and so infinite possibilities, and that Eternity is the fulfilment of all possibilities. You remember one definition that Christ gave of God—that with God all things are possible. God is not in Time but in Eternity, outside Time, having nothing to do with Time. That is why, in order to understand aright what is above us, we have to get rid of Time in our thoughts. We have to get away from Time altogether in order to reach a level of ourselves that is above us. Time and space prevent us from reaching a possible and actually existing higher level of ourselves. A man must be re-born out of Time and Space—for his mind, if awakened, can understand and reach to a higher dimensional world in which there is no Time and all *is*—not *was*. That is why we have to start with the realization that all our life lies living in the invisible 4th Dimension and that the past is living. The past *is*—not *was*—and so can be changed. *I can change my past by working on myself now.* You can change the past as well as the future *now* if you remember yourself and cease identifying with a typical path that you usually follow as, say, in judging others. So what we do now in order to gain new knowledge so as to understand how to think in a new way—by making new connections, for that is the start of all change of Being—is truly important. Among other things you begin to think in a new way if you think of passing time as an illusion. What is the reason of this illusion? One reason is due to these rolls in centres of which we were speaking, apart from what was said earlier. When they turn they give the sensation of the past, of what *was*, and so we think of the past as non-existent, dead, and irremediable, and from that derive an entirely wrong feeling of ourselves—yes, from that and a hundred other things. Rolls are necessary—otherwise we would have no memory. But memory is not new meaning, new inspiration. It is not the same as consciousness in the 4th Dimension which is sometimes experienced when the carbon dioxide in the blood reaches a certain concentration. Then there can be direct access to the 4th Dimension of Time. A certain kind of breathing can result in this. It is then like going to Paris, instead of remembering about it. Paris, is, not was. If you could see rightly into a person's brain, you could see, say, an illness coming. The brain is strung on to Time like a ring sliding along a rope. It is a machine passing through Time—through one of the possible lines of Time—and there is left in it a slight deposit on these rolls. This is memory. Memory is slight. We remember very little. We mis-remember or forget nearly everything. But in the 4th Dimension itself, apart from memory, all our life stands just as it was in every detail of thought, feeling, sensation, movement, perception and action. At death all the life together—the entirety of the life—forms a certain kind of food and according to its quality it is absorbed either by what lies below the Earth in scale of creation—namely, the Moon—or by a higher level—namely, the Sun. So we are not our bodies, but all that is laid down in our lives apart from memory. We are our total lives from birth to death. This is our Time-Body. It is all present, all there; and if I work on myself now, observe myself, see where I am identified, see what accounts I am making against others, how I justify myself and forgive no one, how I think only how others are wrong, how I judge people mechanically without seeing into their lives or seeing how self-satisfied and complacent I am, how I am not at all what I imagine—in fact, if I begin to work on myself from the esoteric ideas of this Work which seek to transform us, then I may be able to change my Time-Body by getting on to another level of Time, on to another line where everything in the past is altered—so that when I re-enter my life at the moment of birth I find things are different and even remember my previous recurrence, possessed perhaps of a strange feeling of familiarity—of having been there before. This is because when real memory is opened, at death, when the book of our life is opened—not only what others did is recorded, but your own smugness, your own meritoriousness, your own cruelties and dislikes, what you did, what you felt, and thought, are also recorded. This is too strong medicine to bear, save by long, sincere, uncritical self-observation. So instead of such a powerful degree of direct consciousness we are mercifully given memory on rolls and are not allowed to have access to real memory, which only Conscious Man can bear and has. We, as mechanical people, groping in the dark, could not bear such an intense light. Gradually, however, by work on oneself, this range of consciousness increases, and with it our Personalities begin to lose power—and Essence begins to develop.

You can catch perhaps a glimpse of what I am speaking of—namely, how little we can trust to the memory deposits on rolls in centres. If people only realized that what they call absolutely certain memory is not certain and that, in fact, they cannot trust memory on rolls in centres and that what they are sure happened did not happen as they remember—it would lead to a freeing of themselves from the brain-machinery and as a result a loosening of everything in them and a new feeling of themselves. This Work, from many different angles of approach, is to free a man, a woman, from their habitual, rigid, set feeling of themselves, and eventually create a new sense of 'I', a new feeling of oneself. How many evil accounts against others, how many bitter grievances, are kept alive against others on the basis of this faulty memory on rolls, which, if we could experience real contact with the Time-Dimension, would utterly vanish. But few are yet prepared enough by the Work to begin to see and bear what really happened. If we had real memory we could never have negative emotions against others. But as we are we have to begin the other way round—that is, to notice and separate from our negative emotions. This is called "preparation of lower centres for the reception of higher centres." Higher centres work in higher dimensions. They embrace the whole life.

Great Amwell House, October 19, 1946

A NOTE ON PERSONAL WORK ON ONESELF

When we are identified we do not remember ourselves. In the method and practice of the 4th Way the attainment of the 3rd State or level of Consciousness is made a central theme. Self-Remembering, Self-Consciousness and Self-Awareness are some of the characteristics of the 3rd State of Consciousness. I would add as a commentary Self-Recognition or recognizing oneself. When we identify we drop to the second level of Consciousness. What results? A number of related things then result. We fall asleep. We come under the Law of Accident. We serve Nature and the influences created by life— namely, *A* influences. We are under the power of whatever we identify with and lose force to it. The inner work of the organism is altered. We forget our aim. Consciousness contracts. Our associations receive energy and former things return. All this and much more results from identifying. Viewed on a great scale in the light of the Ray of Creation and the Side-Octave from the Sun, when we identify we shut ourselves to influences coming down from a higher level and open ourselves to those coming from beneath us. That is, we feed the Moon. The more we identify the more we feed the Moon. A person who enjoys negative emotions is an example. Identifying is dirt. Has the vision of the world being filled with useless suffering—that is, useless to any development —yet come to you in internal experience? Yet useless suffering is useful for something else, for everything is useful to something or for something. At different levels everything is used. If a man makes no effort to awaken, what energy he has for awakening will be used elsewhere. It will be given to others. Christ said: "Unto everyone that hath shall be given, and he shall have abundance, but from him that hath not, even that which he hath shall be taken away." (*Matt.* XXV 29.) Nothing is wasted, although to us it looks as if it were. Everything is "food" for something else. The useless sufferings of mankind and all its identifyings form food. They are collected from the sensitive film

953

surrounding the Earth and transmitted to the Moon. So we realize that a man in a state of Self-Remembering and a man in a state of sleep are two quite different people although they may be sitting next each other. They are not sitting next each other in the vertical scale of Being. Psychologically they are separated by an immense distance— not a distance in space but a distance in Being. When people identify with everything, both with themselves and with life, they do not understand the Work. Let us take identifying with oneself. Oneself is a multiplicity of different 'I's. When a person identifies with every 'I' that comes round in the turning circle of 'I's, he is not working on himself. This thing we refer to as "ourselves" is exactly what we have to observe. It is a series of 'I's that successively take charge of us, and to which we always say 'I'. By saying 'I', by thinking it is always *oneself* and so taking oneself as *one* self, we are continually identified, continually asleep.

How and in what way does the fine edge of the Work enter, so that all this mechanical state of things begins to be altered? By realizing through directed observation that one is not one person but many different people. One is not "oneself" but "many selves". Some may say that this has been often said before. Yes, and it will often be said again. Why? Because unless we are constantly reminded of it we completely forget where the practical work on ourselves starts from. It starts from separating from certain kinds of 'I's. Can you hear what is being said? Work on oneself starts from separating from certain kinds of 'I's. But how can you begin to separate from the power of any 'I' unless you observe it in action? In the Work the object of observing oneself is to become aware of certain kinds of 'I's that feed the Moon and then to go with them less and less—that is, to identify with them less and less—not take them as 'I'—that is, to separate from them. Here the starting-point of the Work lies. Unless you have come to this realization, the Work and its meaning remain obscure to you. You do not grasp what it is about. You remain negative, distressed, unhappy, miserable. You can see no connection between what the Work teaches and your own states. You believe every state of yourself. You believe every 'I' that momentarily takes charge of you—that is, you identify with everything in yourself. You do not grasp where the secret of the Work lies—namely, in not taking too much notice of and not identifying with your negativeness, your distress, your unhappiness, your miserableness. You need not identify with them, need not consent to them, need not say "I am negative", for they are 'I's that love to destroy you, that love to poison you.

As was said, when you identify, you are asleep. Negative 'I's wish to keep you asleep, for when you are awake they have no power over you. People say: "Oh, that may be true, but I have a very good reason for being negative." In this way, negative 'I's continue to have full sway. They provide the reasons. The Work says that all negative states, no matter what the cause of them may be, are wrong, and must be separated from. Try to ignore the cause. We have, the Work says, a right not to be negative and we must fight with all our strength of mind and through the truth of the Work for this right which is ours and which we lost by imitating others. Must you take things in the same mechanical way? If you do not see how else you can take them, then again you do not see where work on yourself lies. Put it in this way—must we always behave mechanically? Is it not possible to behave more consciously to life, to ourselves and to others. What does that mean? It means we know already by self-observation how we take an event, a situation, a person, mechanically, and that we do not identify with this typical mechanical way of taking them but (1) separate from it and (2) if possible consciously try to find a new way of taking them. This is work on oneself and this leads to change of Being—to new Being. There is plenty of new Being, so to walk in old Being is unnecessary. But we are jealous of old Being and do not wish to have new Being—or rather, we wish to have new Being and retain old Being. But we cannot go to Paris and remain in London.

Now to return to this open secret that the Work is always teaching us and we take so long to see. If you say "I am negative" you cannot separate. If you see the 'I' that is producing a poison gas of negative emotion then you can say "This is not I". Again, you should not say "Need *I* take the event in this way?" The point lies in observing that an 'I' in you is taking it that way and you are identified with that 'I' and need not be. So you step back from that 'I'—separate from it— and standing behind it watch it taking the event in that way. So gradually you step behind the Personality-Machine and see it as a cage of 'I's and no longer as you. You begin to strip it off like a lot of coats. Then Steward comes to prepare the house for Real 'I'.

Great Amwell House, October 26, 1946

ESSENCE AND PERSONALITY

To-night we speak again about Personality and Essence because all self-observation leads into that question anew at different stages— "What in me is Essence? What is Personality?" It might be said that Personality is the grown-up side and Essence the ungrown side of ourselves. The point however is that the grown-up side is not really ourselves. It fits like a tight costume round us but can under certain circumstances be stripped off. The real person then appears, quite unlike what the Personality made him appear *to himself* and *to others*. Why is so much said in this Work about the necessity for Essence to grow? Essence cannot be stripped off. The real person, the person that remains after Personality is removed, is the Essence. A person may

955

have a noble Personality. But this is not the real person. When the safeguards and restraining influences of life are removed and all fear of exposure or loss of reputation or the consequences of the law are done away with, what lies behind this noble Personality emerges. That is, ungrown, undeveloped Essence appears. We must not imagine that Essence is wholly beautiful and charming. The real man appears separated from the Personality that has surrounded him hitherto. People do not understand how, if certain outer restraints and fears were removed, they would not lead the careful lives they do. They do not understand that their behaviour is not from *within*, but is caused by external circumstances. That is, they do not see that Personality is active, but not Essence. Now we know that Essence manifests itself openly and uncovered until about three or four years of age. Then Personality begins to surround Essence, masking it, and takes charge. Personality is formed by imitation and education, by praise, by fear of consequences. But it is not the individual himself. The real person— the Essence—remains covered over and passive. Now whatever is done by Personality is done through the force of external circumstances. That is, it is done from without, not from within. In this sense it is unreal—not the real person. Let me repeat: "What is done through Personality is done through the force of external circumstances." That is, life drives the machine of Personality. External circumstances make you act as you do. You may imagine you are free. But you are not free. Whatever you do is due to external circumstances acting on your particular kind of acquired Personality. Notice how external circumstances put people in great or small positions. It is not them. It is the force of external circumstances. All the time we say 'I' to what we do, as if we were doing it. We do not suspect, save through genuine self-observation, that it is external circumstances acting on Personality that make us do as we do. It is not *I* from within doing it. Ordinarily, what you think is really your 'I' is only a collection of 'I's in the Personality that are for the moment in agreement responding to outside impressions —that is, responding to external circumstances.

Let us go back to what was said—namely, that what you do is not from Essence but from Personality. Now suppose in some way you could act only from undeveloped Essence; it would be foolish, even not human. So here lies the paradox of Personality and Essence. To be able to act from Essence requires a development of Essence. The Work teaches that the first step to bring about the development of Essence is the formation of Personality. It then says that for Essence to grow, Personality must become passive. To say that Personality must teach Essence is one way of putting it—a way I have always thought a wrong way of putting it. I would rather say Essence must learn from Personality. The esoteric problem—the task of the Work—is how to make Essence grow. It does not grow from itself save to a point. Something else is necessary. This is the central idea and explains why esoteric teaching—religions, and, in fact, all *B* influences exist. How to make

Essence grow is the real esoteric problem—how to make the real grow in us so that there is no duality of acquired Personality and born Essence. The difficulty is that Essence cannot be *compelled* to grow. No external compulsion can make Essence grow. You cannot compel a small child to grow essentially. Why? Because each child is a self-developing organism by creation. That is, it can only develop itself. Since Essence cannot be persuaded directly, by outside force, Personality is formed round Essence. This is the first step in the scheme for Man on Earth, coming down from the Sun-Octave. The trouble is that Man stops at that point—namely, he has a Personality formed for him and then identifies with it and takes it as 'I'—as himself. For this reason he suffers from inner disharmonies all his life. He does not know he is half-formed. For this acquired Personality may give no outlet to Essence. A very strict upbringing means a very tight, rigid Personality and so the making of Personality more passive becomes a formidable problem. Yet the point remains that, unless Essence grows, the man is a failure esoterically. He is perhaps a very good man—but mechanically so. He is not really a good man but an acquired imitation of one. The mechanically good and the mechanically bad are therefore seen as the same in the light of this Work. Only understanding can make Essence grow and this can only enter a man through new knowledge that comes in first through the Personality. So Essence can only grow through new knowledge—a special knowledge that is, in short, esoteric teaching. And this must first come in *via* the Personality—from outside—from peculiar external circumstances. The Personality transmits it. It means the death of Personality eventually. But Personality does not know this. The new knowledge has a force behind it not derived from life. Mr. Ouspensky used to repeat again and again that it is impossible to escape from Personality and buffers save through a special force and that we have not this force ourselves. We have to get in contact with this force. Then Personality can gradually become passive when it must, so that Essence can grow. Then it becomes a matter whether *you* wish to follow understanding or not. Essence is lazy—like all primitive peoples. Laziness is a very deep powerful thing. That is why the Work says that once you really *understand* why a thing is wrong and still do it, you in a real sense sin—that is, miss the mark. In connection with Essence, Mr. Ouspensky once said that, from the standpoint of the astral or planetary world, Essence is often more or less like an animal, and that *essentially* there are very few *human* beings at this level. He said that Humanity scarcely exists at a higher level—when stripped of all pretence and quite naked. Now if we do not steal, from ourselves, no matter what the circumstances, it is essential. If I do a thing because no one is looking, or I wish a reward or praise, or from fear, it is not from within, but from outside—that is, from external circumstances, from Personality. It is not real. When stripped of external life what will I be—when Personality is removed? What remains that is real? I advise you all to think about this problem that arises from the fact that Man is created to be a self-developing organism. You will see how all external compulsion and social systems of that kind will never develop Man and will, in fact, separate him from Essence completely. All the long process and living of the Work is to pass from Personality to Essence, bringing to Essence the gifts Personality has acquired. Sooner or later, somehow or other, somewhere or other, we are unmasked, and Essence is revealed as ourselves. Do you recollect the masked balls of a former age? At midnight we had to unmask.

Great Amwell House, November 2, 1946

A NOTE ON BURIED CONSCIENCE

This Work is about reaching a higher level called the Third State of Consciousness. This level exists in us as a possibility. The second level of Consciousness, the level of so-called waking Consciousness, in which we spend our lives, is a level below the third level. All forms of thought, all emotional reactions, all feelings of oneself, the way one takes things ordinarily, belong to the second level. We seek to reach the third level. About what can we be quite sure? We can be quite sure that at the third level the way of thinking and feeling, the sense of what is important and unimportant, will be utterly different. Another order will be reached. The third level is experienced by many during their life-time as a flash, a momentary experience. They are for the moment without any time-feeling, and so without any sense of identifying. Troubles, cares, anxieties, all their sources of being identified, lie far below them. But these moments are not enough. They merely indicate something possible to reach. Work is about separating from everything that does not belong to this third level, which is our real aim. People say: "Why should I work?" Or they say: "What does this Work mean?" This Work is based on real knowledge which concerns how the attainment of this third level is possible. For example, why should you not identify fully with everything? The answer is that if you do, you will get nothing from the Work. You serve yourself as you are; you serve life; you serve nature. Therefore you are used by the cosmic forces that seek to keep you asleep. Now a person may say: "I will not serve this cosmic purpose. I will not give way to useless suffering. I will not identify myself with negative emotions. I will become conscious." But he can do nothing by himself. In the first place, new knowledge must be given to him, and in the second place, when trials come, as they always must, at certain periods, he must use them practically—that is, he must really be able to think in a new way about his trials. New knowledge cannot be put into old bottles—that is, into the old mind. Understand that a higher level of

Consciousness means another way of thinking, not the old way stepped up. The freeing of the mind from its old habitual ways of thinking, the freeing of oneself from one's old mind and its ways of thinking, the freeing of oneself from one's habitual emotions, takes place by stages —often at long intervals. It is comparable to climbing a stair, each step exhausting one's energy for the time being. Each person is given his own octave or staircase of development and what may be easy for one person is not necessarily so for another. But the sum-total, the quantity of effort necessary for reaching internal freedom, is the same for everyone. No one is better off than another person. To be given advantages, for example, will not help in the long run. Just where you have been helped will become eventually the most difficult place where you have to help yourself. And here you must remember two things—namely, the esoteric saying that the more you are given the more is required of you and that if you are told things beforehand that you should have found out for yourself by observation, you may think it is a help—as, for instance, being told your Chief Feature before you have even caught a glimpse of it—but it is not a help. Actually, it will make things far more difficult. It interrupts a gradual inner process of unfolding, of seeing things for yourself and seeing for yourself how something in you is wrong and hinders you. You may be sure that once your evaluation of the Work is strong enough and you hear it enough and reflect upon it enough, you will see gradually unfolding the mystery of your own development. This mystery is different in each person. That is why it is so important not to compare yourself with other people. A great deal of negative emotion arises from comparison. Remember always that the Work is equally difficult for everyone and that it does not become easier. It is always difficult. And yet it is not too difficult if one will remember enough and maintain a certain inner strength of will in regard to it. The greatest force that we can create in the Work is understanding. A man must build his inner Work on himself up on the affirmation of the moments of understanding that he has had and not let himself be shaken too much by outer events, whether in the Work or in life, that seem to contradict what he understands himself. In no other way can the individual development take place. A person's understanding is his own growth of understanding and cannot be borrowed. I cannot borrow someone else's understanding but I may borrow his knowledge and through applying it to my being come to a new understanding, and yet his understanding and my understanding are two different things. They are both unique, individual. For example, I cannot borrow my teacher's understanding but he gives me knowledge through which, when I apply it to my being, my own understanding grows. Remember that a growth of understanding can only come when new knowledge is applied to your own being. Knowledge and being together constitute our level of understanding. It would be no good my trying to imitate what my teacher does. That would be external imitation and would become part of the False Personality.

For example, if my teacher does not express negative emotion and I imitate him, I understand nothing about negative emotion. My imitation is external. But if receiving knowledge from my teacher that I must work on the negative part of my Emotional Centre and that in order to do this I must observe my negative emotions uncritically and fight not to identify with them and see the reason why for myself, then I may also begin not to express negative emotion just as my teacher does not. But this would no longer be from imitation. It would be from myself, from the growth of my own understanding, from the same experience as my teacher underwent.

In this Work we are taught to work on the Intellectual Centre and on the Emotional Centre first of all. To begin with, we must work on the Intellectual Centre by taking in a new supply of ideas and arranging them in our minds so that we begin to think in a new way about everything. This alters connections in our minds. If the ideas of the Work do not influence our thinking at all, if we never really think from the ideas of the Work about ourselves, about other people, or about life, we will then be always following our habitual minds, our habits of thought. The first place that has to be altered in order to undergo a change of being is the mind itself. That is, the way we think. When we observe the Intellectual Centre, we observe our thoughts and notice how we say 'I' to our thoughts; but these habitual thoughts must be seen as habitual thoughts, as machinery. For example, need you think in this way that you are doing at present? This is the first challenge that you have to make to yourself if you want to change. Need you think in the way you are thinking at this moment? Challenge the thought. The thought is automatic. Did you go with it? Did you identify with it? Bring the Work up into your mind and try to see whether the Work teaches you to think in this way. Try to bring the system of thoughts, of ideas, that the Work teaches as knowledge to us, into your previous form of thinking about yourself or your habitual way of thinking about other people, or your habitual way of thinking about life. If you cannot do this, it means that you are identified with your mechanical thinking which you have got haphazard from your upbringing. Are you sure that all these thoughts that you have gained from your upbringing are of any use at all?

Now to think from the ideas of the Work requires an effort of internal attention. This Work is to make us think in a new way. That is why you have to be reminded so often and for such a long time about what the Work teaches in order that eventually something takes place in you, something quite definite and difficult to define, when you no longer think habitually, but begin to think from what the Work has been saying to you for years. When this happens, the Work is born in your mind and you undergo a change of mind. A new set of ideas, a new set of associations, is formed in the mental part of you. Then a long struggle takes place between your ordinary thinking and Work-thinking. It is as if the brain itself had to be altered in all its connections and re-framed and re-connected on the basis of the knowledge of the Work. We think from such knowledge as we have. But this Work is new knowledge and we have to begin to think eventually from this new knowledge about ourselves—and that is a great subject—and finally about life and what it means—and that again is a great subject. Once the new thinking coming from knowledge of the Work begins to connect itself with our minds we have moments in which we see things and understand things in a completely different way from what we usually do. Then we fall asleep and think in the ordinary way—that is, we are subject to oscillations, often very violent. Now if we were always in the Third State of Consciousness we should always think from the knowledge of the Work. This would govern us and everything would be quite easy then. We might simply withdraw into this new kind of thinking and meditate on it, as happens in some forms of Yoga. But the trouble is that we also have an Emotional Centre which for a long time does not obey our thoughts and so it is necessary to work at the same time on the Emotional Centre in connection with the new knowledge of the Work, and the first thing that is emphasized is that we must work on our negative emotions. Why should we work on our negative emotions? This is a very good question to ask oneself in all inner sincerity, and here the mind will help if the strength of the Work-ideas is beginning to form a new mind which has a small will of its own. The Emotional Centre is the seat of our ordinary will as it is and the negative part of the Emotional Centre is especially so. The small Will from the change in Mental Centre is not sufficient to control the will of the unredeemed Emotional Centre for a long time. The will of the negative part of the Emotional Centre coupled with the will of the physical body forms a very powerful antagonist to the Will that is formed through the Work in the emotional part of the Intellectual Centre. But although we witness constantly our complete failure in controlling our negative emotions, or, let us add, the will of the body, yet if the relationship to the Work and the valuation of its ideas are strong enough, there remains always in spite of constant defeats something in the background which does not consent to all that is going on. I do not think I have mentioned here, in connection with what the Work says that the knowledge of the Work must become emotional, that the first place in which it can become emotional is in the emotional part of the Intellectual Centre. As I said, it is here that the new Will of the Work is formed first of all. The problem then is the negative part of the Emotional Centre itself in which exist 'I's that are very powerful and do everything they can to fight every form of belief that we possess in regard to this Work. Now if we had not got *Buried Conscience* the situation would be hopeless. The negative 'I's in the Emotional Centre would always have the victory. The secret is however that in the Emotional Centre there is Buried Conscience and this is awakened by the emotional part of the Intellectual Centre when the ideas of the Work have entered the mind and become emotionally felt—not only as what is Truth but as what is

Good. This awakens the Buried Conscience in the Emotional Centre itself. The Work teaches that Buried Conscience exists in everyone, quite apart from acquired Conscience, which is a matter of local upbringing. But for this Buried Conscience and the awakening of it in the Emotional Centre through the new mind and its new Will, we should indeed be in a hopeless position. But fortunately, as it is, every emotional perception of the truth of the Work coming from the Intellectual Centre arouses this Buried Conscience in the Emotional Centre and then the Emotional Centre itself fights against its negative emotions.

Now if you do not keep the Work strong in your mind and renew it continually at least once a day, or at least often, if you do not re-arrange everything in your mind at intervals so that you are thinking from the channels of the Work and their connections, this awakening of the Buried Conscience begins to cease and then you find yourself alone. When you feel alone like this, you must think of the Work, as, for example, go over what was said at the last meeting and refresh your mind with it. This is a form of Self-Remembering in a practical way and it will send a current of force to Buried Conscience in the Emotional Centre which alone can cast out your devils. It is not as if you do it, nor must you think that you can do it, but if you do what you can do, then something will help you which is not you and which you must never ascribe to yourself. We get into a bad state often because we ascribe everything to ourselves, just as we ascribe our merit to ourselves, just as we ascribe our good to ourselves, which means of course that we inevitably ascribe our evil to ourselves. One must ascribe neither good nor evil to oneself—otherwise one stands in the way of one's development. The Work is an instrument first of all—a mental instrument—which must be used to put our thoughts in the right order, to get things straight, and if we do this with the memory of our past experience in the Work, this effort to re-arrange internally will stimulate this Buried Conscience in the Emotional Centre which can fight all negative emotions and cast out every devil in us. You cannot overcome a negative emotion directly. It will only get stronger as a rule. But you can through your mind, through arranging the Work in your mind, touch the emotional part of the Intellectual Centre, which in turn awakens the Buried Conscience which will attack by itself the negative emotions. The power of Buried Conscience derives from the Higher Emotional Centre. You must remember that the Work teaches that Man was once in touch with Higher Centres but went to sleep. He once knew what to do directly but now, in this state of sleep, he can only get to where he was by indirect methods. All that is left now is *change of mind*. Change of mind starts the whole possible recovery. That is why Christ taught always μετάνοια change of mind, as the first thing—not repentance, but change of mind. Unless the mind changes, whereby the attitudes change, everyone will always be just as he is, whatever effort he makes in the way of starvation, self-denial, and so on. With the same attitude, a man will always remain the same. As long as a man thinks in the same habitual way, he will remain the same. The Work can actually teach a man to think in a new way, I repeat, about himself, about others, and about the meaning of life. With this change of mind his attitudes will inevitably change. If your attitudes have not changed then *you* will not change and you can never change. If, for example, your attitude is that you are a fully conscious man and that you are a unity and you have a permanent Real 'I' and an inflexible will and that you *can do* and so on, then these attitudes and this way of thinking will fix you always in the same psychological place as you are in and no new development is possible. But if your attitudes change through new thinking, through the ideas of the Work, from esoteric teaching, then you can change, because you will begin to arouse Buried Conscience which cannot work in you as long as you have all these false notions about yourself, about others, and about life, and ascribe all to yourself. It is exactly this new thinking, this μετάνοια, that the Work can give us, that when emotionally felt arouses into activity the Buried Conscience which then begins to help. So you will see how important it is to keep the Work mentally living in oneself not only by constant outer reminders of it but by your own deeper inner thinking because, as you know, this Work is a rope let down that you have to jump to catch hold of. No doubt sometimes one need no longer jump but as we are it is necessary to jump—that is, to make a certain kind of effort every day to jump up to the Work. If you ask me: "What is this effort?" I will answer that I have said in the paper what this effort is. I will put it in reverse form: If you use the Work merely as a means of occasional chats then you are not making this effort.

Great Amwell House, November 11, 1946

INNER CONTRADICTIONS

It is said in the Work that if a man or a woman throughout the whole of their lives were to feel all the contradictions that are within them, they could not live and act as calmly as they live and act now. They would have continued friction and unrest. One of the problems of mankind in general, and perhaps particularly of modern mankind, is that contradictions are not realized. As a result, human psychology remains at a low state of development, and since the development of mankind as a whole depends entirely on the development of each individual, it does not seem likely that any genuine development is possible—for the present at any rate. For that reason, we cannot expect any world-settlement. The level of being, the Work teaches, attracts the life—that is, you attract your problems and typical situations because of your level of being and if you seek to change things you must begin by working upon and changing your own being—that is, the kind of person you are. Then your outer problems and typical situations will change. When you notice this is the case, you can be sure that some changes in being have taken place. Change of being, however, is difficult, and needs hard work and patience, and since it can be said that mankind, again perhaps especially to-day, does not work on being, or even disregards it, the same form of life will be attracted—or even a worse form—and all attempts to ameliorate human existence based on external changes will necessarily fail, since mankind remains the same. But a single individual can change his being.

Therefore let us speak again about change of being only from the angle of contradictions. A man's being, a woman's being, cannot change beyond a certain point, unless contradictions are seen. To change your being you have to begin to realize contradictions in yourself by direct, uncritical self-observation. Or, to put it the other way round, when you begin to see contradictions, your being is altering, perhaps owing to another line of work. The Work shews us that our present level of being is kept where it is by very powerful factors. I mention to-night only *pictures* and *buffers*. Pictures of ourselves prevent us from seeing what we are like. To take one common enough sort of picture—you have, let us say, a picture of yourself being kind, just, self-sacrificing and full of good will. You live, or rather float, in this rainbow-picture, in this illusion. You do not realize that you are often cruel, selfish, unjust and sometimes full of evil will. That is, you do not see contradictions in your being. Now in such cases you do not see your evil but project it on to others. That is, what you do not see in yourself you see reflected in the other person. Until you accept your evil you will remain floating in this absurd and romantic illusion—in this picture of yourself which has nothing to do with truth and is, in short, composed of imagination and lies. In this state, a man's being is prevented from development by this contradictory situation in him.

Now only truth can lead us into the light and only the light coming from realized, accepted truth can cure us. Lies only make us more distorted in our being, more disharmonious, and internally more ugly. Certainly we should, after some years' work on being, practically cease to have any active pictures of ourselves—I say, we should. If so, it means a corresponding development of being. But when we come to buffers the matter is more difficult. A buffer is a silent thing, comparable to a little wall intervening between two contradictory things, both of which we can be conscious of, but only one at a time, not simultaneously. By the action of a buffer, a person is now conscious in what lies on one side of the buffer and then very swiftly and smoothly is conveyed to the other side of the buffer without any shock—that is, without any sense of contradiction. Yet these two sides, if brought together suddenly, would appear so wholly contradictory that a violent shock would result. So the Work says that if a man or woman were continually to feel all the contradictions that are within them, they could not act or live as calmly as they do. Actually the sudden removal of all buffers, if it were possible, would drive a person mad. He would lose all idea of himself.

Now I advise you not to waste too much time on discussing exactly what a buffer is. It is too easy to get so identified with a word that one cannot look beyond it to where it is pointing. Words—Work-words —are sign-posts. The Work-term *buffer* points to the whole question of contradictions in us—that is, to what is in consciousness at a given moment and what is in the dark and opposite in sense and meaning to what is in consciousness. Now an increase, an enlargement, of consciousness, which is the aim of the Work, would result evidently from bringing the dark into the light. At the same time this would be necessarily accompanied by an alteration in our feeling of 'I'. What we call 'I'—our idea of 'I'—would change. If you reflect for a moment you will see the reason why this would inevitably follow. Contradictions keep our being where it is. Realizing contradictions through inner work changes being. If being changes, the feeling of 'I'—of what I am —the idea of myself—changes. Therefore I become another person and begin no longer to recognize myself as I was. Some people take this negatively but they are quite wrong. How can you become another person if you still persist in being the same person? Now it is said that whenever a buffer is seen it can never re-form—that is, when a contradiction due to a buffer disappears and both sides are accepted simultaneously a real change of being takes place. Instead of being conscious on one side and then on another side, which is a duality, two sides come together and form a unity. But in that case neither one side nor the other remains the same. A third thing is made which is not Yes *or* No but Yes *and* No. This is one of the first steps towards unity of being because our being at present is, as it were, a duality divided into an accepted side and an unaccepted side, into a light and dark side, or rather, I would say, into a side which for the moment is in consciousness, the other side being in darkness, and then into an opposite side in which the side that was in darkness now comes into consciousness and the side that was in consciousness now comes into darkness.

Mr. Ouspensky once represented this on the board in the following way. He took a centre as a circle and superimposed upon it another circle in which a section was cut out as follows:

This superimposed circle is turning all the time and the part of the centre or the 'I's in this particular part of the centre become conscious only where the action lies. As a result all the rest is in darkness and therefore we go with those 'I's which the section exposes at a given moment. Our task is, as it were, to remove this superimposed circle so that all 'I's can enter into consciousness at the same time if called upon. Mr. Ouspensky said: "In ordinary life we are only conscious in a very small part of ourselves. Real Consciousness is being aware of everything together." And, quoting Mr. Gurdjieff, he said: "Real Consciousness is a state in which a man knows all at once everything that he in general knows and only in this state can he see how little he knows and how so many contradictions lie in what he knows."

Now Conscience, Real Conscience, which at present is buried in us, is to *feel* everything together. And this Conscience is very necessary in making relationships with people in the Work. To make relationships in the Work means to be able to *feel* everything together, both the bad sides and the good sides of a person. Real Consciousness is to *know* everything together.

Enough has been said in this short paper to give rise to discussion. Now please let nobody start off by saying: "What exactly is a buffer?" A buffer is what prevents contradictions from being seen and merely points the way to this great branch of personal work—that is, work on *oneself* in order to change *oneself* by realizing contradictions in being. Remember that this Work is to change you and unless you see that you should change, and wish to know *how to change*, it is useless to attempt to connect yourself with this Work. Let no one who is content with himself or herself ever try to enter into this Work. Such people are already *dead*. This Work is for those who wish to awaken from the dead.

Great Amwell House, November 16, 1946

A NOTE ON FALSE PERSONALITY

It is said in the Work that to be awake is to have no False Personality. The more one is in False Personality and all the consequences resulting from meeting daily life through False Personality, the more one is asleep; while, on the contrary, the less one meets daily life through False Personality, the more one is awake. We understand that False Personality is composed of imagination—of false ideas about oneself. Some people think of False Personality as being something blatant, loud and boasting. But this is wrong. False Personality in one person may sing: "What a fine fellow I am", and in another person sing: "Poor little me". But the action on Being is the same in both cases— that is, its power to produce disharmony in Being is the same and the effort necessary to bring it face to face with facts about oneself equally difficult. The object of uncritical self-observation is to collect facts about oneself. For this reason Observing 'I' must not be right in front of oneself in the sphere which False Personality influences but further back. The power of self-observation increases as Observing 'I' moves more internally. This partly depends on the deepening of feeling or valuation of the Work when surface enthusiasms are seen through. We spoke recently of this Work forming itself in the Intellectual Centre as some transmitting instrument that Higher Centres can touch eventually, built up gradually until all its parts are in order. This is done by two things—effort of thinking in a new way and valuation. Valuation lies in the emotional part of the Intellectual Centre at first; this, it was said recently, begins to awaken Buried Conscience in the Emotional Centre itself. During this process Observing 'I' moves inwards more internally and begins to pass ultimately into Real Conscience. It is like John the Baptist coming before Jesus. First it is necessary to have right Magnetic Centre. This can bring us to the Work but cannot hold us in it. Then comes Observing 'I', and through it the application of the teaching to oneself. Then one observes oneself in the light of the Work, not in the light of the past or social life. Then finally Real Conscience begins to appear as Steward. Now nothing of this can happen as long as False Personality is in the forefront and governs being. So it is necessary to think about what False Personality is in oneself, and not assume one knows what it is. As said, it takes many forms and yet is the same thing. It is false—a lie—that one insists on telling to oneself. One is then governed by a liar—in fact, by a *Hasnamous*. It is said that the chief cause of giving wrong impressions is False Personality. This hint can help in one's search for it. But to me it seems that the most terrible things about False Personality are the narrow judgments it makes and the tight fixed attitudes in which it imprisons us. You might think that a rigid, inflexible life has nothing to do with False Personality. In that case you have not understood enough about False Personality and its different forms in people.

Now only the full power of the Work can redeem us from False Personality. If you *feel* the Work as truth, apart from thinking it is true, then you let into you the only force that can weaken False Personality. Consider some of the things the Work says—such as "Man cannot do", "Man is a multiplicity and not a unity", "Man has no Real 'I'," "Man is not conscious" and "Man is asleep". Such teachings, if deeply felt, surely cannot be acceptable to False Personality? On the contrary, if *their meaning* is deeply enough felt and realized through one's own observation of oneself, they make the existence of False Personality impossible. That is, they lead to awakening since, as was said, to be awake is to have no False Personality.

Some of you will remember that recently we began to touch on the meaning of that strange remark in the Gospels: "Judge not". But is it so strange? How can you judge when you begin to realize your own nothingness? The Work teaches that a man, through self-observation, must come to the point of realizing that he is nothing—that not only he really *knows* nothing, but *is* nothing. This is not acceptable to False Personality. All real work on oneself leads from one sense of nothingness to another and deeper sense of one's nothingness—not as a sentimental idea coming from the rapid adjustment of False Personality, not a pretence—but, though momentary, an actual, and overwhelming realization. How can *nothingness* judge anybody? You know, it is also said in the Gospels: "With what measure ye mete, it shall be measured unto you." What does this mean? It means on one side that as *you* judge so shall you be judged—that is, having spent a life-time in judging others, through your idea of your superiority, through False Personality—then you shall be judged yourself. By whom? By yourself—by your own False Personality. That is at least one haunting reason why it is necessary to see and separate from False Personality as quickly as you can. The Pharisees were full of False Personality. That is why they were attacked by Jesus. It is just the same in this Work. The False Personality is the Pharisee in oneself that judges everyone. Now in this Work—in the Second Line of Work—that is, work with one another—we should not judge. The Work never speaks of judging. It speaks instead of understanding and external considering. In this Work we have to learn how to hold one another, include one another, not murder one another. And is not all murdering due to judging—as if one were superior?

Great Amwell House, November 23, 1946

THIRD FORCE

We speak to-day of the Neutralizing Force of the Work. In one of the diagrams it is said that the part of a human being that can grow remains inactive as long as Life is the Neutralizing Force. Life as the neutralizing principle keeps Personality active and Essence passive. So it keeps that part of Being that can grow, inactive. Man is then unfinished, incomplete, not a real being, having an outer part developed and an inner part undeveloped and often quite at variance with the outer part. Therefore from the standpoint of this teaching (and all esoteric teaching of the past) life does not develop a man internally but only outwardly in appearance—that is, exoterically, which means outwardly, and not esoterically, which means inwardly. To develop internally a human being must be given special knowledge that only indirectly concerns life and its affairs—how to get on, how to be a success, etc. This knowledge teaches him what he is and what he can

968

become internally and shews him how, esoterically—that is, internally —he is nothing as yet as he is, and that if certain outer fears and restrictions that exist in life and act as bonds were removed, he has no inner bonds that would hold him together, and desires would break out and he would dissolve, disappear, cease even to be the outer resemblance of a man. In that case, every higher influence reaching him, having no inner plane to act on, will pass straight through and downwards into every form of inhumanity. That is the situation—namely, *outer* bonds hold Man together. But, as the Work teaches, acting against the forces of barbarism, which surround every culture and seek to swallow it, the forces of Conscious Man act on Earth, through which cultures are established, and resist for a time this inevitable encroachment. Every manifestation of culture lasts only for a time and belongs to higher influences reaching mankind and opposing the lower influences of barbarism. These forces belong to the Neutralizing Force or Third Force that the Work speaks of in connection with the making of Personality passive whereby Essence can begin to develop. Once mankind in general has a developed Essence the forces of barbarism would cease to act on the Earth among men and everything that is argued about and fought about would cease. That is, war would cease, because those extra-terrestrial influences that cause war would act on a developed Essence quite differently from an undeveloped Essence and be received by an inner plane in Man.

Now what does all this mean? It means, to begin with, that we cannot do this Work and get results from it unless we have *background*. Unless there is a background bigger than oneself, one cannot feel the Work, and so it cannot fall on the right place, the right parts of centres, within us, which is only possible through right valuation. It is not a moral question, but an intelligent, practical question. For example, if I try to turn on a light, where the switch does not exist, I cannot get light. I am in the wrong place—here, I mean, in my own house, in the house of myself—and I speak not of physical, outer light, but the light of understanding, which is inner light. All the great diagrams of the Work, starting from the Ray of Creation, with their inexhaustible meaning, are to give us background and so to open up unused parts of centres. Great background gives great force and great understanding. It is beyond our small selves. The Work gives this scale in regard to this question:

Greater Mind
Psychological Mind
Logical Mind
A-logical Mind

Mr. Ouspensky said that unless a man realizes that Greater Mind must exist, he cannot reach Psychological Understanding. Logical Mind may explain everything in terms of itself, starting from the observable world of matter. But it has no greater background and so keeps a man where he is. Only the feeling of a greater background can change a man, because it opens Greater Mind in him.

When a man begins to realize that life cannot be explained in terms of itself and if taken thus has no meaning but becomes a torture to his reason, then the cure lies only in reaching another and deeper interpretation of life—namely, that there is something over and above visible life—another meaning of the whole matter. This is exactly what the Work teaches. Life in terms of the Great Ray for Man on Earth, as a part of the inserted amplifying machine called Organic Life, means nothing. He is chaff. His real meaning is only derived from the Side-Octave from the Sun, about which we recently spoke again in connection with Man serving Nature or Man serving the Work. Here, in the Work, a man, a woman, gradually find their real significance— that is, provided they have something early in themselves that can respond to esoteric teaching or have come to the end of life and finally have become certain there is something else. Such a man or woman belongs to the category of *Good Householder* as defined by the Work— namely, one who has done all duties and is responsible and remains so but does not *believe in life*. This is the stepping-off place. In such a case, the man, the woman, views life differently. Life ceases to be an *end* in itself. Life and its situations become a means to work. Then every experience is taken as an experience in itself—an experience in nonidentifying, for example—and *results* in life are not looked for. The whole point of view alters. This is the beginning of *Psychological Mind*. Then this man, this woman, is no longer controlled by the Third Force of Life—the Neutralizing Force of life—but by the Neutralizing Force of the Work, this other 3rd Force that can change the inner balance so that no longer is Personality active and Essence passive, but Essence becomes active gradually and grows, and Personality becomes passive and gradually diminishes. Such a person is no longer a mechanical person worked by life. He or she begins to leave the mechanical circle of Humanity. They begin to become more balanced by the very operation of psychological understanding upon them. They no longer take violent sides, for, owing to psychological understanding, they see both sides together. So their judging changes—first, their judging of themselves—for mechanical self-judgment keeps us unbalanced, which is why we have to observe uncritically. Then they understand others and do not judge them—an incalculable freedom. Such people now pass from logical understanding, which divides everything into "Yes" or into "No", and so into judging. The two halves of them, the dark and light, become intermixed. They understand a remark of the Work in its right setting and on its right scale. They realize they have scale in them (as they had from birth). Another light of understanding shews in their minds and brings things into a harmony impossible for the logical mind —that is, the formatory mind, which cannot by its function and structure, which is to divide everything into "Yes" and "No", possess the third harmonious uniting force of the Work. You remember the Work says that the Formatory Centre is Third Force blind. The Work-force is meant—this Third Force of the Work. Now when the great meaning of esoteric teaching enters the mind, it shifts the position of all things within and gets them in the right order. It gives birth to μετάνοια, to mental change, to psychological understanding. John the Baptist had formatory mind and his religion was "Thou shalt not". So Christ said he was "the greatest of those born of women, but that the least in the Kingdom of Heaven was greater than he". Why? Because there can be no approach to the higher level—to the "Kingdom"—save through psychological understanding—that is, without greater background. He had not psychological understanding and so was worried because Jesus did not fast. The Work therefore gives us this tremendous background in a few diagrams, which are inexhaustible in their density of meaning, to let in psychological understanding. Therefore it is said that unless we believe in Greater Mind, the Work cannot work in us, for otherwise, unless we believe in Greater Mind, we cannot reach psychological understanding.

All this gives us the beginning of another 3rd Force distinct from life and only this other 3rd Force can change being and lift us to a new understanding. A man by himself cannot add one inch to his stature—that is, as he thinks. New knowledge and new thinking are needed. But the Work, if *felt* emotionally, can do so, even apart from oneself and one's own small endeavours, for it puts us in touch with the tremendous transforming forces that come from Higher Centres and opens us to them gradually as we can bear it. For it destroys gradually nearly all that we were and thought and felt. To be re-born one cannot be what one was. That is obvious. One cannot change and be the same. Life keeps us the same. The Work seeks to change us and tells us what to separate from in order to change.

Great Amwell House, November 30, 1946

A NOTE ON EFFORT

The Work speaks of the necessity of effort. Strictly speaking, it says that it is necessary to make right effort. The method of Sly Man is to make right effort: he sees what particular effort is necessary at a particular time, and when things are too easy for the time for him, he creates difficulties for himself, as, for example, by doing things in the most difficult way. In life, acting mechanically, we do things in the easiest way, which is always the most mechanical way. In making effort in the Work-sense, it must be understood that anti-mechanical effort is meant. So the Work begins with general instructions on the practical side to work against one's mechanicalness. This gives new impressions. How can one cease to be a machine if one always behaves mechanically? Man is a machine but his transformation into a conscious being is awaited. So his general task is to work against his mechanicalness. This needs special kinds of interesting efforts, for his mechanicalness lies in all centres. Therefore efforts are in three main directions. What did you make effort against yesterday? Against the inertia which prevents you from thinking distinctly? Against pleasant and unpleasant day-dreaming? Against general distaste? One can always notice the stale flavour of mechanicalness within one and the fresher feeling that comes from a new impression which even a short, real Work-effort can create. In this connection I remind you that G. said it is necessary to move the brain once a day—apart from the bowels. In a large sense, people avoid extra and interesting effort and remain heavily at the level of mechanical effort—that is, what they are compelled to do by external circumstances—that is, as machines. Now Work-effort is *not* what we are compelled to do by external circumstances. The Work and Work-effort belong to something extra, outside nature, outside life—something very interesting. In this connection mechanical life-efforts, that external circumstances dictate, can be taken interestingly from a Work-attitude and no longer seem at variance with the Work. Let us speak first of this. How can you turn mechanical life-effort into Work-effort?

The secret lies in taking your life as an *exercise*. To do this interesting thing, a certain vision of life is required. All the background of the Work, all the teaching about the Cosmic Ray, the Sun-Octave, and the significance of Man, can give this vision, if you know it well mentally and then imagine it so that it better connects with the Emotional Centre. To know what you know, you must also imagine it with directed imagination. Then you see your life as a miraculous adventure—that ceases to be so once you identify with it. Then it is all spoiled and life no longer becomes your teacher but your taskmaster, your Pharaoh. It is only when we lift ourselves, when we can take life as this interesting *exercise*, that life can become our teacher. In other words, only through this vision that the Work gives, which separates us from the full power of life, can life change into what it should be—into, as it were, an intelligent person. With this attitude we gain the sense of being *in* life, not *of* life or caused by life, and this is a preliminary to that form of Self-Remembering where the three factors, (1) the seen object in outer life, (2) my observed reaction to it, and (3) I myself, constitute a triple simultaneous consciousness—a full triad—that is, a being conscious in 3 forces at the same time. It is clear that the usual state of being always identified with life and its worries can never give such results. This vision, therefore, which I have mentioned, is one belonging to a right development in the understanding of the Work, which is to lessen the power of life over us. One must get this vision—in which the centre of gravity of the whole Work lies—a vision of the Work that lifts us above life—in short, this Rope which we have to catch hold of. *Hold this Rope*, when you catch it.

O. said that what people find difficult is that the Work changes as you understand more. What *was* said may be no longer said, but something different. For example, you are told at first in making effort in the second line of Work *not* to try to like one another, *but* to stop dislike. This is one kind of anti-mechanical effort. This is surely very clear. *It can be done.* You *can stop* disliking. If done, it leads, almost without our being told, to the next effort in scale, in ascending octave, "that we have to like what we now dislike." There is great density of meaning in this sentence. It applies to outer and inner—to the object and to oneself. Now you can do nothing of all this if you are too externalized, too far out, too far in front of yourself, too identified with seen objects, with life, seeing everything outside you, and so a mere sense-machine. You have to see that a person is not outside you but is your *idea* of him, your imagination of him, your reaction to him (or her), and not the object you see *via* your senses. Here begins the real effort as regards the second line of Work—work, that is, about relationship, work about enduring without negativeness one another's unpleasant manifestations. Only in this way can an accumulator be made among ourselves that eventually gives force to all of us. For one person can, if a Work-group is established, give force to another, without knowing it, simply by working against his or her mechanicalness privately.

I will here remind you of what the Work says of life. It says that under the 3rd force of life, things always divide, disunite, and are at war—as life shews us. One party splits into two mutually hostile parties and so on. Now the 3rd force of the Work unites. It holds people together who in life would at once split and hate one another. Through the 3rd force of the Work—and, let me emphasize—the work done by each person on himself or herself in the light of the Work—an accumulator can be made, by uniting people in a common understanding through a common language. The supreme effort that has to be made in the Work is to *feel the Work*. Seek the Work first, fight for it, keep it alive—and then all the rest follows. Remember that all temptations in the Work-meaning are about feeling, valuing, cherishing the meaning and reality of the Work, of Esotericism. This is faith—a thing requiring much and constant effort of mind—an inner daily action in both mind and heart. Faith is what is unsupported by the evidence of the senses—by seen visible life. Now in ordinary seen life, where people, even religious people, do not *practically* work on themselves each day; they accumulate a substance which cannot lead to unity. For example, they criticize one another, talk scandal privately, slander each other secretly and hate each other—in short, make every kind of internal account against one another. They are mechanical people, and just because they do not work they remain mechanical. As a result, there is formed a thick, heavy, psychological substance which G. called by one of his strange words—something like Tzarvarno. "This substance," he said, in so many words, "accumulates in life and makes all right relationship impossible. This substance has no Holy Spirit in it. It is dead." He said it was due to the unnatural outward and inward manifestations of people to one another and was an accumulation of evil actions, thoughts and emotions, of which people do not understand the consequences. The Work calls it simply "making internal accounts." Now remember, the slightest, unworked-on "evil" towards another mounts up and makes this thick, dead substance. Where? In oneself. One may suspect how often illness is due to this dead substance, daily formed. Now everything the Work teaches us to practise, to make effort about, is to prevent this heavy dead substance from forming itself. A good daily and nightly incinerator for negative states is necessary.

To keep the Work alive one must make effort. I have spoken of effort in regard to the 2nd line of Work. First we must make effort to stop disliking. This is more easy than you might think, once you have some self-observation and see your mechanical disliking. Then I spoke of the second note in this effort: "that we must like what we dislike". To like what we dislike is one great key to giving up useless suffering. This releases us from our cramped judgment of others. Through this we begin to feel "nothingness" rightly. One, as it were, pushes off from the shore of oneself into the unknown—into what seems nothingness—where only the Work can meet us. The Work cannot meet us if we are full of our usual Personality.

Great Amwell House, December 7, 1946

EFFORTS AGAINST CERTAIN 'I'S

Everyone comes to a point in the Work where efforts against certain particular 'I's that wish to maintain their power are necessary. These 'I's are hostile to the Work, only they often disguise themselves cleverly. In connection with all this we must get back to principles. Let us recall that from the standpoint of Esotericism—that is, real psychology—a man, a woman, is not one but many—a crowd of different-sized, different-aged and differently-dressed people marching along in disorder. In this crowd are people of all kinds, pleasant, unpleasant, educated, uneducated, sick and healthy, polite and rude. One or two or several of these people may be interested in the Work-ideas. The rest may either not hear what they say or tell them they are fools, and so on. All these voices can be heard talking within one at any time if one observes oneself. Now to say 'I' to them all is to identify with them and that means not a single thing can change in us. We are then stuck to ourselves and cannot shift from what we are. That is the general

974

principle and it is just as well to repeat it to ourselves often and keep on re-seeing what it means.

It is called the doctrine of 'I's. It is fundamental. It is directly connected with the teaching about the level of mechanical Man's being —namely, that his being is characterized by multiplicity and is devoid of unity. It must be realized personally by self-observation—by the First Line of Work, work on oneself. Now people may try genuinely to work on themselves but try to do so without any observation of 'I's. They take the whole mass of themselves as one, as 'I'. It is impossible to work on yourself if you take the whole mass of yourself as one, as 'I'. Of this we have to be continually reminded. Have you seen a view of yourself marching along as a crowd of 'I's, some good, some evil, some in tatters, some over-dressed, some well-meaning, some slanderous, some brave, some self-pitying, some intelligent, some stupid, some a little developed, some undeveloped, and childish, and so on? This marching column, marching anyhow, now some leading, now others, this haphazard crew, *is leading one's life for one*. This is a phrase in the Work not used recently. I was reminded of it by a letter I received from a person once in the Work years back. He wrote: "There was much in the Work which I did not understand, but a small fragment, a phrase you used, touched something in me and has haunted me ever since—a partial understanding of what you meant when you said that one contains within oneself a group of conflicting 'I's which lead one's life for one." He said he had begun to realize, on looking back, that he had never led his own life, but that he had been compelled to lead a life that these 'I's in him insisted upon his leading. Now it is these 'I's that lead our lives for us, arrange things for us, make us do this and that and think and say as they please and make us dislike and like as they dictate—and the trouble is that we take them all as 'I' and believe that this is 'I' myself liking and 'I' myself disliking. To realize, to attain the realization that one need not go any longer with an 'I' or believe it for a moment, is a great release. It is the beginning of inner freedom. It is a definite move, however small, in the direction of Real 'I'. Often we have, leading our lives for us, some unpleasant 'I's that take pleasure in making us unhappy. They are clever at pretence. For instance, they say in a sweet sad way—or rather make one say such things as: "If only I had met this Work before, it would have made such a difference to my life." They induce this thought and one simply thinks it is one's own thought and so that it is true. 'I's induce thoughts in us and we take them as our thoughts. Negative 'I's—that is, 'I's that can only breathe properly when one is negative— are very clever in this respect. When you are in a reasonable state they wait until they can induce a thought that makes you negative. Then they feed on your negative state. It is all so simple and clear once one has begun to understand practically about 'I's and has lost the illusion that one is an actual person.

Now I will continue from the last paper on "Effort" and speak

975

further on mechanical liking and disliking. It was said that first we have to make effort in regard to stopping internally mechanical disliking and it was also said that this is not so difficult to do, once one can notice it at work by observation. One says "Stop" to it. One makes "inner stop" in regard to it, without arguing or self-justifying. Or, to put it another way, one stops inner talking about it and practises inner silence. This you can all do. It was then said that we have next to begin to like what we dislike and it was added that this leads to the right feeling of *nothingness*. For the Work cannot reach us if we are full of self-feeling, full of our importance, our egotism, our sense of being right. It enters what is lowest, most despised, where we are nothing, not something. It is near when we feel we do not know, not when we feel we know. In general, the more Personality is passive, the closer are the influences of the Work, and it is closer to the passive parts of Personality rather than the active. We are told that to like what we dislike is the quickest path to giving up one's suffering. We are told that our suffering is the only thing we can sacrifice. The Work says we must sacrifice our suffering. Now how can liking what we dislike rid us of the mass of useless suffering stored up in our Time-Body, that all have, whatever they may say? What can it possibly do to those many 'I's that all enjoy suffering—and indeed often nearly eat a person up—or give rise to recurrent attacks of suffering which the Instinctive Centre loathes and which are the source of so much physical illness? If there is anything in the earlier stages of the Work that characterizes the Way of Sly Man more than liking what one dislikes, I do not know it. This is being sly, this is being clever, this is being intelligent—this is right effort. Suppose a man more or less dislikes everything and everybody—what then? Think for yourselves. Will he feel his own nothingness or will he make internal accounts? He will be full of complaining. Everything will be difficult and restricted for him. He will certainly be hard to please.

Now all this applies to oneself and has to become a subject of self-study. For example, a person whom one dislikes should become a matter of genuine interest—and here one will have some real work to do—some real conscious observation and non-identifying and finding the same qualities in oneself—in fact, all that the Work teaches. When you find a person who obviously dislikes you there is another task for personal work. Notice what he dislikes in you if you can. Remember that we have to thank those who make it necessary for us to work on ourselves. Work does not mean behaving mechanically—as we please —but behaving more consciously. If we are going to let those 'I's who hitherto have led our lives for us take on this Work we shall indeed find ourselves in a state of confusion. At the Institute in France what we were in life scarcely counted. Personality was scarcely allowed to exist. Why? Because the object of the Work (and of all esoteric teaching) is change of being. How can being change if the 'I's that have always led your life for you still remain in full power? No, change of being means change of yourself and change of yourself means that other 'I's —'I's that wish to work and understand and eventually form Deputy-Steward—come forward and take charge. So the time comes, as was said, when efforts against certain particular 'I's that wish to maintain their power and are hostile to the Work have to be made. Many of these 'I's belong to the life-notion we have of ourselves—that is, to the False Personality. Others belong to the formatory centre and others elsewhere—e.g. to past hatreds. The Work is easily strong enough to overcome them once it has really got into one's mind and made one think anew. First get inner attitude to the Work right—then everything will follow in the right order.

Great Amwell House, December 14, 1946

OUR PSYCHOLOGICAL COUNTRY

Someone said recently: "How is it that we can have the same experience?" I answered that when a person has the same experience as another person it means that they have both been in the same part of psychological space. As this was not understood, I will try here to explain the idea further. It is well-known that in respect to books having a mystical quality, as it is called—that is, containing *B* influences, however ancient—we find many similar ideas and experiences. Historically speaking, in countries widely separated by space, by time and by language, we find records exist that are similar in trend and are not simply concerned with matters of life. It might be said that most ancient manuscripts are of this kind. Whether this is so or not, it is not surprising if it is so, since all literature started from the Conscious Circle of Humanity and, passing into the world, became *B* influences. The reason for this is that the level of mechanical Man is such that *C* influences—or direct conscious teaching—cannot be grasped. So only a distortion of real teaching is possible in written form, and "either-or"—"Yes-or No"—substituted for the new mind of Third Force that lies between the opposites—namely, the mind that can think in terms of *Yes and No* and is not chained to the opposites of "Is it true?" or "Is it not true?" The ordinary mind is, of course, formatory centre which is Third Force blind and only creates disturbances.

In life, in physical space, we visit the same houses, the same places— provided we *actually* go to them—Paris, Brighton, and so on. It is the same with psychological space. But psychological space is not visited by the physical body, but by the mind, the emotions and the sensations —that is, *via* the centres. This invisible world is as real as—and becomes far more real than—physical space. So I have taught you in commentaries about the idea of your having a psychological country. Where

977

are you now in *that* country? For although you are in the same *place* in a physical sense—say, in 5 Heath Row, N.W.12—you can be in a vast number of different places in your psychological space, in your psychological country—and it is where you are in that psychological country that begins to matter so very much as you realize what the Work teaches. The Work is about your *inwardness*—where you are inwardly—namely, in this great inner country on to which centres open.

The Work expresses this idea by speaking about centres and different parts of centres. For example, one may be in a wrong centre for the business in hand—or in a wrong part of a centre. It is your position in your psychological country that matters. One should ask oneself: "Where am I?" And this question does not relate to outer sense-given space but to that inner space of which only self-observation can make you conscious. It is in connection with this that the Work teaches so much about that psychological position called the negative part of Emotional Centre. This inner psychological invisible country, in which we really live our lives, has good and bad places. It has in it heaven, hell and an intermediate place. When we are in the negative part of Emotional Centre, we are, inwardly, in hell—or at the mouth of hell. And if we identify, if we consent, if we make internal accounts, if we have no idea of cancelling them and neither realize where we are internally nor know what we have to do—namely, especially remember ourselves—then we have no Second Body—no inner intelligent sense of our direction in this inward spiritual world—and fall into every ditch, never understanding that the Work is to teach us *where we are* internally.

In these different localities in inward space, we will get what is there—i.e., in slums we will be knocked on the head. One usually walks in "unpleasant places" and expects outer life to be nice and pleasant. How can this be possible? How can you expect things to improve if you are walking about all the labyrinths, the squalor, the vast, dark city of the negative part of Emotional Centre? Only by sincere self-confession, only by sincere self-observation, can you be aware of where you are dallying internally, in your psychological world, your inner world, however you pretend with a bitter smile that you only have the best intentions. Then you lie and your smile is tainted.

Now where you are in this inner psychological country is not necessarily due to you. Things turn: life is a turning circle. The wheels turn, like the Enneagram. Everything comes round again. But when you find yourself in a bad place and see where you are, through the development and inner light of Real Conscience, you only get out through *valuation*. The work, if valued, can get you out, unharmed, from many unpleasant places that you have to endure for a time. It is just like external life. If you value living in a pleasant place and happen to be in a bad place, you will tolerate your situation without identifying for a time, and you will not buy a house in the bad spot, but wait till you can get a better house. This is called "not saying Yes to your bad states". For remember *state* psychologically is *place* physically. Every internal *state* is a *place* in the great psychological world of heaven and hell. Because this internal word exists, so can you be in the same part of it as someone else has been. So you have the same experience. And if you have been in a wonderful place in this inwardly-touched world, so you can share your experience with another who also has been there and seen the same things. This is why there can be a similarity of experience.

Great Amwell House, December 21, 1946

ON FINDING SOLUTIONS

On one occasion Mr. Ouspensky was speaking of someone whom he described as a violent just man. He said, in so many words: "He believes that there are final solutions for everything. This makes him violent. He does not realize that everything is turning and changing, that Man cannot do and that there are no final solutions. If there were, life would cease to be life. It would be death. You must understand that life is a perpetual-motion-machine. The same problems come round again and again and people try to solve them, to find final solutions to them, and no one can. How could they? We have to realize that the main life-problems are insoluble. There is only one solution to all problems and that is change of attitude." I said to him: "You mean that one must always start from oneself?" He said: "Yes, because you cannot change life, so why start from life, from the other person, and seek first to change him? But you can change yourself, and so change your reactions to life. Change of attitude changes the way life touches you. Attitudes connect us with outer things and make them important or unimportant, according to the kinds of attitudes we have been taught. So we get bound to unimportant things and take them as important—as if they were our whole life—and things that are really important we neglect."

In this connection, it is clear that Mr. Ouspensky emphasized what the Work means for a person who has begun to understand its direction and import. One has to start with oneself. It is this "oneself" that has to be changed. The Work is not about outer but about inner things—things in oneself—and therefore it begins with self-observation. In beginning with self-observation it lays its stress on *you*—on what you are like. Life, from the teaching of the Work, is a vast interknit machinery in which everything happens. So it removes all emphasis from life, from what happens, from how people behave to you, and lays the emphasis on what kind of person *you* are and how *you* take things.

Now as regards this thing called *you*, it teaches that it is a mass of acquired associations and buffers, a mass of acquired attitudes and so of acquired mechanical reactions to life. These attitudes, these reactions, can be changed. You need not react in your typical way. You need not feel depressed, negative, or violent, as you ordinarily do. It is your psychological machinery that makes you do so. Life need not have the ever-recurring, same effect upon you that it habitually has and that you take for granted as right. The habits of taking life as you do are because you have a locally acquired stamped machinery. But you can alter it if you begin to observe how you mechanically take things and realize your mechanicalness and have eventually sudden flashes of insight whereby you realize how you are always taking things mechanically and need not do so. Then you begin to see what the Work is about—i.e. self-change. The truth is that people do not see what "personality" means. It means the acquired side of yourself—and it is this that has to be made passive—namely, this mechanical way of taking life, people and yourself. This is certainly a great truth that few can meet successfully, being so convinced of their own rightness in all things. When a new person is brought into this Work I first of all think: "Can this person ever see himself or herself and begin to work on themselves, or are they crystallized in life, in their attitudes and in their estimate of themselves?" One notices how they talk, one encourages them to talk as they habitually do, and then eventually one can tell either that they will never be able to separate themselves from what life has made them, or that they might to a slight extent, or that they might even go further and actually begin to change their being.

Now if a man cannot possibly *see himself,* if he is so glued to himself that he cannot observe what he is glued to—then he cannot do this Work internally, although he may do sufficient externally if he has being on the level of Good Householder to work externally—that is, serve the Work and its outer discipline. And a person who does this faithfully may be given gradually, by the power of the Work, in measure that will not injure him, the beginning of insight into what he has hitherto taken as himself. I say, gradually, because a man without inner life, if he were to be suddenly detached from all he values and prides himself on, would be completely smashed. Having his foundations in life, and having nothing else, he would collapse under the vision of a higher level of himself and another order of things.

Now to come back to this question of finding solutions. The Work teaches that the solution of things lies ultimately only in yourself—in how you take things. Let us take the question of liking and disliking, that many do not understand yet. First you are told, in the Second Line of Work—that is, in relation to others—that you have to start with yourself and stop *disliking*. As was pointed out, this can be done. How? By noticing where the impression of a person whom you mechanically dislike tends to fall on centres and not identifying with it. Yes—it enters and stimulates its typical reaction. But if you know anything about self-observation, you already have a space of time in you—a pause—before the impression can get fully into the centres and have its full mechanical effect. Self-observation opens a little room, a little space, and time, between the incoming impression and its lodgment in the place that habitually receives it and reacts to it. Self-observation begins to make an inner life in a man. Eventually he undergoes a growth of Consciousness in this way—namely, that Consciousness begins to intervene between the impression and the reaction. The man himself begins to stand between outer life coming in as impressions and his psychological machinery lying in 'I's and rolls on centres. *He* intervenes. He then begins to take life—that is, impressions—consciously, so he can stop dislike. And so often the solution lies just in this —to stop mechanical disliking.

The next point is that when you have this pause in you, this momentary consciousness in a new place—you can begin even to like what you dislike. As was said, if you can stop mechanical disliking— the common source of loss of force and negativeness—by catching the impression of the disliked person before it fully engages the acquired machine you take as yourself—then this work on yourself will lead you to the possibility of sounding the next note in this octave—namely, of beginning to like what hitherto you so easily, so continually, so unchallengeably, so automatically, disliked. One must shift oneself from what one is. And if you continue to dislike mechanically you cannot shift yourself. All mechanical reactions to life, to others, keep you exactly where you are. Remember, work on yourself must be accompanied by work in regard to others. Work means conscious work—i.e., not behaving mechanically. And here I might say that the most deceived men or women are those who always say, parrot-fashion, that they always consider others and put them first—as if one could mechanically, by habit, do such a thing, which requires the highest conscious effort constantly, yes, every day, renewed. In beginning to like what you dislike, start with a person you know. First, stop disliking. Then see for yourself what happens.

Now take yourself. You have quarrelled with someone. What is the solution? Where are you going to start from, if you really wish to work consciously? With the other person? Certainly not. *It is your fault*, so start with yourself. What is wrong with *you*—not with the other person? The solution lies *with* and *in* yourself. In this Work everything must be turned the other way round. It is *you*—not the other. So long as a person sees the solutions of his troubles only in new arrangements of people, in others, in things, he will be negative. As a result, his mind will be dead—that is, he will not be able to think aright. Negative emotions prevent the mind from working rightly. Instead, a person indulges in negative recriminations—which is not thinking. Is it not extraordinary how people spend their lives in vague negative recriminations? No, one must begin with oneself in all one's own troubles. Start from what you take as *you* and observe this thing you take so glibly as *you yourself*. Do not start with the person whom you think to be the source of your misery. Then you will see how the Work is like that esoteric myth of Perseus who had to slay the Gorgon of hatred and all negativeness, who, if you looked *once* at her, turned you to stone. So Perseus, by looking at her with a mirror—that is, the other way round—and so seeing her in himself—slew her and released from her Pegasus, the horse, which means, in esoteric symbolism, the mind, on which he mounted.

Great Amwell House, December 28, 1946

FEELING OF I

On one occasion Mr. Ouspensky was asked: "What is the right feeling of oneself?" He answered that this question belonged to what he had spoken of earlier—namely, "the wrong feeling of 'I'." He said, in so many words: "In this Work one must separate oneself from pictures, from 'I's that like to suffer, from internally considering 'I's, that enjoy negative emotions, that justify their past, and so on. A person may have a stereotyped wrong feeling of 'I' and through this everything is wrong in him or her. Only by observing that he or she has wrong feeling of 'I' and separating from it can they expect to begin to have right feeling of 'I'. For example, how many people simply hold themselves too tightly, too rigidly, and do not observe it." On another occasion he was speaking on the same question and said that wrong feeling of 'I' is always due to buffers, which give a one-sided feeling of 'I'. "For a man to feel himself rightly," he said, "he must have Real Conscience, which is to feel all together, and no one can have Real Conscience if he is full of buffers. Such a man or woman sees only one side, only *is* one side of themselves. Real Conscience is the same for all people and has nothing to do with different moral or religious systems. It is a general and permanent phenomenon given to us, but now buried in everyone—that is, in sleeping humanity. The esoteric problem is how to awaken it. Man has fallen asleep and because of this world-state of sleep, he has lost touch with all that is of the most importance to him, all that could help and guide him aright. As a consequence, all sorts of religious theories and methods of education and social experiments have replaced what alone could truly shew him what he has to do, and how he should live and what he is. If a man begins to know what he is, he begins to have right feeling of himself. Only Real 'I' can ultimately give a man right feeling of himself in the full sense. But Real 'I' and Real Conscience are not far distant from each other. A man asleep can only have an artificial feeling of 'I', according to what he esteems himself on. It will be a false feeling of 'I'

982

—and one that he may suffer from all his life without realizing it. He has buffers in place of Conscience. Real Conscience is only possible in the absence of buffers."

Let us take to-day this phrase used by Mr. Ouspensky: "If a man begins to know *what he is*, he begins to have the right feeling of himself." This Work is about self-knowledge. You all know that over the Temple at Delphi, where esoteric teaching existed in the days of ancient Greece, was written above the portal: *"Know thyself"*. Now no man, no woman, can know themselves, unless they begin with direct impersonal, un-critical self-observation. Why should this change the usual feeling of 'I', the usual feeling of oneself? Because by this uncritical, impersonal, almost remote observation of oneself, one begins to see that one is quite different from what one has hitherto taken oneself as. One's usual feeling of oneself, feeling of 'I', does not fit what one is. Understand that you may have had all your life a totally wrong feeling of 'I' and this wrong feeling has stopped all further growth in yourself and probably spoilt your life. You have become fastened to an error, a mistake, something not real in yourself. As long as life is the neutralizing force, you will be unable to tear away this totally wrong, not real, feeling of yourself, with which you meet your daily existence and other people. Only through self-observation done through the strength of the third force of the Work will this fixed life-produced feeling of yourself begin to change. And what a relief it is to find that you have been trying to lead your life with an utterly wrong set of 'I's, with the wrong, generally dominant feeling of 'I'. It is a marvellous thing to find you can move in new directions internally and escape from this spurious invention of yourself. Just say to yourself: "Why am I always like this? Why do I always feel this? Why, in short, am I always the same fixed person, with the same points of view, the same attitudes, the same little unpleasantnesses, the same judgments, the same dreariness, the same criticisms, the same thoughts, the same reactions?" Now you know this is called: "The realization of one's mechanicalness"—and this again is called: "The first stage of Self-Remembering." Why? Because it means that a person who begins to see internally his or her mechanical-ness has already separated *something* from what they have taken them-selves complacently as. Something different from themselves has appeared in their inner world. This is the beginning of development —that development which begins with Observing 'I', and leads to Deputy-Steward—and then to Steward and at last to Real 'I'. Is it not extraordinary to reflect that we are not Real 'I', but false 'I', and that what we are and take ourselves as is all invention? Is it not tragic that all these wrong feelings of 'I', these wrong feelings of what oneself is, these inventions of ourselves, lead our lives?

Now there can be no change of being without an alteration in the ordinary feeling of 'I'. The Three Lines of Work speak of this—work on oneself, work in connection with others and making new relations with them, and work for the sake of the Work itself. To remain the same, to have the same outer manifestations, to feel the same feeling of 'I', means simply that one is not following any of the three lines of Work. Sometimes an overwhelming sense of the Work may alter a person. Sometimes a realized self-observation may alter a person. But if you have still the same feeling of 'I' you have not yet changed being.

Great Amwell House, January 4, 1947

POSITIVE IDEAS IN THE WORK

I

It was said recently that one should not do anything negatively. In this age it might be said that in the world people tend, as a whole, to do things negatively. For example, factory workers do not, and indeed cannot, take pleasure in their work—that is, the emotional part of Moving Centre is not used, so they have to have music and so on as a substitute. The Moving Centre works infinitely better when the emotional part collaborates. Then a person *takes pleasure in his movements*, in the skill of his hands, etc., and he becomes a craftsman through the guidance of the emotional part—that is, of emotional cognition. We spend a great deal of our time in being negative and doing things negatively without noticing it. The difference is between going to, or being dragged to, something. If you go to a thing from yourself you work at it positively. Otherwise it works you and that is one form of doing things negatively. One source of this is when we doubt. The Work is always tempting us and so making us negative. *Temptation is when we doubt the end*. It is easy to give up, to think things useless—that is, to think negatively. One has to say to oneself: "*I can work*"—and say it further and further inside oneself. People do not recognize it as temptation. Here is an example in a letter on the subject: "I have noticed that temptation can be met *if it is recognized as temptation.* I had an example last night. I was about to fall into a well-known Slough of Despond, doubting the end, and then it suddenly struck me that it might be temptation and that perhaps it was not inevitable and that perhaps one need not go into it, if one had some help. In the end I went to sleep quite peacefully." We must live with a plan, noticing ourselves in regard to it. If there is no aim, no plan, no individual direction, there is nothing to notice, nothing to work on. We remain where we were, for then we do not act consciously in our relation to our inner world and what we allow to go on in it, and in relation to the world of others who are mirrors to us. Self-Remembering increases the force of consciousness. The act of Self-Remembering, as, for example, remembering distinctly one's plan, one's aim, in the midst of some difficult situation, actually creates new energy. It is like the light becoming much brighter, as if the central station had increased the current. And this is just what it is. We get connected up inside again and the Work then can give us force. Falling asleep, letting smouldering negative states grow unchecked, breaks up right connections. The whole plan and system of the Work is simply to give right inner connections so that force from higher centres can be received. The act of Self-Remembering, in a full sense, includes all the Work, all its teaching and new ways of thinking, all one has learned from it, all that one has gained from it, all that it means, all the insights, all the new experiences —all this together. Then right connections open up again and new force passes through one. What does this force do? It overcomes the negative mess of life, which people are always accumulating, which forms wrong connections. It increases consciousness—which is light. Through this light one sees everything more clearly, just as if you turn on the light in a room in which you have been blundering about and knocking everything down in the dark. Yes, Self-Remembering gives new light. This light is consciousness, increase of consciousness. The Work is to increase consciousness.

Now to have more consciousness requires a not going to sleep inside, for that is to invite and encourage darkness. Going to sleep means not doing anything in any of the three lines of Work. You neither work on yourself and your personal ambitions and desires, nor with others, and on your mechanical contempts and dislikes of them, nor do you value the Work itself and keep its ancient worth alive, between your two hands, as a delicate thing. Do you expect this ancient Work to give you straightway the highest consciousness and understanding? That would be trivial, and would point to a tedious level of being. The Work means work—inner work—many inner and outer readjustments —many self-realizations and slow difficult periods during which you *will* the Work, as a small guarded plant, between your two hands, and keep your eyes on it enough. That means your attention and the two hands mean inner and outer consciousness—consciousness of yourself and consciousness of others. This plant begins to die if you do not look at it enough. G. compared it with an egg hatching out that you must not allow to get too cold. One ancient teaching says: "not more than 8 hours." Well, it is something like that. For people who only think of this ancient Work once every week at meetings everything has to be taught again. They do nothing themselves in the first, second or third lines of Work. They have no internal heat, no esoteric faith, only life-faith. They expect to be warmed up by others. This is a poor state of being and understanding. "What," said Mr. Ouspensky once, "have you done since the last meeting? What have you seen? What have you understood? What have you noticed?" Silence was the answer. Now we know that as long as a person is himself and delighted with himself, as long as he takes himself as himself and is satisfied, as long as he cannot by self-observation begin to separate himself from what he has up to now taken as himself, he cannot change his being. He will *be* as he has *been*—that is, his being will remain the same.

Now to change being it is necessary to have *positive* ideas. Let us speak of this. It was once said by Mr. Ouspensky: "The state of humanity can be compared with the following octave":

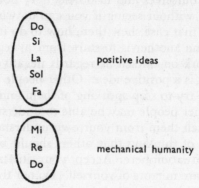

Mr. Ouspensky said: "Mechanical man can be compared with the notes *Do, Re, Mi*. He cannot get to the notes *Fa, Sol, La, Si, Do*. For what reason? Because mechanical humanity has not got positive ideas. Only positive ideas can make mankind pass the place of vacuum, of nothingness, the place where collectivism, crowds, medals, examinations, are no good at all. What makes a man want to go on? He wants to rival someone else. Mechanical men cannot get beyond this because life as third force cannot get them beyond this. You have to pass the place where life-things are no good. Probably it is impossible on this planet for humanity to reach this stage. Only individuals may reach it. The Work is a special forcing-house to produce in people positive ideas without which they cannot pass from *Mi* to *Fa*."

To change being, to grow, to fulfil oneself, a certain inner *positive* pressure of attention is necessary. One must have positive ideas. One must wish to change. This has two sides. One understands from the Work that one's life on Earth means that one has something quite definite to do or else one would not be here. That is a positive idea. The other side is that one finds in oneself many undesirable things that one is vaguely aware of and sometimes uncomfortable about. This side must become a positive idea and not a negative one. It is easy to find fault with oneself in a certain way. This is a negative idea. Through right self-observation one sees what one has to alter. Then the negative idea becomes a positive idea. No one can change through negative ideas—through vague self-accusations, for example, or through a certain kind of miserableness. All this is negative. Do not listen to miserable 'I's that love to drag you down. "There is much in everyone," said G., "that seeks to destroy him." Further it must be understood that as

986

long as a man thinks he can do he is acting from a negative idea. His third force is life.

Now it is necessary to wake up and feel the shock of the Work-teaching and see that the cause of all negative emotions and states is in you. It is useless to look at the outer cause of them. You must separate from them. And also recollect that negative states create only negative states in ourselves and in others. Try not to speak to people as if they *could do*, without seeing if you can do what you blame them for not doing. In that case shew them how to do it themselves. To be negative and blame another is to start from a negative idea. To see that one must work on oneself as regards negative emotion and stop identifying with it is a positive idea. Other people cannot *do* any more than you can. So try to stop speaking of them and criticizing them as if they could. Other people may be able to understand—if you understand and can teach them from your own understanding. Do not live in a frozen world of thinking that others should be different. This is the ordinary life-situation here. Accept your situation intelligently and remember others are mirrors of yourself. Do not think what you see in others cannot possibly be in you. God is what you need. Begin with your neighbour. He shews you what you need—that is, what you need to see in yourself and become conscious of. We all need to become more conscious. All Work requires force. People have not enough force because they have not distinct positive ideas about the Work and what they are doing and what it means in life. The more you feel the Work, the more force of consciousness is possible for you—that is, consciousness above that required for serving life, serving nature. Everyone can become more conscious—that is, have more force. But this is only possible by following all this ancient Work teaches. One must work for it—pay for it. If you prefer sleep, sleep. If you wish to awaken, work.

Great Amwell House, January 11, 1947

POSITIVE IDEAS IN THE WORK

II

Let me repeat again that we should not do anything negatively. Whatever you do or rather, have to do, do not do it negatively. Last time this was spoken of, together with the subject of positive ideas and how Man in general is kept at the notes *Do, Re, Mi: Do, Re, Mi,* over and over again. Real development is impossible because he does not possess sufficient positive ideas to jump and reach the note *Fa* and so approach the sphere of Conscious Man. Now it is obvious that if we do anything negatively we have not a positive idea connected with it. Looking at life, we find considerable reasons for having negative ideas about it. The most of literature is negative, the most of poetry is negative. History is a history of crime, and so on. How, it might be said, can we have positive ideas under such circumstances? Only by a new set of ideas—another range of ideas.

Negative ideas have very great attractive power. A negative idea, such as that the Universe is meaningless, can draw millions into its vortex and hold them as in prison. This takes away the chance of individual growth from them and so renders them subjects for mass-suggestion. This is the effect of negative ideas—namely, to destroy individual importance and meaning and inner individual thought and make a man dependent on the outside and so more and more under the power of external life. We here catch a glimpse of the meaning of negative ideas as distinguished from positive ideas. A positive idea puts a man less and less under the power of the outside, of external life. You remember that it is constantly repeated in the Work that as long as life is the Third Force, you cannot change. That is, this inner development, possible for Man, which all esoteric teaching is about, cannot take place. The Work says that unless a man has undergone his destined development he remains in the experiment of creating a self-developing organism on Earth, as distinct from the animals and plants, etc., that form the main bulk of Organic Life. Life, as Third or Neutralizing Force, keeps outer Personality active and inner Essence passive. Yes, but one must begin to ponder for oneself as to what this means. The real man remains undeveloped by life. Only another force, coming from another direction and having another range of ideas, can bring about the lessening of the life-formed Personality, with its craving for visible rewards, and lead to the stirring and awakening of the inner man—the essential man—the development of which is the object of esoteric teaching.

Now, to interrupt the theme for a moment—what does esoteric mean? In the New Testament the outer man and the inner man are spoken of. The outer man is called the exoteric man, the inner man the esoteric man. What does this mean? The outer man, the Personality, may be well-trained and will never steal, let us say. But if all fear were removed, he would steal. But if the inner or esoteric man were developed, he would not steal, understanding why not. He becomes internally responsible, That is the difference. If the inner man were developed, no police would be necessary. Now, in us, life develops the outer man, but not the inner man. Esoteric teaching is therefore about the development of this inner, as yet undeveloped, Essence—the esoteric man. Then, whatever happens in outer life, a man behaves rightly— from himself, internally. In the Greek, εξω means *outer*: and εσω means inner. Esotericism therefore is a teaching applying to the inner man— to what you are in yourself, apart from external restraints and fears. So the Work starts with self-observation—that is, observing your inner states and what you are like. It does not start with external observation as does Science.

A man, a woman, in this Work, must learn by self-observation that what they seem to be, what they pretend to be outwardly, is not what they are internally. Realizing this, they begin to suffer from the sense of contradiction. This is useful suffering. The outer and inner must conform eventually and become one—a unity. Man asleep takes himself for granted as a unity. When he begins to observe himself, he realizes he is two in the broadest sense—that is, what he pretends to be and what he is. Then he must eventually become a unity. Then outer and inner are the same. This is the first step. To be kind to a person outwardly and hate and murder him inwardly is the ordinary state of Man asleep. In this psychological state *nothing* can change in the man. He is a failure in the experiment of self-development.

Now to return to positive ideas. "Unless", said Mr. Ouspensky, in so many words, "Man believes in Greater Mind, he is useless for the Work. To believe in Greater Mind is to have a positive idea—and without positive ideas no one can develop. A man who thinks he is isolated, independent, that he knows and that he *can do* with his limited finite mind, with all its ignorance, starts from active *Do*, and then describes a descending octave and so perishes. History is full of such examples. To think one can do is to start from a negative idea. To realize one *cannot do* and to study how to do and what is necessary is to start from a passive *Do*—that is, to begin an ascending octave." Mr. Ouspensky used often to talk in this way.

You might very well think that the idea that you *can do*—can, for instance, reform the world, change other people, and so on—is a positive idea. On the contrary, it is a negative idea. It is as negative an idea as if you were to think that you could, without any very special knowledge, operate on a man's brain. In this Work, people who think they can do are called Lunatics. Mr. Ouspensky once asked Mr. Gurdjieff what a man has to do to assimilate his teachings:

"What *to do*?" asked Mr. Gurdjieff, as though surprised. "It is impossible *to do* anything. A man must first of all *understand* certain things. He has thousands of false ideas and false conceptions, chiefly about himself, and he must get rid of some of them before beginning to acquire anything new. Otherwise the new will be built on a wrong foundation and the result will be worse than before."

"How can we get rid of false ideas?" Mr. Ouspensky asked. "We depend on the forms of our perception. False ideas are produced by the forms of our perception."

Mr. Gurdjieff shook his head. "Again you speak of something different," he said. "You speak of errors arising from perceptions but I am not speaking of these. Within the limits of given perceptions Man can be more or less deluded. As I have said before, man's chief delusion is his conviction that he can *do*. All people think that they can do, all people want to do and the first question all people ask is what are they to do. But actually nobody does anything and nobody can do anything. This is the first thing that must be understood. *Everything happens.* All that befalls a man, all that is done by him, all that comes from him—*all this happens*—and it happens in exactly the same way as rain falls as a result of a change in the temperature of the atmosphere, as snow melts under the rays of the sun, as dust rises with the wind. Man is a machine. All his deeds, actions, words, thoughts, feelings, convictions, opinions and habits are the results of external influences, external impressions. Out of himself a man cannot produce a single thought, a single action. Everything he says, does, thinks, feels—all this happens. Man cannot discover anything, cannot invent anything. It all happens."

Great Amwell House, January 18, 1947

FURTHER NOTE ON POSITIVE IDEAS IN THE WORK AND REVERSAL OF SIGNS

A positive idea may be tentatively defined, in these commentaries, as an idea that lessens Personality and increases Essence. It was said last time that the idea that "Man can do" is not a positive idea, although most people would say it was. But the idea that Man can do increases Personality. It is exactly what Personality thinks. The Work says: "Man cannot do." And this is a positive idea. Why? Because it lessens Personality, whereas the idea that Man can do increases Personality and therefore is a negative idea. Personality has no life of itself. Only what has life of itself can do. For example, we have no ideas of our own. All rolls and combinations of 'I's form Personality, all records on rolls made from impressions, all buffers, attitudes, pictures, all this makes up the machine of Personality. With this absurd machine we move about, believe in ourselves. Yet we cannot think a new thought. We can only compare, copy, alter. This machine, which is dead, surrounds Essence which is alive, but inarticulate, undeveloped. A man with developed Essence, a man who has undergone this reversal of signs, Personality active and Essence passive to Personality passive and Essence active—such a man belongs to Conscious Humanity and such a man can do. He is re-born. Such a man has real Fate, for Fate is of Essence, and mechanical law belongs to machines—that is, to us. Ordinary man is under Accident, not Fate. Now we realize what is meant by the positive idea "Man cannot do", when we begin to become conscious of our own mechanicalness. A machine does not do. It has no choice. This is one of the definite increases of consciousness possible for us and expected after a certain time. Time is measured in the Work. This Work is about increasing consciousness in many definite directions. Consciousness is light—not physical light but psychological light, which gives a new power of seeing everything. As Man is, he is in darkness—quite literally. He is in psychological darkness. He is not conscious. To realize—to begin to realize—that one is mechanical and not really alive is a shock. This shock belongs to the zone which in the 3-storey factory, fed by impressions, air and food, is called the region of the First Conscious Shock. This shock a man can give himself. Here he can do. Man can work—with the help of the Work. But first he must form Observing 'I'. Observing 'I' is the result of this Work and of the ideas taught by it. The more you see the strength of the Work the more you can observe. Only through the Observing 'I' formed by this Work and its positive ideas can a man observe himself deeply enough to realize his mechanicalness as a psychological fact. He then sees that the whole matter and meaning of life lies in himself and his relation to himself. Hitherto he has been identified with what is not him—with Personality—and so not with his Fate. Now he begins to separate. In short, he begins to awaken from sleep, from Personality active. So the realization that he is a machine and that he cannot do has a positive result, although it seems a negative idea. It brings him a step toward that reversal, that interchange of signs between Personality and Essence. For we have tentatively defined a positive idea as that which lessens Personality and increases Essence.

So let us again refer to the great diagram—the condensed formulation—of what is necessary if we wish this Work and no longer believe in life as an end in itself.

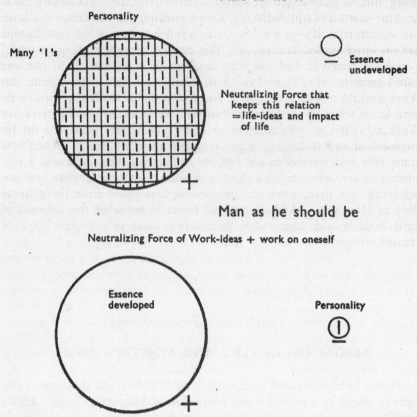

One can see without difficulty that a reversal is necessary for a man to be "re-born"—or reach his inherently possible development. For according to the Work everyone is born a self-developing organism—that is, capable of a further step, individually, in his evolution. But for life-purposes—i.e. to serve Nature—this is not necessary. Man asleep serves Nature. The Side-Octave from the Sun—that is, from that internal psychological level represented physically and externally by the natural and quite dramatic Sun—has sown Man on Earth to contribute to the pain-factory of Organic Life, but has given Man the inherent possibility of raising his level of Being in such a way that although he, as a body, is on the Earth, psychologically he is at a higher level. The psychological man, that is, is at a higher level. As you know, a man is first his body and then his psychological body. The Work is always making the second psychological body and for this new ideas and the practice of them are necessary. Now all the ideas of the Work are positive in exactly this sense—namely, if followed they lead to the formation of a psychological body. As Man is, from the action of external life, he has no organized psychological body. His level of being and his knowledge are such that internally, psychologically, he is Legion—a mass of contradictory 'I's—a multiplicity—in fact, a machine run by external life—a machine which is a function of the outside and has no inner life of its own. All this cannot be pondered on enough. You have heard it, but not seen it. You have listened to it but not found secretly what it means. I will only add that if you value the Work and do not nibble at it, if you feel it emotionally, you will very soon know what the 3rd Force of life is and what the 3rd Force of the Work is. That is, you will get to know practically what it is to be mechanical and what it is to begin to behave consciously. When you know this as a psychological fact for yourselves, then you will know when you are behaving as a man, a woman, asleep, and when you are behaving as a man, a woman, beginning to awaken from the general sleep of Humanity. And so you will begin to see what this reversal of signs implies and understand practically what this ancient idea of "being re-born" means.

Great Amwell House, January 25, 1947

MAGNETIC CENTRE AND POSITIVE IDEAS

It has been often said in the teaching of this Work that one of the signs of Being in a person is the possession of Magnetic Centre, which signifies the power of seeing things on different levels. A sense of scale in regard to the meaning of Magnetic Centre has nothing to do with a mechanical sense of scale. For example, an emotional type—e.g. an artist—has a sense of scale about art and usually a very jealous one. Or an intellectual man, a No. 3 man, has a sense of scale about intellectual things, and again is very jealous. But this is not the scale that Magnetic Centre gives, which is a scale outside life. For example, let us take a No. 1 man, who judges everything from the viewpoint of physical prowess. He meets a No. 2 man who is, say, an artist. He feels nothing from this artist because he has no sense of scale. He cannot understand that this artist, who perhaps contributes to the culture of life, is superior to him, because he judges him from his physical power, and so on. That is, he sees nothing higher than himself except in visible people who are taller or shorter or more powerful than himself. So he derives his feeling of scale from the physical senses. Magnetic Centre, however, means the power of seeing beyond our mechanical fixations. It means the power of seeing that there is something far higher than oneself—whether one is No. 1, No. 2 or No. 3 man.

Speaking in general, a man who possesses Magnetic Centre is at a higher level than one who does not—because he can see higher and lower. There are, however, different qualities of Magnetic Centre. Sometimes people have what Mr. Ouspensky called false Magnetic Centre—and sometimes they have multiple Magnetic Centre—that is, they have many small, weak Magnetic Centres. As a result, they run after every variety of magical and pseudo-occult practice, every kind of mystical cult, or even join end-of-the-world societies, or spend their time in measuring dark passages in the Pyramids and explaining everything by them. Such people have no right sense of scale. Right Magnetic Centre does not lead in this direction. But both in a man with wrong or false Magnetic Centre and a man with right Magnetic Centre, there is the belief that there is *something else*, another idea of life, and that life cannot be explained in terms of itself. This is a positive idea. Now Man, being created a self-developing organism, as the Work says, cannot fulfil himself unless he finds out how to develop. He may feel he cannot explain the Universe or that he cannot explain himself, or both. In any case, the sense of mystery enters. This feeling, this continual awareness of the inexplicability of everything is one of the signs of right Magnetic Centre. Curiosity, ambition to be great, the excitingness of so-called occult knowledge and the belief that one can get something for nothing have to do with small 'I's and with the self-emotions. But the sense of mystery goes beyond all self-love. It decreases Personality. It makes a man feel his nothingness. So it connects him with positive ideas, for anything that renders Personality more passive and Essence more active has connection with positive ideas. For this reason God, as Absolute, is a positive idea. The Ray of Creation is a positive idea. The Conscious Circle of Humanity is a positive idea. The idea that we are all asleep and must awaken is a positive idea.

Let us recall once more the teaching of the Work about Magnetic Centre. It says that Magnetic Centre brings us into the Work but cannot keep us there without our own efforts. We have to work on ourselves and in contact with a system that tells us how we have to work. We have to will this Work. To attempt to do this Work—such as the practising of non-identifying—without willing the Work cannot give any result. Will starts from affection. Will, if you come to think of it, is love. One emotion can overcome another if strong enough. The centre of gravity of Will lies in the Emotional Centre. It is worth reflecting on this oneself. But although a man may have right Magnetic Centre, which should lie in the intellectual part of the Emotional Centre, it is only introductory. If he is led to a teaching connected with the Conscious Circle of Humanity by means of it, his task is only begun. He has to turn his sense of mystery, his seeking, his cravings, his lack, into something real—into practical and practised work, and the more he values emotionally the more he is given help. If he has the strength to catch the rope overhead then not only is he working but the Work works on him. It begins to teach him, in periods of silence, in those gaps in one's mechanical life when usually everything is a blank or boredom. Above all, it enters when one has separated—that is, not identified—with

one of the hundred and one daily things that keep us asleep and seem
so great through identifying, which is an enormous magnifying lens.
People like to make a problem of everything, to be worried, and, like
flies, get stuck on every little fly-paper-event. One may have no idea
how it is possible to avoid these fly-papers—that is, unless one takes the
Work simply and applies it simply, almost at every moment. What an
up-rolling of care can then take place and how these things adjust
themselves and fall into their right place.

Diagram of Magnetic Centre

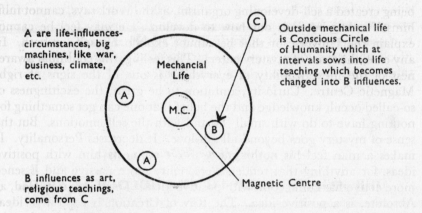

A are life-influences-
circumstances, big
machines, like war,
business, climate,
etc.

Mechancial
Life

Outside mechanical life
is Conscious Circle
of Humanity which at
intervals sows into life
teaching which becomes
changed into B influences.

B influences as art,
religious teachings,
come from C

Magnetic Centre

Some people do not distinguish the difference between *A* and *B*
influences. They take everything in life in the same way and on the
same level. Others recognize *B* influences and are affected by them and
a few even make an effort to find out more. This is due to the quality
of Magnetic Centre. They seek. Only a few seek from themselves.
Memory, due to recurrence, may make Magnetic Centre very strong
from earliest times. In a sense, contact with the Work may create
Magnetic Centre in those who seem not to possess it. If so, in recurrence, they will recognize the Work when they hear it again, for everything repeats, everything returns, in the circle of one's life. However,
the Work simply says that Magnetic Centre is acquired and is due to
the early influences a child has been under. To-day it is ceasing to
exist—that is, the level of Humanity is dropping. Positive ideas, in the
Work-meaning, are being replaced by negative ideas. As a consequence,
all those higher parts of centres, that we are furnished with just because
we are self-developing organisms, are not made contact with, not used,
not given food. Man more and more is living in the basement—not
merely literally—and in consequence change of Being is being made
impossible, for only positive ideas can change Being. Since change of
Being—that is, self-development—is the real idea of Man by his
creation, his individual meaning is being lost. If we change Being, even

a little, as not disliking so easily, not identifying with every worry, our life alters. Unless we change Being the taste of our life and our actual life-situations remain nearly the same. Without positive ideas—that is, without contact with *C* influences *via B* influences—all the real meaning of Man perishes. He is cut off from influences that could change him. So he becomes wholly under the power of *A* influences. He then serves life and the big machines of life—politics, trade, war, mass-exercise, mass-propaganda, etc. He will not possess Magnetic Centre. He will not seek positive ideas. His inner mind is shut. His inner life dies, and, esoterically speaking, he becomes useless, meaningless, dead. Much was said in the Gospels about the quick and the dead and many warnings were given about Man being cut off, which can be understood far more distinctly from the Work-ideas. On the other hand, a culture comes to an end, and has to be destroyed, and the flood comes—namely, barbarism, violence, loss of truth. Then an Ark is made to survive the Flood and keep alive knowledge for the next culture. What do you think of this time in the light of these ideas?

Great Amwell House, February 1, 1947

OUR RELATIONSHIP TO PSYCHOLOGICAL SPACE

STATE = PLACE

Some of you have heard it said that while everyone is somewhere in physical space, at the same time he or she is somewhere in psychological space. It is obvious that a living person as regards the physical, visible body must be somewhere in physical space—in some distinct place. But unless you reflect on the matter, it is not so obvious that everyone is at the same time in some distinct place in psychological space. Outwardly, by our external senses, we can observe where we or others are in visible space. This Work is to train us to observe where we are internally—in this psychological space that all esoteric teaching is about. Each of us dwells somewhere in a vast psychological country, the same for everyone. In this inner psychological space, only apprehended by the inner senses, it is possible for a man or woman to spend their lives in a very bad part of it, without ever realizing it. In the Work we seek to change our *habitat* internally. For example, the cultivation of negative emotions, the love of negative states in general, puts us in a bad part of this vast, inner psychological space where the spirit of a person dwells. That is, we can live physically in comfort and psychologically in a wretched part which, if it were represented by visible space, we would be horrified at and seek to leave at once. Suppose a person's favourite, most habitual psychological activity consists in internal considering, in blaming, in

996

making accounts against others, in violence, in feeling upset by every life-event, in being negative and so on, then such a person inhabits psychologically, spiritually, a bad place internally. He or she dwells, *inwardly*, in a bad place, however healthily outwardly. How then to get out of it? *First, by observing that it is so* and acknowledging it. Then by work on oneself on non-identifying with one's states. Remember *State* is *Place* in this inner invisible realm which is psychological space. Whatever state you are in, there you place yourself. Suppose you have mean, narrow thoughts and instantly you were to find yourself physically in a mean, narrow street. That would certainly give you a shock. This does not happen in physical space—and just as well. But it happens in psychological space always and instantly. So reflect again on the saying that *State is Place* internally. Whatever state you are in, so you are in a certain place internally, psychologically. This must become as real to you as what would be corresponding in outer space—where at least we learn not to walk in mud and filth. Negative emotions are mud and filth. Psychologically, they correspond to literal mire and filth.

As has been said several times, we live in what is invisible to others. Our bodies are in visible space, but our thoughts and moods and fears and anxieties and feelings are invisible and constitute where we dwell in the psychological world. It is in this psychological world that we really live. So it has been said that we are all invisible. Through our visible bodies we try to signal to one another in a clumsy way. But actually we are invisible and nearly unknown to one another. This is very strange. Yet the more you reflect on it, the more will you see that it is true. We do not live in the external sense-given outer world, but in an invisible, inner psychological world. If we are in the same place in the psychological world, however, we understand our signals better and perhaps even do not have to signal in the usual manner. That is one reason why this Work teaches us to learn a common language and practise a common work, a common discipline. Then we are closer in psychological space. In this space, in this psychological or spiritual world, there are definite places where it is possible to receive help. I do not think, as we are, that it is possible to be in two places at the same time, either in the world of physical space or the world of psychological space. In this connection the Works says merely that it is impossible to cross a river in two boats. When one comes in contact with a teaching that comes from a particular psychological place, that has been reached by others who have laboured in the past, then if the teaching is valued and *followed* it leads to that place where, on the way, one begins to get help. Another reality and another meaning begin to shew through what one has hitherto taken to be the *only* reality and meaning. Every form of esoteric or inner teaching is a *way* to a place. For example, Christ calls himself a *Way*. Only when it is followed to the end can a person be transformed into a Christian. Yet people *begin* by imagining they are Christians.

Now if a man has no Magnetic Centre, no sense of scale, and there-

997

fore no positive ideas, he cannot reach those desirable parts of this psychological country of which we have been speaking. What in our machine, our apparatus, corresponds and relates us to this country? Centres and parts of centres do. They open into different places. Higher parts and lower parts of centres touch different levels in this psychological country—for it is a country of levels, higher and lower, valleys and mountains. For example, if one lives in little 'I's, in negative 'I's, in minute thoughts, in minute self-feelings and self-satisfactions, and so on, one lives in poor dismal valleys internally. *State is Place.* Bad states put a man, a woman, in bad psychological places. It is just like that—just as practical as that. But it is worth thinking about often—that is, once you begin to feel, even faintly, responsible to yourself or your states and cease to say, or think secretly, that it is somebody else's fault. "Remember", the Work says, "that you come here to contend only with yourself. Thank any who give you the opportunity to do so." But it is not only a question of coming here—the idea runs through all the Work, wherever you are—"work on yourself", whether here or elsewhere. Observe yourself. Consider what the Work tells you to observe. Then work on yourself through the material you have collected by observation. But people identify so much with their states. Something makes a person, say, feel miserable. Does it occur to the person that this is exactly where one can work? No—the person simply is miserable, totally identified with the mood. Whereas an inner relaxing, an observing of the thoughts and the feelings and the posture, a remembering of something said in the Work, and perhaps in a flash the mood has vanished or perhaps it gradually lifts. Why? Because you are observing it and so are not it. But if you want the state and enjoy it in this curious way that we do—that is, love our negative states—then how can it disappear? So many *will* misery or anxiety. To love is to will: we do what we love to do. To be negative and to hate are easy: to hate to be negative is difficult. First, we must feel that in this Work we have a right not to be negative. That is a very deep remark. It is not the same as saying that in the Work we have no right to be negative. The pain-factory of life demands negative states from sleeping Humanity. Only the Work gives us the *right* not to be negative. The Work has paid for us in that respect. Others have paid. Is it not a pity that we cannot observe our evil states instead of being them and taking them as ourselves? How shall we ever find the principle of unity in ourselves if we take our changing states as 'I'? To do so seems to me not to understand the Work—not to see where it begins. The Work begins in you —not outside you. It begins in studying where you are now in this inner psychological space. It is not merely that the Kingdom of Heaven is within you. This has many mansions. It is to see where you are now internally. The Work shews you where you are. This is self-study. This is practical work.

A NOTE ON SELF-JUSTIFYING

One of the many definite things we are told by this Work to observe in ourselves, and specifically to work against, is self-justifying. What does self-justifying mean? It means always putting yourself in the right. To justify one's action, for example, is to vindicate oneself, to shew to others that whatever one did, it was reasonable, right, proper and just. When you justify yourself, you start from the picture of yourself as always good, honourable, just, upright. To justify oneself is to exonerate oneself, to explain to people how one was not to blame, how one was misunderstood, how one acted from the best motives, and so on. If you have begun to observe self-justifying, you will realize what a prodigious quantity of psychic energy is used every moment by the human race in this useless activity. The man or woman can never be wrong. People feel themselves always right, whatever they do or say. Nothing penetrates them. Nothing can rouse them from the deep sleep in which they prefer to exist. This' becomes a serious matter, however, if a person wishes to awaken.

Now it is useless to speak of self-justifying to people unless they have tried to observe it in themselves. Suppose a person is suddenly asked why he is so negative? Probably he will either indignantly deny that he is negative or say that he has good reason to be. In both cases, he justifies himself—that is, he justifies his negative emotions. You can justify yourself by denial, or by finding an excuse such as blaming others. But the root of the matter lies in this picture of always being right and so never being actually in the wrong. Here a very powerful force is at work to keep us asleep in illusions about ourselves. As a consequence, we are then never at peace internally. On the contrary, we are at war—with ourselves. For there is that in us that knows we are in the wrong and that in us that refuses to admit it. Here the two Giants, Pride and Vanity, come in, but it seems to me that it is chiefly Pride. But that is a matter for personal observation. Vanity may make pictures of oneself and Pride defend them. But whatever the case is, the fact remains that some very powerful force lies behind the act of self-justifying and that this force does not give us any inner stability and so no inner peace. A man or woman may, say, not sleep all night simply because of something they will not admit and accept, and instead they justify themselves. Yet one real act of uncritical, sincere self-observation, one search through their inner rooms for the missing piece of silver —that is, the missing truth—will clear everything up. The tension relaxes. A real act of self-observation has been made. Something not admitted and so not properly conscious has been allowed to become fully conscious. All inner strain and tightness suddenly vanishes. Why? Because instead of the crowding voices of self-justifying—and here it is oneself justifying oneself to oneself—observation, acknowledgement and acceptance have been carried out. In other words, an act of real work has been done. The pill has been swallowed.

Let me talk once more of this pill that Sly Man makes and swallows in the 4th Way. Sly Man does not sit on his haunches for years with his arms outstretched. He does not starve for weeks or deep-breathe for days. He observes himself and sees what he has to do with himself now to change his machinery—his present Being. He is clever—like the wise virgins in the parable. (In the Greek the word translated as "wise" means "clever".) He works on what it is immediately necessary to acknowledge and accept in himself without Pride or Vanity. So he is sly, clever, intelligent. He makes a pill and swallows it. Now if he always justifies himself, how can he make this pill and swallow it? The Sly Man does not strive to keep up with himself as he imagines he is. He notices distinctly that he lies, for example. He observes it over a period and does not seek to disguise it to himself, to justify himself. He notices it, sees it, acknowledges it, accepts it, and so swallows this particular pill. Then he must digest it. It tastes bitter in the mouth. But once digested it becomes sweet.

When we justify ourselves nothing comes home to us. We keep, as it were, a half of ourselves from entering consciousness. We live on one side. This is due to those extraordinarily difficult things to observe called in the Work *buffers*. The more buffers, the more self-justifying. But once the other side of a buffer is observed, acknowledged and accepted, the buffer can never re-form itself. We lose a particular idea of ourselves. We gain a broadening of consciousness. Thereby we reach a higher level of Being. This seems paradoxical. It seems paradoxical to say that if you will accept what you disapprove of you reach a higher level. People imagine that by increasing their sense of self-merit and virtue, they get higher. On the contrary, they descend. This is worth thinking about.

Great Amwell House, February 15, 1947

NOTE ON TAKING IN NEGATIVE IMPRESSIONS

When you take in a negative impression it increases 2nd Force in you. You can say simply that it makes everything more difficult. People often make difficulties about everything—in fact, making difficulties may belong to their Chief Feature. Every person has a Chief Feature, on which everything rests. It is compared with a central axle round which everything in the man or woman turns. When a person tries to forget himself and only remember what his aim is, Chief Feature interferes. In every decision, Chief Feature decides. In short, in regard to changing oneself, changing one's Being, it constitutes the greatest 2nd

Force in us. Every manifestation is the meeting-point of three forces. First, Second, and Third Force. First Force is called active and 2nd Force is force of resistance to active force, or opposing force. This 2nd Force is in all things, even in the imagination and phantasy where at least we might suppose we can do as we like. But for this force of resistance, everything would be without restraint, without brakes, without the necessity of effort, without form—but to say this is absurd, for nothing that exists, nothing that manifests itself, is without 2nd Force. Now when a man makes as his aim change of himself, his Chief Feature stands up as 2nd Force to resist him. But people do not see that they have 2nd Force in themselves. They see it always as outside themselves.

Let us return to the opening remark. I said that when you take in a negative impression, it increases 2nd Force. Let us try to see why this is so and how as a result it can hold people back in the Work without their realizing what it is that does this. I mean that a person in this Work, the object of which is increase of consciousness and so change of Being, cannot proceed beyond a certain point unless they halt negative impressions of others. In the first place, taking in and accepting negative impressions of others, of life, of everything, feeds the negative part of Emotional Centre. This part of Emotional Centre has to be starved, because it is like a disease in the Emotional Centre. The Emotional Centre, if a man or woman works against this acquired part, can transmit meaning from Higher Emotional Centre. You can call it inspiration, meaning, worth-whileness, something different from life, some inner source of life and of being happy—a weak word—and yet quite true. Since we were all born amongst sleeping people—since Papa and Mamma and all the rest were asleep, we become infected by negative emotions. We inhale the atmosphere of those around us from birth —and people are negative and governed by negative emotions. So in our acquired Personality we have formed in us a spurious centre called the negative part of Emotional Centre. At birth the Emotional Centre has no negative part. So we acquire negative emotions. This is a blessed business, because if negative emotions were born in the essential Emotional Centre, we could never separate from them. That is the teaching and you can see what it means if you reflect. The validity of being negative is not *essential*. It is a matter of the acquired Personality and so a disease. So you begin to see perhaps after many years what it means when it is said that we have a right not to be negative. This is a marvellous insight—a real awakening—a beginning of change of Being.

Now when we take in and accept a negative impression of another person it increases the strength over us of the negative part of Emotional Centre. But not only that. It comes back on us—namely, that representation of the person in us becomes negative. Each person we know exists in us as a representation as well as outside us as an object of the senses. The external world is reflected in us through the senses *via* the nervous system, the nerves and their impulses, and represented in us as

1001

people, things. If you take in a negative impression of a person that you know well, *that person in you* becomes negative *to you*. For example, you say you love X. Then you see X and think how silly he is. X in you then becomes negative. You may have a nightmare about X—how he hates you and wishes to murder you. Why? Because you have murdered X in yourself. So taking in negative impressions of others increases 2nd Force in you. It increases enemies in you. It can become a serious matter in the Work to take in negative impressions of others in the Work.

Now if you have cleared a portico, a hall, a space in yourself by self-observation so that you can see a negative impression coming in and are able not to let it enter freely, not to identify with it, not let it go where it wishes, not say 'I' to it, then you keep clear of the mechanical result of that impression. This is magic. This place is what all must make in their inner world. It is just as if we open the physical door in the external world and find an evil man and let him in—or shut the door and lock it. It is just the same thing in the internal world. But if we may not have made this clearing, this portico, not made doors and locks, we are at the mercy of outer life, having nothing in us to prevent its continual effect. But when you realize that outer life and people and things come in only as *impressions, via* the senses, then if you have made this inner space or clearing in yourself, you can allow to enter and accept some of these impressions and reject others. *This is taking impressions in consciously.* This is called the *First Conscious Shock*—when a man, a woman, begins to be a man, or woman, for the first time—whatever they are mechanically in life. This is the *beginning* of being *Conscious Man.* Now if you take in and accept the endless, jealous, envious, unhappy, and so negative impressions of events of daily life and other people, you are just a mechanical person—although you may be a General or Prime Minister. You are a function of life, driven by life. There is really nothing conscious in you. So the Work says you have no psychology. "How can a machine have psychology?" said G. "Machines are machines, some good, some bad. A man must begin to awaken before I can speak to him of psychology. As he is mechanical, whoever he is, I cannot speak to him. Psychology refers to real people. Ordinary people, people in life, who have been made by life, whoever they are, are machines. What *psychology*", he emphasized this word, "can there be in relation to machines? For the study of machines, mechanics is necessary, not psychology. That is why we begin with mechanics. It is yet a long way to psychology. We begin with the study of the machine—of the man-machine, of the man who has the illusion he is not a machine."

ON REALIZING THAT ONE IS NOT CONSCIOUS

On one occasion Mr. Ouspensky was speaking of the various attempts made by the Conscious Circle of Humanity to raise mankind to a higher level of Being. He said in so many words: "But for the work done on mankind by conscious men we would be nothing but barbarians. Always behind culture is the threat of barbarism and always conscious men are sowing, at intervals, influences into the world to lift Man above the state of barbarism. These efforts take different outer forms, and can only be given at times, but always are the same eventually." He said G. had spoken of teachings in the past based on faith, on hope and on love. G. had said: "All these systems have had their influence on mankind at different periods of history. Faith, hope and love have all been tried. But if you were to ask me about this system, I would answer you by saying that it is based on consciousness. In this system that I teach the emphasis is not on faith, or hope, or love, but on consciousness. For this reason I begin by saying that Man is not yet conscious, although he believes he is. He believes he is conscious. He believes that all he does and says is done and said in a full state of consciousness. But this is not the case. Western psychology, as contrasted with Eastern psychology, starts from the idea that Man as he is is fully conscious and that there is no further state of consciousness possible for him. This is where Western psychology is at fault. A man, as he is, is not fully conscious. What he calls consciousness is not, in my sense, consciousness. From the standpoint of the system that I teach, Man is in the illusion that he is already conscious, whereas actually he is in a state of sleep and he lives his whole life in a state of sleep."

At some other time G. spoke of hope as a basis of teaching. "People", he said, in so many words, "may base themselves on hope. They hope for after-life, or they hope that some promised Messiah will come and do everything for them. But they do all this in a state of sleep. They do not understand that all *real* teaching about Man and his possibilities refers to the actual state of Man now—as he is and what he can become —and not to some future state or some eventual progress. For that reason if you ask me what this Work promises, I will answer you by saying that it promises nothing. A man must begin by realizing what he actually is now. He is not yet conscious. When he sees this, he must begin by remembering himself. If a man could remember himself he would be at a higher level of consciousness. He would be no longer asleep. As a result, many illusions would fall away from him and everything would appear in a new light. If he went on he would reach a state of consciousness above that of Self-Remembering—the state of Objective Consciousness. In that state he would see things as they really are. He would then be awake. A man can merely hope for Objective Consciousness, but hope will not give it him. He has to work on himself here and now, and not hope that he will be given it in some other existence. So this system promises nothing. But if a man works, he will get something. Let us say, he will receive leather with which to make shoes. But he must make the shoes himself, so that they fit him. They must be his own shoes—not borrowed shoes."

Let us speak to-day about not being properly conscious. You know that it is impossible to *understand* the Work without doing it. One hears that one is not properly conscious and hears it again. One may then think that one knows all about that matter. Yet one *understands* absolutely nothing about it. Why? Because one has not observed and so seen for oneself that one is not properly conscious. Here a curious state exists. One still has the illusion that one is fully conscious and says and does everything consciously and behaves consciously at every moment and then one hears from the teaching of the Work that one is not conscious. The two teachings lie in the mind without arousing just what should be aroused in oneself. This happens because a person does not apply what the Work teaches to himself or herself. People just listen to the Work and nod their heads. They may hear it a little. But it is necessary to hear *and do* the Work. When by uncritical observation of yourself, instead of this heart-rending continual critical observation of others, you notice that you speak without being really conscious of what you are saying, and all the rest of it, you begin practically to realize that you are not properly conscious. You see the truth of the Work internally. If the whole world were properly conscious all wars, political lies and so on would cease. Can you catch a glimpse of what it might mean to live amongst more conscious people? Can you see why you cannot? Can you see that an increase of consciousness, which is the goal of the Work, and which begins by making yourself more conscious of yourself to yourself by self-observation, would lead to an entirely different life? Here, for instance, you always get offended or hurt or in a rage or depressed because of a constantly recurring trivial situation. Others will tell you that you always *mechanically* (that is, not consciously) behave like that. But you won't believe it. You will justify yourself. In other words, you will refuse to become more conscious of yourself, of what you are like. Once we see for ourselves a thing recurring in ourselves through the inner sense of self-observation, we are gradually freed, gradually made less and less under its power. Why?—*through the increase of consciousness*. All increase of consciousness renders mechanical behaviour less dominating. Consciousness is light. Mechanicalness is darkness. Things happen in the dark that cannot happen in the light. Self-observation is to let a ray of light into all that which we take for granted —namely, the illusion that we are fully conscious and always behave consciously. What an illusion! Can you think of a greater one?

Now as regards *doing* this Work and not merely listening to it—to do this Work requires effort. Only people make a great mistake in thinking, for example, that effort means that they should get up earlier or dig all day or give up smoking and all that. Effort in the Work is psychological. It is all about not identifying and Self-Remembering. Effort in the Work is all about observing oneself—observing 'I's in oneself and not going with them. Effort in the Work is about being sincere to oneself and so knowing what one's motives really are, and not pretending. Effort in the Work is about remembering oneself and not becoming at every moment identified with everything and everybody. Effort in the Work is to stop inner talking. Effort in the Work is not to let negative impressions fall where they mechanically would fall. Effort in the Work is not to pile up internal accounts against others, but to try to see in yourself what you blame in others—as, for example, unkindness. All effort in the Work is passive. Self-development starts from passive *Do*. Effort is something very quiet and deep and clearly seen. It is not noisy, not pretence. It is not contracting muscles and thrusting chins out. Effort in the Work is about effort on your inner states, where you are in your psychological country. All effort in the Work is about becoming more conscious of yourself to yourself. All effort in the Work is about seeing where you are inside—in what place internally in this vast psychological country—and separating yourself from the innumerable bad places in that country. Remember that to move away from a bad inner state is only possible by non-identifying. An ordinary mechanical man or woman is totally identified with his or her inner state at each moment. A person who begins to work begins by knowing what it means to non-identify with the bad 'I's that inhabit those states —those 'I's in you that live in slums. He then begins to know what the Work means and therefore what can lead to change of Being. If you believe in all your states and moods and thoughts and feelings, if you say 'I' to all your 'I's, then you are totally identified with yourself and so are not properly conscious of yourself. To be conscious of a state, to observe it, means you are not that state. *This is the secret*—the first secret of esotericism. Yet people say: "How can I change my Being?" Hear and *do* the Work. Do and practise what it teaches on yourself. Then you will get gradually to another level of Being. So think what practical work is clearly taught in this Work. Begin with what the Work tells you to begin with, and so do not keep asking: "What shall I do to change my Being?" The Work tells you how to begin. But have you ever thought of following it practically—of actually doing it now? The subject of this Work is not the blackboard: it is you yourself. You are the subject of the Work. How many times have you been negative to-day? And how many times have you noticed it and not identified with it? Have you lifted yourself even once to-day out of your mechanical moods? Even an act of noticing a negative state, of observing that you are negative or speaking negatively, separates you a little. Sometimes this moment of self-observation will change you for the moment completely. A sufficient number of such Work-moments may change you, not for a moment, but for all your life. "Nothing", said Mr. Ouspensky, "is more easy and more useless than to be negative all day long. People get negative, say, because life is not going as they think it should. If they only understood they would know that life is going in the only way it can and that nobody can do. This realization might help them. Of what use is it to expend all one's energy in being negative about life when it is all happening in the only way it can happen? This is sleep."

Great Amwell House, March 1, 1947

WORK ON UNDEVELOPED FUNCTIONS

One can use life or be used by it. When a man is used by life he is food, used by a plane of life below that of Earth. Everything is food for something else. Everything feeds on something else. When a man uses life consciously, he becomes food for a plane above the level of the Earth. The reason is that if a man lives more and more consciously he develops, whereas if he is used by life he does not develop. The illustration employed in the Work is that if an acorn lies and rots on the ground it is eaten by pigs, but if it grows into a tree it has another destiny. Oak can be used—eaten—to make a house, but not acorns.

To develop, a man, a woman, must cease to be one-sided, cease to live in one small part of vast centres. Everyone who is in any sense near the level of Good Householder—that is, who has some reasonable, responsible, trained adaptation to external life—has a small developed part that is used for everything. It is like using a saw for everything, such as driving in nails, or writing. To develop is to become less and less one-sided. One must explore one's own country and travel abroad in it—yes, go to Paris in oneself, let us say. Unfortunately people get fixed and stiff and do not get behind themselves, so that they may see where and how they have got stuck to one thing, one idea, one picture of themselves, one point of view, one outlook, one set of phrases, and one judgment on everything. For the first half of life or so, the function most used by the acquired Personality that relates them to the world is sufficient. They remain apparently well. A time comes when the other functions belonging to the other centres need expression. That is, the machine urgently needs balancing. The unused functions begin to project themselves on to others. One's own limitations are seen as being only in others. So they have to be brought into consciousness and thus prevented from unconsciously going out into others. Undeveloped thinking, for instance, needs to be observed and made more and more conscious to oneself. I am speaking of a person in whom thinking is the least-used centre—say, a 123 man. He will then see that it is not the other person who is so intolerably stupid, but himself. Unless he does this, the same situation will occur repeatedly. For what lies in us, beyond our slight range of consciousness, acts very powerfully and quite against our small sphere of will. So the Work emphasizes the importance of increasing our consciousness of ourselves. Notice when you are behaving in a way that surprises you. You may be sure that an undeveloped centre is discharging energy through you—that is, discharging it in a silly infantile way. Infantile here means undeveloped. People ask: "Is Essence bad?" It is not developed. A thing not developed can be bad—impulsive. When developed it passes into its own intelligence and use. Everything in us not developed—that has never been given a chance to develop—can act in an undifferential way—in a purely violent, impulsive way—and so seem bad in itself. It is not bad in itself. It is simply in prison.

As said, a man, a woman, may get on reasonably to a certain age by means of the comparatively developed function in Personality. Then the need for the recognition of the other sides becomes urgent—not in human-animal types, but in people who have more in them. These other sides require a new education. This Work is called a second education. One of its main ideas is to open up other centres—to become No. 4 Man—Balanced Man. But rigidity easily prevents this. So one has to begin to think about this point. Even after, say, about 30, one has to begin to see other sides of oneself and consider them. An ordinary man is No. 1—in Moving Centre—or No. 2—in Emotional Centre—or No. 3—in Intellectual Centre. In each case he will—or she will—come to the end of that function in middle life and lose the way —lose meaning. Then all sorts of troubles arise. The solution lies in themselves. The Work is about this developing of undeveloped parts. The dark side of us is not only what one refuses to admit about oneself, but what one refuses to use. Each centre is a mind, giving a quite different view. All the views are necessary. So a man must work on not only what he is now in this small one-sided being, and improve *that*, but let in new ways of understanding and new interests. So here we have and may have many things for people to do that in life they would never dream of doing. There is Intellectual Centre, Emotional Centre, Sex Centre, Moving Centre and Instinctive Centre. All should co-operate *successively* in the full man or woman. Then there are no contradictions.

This is a brief note, but if there are enough questions I will return to it. I will add that the Work will make it possible for you to use new growth in yourself, but life will not. Effort—to speak of it again—that is right is to learn something new, understanding that thereby you will open a new source of energy—a new centre. Personality puts a man in prison eventually. He "dies" soon—psychologically. The Work begins to get a man out of prison. But first he must be good at something. That is why for some it is necessary only to work on considering, negative emotions, and non-identifying, and not to try to take up what does not lie in the direction of a person's first early contending with life. The Work helps very much in life. Some intelligence is necessary. Afterwards, it helps in another way. Work is different at different ages.

FURTHER NOTE ON UNDEVELOPED FUNCTIONS

If we had all our ordinary centres developed our entire life would be different. I am not speaking of Higher Centres for, as this Work teaches, Higher Centres are fully developed and working in us all the time. But we cannot hear them. We are non-receptive of their vibrations, our ordinary centres being both in a mess and also not rightly developed. For example, the state of Emotional Centre is such that it is impossible to hear the continual meanings coming from Higher Emotional Centre and this is due to its being choked up with useless negative emotions collected since early life chiefly by imitation.

Let us speak about the Instinctive Centre and what can be developed in connection with it. One function of Instinctive Centre is sensation. What would you conceive to be a development of sensation? Now every function can be directed outwards and inwards—that is, be connected with external attention or internal attention, to use the Work-terms. Here I speak of a development of the function of sensation when turned outwards. Suppose you never notice anything outside you with any kind of precision. You never notice, say, how maps go, or the shapes of different trees, or forms and arrangements of things. You say: "I really cannot remember how it went exactly." In such a case outer sensation is undeveloped. There was an exercise for this—noticing a number of objects for a short time and then describing them in *detail*. This develops attention in sensation, turned to an outer object. That is also why drawing and painting are useful and can refresh one. The use of a rarely-used function always refreshes. The constant use of the same main function exhausts. There is a wealth of new ground in everyone. But people will traverse the same worn paths. For this reason the Work begins with change of thinking. "This Work," it is said, and repeatedly said, "is to make you *think in a new way*. That is the beginning of the whole matter." Now all the ideas of the Work, if learnt and assimilated over a period of years, open up the mind in new directions and alter one's whole way of viewing things. That is, this Work develops a person's thinking. In fact, people learn to think. This general idea stands at the head of all talks about functions and new development of centres. The Work, by changing the thinking, makes it possible for other changes to take place. If one's mind remains just the same, if one's views and prejudices remain just the same, so will one's thoughts remain just the same, and everything in oneself will be just the same. The magic of the Work starts from new ideas for thinking with. The Work begins by shifting the mind from its mechanically set position. Everything else can then shift a little. Yet is it not strange that people always think they can change if they wish. They imagine they are free, but find excuses, not seeing that only a new force—a new set of ideas—coming from another direction, can make it possible for any change to take place. So remember that in all these and subsequent talks about development of centres, it is assumed that the first necessary condition is fulfilled—namely, contact with a conscious teaching that can make it possible to change the mind. I remind you again that the Gospels start from μετάνοια—change of mind.

Let us take emotional perception. Some have this rather than perception through sensation. Emotional perception is connected with the emotional parts of centres, especially with the intellectual part of Emotional Centre. This is very quick and a thought perceived through this part in a second may take many hours to write down. The intellectual part of Emotional Centre is open to Higher Emotional Centre and capable of receiving in a fragmentary way its vibrations of higher meaning. The working or vibrations of a psychic centre become conscious to us as meanings on different levels. Where with a lower centre we see only one meaning, we see many interblending meanings with a Higher Centre. Using our ordinary more or less mechanical parts of centres we see very little meaning. That is why we feel a staleness in experiences. But a flash of higher meaning, which, by work on oneself according to what is taught, is always possible, gives an entirely new range of meanings. We see things in a new way—our problems, and so on. What was ordinary and dull seems transformed. This Work is to *transform* impressions. So try not to see everything as you mechanically do and not to identify with your usual way of taking things. Step aside *from your habit of seeing everything*—first by noticing how you take things daily. Each centre and part of a centre can see the same thing in quite new ways. *Now if all centres were working in us everything could be seen in many different ways.* Take thinking: thinking is a function of Intellectual Centre. Now take feeling: feeling is a function of Emotional Centre—it sees a thing, a problem, quite differently from the way in which thinking does. The two are incompatible—that is, they can never meet. One thinks about a situation: then one should if possible be able to feel about the *same* situation. You will never bring thinking and feeling to the same state or point of agreement. So each centre gives a different interpretation of situations. One has then to learn to use both interpretations in this case. At this point the *individuality* emerges which can take something from thinking and take something from feeling and make some resultant, some harmony, some decision. This is the harmonizing of the centres. But it is only possible by not identifying with *one* centre and its functions and excluding the rest.

Is it not true that at different times the same problem looks different? Do not think this is weakness of so-called will. It is the beginning of growth—the seeing of the same situation from many sides. To follow one function exclusively and its judgments—say, thinking—is to be a slave to one centre—that is, to be one-sided. For that reason the Work speaks of being Balanced Man, No. 4 Man—that is, a man in whom all centres can be called on, with all their different meanings, their different interpretations, of the situation. It is like a guitar with many strings.

To pluck one all the time is not to reach any harmony. A Balanced Man can reach his own harmony—seeing a thing through one centre in this way, through another centre in a different way, and so on—and making a resultant or harmony of all these different viewpoints. This is Balanced Man. But an unbalanced man sees through only one window, one part of a centre. He therefore has no breadth of Being. He is narrow—a man using one tiny function for the whole meaning and interpretation of life. Such a man may seem to have great strength and inflexibility in life. Yet from the Work point of view he is the weakest man, the most mechanical man, the most one-sided man. One-sidedness in the Work is a sign of weakness of Being.

Great Amwell House, March 22, 1947

PERSONAL REALIZATION THAT ONE IS A MACHINE

On one occasion Mr. Ouspensky was speaking with his teacher. He asked: "How can one stop being a machine?" The answer was: "Ah, that is a real question. If you asked such questions more often we might perhaps have got somewhere in our talks. It is possible to stop being a machine, but for that two things are necessary. First, it is necessary to know, to realize, that one is a machine, and second, to know the machine itself and its possibilities. A machine, an actual machine, does not know itself and cannot know itself. If an actual machine were to know it is a machine it would then no longer be a machine." Such conversations were always about the fact that Man as he is, asleep and driven by life, is a machine without seeing it, without realizing it, but that if a man begins to observe himself and to become conscious of himself he can eventually cease to be a machine. In this teaching, this *double* view of Man is always emphasized—mechanical Man and Conscious Man. All those scientific doctrines that teach that Man is a machine are correct. But where they cease to be correct is in not understanding that Man can cease to be a machine and become conscious. As was said, an actual machine, say, an engine, cannot ever know it is a machine, and so must remain the machine that it is until it is worn out and broken up. Scientists may create a robot—but not a conscious one. "There is not a single theory about Man," O. once said, "that has not its truth. The theory that Man is a machine is true on one scale. It is relatively true. But it is not true on all scales. To see all truth, to see the whole truth, or to begin to see what people call the whole truth, is a matter of seeing scale, and this requires a development of consciousness far beyond the so-called waking consciousness that Man takes as full consciousness. In the light of full consciousness what ordinarily appears as contradictory ceases to do so. Things fall into their right places in scale." "What is a sign of a development of consciousness?" I asked him. He said: "As I said, a development of consciousness means the power of being able to think in different categories, to see things on different scales and so to think in different categories." He went on to speak of Man himself being on different scales and how the taking of mankind as all similar, on the same level, was a sign of undeveloped consciousness. As I remember that conversation with him very clearly I will give some of the rest of what he said. Looking across at me he said: "You do not realize different categories of thinking, different scales, different being. You take people too much as the same. You know this Work divides mankind into seven kinds of Man. Men No. 1, 2 and 3 are machines. They are each one-sided in their own way. Man No. 4 is balanced. Men No. 5, 6 and 7 are conscious. As long as you think as you tend to do, you will not be able to understand this. I mean, that unless your thinking changes, your consciousness will not change and you will then tend to take things on the same level, on the same scale, when actually they are utterly different and have no connection." He went on to say how this power of seeing that things are on different scales was essential for the gaining of force from the Work and maintaining the strength of it in oneself. "This," he said, "is what is meant by evaluation of the Work. Unless it is constantly renewed the Work falls down to the ordinary level of life and becomes drained of its force." I called it to myself afterwards the *vertical* feeling of the Work. Scale is vertical—above and below. All Self-Remembering should be accompanied by this feeling. The Ray of Creation, when held in the mind, can by itself produce a change of consciousness, because it is supremely a vertical diagram of scale, of different categories, of different levels. What else can cure us of small emotions and thoughts, which spread over the day like a fungus?

Let us now take the realization that one is a machine. Who yet has begun to suspect that he or she is a machine? It begins when we can take photographs of ourselves. A photograph is not a single observation but a series of observations of oneself over a period. One becomes aware of something separating from what hitherto was the undigested mass of oneself, covered over with advertisements and pictures of oneself. One is startled to catch a glimpse of this photograph which does not correspond with any of the pictures one has used of oneself. Pictures of oneself and photographs of oneself are totally different things. They can never agree. One has possibly an uneasy moment. It is as if a ray of light had got into the dark-room, where one spends one's time in developing these often sad but always agreeable pictures, and thrown an image of something unknown on the wall. "So I am not what I thought," one mutters. Exactly. One now becomes negative in many ways. For every moment of slightly increased consciousness, every experience of seeing oneself as machinery—that is, of awakening —is usually followed by a host of 'I's that wish to keep you in their power and make you fall asleep again. I am not speaking of those moments of awakening that leave you silent, and even terrified.

Now this Work helps you according to where it is in you. It is designed to be in the highest parts of centres. Here it can withstand the attacks of negative 'I's and so a man can awaken eventually if he renews his evaluation often. One must light a fire. It is bad to sleep too long. Is it not true that we all have dangerous negative 'I's, so often not quite detected, not seen for what they are, that seek to make us "feed the Moon"—that is, follow the endless labyrinths of useless suffering? Even the near presence of them can darken everything. So one must work, search and find something able to resist—something actually designed to break the power of them. Life made them and so life cannot break them. That is why Man, seeking to awaken, must have help from another source than life. As a machine formed by life he will have the poison of negative states. All mechanical mankind has this. Only Conscious Man can help him—the man who has given up poisoning himself. All this Work coming from Conscious Man is to do with breaking the wrong power of life over us. The worst power of life is the infection of negative emotions. It is something quite terrible. Have you yet reached that stage when you know it is quite terrible to be negative—even quite quietly, to oneself? But the Work—that is, conscious teaching—is stronger than life. If it were not, we would have no culture on the Earth, no literature, no art, nothing civilized. Now if one wishes to realize one side of one's mechanicalness, observe negative states. This takes a very long time, because one keeps on justifying them. If you justify everything in yourself, all you think and feel and do, of course you will never see that you are a machine. Have you realized this? Seeing that one is a machine therefore demands not justifying. But that means letting go very much vanity and conceit —many pictures, buffers, attitudes, etc. You see, therefore, that it is complicated, one thing depending on another. One cannot just step out of oneself and become a different person. But one thing helps here. No one can endure the idea that he is a machine. That is one reason why we justify ourselves. Scientists say we are machines—but if you say to a scientist that he is a machine, he is annoyed. Now because we have this feeling of dislike of being a machine, we have therefore something in us that does not wish to be a machine. This is an interesting fact. Think about it for yourself. But next time we will speak more of this machine that one is without knowing it—this typical way one has of taking everything and responding to it typically like a machine. It is quite wonderful to realize one need not be this typical life-stamped machinery.

Do you think an ant, if asked, would admit it is a machine?

MECHANICS AND PSYCHOLOGY

Last time a short commentary was read on realizing that one is a machine. It was said that the realization that one is a machine and that one acts mechanically is profoundly distasteful. The illusion that we are fully conscious of everything we do or say is very strong. As a result we justify even our most automatic behaviour. We explain away everything—how we really meant to say this or do that. In this way we avoid seeing in what way we are machines. For if you justify yourself in everything—that is, put yourself in the right—you will never admit that you act quite mechanically and are not properly conscious. Yet sincere, uncritical and direct self-observation will shew you that you are not. This brings about a new emotional state. There are certain emotional experiences that are necessary in the Work and they come in a certain order and arise from contact with it over a sufficient period. These emotional states overcome the emotions belonging to or supporting False Personality. They are painful to the self-conceit and self-valuation in general. It is, of course, the self-conceit that justifies our mechanical behaviour and prevents us from seeing that we are machines. G. once said: "One emotion can only be conquered by another emotion." Now you might not suppose that glimpses of the fact that one is a machine give rise to any useful emotion. On the contrary, you might expect only negative emotions to arise. The strange thing is that this is not the case. The feeling of helplessness and the feeling of nothingness that come from the realization that one is a machine have nothing to do with negative emotions. At the back of negative emotions lie anger, violence, suspicion, bitterness, internal accounts, and so on. But behind the emotion arising from the realization of mechanicalness lies peace. And it is this emotion that can overcome negative emotions.

Now once you begin to feel negative emotions are mechanical—to feel for yourself by inner taste that this is so—you deprive them of a great deal of their power. Inner taste is the first sign of Buried Conscience. Unless we had this deeper emotional perception, we could never feel that negative emotions are undesirable. And if, in addition to this, you can see for yourself that they always *lie* and do not present things in a true way, but twist and distort everything, then you will not suffer from their continual dominion over you as most people do. I mean, of course, provided you do not fall fast asleep. For if you *feel* they are mechanical and *mentally see* they tell lies, then you are using two centres consciously and that makes something very powerful that can resist the great power of mechanicalness. It is these quiet emotions and insights and perceptions of truth that have the greatest healing power and help us against the tyranny of the machine—which all this time we have assumed is oneself. But this machine—oneself—is not really oneself. In the grip of it we lead the most stupid and even idiotic lives. The Work is to awaken us to a new behaviour, apart from this stereotyped machine-behaviour. Remember—one can take everything *in a new way*. Yes, I assure you that you can take every life-situation, every life-event, in an entirely new way—if you see how you have hitherto taken it as a machine. Once this begins in you, you begin to have a *psychology*. An ordinary machine-man has no psychology. G. said once, in so many words: "Why speak of ordinary man asleep as having a psychology?" An ordinary man asleep is a machine, with buffers, attitudes, and pictures of himself, that remain the same. For such a man, a man asleep, a man not conscious, to use the word *psychology* is absurd. He has no *psychology*. He is a machine—and for the study of machines only *mechanics* is necessary. But if a man begins to struggle with his machine, if he begins to see he is asleep in this acquired machinery, then such a man begins to cease to be this machine that life and upbringing has made him and then, in such a case, we might begin to speak of *psychology* and not mere mechanics."

Very often I used to ponder G.'s remark: "What does it mean to have a *psychology* and not merely a machinery?" On one occasion, in speaking to O. about this, he said, in so many words: "You know that all this Work—and all real forms of esoteric teaching—are designed to make it possible for a man to begin to feel the influences of Higher Centres. These centres, the Higher Mental and the Higher Emotional Centres, correspond to what is called Greater Mind. But you must remember that logical thinking, based on the senses turned outward to the external world, does not put us in touch with these Higher Centres, which exist in everyone and are fully developed and send their influences down to us. Our trouble is that we have not any receptive apparatus to hear them with. For that reason one definition of this Work is: "the preparation of lower centres for the reception of the influences coming from Higher Centres. All that this Work teaches practically —namely, self-observation, non-identifying, Self-Remembering, not making internal accounts, not internally considering, not justifying, not going with negative 'I's, not being depressed, making Personality (especially False Personality) passive, separating from negative states, breaking buffers, destroying pictures, seeing ingrained attitudes, and not accepting them, stopping wrong imaginations, in fact, all that this Work teaches, is to purify lower centres for the hearing of Higher Centres. When a man wishes to keep in touch with this Work which really means to keep in touch with any moments of insight or Self-Remembering that he has had, from Higher Centres, then he begins to have a *psychology*."

I then began to understand that when G. spoke of a man who had a psychology and not merely a machinery, he meant a man who had begun to strive to reach a higher level of himself and that all this Work is exactly about this—namely, to get in touch with this higher side in him and find out by personal experience what cuts him off and what increases his contact with this higher level. Then I better understood the Work-phrase used in connection with a question: "What is right and what is wrong?" The answer was and is: "All that puts you more asleep and makes you identify more is wrong: all that awakens you is right."

Great Amwell House, Easter, April 5, 1947

NEUTRALIZING FORCE—TRIADS

On one occasion I was speaking to Mr. Ouspensky and he interrupted me by saying: "Why are you so tragic?" I was naturally very surprised to be told that I spoke tragically. You know now perhaps how people tend to speak about their lives and difficulties tragically, and what this tragic sense can drag people down to. I said I did not think I spoke tragically. He said: "Yes, you do not see it yet. But this is a sign of a bad neutralizing force to speak from. One must learn not to be tragic."

This was long ago, when early meetings were being held at the time in Harley Street. I remember the place, the people, even the expressions and postures, but I got nothing from what he said except resentment. That is to say, I had not become in any way conscious of speaking tragically. All I felt was being hurt and surprised. Certainly, looking back, I see I did speak tragically. Tragedy, speaking tragically, is a very fond self-luxury, that can attach itself to everybody. Everything can be taken in a tragic, dramatic, negative way—that is, one invents oneself, say, as a tragically suffering man or woman. However all this must later on become conscious to oneself. Then it is overcome. For to make a thing *fully* conscious to oneself is to overcome it. It is only the semi-conscious or not-conscious that has power—the not-yet-quite-seen, the not-yet-really acknowledged. I often thought about what Mr. Ouspensky said in regard to it: "Being tragic is a sign of a bad neutralizing force." At the time I understood next to nothing about this term "neutralizing force" and, as I said, I refused to admit that I spoke tragically. In fact, I would then never have admitted I had any self-pity or vanity. Such a state of sleep is possible.

To-night I am going to speak of triads and so therefore of neutralizing force. Let us begin with the general idea of triads as the Work teaches. The Work teaches that every *manifestation* is the result of 3 forces, active, passive and neutralizing. For any *one* manifestation to take place, *three* forces are necessary. No manifestation can take place without the co-operation of 3 forces. Everything that manifests itself is due to *three* forces. We see a manifestation and think it is one thing. But it is not due to one thing but to three things—that is, 3 forces, meeting at a point, which produce the manifestation. Therefore, every manifestation is a complex thing—not one thing, but *three* things in a certain balance.

Now in order to understand as simply as possible how every manifestation is the result of 3 forces and not one force, let us begin with the idea that you want something and let us call the wanting of something active force. Now simply wanting something will not lead to your having it. This fact makes many people early sick at heart. They say "if only", and so on, and become negative. The world is full of imbeciles of this kind who simply want something and, not getting it, become sick-hearted and so tragic. Now if you want something, you have to calculate on the existence of 2nd force, or passive force, which is the force of resistance to what you perhaps quite simply and innocently want and expect to be given. This 2nd force meets everything that you *want* at every turn, at every point. So the Work teaches that if you want something—if you make an aim, say—you must calculate this 2nd force which will at once oppose what you want, what you aim at. You have, say, a phantasy, the idea that you will be a wonderful woman, adored by every man, or a wonderful man, adored by every woman, and so on. Yes, in phantasy this is easy. People are absorbed in similar phantasies all day long. But to make phantasy equal to reality takes time and effort. Why? Because in phantasies there is no 2nd force, or very little, let us say, for here something else comes in that is very interesting. I will say here simply that no phantasies are quite satisfactory and 2nd force appears in many ways.

Now in reality, if you want something, you will inevitably have to meet the opposing force to what you want—that is, 2nd force or force of resistance to what you want—and contend with it. Let us say that you wish to make everyone converted to your own idea of life and to make them think as you do. Take this as first or active force. You advance into life and meet with perhaps indifference or derision or criticism or contempt. You become disappointed or tragic or full of self-pity. Why? Because you have not calculated the effects of 2nd force. What is 2nd force here? Well, you can see what it is. People are not interested, they do not believe you, they are satisfied with what they have, so other people are 2nd force. So you fail and become tragic, misunderstood, and so on. Yes, but why? Because you want something and do not see how 2nd force will inevitably appear and inevitably oppose what you want. People call it the devil. But it is the Trinity—the 3 forces at work—active, passive and neutralizing.

Now the relationship between 1st and 2nd force is established by the nature and quality of 3rd force. The 3rd force brings the 1st and 2nd forces into connection and so it is called sometimes connecting force. You will now see why O. said to me that "speaking tragically is a sign of a bad neutralizing force." A bad neutralizing force will relate me badly to 2nd force—to all that is opposed to what I want. Everything will then overcome me.

When active force—and here we are calling it *what you want*—has a bad or wrong neutralizing force with the force of the opposition—that is, 2nd force—then 2nd force becomes active force. The whole triad is reversed. The two forces, active and passive, reverse their rôles. Instead of using 2nd force through right or clever connecting force, to work out practically the end or aim contained in active force, the triad reverses, and opposing force becomes triumphant—that is, it turns into active force. Now this can happen all the time to everyone because for one reason people want what is impossible save in phantasy. We are told in this Work not to make too many requirements. If you make many requirements then you will, in so many words, be up against life all the time—that is, up against that aspect of life which is 2nd or opposing force. You will never learn anything, never gain by experience, because there is no effort to deal cleverly with 2nd force.

You will see now that second force is necessary for the development of individuality—that is, how you individually and from yourself deal with the inevitable 2nd force. If you deal cleverly with this 2nd force it will give you results and, instead of being simply a blind, opposing force, will become gradually what you want. You do not instantly become negative when opposed. You try this way and that, and gradually this formidable opposition yields and becomes what you want—or, let us say, rather, what is possible in your wanting. Then active force as what you want—and let us bring in here the idea of what you will—by modifying itself attains through a right neutralizing force its aim. G. said: "Patience is the Mother of Will." That is, Will, passing through patience as 3rd force, attains what it wants. But to will, to want, blindly, is not clever, and leads only into a hard, uncompromising force of opposition—that is, into a reversal of the triad, and so to negative states. In the Gospels Christ spoke a great deal about *cleverness* in dealing with life and its situations. To-night we will go no further but later on return to this subject—namely, a clever neutralizing force.

Great Amwell House, April 12, 1947

ACCIDENT AND FATE

From one point of view the Personality can be thought of as the outer man and the Essence as the inner man. We know that in the growth of a child Personality gradually surrounds active Essence and becomes active, while Essence becomes passive. This first state of development usually persists throughout life and is sufficient for life-purposes. But a further development is possible and it is of this further development that esotericism always speaks, and that this system speaks.

It consists in a *reversal*. In fragments of past literature coming from schools connected with fully developed—that is, conscious Man—you will often find references to some reversal that is necessary before Man reaches full development. Man adjusted to life, Man with Personality active and grown, and Essence passive and ungrown, is not yet a fully developed Man according to esoteric teaching. A great deal of confusion arises in people's minds because this idea is not grasped distinctly. Life develops Man up to a point, but cannot bring about this reversal in him that leads to his further and full development.

In the brief condensed language of this system the reversal is formulated as consisting in making Personality passive and Essence active. Now education does not bring about this reversal. Education increases Personality and so moves Man further and further away from his Essence. Simple folk can live closer to Essence. It might be said that to-day the world is suffering from a wrong, one-sided development of Personality. If by magic or dire stress everyone became simpler, it might seem like reversal. But the reversal spoken of in esoteric literature, say in the Gospels, where it is called re-birth, is only brought about internally in a man's own experience with himself and not through a change of circumstances *outside* him.

You must remember that your usual life and its ambitions and interests can be taken away from you and if you have nothing else you feel indeed lost. For example, in illness force *may* be drained from the Personality and the quality of Essence appear. Personality is the machine through which you adapt to life and feel its influences and attractions. We may suddenly by illness be faced with another kind of life. Yes, but what kind? O. said some illnesses were to open something in us that health and success could not. If we already have a slight internal life apart from our outer life we have something to fall back on. I said that from one point of view Personality can be thought of as the outer man and Essence as the inner man. If a man is only developed in the outer side and has no inner development he is called in the Work a machine driven by outer life and its turning wheel of changing circumstances. Yet the Work also teaches that Man was created a self-developing organism and that full development consists in a development of Essence, or the internal man, further upon the first development of the Personality or outer man, which gives a relation to external life and its affairs. All esoteric teaching, such as that found in fragments in the Gospels, is clearly about the development of the internal man. Very little is said about the development of the external man, the business man, the professional man, etc. It is the second development that is emphasized. But, as was said, people mix up the two. Christ did not say he came to make everything nice and satisfactory on this Earth. He said: "Think not that I came to send peace on the Earth: I came not to send peace, but a sword." (*Matt.* X 34.) The conditions of the second development—the reversal or re-birth—are the important things. A smug, settled earth without acute internal struggle

1018

and searchings and contradictions on all sides could hardly be expected to produce the conditions for the second development which is internal, individual, and a matter of one's own most real and deepest thoughts and essential feelings.

Yet few people think much about what their existence means save in terms of their external man and his needs. Now to think about one's life from the internal man is a quite different thing from thinking about it from the external man. You all know, whether perhaps of yourself or others, how it is possible to have a somewhat pious and religious, even holy, external side and perform various acts to give a good impression, and yet in the internal side there is nothing whatever that corresponds. In such a person—that is, in short, in all of us—there is an almost total severance between the outer and inner man: and the outer dominates the inner. It is the inner man developed who should dominate the outer man. If a man acts sincerely from himself the case is different.

Now as long as a man's outer side or Personality is active and takes the lead, especially from the idea that it *can do*, the man is under the Law of Accident. That is, anything, however meaningless, can happen to him. When the inner man or essential man becomes active he is under the Law of Fate and then what happens is significant for him. Personality is under the Law of Accident: Essence is under the Law of Fate. This is expressed in the Work by saying that Essence is (to begin with) under the Laws of the Planetary World—that is, 24 laws—and that Personality is under the Law of the Earth—that is, 48 laws—and it is added that False Personality is under the Laws of the Moon—that is, 96 laws. There is, therefore, a point in us called Essence, that is under fewer laws than all that belongs to Personality or False Personality. It is to become more conscious in this point that we work on ourselves and our inner life. When a man remembers himself, he is under 24 laws. When he is asleep in negative emotions, etc., he is under 48 or 96 laws.

Great Amwell House, April 19, 1947

ON PSYCHOLOGICAL THINKING

When people no longer believe in Greater Mind and the existence of any form of knowledge and truth higher than materialism and what is evident to the senses, they are mentally shut. One characteristic of a shut mind is the absence of Magnetic Centre. In that case, no influences, apart from those of the life of the world, can be received, because then the first necessary receptive apparatus is missing. The mentally defective person, in this sense, cannot either let a ray of light into his inner darkness or ever change the relationship between

Personality and Essence. Life must remain his Neutralizing Force. That is, no reversal within him can take place. He remains, to use a phrase of the Work, an *unfinished house*.

Now the Work says that we must create our lives. It also says repeatedly that its teaching is to make us think for ourselves. Can we suppose then that we can create our own lives if we have never thought for ourselves? Everyone on reflection can see that the human mind, by its mechanical way of working, contributes to its own early enslavement. That is, it very easily forms acquired habits of thought, associations, attitudes, borrowed beliefs, opinions, and so on. So it fixes itself at an early age unless impressions are taken in voluntarily.

A person fixed in this way does not think for himself and cannot therefore create his own life. If we follow general views and standards and conventional family or racial opinions, etc., we do not create our own lives. Life creates our lives. If everyone had reached his inner goal and had become conscious in Real 'I' instead of in the many acquired 'I's of Personality then he would have created his life. He would be a house completed—or, as the Work puts it quite simply, he would be a *Man* and not a machine. To-day we can watch on all sides machines trying *to do*, not men trying to do. But it is better to observe the continual struggle in oneself between more mechanical and more conscious 'I's. More conscious 'I's—that is, 'I's that wish to grow, to remember, to understand for themselves and form Deputy-Steward, are kept down, often sternly, by mechanical or dead 'I's with old voices, corpses in one's Time-Body.

It is a mistake to sacrifice psychological thinking. It is an ever-repeating tragedy in the world of sleeping humanity that psychological understanding is put to death by logical and literal thinking. This is one meaning of the crucifixion. You can see all through the Gospels that Christ was teaching *psychological thinking*, something new. That was why he used parables and not commandments of stone. John the Baptist could not understand him because he was of the old literal, dogmatic, harsh, merciless school, and so clad in camel's hair and leather—for what you are clad in means, in psychological language, what truth you wear, what your mind wears. Now no one can create his own life unless he can reach the level of psychological thinking. Four mind-levels are given in the Work:

Greater Mind
Psychological Thinking
Logical Thinking
A-logical Thinking (e.g. superstition)

In many ancient symbolic drawings of Man, he is first represented as lying asleep on the ground, horizontal. At the last, through the operation of a Third Force different from life, he is represented as standing up with his eyes open. But to stand on one's feet and to awaken—that is long work, and, if a man cannot even begin to think psychologically, it will be impossible. He will insist on everything being put down for him in black and white so that the logical formatory mind can get hold of it. He will not jump to catch the rope overhead but will make requirements. But no one has ever reached a higher level of Being by means of that interpretation of one's meaning on Earth given by the formatory centre. One might almost say the reverse—namely, that formatory thinking, so much taught and emphasized to-day, can pull down the level of Being. What does psychological thinking mean? In the first place it has three forces in it, while formatory logical thinking has two. In the second place, it is not seated in the moving parts of centres, but in the higher divisions, turned towards Higher Centres themselves.

To free ourselves from the laws we are under on this planet inevitably, a man, a woman, must *think differently*. Yes, think differently from all ordinary life-thinking. It is so easy just to think as everyone thinks. Mob-thinking is easy, whatever your social mob is. But to think for yourself, to begin to create your life, is only possible through utterly new ideas. This is the function of esoteric knowledge—to make a man think in a new way. Mere reaction to life-thinking is useless. To become a Radical in opposition to a Tory, etc., etc., is not thinking in a new way. Merely to go against everything your parents taught you is not thinking in a new way. It is life-thinking—pendulum-thinking—in terms of the opposites that the pendulum is always ticking between. That is not new thinking, nor can it produce in us ideas and thoughts that can create our lives—that is, lead to the Master—that is, Real 'I'— entering the carriage and telling the Driver where to go.

Now the idea of the Conscious Circle of Humanity, the idea of Greater Mind, or, to put it in terms of the Gospels, the Kingdom of Heaven, that is a new idea belonging to creating one's life. Connected with this, and oppositely, the idea that Man is asleep on this planet and can do nothing unless he awakens—that he is definitely hypnotized —is a new idea. Again, the idea that one has no Real 'I' is a new idea. The idea that Man—that is, you—is not properly conscious, the idea of being identified and so asleep, and all the teaching connected with it, the idea that Man—that is, you—is governed by negative emotion— all this is knowledge that really makes a person with Magnetic Centre begin to think in a new way—that is, it leads to μετανοια—change of mind. This makes the possibility of creating one's life, and only such ideas, coming from a higher level of Being, can alter us and create a new person. That is, only contact with the 3rd Force of the Work— the influences coming from Conscious Man, from Greater Mind, and thinking from the ideas given by them, can enable a person to *create* his life.

Now the ideas, the knowledge, coming from Greater Mind, cannot be understood logically. On that level they are split into opposites, into contradictions. Logically a thing is either right or wrong: psychologically it can be either right or wrong *relatively*. Relative thinking, in the Work-sense, means thinking of the Part in relation to the Whole.

To think *relatively*, it is said, one must know something of All before one can think of a detail, a part. The Ray of Creation, for example, gives us our Earth in relation to All—to the whole Ray—and this at once alters our thought of the Earth.

Now to think of yourself from yourself is one thing, but to think of yourself from what the Work teaches is another thing. To think of yourself from what the Work teaches is to begin to think psychologically.

Great Amwell House, April 29, 1947

FURTHER NOTE ON PSYCHOLOGICAL THINKING

Let us try to understand again what the Work means by psychological thinking and find examples. In his introduction to his last book O. says that logically machine-guns are excellent, but psychologically they are wrong. Nowadays we might easily apply this idea to atom-bombs. Logically, they are excellent for totally annihilating the enemy, but psychologically they are all wrong. Now what does this mean? Can you see what is meant? Let us reflect. To-day war is openly avowed to be total. Everything that remains human and decent in war, we are told, must be eliminated. Total war is total destruction, without mercy or pity. Logically, this is an excellent argument. If, they say, you are going to have war, let it be total war. Let us invent machines by our logical science that will, at one instant, destroy a continent. And some add that this is the only way to end war.

Now one object of the Work is to teach us psychological thinking, and *one* out of many aspects of the teaching in this respect is about *external considering*. Let us think about what external considering means. It means, in a word, putting yourself in the position of another person. In the Gospels it is called "love of neighbour"—a phrase perhaps which does not to-day conduct much meaning, but which if properly translated, would mean "be conscious of your neighbour"—for what is translated as "love" is very close to the supreme idea of this Work—namely, to become more conscious, to enlarge our consciousness—in fact, to become Conscious Man. The *Conscious* Circle of Humanity—as the Work terms it—is composed of people who, in comparison with us, are fully conscious. To be fully conscious implies, amongst many things, to be conscious of oneself and of the other person. External considering means to be conscious *in* the other person—to put your consciousness, so to speak, into the other person—so that you see *from him* what he feels *about you*. That is, you can see, let us say, why he dislikes you. But that is impossible unless you have become conscious of yourself. By that means one sees oneself in others and others in oneself. This ends violence. And so it ends mass-killing by machines. O. once said that

1022

machines make war. He said it is as if they insist on being used and Man, being asleep, and having no real will, has to obey their will to be used. The idea is worth thinking about—that is, if you have any time to think for yourself in the increasingly hurried stress of life. The idea, of course, belongs to the great idea of the Work that Man himself is a machine and can do nothing, unless he reaches a higher level of consciousness and comes under better influences and so is helped. Now to put yourself completely in another person's situation, with conscious knowledge of yourself as a starting-point, is one example of thinking psychologically. You will lay aside the machine-guns. Violence only breeds violence. Consciousness takes away the *desire* for violence, for how can you be violent with, as it were, yourself—that is, when you recognize that the other person is yourself and has the same fears and pain? This is by way of commentary and I put as an example of *psychological thinking*, based on this remark of O., that the use of machine-guns is no doubt right on the logical level but does not belong to the level of psychological thinking and is not right on that level—that is, a man who thinks on the psychological level cannot use them, just like that, or any other mass-destructive machinery.

Now no psychological thinking is possible if there is no belief in Greater Mind. Let us put the different categories of thinking on the board again, one below another. First comes Greater Mind. This mind is beyond our mind. It thinks not only differently but in an *entirely* different way. Now we can guess one way it thinks—namely, it thinks always *relatively*. That is, when we, with our scarcely conscious minds, think of *one* thing, of *a* thing, separate from anything else, Greater Mind thinks of that one thing in relation to the whole thing of which it is a part. Now our thinking, to take one example, can scarcely get beyond our national country. The existence of the world as a whole, of which our country is a small part, and of our country as a small part of the whole world, does not enter consciousness as a *sine qua non* of even beginning to think rightly in this respect. "In relative thinking", O. said, "it is necessary to know something of the whole before one can think rightly of the part. This is the right definition of relative thinking and it is what I mean when I speak of relative thinking to you." He added that only a little may be known of the *whole*, and far more of the part, but that, unless the two were thought of in relation to one another, the thinking would be wrong. He observed that we live in a related Universe—a Universe in which everything is related with everything else and everything influences everything else, and nothing can be taken separately, isolated from the rest. It is just the same, he said, with the body. Not a single part of the body is isolated, a thing by itself. To understand a small part of the body, such as the thumb, something must be known of the whole body, and the part thought of in relation to the whole. First the thumb has to be thought of in relation to the hand, and to the four fingers which are useless without the thumb, and so to the arm, etc. We can therefore be sure that *Greater Mind*,

1023

although its mode of thinking is quite different from ours and it is another kind of mind altogether, always thinks relatively and that, to it, everything is seen to be related to everything else. Again, we may be sure that Greater Mind, thinking relatively, can be conscious in all 3 forces, and certainly in 2nd force, and calculate when and how it will appear if such-and-such a thing is done. Many things, therefore, that mechanical man reacts to without consciousness, must appear sheer insanity to Greater Mind. In short, our wisdom must appear sheer folly. So it is said in sacred writings: "For the wisdom of this world is foolishness with God"—God meaning Greater Mind.

Now we shall speak for a moment of Higher Centres, and Greater Mind, and fully Conscious Man together. You have heard that the language of Higher Centres is not logical language, because it has *three* forces in it and cannot be understood at the logical level. The ideas of Higher Centres do not fall on lower centres but are altered. This is one reason why *C* influences—coming direct from Higher Centres or Conscious Man—are inevitably distorted in passing into life and so become *B* influences. Think about this for yourselves and see why this must be so. Higher Centres do not think in terms of Yes-or-No: they do not think from opposites as does the formatory or logical mind. Their range of thinking is of another order in which *there are no* contradictions. To make contact with Greater Mind, a man must understand that his logical formatory thinking will prevent him. A logical man *cannot* understand this Work. He must "jump" from that formatory arguing level and catch "the rope suspended above his head." He must first begin to distinguish between psychological meaning and logical meaning. For example, when it says in the Lord's Prayer: "Give us this day our daily bread," the logical thinking takes this as literal bread. But it does not mean literal bread. Notice that the prayer begins with the *idea* of Greater Mind—namely, "Our Father in Heaven". The bread prayed for is meaning from Greater Mind. In the Greek the word translated as "daily" is a word not used anywhere else which has nothing to do with the baker delivering bread every day. Now if a person begins to see the world and himself in the light of esoteric teaching—that is, in the light of this Work—he begins to awaken. Then he prays for that which will help him to awaken and keep him awake daily. Now you understand that in the above example logical, literal thinking will take "Bread" as bread. If there be a God it is surely perfectly logical to ask him for daily, physical bread. The point is that the prayer does not mean this. It means something *on a different level* that can only be understood by psychological thinking and you will see that it is all connected with the general idea of the Ray of Creation, of Greater Mind, of the Conscious Circle of Humanity, of Man awakening and getting in touch with higher forces that will help him to undergo his destined internal development. In other words, praying for his so-called daily bread means praying for the force, the influences, that will enable the spirit of Man to awaken and open his eyes and stand upright on his feet on this Earth where everyone is asleep and spiritually horizontal and yet imagines he can do. That implies that he imagines he knows what right and wrong is and can ensure it. I will end this brief commentary by saying that another example of psychological thinking is concealed in this statement: "Whatever keeps you awake is right: whatever puts you to sleep is wrong." This gives a new idea of right and wrong—a psychological idea, not a literal one.

Great Amwell House, May 3, 1947

A NOTE ON EXTERNAL CONSIDERING

A quite natural question was asked at one of the sub-groups in connection with the last paper: "Can external considering be entirely divorced from internal considering?"

External considering is always conscious. It is anti-mechanical and so requires conscious effort. Internal considering is always mechanical and so effortless—that is, not conscious, but the work of the machine. To put yourself consciously in the position of another person and see *yourself in him* and *him in yourself* is a conscious act requiring conscious effort. Internal considering goes by itself and is mechanical. Just cheering up a person who is miserable is ordinary human and reasonable behaviour, but if it is a question of the Work—and here the Second Line of Work comes in—you have to listen to the person internally and find the corresponding thing in yourself—that is, to reflect the person in yourself as by a mirror, finding the same thing in yourself and not denying it, and then the other person will undergo a change of state without your saying anything. You do not blame but accept and by doing this you make room for the other person to alter. We have, in the Second Line, to make room for others. This is quite different from helping the person in the ordinary sense, which is simply the blind leading the blind. External considering demands listening internally and finding the same thing in yourself—that is, if you have sufficient self-observation and self-knowledge. You cannot influence others if you do not know the other person in yourself.

External considering is seeing the state of a person and remembering that you were in that state, because in the Work everyone passes through the same states as, say, an older, intelligent person has passed through and remembers. Intelligence means seeing the truth of a thing. As I implied, the mere finding in yourself of this state of the other person, without saying anything, will help the other person. External considering is a deep internal act and is based on an increase of conscious-

1025

ness—that is, on love—for all real love is consciousness of another person's difficulties through finding the same difficulties in yourself. Conscious love is not blind. This makes a new neutralizing force—a Work-force. So in a sense it is done in silence—internally. It can be done, even if you are not in the presence of the other person, by inner work and by always finding the same state in yourself for which you might tend to blame the other person and perhaps nobly try not to, and call it self-sacrifice. This is useless suffering. But when you are externally considering, which is inner, you must not shew it outwardly —otherwise it becomes condescension and so goes into False Personality. To imagine *you*, as you are, can help another is always condescension. That is, it is based on the idea that you know better. You can, by sitting in your room and doing this inner work of external considering, this consciousness of your Work-neighbour, actually change the state of that person at a distance, but only by becoming conscious of the same state in yourself and so seeing him or her in yourself. So you climb down, as it were, and do not feel superior.

People will say: "Why is external considering called *external* and internal considering called *internal*, if the act of external considering is internal? " Reflect for a moment, and you will plainly see why. In external considering you put yourself in the position of an external person, an outer object—namely, the other person. In internal considering you think only of yourself. The first is objective, the second is subjective. We do not see people objectively: we see them subjectively —that is, as we imagine or expect them to be. We all do violence to one another by not realizing this. In this sense, people can be mutually destructive of one another.

Now the 4th State of Consciousness is called Objective Conscious ness. The four States of Consciousness as given by this Work are:

4   State of Objective Consciousness
3   State of Self-Remembering
2   State of So-called Waking Consciousness
1   State of literal Sleep—physical Sleep

These are the 4 States or Levels of Consciousness as given by the Work and we first strive to reach level No. 3. To reach State No. 4 a man must pass through State No. 3—otherwise he will get nothing, recall nothing of a sudden touching of State No. 4. What can we understand by State No. 4—that is, the State of Objective Conscious-ness? The first answer is that in this state we see things as they really are. But this definition does not satisfy the mind. Naturally it cannot, because no one can describe a higher state of consciousness to another person who has never touched it. Unless we have touched the state of Objective Consciousness we cannot apprehend it, just as a man sensible of a three-dimensional world cannot apprehend how things would be in a four, five or six-dimensional world. For instance, he cannot appre-hend the idea of his Time-Body—that is, that all his past life is living. But he can begin to understand, however vaguely, what Objective

Consciousness *might* mean. Take what was said: "It is seeing what things really are." The best analogy is a mirror. A good mirror faithfully reflects the outer scene. It distorts nothing. It is not jealous. In a word, it has no subjectivity. It shews you just what you look like. People say that a mirror does not lie. Now if we could squeeze out our sentimentality, our imaginations based on False Personality, our negative, subjective states, our so-called ideals and a thousand and one other things, including our lovely pictures of ourselves, ingrained hostile attitudes, typical mechanical reactions, buffers, prejudices, vanities, and, in short, all the Work teaches us to work against and separate from, then we are approaching the state of seeing things as they are. Now to see another as he or she is demands one absolutely necessary preliminary —namely, the necessity of seeing what oneself is like. The more conscious you are of yourself, of what you are like, the more will you see others objectively. For self-knowledge, gained through the practice of self-observation over a long time—in fact, all one's life, after one meets the Work—leads to you yourself becoming more and more objective to yourself. The import of self-observation is to make you an increasing *object* to yourself—that is, to make this thing to which you have been a slave, this thing you have accepted as a whole without question— namely, "yourself"—more and more objective. If I see something in myself it is no longer me—that is, subjective—but becomes an object to me—a thing separate that I can see as distinct from what I regarded as myself. The part of you that begins to see yourself as an object retreats inwardly until finally it leads to Real 'I' which lies inward and is your real self and is unobservable—that is, it is an experience that cannot be further made objective or analyzed. It becomes close to but not actually "I am that I am". Then a man is master of himself and is no longer in multiplicity but in unity. This state is very far. But it is quite real, quite true.

This idea is expressed in the Work-diagram that begins with Observing 'I' and leads up to Master. Let us look once more at the diagram:

> Master. Real 'I'
> Steward
> Deputy-Steward
> Observing 'I'

One clear thing that this diagram indicates is that unless a man or woman establishes Observing 'I' in themselves nothing can take place in regard to their full development—which is the passage from the state of many contradictory 'I's that belong to the so-called Waking State of Consciousness, upwards towards the attainment of Real 'I', which is, as it were, awaiting oneself. But taking what is not oneself as oneself can only lead to endless sleep and negative states. So a man who attains to his real goal—namely, becoming conscious in Real 'I'—is objectively conscious—that is, he attains the 4th State of Consciousness.

Let me quote now in brief what O. said about the preliminary state which leads to Objective Consciousness. In his experiments on himself, quoted in "Experimental Mysticism", he says he reached a state in which the ordinary sense of 'I' vanished. He says: "I understood that with the usual sensation of 'I' all usual troubles, cares and anxieties are connected. Therefore, when 'I' disappears, all troubles and cares and anxieties disappear . . . I saw how terrible it is to take on ourselves this idea of 'I' and bring in this idea of 'I' into everything we do—as if we all called ourselves God. I felt then that only God could call himself 'I' ".

Now the more you make yourself objective to yourself the more you lose the ordinary, usual, worrying feeling of 'I'. This is a sign that one is moving towards a different level of consciousness, the highest of which is Objective Consciousness.

Great Amwell House, May 10, 1947

THE BODY AND THE DIFFERENT MINDS THAT ACT ON IT

I

On one occasion G. said that amongst the many illusions which influence us deeply and keep us in that remarkable daily state of consciousness, which we take for granted as full consciousness and which the Work calls sleep or so-called waking consciousness, is the illusion that we have *one mind*. We call the functions of this mind conscious. Imagining thus that we have one mind and that the functions of this mind are conscious, we completely misunderstand ourselves and therefore completely misunderstand everyone else. When this teaching was first given it was said: "I want to explain to you that the activity of the human machine—that is, of the physical body—is controlled not by one but by several *minds*, entirely independent of each other, having separate functions and spheres in which they manifest themselves. This must be understood first of all, because unless this is understood nothing else can be understood." Now when I first heard these words I realized that hitherto I had always thought that we possessed only one mind. It had not occurred to me, for example, that what we call feelings are also the manifestation of a mind different from that which thinks, and that feelings have a cognitive value—that is to say, feelings have knowledge value. Or, put in another way, you may *know* something through a feeling which you cannot know through a thought—that is, through the thinking mind

To *know* with what we ordinarily call the mind and to know with the feelings are two totally different kinds of *knowing*. Now a man who trusts only *that* mind called the thinking or intellectual mind can form many intellectual theories as to what is absolutely right or wrong. But the conclusions of the intellectual mind may be completely contradicted by that mind whose functions belong to feeling. Intellectually, I may prove to myself that such and such a thing or viewpoint is right. But when I am conscious of any feeling about the matter I may be not quite so sure and I must modify the working of one mind by the working of another mind, called feeling. You can see the strength of the illusion that we have only *one* mind on every side to-day.

Now let us take the diagram of the different minds in Man that can at different times control the human machine—that is, the body, which is the visible apparatus for the invisible minds and so the visible representation of the different minds by means of sense-perceived speech, intonation, movement, expression, posture and action, etc. Man, in the Work, is taken as a 3-storey house:

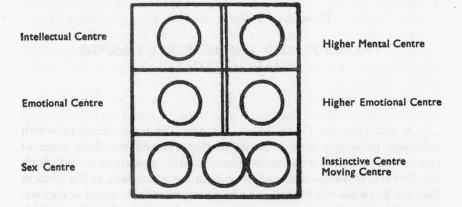

Intellectual Centre — Higher Mental Centre

Emotional Centre — Higher Emotional Centre

Sex Centre — Instinctive Centre / Moving Centre

You will see that in each storey of Man's 3-storey house he has different centres. Now each centre is *a different mind*. Each centre, a different mind, views the same problem quite differently. Each centre is a mind that sees the same thing in a different way. On one occasion, in speaking of this, Mr. Ouspensky said, in so many words: "Man is like a house with windows opening on to different sides. You look through a window facing south, and then through a window facing north, and then east, and then west. You believe at first that only the view of things that you get from looking south can be true—the truth as we call it. But looking through a window giving on the north you see a quite different aspect and then think that must be the truth, and so on. Actually, a balanced man, who can use all ordinary centres, can see as it were out of all windows. He realizes the truth as that which is transmitted severally from each window and then joined into a whole view by 'remembering'". He added later that it also might be compared with walking round a house. One sees first one side, then the other and so on—and so gains a whole idea of the house, not a one-sided view of it.

As you know, the Work teaches that there are three kinds of Mechanical Man—that is, Man asleep and serving nature. The first has his centre of gravity in Instinctive and Moving Centre and he is called No. 1 Man. The second has his centre of gravity in Emotional Centre and he is called No. 2 Man. The third has his centre of gravity in the Intellectual Centre and he is called No. 3 Man. Man in the Work is divided into different categories. No. 1, No. 2, No. 3 men are all *one-sided*—and so see everything subjectively and always quarrel with one another. To-day you see the tragedy of mechanical, one-sided men trying to understand each other and come to agreement. One is looking at the view, say, from the south window, the next from the north window, and so on. How can they agree? Each uses *one* mind only and so sees everything differently from the others. Now the development of Man—the inner possible development that all esoteric teaching is about—can begin with the further development of only *one* centre. No. 1 Man—Instinct-Moving Man—can undergo a severe discipline in order to get Will over the Instinctive and Moving Centres. This, the Work calls "The Way of Fakir". No. 2 Man—Emotional Man—can be subjected to severe discipline in order to get Will over his emotions. This is called "Way of Monk". No. 3 Man can undergo severe training to control Intellectual Centre. This is called in the Work "Yogi-Way".

These are the 3 Ways. But there is a 4th Way. This Work—this teaching—is about the 4th Way. What is one characteristic—out of many—of the 4th Way? In the 4th Way, which is rarely met with and enters the world only before some crisis is impending, work is done on all centres at the same time. That is, a man in the 4th Way seeks to reach the level of Balanced Man or No. 4 Man. He seeks to use and learn how to control not one centre but three centres—namely, Intellectual Centre, Emotional Centre and Instinct-Moving Centre. For the moment let us leave the question of the control of Sex Centre, save that it can be said that without becoming conscious in the three other centres, realizing what they need and what they demand in the way of force, it remains impossible to understand how to relate the manifestations of Sex Centre rightly. I speak from the angle of balancing of forces. One centre can take too much force.

We have, then, briefly put, a system of teaching called the Work that begins with the study and observation of the 3 centres, Intellectual, Emotional and Instinct-Moving. Now the Work as taught so far begins with the observation of the thoughts and the emotions or feelings as quite distinct. One of the first things taught is that a man, a woman, must observe that different centres exist in them and that they are not one person. They must begin by *self-observation* to become conscious of their thoughts *and* of their feelings and know distinctly whether they are thinking or feeling. To merely feel everything, when it is necessary to think, is wrong. Merely to think when one should also feel is wrong. Merely to think and feel without corresponding action from Moving Centre is wrong. Merely to act without thought or feeling is wrong. We seek in this Work to live more consciously and to live more consciously requires internal self-observation which leads to self-knowledge. One must first be more conscious of oneself—of what one is like. Do you always feel instead of thinking, or vice versa? To realize by internal observation and self-awareness that one is not *one* mind, but, to begin with, *three* minds, changes our self-sufficient, taken-for-granted view of ourselves—that is, begins to awaken us. The balancing of all the different viewpoints, of the different minds, begins the Work of *transformation of Being. It begins with not identifying with one point of view*, with *one* mind, with *one centre*. This is difficult work—over a long period. But it leads in the real, inborn direction of Man—namely, inner development.

As you know, the Work teaches that Man is an experiment on this planet. He was created a *self-developing* organism, as distinguished from the animals and plants which are given their lives *via* the mind of Instinctive Centre. Man as a 3-storey being has a certain inner task, which has been spoken of in different forms, religious or otherwise, from the beginning of history. This inner task is inner development. This Work, which cannot be given in a nut-shell, is about what to do, what efforts are necessary, what is allowed in respect of this inner possibility destined-by-Creation, where a man, following by practice the teaching of this Work from sincere inner evaluation—that is, love of it—eventually can reach the state where the two Higher Centres or minds begin to influence him directly and then he passes under a control that fulfils his inborn meaning, and no longer serves nature blindly, as does sleeping humanity. He is then awake.

Now in this brief commentary let me add that to awaken from sleep: (1) a man, a woman, must realize that they are asleep and that they do not remember themselves, and (2) they must see that the state of their Emotional Centre is very bad—that is, that they know little else emotionally than *negative* emotions—that is, unhappy, jealous, bitter or simply unpleasant feelings. About the practice of *Self-Remembering* much has been said and will be said. The purification of the ordinary state of the Emotional Centre—that is, the separation from negative states of feeling and many associable unpleasant things—this again is a subject in the teaching of this Work, which, however often talked about, must become so real a fact, so genuine a task for everyone connected with me, that it can eventually be remembered and understood without constant reminders. No inner development, no inner attainment to Real 'I', is possible unless a man, a woman, practises Self-Remembering and non-identifying with negative states. If people do neither, they become in time useless to this Work. Remember that in this Work "Time is measured."

THE BODY AND THE DIFFERENT MINDS
THAT ACT ON IT

II

Last time when we were speaking of the different minds that can control the physical body of Man, the following passage was read: "I want to explain to you that the activity of the human machine—that is, of the physical body—is controlled not by one mind but by several minds, entirely independent of each other and having special functions and spheres in which they manifest themselves. This must be understood first, because, unless this is understood, nothing else can be understood." Now, as I said, when I heard this the first time I realized that I had always thought we had only one mind and probably you think the same. That is, you conceive of yourself having one mind controlling the body and have never thought that you have more. Actually, you have seven minds. These minds act through the seven centres in Man and can control the working of the physical body. First we have five, so to speak, ordinary minds, acting through the five ordinary centres:

Intellectual Mind acting via Intellectual Centre,
Emotional Mind acting via Emotional Centre,
Sex Mind acting via Sex Centre,
Moving Mind acting via Moving Centre,
Instinctive Mind acting via Instinctive Centre.

And second, we have two super-minds with which we are not in touch, save under exceptional circumstances when Personality is passive. These minds are:

Higher Emotional Mind acting via Higher Emotional Centre,
Higher Mental Mind acting via Higher Mental Centre.

These latter two centres each speak in a special language that is not understood by lower centres. This is the reason why we find, say, in Holy Scripture, many strange compositions that can only be understood psychologically and have no meaning if taken literally. In the Bible the Creation of Man at the beginning and the Judgment of Man at the end are in the language of Higher Emotional Centre.

Now, as was said, we have to understand that different minds control us and that unless we can understand this we can understand nothing about ourselves. This teaching or, as it is called, this Work, is self-study by means of following a definite system of self-observation —that is, we are told what to observe in ourselves and what to separate from. To begin with, we have to observe centres in ourselves and notice how they work in quite different spheres and see things quite differently. Intellectual Mind sees things quite differently from Emotional Mind; Sex Mind sees things quite differently from both Emotional Mind and

Intellectual Mind, and so on. But let it be said now that actually the three centres in the lowest compartment of the human machine need not be opposites and can combine and so form a triad. That is, Active Force, Passive Force and Neutralizing Force can be conducted by each alternately in conjunction with Sex Centre, Moving Centre and Instinctive Centre. But it must be emphasized that this does not apply to the other centres and that the teaching as given to us so far only speaks of Sex Centre, Moving Centre and Instinctive Centre as *capable* of forming a triad and not being opposites—that is, of being able to relate themselves together in such a way that each one conducts one or other of the three forces.

Now let us by way of comment notice a few points about centres that can be viewed by trained self-observation. Each centre has its own sphere of activity—e.g. the work that Moving Centre can do is quite different from that of Intellectual Centre. It is possible to observe that when you are in one centre you are not necessarily in another also. A decision made in one centre does not have any power in the sphere of power of another centre. Now it is true that we spend most of the day in a vague, unfocused state, in which a stream of mechanical inner talking and phantasy goes on endlessly. This is called being between centres. When we are *in attention* we are in a centre. But one centre does not know another. They are different minds. Their modes of doing things are quite different. A harmonized man—a man No. 4— knows the difference of different centres and stands as it were in the midst of them and can speak to them all. But, as we are, we do not possess this inner state of Being, which belongs to our further development, and is definitely a higher level than we are at. The developed man, the man needed to-day, the level we strive for, is not the usual one-centre man, whether No. 1 or Instinctive Man, or No. 2 or Emotional Man, or No. 3 or Intellectual Man, but Man No. 4, and that is the general aim of everyone in this Work. For in Man No. 4 all centres are accessible to him, according to his circumstances.

Now each centre has its own truth. So there is not one truth, but the truth of each mind, and the whole makes up truth. I said that a harmonized man, a balanced man, knows and understands the language and needs of the centres. So he knows *which centre to use at the right time* and gives, as it were, what properly belongs to a centre. That is, the letters, the impressions, go to the right address. But G. compared Man as he is—that is, Man asleep in himself, ordinary Man, one-sided Man, one-centre Man, Man not yet awakening, Man driven by outside forces, Man-Machine—such a man G. compared with a big business office in which sit three big bosses in different rooms. They do not know one another and all business communications come through an uneducated secretary who lives in a little office with two or three standard reference-books. She does not even know what the business house is for. She sends the incoming letters—impressions—up to the house just as takes her fancy and the bosses cannot make head or tail of most of them. That is, what should have gone to one centre goes to the wrong centre and so on. This is one of the pictures that has been given, in the original teaching of the Work, of the state of ordinary mechanical Man—that is, Man or Woman asleep.

*　*　*

Now, the paper having been read, let me speak of what it is all about. It is necessary to bring things down to a certain level for us to take things in. In the first place, do you begin to see you have different centres and also that they tend to work as opposites? Each centre has its own hunger. Have you seen from yourself that you have different hungers? That should make you reflect that you are not one person, but many persons. There is the hunger of Instinctive Centre, the hunger of Sex Centre—and, more difficult perhaps to notice—the hunger of Moving Centre—that is, the desire to make something, or take exercise. There is also the hunger of Emotional Centre—say, to be appreciated. And the hunger of Intellectual Centre—the hunger to know. All these hungers are different. In Balanced Man each does not dominate and exclude the others, for Balanced Man stands in the midst of the hungers of different centres and does not go only with one. This is the harmonized or balanced Man. Do you think you have already reached this stage—this level of Being? I can assure you that if you think so it is nothing but a very complacent picture of yourself that will only be destroyed by sincere self-observation. A man or woman who feels that as they are they are *all right* and even better than others—such people are asleep in themselves and to themselves. In short, they are asleep. Now this Work is about awakening, not about continuing in the general sleep of Humanity.

Great Amwell House, Whitsun, May 25, 1947

A NOTE ON UNDERSTANDING

We have noticed that in this Work Man is taken from many different aspects and studied in different ways. From one aspect it is said that Man has two sides—the side of his knowledge and the side of his Being. In this connection one of the practical things we are taught is to get knowledge of our Being. Now self-observation is to get to know oneself—to make one objective to oneself, to become *conscious* of oneself. One can get to know one's knowledge and one can get to know one's Being. I will not speak to-day of getting to know one's knowledge save to say that later on one finds that the degree of knowledge we have hitherto imputed to ourselves falls very far short of our

1034

imagination and that the gaps in our supposed knowledge are very wide.

Now to gain knowledge of one's Being is one of the earliest things emphasized in the Work. On one occasion it was said that we must work on:

> Knowledge of our Being
> Self-Remembering,
> Non-Considering,
> Non-Identifying.

Without knowledge of our Being, it is impossible to work on Being. Part of our Being is under the 12 influences coming from the cosmic level of Being represented outwardly by the visible Sun; part is under the 24 planetary laws; part is under the 48 laws of the Earth; and part under the 96 laws of the Moon. The worst spot in our Being under the most laws is the negative part of Emotional Centre. In this respect one sign of a higher level of Being is the capacity to bear the unpleasant manifestations of others. One does not continually get negative with other people. Another sign of a higher level of Being is possession of Magnetic Centre which means the intuition that this life is not explicable in terms of itself—or, what is the same—the power of seeing that two sorts of influences exist, *A* and *B*.

As a man gets to see himself more objectively—that is, to have direct knowledge of his Being—he is liable to be attacked at intervals by special kinds of subtle negative emotions. He or she cannot be helped save through individual struggles. These situations are necessary to bring forward the individuality or Real 'I' with which one's usual level of Being is not in contact. Our ordinary Being lacks unity. Real 'I' when it emerges harmonizes the different centres and 'I's. It brings about unity in multiplicity. Now only individual struggle brings Real 'I' out. It is you centrally yourself, and quite alone, that has to believe and apply the Work. To do it from another side of yourself is not individual—as to do it because you ought—from some orthodox notion, etc.—is not central. Perhaps you can see what is meant by what I will call central effort. The place where you make effort from must be genuinely yourself. If I imitate my father, I will follow his example in myself and then the individuality will be in his hands—in this psychological imitation of him in myself. The father in us will then have the power. This may seem very obscure. Yet I assure you it can be understood if you think of yourself as having many different groups of 'I's which form roughly distinct personalities, all of them forming the Personality as a whole. They are not us. They have, as Christ said, to be hated—as not being us. Full Being can be thought of when the Driver is on the box, the horse harnessed, and the Master sitting in the Carriage. We must realize that this situation can never occur unless we see clearly that we have to make effort ourselves and to work ourselves, from ourselves, by transforming life, and every day we must make a real Work-effort from our own understanding—that is, take the mechanical effects of life in a new way. Now in regard to Knowledge and Being and its relation to Understanding, a paper from a lecture by Mr. Ouspensky will be read:

"I will speak to-day about understanding. What is *understanding*? Try to ask yourselves this question, and you will see that you cannot answer it. This means that you have never thought about it. You always mixed *understanding* with *knowing*. But to know and to understand are two quite different things. First of all, understanding must be divided into two parts. You can understand a thing or a problem, or an idea, and you can understand a man—i.e. what he says to you. We will leave for the moment the case where you can understand a man without his saying anything, because it is only a development of the same idea. In order to understand a thing, an idea, or a problem, you must know all that refers to it, or as much as possible. For instance, suppose I shew you an old Russian silver rouble. It was a piece of money the size of a half-crown and corresponding to two shillings and a penny. You may look at it, study it, see which year it was coined, find out everything about the Tsar whose portrait is on one side, weigh it, even make a chemical analysis and find out the exact quantity of silver contained in it. You can learn what the word 'rouble' means and how it came into use. You can learn all these things, and probably many more, but you will never *understand it and its meaning*, if you do not find out that before the War its purchase-power corresponded in many cases to a present-day English penny farthing. If you find this out you will *understand* something about a rouble and also perhaps about some other things, because the understanding of one thing immediately leads to the understanding of many other things.

"Now if we ask ourselves what does it mean to understand or not understand a man, we must first think of a case where we speak different languages from a man and have no language in common. Naturally we cannot understand one another. We must have a common language or agree on certain signs or symbols by which we will designate things. But suppose during a conversation with a man you disagree about the meaning of certain words or signs or symbols. You again cease to understand one another. From this follows the principle that *you cannot understand and disagree*. In ordinary conversation we say very often: 'I understand him but I do not agree with him.' From the point of view of the system we are studying this is impossible. If you understand a man you agree with him: if you disagree with him you do not understand him. It is difficult to accept this idea and it means that it is difficult to understand it.

"Let us try to understand more clearly what understanding is. There are two sides in a man which must develop in the gradual course of his transformation. These are: his *Knowledge* and his *Being*. I have already spoken many times about the necessity for the development of knowledge, particularly self-knowledge, and you can easily understand the idea of different levels of knowledge and the relativity of knowledge.

1036

What people do not understand in most cases is the necessity for the development of their Being, or the possibility of very different levels of Being. Now, what does *Being* mean?

"A Russian philosopher, Vladimir Solovieff, used the term '*Being*' in his writings. He spoke about the being of a stone, the being of a plant, the being of an animal, the being of a man, and the Divine Being. This is better than the ordinary concept because in ordinary understanding the being of a man is not regarded as in any way different from the being of a stone, a plant, or an animal, which *exist* exactly as a man exists. In reality they *exist* quite differently. But Solovieff's division is not sufficient. I have already explained that from the point of view of the system, Man is divided into seven concepts: Man No. 1, Man No. 2, 3, 4, 5, 6, and No. 7 Man. This means *seven* degrees or categories of Being; Being No. 1, Being No. 2, Being No. 3 and so on. In addition to this, we already know still finer divisions. We know that men 1, 2 and 3 can also be very different: they may live entirely under influences 'A'; they may be equally affected by influences 'A' and 'B'; they may be more under influences 'B' than influences 'A'; they may have 'Magnetic Centre'; they may have come into contact with influences 'C'; they may be on their way to becoming men No. 4. All these states mean different levels of *Being*.

"The idea of Being entered into the very essence of thinking and speaking about Man in *religious thought*, and all other divisions of men were regarded as unimportant in comparison with this. Men were divided into saints, righteous men, good men, bad men, sinners, repentant sinners, unrepentant sinners, heretics, unbelievers, and so on. All these definitions referred to the difference in Being. In modern thought people pay no attention to Being; on the contrary, they think that the more discrepancies and contradictions there are in a man's Being, the more interesting and brilliant he can be. It is generally, although silently, admitted, that a man can be given to lying, that he can be selfish, unreliable, even perverted, and yet be a great scientist or a great philosopher, or a great artist. Of course this is quite impossible. This incompatibility of different features of one's Being, which is generally regarded as originality, in reality means weakness. One cannot be a great scholar or a great thinker with a perverted or an inconsistent mind, just as one cannot be a prize-fighter or a circus-athlete with consumption. The idea that a really good professor must always forget his umbrella everywhere needs revising. At any rate from the point of view of schools the professor would have been advised first of all to learn not to forget his umbrella.

"I hope it is now clear what *Being* means, and why it must grow and develop parallel with Knowledge. If Knowledge outgrows Being or Being outgrows Knowledge, it always results in a one-sided development, and a one-sided development cannot go far. It is bound to come to some inner contradictions of a serious nature and stop there. Some time later we may speak about the results of one-sided development, but happily they do not often happen in life and we can leave them now.

"We return now to the question of understanding. Having explained the difference between Knowledge and Being, and the connection between the one and the other, I can definitely say what understanding is. Understanding is the *arithmetical mean* between Knowledge and Being. You know what an arithmetical mean is? It is a quantity lying between two other quantities. For instance, if you take 25 and 15, you add them together and get 40: divide 40 by 2 and you have 20. 20 is the arithmetical mean between 25 and 15. This explains the necessity for a simultaneous growth of Knowledge and Being. The growth of only one of them will not increase enough the growth of the arithmetical mean. This also explains why to *understand* means to agree. People who understand one another must have not only an equal Knowledge, but they must also have an equal Being. Only this gives a possibility of understanding. Another wrong idea which people have had always and which particularly belongs to our time, is that understanding can be different, that people can understand the same thing differently. This is quite wrong from the point of view of the system. Understanding cannot be different. *There can only be one understanding.* But at the same time people understand things differently. How can we find an explanation for this seeming contradiction?

"In reality there is no contradiction. Understanding means understanding of a part in relation to the whole. But the idea of the whole can be very different in people according to their Knowledge and Being. This is why the system is necessary again. People learn to understand by understanding the system and everything else in relation to the system. Complete understanding of the system together with complete understanding of everything in relation to the system makes the understanding of Man No. 7 which is the only one full understanding possible. Speaking from this point of view there can be no other understanding, only different approximations to this understanding. But, speaking on an ordinary level, without the idea of a school or system, there are as many understandings as there are people. Everyone understands everything in his own way or according to one or another mechanical training. But this is all a subjective understanding. The way to objective understanding lies through the system and the school."

Great Amwell House, May 31, 1947

ON VIOLENCE AND UNDERSTANDING

I will contrast Violence with Understanding. Violence is the anti-thesis to Understanding. All violence has its roots in not understanding another. It is said in the Work that understanding is the most powerful force we can create and also that we have to create our lives. So we have to create understanding. Suppose you feel violent towards another person, and then let us imagine that you get to know and understand that person. You will no longer be violent. Now it is also said in the Work that all violence has its root in negative emotion. I said above that all violence has its root in not understanding. There is no contra-diction in this. It means simply that negative emotions do not lead to understanding but to violence. The more negative you are the less you understand and the more violent you tend to be. And since the Work says that understanding is the most powerful force we can create, it is clear that continual indulgence in and enjoyment of negative emotions can only create negative things. Understanding is a positive thing. So negative emotion cannot create understanding but only misunderstand-ing. Misunderstanding is not a positive thing. Some people even love to misunderstand. But this is simply to love negative emotions, for negative emotions never speak the truth. They are liars—often very clever liars—but always liars. If you are in a negative state, then everything is distorted and you understand nothing or misunderstand everything. Truth can be twisted into a thousand semi-truths—as, for example, someone said something to you but because you hate the person you twist it, leave out a bit, alter the sequence, and then you have a lie and not truth. Yet something in you, if you listen, tells you that you are lying. What tells you is Buried Conscience which is the herald of Higher Centres, as John the Baptist of Christ. Unless we had something in us that can, as it were, chemically, taste negative emotions, our case would indeed be hopeless. But after a time, through self-observation, you can tell, or rather, you are told internally, when you are negative, because a deep unhappiness goes with it. Otherwise we would have to learn everything inner by copy-book and blackboard. Fortunately, being born self-developing organisms—as the greatest experiment so far—we have inner senses and materials in us for this development. That is, we can create understanding, the most powerful thing.

Now the Work says a man is his understanding. He is not his size, his money, position, birth, strength, or his prestige, or distinctions, or religion. A man is his understanding. So a man, a woman, who under-stands little or nothing, is, from the standpoint of the Work, of no value. It is worth while reflecting on this, especially to-day, when there is a danger of a general loss of understanding over all the Earth. Now, before mentioning again the Work-definition of Understanding, I will

1039

say, by way of commentary, that to understand one must learn, and learning is to perceive in oneself the truth of a thing that one is taught —that the thing *is so*. This leads to understanding. The Work teaches that knowing and understanding are quite different. I may know many things, but may never have perceived in myself the truth of any of them. In that case, I do not understand what I know, though I may retain it in my memory. The Work says that Understanding is the arithmetical mean between one's level of Knowledge and one's level of Being. If one's Knowledge is represented by the number 20 and one's Being by the number 10; then if we add 20 and 10, it equals 30. Divide by 2 and the result is 15. 15 is the arithmetical mean between 20 and 10. This would mean that I understand only a part of what I know.

Now have you reflected for yourselves on why Being is necessary for Understanding and why Knowledge alone does not give Understanding? When a man perceives in himself the truth of something he has come to know—let us say, that mankind is asleep—he then receives this truth in himself and acknowledges it. But only when he sees the truth of it in himself. It then combines with his Being. It is Being that *receives* Knowledge and transforms it into Understanding—otherwise Knowledge remains chiefly in the memory and does not affect the man himself as a man. The quality of the reception of Knowledge therefore depends on the level of Being. Low Being can receive little or nothing and Knowledge given to low Being can only be used in a wrong way and not rightly understood. This is the problem of Knowledge and Being. We have to be constantly reminded of it. It is, in fact, one of the greatest problems that Conscious Man is faced with in trying to lift mankind to a higher level of development. Knowledge alone cannot do this.

Now we will return to work on Being as taught in this system. We have to work on:

> Knowledge of our Being,
> Self-Remembering,
> Non-Identifying,
> Non-Considering.

By self-observation, according to the discipline of the Work, we come to Knowledge of our Being—namely, that we do not remember ourselves. By the same means, we come to the Knowledge that we identify, and of what we identify with, especially. Finally, we begin to know what our chief forms of internal considering are. All this is knowledge of our Being. There are also other things that we have to observe and get to know, but we are only speaking now of those mentioned above. To become conscious of these things "saves time". I refer to the self-evolution that is required of everyone. A person not conscious of his Being cannot change. There is a Way called the Way of Good Householder. But this is very long. One should work—while it is day. (Things have to be brought to the light to change. Light is consciousness.)

Now I will add to the list knowledge of one's negative emotions. In O.'s teaching of this system he particularly dwelt on this part of it and the importance of first observing and then separating from one's negative states. In this connection he spoke of violence and how violence destroyed everything in us like an outbreak of fire, and how one moment of violence could put a person back to the beginning. He indicated early that the 4th Way was not lady-like and could produce violence in people, but always said that one has to understand why things are said and done as they are. To react with violence is the easiest of all things. To understand is the most difficult. I said last time that external considering is essential for understanding anyone. It has two sides, putting yourself in the position of the other person and putting the other person in your position. Now it might be said that when you get violent you come to the limit or end of your Being. Capacity for endurance is a sign of Being. Small Being, which only loves itself, soon reaches its limit and becomes violent. In violence one is totally asleep and has no understanding. The overcoming of violence is one of the things spoken of in the Work. The more you see others in yourself and yourself in others, the more understanding and the less violence you have. And the more you realize as a fact your own nothingness, the less violence. In the Gospels this is called Consciousness of Neighbour and Consciousness of God.

Great Amwell House, June 7, 1947

ON CENTRES AND PARTS OF CENTRES

The mechanical reception of impressions can only feed mechanical parts of centres. But when impressions are taken in, say, with a sense of wonder or delight, they fall on emotional divisions of centres. When they are taken in by directed attention and individual mental effort they fall on intellectual divisions. Now a negative impression will go to its proper place—namely, negative parts of centres. Impressions taken in of a person one freely dislikes will feed negative emotional part. This then becomes stored with energy and will discharge itself on anyone from a trifling cause—i.e. one will become violent over nothing. Negative literature and films of crime, violence, hatred, etc., if identified with, all feed the negative part of Emotional Centre and store it with energy. A negative book can do this—if one reads it with identifying. So we have to learn to take impressions in more consciously and not identify with negative impressions. Learn to be very careful in all this. This is a form of Self-Remembering and the energy it uses is drawn out of the negative impressions. People imagine, however, that when they are alone or no one is looking, they can indulge in as many negative thoughts as they like. In this way they increase the material for making negative emotions, which sooner or later will wish to rush forth and attack someone and hurt them. All negative emotions desire to hurt, and at the bottom of them are unlimited forms of violence. Continually *making accounts* against others stores up big material for the manufacture of negative emotions which if they cannot attack others attack oneself. The only remedy is not to consent to negative impressions—that is, to be sufficiently awake to prevent these impressions from automatically going right home to the negative part of Emotional Centre. I speak of outer impressions and also of inner impressions derived chiefly from thought or memory or imagination. The uncontrolled working of imagination can feed negative emotions strongly. That is why they go on and on. You can always tell if you have identified, and so let pass a negative impression, if you can listen to your inner state. We are supposed to have a good filter—that does not eventually let pass any infectious poisonous germs. Yes—but have you realized this? Have you begun *this* aspect of the Work on yourself? Or do you let everything pass unfiltered?

Now what can we understand practically of all this? We have to understand that impressions can fall on different *parts of centres* and that impressions of outer life, of people, etc., coming in *via* the senses, can be directed and need not fall always on one sore place. We actually have the power, if we develop it, of conscious effort to make impressions fall on *new places* in ourselves. Now there are very many new places in us, scarcely used. For this reason we will study our Being again from the angle of centres and parts of centres. It will then be possible to grasp better how our Being, as it is, is on different levels—some parts being more mechanical and so lower and some less mechanical and so higher in level. A man who lives wholly in mechanical divisions of centres cannot change his Being. The first step is self-observation. This is never mechanical—that is, a man or a woman cannot observe themselves mechanically. It requires directed attention to observe oneself and attention requires consciousness, or rather, the act of attention puts us at once into more conscious parts of centres. It is the same with Self-Remembering. No one can remember himself mechanically. Full Self-Remembering requires full consciousness. In this connection O. spoke as follows:

"Now we must return again to the study of centres and to the study of attention and Self-Remembering which are the only ways to understanding. Besides the division into two parts, positive and negative, which, as we saw, is not the same in different centres, each of the 4 centres is divided into 3 parts. These 3 parts correspond to the divisions of centres themselves. The first part is "mechanical", including moving and instinctive principles; the second is "emotional"; and the third is "intellectual". The following diagram shews the position of parts in the Intellectual Centre:

Man as a 3-Storey House

Intellectual Centre

Intellectual Part

Capacity for creation, construction, invention, discovery.

(works by controlled attention, kept there by effort.)

negative part of intellectual part

Emotional Part

Desire to know and understand.
Pleasure of discovery

negative part of emotional part

Moving Part
(apparatus replies to questions, etc.)

Intellectual Part { shrewdness, craftiness, cautiousness.

negative part.

Emotional Part { curiosity, inquisitiveness, undirected imagination.

negative part.

Moving Part { mechanical repetition of words and phrases

negative part.

"The centre is divided into positive and negative parts, and each of these two parts is divided into 3 parts, so that the Intellectual Centre actually consists of 6 parts. Each of these 6 parts in its own turn is divided into 3 parts: mechanical, emotional and intellectual. But about these we will speak later, with the exception of only one part, mechanical part of Intellectual Centre, about which I will speak presently. The meaning of the division of a centre into 3 parts is very simple. A mechanical part works almost automatically: *it does not require any attention*. But because of this it cannot adapt itself to a change of events and continues to work in the way it started, when circumstances have completely changed. In the Intellectual Centre the mechanical part includes in itself all the work of *registration* of memories, associations, and impressions. This is all that it should do normally—i.e. when other parts do their work. It should never *reply* to questions addressed to the whole centre, and it should never decide anything, but unfortunately it is always ready to decide and it always replies to all sorts of questions in a narrow and very limited way, in ready-made phrases, in slang expressions, in party-maxims, etc. This part has its own name: it is called 'formatory apparatus' or sometimes 'formatory centre'.

"It is possible to distinguish 3 parts in the formatory apparatus: mechanical (purely automatic) like mechanical repetition of some words heard or read, emotional (curiosity, inquisitiveness and undirected imagination) and intellectual (shrewdness, craftiness, cautiousness). Many people, particularly people No. 1, live all their lives with 'formatory apparatus' only, never touching other parts of their Intellectual Centre. For all immediate needs of life, for receiving 'A' influences and responding to them, formatory apparatus is quite sufficient. They are stereotyped people—just machines.

"The emotional part of the Intellectual Centre consists chiefly of what is called an intellectual emotion—i.e. desire to know, desire to understand, satisfaction of knowing, dissatisfaction of not knowing, pleasure of discovery. Work of the emotional part requires full attention, *but in this part of the centre attention does not require any effort*. It is attracted and kept by the subject itself.

"The intellectual part of Intellectual Centre includes in itself a capacity for creation, construction, invention and discovery. It cannot work without attention, *but the attention in this part of the centre must be controlled* and kept there by will and effort.

"This is the chief point in studying parts of centres. If we take them from the point of view of attention we will know at once in which parts of centres we are. Without attention, or with attention wandering, we are in the mechanical parts; with the attention *attracted* by a subject of thought or consideration we are in the emotional part; and with the attention controlled and kept on our subject by will we are in the intellectual part. At the same time it shews the way to higher parts of centres. By studying attention and trying to control it, we compel ourselves to work in higher parts of centres, because the same principle refers to all the centres equally, although it may not be so easy for us to distinguish different parts in other centres.

"Let us take Emotional Centre. I will not speak at the present moment about negative emotions. We will take only the division of the centre into 3 parts: mechanical, emotional and intellectual. The mechanical part consists of the cheapest kind of ready-made humour and the rough sense of the comic, love of excitement, spectacular shows, pageantry, sentimentality, love of being in a crowd, all kinds of crowd-emotions, and all kinds of lower half-animal emotions, unconscious cruelty, selfishness, cowardice, envy, jealousy, and so on. The emotional part may be very different in different people. It may include in itself religious emotion, aesthetic emotion, moral emotion, and may lead to *Conscience*, but with identification on its negative side it may be something quite different—it may be very cruel, obstinate, and cold, and jealous, only in a less primitive way than the mechanical part. The intellectual part (with the help of the intellectual parts of the Moving and Instinctive Centres) includes in itself the power of artistic creation. In cases where the intellectual parts of the Moving and Instinctive Centres, which are necessary for the natural manifestation of the creative faculties, are not educated enough or do not correspond to it in their development, it manifests itself in dreams. This explains the beautiful and artistic dreams of otherwise quite inartistic people. Also the intellectual part of the Emotional Centre is the chief *seat of the Magnetic Centre*."

Man as a 3-Storey House

Emotional Centre

Intellectual Part
Chief seat of Magnetic Centre Artistic Creation
negative part of intellectual part

Emotional Part
Religious emotions, aesthetic emotions, moral emotions, may lead to CONSCIENCE
negative part of emotional part cruelty, obstinacy, coldness, jealousy

Moving Part	
Intellectual Part	resultant of small desires, little daily " wills ".
	negative part.
Emotional Part	All emotions relating to one's likes and dislikes. personal emotions.
	negative part. jealousy, envy.
Moving Part	mechanical expressions of emotions, laughing and crying, cheap humour.
	negative part.

FURTHER NOTE ON VIOLENCE AND UNDERSTANDING

VIOLENCE AND FEAR

We spoke recently about understanding and how it is the most powerful force we can create. Force by itself without understanding naturally will tend to pass into violence. When a man acts through violence, he acts without understanding. Violence lies in the self-will. Now when a man acts through his understanding he acts from the best in him in regard to his level of knowledge and his level of being. The quality of his will, which chiefly belongs to the side of his being and in a mechanical man is the resultant of his feelings and desires, and the quality of his learning, which chiefly belongs to the side of his knowledge, will determine whether under any given circumstances the man will act from violence or understanding. We can probably agree that we know better than we act. This means the level of being, which is that which acts, is lower than the level of knowledge, and so we often act from violence.

Let me remind you again that in the Work people are looked at from two sides—the level of their knowledge and the level of their being. It is useful to look at everyone from this angle, especially at oneself. The question is not merely: "What does the man know or where has he been or what job has he?" but also "What is he like? What kind of man is he? Is he, for example, quarrelsome? or conceited? or un-reliable? or a thief? a liar? a slanderer?" For all these belong to the *quality* of being. Now it is difficult and at first impossible to observe oneself when one is in a state of violence because, as was said recently, when one is in a state of violence one is completely asleep. One can, however, observe the state afterwards to a certain extent. The Intellectual Centre will probably remember some of the expressions used and the Moving Centre will have recorded some of the gestures. But you will not be able to recall the emotion itself. When you pass out of a particular emotional state it seems remote, even unreal. When you pass into it again nothing is closer and more real. Take, for example, the state of fear, because we have to speak briefly about it. We know how, when we are not in a state of fear, fear seems unreal. Just think what things would be like if we could remember in the Emotional Centre the horrors of war and feel the emotions again at will. But we cannot—and so everything goes on as it does. Ah, if we could in our personal life remember at will some healing emotions that visited us.

Now there are, broadly speaking, two kinds of fear. There is instinctive fear—that is, fear originating in the emotional division of the Instinctive Centre. This is present in us and in all animals, but of course differently orientated. This fear is stimulated only by the direct sensory impression of danger. It excites a secretion from the adrenal glands and releases material that activates the muscles—either for attack or for defence. This substance, *adrenalin,* although constantly manufactured in small quantities under normal safe conditions, and in excess under abnormal unsafe conditions, can in a certain disease called Addison's Disease be absent. In this case, the man is inert muscularly —practically unable to perform any muscular action. This is nothing to do with being lazy. From the angle of the Work, 3rd Force is lacking. Now there is another origin of fear which does not arise only when the senses recognize danger. This fear is situated in the Emotional Centre and so is intimately connected with emotional imagination. Imagination is not nonsense—except in a literal sense—i.e. not springing from sense. It is a very powerful thing. It is useless to say to a person: "It is nothing but imagination." To say a thing like that merely shews your ignorance, your lack of psychological understanding—for imagination, undirected imagination, exerts an incalculable influence on sleeping humanity. Suppose a person is always imaginatively afraid. This arises from the Emotional Centre. He is afraid he may be buried alive, or afraid he has a serious illness, or afraid he will be suddenly attacked, or afraid he will fail in his exams, or that he may lose his money or position, and so on. All this is *fear* arising from the Emotional Centre and of course it is negative—that is, it arises from the manifold activities of the negative part of Emotional Centre. It is not based on an actual sense-given situation. A rabbit, seeing a dog, dives into the burrow. Its fear is from the Instinctive Centre—a direct response to a sensory stimulus. After a time, the rabbit emerges again. Just imagine if rabbits had emotional imaginative fear! They would never appear above ground. It is wonderful how they do. But this is not bravery.

Now fear in Man leads to violence in many different ways. It could be said that a man may be taught to control *instinctive fear,* especially by discipline, but that to control emotional fear is far more difficult. It is indeed impossible, unless he has a form of faith, vision and belief, through which he knows that he can do nothing and be nothing by himself, and that as long as he remembers himself he will be helped, realizing that his life is not from himself. This faith, this belief, this vision, is called "catching the rope" in the Work and it heals the Emotional Centre. But if a man ascribes his life to himself, if he attributes everything he does—even digesting his food and making his heart beat—to himself, then his Emotional Centre is necessarily all wrong and, in fact, upside down. It is not internal considering that will lift fear, but external considering. He knows only self-emotions. He loves only himself. It is not this love that is meant in the phrase: "Love casteth out fear". As I said, it is not internal considering that will lift fear, but external considering. I will ask once more: "How do you move? How do you think? How do you feel?" In short, the Emotional Centre is wrong unless it is increasingly susceptible to the feelings that come from ideas such as that we did not create ourselves and that this life is not explicable in terms of itself. Now, all the emotions opened up by sufficient contact with the Work begin to purify the Emotional Centre and lessen fear. That leads to the elimination of fear—and so to the gradual cessation of violence arising from this source. A man who only believes in himself must obviously have many unnecessary fears which may lead to violence. He will naturally suspect others. Suspicion gives rise easily to violence. With the decline of vision to-day there is automatically a rise in suspicion and fear on all sides. You know the kind of man who suddenly walks up to you and says: "You are not laughing at me, by any chance?" Now such a man, believing in himself, attributing everything to himself, admiring himself, and having many amazing pictures of himself, will tend to violence because, for one reason, he cannot laugh at himself. If one were to say to him: "I am laughing at an 'I' in you, but not at you", I am afraid you would measure your length on the floor.

Now as regards the purification of the Emotional Centre. Since we ascribe everything to ourselves, even our brains, we have only self-emotions. Self-emotions may lead eventually to violence. I advise some of you to read Mr. Ouspensky's chapter on the emotions in his first book "Tertium Organum".

Now on the practical side—*all this Work is about making what lies in your Being more and more conscious*—that is, bringing out into the light of consciousness what has always acted mechanically in you so far and perhaps spoilt your life. In this respect it is useful to observe what kind of *fear* makes you *violent*. Do you fear not to be properly treated, for instance? (I am not speaking of instinctive fear). If you begin to see the connection between some forms of violence and some not hitherto realized or acknowledged fear, then you will find that this connection, exposed more and more to the light of consciousness (by means of self-observation) will operate less and less powerfully. In other words, whereas you reacted mechanically, now you see and begin to act consciously. This is a change of being.

Great Amwell House, June 21, 1947

COMMENTARY ON PSYCHO-TRANSFORMISM

We return once more to the idea of psychological transformation. We must understand that the main ideas of this Work come round in a rotation. They cannot be spoken of all together, so a rotation is necessary. This Work has been tentatively called psycho-transformism. To-day we speak again about psycho-transformism, in order to understand more what is meant by the term. A man, a woman, by means of Self-Remembering can *transform* their lives. They cannot transform life itself, but their own lives, their relationship to life. You cannot change life itself, the recurring circle of events that constitute life and history, but you can change your relation to them by changing your attitude to them. This is one aspect of psychological transformation—or psycho-transformism. But to effect it, you must change your attitude to yourself. You cannot, by having the same ideas about yourself, change yourself, and if you cannot change yourself you cannot change the effect of life upon you. One has heard this said repeatedly. But one does not perhaps yet see what it means. It means, if you remain the same, life for you will be the same, and then the question of psychological transformation does not arise. That is, it is not for you—so I suggest you do not bother about it. However the whole Work is about self-change. If you think this is an extraordinary idea, then, I will add, do not bother about the Work.

Now the Work begins with you yourself. It starts with the observation of yourself—that is, with drawing slowly into consciousness of yourself all sorts of things that belong to your Being of which you are unaware. This alters your idea of yourself. A man must "know himself." That is, he must become more and more conscious of himself—so conscious, in fact, that, for example, when he is talking he is conscious of which 'I' is speaking and can notice what it is saying and not identify with it. This is inner separation. This is especially difficult, in this case, because when we are in action we are usually most asleep—that is, least conscious—and one of our commonest actions is talking. If you do not believe it, watch another person using one of his typical gramophone records, such as his adventures or successes, before a new audience. Talking is the most mechanical action. But one can be conscious of this most mechanical action. One can observe it while it is going on. Then one is conscious of what is mechanically going on. This seems paradoxical. But try it and see for yourself. It needs a very light touch. The first object is to observe oneself *without* criticism. We are told to observe, not stop. So one can observe one is talking mechanically and, as I said, notice which 'I' is speaking, without checking it. If you begin to criticize it, it will stop, and so you will learn nothing further. In this commentary, I will call this the first necessary stage in psycho-transformism—this developed power of being conscious of one's mechanicalness and not stopping it. If you keep on trying to stop things, you cannot see them. Our aim at first is not to stop, but to see, to become conscious of. Now, in this connection, as you know, the Work teaches that the *realization of one's mechanicalness* is one of the first real experiences of Self-Remembering. It is easy to see why. Hitherto you have taken yourself seriously. You have identified with everything in yourself, with family, money, position, etc. You have said 'I' to everything. Then there is a brief vibration of *greater consciousness* and you suddenly see that all you took so seriously as yourself is machinery and *not you*. You then realize your mechanicalness. Now this introduces us to the idea of psycho-transformism. Self-change is not possible if one can be only what one is. I mean that, were what we are all that we could possibly be, no transformation would be possible. But the Work says we are only at the beginning of ourselves, and calls us seeds. Take our consciousness: the Work says we are not conscious and that Western psychology makes a fundamental error in taking Man as a conscious Being. There is a ladder of Consciousness. We seek the next rungs—called the State of Self-Remembering, Self-Consciousness or Self-Awareness. As we ascend this ladder everything changes. It is a magic lift. Imagine a seed in this lift. If it ascends it becomes a tree: if it descends it becomes a seed again. This is clearly not a 3-dimensional lift. In 3-dimensional space one goes up and down and remains the same, save perhaps for being worse-tempered than ever.

When we know this magic lift, which is in everyone, we know that going up in it requires the greatest care and valuation and that everything false in us can make us fall straight down instantly. I will put it more simply. You cannot rightly go up to a higher level of Being if you go up clinging to all the false notions and values that belong to a lower level. For example, if you cannot stop wanting what you *think* you want you certainly cannot go up with intelligent experience in this magic lift, and so you render yourself liable to be suddenly hurled down. This means no real valuations save those of False Personality. All this belongs to the Work teaching about Magnetic Centre and sense of scale. Of course, if everything is the same to you—as when you only want to be a popular success whether in life or in the Work—then you have no sense of real inner valuation and so no sense of scale. Then it is as if your inner lift is not present and instead there are precipices, height and depth without means. Now the lift is *means* between height and depth and at every floor it stops and we should realize new feelings and insights: and so we can be *taught*. But some cannot even be taught, simply because they live in the conviction that they are right and know all to be known. Just imagine the state of a man who in this way cannot see that his minute knowledge compared with his ignorance is incommensurable. Yet people live in this illusion—that is, under a definite hypnotism among the many forms of hypnotism that act on humanity to keep them asleep.

Now the realization of one's mechanicalness and the realization of one's ignorance—for all knowledge leads into mystery—these two realizations are necessary for any transformation of oneself to take place. Why? Because they weaken the hold of the acquired Personality. Unless the grip of the Personality is weakened no psycho-transformism is possible. In other words the background of one's mind must change and a new, deeper thinking begin. This changes the attitude to life and the attitude to oneself. Attitudes begin in Mental Centre. Change the mind, and attitudes change. And to change the mind the habitual little meagre ways of thinking must change. This Work is to make us *think in a new way*. Why? Because only in this way can we change attitudes. Mr. Ouspensky said: "If attitudes do not change, nothing can change in oneself."

Now let us come, as it were, from background more into foreground. How by practical work can a man begin to transform himself? I said just now that if you cannot stop wanting what you *think* you want you cannot really change. I will give a simpler example: an obstinate man has a picture of himself as being a very reasonable man. After, say, a considerable time—several years at least—he begins to suspect his picture—that is, what he was not conscious of before begins to enter his Consciousness. He begins to be conscious of the self-fact that he really is obstinate and finally sees it is so. What is the result? By this *increase of consciousness* his Being changes. That is, a small transformation of Being takes place. It may not be merely small—it may mean that many other things in his Being can readjust themselves—especially if unrecognized, and so unacknowledged, obstinacy has anything to do with his Chief Feature. If so, the whole man will begin to change—that is, undergo a transformation.

Now, another example from a different angle. You take a thing, an event, always in the same way. You always react mechanically to it. You have no idea that although you cannot change the event in life you can alter the way you react to it. I can only say, as I have said often before, if you can see it this means by experience you have something of great value in your hands. However, people are so glued down to the familiar that they almost resent the idea of taking things differently. There is always this hurt feeling in the Work. In the Gospels it is called "being offended". Most people who met Christ were very offended. Now if you could start the day from the sense of the utter mystery of your life you would begin to understand something about psycho-trans-formism. But you pick up your to-day self from your yesterday-self and so carry on everything as before. You think that the familiar is right and so remain the same. You do not understand what was meant when it was said that those born of the spirit are unpredictable. Now if you worship the same, you transform nothing. You turn even what might be new into the old. In that case, certainly, you do not remember yourself and you remain a machine. You remember only the wrong self —what is not you. So you carry all the negative states of yesterday into to-day untransformed.

INTELLIGENCE AND INSTINCT

A question was asked recently about the difference between *instinct* and *intelligence*. Now one definition of *intelligence*, used in the Work, is that it is the "power of adaptation". In animals, birds, and insects instinct may be highly developed and yet little or no power of *adaptation* may be present. For example, a bird, say, can only make its nest in a certain way and if interrupted has to start all over again from the beginning—that is, from *Do*. Instinctive Centre seems to work in nature directly by the Law of Octaves—the stage *Do* leading to and exciting *Re*, and the stage *Re* exciting *Mi*, and so on. In biological science, the characteristic "all or nothing" is sometimes applied to the working of the instincts. That is, there is nothing *adapted*. So, in other words, the power of *adaptation* is not a marked feature of the Instinctive Centre. To act instinctively is therefore not the same as intelligence.

Now it has been noticed that the power of adaptation is related to the size of the brain. A living creature with a very small brain and therefore comparatively few brain-cells has little or no power of adaptation, although it may perform most complex movements and make complex things. Now every living thing has its own special form or pattern of Instinctive Centre which is its life-director and gives it meaning. It would be no use creating an animal without creating a life for it to live. The animal would be meaningless. The Work says that Instinctive Centre at birth in us is not blank, as, say, the Intellectual Centre, but is highly developed and gives us our early meanings. The Instinctive Centre, then, may be thought of as being similar to a particular disc inserted into the body, just as a record is into a gramophone. The "tune" on the record is already written on it. The form of the body in each creature is of course adapted to the record. It would be odd and amazing if the brain of a fly were inserted into a dog. Now the size of the brain is connected with the quantity of association-areas, as they are called, and it is upon these so-called silent areas that the powers of adaptation depend, in contrast to compulsory single-track instinctive behaviour. There are vast nerve-tracts and millions of fibres ascending to the brain which carry inwards all the sense-impressions from the external world. There are vast nerve-tracts and fibres that descend from the brain and which terminate in the hundreds of thousands of muscle-bundles that produce action. Between these two sets of nerve-tissues lie the association-areas, owing to which a stimulus coming from, say, a prick of a pin, need not follow *only* one track and cause, say, a cry. We must remind ourselves that there are about 14,000 million separate brain-cells or small minds in an adult European, each with about 100 connections with one another. This is the physical basis of associations and associative pathways. We, of course, use only a very few—so much of the brain seems useless. In short, we have *far more* than we need for ordinary life and this is surprising if the modern theories of evolution by mechanical selection are correct. If we have extra, how can that be mechanical selection? All these associative paths, these brain-cells that endure for our life-time, as distinct from body-cells, form the underlying basis of the power of adaptation. To-day we will speak briefly of associations and adaptation and the connection of these with Work-terms, Self-Remembering and thinking in a new way—that is, μετάνοια, so much used in the New Testament and so badly translated as *repentance*.

In this Work we are studying through the method of *self-observation* to become increasingly conscious of how we take things as we are now. This is the first step—to know oneself, to become aware of one's mechanicalness which one always accepts as "oneself"—that is, to realize that we react in the same way. But in this Work we are also studying how *not* to take things in the same way. This is the second step and it is called Self-Remembering. It is called the First Conscious Shock that we can give the human machine and it depends for its application on a *development of consciousness* at the point of reception of impressions, and its starting-point is *self-observation*. A man who can be conscious simultaneously of the exciting stimulus coming in, say, a person, and the mechanical response, is already at that level of consciousness called in the Work the State of Self-Remembering. This is a higher state of Consciousness. In general, Man is asleep in his mechanicalness and so the world is as it is—that is, Humanity is asleep. Now if the stimulus arising from without always calls up the same reaction, the same response, the same feelings and words, from within, it can be said that such a person is not *intelligent*. Why? Because he has no power of adaptation. The same associations are followed, the same reply is made. You may ask: "Oh, we all know such people." But *you yourself* are like that. You are a machine too and only by struggling to reach another level of consciousness can you cease being the machine you are.

Now when you take in impressions voluntarily the associative paths they follow are different from the paths followed when you take in impressions involuntarily. In this Work we gradually learn to take in impressions more and more consciously—that is, to take in impressions voluntarily. What does this mean? Voluntarily means this: "I see myself taking in this impression in this way and notice what response it makes." If you are in that state something is added to your way of living. This is the beginning of understanding what the Work is about. If you have got so far you have already a priceless pearl. You realize you need not take things as you always have taken things. This is the First Conscious Shock. This means you have intelligence—that is, that you can change your automatic way of behaviour. In other words, you can *adapt* yourself to changing external life and not be held down to one path of associations.

A NOTE ON RELATIONSHIP

Relationship depends on Attitude. With wrong attitude to another you cannot have relationship. Attitude depends ultimately on three things:

(1) Attitude towards yourself,
(2) Attitude towards life, which includes the other person,
(3) Attitude towards the Universe.

The interesting thing is that your attitude towards the Universe is the determining factor. For example, if you believe the Universe is meaningless and merely happened, then you cannot change your attitudes. Since attitude is part of your Being, it follows that you cannot change your attitude, unless you begin to change your Being—that is, the kind of person you are.

In this Work we study a created Universe, descending in a Scale from the Absolute, that is fullest meaning, through successive lower levels of more and more partial meaning. It is for this reason that the Work speaks so much about the importance of levels, and about reaching a higher level of Being—and in this respect it says that there are *more* conscious people and *less* conscious people. It does not speak of Man as one and the same, but of Man on many different levels. It speaks of different circles of Humanity, mechanical and conscious.

Mechanical people cannot understand one another, and therefore cannot make right relationship to one another. Relationship depends on a common understanding. We notice that this is to-day the problem. In the circle of mechanical humanity people do not understand one another. For this reason the circle of mechanical humanity is called "the Circle of Confusion of Tongues" or "Babel". To-night I cannot speak of relationship between mechanical people—that is, people asleep —because it does not occur as a conscious act. It depends entirely on circumstances. I wish to speak only about relationship between two people who are studying the common language of this Work and who can therefore begin to understand one another and so make a conscious relationship. No right relationship can exist save through common understanding. The keynote of relationship is understanding. Now the first thing we have to understand with regard to relationship is that we start off as mechanical people, as different kinds of machines. To begin by self-observation to see that one is one sort of a machine and so always reacts in the same way, helps us to understand the other person who is *also* a machine and who always reacts in the same way, though differently from the way we react. This is the beginning of conscious relationship—namely, the gradual realization that we are both machines. The next stage is for both of us to practise this Work in relationship to one another. Some people, even after hearing this Work for many years, never practise it in relationship to one another. They go about asking what they should do, when all the time they are being told, for example, of the importance of not identifying with negative emotions, but they never practise it. This is because they do not yet feel the Work strongly enough—that is, emotionally enough. It is not yet real. And also this is due to the fact that they never observe themselves from those points of view that the Work teaches them to observe themselves from. In other words, the Work is outside them, mere words and diagrams. They may think that they work on themselves but they work only in imagination. In short, they cannot divide themselves into, in my case, "I" and "Nicoll", or, in your case, "you" and "Smith"—if your name is "Smith". Now unless you can divide yourself into an observing side and an observed side you cannot do this Work. Why? Because you take yourself for granted. If your name is Smith, you take Smith for granted, and probably have many pictures, admirable, of yourself. These self-pictures will fortify Smith and therefore you will always find fault with everyone except yourself. Such a man will identify with his False Personality and his pictures of himself, with everything he has acquired, with all his buffers, his prejudices, all his attitudes, in fact, with everything that constitutes Smith. To all his contradictory 'I's he will say 'I'. Now from the Work point of view such a man is in deep sleep. He may be tolerably placed in life—that is, in sleeping Humanity—but for such a man the Work is useless. The Work is about a further possible development latent in everyone and this development begins with a certain "technical" self-observation along certain lines carefully laid down for us. Only by following the Work can a man begin to change himself, to separate himself from what he has hitherto taken as himself. And only in this way can a man begin to have a *conscious* relationship to others who are working along the same directions as he is. You will see I am talking about relationship from the Work point of view and not from the life point of view. To see in yourself what you criticize so easily in another person is to begin to make a conscious relationship.

There are three lines of Work: (1) work on oneself, (2) work in regard to relationship to other people in the Work, and (3) finally work that helps the Work in general. The first two lines are really all to do with conscious relationship, which, as I said, is based on mutual understanding through the study of a system such as this Work which enables you to speak to one another in the same language and not in terms of Babel—i.e. the usual rows. Conscious relationship is a very wonderful thing, however imperfectly it is carried out by us at present. When two people are trying to make relationship through a common understanding of the Work it will be quite certain that they will find the right way both to behave and act towards one another. In other words, the Work will shew them what to do. There is a phrase, sometimes used: "The Work will find a way"—but this applies only to those who work on themselves.

Now I will add one practical thing more. If two people cherish—in fact, love and dote on—their negative emotions and keep on making mutual inner accounts, one against the other, they will never make relationship. Why? Simply because neither of them is working. Once you begin to have negative emotions against another person, whom you say you love, and enjoy them secretly, you are making it impossible to have relationship. Love is cancelling all debts. In this Work we are supposed to be able, after a time, to "non-identify" with our negative states and not believe in them. This is transcending the situation by work on a higher level. It is not finding a *solution* to the situation—it is *transforming* the situation—through all the new ideas and force that this Work can give. But if your narrow self-attitudes remain the same, nothing can change. The assimilation of the new ideas of this Work and all the new viewpoints it gives, changes your *mind*, and since the primary seat of our attitudes lies in the mind you will realize what was said at the beginning, that only by new knowledge can your attitude change. In that esoteric volume, called the New Testament, where only hints and scraps of esoteric teaching are given, it is taught that a man must "change his mind" before he can heal himself. Unfortunately the Greek word is translated as "repent". It means really that a man, a woman, must change their whole outlook and way of thinking if they themselves wish to be different. Now as long as your Being is what it is, as long as you are the same person, you will attract the same life. Your Being, the Work teaches, attracts your life. That is, whether you marry someone else, or go to the colonies, etc., if your *Being* remains what it is, it will attract the *same* life, the same troubles, and so on. A new life is only possible by work on oneself—for this can change your Being. But if you remain a fool, as G. said once, you will always attract all that belongs to being a fool.

Great Amwell House, July 12, 1947

AIM

In speaking about aim and having aim in this Work it was said on one occasion that there are three kinds of aim. First there are *invented* aims. An invented aim has no practical meaning. A man, for example, might make it his aim to count the numbers of words beginning with the letter R in the Bible. And not only that, but he might seriously think that this would be a Work-aim and would make it possible for him to become more conscious. Second, there are *imaginary* aims. An imaginary aim is based on imagination about oneself. A person, for example, who imagines he is a good, kind man, makes it his aim to be still more good and kind. That is, he starts from a picture of himself, and all pictures of ourselves are formed out of the imagination. Again, imaginary aim necessarily goes with imaginary work on oneself. People may imagine they observe themselves and work on themselves and it is all imagination. Actually, they neither observe themselves nor work on themselves. Third, there are *real* aims. There is only one possible source of *real* aim. Real aim must grow out of one's own self-study in relation to the instructions given by this Work. If a man studies himself along the lines laid down in the Work he will eventually begin to catch sight of what his real, individual aim must be. Remember that one man's aim is not another's in the Work. Although the method of self-study is the same for all in the Work, it is clear that a No. 1 Man whose centre of gravity lies in the Instinctive or Moving Centre will have to work on himself differently from a No. 3 Man whose centre of gravity lies in the Intellectual Centre. Each, to become balanced, so that all centres can be equally used, will seem to move as it were in an opposite direction. But the supreme aim of the Work, to awaken, will be the same for each of them.

At first, invented aims are necessary in order to see how difficult it is to keep them and how mechanical we are without realizing it. For instance, a man decides not to sit down until six o'clock. Of course, this is merely an invented aim. But in trying to keep it he will observe how many different and contradictory voices speak in him and **he** will begin to realize that he is not one 'I' but many 'I's, and many **other** things that the Work teaches him, which he has not yet realized **in** practical experience. For if a man, a woman, do not apply the Work to themselves, they never advance an inch, and quite naturally. To experience and so begin to understand this Work, self-observation is absolutely necessary. Invented aim is an *artificial* aid to self-observation in the early stages. Imaginary aim is useless unless one can observe it and see how absurd it is in comparison with the direct knowledge of oneself gained by uncritical self-observation and the special quiet memory that is formed in consequence.

Real aim, as was said, grows out of one's own study of oneself. It changes, at different stages of the Work, for what has been done it is no longer necessary to do. Each stage opens a further stage, as in the case of a journey. So real aim changes but some things remain. A man, for example, must *always* remember himself, although his way of doing so may change. At first, by self-observation he realizes he does not remember himself, and realizing all that the Work says about the necessity of reaching the 3rd State of Consciousness where only help can reach us, his aim becomes that of trying to find out for himself what Self-Remembering is. This arises out of his self-study by observation, for he has seen he is asleep and does not remember himself. This is real aim, because it is based upon what the Work teaches and upon what he has seen for himself in the light of the Work and the insight it gives. In that case, that man may expect a result. But a man who makes always invented aims that have no relation to what he needs to awaken cannot expect any result. He does not know how to ask and unless we know how to ask we cannot receive. When we begin to notice what puts us asleep we are nearer the possibility of asking aright—that is, making real aim. For aim is really request to which we desire response.

Great Amwell House, July 19, 1947

FURTHER TALK ON ESSENCE AND PERSONALITY

Essence is what we are born with: Personality is what we acquire by contact with outer life. Essence is internal to Personality. Personality surrounds Essence. It forms the outer man, as it were, and Essence forms the inner man. The relations between the two are very complicated. Both are necessary, for Essence, the real part of us, cannot grow beyond a certain point without the aid of Personality, the artificial part of us. One interesting thing is that the Work teaches that these two parts of us are under different laws. Everything that exists is under laws. Personality is under what is called in the Work the Law of Accident and Essence is under the Law of Fate. We begin life under the Law of Fate, but soon pass under the Law of Accident. But we should, in later life, pass out of the Law of Accident and come again under the Law of Fate. These phases correspond to change of sign— that is, at first in early life Essence is active; then it becomes passive, while Personality is forming ; finally it should become active again at the expense of Personality. Thus one's task in general in the Work is, after Personality is formed, to make Personality passive. If you remain in older life dominated by all the opinions, prejudices, buffers, attitudes, pictures of yourself, etc., that you have acquired in Personality, Essence cannot grow. The unreal side of you gains the victory. Also you remain under the Law of Accident. That follows from the unrealness of oneself and from continuing to do unreal things. One remains then an imitation or invented man or an imitation or invented woman. Not only so, but all the worries and anxieties imitated by the Personality torture the life. People then cannot see how many useless efforts they make and how they rush after meaningless things. Essence cannot deceive itself, because it is real. But Personality can deceive Essence. A man may pretend to himself that he only wishes to help, say, the poor, and Essence thinks it is so. But Personality wishes to gain power and cares nothing for the poor. That is, the outer man deceives the inner man. The power of distinguishing between real and unreal things is lost in this kind of mill-race in which so often it seems that the ideal is to "waste no time", etc. Waste no time for what? Now hurry, strain, worry, anxiety, a wrong sense of duty, a constant inner uproar and all such states lead only to wrong efforts in useless directions, and strengthen the hold of Personality. Finally they destroy all connection with

1059

Essence and the person becomes a sort of worried empty shell. For these states are all illusions, all forms of hypnotism, all little tricks used by those influences that seek to keep Man asleep on this Earth—and which they do so successfully. A great cleansing of oneself from Personality is required in this Work from those who can *hear* it. If your name is Smith, then you must work against Smith, for that is the name of your Personality which is active. For this reason you will find it necessary really to study and obey what the Work tells you to do and so apply it to yourself. Smith will be under the Law of Accident. By beginning to make him passive through the power of this Work you will draw force into Essence and it will be able to develop. Essence is under the Law of Fate. A new growth of Essence is something that can never be taken away from you. It can only happen through what is internally and genuinely seen and done and never through the external action of life. A new growth of Essence is not something which one knows or plans. It takes place when the falseness of Personality is weakened by genuine inner perception of its unrealness. It means a change in the level of Being. So the life cannot repeat itself as before since, if Being changes, it will attract a new life. But if it does not change, it will attract the same life.

Now I will quote part of a talk on Essence and Personality given by Mr. Gurdjieff and recorded by Mr. Ouspensky. It begins with a brief reference to the subject of Will. Mr. Gurdjieff is speaking:

"The question of Will, of one's own will and of another man's will, is much more complicated than it seems at first glance. A man has not sufficient will *to do*—that is, to control himself and all his actions—but he has sufficient will to obey another person—or obey the Work. And only in this way can he escape from the *Law of Accident*. There is no other way.

"I mentioned before about *Fate* and *Accident* in a man's life. We will now take the meaning of these words in more detail. Fate also exists, but not for everyone. Most people are separated from their Fate and live under Law of Accident only. Fate is a result of planetary influences which correspond to a man's type. We will speak about types later. In the meantime you must grasp one thing. A man can have the Fate which corresponds to his type but he practically never does have it. This arises because Fate has relation to only one part of Man—namely, to his *Essence*. It must be understood that Man consists of two parts— *Essence* and *Personality*. Essence in a man is what is his own: Personality in a man is what 'is not his own'. 'Not his own' means what has come from outside, what he has learned, or what reflects all traces of external impressions left in the memory and in the sensations, all words and movements that have been learned, all feelings created by imitation —all this is 'not his own', all this is in 'Personality'.

"From the point of view of ordinary psychology, the division of Man into 'Personality' and 'Essence' is hardly comprehensible. It is more exact to say that such a division does not exist in psychology at all.

"A small child has no 'Personality' as yet. He is what he really is. He is 'Essence'. His desires, tastes, likes, dislikes, express his Being such as it is. But as soon as so-called education begins, 'Personality' begins to grow. 'Personality' is created partly by the intentional influences of other people—that is, by 'education'—and partly by involuntary imitation of them by the child itself. In the creation of 'Personality' a great part is also played by 'resistance' to people around him, and by attempts to conceal from them something that is 'his own' or 'real'.

"Essence is the truth in Man: Personality is the false. But in proportion as Personality grows, Essence manifests itself more and more rarely and more and more feebly, and it often happens that Essence stops in its growth at a very early age and grows no further. It happens very often that the Essence of a grown-up man, even that of a very intellectual and, in the accepted meaning of the word, highly educated man, stops at the level of a child of five or six. This means that everything that we see in this man is really foreign. What is his own in Man, that is in his Essence, is usually only manifested in his instincts and in his simplest emotions. There are cases, however, where a man's Essence grows parallel with his Personality. Such cases represent very rare exceptions, especially in the circumstances of cultured life. Essence has more chances of development in men who live nearer to nature in difficult conditions of constant struggles and danger. But as a rule the Personality of such people is very little developed. They have more of what is their 'own' but very little of what is 'not their own'—that is to say, they lack education and instruction, they lack culture. Culture creates Personality and is at the same time the product and the result of Personality. We do not realize that the whole of our life, all we call civilisation, all we call science, philosophy, art, politics, is created by people's Personality—that is, by what is 'not their own' in them.

"The element that is 'not his own' differs from what is Man's 'own' by the fact that it can be lost, altered, or taken away by artificial means. There exists a possibility of experimental verification of the relation of Personality to Essence. In Eastern schools, ways and means are known, by the help of which it is possible to separate Man's Personality from his Essence. For this purpose they sometimes use hypnosis, sometimes special narcotics, sometimes certain kinds of exercises. If Personality and Essence are for a time separated in a man by one or another of these means, two beings are as it were formed in him, who speak in different voices, have completely different tastes, aims and interests, and one of these two beings often proves to be on the level of a small child. Continuing the experiment further it is possible to put one of these beings to sleep, or the experiment may begin by putting to sleep either Personality or Essence. Certain narcotics have the property of putting Personality to sleep without affecting Essence. And for a certain time after taking this narcotic a man's Personality disappears, as it were, and only his Essence remains. And it happens that a man full of the most varied and exalted ideas, full of sympathies and antipathies, love and hatred, attachments, patriotism, habits, tastes, desires, convictions, suddenly proves quite empty, without thoughts, without feelings, without convictions, without views. Everything that has agitated him before now leaves him perfectly indifferent. Sometimes he sees the artificiality and the imaginary character of his usual moods, or his high-sounding words, sometimes he simply forgets them as though they had never existed. Things for which he was ready to sacrifice his life now appear to him ridiculous, meaningless and unworthy of his attention. All that he can find in himself is a small number of instinctive inclinations and tastes. He is fond of sweets, he likes warmth, he dislikes cold, he dislikes the thought of work, or, on the contrary, he likes the idea of physical movement. And that is all. Sometimes, though very seldom, and sometimes when it is least expected, Essence proves fully grown and fully developed in a man, even in cases of undeveloped Personality, and, in this case, Essence unites together everything that is serious and real in a man.

"But this very seldom happens. As a rule Man's Essence is either primitive, savage and childish, or else simply stupid. The development of Essence depends on work on oneself.

"A very important moment in the work on oneself is when a man begins to distinguish between his Personality and his Essence. A man's Real 'I', his individuality, can grow only from his Essence."

Great Amwell House, July 26, 1947

THE IDEA OF PAYMENT IN THE WORK

On one occasion Mr. Ouspensky said: "If we attain happiness before we have paid for it, we shall not be able to keep it. We shall lose it and what was happiness turns into pain. We must suffer first and suffer *now* to be free from everlasting suffering. And by suffering in the Work-sense is meant that suffering that goes with the effort to give up one's mechanical suffering, to give up useless suffering." "How can this be done?" was asked. The answer in so many words was: "By not identifying with one's suffering. Nothing is more easy than to suffer. Everyone suffers. But this kind of suffering is not conscious but mechanical and simply leads to endless unhappiness, and indeed can become a bad habit that cannot be conquered. All this useless suffering belongs to the pain-factory of Organic Life that cares nothing for Humanity. It is an energy used by something else. No one evolves, no one becomes more conscious by identifying with useless suffering. Some people suffer if they cannot have their own way even in the smallest detail; even if it rains when they want to go out they suffer. So everything becomes an increasing burden.. They are only happy, so to speak, when they are ill."

Mr. Ouspensky said many other things at different times about the necessity of giving up our suffering. One thing was that when people speak of sacrificing themselves, or ask what they should sacrifice, they speak as if they had something real to sacrifice. He said people have very big ideas about themselves, but really they have nothing of their own to sacrifice that is worthy enough to be called a sacrifice save their suffering. "If only," he said, "people would observe their suffering, whether they shew it or endeavour to conceal it or nurse it in secret, and would begin to sacrifice it, they would change their level of Being and find themselves internally in better company. But it is extraordinary how people cling to their suffering and seem to feel they would cease to have any personal identity if they gave it up."

I asked him whether, if Humanity were at the third level of Consciousness, which it was born with a right to be at, the world would still be full of useless suffering. He laughed and said: "How could it be? People would all remember themselves and so would not identify. Everyone has a grievance. Think of all the negative emotions with which people identify—despair and horror and depression and dislike and worry and hate and a hundred others. They do not see that all this is useless suffering and that they cannot have happiness while they are behaving like that. They are not fit for it. But if they pay long enough beforehand by work on themselves, and learn how not to identify with their bad moods, and separate from them, then they may reach happiness—yes, on this Earth", and he added: "A man sitting in this room, appearing just as others, can be in a quite different inner state and experience quite different emotions and thoughts from everyone else and yet shew nothing outwardly unusual." Often Mr. Ouspensky emphasized that there were better states of ourselves and that everyone knew it. Asked once what the Work is all about, he said: "It is about reaching a better state of oneself, learning how to, learning what efforts are needed and what to avoid and knowing how to maintain it. Reflect on all the Work-teaching practically, if you have not done so already. Begin to make an effort to see what it is about. It is not very difficult. Why, for example, does it speak so much about not identifying with negative states? You must understand," he said, looking on us all, "that a negative state is not a *better* state of oneself. It is a *worse* state. But some of you do not yet understand."

At the time these words of Mr. Ouspensky seemed to awaken something in me. Although I had heard so often about negative states, it had not come home to me with any depth that *I* was so often negative and that in a negative state one was not *better* but *worse*. Negative states seem to possess an energy of their own and one tends to feel more vivid and alive when one identifies fully with them—that is, plunges head over heels into them. Only later does one see that this apparent accession of energy is due to a contraction of the whole being down to a few narrow, exacting and often relentless 'I's. Then when one has escaped, say, for a time, from their tyrannical power, one tastes the difference.

1063

When one can taste the difference then one has started to understand what the Work is about—namely, reaching a better state of oneself. The Work assures us that this is possible and gives many ideas, diagrams, etc., concerning this. But it promises nothing. It says that if you value the teaching, listen to it, and apply it to yourself with sincerity in daily life, you will get results. But each of you must understand that the Work is not going to do *your* three lines of Work for you. In any case, it would be impossible. You cannot make an effort for someone else who should make it.

Great Amwell House, September 6, 1947

SEPARATION AND SELF-REMEMBERING

The energy of impressions is used up by the psychic machinery. I will ask you a question: "What is the difference between a mechanical and a conscious man receiving impressions?" The answer is that in a mechanical man, No. 1, 2 or 3, the energy of impressions is not transformed. It is used up in turning rolls or centres, in stimulating different 'I's, in negative states, and in all those mechanical reactions, attitudes, pictures and thoughts and feelings that men and women insist on taking as their real selves. In a more conscious person, one who can separate, this energy derived from incoming impressions is not wholly used up in working the mechanical psyche, but can pass it and become transformed into a higher energy. How is this possible? By Self-Remembering. This is called the First Conscious Shock. Mechanical people—that is, men and women in general—do not give themselves the First Conscious Shock. They do not remember themselves. For this they pay many penalties—that is, they are under the Law of Accident and they, asleep themselves, dwell among sleeping people who cannot understand one another; nor can they attract the help necessary for them. Help cannot reach the 2nd State of Consciousness: it can only reach the 3rd State—which we pass into when we remember ourselves. We cannot realize what penalties people on earth pay for not remembering themselves, save through studying ourselves when asleep.

All the absurdities and cruelties of life, all the waste and imbecilities, all the vain-glory and insincerity, all the lies, all the pretence and falsities and misunderstandings, are due to *one definite cause*, as this Work teaches—namely, people do not remember themselves. In consequence, they are driven, as by a belt, by constantly changing outer circumstances, war and peace, and so on. Life is constantly changing circumstances. What is it in us that thus is driven? It is the external, acquired side of us, called Personality. We have an outer and an inner man, an

1064

outer and an inner woman. If the inner were developed in each of us —the real, essential part—all life would be different and we would no longer be at the mercy of changing outer circumstances, now having something internally stable. But for this to take place, the practice of Self-Remembering is necessary. When a man and a woman remember themselves, they are no longer Smith, or Mrs. Smith, Robinson, or Mrs. Robinson, Brown, or Mrs. Brown. In Self-Remembering one does not remember the Personality, acquired by religion, education and example, but something behind all this *acquired* part, which surrounds Essence and is different in different people and nations so that they can never agree. For one man merely to remember that he is a Mohammedan or a Sikh or a Hindoo, another that he is a Christian, another that he is an Arab, another that he is a Jew—or again that he is an aristocrat, or a doctor, or that he is a labourer, or that he is rich or poor, good-looking or ugly—all *that* is not to *remember onself*. Each man, each woman, has at the back of them, deep to Essence within, Real 'I', that is neither Mohammedan, Christian, Jew nor Arab, aristocrat nor poor man, good-looking or not. So the Work teaches that when a man or woman comes to the point of realizing his or her own *nothingness*, then this nothingness attracts Real 'I'. For if you are over-swelling with yourself and your virtues and value, how on earth can you come in contact with *anything* real? So Self-Remembering, which is endless in its different forms, can never be based on your self-merit, but only on a gradual feeling—profoundly emotional—and by that is meant the inner perception of the truth about yourself—of your own unreality which hitherto you have taken as yourself. So the Work talks of Imaginary 'I' or False Personality, and teaches in so many ways that this Imaginary 'I', with which people advance into life and which continually they suffer from, must be made passive. I remind you again of what we were told in France: "Personality has scarcely any right to exist here." Just reflect what that means.

Now in regard to separation by non-identifying, it is said that in separating, say, from a negative emotion—that is, struggling not to identify with it—you must at the same time try to remember yourself, remember your aim, and remember all the Work means to you so far. Then the force withdrawn from some typical reaction by separation *passes into Self-Remembering* and so does not flood some other mechanical reaction. This is the beginning of the transformation of the energy of impressions. That is, *Do* 48 passes into *Re* 24 and eventually into *Mi* 12.

This short paper is written because of a difficulty that arose in a sub-group recently. A paper was read in which the following sentence appeared: "The Work says that we must struggle every day with identifying and that this struggle takes very many forms, and very many directions. For example, a man may through his observation realize that he identifies with someone, and may for a time separate himself from that particular form of identifying. But he will begin to identify with something else far more." It was said in the report: "We all felt at a loss to understand why he should pass into a greater state of identification subsequent to having observed and separated from one state." The answer is that if you take force away from one mechanical reaction it will pass into and strengthen another mechanical reaction —*unless* you remember yourself and all the meaning of the Work and your aim, and so give it a definite direction. If you do, the force of the Work in you will increase—i.e., you starve yourself to increase the power of the Work. There is another power apart from your own self-ascribed power. The power of the Work demands a sacrifice of the self-ascribed power. To starve yourself to yourself is useless. If you starve a negative 'I' by not identifying and that is all you do, the force liberated will go to some other negative 'I'. But if you give the force abstracted from the negative 'I' to the whole sense and meaning and valuation of the Work, it will be absorbed and stored by all those 'I's which lead eventually to Real 'I'. People fast or starve to increase their merit. They perform rituals, etc. But there is a phrase in the Old Testament where God says: "But have ye fasted unto *me*?" To fast, say, from negative states *for the sake of the Work* means that the power of the Work will increase in you. To obey the Work is to fast unto the Work. But all this is very deep and internally sincere.

Great Amwell House, September 13, 1947

THE INNER MAN

"If thy right eye offend thee, pluck it out, and cast it from thee: for it is profitable for thee that one of thy members should perish, and not that thy whole body should be cast into hell.

"And if thy right hand offend thee, cut it off, and cast it from thee: for it is profitable for thee that one of thy members should perish, and not that thy whole body should be cast into hell."

(*Matt.* V 29, 30)

How difficult it is to grasp what this means as long as the literal sense dominates the mind. Of what use to pluck out the right eye or to cut off the right hand as perhaps some fanatics have done? It is the psychological meaning that matters. What does the eye mean in the ancient language of parables? Christ said: "The lamp of the body is the eye: if therefore thine eye be single, thy whole body shall be full of light; but if thine eye be evil, thy whole body shall be full of darkness." (*Matt.* VI 22.) But in saying this it is not meant that the literal eye is the lamp, but the psychological eye. What is the psychological eye? It is the eye of the mind. It is how one sees things mentally, not physically. When a man says: "I think I see what you mean," he does not refer to his physical eye, but to the eye of his mind. That is, he means that he thinks he *understands* what you mean. So to transform literal into psychological meaning, when Christ says that the eye is the lamp of the body, it could be written: "The understanding is what illuminates the mind." According to the quality of the understanding, so is the mind illuminated with meaning. A low level of understanding therefore makes the mind dark. The mind will be in darkness because the understanding is undeveloped or negative.

* * *

Why is the right eye to be plucked out if it offends? The *right* eye and the *right* hand, if they offend, are to be got rid of. Why not the left eye and hand? The right hand is ordinarily the more conscious. The more conscious side of a man is the external man, the side he makes use of most: the less conscious side is the inner, deeper man. If the external man offends or causes offence, in relation to the inner, deeper man, then that which offends in the external man must be plucked out or cut off. Why? Because these two men must become one.

The outer man is formed by contact with outer life, to adapt to life. If we understand this, then it is apparent that the *left* eye and *left* hand could not be plucked out or cut off, for they belong to the inner man. Esoteric—that is, inner—teaching is about the development of the inner man, to make it possible for it to control the outer man as a good rider controls a horse so that they become one. In so far as the acquired views of the external man (the right eye) offend the growing understanding of the inner man, or the actions of the external man (the right hand) do the same, then it is a question of plucking out or cutting off what offends in the outer man—the man acquired from life. For a man can only grow from his own understanding, which is inner freedom, and not from his acquired views.

A man with only an outer side developed towards life is a *half-man* —a one-sided man in the sense of a man cut longitudinally in half. He has one leg and arm and half a brain. There are two sides to a man, a right and left, an outer and an inner. They have to be joined together to form the entire man. The faculties that turn us towards life and those that turn us towards the soul need equivalent development. The *lost half of us*, by remaining lost, renders our existence a *half*-existence. So we live with half-meanings. There is an incredible lack of meaning in each day that we arrange for by forming habits from which we derive meaning at secondhand. The external man—and so the external mind —is open to the ambitions, cares, and worries of life. This external mind, however well-formed, does not and cannot unite with the other side of the man. By a change in circumstances it can be brought to nought—and the man perhaps dies, having nothing else. Life is a picture of people fighting to keep the external man alive. One mistake, major or minor—and the man falls. Why? Because all the meaning of himself is in what is outside himself—in the external man which is not the real man.

Self-esteem, self-liking, self-approbation keep the external man active. When a man begins to see what he is really like, the false idea of himself diminishes. This makes it possible for the inner, real but undeveloped side to grow. But as long as a man believes in what he imagines himself to be this is impossible. In this connection there are many spurious ways of saying that one is bad, headstrong, and so on. All this rests on the vanity of self-approbation and is not *really seeing* what one is and knowing it. To say easily that one is bad, etc., is not to feel its truth. Once a man begins to see straightly what he is like, he is silent about himself. The danger then is that he may kill himself unless he is shewn that this is a necessary and definite stage in his inner development.

Great Amwell House, September 20, 1947

NOTE ON SELF-OBSERVATION

OBSERVATION OF ONE'S MECHANICALNESS

Realizing that your ways are not the only ways, that your views are not the only views, that your opinions are not the only opinions, that your values are not the only things to value and that yourself are not the only possible yourself—all this is necessary in the path of self-change. Why? Because it weakens Personality. But for it to do so, the realization must be genuine—a matter of direct inner perception. Let us imagine a man called Mr. Amwell. He says: "I have observed myself, but I do not see how that helps. I have observed what I say, for example, but I do not yet understand why I should do so." In short, Mr. Amwell—who I hope is actually an imaginary person or otherwise in these days I shall no doubt be liable for libel—I say, Mr. Amwell does not realize what idea lies behind the Work-teaching concerning self-observation. He does not see why it is necessary. No doubt he has never said to himself: "Now I wish to change this or that in myself." He does not see why he should observe himself. Now the Work says, for instance, that self-observation is a method of self-change. It says this quite early. Mr. Amwell says he observes himself, and cites as an example that he observes what he says but does not see why he should. He says it makes no difference to him. He adds that it does not change him in any way and so he cannot see why he should observe himself. Clearly he hints that it is a waste of time. Let us suppose a conversation is held with him by the Work itself. The Work says to him: "I notice, Mr. Amwell, that whenever Tennyson is mentioned you say he was no good as a poet." Mr. Amwell says: "Yes—that is exactly what I always say." The Work then asks him: "You dislike hard-boiled eggs, I believe?" Mr. Amwell says: "Yes, I always tell people that. It is quite true." The Work then asks him various similar questions to which Mr. Amwell replies in a similar manner. Maybe there might be one, resembling Mr. Amwell, who, candidly understanding himself, would add that he is a little aware that he does say the same things over and over again and may bore people. But even so there is a considerable step between such a confession and the deeper recognition that he is *mechanical*. He is fixed—crystallized—but does not see it. A man, a woman, can be very satisfied with their mechanicalness, not because they see it as mechanicalness, but because they see it as their own intelligent conscious selves. Long before they get to opening their lips, their audience knows exactly what gramophone record is going to utter such solemn truths as that they dislike Tennyson or hard-boiled eggs.

Now one of the first things taught in this Work is the necessity for realizing one's own mechanicalness through uncritical self-observation. A man, a woman, very early can become almost completely mechanical. They say the same things over and over again, they feel the same feelings, they do the same things. And it is almost as if they dislike the very idea that they should not continue to be such machines, such bits of sheer mechanicalness, and awaken from their sleep. They are always upset by the same events. They are always prejudiced towards the same people. They like or dislike almost automatically. And, however it may seem outwardly, if anyone touches them beneath the skin, there is found a calm self-esteem that is apparently the explanation of their mechanicalness. That is, beneath the surface they strongly approve of themselves however they apologize for themselves. Here there is a lack of connection which results in a certain psychological blindness. For example, if a person easily says he or she is no good, it means often that it masks something quite different, such as conceit. There is a lack of connection, due to a lack of long and sincere observation. The man, the woman, do not see what they are like on both sides, right and left. They live in compensatory pictures—often really too modest to be tolerable to others who sense their other side, which is contradictory. All this, of course, applies in very complex ways to all of us—namely, these inner and outer contradictions. A man may seem outwardly conceited and boastful and within himself feels poor and inadequate and vice versa. But the opposites are mixed in us in a very strange way.

Now a man should observe what he observes. To observe is difficult. It needs a conscious effort. You cannot observe yourself mechanically. That certainly will change nothing. But, in such a case, if you become cleverer, you will begin to observe that you always observe only two or three things over and over again. This will not separate you from your mechanical self. For has not observation now become a very part of your mechanical self? The function of Observing 'I' is to move inwards, more and more deeply, so that more and more of yourself can

1069

be seen by it. If Observing 'I' remains on the surface of yourself it cannot perform its real task, which is to make a man more and more objective to himself, more and more aware of what he has hitherto calmly taken as himself. If self-observation is truly carried out and not blocked by some strong attitude or picture that the man or woman cannot observe, then it leads to seeing bits of one's life and behaviour all together. This is called taking photographs of oneself. "One has", it was once said, "to take a number of full-plate photographs of oneself and keep them in an album and often look at them." Yes, this will certainly begin to change you. It will change the typical feeling of 'I' that you reside in—the usual sense of yourself. For unless *that* is altered, nothing can alter.

To return to Mr. Amwell—one wonders if, for instance, he observes not only what he says but, let me say, his vanity, negative states, suspicions, jealousies, laziness, his queer pictures of himself, his imitated attitudes, his fixed opinions, his buffers, his internal considering, or indeed anything that the Work teaches him to observe. If not, he will have no real photographs of himself. His album will be empty. Also he will never reach the state, possible for all who genuinely work—who genuinely value and apply the Work to themselves—namely, the state in which it is given to one sometimes to stand aside internally, to be separated, and to watch the stream of moods, passion, negative thoughts, worries, hatreds, depressions and bitterness, with which one is usually wholly identified. So he or she will not be able to understand, for example, the following quotation I give you from a recent letter: "Lying in bed in the morning I saw thoughts coming in, jealous thoughts, anxious thoughts, sad thoughts, self-pitying thoughts, which followed one another, and seemed to pass through my mind and then went out again, and they were nothing to do with me at all." Now to have this experience means that you begin to realize what is inner freedom. You have heard it sometimes said that this Work is to give inner freedom. But if a man cannot understand what self-observation is or if he has always identified himself with everything he has observed, if he has always said 'I' to it—how can he ever reach the state illustrated in the above quotation? Try to see what is meant here for yourselves.

DIFFERENT 'I'S

A recent question was as follows: "What does it mean that we have many different 'I's in us?" This question is a good question and everyone in this Work should often ask it of themselves. "What does it mean that we have many different 'I's in us?" The Work teaches that we are not a unity, a oneness, but a manyness, a multiplicity. It says in so many words: "People imagine they are one, a single 'I', and that they remain always the same. That is, they imagine that they have one thing they call 'I' and that this 'I', that they imagine they have, always behaves in the same way." Now the Work calls this *Imaginary 'I'*. That is, people who imagine they have a real, permanent 'I', that always behaves in the same way, actually have Imaginary 'I'. They imagine they have a real, unchanging, permanent 'I'. But by imagining they have, they have only Imaginary 'I'. They imagine they have a real, permanent 'I', but have not. In place of having a real, permanent, unchanging 'I', they have Imaginary 'I'. And by clinging to this belief, they cannot ever attain to Real 'I'. Why is this? It is because if you imagine you have something, you will not want it. Imagination can supplant reality and does. Imagination works in nearly all the centres, and supplants what is, or could be, real. If I imagine I have cigarettes in my drawer I will not go out to get some.

Now the Work is about destroying illusions about ourselves. What is an illusion about oneself? One illusion is exactly that we possess a real, permanent, unvarying 'I'. The Work calls this illusion Imaginary 'I'. It is a very good name for it, and when you begin, through self-observation, to realize that you have no such real, permanent unchanging 'I', you are beginning to move in the direction the Work leads you into. What is that direction? It is the direction, the journey, to finding Real 'I'—the 'I' that people imagine they possess already. People have no Real 'I'. That has to be earned by hard and long Work. People have many 'I's—not one. They are not a unity, but a multiplicity. Everyone has many different and contradictory 'I's, to each of which the value of 'I' is given. Through everyone's mouth many different 'I's speak at different moments. But all this is taken both by the speaker and by the person hearing him as *one 'I' speaking*. Yes, the same mouth is speaking, but not the same 'I'. Unless we begin to see these different 'I's that speak in our name we cannot change. Why? Because we cannot separate from them. We take them as ourselves.

When by self-observation a man or woman begins to realize that he or she is not one real, permanent, unchanging 'I', but is many different 'I's, they begin to lose an illusion they have hitherto been under. That is, they begin to move inwardly towards Real 'I'. Real 'I' has no illusions. Now one 'I' may promise something. But the next 'I' called up by circumstances knows nothing of this promise or does not agree with it. All this you must observe and notice in yourselves. Fortunately—or unfortunately—between these different 'I's there are partitions or buffers. These prevent us from seeing our contradictions. The Work says: "If a man had not these buffers—if these buffers were destroyed suddenly—he would go mad." Why would he go mad? He would go mad because he would become conscious of all his contradictions. To begin to understand all this it is necessary to be able to observe *for yourself* (not because you have been told on the blackboard) that you are not one 'I' but many different 'I's that take charge of you at different moments and that are often quite contradictory.

Now try to discuss this Work-teaching of different 'I's and try to give examples based on real self-observation. Kindly do not begin to ask what Real 'I' is. Begin with the plain fact that you have not got it, but in place of it you have many different 'I's, to all of which you say 'I', thus having only Imaginary 'I'. In connection with this teaching that Man has many different 'I's which, if he aims at internal development, he must observe and see that they are *not him*—not 'I'—the Work compares Man mechanical, Man asleep, to a House in Disorder. The House is full of servants. But there is no Master. Each of the servants uses the telephone and speaks in the name of the Master. Such is the inner state of Man.

Great Amwell House, October 4, 1947

FURTHER NOTE ON 'I'S

'I's and Levels of Being

Last time we spoke of different 'I's in us and how we are not one person but many different persons and how unless we realize this by direct self-observation we can never begin to understand ourselves or other people. In this connection we spoke of Real 'I' which it is the aim of this Work to reach, in place of having our centre of gravity in Imaginary 'I' that is the source of so much misery and misunderstanding. Just figure to yourself two Imaginary 'I's marrying each other. The dream-man marries the dream-woman and so on. All this, of course, can lead nowhere save in romantic novels which usually and wisely end just when the imaginary hero marries the imaginary heroine —obviously a difficult starting-point suggesting difficult situations in the future. It was also said last time that occasionally, even in ordinary mechanical life, we may experience a momentary trace of Real 'I'. As was said, this may happen in cases of extreme fatigue, as in war, when suddenly an access of force comes, or in great danger, also in many strange ways that cannot be classified, but produce the same result.

By contrast, the usual life of sleep that we are immersed in, when we identify with everything outside us, and inside us, has an utterly different taste from those brief, calm but rare moments of touching Real 'I', which in the Work are called "moments of awakening from sleep" or "moments of Self-Remembering". The very undeniable difference in inner taste, in emotional quality, between our ordinary and these exceptional moments shews us that there is within us some other level of consciousness, some other centre of gravity and some other level of experience—and clearly a higher level—that we do not customarily know. Now in this Work, as in all esoteric teaching, it is said that to reach a higher level of ourselves, to make contact with 'I's that do not exist, so to speak, in the basement of the house of our being, efforts on oneself have to be made. We are told what efforts have to be made very clearly. For example, to take one line, we are told that a man must observe himself, he must observe that he is not one but many, that he must by practical work destroy the illusion that he has Real 'I', he must get to know by observation some of his prominent 'I's that hitherto he has mistaken for himself and not identify with them—that is, not say 'I' to them—because what in you you say 'I' to chains you to it. Once you say 'I' to any thought or feeling it has power over you. In hysteria, the victim identifies with every sensational and horrifying thought. There is no power of self-observation and separation. It is something like thinking that a snake in the grass is you and so not being able to separate object from subject. There is a mystery here which goes very deep and cannot be entered into now—save to say that this Work teaches that mankind is under a definite hypnotic force to keep it asleep and prevent it from waking up. I will give one hint of this from another esoteric source. It is said in Isaiah: "The Lord hath poured out upon you the spirit of deep sleep, and hath closed your eyes. (*Is.* XXIX 10) And in the New Testament: "This people's heart is waxed gross, and their ears are dull of hearing and their eyes they have closed, lest haply they should perceive with their eyes and hear with their ears, and understand with their heart . . ." (*Matt*, XIII 15) This Work merely says that Man is asleep and that we are born asleep into a world of sleeping people who are kept asleep and spend their time in killing one another. Now the realization that we are many and not one, that the quality of our Being is characterized by multiplicity instead of unity, belongs to a stage in the journey called "awakening from sleep" which can end in a man being born again—that is, finding and becoming Real 'I'. What then undertakes this journey? Those 'I's in a man which have the most understanding. We come, then, to the idea that our different 'I's are not on the same level. Some 'I's are very small in understanding—very mean, very poor, envious and stupid. Some 'I's are bigger, and so on. When a man begins to hear the Work with both ears, and to observe himself in accordance with its instructions, there gather around Observing 'I' all 'I's who wish to understand more. This collection of 'I's is on a higher level than the 'I's that deal with everyday life and its affairs. This collection of 'I's that form round Observing 'I' is called Deputy-Steward and if they are strong enough to persist and fight against all these negative and disbelieving 'I's that attack them a further stage is reached called "Steward". This is the herald of Real 'I'. So we can put them in this way: Observing 'I', Deputy-Steward, Steward, Real 'I', in order of ascent.

I said last time that one should try to observe and study the history of different 'I's in ourselves. Some people undertake to write their biographies. But in their autobiographies they always take themselves as one 'I', moving through Time. They should write instead the history of different 'I's in them. Now our most mechanical 'I's live in small parts of centres—in the basement of oneself. They are usually quite unintelligent and have no understanding. They belong to the lowest level of our Being. They take charge of us most of the day, speak through our mouths and call themselves 'I'. They are rigid, always saying the same things in the same way. Towards the end of life it is often noticeable how the better and more understanding 'I's in a person get disconnected and there remain only the most petty and tiresome 'I's. This is impossible to understand unless we realize that a person is not one 'I', but many 'I's, and that these 'I's are on different levels, as on the wires on a telegraph-pole. In this Work one should aim not to go always in company with negative, weak, vain, poor 'I's, for they spoil everything, and produce bad, inner states. It is a common thing that while we have no power of making ourselves happy we have considerable powers of separating from unhappy states once we begin to understand what self-observation and non-identifying mean. But all this belongs to awakening from sleep so perhaps it is not so curious in view of that goal.

Great Amwell House, October 11, 1947

THE WORK-OCTAVE

I

The first note *Do* of the Work-Octave was once defined as "Evaluation of the Work-Ideas". Since the Work-Octave is an *ascending octave*, the next note is *Re*. This was defined as "The Application of the Work-Ideas to oneself". The third note *Mi* was defined as "The Realization of Personal Difficulties." Now the next note *Fa* lies beyond the "place of Missing Semi-tone". This means, psychologically, that a special shock has to be given here to reach the stage of understanding represented by the note *Fa*. In this connection it was said previously that *Do* must sound strongly enough, to begin with. That is, the "Evaluation

1074

of the Work" must be great enough to give sufficient strength for anyone to pass the note *Mi* and reach the note *Fa*, apart from other things. It is obvious that if a person lightly esteems the Work, or cannot understand anything about it, or thinks in his secret, internal side that it is nonsense, and so on, then he will not value it. So he will not apply it to himself or be able to pass to any degree of self-realization by its means or sustain anything coming from it adverse to his self-esteem.

We will speak later about the third note *Mi*—defined as "The Realization of Personal Difficulties". Now between this note *Mi* and the note *Re* beneath it, defined as the "Application of the Work-Ideas to oneself", lie all the processes *of connecting the Work with what one observes*. If we connect the Work with what we observe, then things become arranged in right order in us. (This must be understood. The Work, not Life, sets things in right order.) As we are mechanically, things are in wrong order. Unimportant things are made important, and important things are made unimportant. On one occasion Man was compared by G. to a three-roomed flat in which wrong articles of furniture were mixed up with right ones in every room. Since in life we live by false values and endless lies, this is inevitable. One definition of truth is right order. That is, when things are arranged in their right order, *there* is truth. The body is built up and integrated in this way—the more important parts being served by the less important, the brain itself being the highest and so the most carefully nourished and protected and served by all other organs. So in the Work, the Law of the Octave is sometimes called the Law of Order of Manifestation. It is evident to you that things can be connected in right or in wrong order. If in right order, there is truth: if in wrong order, there is something false. What is a lie, but things in wrong order? It is interesting to reflect on this aspect of the Law of the Octave (or the Law of 7—both terms being used). In the Work-Octave it will be seen that unless *Do* sounds first strongly enough, *Re* will never be reached. Without *Do*, *Re* cannot sound, and without *Re*, *Mi* cannot sound. One note depends on another. No note can possibly exist by itself. So unless at *Do* there is some real evaluation that increases, the further notes will sound weakly and everything will die out. But all three notes can strengthen each other, once they start sounding, through the practical verification of the Work, whereby we internally see its value more and more. When this is the case, the gap between *Mi-Fa* may begin to be bridged and the note *Fa* begin to sound. This note *Fa* is always a *new thing* in one —as if another being with a new understanding had begun to grow in one's being.

*   *   *

In every aspect of life, whatever people may study for their living, it is difficult and rare to reach the note *Fa*. A pianist may get as far as *Do-Re*, or even to *Mi*—but rarely further. The note *Fa* is not struck. That means simply that the pianist is a *Do-Re-Mi* man and so nothing is unique; nothing, save perhaps technique, is exceptional in his playing. The same applies to every branch of life. In whatever branch of life you are, to strike *Fa* means at once that you are at a far higher level than others are. The reason is that the person has made some curiously indefinable individual effort that lifts him beyond this gap, this missing semi-tone, and establishes him at the note *Fa*. No teacher can do this for the person. It is, as I say, a curiously indefinable effort that only the man from his deepest sense of *himself* can make. Imitation will never do it, for that only increases Personality. In brief, in some way Essence is touched, which can in turn touch Real 'I' and then the man *is* whatever he does, or whatever he does *is* the man.

Of course, if a man has, in a previous recurrence, learned something that Essence can remember, then Essence will remember earlier, in his next recurrence—a fact that explains many curious things about those to whom by common consent genius is attributed. In such a case, the note *Fa* will be struck early, and the notes *Do, Re, Mi* passed quickly. It is surely obvious to even the most formatory material mind that it is impossible to explain the lives of some people in terms of *one* life. I have often thought this is clearest in the case of some musicians.

*   *   *

Let us return to the note *Mi* in the Work-Octave defined as the "Realization of Personal Difficulties". At this stage of the Work, represented by *Mi*, one's consciousness has increased to the point of one's becoming more aware of the kind of person one is. Now the realization of personal difficulties must not merely depress one or make one negative. To take *Mi* in that way is not connecting the Work with what one observes. To realize as a fact that one is not the perfect man or woman that one imagined hitherto, belongs to the necessary action of the Work which is to increase consciousness. The Work says: "Find out facts about yourself by self-observation." An increase of consciousness reveals what you are. You realize, for example, after some years, that you are not one, but many different contradictory 'I's, all with different desires. In that case, you have begun to escape from the hypnotism of one form of imagination and *so have become more conscious*. A man or woman, hypnotized by life, full of illusions and self-satis-factory phantasies, is not conscious. Remember also that self-observa-tion is to let a ray of light into the inner darkness of *yourself*. Yes, you yourself. To realize one's personal difficulties is a state comparable with the Driver awakening from his drunken sleep in the inn and going out and seeing the wretched state of his horse and carriage. If, at such a stage, *taking my own case*, I can think *from the Driver* and *not from Nicoll* I may have a chance of hearing *Fa* beginning to sound in me. This is a new feeling of myself—not the feeling of Nicoll. The *Driver* can understand the Work, while *Nicoll* cannot. I refer to my own case. It was once explained to you that positive ideas are necessary to *lift* a man from *Mi* to *Fa*. The first requisite for Positive Ideas is the belief in "Greater Mind"—or the Ray of Creation. The ideas of this Work are Positive Ideas. In life we can notice the increase of negative ideas accompanied by the increase of negative views and negative emotions. Now all these 'I's that wish to work are present at the note *Mi* as well as the consciousness of one's personal difficulties. You will see clearly that this stage represented by the note *Mi* cannot be reached if a man takes himself as *one*. The 'I's that wish to work are not the personal difficulties, for example. They must be seen as quite distinct from 'I's that, say, do not wish to work. The 'I's that wish to work wish to go up to *Fa*. All this means that a man must see and tolerate his multiplicity. Where one was narrow and contracted to the illusion of oneness one is now an expanse of many people where choice is possible. In other words, the inner state as regards the Work, represented by the note *Mi*, is a very *wide one*, due to a broadening of consciousness. It is like looking over a wide garden and seeing what is useless and what is useful. What are you going to select? Which 'I's will you go with? Remember you can do nothing unless you choose the right 'I' to go with. If you go with 'I's that drag you down, you will be dragged down. And again, if you have no idea of inner separation—of separating from uncomfortable, vain or deceitful or bad 'I's—if, in short, you say 'I' to *everything* taking place in you—then you cannot sound *Mi*—and so you cannot grow. Your level of Being will remain where it is and you will attract the same life as before.

Some people cannot reach the note *Mi* because they do not observe themselves over a sufficient period. I quote from a recent letter: "If one observes oneself over the period of a week, it is possible to discover what one's personal difficulties are, because during the space of a week they are bound to recur. One may go through a day without noticing them, but one cannot get through a week without coming up against them, even if one goes away into different surroundings. I have noticed three things that make me lose force. (I also noticed several ways of getting force.) The same three things may not all recur next week, but probably one of them will, or two, or perhaps even all three. And they are the same things that have always spoilt one's life."

When a man, a woman, reach sufficiently the stage of understanding of the Work called the note *Mi*, through a strengthening of the notes *Do* and *Re*, then they are close to receiving help from the Work. If they will be passive to their faults and difficulties, acknowledge them and separate from them, then, as was said, the note *Fa* may begin to sound in them. But, as was said, this note is an utterly different feeling.

It is something delicate and new. Yet this is the beginning of meeting Real 'I' which is nothing like what they thought was Real 'I'. It is possible to say that some may not accept this new feeling of what they are.

THE WORK-OCTAVE

II

We are taught that an *ascending octave* starts with *Passive Do*. The Work-Octave does not start with work but with valuation. It does not, for instance, start with thinking one can do and all the consequences that arise from that illusion. To think one can do—to think, for example, that one can easily change one's Being and become different and behave differently if one wants to—is to think from *Active Do*. What does it mean to start from *Passive Do*? Some people think they can do anything by force. They think perhaps that they can compel people to believe in God by violent measures and through fear of consequences. This is starting from *Active Do*. It is starting from the wrong attitude. To start from *Passive Do* is an entirely different thing. It is very interesting to study at different times what it means and how one continually tries to start from *Active Do* and continually fails because one has not begun rightly. As was said, the Work-Octave begins not with doing but with valuation. Since it is an ascending octave it must start with *Passive Do*—for all ascending octaves start from *Passive Do*. In this case, then, the valuation of the Work must constitute a *Passive Do*.

Now your whole attitude towards a thing you value is quite different from your attitude towards things you do not value. That is to say, your psychological state is quite different in each case. You must understand that a wrong psychological state is just as real in its effects as trying to open a door with the wrong key. Valuation of the Work is the right psychological state to begin with. Through valuation a thing becomes precious to you. Through valuation you care for and remember a thing. Through valuation you have patience to find out more about it. Through valuation, if it is great, you regard yourself as of secondary importance in comparison to what you value because what you value is greater than you. The Work is greater than oneself and so the approach to it is through valuation. There are many parables about valuation such as the parable of the merchant who sought "goodly pearls, and having found one pearl of great price, he went and sold all that he had, and bought it," and the parable of the man who found treasure hidden in a field, "and to his joy he goeth and selleth all that he hath, and buyeth that field." You can understand from them what valuation means and so what starting from *Passive Do* means. The Work says that a man must believe in Greater Mind. To me it was evident at an early stage that this Work, this system that we study every day, came from a mind far above ordinary mind, and one that was possessed of a knowledge beyond human knowledge. So when we were told that it was useless doing this Work unless one believed in the existence of Greater Mind, no difficulties arose in me, because I had already come to the conclusion that the system came from Greater Mind—that is, from Conscious Humanity. Now if a man feels he knows better than the Work, he cannot do the Work, because he cannot sound the Note *Do*. To start from the Note *Re*, which is the application of the Work to oneself, to make *Re* into *Do*, is impossible. I mean, it will lead nowhere. The man is starting from the wrong place *in himself*. He is putting the valuation of himself before everything else. He thinks he knows and he thinks he can do. He does not see that he knows nothing or that such knowledge as he has contradicts itself, nor does he see that he always does the same things over and over again. That is, he does not realize that his "doing" is simply the result of mechanicalness. He imagines he is fully conscious, has Will, can do, and so on. You have heard sufficiently often how all these illusions have to be broken. *How?* By a man slowly seeing *for himself* that they are illusions and that hitherto he has been sitting in a public house drunk with dreams about himself. This is called beginning to awaken from sleep and there is a strange harsh taste connected with it, quite unlike any of the tastes of life.

Now if a person does not value, and ascribes everything to himself, his work will lead nowhere, because, as I said, the man is starting from the wrong place in himself. He is starting from False Personality. You will remember that what is done from Personality is done through the force of external circumstances. External circumstances make you act. You are not free. That is, you *cannot do*. External circumstances acting on your machine cause it to react. This is not *doing* in the Work-sense. The machine does, not you. In fact, there is no *You*—that is, no Real 'I'. What you call 'I' is nothing but a changing collection of 'I's in the Personality acted on at the moment by external circumstances. To begin *to do*, one must *stop* the reactions of certain 'I's—that is, *not do*. All you can *do* is to remember yourself.

To continue—if there is little or no valuation of the Work, it cannot begin in the right place. It is a practical question, like sowing seed in the right place. Of course, valuation increases as *Re* and *Mi* sound stronger. But if you have possessed Magnetic Centre the Note *Do* will sound early and clearly. Things will get cold, however, unless you constantly return in your mind to the Work and relate each day to your self-observation and to all you remember and to what you want. For what you want will gradually get more and more distinct.

1079

Now to turn to the Note *Re*—at *Re* you have to learn all the Work teaches, to learn the language of the Work, and to apply it to yourself. This takes a long time—in fact, one's life. Application begins with self-observation—and you will not keep conscious of yourself in this respect unless your valuation is strong enough to supply you with the necessary emotional force to make effort every day from your understanding. We all need to work. But do not criticize another's way of working. If you must criticize, begin with yourself. It is not merely that people have to learn the language of the Work: they have to learn the meaning. It is not the words, but the meaning. And you can only learn meaning by seeing the truth of it for yourself—because interiorly we are all open to truth, while exteriorly we are all open to lies—that is, to life.

Now let us touch the Note *Mi* for a moment. Here you realize, on a wider and wider scale, the city of yourself, of which you took yourself as the sole inhabitant, and the Note *Fa* becomes possible—not in all probability as you may have conceived. And it is here that you learn to speak and understand the language of the Work. Here, for instance, you know you cannot do, and here you know that others cannot do, and so you do not speak always as if you or others could do. This already is a great difference in you. And because you know and understand yourself better and have lost many conceits, you know and understand others, and cease to judge them. It is when you have reached this stage that the Work itself may begin to speak to you internally, because you have learned something of the language in which it speaks. This is why the Note *Fa* becomes possible.

Great Amwell House, November 1, 1947

THE WORK-OCTAVE

III

For right valuation the Work must become *emotional*. A man, a woman, should begin to see *for themselves* the truth of the Work. Why? Because otherwise it cannot become emotional. That is, it cannot touch the Emotional Centre. If it does not, it merely remains in the external memory of the formatory part of the Intellectual Centre. It is a detached memory, not affecting one's life. It is a memory comparable, say, to remembering the dates of battles in history. It is not yet a part of oneself. Now it is sometimes said that one of the supreme objects of the Work is to awaken the Emotional Centre. What can it mean to *awaken* the Emotional Centre? As we are, the Emotional Centre is in a very bad state. It is "impure". Let us speak of this impurity. No one who has begun to sound the Note *Re* of the Work in his or her life

—that is, to apply sincerely the ideas of the Work to themselves through self-observation—can possibly deny the great power of negative emotions. The Emotional Centre is impure, first of all, from the terrible mass of negative emotions that govern us and all mankind. I remind you again of what the Work says—that it is not desires of sex or of power that govern the world, but negative emotions. And this applies to each of us. We are taught that the Emotional Centre is born in us free of a negative part. But since we are born amongst sleeping people, all deeply under the power of negative emotions, we acquire in a short time a negative part of the Emotional Centre, which increases more and more. This, then, is one of the *impurities* affecting this centre, which if it begins to work aright marvellously supplies us with what we lack and gives an inner source of force that I cannot explain to you in any words. As it is, we have a marvellous inner source of negative emotions and general unhappiness. So work—real, practical and hard work—against negative emotions, by non-identifying with them, not consenting to them, not going with them, not believing them, separating the feeling of 'I' from them—is necessary.

Now it is impossible to pass from the Note *Mi* to the Note *Fa* in the Work-Octave if one believes in one's negative emotions. Only the realization of the truth of the Work can make it possible to pass from *Mi* to *Fa*—that is, for help to be given you to do so. You have to see by self-study that negative emotions always lie and pervert the truth. They take everything as they wish to take things. Negative emotions distort everything. They malform, they twist, they deny, they hate— for at bottom all negative emotions lead down to hate and violence and so also to fear. Hate, violence and fear form a typical triad of forces and each one depends on the others.

As a result of this distortion that negative emotions produce in oneself, several forms of lying result. And again it is necessary to understand that no one can pass from the Note *Mi* to the Note *Fa* unless they know all about how they lie and have observed lying in themselves. There are many forms of lying that the Work speaks of. One that is comparatively harmless is writing or telling something that happens in a way that puts you in a good light. But there are some very evil forms of lying that spring from deep-seated negative states that are not acknowledged and are surrounded by clouds of self-justifying. If they are not acknowledged the person concerned can only sound a very poor *Mi*. He does not know himself and, as is often the case, absolutely refuses to broaden the consciousness of himself to include his lying. Sometimes this is due to some extraordinary self-satisfactory picture of himself being just and honourable and all the rest of it that prevents him from this necessary increase of consciousness, only gained at the cost of his vanity. Remember in this connection that every time we say 'I' we are really lying. Which 'I'? We all for a long time say 'I' with such emphasis and confidence, as if Real 'I' controlled all we do and say and think and feel. But if we sound eventually a broad *Mi*, such illusions are no longer powerful. We have, in short, to come to accept, to endure, what we are, which is the only way to accept and endure others in the Work.

To return to the question of the impurity of Emotional Centre—there is another impurity which is best illustrated by what Mr. Ouspensky wrote about it in "Tertium Organum". I will make the following quotations and then leave the matter for discussion, emphasizing the observation: "It is impossible to *know* through impure emotions."

Mr. Ouspensky wrote: "Impure emotion gives obscure, *not pure* knowledge, just as impure glass gives a confused image. Pure emotion gives a clear, pure image of that for the knowledge of which it is intended. This is the only possible decision of the question. The arrival at this conclusion saves us from the common mistake of moralists who divide arbitrarily all emotion into "moral" and "immoral." But if we try for a moment to separate emotions from their usual moral frames, then we see that matters are considerably simpler, that there are no *in their nature* pure emotions, nor impure *in their nature*, but that each emotion will be pure or impure according to whether or not there are admixtures of other emotions in it. There can be a pure sensuality, the sensuality of the "Song of Songs" which initiates into the sensation of cosmic life and gives the power to hear the beating pulse of nature. And there can be impure sensuality, mixed with other emotions good or bad from a moral standpoint but equally making muddy the fundamental feeling. There can be pure sympathy, and there can be sympathy mixed with calculation to receive something for one's sympathy. There can be pure love of knowledge, a thirst for knowledge for its own sake, and there can be an inclination to knowledge wherein consideration of *utility* or *profit* assume the chief importance.

"In their outer manifestation pure and impure emotions may differ very little. Two men may be playing chess, acting outwardly very similarly, but in one will burn self-love, desire of victory, and he will be full of different unpleasant feelings towards his rival—fear, envy of a clever move, spite, jealousy, animosity, or schemes to win, while the other will simply solve a complex mathematical problem which lies before him, not thinking about his rival at all. The emotion of the first man will be impure, if only because it contains much of the mixed. The emotion of the second will be pure. The meaning of this is of course perfectly clear.

"Examples of a similar division of outwardly similar emotions may be constantly seen in the aesthetic, literary, scientific, public, and even the spiritual and religious activities of men. In all regions of this activity only complete victory over the pseudo-personal elements leads a man to the correct understanding of the world and of himself. All emotions coloured by such *self-elements* are like concave, convex, or otherwise curved glasses which reflect rays incorrectly and distort the image of the world.

"Therefore the problem of emotional knowledge consists in a corresponding preparation of the emotions which serve as organs of knowledge. 'Become as little children . . .' and 'Blessed are the pure in heart . . .' In these evangelical words is expressed first of all the idea of the purification of the emotions. It is impossible to know through impure emotions. Therefore in the interests of a correct understanding of the world and of the self, man should undertake the purification and the elevation of his emotions."

Great Amwell House, November 8, 1947

PERSONALITY AND ESSENCE

or

OUTER AND INNER MAN

or (in my case)

NICOLL AND 'I'

When you act from the Work-teaching—as, for example, you do not speak scandal when you might—then you act beyond the pleasure-principle. If you do only what gives you pleasure, you do not work on yourself. Only then the question arises—what gives you essential pleasure and what forms of pleasure are due to *False Personality*? You all know by now that the man who acts always from a desire to produce a good impression, to add to reputation, to be well-thought-of, acts only from his outer side—that is, his false, world-turned side. Inner goodwill he has none. He does nothing from his interior side. So he is acting his "goodness". The central attack of Christ was on the Pharisees—that is, *you* and *me*—not people who lived 2,000 years ago. As has been so often said, the Pharisee in you is the False Personality that does everything for the sake of every subtle form of self-glory—even to fasting and praying all day, like the hypocrites mentioned in the Gospels who "love to stand and pray in the synagogues and in the corners of the streets." (The word "hypocrite" comes from the Greek ὑποκρῐτής, which means an actor on the stage.) Yes, this is the tragedy of so many people who regard themselves as devout and so on. They are not so, interiorly, in the inner man, the inner woman. If all outer social restraints were removed they would neither fast nor pray. That is, everything they do is *impure*. This is well illustrated in the parable of the people who prayed. This parable was spoken "unto certain which trusted in themselves that they were righteous, and set all others at nought."

"Two men went up into the temple to pray; the one a Pharisee, and the other a publican. The Pharisee stood and prayed thus with himself, God, I thank thee, that I am not as the rest of men, extortioners, unjust, adulterers, or even as this publican. I fast twice in the week; I give tithes of all that I get. But the publican, standing afar off, would not lift up so much as his eyes unto heaven, but smote his breast, saying, God, be merciful to me a sinner."

(*Luke* XVIII 10-13.)

You have heard all this before. Very well—but have you observed it *in yourself*? For this Work starts from *self*-observation—a long journey. That is, it is internal—its direction is inwards: its result lies only in *self*-revelation, in seeing and acknowledging what is not *really* you, not this imagined *you*—and ending up with the reaching of that inner goal that all esoteric teaching speaks of and which Christ calls "the Kingdom of Heaven, which is within you." He adds, of course, that you have to be re-born, before this is possible. The Work says: "Personality must become *passive* before any inner development can take place." Yes— and do you see it is the same idea? At present, say, in me, Dr. Nicoll is active. And in you, if your name is Smith, Mr. Smith is active. Now, in my case, Dr. Nicoll, and, in Smith's case, Mr. Smith is the Personality and especially the False Personality to which he attaches such value and so is so hurt and offended by life. I will once more remind you that we are born with Essence which is pure but not developed. Then, born in a world of sleeping people who tell lies, Essence stops growing (it can only grow through truth) and becomes surrounded by *acquired* Personality, typical local attitudes, etc., by imitated things, not real things, not internally-seen truth. So a man becomes a disharmony. Why? Because his truth is all wrong—his taking of himself is all wrong—his very feeling of 'I' is all wrong. He has lost his inner relation to himself and developed a *false realness*. This is False Personality. We are all in this *False Realness* and all feel lost and wish to return. We are nostalgic. Yes—but where, to what, do we wish to return? Perhaps you know, or imagine you know: perhaps you have never had this feeling which goes inwards *rightly* and have taken it *outwards* as dislike of everyone and everything, and discontent, and all the rest of the feelings of not being properly treated. Yes—then indeed you are in disharmony—that is, you are taking everything wrongly, including even your darling self.

Now this *return*—this place we deeply, nostalgically wish for—is not possible to realize unless a man, a woman, knows something as to what it is necessary to do about it. Instructions are scattered about in the Gospels, not in the right order. On this point the Work teaches us that a man must first *awaken* before he can *die* and that he must *die* if he wishes to be re-born. Our work here is about *awakening*. A man must awaken to the multiplicity of his being, to his negative emotions, to his internal considering, to his continual identifying with everything. He must awaken to the different 'I's in him that always speak in his name. He must awaken to his inner contradictions—in fact, he must reach the note *Mi* in the Work-Octave called "realization of personal difficulties". All this is necessary before a man can "die", because otherwise he does not know what to die to and may even attempt to die to the wrong things. In this connection, you will remember how sometimes the Work speaks of going against one's *mechanicalness*. You must understand that if we seek to live more consciously we cannot simply live mechanically all day long, if we are doing this Work. You know how the Work speaks of people being asleep and yet imagining all the time that they are fully conscious of all they do. One therefore has to realize the fact that one is not properly conscious—or, as the Gospels say— *awake*—a painful matter. So it can be said that the study of this Work enables one better to understand the Gospels in this inner sense. So this Work is called Esoteric Christianity. "Esoteric" simply means *inner* and "exoteric" means *outer*. A parable has, for example, an *inner* meaning. The widow's cruse and the oil do not mean an actual cruse and oil. In order to start on the inner journey so that one *returns*, inner meaning is required, and so self-observation is necessary. One must see False Personality and see it again and again and again for days, months and years—until one begins to separate from it interiorly and no longer says 'I' to it, no longer takes it as 'I', and no longer puts all one's psychic force into it. And all this time you will be hurt and hit—if you are in the right atmosphere. Then at last False Personality is passive. This new state is the beginning of that journey of which we speak.

Great Amwell House, November 15, 1947

ON HEARING THE WORK

On one occasion G. said of someone: "He cannot hear". On another occasion he said: "He is always out". In this commentary I will speak first of hearing. Of course, literally, to say that a person cannot hear means that he is deaf. But G. did not mean a physical incapacity of the ears because the man could hear as well as anyone else. He meant that the man could not hear psychologically. Everyone who has been in the Work for some time must have had experiences of hearing something for the first time which had been often said before. Now why cannot we hear psychologically something said the first time? The answer is: Because of our level of understanding, which depends on our level of Being. To hear in the sense G. used the word is to perceive the meaning of what is said. But our perception of meaning depends on our level of understanding and this depends on a certain ratio between our level of Being and our level of Knowledge. Our general level is characterized by the state of sleep. Being asleep, we cannot hear. When we begin to awaken from sleep we hear better. Some, having heard a little better, prefer to go to sleep again and either no amount of shaking will make them awaken, or they wake up for a time again and then sleep. This process is like going up and down on a ladder and happens to us all. Now you are more awake and hear better: then you are more asleep and hear nothing. It is necessary to be patient with oneself. The Work is stronger than life, and if we had sufficient reception of the Work—that is, if we heard its meaning fully enough—then we would perceive for ourselves that the Work is stronger than life and its sleep. But our power of reception of the Work is small and so life and sleep seem more powerful and overcome us continually. This is not because life and sleep are stronger than the Work: the reason is that our capacity to receive the esoteric teaching of the Work is small. Is it not extraordinary that sometimes people do not understand even this, and, as it were, blame the Work? Now to *hear* means to receive, to take in. A man therefore who cannot "hear" is a man who cannot take in, cannot receive the ideas of the Work. He has no bowl, no cup, no containing vessel. He is convex. There is in him no room for anything save himself. It is said in one ancient fragment of esoteric teaching that a man secretly is a cup upside down and that it is required of him to turn this cup upwards so that it can receive something and hold it and so retain it. We must all admit that even when we have "heard" something—that is, received some small new vision of things—we find it difficult to hold it, and so to retain it, so quickly does the cup turn down again to the power of life and sleep. This is when the real struggle of Work and Life comes in—namely, the fight between psychological and physical meaning, between what the Work stands for and what Life stands for. This is where all real temptation begins. Notice the allegory about the temptation of Christ. He was asked by the Devil—that is, Life—to turn the cup downwards and so worship the power of external life and all its spectacle and glory and power:

> "And he (the devil) led him up, and shewed him all the kingdoms of the world in a moment of time. And the devil said unto him, To thee will I give all this authority, and the glory of them: for it hath been delivered unto me; and to whomsoever I will I give it. If thou therefore wilt worship before me, it shall all be thine."   (*Luke* IV 5-7.)

To return to "hearing": a man cannot hear the meaning of the Work if he is full of himself because in that case he has no "cup"—that is, nothing in him to receive the teaching of the Work. He is already in need of nothing. With the complex inner arrangements of self-estimation, buffers, attitudes, pictures, self-justifications, vanity, pride, and all the rest of it, there is absolutely no room for anything to enter. So the Work starts with self-observation, uncritical and sincere. Why? In order to make room for something else. For when a man through self-observation realizes something of his true condition—when, for instance, he begins, even slightly, to realize he is *mechanical* and not a man, he loses something of his hitherto untouched self-sufficiency. This *at once* makes room. Yes, makes room in the inn. For in the parable of the Birth of Christ, there was no room in the inn—which means that esoteric teaching, given as it has been through the ages, has always found "no room in the inn"—the inn being something in a man very close to the highroad, yet a little apart, that might receive strangers. The ideas of the Work are exactly strangers—strange to one's ordinary thoughts and ideas. Now it is only through Work self-observation, over a long time, that room can be made in a man, a woman, for the knowledge of the Work to enter and begin its gradual, successive, not noticed transformations of Being. Then a man begins to *hear*, who hitherto, with the cup downwards, has been deaf and so "heard" nothing beyond life and sleep.

* * *

Now let us speak of the man, the woman, who is "never at home" or "always out". This refers to those who have no centre of gravity in themselves. They live, as it were, outside themselves, and indeed this is not surprising because they have no home, or only a haunted home. It is impossible, therefore, to have any kind of serious conversation with them, for a man must be at home before you can talk to him. They will not meet themselves, but avoid themselves, as if they were afraid to look, and they hurry away both in their minds and in their speech from anything that might involve themselves. If you ask them a question about themselves they escape from it and you can see them as in a vision fleeing away across the plain to some distant crag or forest to conceal themselves. Or they answer in some agitated or strained way. In fact, it is possible to give many other descriptions of the person G. describes as "never-at-home", and so it is, for us, a matter for observation and self-observation. Fear, of course, and therefore tension, must play a strong part—but what kind of fear? This again is for observation and self-observation. But I have given you two examples of the way in which G. formulates a person. I was always interested in his simple way of expressing things in people's psychology. He said that the practice of relaxation was necessary for a person "always out".

Why did he say that the practice of relaxation was necessary for a person whom he described as "always out"? I should say that one reason lies in the fact that a person without a centre of gravity, a person who is not there, never there, always out, is strained in his muscles, and so the practice of relaxing his muscles puts him—or her—more into themselves. This is an example of starting from Moving Centre, in order to control Emotional Centre. Apart from this G. always said that there were two supreme things in the Work-discipline—to *remember oneself* and to *relax*. The practice of relaxing, he taught us, begins with inner attention, so that Consciousness can be placed in each part of the Body. He said: "Begin with the small muscles of the face." I will

1087

add that both G. and O. taught us to remember ourselves for only a very short time at a time, and, as far as I remember, G. indicated that relaxation must only be for a short time at first. This must be right, because placing the internal attention into different parts of the Body requires force which is soon easily exhausted.

Great Amwell House, November 29, 1947

CENTRE OF GRAVITY

SUN, MOON, AND STARS

A question was asked at one of the Groups recently: "What is Centre of Gravity? How to define it?"

*   *   *

It is necessary to review the different senses in which this term is used in the Work. As in everything in the Work we have to distinguish between a *mechanical* Centre of Gravity and a *conscious* Centre of Gravity in oneself.

(1) *Life as Centre of Gravity.* Here come in the categories of Man— Man No. 1, 2, 3, 4, 5, 6, 7. In the case of Man No. 1, Man No. 2, Man No. 3, "centre of gravity" is used to signify the centre chiefly used in the approach to life. That is, in the case of Man No. 1, his life-centre of gravity is either in Moving Centre or in Instinctive Centre. Man No. 2 approaches everything *emotionally* to begin with—that is, by liking-disliking, and so his life-centre of gravity is in Emotional Centre. Similarly, Man No. 3 approaches everything theoretically, intellectually, so his life-centre of gravity is in Intellectual Centre. These are the life-centres of gravity of *mechanical mankind* and by reason of these differences Man cannot agree with Man. This is therefore called in the Work: "The Circle of Confusion of Tongues" or "The Circle of Babel" or simply "Life". By contrast the Conscious Circle of Humanity—No. 5, 6 and 7—understand one another.

(2) The next meaning of Centre of Gravity is used in connection with work. The passage from the mechanical to the Conscious Circle of Humanity is impossible without the help of something *different from Life* and its daily stresses and strains. So the Work is called a different 3rd Force from Life. Let us speak of this second meaning of Centre of Gravity which must begin with "Point in the Work"—that is, a

1088

genuine feeling that the Work is important. A point in the Work begins with evaluation.

*　　*　　*

The gravitational force of the Moon is strong enough to affect the movement of tides, etc., on the Earth. Now the Work teaches that, as we are, the "Moon" acts psychologically on us. The external Universe, represented physically by visible Sun, Moon, Stars, etc., is also within us—not physically, but psychologically. So the Work, speaking psychologically, says: "We have to make Moon in ourselves." Man is a microcosmos—but not fully—living in a macrocosmos. The physical, visible Man and the physical, visible Universe are represented also or another scale—that is, a psychological scale—not complete in Man. The Moon, physically, literally, is lower than the Earth; the Sun is higher; the Galaxy is higher, and so on. But this external symbol of the seen Universe is, the Work says, in us psychologically. That is, when it is said that Essence comes from the stars, it means, psychologically, that Essence comes from a high level. Can you grasp that the external, visible represents the internal invisible? As within—so without. Yes—but do you see? There are scales in the visible Universe—and scales in yourself, corresponding. If you had solar Consciousness then you would be at the divine level of the Sun—represented outwardly, visibly, in the scalar structure of the outer world as the literal, physical Sun—but *not* the inner psychological Sun only present and contacted within, through inner Consciousness. I speak here of Higher Centres. People all through the ages have worshipped the external, physical Sun. Here the difficulty arises of separation of literal and psychological, of material and spiritual, of outer and inner—a difficulty which for all who persist in holding to the Work will finally cease and a marvellous inner world of experience open up. Man is born in the vast Universe composed of myriads of Moons, Suns, and Galaxies. He is inevitably stamped by it, as by his Mother. But it is represented *in him* as a ladder. In the Ray of Creation, which is a ladder, is shewn how one traces down, from all other possible Rays, *our* Ray, *our* Sun, *our* Planets, *our* Earth, *our* Moon. An enormous machinery is apparent. But, abstracting from the physical representation, the Universe is partly in Man, as well as outside him. So the Work speaks of our Moon psychologically, as a powerful influence in us, the influence of forming intractable habits.

"The action of the Moon," Gurdjieff said, in so many words, "is like a weight. It controls Organic Life, which covers the surface of the Earth as a sensitive film. It is like a weight on a pendulum. Its influence is to keep everything where and as it is. It uses Organic Life as its food. From this point of view life on Earth is a pain-factory." Early in the Work, Mr. Ouspensky said to us: "It is necessary to make Moon in oneself. Try to see what is meant." What can this mean? It means that we must make something in ourselves that will resist the influences of life. Some ancient writers called this escaping from prison. As

1089

machines we are driven by outside life. We are functions of life. We react to everything as machines do. First we have to see this is so genuinely, not extravagantly. The gradual realization of this mechanicalness of oneself is the beginning of awakening. Remember only you can awake to yourself. I cannot awaken you. If we could change our responses to daily impressions, if we could resist the customary effects of daily life upon us, we would be creating "Moon in ourselves". We have, therefore, as it is taught, to *isolate* ourselves from the effects of life on us—*not from life*. If we do not, if we live mechanically—and by now some should really know what is meant by that and understand that one can sit in a chair doing nothing and yet think and feel mechanically —if, I said, we live mechanically, then "Moon eats us". It takes all our energy, especially when we are negative. Notice it is your *way* of taking life you have to work against. That requires long self-observation.

Now you have often heard that each act of non-identification saves energy. It is *anti*-mechanical. And if it is accompanied by Self-Remembering it actually creates a higher kind of energy and so an increase of Consciousness. Now there are three main things which help to isolate us from the personal effects of life upon oneself—Self-Remembering, Non-Identifying, and Non-Considering. All this creates "Moon in oneself". Going against habits does the same—but it is best to begin with psychological habits, such as the habit of being negative, the habit of being asleep, the habit of making inner accounts, the habit of hating, the habit of being sorry for oneself, and so on, for, of course, the more you hate, the more you feel sorry for yourself.

The Work says that Man on Earth is under many influences. The Earth is under 48 orders of laws—that is, influences playing on you like shifting spotlights. It also says that the Moon is under 96 orders of laws. To be under the Moon is to be under the greatest possible mechanicalness and, as you know, this is the case in a man, a woman, who is fast asleep, governed by every form of negative emotion, hate, internal considering, and so on. By work on oneself one can come under fewer and better influences or laws. This is why we work on the lines laid down in the practical teaching of the Work. As a result of obeying them one rises in the "Ladder of Being" represented by the Ray of Creation. But this rising is only possible through *sacrifice*. To behave as you always do, and expect to rise, is impossible. One must, to begin with, *sacrifice one's suffering*. All self-pity, all self-cradling, vanity, secret, absurd fears, all self-sentimentality, all inner accounting, all pitiful pictures, all sighs, inner groans, and complaints, must be burned up in the fire of increasing Consciousness. Remember there is no justice under higher laws such as we understand justice. Higher justice, heavenly justice, is to *work on yourself*, so that when you die you have no accounts. The question only is then—in spite of all these difficulties you may mention: "What have you done *beyond* yourself?" So it is said elsewhere: "Ye shall be judged every man, every woman, according to

your work." I would add: "What situations have you transformed?"
Yes, this is worth-while reflecting on, and as deeply as you can—if you
can as yet even reflect at all on this thing that you cling to and so
wrongly take as "yourself" and on what it is doing to you in the way
of unhappiness. Remember what has been so stressed—what you react
mechanically to, what you take impressions *on, is not yourself.* It is the
machine. It is something that is *not you.* Can you in the midst of a
negative scene say: "This is not I?" If so, you eventually can relax to
an extent that I simply cannot describe to you. Only non-identifying
gives inner peace. Understand that real experiences in the Work cannot
be described to another who has not reached the level of them. It is
like trying to describe the taste of something lovely that another person
has not tasted and perhaps can never taste.

Now in the supreme sense, when we begin to "make Moon in
ourselves" we are making a *Work-Centre of Gravity* distinct from life.
Only a third force different from the third force of life can do this for
and in us. Only a psycho-spiritual force can do it, derived not from
life and the dull, heavy, habit-forming mechanizing influences of the
"Moon" but from those more graceful who have gone before, up the
Side-Ladder to the Sun, and left us memorials of the way to follow
them.

This is the first and greatest idea about forming "centre of gravity"
in oneself. Only with this "centre of gravity" can a man reach that level
of being called No. 4 Man—a man in whom all centres begin to work
and who is given the unique insight and revelation to see that things
appropriate to each centre are not contradictory any more than Autumn
is a contradiction to Spring.

Great Amwell House, December 6, 1947

COMMENTARY ON INCREASE OF CONSCIOUSNESS

WORK-IDEA

According to the teaching of this Work we are at the second level
of consciousness, designated the so-called Waking State in which people
hate and kill each other in the name of some theory, etc. The Work
teaches that mankind, being at this level, which is not proper consciousness, suffers in accordance with this state, and is used for other
purposes than are beneficial to it. It says, before anything can become
better, mankind—or a sufficient number of people—must reach the
3rd level. Otherwise no real change in the affairs of mankind can
occur and Man will continue to swing between the opposites, war and

1091

peace, etc. In short, we here—each one—must undergo an *increase in consciousness*. The 3rd level of consciousness—where outside help can reach us—is called the level of *Self-Remembering, Self-Consciousness* or *Self-Awareness*. We seek to reach this level. Of course, in common fairness, everyone should. Well, start with yourself. Can you wake up a little? How, then, can we individually, through personal work, undergo an *increase of consciousness*?

Now we come to a commentary on this central Work-idea of becoming more conscious and the consequences of remaining asleep in the 2nd State.

COMMENTARY

One direction of increasing consciousness is making yourself more conscious to yourself. We spoke recently of the person who "could not hear" and of the person who "was always out". As several people found the comments made on these two definitions given by Gurdjieff useful, let us speak about the person "who always makes difficulties". On one occasion Mr. Ouspensky said to me: "You always make difficulties". I was surprised. I thought at the time that this was really an absurd thing to say about me. It seemed so obvious to me then that it was O. who always made difficulties. I never made them. So I was not only surprised, but offended. Probably, I thought to myself: "What? Can he really mean that? Can he believe it is true, when for several months or years I have been carefully pointing out to him how difficult *he* is, and what difficulties *he* makes for me?" Now I take this example in order to illustrate how, unless one becomes conscious of something in oneself one cannot see it, cannot understand how it can possibly apply to oneself and so cannot change it. Is it not clear that if you are not conscious of some quality in yourself, you are therefore not aware of it and therefore cannot believe that you possess it, if someone else happens to point it out to you, and so you cannot change it? Consciousness and change are inseparable. A person has two things: a physical body and a psychological body. The knowledge of both is extremely faulty and erroneous. So people collide daily with one another.

Now let us take only the psychological body—a person's psychology —your own personal psychology, through which you relate yourself to another person's psychology. A difficult matter indeed because you are not aware of your own psychology, nor is the other person aware of his or her psychology. Both have a thousand and one things in them that they are unconscious of, that they are not aware of, and yet that manifest themselves all the time. This is the general state of "Man asleep". So the Work starts with "self-observation". It says that it is necessary to "know thyself"—to quote the inscription written over the portico of the ancient Greek temple of Delphi, where there was an esoteric school that had clairvoyance and which was acknowledged throughout the North-Eastern Mediterranean some four thousand years ago. Yes, before we can *start*, we must know ourselves much better than we do in the running stream of life: and out of that knowledge we must become more responsible to one another and to ourselves. Otherwise we do not really exist individually.

Some time ago it was asked: "What is psychology?" The answer was: "Psychology can be said to be what you are not aware of." At that time we were speaking of the dark side of ourselves—by which is meant the side of ourselves that we do not see, are not aware of, and so do not acknowledge. Understand, you can be what you are not aware of. Yet this side acts all the time—and the tragedy is *we do not see it*. We *are* it, without knowing it, without having become conscious of it. So the Work says: "Self-observation is necessary. It lets a ray of light into the inner darkness of ourselves." What is this ray of light? This ray of light means the light of consciousness, for consciousness is light, not sunlight, but spiritual light, psychological light. And the inner darkness means all that side, all those qualities, that we are not conscious of, not aware of, and do not acknowledge. What is the result? What happens when—to take the example of myself—I cannot see that *I* make difficulties? I do not see it is myself, am not conscious of it, and so do not acknowledge it. Instead, I see it in another person. I see only that O. makes difficulties, not me. The fault is in him, not in me. This is "psychology". To borrow a word from my first psychological teacher, Dr. Jung—he said: "We *project* on to others what we cannot accept in ourselves." Yes—you all know the jealous person who, not accepting his or her own thoughts of infidelity, projects them and accuses only the other person. Is this not the simplest example of what "practical psychology" means—and therefore of the necessity of self-observation and the gradual accepting of what is in oneself? Unfortunately, it is a very difficult thing to become aware of what we project on to others, in the way of suspicion, slander, accusation, offendedness, dislike, hate, and all the rest. There is a machinery of buffers, attitudes, associations, negative emotions, pictures, considerings, vanities, and false personality, that is very powerful and serves to keep us asleep in the grip of mechanical life, from which so few have the courage and clear thought to awaken at all costs. In other words, we do not see ourselves without long effort. We remain not conscious of ourselves, unless we work. We project on to others what we should see in ourselves, if we retain the illusion that we are fully conscious. So the Work speaks of the necessity of an *increase of consciousness*, before a man can change. "Man," it says, "is not yet conscious. He attributes consciousness to himself. He does not realize that he is not yet conscious. A conscious man knows himself. A mechanical man imagines he does. Now in regard to projecting into others what we do not see in ourselves, remember that this Work says: "We are mirrors to one another."

The object of self-observation, then, is to become more conscious of oneself. The great object of the Work is to lead to a definite and possible destiny—i.e. a definite *change of Being*. So I ask you again: "Can you change anything you are not conscious of?" Obviously, if, as Mr. Ouspensky said, I always make difficulties, and if I am not conscious of it, how can I change it? To this practical point I wish to call the attention of you all. If a person is not conscious of the fact that he or she speaks or acts in a certain way, can that person change it? No—it is quite clear that it is impossible. Now suppose you point out to the person that he or she speaks or behaves in this particular way— what will happen? Most likely you will be accused of unfairness. Why? Because the person concerned has no idea that it is true. The matter is not conscious to the person's mind. It is unconscious. What is the only remedy? The only remedy is for the person after long self-observation to realize personally that he or she speaks or behaves in this or that way. In that case, an increase of consciousness has taken place and something has been added to consciousness. Is this person then the same? No—by seeing, by becoming more conscious, by accepting, by acknowledgement, the person is no longer the same. This is the *way* we follow in this Work. A man who becomes more conscious cannot remain the same. So it is said that self-observation is a method of self-change.

Now in regard to the impossibility of altering anything that you are totally unconscious of—which is obvious—there comes in here the altering something that you are half-conscious of, but will not acknowledge. This latter situation is due to a buffer. If you try to say anything about it to another, you will get probably a violent reaction and a great deal of self-justifying. This is always important and interesting to notice in oneself. It shews where a buffer lies. A buffer intervenes between two contradictory things in you, both of which in a way you are aware of, but not together at the same time.

Let me return to the phrase: "You always make difficulties." For the moment let us leave myself out. What do you understand by a person "who always makes difficulties"? Does this in any possible way apply to yourself? Do you tend to make difficulties and if so, of what kind? Gardeners and cooks, I have noticed in the past, always seem to do so. No doubt, when I noticed this, I was bitter about what Mr. Ouspensky said to me. But perhaps some have a picture of always helping—"lending a helping hand", I believe it is called—without noticing just how often and where you make a great many difficulties and are no help at all. Remember that in all your relationships with others, it is chiefly *what you are not conscious of* that complicates them. Another person may see, say, that you make extraordinary difficulties about your food, but *you* do not see it. Or he may observe that you invariably say *No* when asked to do anything—a point which you, of course, do not observe. On the contrary, you no doubt have a pleasant picture that you always are ready to do anything or certainly would if you had the time. Or again, you may always disagree, and though you are not aware of it, others may be. This is a mode of making difficulties. But there are very many modes, as, for instance, wanting to be first, to have power, and so objecting to everyone and everything that does not give you this facility. This, of course, points to the inability to tolerate the idea that anything is higher than oneself—one of the commonest situations in self-adoration. So it is interesting to observe oneself from the angle of making difficulties and we have to become more conscious in that direction. Remember that acknowledgement gives inner peace.

Great Amwell House, December 13, 1947

COMMENTARY ON AIM

Work-Idea

In the Work it is said that it is necessary to have aim. Without aim, we in the Work drift.

Commentary

In speaking of Aim once Mr. Ouspensky said that there is far aim and near aim. "The situation is like this," he said, in so many words: "Let us suppose a man is climbing at night up a road lit by gas-lamps. As he nears the top he sees a gas-lamp shining and thinks it is close at hand at the top of the hill. But on reaching the summit he sees it is across a valley and many other gas-lamps intervene between him and it. It is the same thing in the Work. We make an aim. But we do not first see all that must be passed through before we can attain it." You can see that Mr. Ouspensky's illustration can be added to—as, for instance, we may find that the distant lamp one aims to reach lies on a branch road so that one's direction has to be altered, and so on. But whatever we add to it, the main idea is that people must have patience and not expect instant results and also look at the quality of the effort they are making in connection with their aim. Aim can only be attained when that which wants it lies deep. It cannot be made superficially—say, from False Personality. Why? Because it is not deep enough.

Now on one occasion, at which my wife and myself were present, Mr. Ouspensky had arranged, many years ago, for Gurdjieff to meet a large number of extremely wealthy, prominent people in London. After dinner, at which I noticed he ate and drank nothing, a meeting was held. Looking round at all these people, after a long silence, he said: "What do you want? If you can tell me, I will answer you whether I can help you or not." No one said a word. It appeared that the meeting was a failure. Yet I have often thought that at that moment, under the magic of Gurdjieff, people became aware of what they wanted as they were, and were ashamed to say anything. Shortly after, the meeting stopped, and everyone talked thirteen to the dozen. Why? Because, for an instant, they had been brought into a state of consciousness that made them uncomfortable.

Now in making aim, one must want it. Often one can make a theoretical aim—say, to be a better man, a better woman. But this is not aim. I would say: "Well, better at what?" Aim must have a definite formulation. To aim to be better in a vague sense, is not *asking*. When it is said: "Ask and ye shall receive," it means to ask something real, something you have seen and wish to change. Often I have given you the example of a person going into a shop—the shop of the Universe—and, going to the counter, the person is asked: "What do you want?" The person hums and haws and says: "Oh, I really don't know—I want—let me see—I want—let me see—I want—" "Yes, *what* do you want?" asks the shop-keeper. The person does not know. That is one reason why the Work teaches you in detail, specifically, what you must observe in yourself and work against. If you went into that great shop and said: "Yes, I want to stop making these internal accounts against others, I want to cease always blaming life and others, always feeling resentful, and thinking that others have not behaved rightly to me, always thinking that if I had had different conditions I would have been marvellous. I want you to *sell me something* to make me see I am wrong, because I dimly see the idea and yet I cannot get hold of it deeply enough." Well, what do you think? That is a real request. Do you think the shop-keeper might hand you something? He might even smile slightly, even nicely. However, supposing he hands you something—nearly always a pair of shoes—then he may say in rather an insulting tone: "You've got to pay for all this. Hand over some cash." And then all your account-making, all your self-pity, all your sense of grievance that you lie on as on a bed in the background of yourself, will probably make you resent this apparent roughness and you will perhaps say: "How dare you speak to *me* like that?"—and the shopkeeper will vanish and you will then be sure that he vanishes in a smell of sulphur. For the Devil is, first, all that you think should but does not pity you. However, the Devil is so often God. No, if you are going to buy help, if you know slightly what it is you want to buy to be of any *use* to you, remember you will have to pay for it. We live in an enclosed Universe. How can you *pay* for getting rid of always being aggrieved, hurt, upset—in short, of making continual, inner accounts? The point is that there are two stages in aim. First, you begin through self-observation to formulate an aim, more or less clear to you. Second, you have to be able to pay to obtain it. Weak people make aim for a day or so and are disappointed when nothing happens. They have no idea of Second Force. They are like people who say: "I would like to be a millionaire, or a Hollywood Star," and when nothing happens and no one notices, they get sick in their souls and give it all up. They have no idea that to get anywhere, either in life or in this Work, requires effort. It requires money to pay for it—that is, effort which earns psychological money—that is, the power to buy from the great shop that rewards effort—especially intelligent effort.

Now if you want a thing in life deeply enough, you may possibly get it after hard work for years. It is the same in the Work. Notice that to really want is to be independent of local, temporary, outside criticism. False Personality depends on what others think of you—that is, an audience. Real aim needs no audience. It is deeper, more genuine, essential. If you make an aim in the Work—as, for instance, not to feel always this background of tears, discontent, of being not appreciated—which is *one* form of inner accounting—then, if you really want not to have it, after some time it will be given you not to have it—usually in short flashes. But only if you really want this aim and have realized what it might mean *not to have it* will it eventually be given you fully. You are tested first. People love their negative emotions. Remove these by magic—then do you think they will praise you? No—they will hate you. This is our curious situation, about which at one time O. talked endlessly. To have a clean, hard bed to rest on is a difficult acquisition.

Now the Work indicates that it does not matter what you *have* been or what you *are*. It asks, in Gurdjieff's quiet words: "What do you want?" Say you are content with yourself. Then you are dead. *You want nothing*—and the Work is about *what you want*—not what you were, or are, but *what you want now*. That is why, as you get older, the Work can mean more and more to you—unless you have settled down long ago into a complacent idea of yourself—that is, crystallized out in some conventional views of what you should be. Work always means new life. So it asks: "What do you want?" and cares little for what you have been or are now.

Now it has been said many times in the Work that a man is not defined by his income, distinctions, social level, the size of his body, or his strength, etc., but by his *understanding*. So you will see that one thing can be added here. A man is not only his understanding, but *what he wants*—and what he wants will naturally arise from the level of his understanding. I sometimes say to you, by way of commentary, that we wish supremely to go "upstairs". Identifying, negative emotions, fixed conventional attitudes, pictures, inner accounts, being always asleep, imagination about yourself, buffers, stupid 'I's, absurd vanity and pride—in fact, all the Work teaches practically—is not allowed "upstairs". We have been taught what *not to be*, what to separate from, what, as it were, *not to wear*—for clothes symbolize inner attitudes—if we wish to reach a higher level. That is why dress is so important—psychological dress. To go "upstairs", as I call it, requires special dress. I mean, a man dressed in his life-egotism will not get far "upstairs". Nor will he be able to buy anything at the great shop of which I have spoken. You see, he will not for a moment believe he is wrongly dressed for the job. He thinks he is worthy of climbing right up the Ray of Creation and meeting the Absolute. I fear he might not be able to do so and have very good reason for saying this. But I admit it takes many long years to realize first that one is not exactly God, and second that one has all this time assumed one was. Yes, it is a difficult situation to meet and a humiliating one that few can face. That is one reason why the Work says that unless you can believe in Greater Mind you can never do this Work. You may exclaim: "But I have never assumed I am God!" Are you quite sure? Did you not always think you were right? Have you not always in action behaved as if you were right and the other person wrong? And perhaps without having observed it, you have felt superior to others. Now in the Gospels which chiefly, on the practical side, are about the Pharisee in us, very much is said about this state of mind and the necessity of realizing as fact, not as a lisping sentimental pretence, that one is *nothing*. The Work says: "Unless a man, a woman, can begin to realize their own *nothingness* as a fact of self-observation, nothing can take place in them." At the Institute in France we were told: "Here Personality counts as nothing."

Now aim made from False Personality only increases False Personality. How long it takes to observe what False Personality is in oneself! Some think that the basic practical work, beginning with life-long observation in oneself of False Personality, negative states, inner considering, different 'I's, fixed conventional attitudes, inner contradictions, special self-imaginations, vanity and pride—those two Giants, as Gurdjieff called them, that walk in front of us and arrange our lives beforehand—as well as the gradual seeing of buffers, pictures, the realization of one's mechanicalness, noticing how you behave and the impression it makes on others—in short, *all* the Work teaches that one must observe in oneself—I say, some seem to think that all this is elementary. They could not be greater fools. This personal work of self-observation *is for all one's life*. Out of it comes the dawning of real aim, which is in its greatest formulation the desire to awaken. In my case I seek to awaken from Dr. Nicoll—and so in each of your cases the greatest aim is to awaken from what you have hitherto called yourself. This is only possible through self-observation. Then people find, specifically, what particular features in themselves keep them identified with themselves and so prevent any awakening from taking place. Then they can begin to see where their aim really lies. Then indeed they can pray—that is, ask for help intelligently. They may get it, but only by paying for it—that is, by the sacrifice of something hitherto precious to them. You cannot get to a new state, to a higher level—that is, you cannot go "upstairs"—unless you sacrifice something belonging to your old state—and deeply from Essence. As you know originally the Work said: "First of all you must sacrifice your suffering." This is a very good aim. But have you ever thought that unless you observe yourself daily you will never see your form of suffering? It takes years and years of work, and if you cannot see a thing in yourself, how on earth do you expect to change it? Can you change what you are unconscious of? So I repeat—that self-observation along the original lines of the Work is the continual task of all connected with my Branch of this Work.

ONE OF THE WORK-IDEAS ABOUT IMAGINATION

WORK-IDEA

The Work says, in speaking of the terrible power of imagination to keep mankind asleep, amongst the many other factors that do so, that people can roughly be divided as follows:

(1) Some people dream their dreams passively;
(2) Some people talk their dreams;
(3) Some act their dreams.

COMMENTARY

One must understand that, in speaking of "dreams", what is meant here is one's forms of imagination, one's day-dreams, one's phantasies about oneself, about what one would like to be taken as, about what one really feels one is—although unfortunately no one seems to take any notice of all these secret ideas of our value.

In speaking on one occasion about imagination, Mr. Ouspensky said: "We have only a few typical forms of mechanical, self-active imagination about ourselves—that is, self-imagination—say, four or five. (I am not speaking of directed imagination.) It is important to make these unconscious forms of imagination conscious and to realize that they act on oneself at all moments." He added, in so many words: "A form of imagination about oneself, allowed to act without our being conscious of it, can spoil one's life. And two people wishing to unite, if their forms of mechanical imagination are incompatible, can become mutually destructive." This means that two people can, owing to the dominance of their different unobserved phantasies about themselves, mutually destroy one another psychologically, even although they wish to come together as far as they know. Remember that one psychology relates itself to another psychology. It is not a question of the visible bodies uniting but of the invisible bodies—that is, the psychologies. A very superficial and tiresome relation comes through bodies trying to unite without the slightest idea that the psychologies must do so. Love is psychological, but it is practically always imagination.

Looking backward on what teaching has been given in the past in the form of fairy-stories, there is the Cinderella phantasy. I heard the other day that a woman was jealous of a certain royal duchess. One might think it inconceivable that one should be jealous of a person one did not know. But if anyone has a strong Cinderella phantasy, then it becomes more understandable. *The phantasy makes one jealous*—not the person. I read somewhere that in mediaeval times at the millenium many women had the phantasy that they might give birth to Christ at his second coming. This does not seem to be a prevalent form of imagination nowadays. The point is that when a phantasy, a powerful form of imagination, has a hypnotic effect, people behave in an extraordinary way—simply because of the form of imagination dominating them at that period. In a discussion with Mr. Ouspensky I once said that history is nearly useless, because no one can ever really record what happens and that recent psychological tests had shewn that everyone reports an event differently and instead of real records we have people's opinions and points of view. He said briefly: "All history is imagination." He meant, I think, that what people think is true about historical people is imaginary—that is, that so-called history is about imaginary people and so history is imagination. I said, feeling a little wicked, "What about dates?" He said: "Oh, yes, dates are facts—nothing else is. And I can never remember dates." And, looking across at me with a smile he said: "When did Charles the Second live?" I said: "The only date that I know is 1066 and I have no idea what it refers to." Now I would add to this that most of our memory of the past, most of our ideas of other people, and above all our ideas of ourselves, are mainly *imagination*. What is the only thing that can master imagination? The answer is *memory*. I do not mean what we ordinarily call memory. I refer to Work-memory—that is, relatively speaking, *conscious memory*—which begins with the conscious intake of impressions through self-observation.

Now to return: let us take the man, the woman, who comes under the category (1)—that is, *some people dream their dreams passively*. Look at the long ribbon-road, at night, villa after villa. Do you think that their inhabitants have not dreamed phantasies? Yes, but they either say nothing or—to come to category (2)—they may talk about them—as, for example: "Oh, if only I could meet so and so. I know he really would understand me." Yes, but if you met a conscious man who understood you he would not be quite what you asked for. Why? Because through imagination you take yourself as what you imagine you are—which *is not* the case. You are not what you imagine you are, and you have got eventually in the Work to realize this. This indeed is the only real stimulus for working on oneself—seeing one is not what one imagines. It is very strong medicine, which only a few can take.

So realization and memory are powerful agents to use. Now the more the mists of imagination clear away, the more you feel Real 'I'. Imaginary 'I' needs imagination to support iself. As long as one's life is governed by Imaginary 'I' it must of necessity be unreal. I can assure you that the gradual loss of imagination, when you accept the controlling influences of the Work, does not lead to any inner impoverishment. On the contrary, it turns one into rich and inexhaustible fields of new understanding, where the plague of yourself no longer exists. As long as one is surrounded by intractable, unchallenged, and even violent illusions (which, by the way, in the face of great danger may fall away completely for the time being) one is stifled by imagination—for all illusions are due to the work of imagination. Take the comfortable well-dressed, self-complacent person, clothed internally in all sorts of vain imaginations—do you think that *that* is a state of being awake? Or is it a state of being asleep? Clearly such a person, man or woman, must be stung into awakening from spiritual death. Here we can see the work of imagination keeping people fast asleep in all sorts of conceits and vanities, and even the continual reverses and tragedies of life will not awaken them. As physical death approaches many life-illusions weaken—leaving what? A man alive, or a man dead, perhaps for years. Only what is real can withstand death. Christ said that only love of God can withstand death. And it is very strange to reflect upon and get to know what is real in oneself. No orthodox catalogue of standard virtues can assist one here, for what is real in a person is unique to him or her. There is no standard yard-stick to measure a man or woman. We are born unique, we are born to awaken, and so we are born to reach Real 'I' in ourselves and Real 'I' is unique in every case. So each must *eventually* follow his individual pathway to Real 'I'. Yes—but there are general truths about how to reach it—and the Work teaches them and they must be obeyed first of all. For example, no one can reach Real 'I' if the love of being negative continues to be greater than the desire to separate from negative emotions. The momentary experience of this separation is freedom. Here one set of emotions must contend with another set of emotions—and for a long time—for only one emotion can overcome another emotion. A man is his chief love. Now if the valuation of the Work becomes stronger—and that means love of it—then it will contend with the love of being negative, and, in fact, with all the Work teaches us to observe and separate from. The Work, in short, will fight for you. Only in this way can Real 'I' be approached. But if one mistakes Real 'I'—if one takes Imaginary 'I' as Real 'I'—then one has not begun to work on oneself and so is a failure in the sense of all esoteric teaching and so in the Gospel-sense, however successful and respected in life one is. One has mistaken the *real* meaning of one's existence on this low-placed planet, on which the dangerous experiment of a self-developing organism is being tried out.

In speaking about imagination we must erect a background from which to speak, so as to see where and what imagination is. Mechanical self-running imagination keeps us asleep. Imaginary 'I' is composed of imagination. Imaginary 'I' must be gradually drained of its force. That is a plain statement of the situation and of what the Work is speaking to us about all the time.

Let us take Category (3)—namely, some people act their dreams—

that is, their forms of imagination. These people are different from Category (1)—namely, those who dream their dreams—that is, do not try to act them. In this connection, watch a man, a woman, in a passive state of imagination. Their eyes are always unfocussed. They seem rather deaf and blind. They have very interesting expressions on their faces—not lively expressions, but rather sad, withdrawn expressions, yet not quite so, because one can see that they have at the same time some deep, inner satisfaction going on within them. What is happening? Their force is being drained by their mechanical self-running imagination. "They are", said Mr. Ouspensky once, "attending a very important cinema-film, which is very expensive." Yes—imagination can satisfy every centre. It certainly can if you notice the fact. But Category (3) are those who seek to act their dreams—try to relate external life to their internal phantasies. The life of uncontrolled imagination absorbs a person and drains force and there is no connection with what we call "reality". The third Category seeks to make external reality correspond with the internal phantasy. So Mr. Ouspensky said that those who *act* their dreams are quite different from those who dream their dreams, or those who talk their dreams. Yet those who act their dreams do so from a phantasy. It is not yet real. That is the point. They have, say, a phantasy of beating some record of speed. They do so—and yet it is not they but their imagination— and that is why one often wonders that they are never content, but try again to beat their previous record. The reason is that imagination is gripping them so that they can never rest, for imagination is insatiable and will not be corrected by experience. Such a man is not doing from his real side what he is doing. He is driven by something not himself —namely, by the power of Imaginary 'I'. He is following an imagination of himself—say, as being the finest, or cleverest, or most polished, or bravest fellow on earth. And yet the tragedy is that all that is real in him does not really want to do that which Imaginary 'I' makes him do. He is, in short, acting his imagination, which is insatiable and which will torment him to further efforts to satisfy his idea, his phantasy of himself. It is the same, of course, with women. So many people, brought up on stories and legends which have filled their imagination, continue in life trying to act these acquired phantasies. All this is Imaginary 'I'. The Work teaches us that Real 'I' exists, but cannot be approached as long as Imaginary 'I' dominates us.

THE STEP-DIAGRAM

This Work-Diagram has not been given for some time. I am going to give it as briefly as possible.

The Work teaches that the creation of the Universe is according to the Law of Three and the Law of Seven and is a descending Octave in which at each level or *note* the Law of Three operates so that each successive manifestation is under more and more laws or forces, from the Absolute down to our Earth and Moon. This is *our* Ray of Creation. The Absolute is under one law—the Will of the Absolute—and so is unconditioned. The First Order of Worlds is under 3 laws, because all manifestation is due to 3 forces meeting at a point and co-operating, as active, passive and neutralizing. The Second Order of Worlds manifested is under the 3 forces of its own manifestation and 3 forces from the First Order of Worlds. The Third Order of manifested Worlds is under 3 laws of its own, 6 laws from the Order immediately above, and 3 laws directly from the First Order —so is under 12 laws—and so on, down to our Earth under 48 and our Moon under 96. You see, therefore, that creation is limitation by scale—the lowest being under most and the highest under least laws. *This is the game.* I mean that we live far down in the descending scale so the Will of the Absolute can only reach us indirectly through increasing mechanical laws. To reach us directly—which would be unbearable—all the instrumental notes in the Octave would have to be destroyed. That is, the laws of the game would have to be abrogated and so everything would be destroyed. That is why it is possible to speak of the Universe as a *game*.

When you realize that the Universe is built on the principle of scale, you can understand that the energies at work in the upper parts of the Ray of Creation are finer than those acting in the lower parts. These finer and coarser energies are called *Hydrogens* in the Work. I am not going to give you the complex diagrams that belong to this idea, but ask you simply to accept that energies are finer and coarser and are called Hydrogens. Comparatively speaking, we know that in the known octaves of physical energies the energy representing, say, violet light is "finer" than that representing red light—that is, of greater frequency of vibration; and passing upwards a little in the scale of these known physical energies, X-Rays are found which are "finer" than violet light, so much so that they can pass through the body; and so on. So one can, by analogy, conceive how the energy of the Absolute can pass through everything. Now you have heard that the centres in Man work with different energies or Hydrogens, according to their speed of action. Formatory Centre works with Hydrogen of a density represented by the figure *48*. Sex-Centre works with a Hydrogen of a density represented by the figure *12*—that is, a much finer energy. Moving

Centre works with *Hydrogen 24*—and so is far quicker than Formatory Centre—actually about 30,000 times, as we notice when running downstairs and suddenly trying to "think" how we are doing it. Instinctive Centre, the wizard alchemist that attends to the inner working of the organism, works with *Hydrogen 24* and Emotional Centre also—or should do so. The Higher Emotional Centre works with *Hydrogen 12* and the Higher Mental Centre works with *Hydrogen 6*. In all these centres *Time* is different—on the principle that "a thousand years (in the sight of God) are but as yesterday". A *moment* of Consciousness in Higher Mental Centre would seem as years of our Time. And so, also, *Time* in each note or level of the Ray of Creation is different. Each cosmos within cosmos has a different Time. 30,000 years of our Time is to a consciousness at the level of the Sun merely a flash. Finally, the Work teaches that the whole Universe is growing, apart from failures in it.

Now we come to the Step-Diagram. This represents the Universe as a strange kind of psycho-physical digestive-tube in which everything eats and is eaten. According to this diagram and its inner significance everything is defined *by what it eats and what eats it*. We eat all sorts of things, but we do not imagine that all sorts of things also eat us, although after a time on this planet we may come to suspect it. Recollect that we are told that, if we are asleep in life, we feed the Moon—that is, when we are identified and negative, and so on. So you see we must grasp that a man may be eaten *in many senses*—not merely physical. Everything is food for something else, and something else is again food for something else. Pain and useless suffering feed the Moon, the body the Earth.

Now we can see in visible nature that life eats life. Animals, birds, fishes, insects, eat each other. We eat them. Or again, a cow eats grass and we eat the cow and so on. If everything living ate the same thing, living creation would be impossible. Things are cleverly fitted in, often into very odd corners. One thing is food for another in very odd ways. So you see that when it is said that everything is defined by what it eats and what eats it, the definition is very interesting. Now we must add one thing to this Work-definition. A thing, the Work says, is defined *by what it eats, by what eats it, and by the medium in which it lives*. A fish and a bird, for instance, live in different mediums. Many fish live on fish and many birds live on fish—but they belong to different mediums. Again, the possible things that may eat fish are not identical with the possible things that can eat birds, and so on.

The Step-Diagram

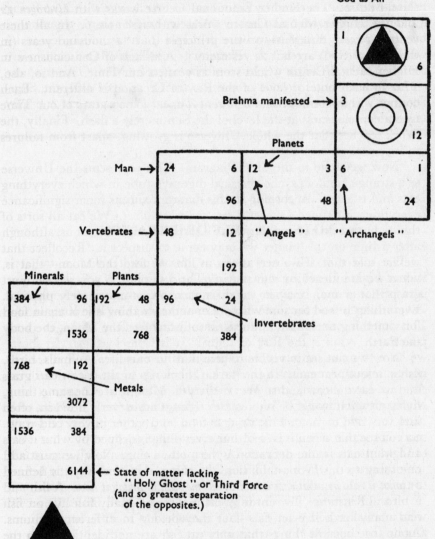

Absolute

Brahma unmanifested
God as One
God as All

1   6

Brahma manifested → 3

12

Planets

Man → | 24 | 6 | | 12 | 3 | 6 | 1 |

96   48   24

Vertebrates → 48   12   "Angels"   "Archangels"

192

Minerals   Plants

384   96 | 192 | 48 | 96 | 24

1536   768   384   ← Invertebrates

768   192

← Metals

3072

1536   384

6144 ← State of matter lacking
" Holy Ghost " or *Third Force*
(and so greatest separation
of the opposites.)

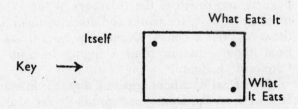

What Eats It

Itself

Key →

What
It Eats

1105

You will notice that Man is taken as *Hydrogen 24* in this Step-Diagram. This means that Man is essentially of this order or quality —namely, *Hydrogen 24*. As such he eats *Hydrogen 96*. *Hydrogen 96* is his food. He does not eat whole animals. And in turn he is eaten by higher Beings, who are represented by *Hydrogen 6*. Now, if you will notice, Man as *24* is eaten by Beings called "Archangels", whose Being is defined by *Hydrogen 6* and not by "Angels" whose being is represented by *Hydrogen 12*. But if Man were *Hydrogen 48* he would be eaten by what are called "Angels" or "Planetary Gods". If Man's being were represented by *Hydrogen 96*, he would be eaten by Man. This is a very curious point—but I do not propose to discuss it. As I said, the Step-Diagram has not been given for some time and I have given it as briefly as possible.

Great Amwell House, January 10, 1948

NOTES ON SELF-OBSERVATION

The object of self-observation, as this Work teaches, is to let a Ray of Light into our inner darkness. The discipline of self-observation is a life-long one, because we do not know ourselves although we imagine we do, and because what we imagine we know is so often wrong. This state is our inner darkness, into which a Ray of Light must penetrate. What is the Ray of Light? It is Consciousness. In short, we have to make ourselves more conscious to ourselves. What we are not conscious of remains in the dark. It belongs to the dark side of us. As you have heard, this Work divides Man into Conscious and Mechanical Humanity. We, as belonging to Mechanical Humanity, need to strive to become more conscious and we begin by becoming more conscious to ourselves of ourselves—that is, by letting this Ray of Light into this inner darkness by the method of uncritical, impersonal self-observation, which establishes Observing 'I' in ourselves and begins to make us slowly objective to ourselves. This changes one's feeling of 'I'. The Observing 'I' eventually collects round it all those 'I's which wish to awaken and when this state is reached of inner re-arrangement among the different 'I's a temporary and substitute Real 'I' is formed termed "Deputy-Steward". The more one studies, reflects upon, and ponders and practises the teachings of the Work, and sees, through inner perception, the truths contained in them, the stronger "Deputy-Steward" will become. Eventually, he attracts in flashes "Steward" from above—that is, from a higher level in himself—and behind "Steward" is Real 'I'.

Now Real 'I' cannot appear if a man is in a state of Inner Darkness. If it were to, the man would go mad. Yet Man was created to reach

Real 'I' in himself and not to go mad. All the above is stating the inner meaning of the Work from one angle. Always remember that, with our limited minds, the Work itself as a whole can only be stated now from this angle and now from that angle. Notice, for instance, we are not speaking of that level of Consciousness called the level of Self-Remembering, nor that further level, the attainment of which gives us Objective Consciousness, with which Real 'I' is connected. We are speaking only of the necessity of making ourselves more and more conscious to ourselves. As we are, we are *identified* with ourselves—that is, not conscious of ourselves. In the Work-sense, *being identified* means not being conscious. And we have recently spoken of how it is in the interests of certain planetary forces to keep Man asleep and use him, by making him *identified*, both with his idea of himself—that is, with his False Personality—and also with every typical event, of which there are only a certain number, which recur and recur until the man awakens to this simple fact and seeks to be no longer identified with all of them. Only the acquisition of *Consciousness*—that is, "light"—can separate us from the darkness of being always identified. If you become *conscious* that you are lame because your shoes do not fit you, you will not groan and sigh and remain identified with this useless suffering. You will observe how you walk and become conscious and begin to make better shoes. But for this to happen one must buy leather from the merchants who sell it and this is not so easy. Conscious Humanity has leather to sell and quite cheaply. But they cannot use violence and insist that Mechanical Humanity should buy it, for this would be against the law that Man is created a self-developing organism. Notice—a *self*-developing organism. To compel would therefore be against the esoteric laws relating to Man and his meaning. He would be *compelled* to develop—and, of course, could not develop at all—even in his slightest intimate and significant communions, say, with the stars and the sea—unless it was permitted and officially approved. Everything real in a man or a woman can only grow through their own will, their own feeling, their own understanding, their own consent, their own internal perception that a thing is so.

Now impressions coming from outside *via* the senses fall on phonograph-rolls in centres and register themselves there. These rolls grow a new skin when filled, yet what underlies is still there and can speak, only most is now in darkness—that is, unconscious. They are really four-dimensional rolls. Let us take a simple example of one of the "dark sides" of oneself. Each of you sings your typical song or songs but does not know it. The Work says: "Try to observe your songs". That is all it says. Do you say you have no songs to sing? Try again —try this time to observe yourself; try to listen; try to notice yourself; try to hear what you are saying. Did you say just now that you never sing? You must be a very exceptional man or woman. You say that you are? Well, in that case, why come here, where no one is exceptional in your sense? I can assure you you sing—and sing very well, probably. You have perhaps two or three good songs to sing, but you are not aware, not conscious of them. They just come out— and perhaps not quite into the open. In any case you may sing them softly to yourself all day. They are always *negative songs*. They spring from the negative part of the Emotional Centre—that part that we have to dig up and level and grow another crop on. Now people do not see how these often not openly expressed songs, if for years indulged in— such as the classical song called "Poor Little Me"—they do not see that these songs, which are so dangerous, so sweet, and so useless, constantly re-infect their inner state. They charm you to a tear—yes, but not merely that—they draw force from you. You know that all negative emotions drain you of force. We were taught in the early days that the constant indulgence of negative states, of self-pity, complaining, dis- liking, the love of being unhappy, of disagreeing as a fine art, and all the rest, is just as if you were to cut an artery at the wrist and let the blood drip all day—and then say you feel miserable.

*   *   *

Now things exist and have power over us because we are not properly conscious of them. The more unconscious a thing, the more power it exerts on us and the more mechanical our behaviour. To bring a thing up into the light of Consciousness is to rob it of its power. For this, long self-observation is needed and much patience with oneself. We observe—but not fully. Full self-observation takes time—years— one life-time perhaps. You have heard how Mr. Ouspensky's teacher said that this Work, which comes from an unknown source, can be called esoteric Christianity. He said that if we really understood what the Gospels were saying, we would see it is just what the Work says. As an example bearing on what we have just been saying about the dark side of us and the necessity of becoming more conscious, I will take the parable about the eye being the lamp of the body. Christ says:
"The lamp of the body is thine eye; when thine eye is single, thy whole body is full of light, but when it is evil thy body is full of darkness. Look therefore whether the light that is in thee be not darkness. If therefore thy whole body is full of light, having no part dark, it shall be wholly full of light, as when the lamp with its bright shining doth give thee light."   (*Luke* XI 34-36)
Here Christ speaks clearly about the importance of "having no part dark" in oneself—the term body being used here for the psychological body. Now to act mechanically is evil and to act consciously is not evil. If we were a unity—that is, single—we would act consciously. But we are not a unity but a many—a multitude of different 'I's which we do not know, do not observe. This is darkness. So the Work speaks so much about letting in this Ray of Light by self-observation into our darkness.

1108

6144

At all times in the Work it is necessary to get things clear, to make right connections, to fight imagination, to struggle with lies and separate from negative states. Everything can be joined together wrongly. Everything, I repeat, can be wrongly connected, wrongly taken, mis-understood, and so on. So an effort of *mind* is necessary to get things clearer for oneself. Notice how one can believe almost obvious lies. Notice scandal and its effects on you. Notice propaganda. In short, notice how easily a man, a woman, can be hypnotized. Our centres work almost in the dark. As a consequence, things pass towards the "Moon", to the region of dimness and wrong, evil, and even monstrous connections, to the place where there is absence of all truth, to super-stitions, to fear yielding to fear, to where everything is half-lit and there is no strength of right reasoning. As was seen in the Step-Diagram, at the bottom of it there is a number 6144 about which it is said briefly that there where it exists is no Third Force. Here First and Second Force—that is, Active and Passive Force, which are opposites—are most widely separated and no right conjoining of them *via* a Third or Neutralizing Force is possible. We can deduce that this will therefore be the region of the greatest improbabilities where nothing means anything and everything is chaos. Now, as the Work teaches, it is necessary to say sometimes: "I *can* work". To say to oneself: "I can work" is a good thing and gives a little shock to oneself. It scatters those stealthy negative 'I's that tend to come in through one's unguarded spots. Of course, if we were properly conscious, if there were "no part dark" in us, the light of Consciousness would prevent any such approach of lying and unpleasant 'I's and nothing would be unguarded. As we are, we have many unlit places that let in all sorts of wrong-minded 'I's that seek to pervert whatever "truth" surrounds us so as to get at everything good both in Personality and Essence. This is a struggle that is worth-while and in it it is necessary to renew the sense of the truth of the Work continually in one's most interior, private, real, almost wordless thought. Now you must understand that in the Step-Diagram, in spite of the semi-physical meaning of the numbers, a man can fall down it spiritually, psychologically—yes—to the bottom of it perhaps —for every diagram in the Work, taken literally, refers in a certain sense to material things and, taken psychologically, to psychological things.

Now we come to another Work-Phrase: "One must create oneself". What then, is it that one must *create*? That is a big question. I will answer briefly: first of all, a mechanical man, who is a machine driven by external life and its events, has not yet created himself, however successful. And secondly, to create oneself one must create something in oneself that can gradually resist life and its effects and keep its inner balance. This latter begins only through some form of truth in which one believes and which one is tested by every day. There is life-truth and Work-truth. So it is said: "Between you and life the Work must stand." This is really the First Conscious Shock, called Self-Remembering—but there are many other ways of defining what that effort called the shock of Self-Remembering means. You can get dragged down, you can get under the power of life, you can get identified with any of the experiences on the turning wheel of the events in life.

Now no one can create himself save through right effort. A man turned outwards who is led by life solely does not *create himself*. His machine works the wrong way round. He will never reach Real 'I' in himself and will not wish to. But let us take a man who can be in life and remember the Work at the same time and apply it. He then leads a double life. And this is exactly the starting-point. He will have to make a certain kind of *effort*. He will see outer life as one thing and *its effects* on him as another thing. He will see both together. This is right effort, and one of the first definitions of the First Conscious Shock. This definition is represented by two arrows⇌. He is conscious outwards and inwards. Something in life depresses a man, say, lack of a nice letter. As an ordinary man not working on himself his situation is just that. He is bowled out by such a typical event. He is identified with his depression caused by this typical event. As a man in the Work he notices his depression and notices what causes it. He notices both his impression and the depression and is not either of them. This is one formulation of right effort. But to do this he must know how to keep more or less awake and not identify with the effects of impressions coming in—that is, with the various events he inevitably and inescapably finds himself in at every moment. To take your life differently you must not try to alter life but begin to notice the effects of life upon you and not simply *be these effects*. If some of you could understand more of what this means, it would help you. There are a certain number of events in life and these are always recurring, not only to you but to everyone else. At this moment, say, 60 million people are depressed because they have not received a nice letter. Yes—and you are one of them, let us suppose. So you are depressed—not only that, but *you* are depression and depression is you. Now right effort here is to notice the cause and notice the effect of the cause in yourself and be conscious of both. In that way you get to real knowledge of your machine. The Work says we are machines—as long as we do not know ourselves. A machine cannot know itself. But a *man-machine* can get to know itself. That is the difference. All right effort is to know our machine and not go always, every moment, with its mechanical reactions. Then something else is created in oneself. Something forms behind this machinery, which you deny for so long, and this leads eventually to Real 'I'. At least this is the way. We are machines because Real 'I' or Master does not control us. Instead we are controlled by the events of life, entering us as impressions. That is, we are not controlled *from within*, as we should be, but from outside things. So we are machines. But we were not made to be machines, but with the possibility of being machines *unless we remember ourselves*. That is, we were made with the possibility of creating ourselves and ceasing to be machines. The starting-point is the observing of one's machinery and realizing that it is *not* 'I' but *IT* that is acting all the time. The machine is acting—or rather, re-acting. This you call 'I'. No, it is the machine. All right effort is about this question—this realizing that what one has taken as *Really Oneself* is not really yourself but is a machinery, a mechanicalness laid down chiefly by imitation in your life. And what tragedies we suffer from this mistake we keep on making about ourselves. I remind you again of what Mr. Ouspensky said. He asked: "What is this Work about?" People said: "To remember", and so on. There were many answers. What was *the* answer? I said: "To make Nicoll passive". He agreed. And I fancy others agreed by the way they stared at me with lorgnettes and eye-glasses. An amusing thought, is it not, to think that some believed that this Work and all the esoteric teaching through the ages behind it was simply to make "Nicoll" passive. Yet, if you reflect, it is quite true—in my case Yes, but it is also true in your case.

*   *   *

Now the Work constitutes a Third Force which is different from the Third Force of Life. We spoke briefly about 6144 as having no Third Force connected with it and said that this means the widest separation of the opposites (since nothing can draw them into co-operation) and the region of the greatest improbabilities. With no Third Force there would be no conjunction. This Work and all esotericism is to attain Unity. At the top of the Step-Diagram is the Unity of the Absolute. Now it is said that the Third Force of Life will not bring about that degree of Unity in ourselves represented by Real 'I' but leaves us in multiplicity, but that the Third Force of the Work leads to Unity. So you can see how this Work with the Third Force it conducts acts in a reverse way and is the antithesis of that psychological region signified by the number 6144. If the Work acts through us we will not go downwards in the Step-Diagram taken psychologically but move upwards. At the top of the Step-Diagram is absolute Unity or God the Supreme, the Greatest Meaning. At the bottom is this state represented by the figures 6144 where everything is meaningless. All right effort is therefore towards this increasing Unity which is only accomplished by increasing Consciousness. The more irreconcilable opposites one has in oneself the less meanings one has to live by. Union of opposites gives greatest meaning. Meaning springs from the conjunction and harmonizing of the opposites brought about through the connecting force called Third or Neutralizing Force. This Neutralizing Force makes the two hitherto hostile back-to-back opposites turn round and face one another and so co-operate and produce something, instead of being at war with each other. When I said to you that you must bring the dark side—the other side of you—the side not conscious to you—into the light of Consciousness, and not imagine that what you admit to Consciousness is all of you, I was speaking of this bringing together of opposites in yourself—of contradictions not acknowledged or even noticed. There is so much to understand here that it is impossible to speak of save over a long time. Yet all this time the Work has been telling you about it in everything it says. All right effort is to increase Consciousness—one's Consciousness of oneself. But many things, particularly buffers, prevent us. We are all angels and everyone is a devil, more or less. We never behave in a rotten way to anyone. Of course not. Yet is not it strange that our Consciousness is not full enough to shed light on both sides of a buffer so that we behold for ourselves our inner contradictions? Well, perhaps it is not so strange when you reflect that Man was made a self-developing organism—that is, to create himself—and that if he never understands this he can drop down to total meaninglessness represented by the figure 6144. And, if you can follow me, total meaninglessness is total darkness. So it is necessary, as was said at the start of the paper, to fight hard.

Great Amwell House, January 24, 1948

ESSENCE AND PERSONALITY

WORK-IDEA.

To-day we speak again of what the Work teaches about Essence and Personality. The Work says we are born as Essence. As very little children we are in Essence. But Essence, which is the real part of us, is very small, primitive and undeveloped. Through our contact with life, through Papa and Mamma and nurses and teachers, we develop Personality which surrounds Essence but does not make Essence grow. Personality grows—not Essence—not the real part of you. Then around Personality there forms False Personality, through which we *imagine* we are real people. Connected with False Personality is Imaginary 'I'—that is, we imagine we have a real, unchanging, permanent thing called 'I'. The Work, however, teaches that we have not got Real 'I', but only Imaginary 'I', and that, although Real 'I' exists in us and can be reached, we are not in touch with it and cannot be as long as we imagine we have it. One of the powers of imagination is to persuade us we have a thing when we have not. I may imagine I have a gun and someone comes and asks me if I want a gun and I say I have one. Then I find I have not one. That is, I imagine I have something valuable and, being offered it, I refuse it because I imagine I have it. Later I discover I haven't it. This is one of the powers of imagination which act universally on Man. As you know, the Work says that mankind is asleep, partly owing to a deliberate hypnotism to keep it asleep, and that if a man wishes to awaken from the Earth-Sleep in which all mankind is used and so made into a pain-factory for other purposes than its own—he must *struggle with imagination.*

Now we come to the Commentary on the above Work-teaching:

COMMENTARY

To awaken from sleep is to grow, to develop. A man, a woman, can only grow and develop internally through positive ideas. Negative ideas put mankind asleep: positive ideas awaken mankind. It was said earlier that one way of defining what positive ideas mean is that anything that strengthens False Personality is not a positive idea. No one can develop inwardly *via* False Personality. The Works says that internally none of us is grown up. It says that if we were war would cease at once. In relationship to our job, to our life-affairs, in which we have been trained, we may appear real men and real women. We look modestly important, we make the right speeches and the right movements. We wear costumes and uniforms, we have carefully arranged faces and expressions, and we manage things as long as they are in the line of our training. But take such a person aside, along a line not familiar, and he or she becomes embarrassed, and uncomfortable or, as is usually said, "out of his depth".

This is the first education—imposed by life—that is, the education of the Personality. This Work is about the second education, in which Personality must be weakened and the real part of us—namely, Essence —grow. And certainly, as most of us already know, this is a very difficult job. But if we seek *new meaning*—and meaning is the most important thing, for we live by meaning—we have to separate from old, worn-out meaning in order to let in new meaning for our existences. Otherwise we die—although our bodies go on living. How many dead walk the streets and sit in clubs. New meaning is only possible for us through *positive ideas.* You will not, after a time, get new meaning from life-ideas.

* * *

There was once upon a time a song—I suppose a vulgar song, no doubt, to some—in which the phrase occurs: "Where did you get that hat?" Let us use this, no doubt, vulgar phrase, as a starting-point. A man is clothed physically by clothes and he is clothed mentally or psychologically by truth—that is, by the truth he follows. The body is clothed by physical clothes and what you think is truth clothes your mind-body. A man, a woman, is first a physical body. I say first in view of the senses. One sees a man's visible body, a woman's visible body, first. But this man, this woman, has also an invisible psychology, quite possibly angelic, and also quite possibly devilish. However, the physical body, the sense-given appearance, may not shew us in the least the nature of the person's psychology. In proposing, say, one may notice a nasty expression, temporarily, but the beauty of the visible body re-assures one and one continues trustfully. However, the nasty expression for a moment revealed the nature of the inner psychology —that is, the kind of psychological body that is attached no doubt to this most marvellous physical body. Is it not strange that, as far as I can see, people have to be over seventy or eighty, before they understand this, in spite of various smart clichés such as "Things are not as they appear" or "All is not gold that glitters" and so on. And then they are too old to remember what it was they wanted to remember, which saves them a lot of trouble. All the same it is a remarkable fact that a man with a heavy frown or a woman with a bitter look, who at the moment of proposing neither frowns nor looks bitter, expects the deep, long causes of that frown and the deep, long causes of that bitter look to vanish through the so-called power of love for ever. So it is not surprising that this Work teaches that *Man is asleep*—and that, notice, includes Woman, who also is asleep in her own way just as much as Man is, only not quite in the same way, I have noticed.

Now I return to the "hat". That part of the invisible psychology or psychological body of a person that is connected with how he or she *thinks* is the "hat"—the thinking-cap. The head thinks—so its covering is what clothes it. A person thinks from what to that person is truth. You think from what you take as truth. What forms of truth you have been taught and accept constitute your "hat". So it is a legitimate question to ask a person, not only: "Why do you think this or that is true?" but "Where did you get that hat?" which equals the question: "Why think like that?" The answer is, of course: "Because I was brought up to think like that". Yes, but another person, brought up differently, thinks in another way—that is, wears another hat, of a different colour or a quite different shape. And so on and so on. Yet each thinks he thinks aright and each thinks he thinks from absolute truth. So everyone wears a different hat—an invisible hat, because it belongs to the invisible body—that is, the person's acquired psychology.

Now are you all fully aware that although you live in visible bodies seen clearly and signal to each other as best you can, and usually very clumsily, you really live in your thoughts, feelings, moods, desires, ambitions, and so on, which are *invisible*? So *you* are really invisible, enclosed in a visible body. Do you see this yet? You may be heart-broken, as the saying is, and yet appear visibly cheerful. Why is it that people cannot take in the idea that they *themselves* live in their invisible side, known only to them through their own consciousness? So look at this vision: here we are visible to one another as physical bodies but almost totally invisible to one another in any real sense. So, being really invisible, you are therefore all alone—not lonely—but alone. This is one thing we have to grasp from height to depth of all the meaning it contains. It is the only thing that saves us from continual self-pity. It is *no-one's* fault that you are not understood—for you are invisible and no-one can know you. Only you can know yourself. So the Work says: "Begin with trying to understand yourself". Yes—a very big task. But it shifts effort to the right place. However, imagination steps in here to keep you fast asleep. It says: "Of course I know myself—of course I understand myself". The answer is: "You do not and as long as you are under this illusion nothing will change for you. Everything will remain the same. You will go through the same troubles, the same unhappiness, and the same tragedies. There is only one way to change all that and that is to change yourself, change your own being and life will change. Try to change life and everything will be the same, even if you go to the uttermost parts of the Earth."

Now here we have one of the *positive ideas* of the Work—namely, "To change things, to change his life, a man must first change himself. And in order to change himself he must find a teaching that will tell him how to do so. He must be willing to be taught new knowledge, new truth, and to begin to think in a new way. If he continues to think from the knowledge he has acquired, he will continue to think in the old way and then nothing can change. Only thinking in a new way can change a man."

Now a life-idea—that is, a negative idea—begins with changing outer life, changing your house, income, servants, and so on. A Work-idea begins with *changing yourself*. This is a positive idea. If you remain the same man, the same woman, wherever you go you will attract the same troubles, the same anxieties. The Work says: "Your *being* attracts your life." If you do not change your being—the kind of person you mechanically are by upbringing—nothing can possibly change for you in outer life. You will always attract the same kind of things, the same situations, the same troubles." So the Work teaches in this second education that one's task is to begin to try to change one's being, and not to try to change outer conditions. This is a *positive idea*.

Great Amwell House, January 31, 1948

INTERNAL CONSIDERING AND INNER TALKING

Part I.—We have to struggle with unnecessary emotions. Energy that goes into unnecessary emotions is lost. You see it is raining and feel, say, a sort of hostility or dislike or slight depression. This is unnecessary emotion. People seem to get caught by everything that does not correspond with their expectations. That is, they identify with the fact that it is raining or cold or blowing a gale, because they did not expect it. They say, "Tut, tut", and feel a little upset. People seem to expect everything save what does happen. Of course, if you expect an unpleasant thing to happen and it does happen, your expectation protects you. Again, if you expect an unpleasant thing to happen and it does not, you are relieved. But, as was said before, most of us seem to have forms of expectation that lead us to expect everything save what does happen. In consequence, a great many unnecessary emotions are made and a lot of energy is lost in disappointment and internal considering—for a person may even internally consider to such a degree that if it rains on his dear little birthday he feels the Universe and all the hosts of Heaven have purposely done it. This is a quite childish attitude and, as anyone can see, must lead to a lot of unnecessary emotions. A weak being results, easily upset.

Now let us speak of internal considering in connection with unnecessary emotions. Internal considering has its source in the Emotional Centre in this sense—namely, that behind it there is always a feeling, an emotion. It *employs* the Intellectual Centre in endless words, inner talking and writing pathetic letters never or rarely sent, but at its root is a feeling, an emotion. What is this emotion that is the source of internal considering? Let us speak of it gently, for all of us, however grand or brave or hard-boiled we fancy ourselves, have this emotion, this feeling, deep within us—unless, by some miracle, the love of God has entered into our hearts and we have come to understand that this Earth is a place of test, and that nothing human can understand us. Take the person who feels that it should not rain on his dear birthday. It pours with rain. He considers. He feels sad. He feels something does not appreciate him sufficiently, that, he is not rightly treated, that something does not understand him. He was so looking forward to it. This, in the Work, is called internal considering. As I said, it is at bottom an emotion, a feeling, although the Intellectual Centre is employed to voice it in millions of words, spoken or unspoken. He puts on a bright face and says it does not matter. Yes—but inside the feeling, the emotion, continues, and many other similar emotions from similar experiences going far back into his past form a core in his Emotional Centre, from which many other forms of internal considering branch out—as, for example, you just miss the bus and somehow it is always like that, or just when you want to see her she says she has to go and see her aunt, or you did want to see that play and they took you to another, and so on. No one, of course, ever listens to what you want. I speak in a trivial way on purpose, because the subject of internal considering is very deep and a serious matter in everyone—for somehow life is foreign to us. Indeed, it is so deep and so serious that the whole range and power of esoteric teaching through the ages, including the strength of teaching latent in the parables in the Gospels—such as "The Prodigal Son"—has not been able to cure Humanity of it. Indeed, Humanity, unless it begins to awaken from sleep and reach the level of Conscious Man, can never be cured of it,

But one man, one woman, may begin to cure themselves of it—by hard work on themselves.

So we have to speak of *unnecessary* or avoidable internal considering. Let us suppose a man does not see his own disloyalty, callousness and malice. He has never observed himself. He does not see that people dislike or avoid him for this reason. He can see no reason why everyone does not adore him. He then fancies people unfairly do not like him. They behave unfairly to him. So he has a grievance. This is internal considering. A man with a grievance is a good example of internal considering. He never externally considers—that is, puts himself into the situation of other persons and realizes their difficulties. On the contrary, he wishes to put everyone he talks to into his situation, to make them realize his difficulties—and a very boring experience it is to hear them, especially if you are a doctor and are forced to listen to him. Now this word *unfair* is, I think, a favourite word in internal considering. Do you see it yourself? Do you not secretly think that everything is *unfair*? If so, you have an admirable source of continual internal considering, and will lose force every minute of the day. I mean, each day will be a failure from the Work point of view. On the other hand, if you observe your typical forms of internal considering and do not identify with them and remember yourself, you will realize that only *you* can help *yourself*, and all this internal considering and sense of unfairness is useless and worse and can only give rise to daily emotions which are unnecessary. But let no-one think he or she is free from internal considering.

Internal considering on one side is defined as making internal accounts against others. You have done a job of work and feel that others have not done a similar job. So you start internal considering —though you may not express it in spoken words. Others do not have to work as you have to. Others do not see what you have done. No one appreciates you—and so on. All this arises from not doing what you have to do from yourself—not *you yourself* willing what *you* have to do. Whatever you have to do, *will* to do it and you will get through the job without becoming negative and so without being tired and without making internal accounts. We have to be reminded of this constantly —and you all are reminded of it constantly, for it is one of the secrets of right work on oneself. Not only that: *it makes force in you.* Perhaps nothing destroys one's understanding of the Work as much as internal considering, this making of inner accounts against others with all the resulting self-pity and damp, negative states, which, as it were, turn one's whole psychological country into marshland filled with venomous mosquitoes.

Now, if I *will* to do what I have to do, I will not make inner accounts against others. But if I do what I have to do and all the time think that someone else should do it and that it is unfair that I should have to do it, then I am making internal accounts. That is, I am internally considering. And this will give rise to endless *inner talking* in myself—

a sort of inner muttering and complaining and brooding, that will go on and on by itself, for the sign of the negative part of Emotional Centre working is that it all goes on and on by itself—a sort of perpetual secret grievance that may spread over and darken all one's inner life. We know that we have to protect our outer life—our bodies—from assault. Yet, even more important, we have to protect our inner psychological life—our psychological body—from assault—and a much more dangerous form of assault. For a man may preserve his outer physical life but not have any idea that he has to protect his inner psychological life. So he gets narrow, hard, sour, stiff, bitter, revengeful, jealous, moody, tiresome, and so on. In other words, he lives in his body, but is dead inwardly in himself. However his body may appear, the Work will say: "This body is alive, but he himself is internally a failure and is dead. He is a walking dead man." All this, of course, applies to women as well. How many dead, Mr. Ouspensky said, walk the streets.

So it is necessary to observe internal considering and notice what it is and try to control it. This will lead to psychological health. Notice your inner talking. Notice what obsesses your thoughts. Taste it and see whether it is negative. Try to struggle with it. Hate it. Try to wake up and do what you have to do *from yourself, willingly*. Only one person can live your life and that is yourself. But are you on the box of your own carriage and have you reins? Otherwise you cannot *will* anything.

You all probably have heard that extraordinary esoteric remark attributed to Christ: "Resist not evil". It has many remarkable meanings. One is to *will* what you think evil, what you think you dislike, what you think should not be. You think you may die. Will it—and you will no longer be afraid. To object to everything is easy. To will what you object to is another thing. If you object to everything you will internally consider all day. You will make internal accounts against everyone. But if you *will* the existence of someone you object to, everything will change—miraculously. If you *will* what happens to you, you will gain force. If you object to what happens to you, you will lose force. This Work is about how to gain force.

* * *

Part II.—You have heard many times that this Work is Esoteric Christianity. Exoteric Christianity—belonging to different sects and rituals and so on—is one thing. Esoteric Christianity connects with all former esoteric teaching and is about the inner meaning of fragments handed on to us, so inadequately, of the teaching of a Conscious Man who taught some 2,000 years ago. Christ was No. 8 Man. But we have very little reported of what He taught and most of what we have in the Gospels is by people who never knew Christ and no doubt added or distorted things, to fit their own views.

Now there is a parable preserved in one Gospel only about internal considering and how to prevent it, starting on oneself. All internal considering arises chiefly from False Personality in people more than anything else. Christ attacked the Pharisee and so on—and the Pharisee who "did all things to be seen of men" is not one of a group of people who lived centuries ago but something in yourself, *now—in you, now—* that is, the Pharisee in you that pretends to be what he really is not at heart. To realize one is almost nothing is to overcome the False Personality, the Pharisee. Now the False Personality blows us up into an enormous self-importance—like that frog in the fairy-story that finally burst. It is this overvaluing of ourselves that causes a lot of internal considering. The disciples of Christ ask: "Increase our faith". Now faith is a force—force to believe beyond the evidence of the senses, force to lift one above one's mechanical reactions, force to understand that there is something above one's limited human understanding, force to do this Work. Christ answers this question of how to increase one's force to understand above one's merely natural understanding by a parable:

> "And the apostles said unto the Lord, Increase our faith. And the Lord said, If ye have faith as a grain of mustard seed, ye would say unto this sycamine tree, Be thou rooted up, and be thou planted in the sea; and it would have obeyed you. But who is there of you, having a servant plowing or keeping sheep, that will say unto him, when he is come in from the field, Come straightway and sit down to meat; and will not rather say unto him, Make ready therewith I may sup, and gird thyself and serve me, till I have eaten and drunken; and afterward thou shalt eat and drink? Doth he thank the servant because he did the things that were commanded? Even so, ye also, when ye shall have done all the things that are commanded you, say, We are unprofitable servants; we have done that which it was our duty to do."
>
> (*Luke* XVII 5-9)

Now notice that it would be quite possible for the servant to make internal accounts—such as "Why should I have to work all day and then serve you who have not had a hard day as I have?"

COMMENTARY ON BEING

Work-Idea

The Work says that a man is not his size or his strength or position or wealth. It says that a man is his understanding. There are two sides to him in this respect—the side of his Knowledge and the side of his Being. According to their development, this forms the man's understanding. A man with great knowledge and bad being will *understand* very little or nothing and misunderstand very much. A man with poor knowledge and good being will again *understand* little but he will understand what he knows. Theoretically, full development of Knowledge and full development of Being will give the fullest possible understanding. Man can have many other things belonging to this subject. To-day I will make some commentaries on *Being*.

Commentary

In a recent question it was asked: "Can Essence be related to Being? Would it be correct to say that Essence is the part of our Being which can be developed?" From a general point of view the Being of a mechanical man is all that he is—that is, his False Personality, his Imaginary 'I', his acquired Personality, with all his different contradictory 'I's, his attitudes, prejudices, etc., and his undeveloped child-Essence. In reference to being many 'I's or "egos" the Work therefore says that the Being of a mechanical man is characterized by multiplicity. He is a many, not a one—but he imagines he is one and the same all the time and this illusion is produced by Imaginary 'I' which blinds him. This is the state of Being of mechanical man. It is not real Being. A conscious man has real Being. Let us examine the point. In what sense, that we can grasp, is the Being of a conscious man different from that of a mechanical man? In mechanical man—that is, in every one of us as we are—there is an absence of unity. As was just said, the Being of a mechanical man—that is, the Being of ourselves—is characterized by a multiplicity of different 'I's. But we do not notice it. We *imagine* we are a single 'I'. We say "I think", "I feel", "I wish", and so on, believing that it is the same 'I' all the time that is acting in us. But we are quite mistaken. It is merely imagination. We *imagine* we have one permanent, unvarying 'I' that acts in us and from this illusion springs the further illusion that we are unchanging and are conscious of all we think and say and do and feel. Yes—and this Imaginary 'I' dwells in the house of False Personality which in turn is built of imagination. This is an absurd yet extremely powerful form of hypnotism acting on us which sincere, uncritical observation will begin to weaken. If so, we are then beginning to awaken to a small extent and as a result our general feeling of ourselves, our feeling of 'I' and our relationship to ourselves and others, will begin to alter. By weakening a fixed idea about ourselves, we have made a little room to change in. But, however absurd, this form of hypnotism is so powerful that it is comparatively rare for anyone to awaken from it. People simply will not see that it is true of themselves. They will not awaken from sleep. So they live their lives with the wrong feeling of 'I'. They cannot for a moment grasp that Man is kept asleep by different forms of hypnotism for purposes that are of no advantage to him. In any case, they are sure they are awake and fully conscious. As was said, even though they quarrel all day long, the realization that one has many different and contradictory 'I's and not one real, permanent 'I' is a step towards awakening. Why? Because a man can no longer live in the illusion produced by Imaginary 'I' that he is one, a unity, an unvarying, constant and consistent individual. Reflect, some of you, on how a man can be an angel in public and a devil at home. Would you call that a sign that he has one permanent, real, unvarying, constant and consistent 'I'? Does it not mean that he has public 'I's and domestic 'I's, totally contradictory? And he has many other 'I's as well. But he imagines he has only one 'I'—fully conscious—that controls him. Is it not rather ridiculous that even quite intelligent people cannot—or cannot bear to—realize that this 'I' they attribute to their Being is entirely imaginary? As I said, it is an absurd illusion but one of tremendous power and few ever escape from it. One reason is that it deprives one of one's vanity to no small extent to realize that it is true. But one has to see it for oneself. To be told it is infuriating. So the Work starts with self-observation. It says in so many words: "Well, see it for yourself. Observe in yourself that it is so. It is none of my business to shew you it is true. You have to see the truth of it for yourself. You are not one but many."

Now we understand that the possibility of attaining unity, of reaching one permanent 'I', is latent in Man and that Man was created as a self-developing organism to attain to Real 'I' in himself and because he has not attained it he is never at peace within himself but always uneasy. To attain this secret goal hidden in him he must begin a long way off by discarding many illusions, many unreal things, one of which is that he already possesses this 'I'. In the case of this illusion he must begin to see the stark truth that he is many and not one and that in a sense there is no such person as himself but something unreal made up of a lot of people that use his name, that he takes as himself.

Now in the case of Conscious Man, the position is different. The Being of Conscious Man is characterized by unity—by the possession of Real 'I'. So his Being is quite different from our Being. He has real Being in comparison to our Being. A conscious man, because he has real Being, *can do*. Having unity, having Real 'I', he has *one* will, and, having *one* will, he *can do*. In our case, having many different 'I's in our Being, we have not one will, but many wills. Each 'I' has its own will and each 'I' wills what *it* wants and what one 'I' wants is different from what another 'I' wants. Having therefore no Real Will because we possess no Real 'I', a mechanical man *cannot do*. It *appears* as if he can do. But circumstances and training acting on him make him do as he does. He cannot help doing what he does. It is mechanical. It is only when he tries to go against his mechanicalness that he will begin to realize its enormous strength. In a conversation with Gurdjieff a question was asked by Ouspensky about what he could do. Gurdjieff said: "*You* can *do* nothing. In order to *do* a man must *be*." I have often reflected on this remark which, like everything Gurdjieff said, is strange, brief, and arresting. In order to *do* a man must first *be*.

From all this you will see that Being in the Work-sense seems to refer to developed Man—I mean, Real Being. We have Being as we are, but it is confused Being, which shifts and alters every moment. Gurdjieff compared the state of mechanical man's being to a glass retort filled with different metallic powders. He said: "At every tap the powders shift. This is what Man is like. Every change of life, of circumstances, every event, every situation, every mood, taps the retort, and the powders move. It is then necessary to put a fire under the retort until the metallic powders melt and fuse together and become one."

Now for this to begin to happen a man, a woman, must *crave* Being. Imagining they have real Being will not help. In fact, since imagination always can satisfy all our lack, it prevents us, in this case, from seeing that we have no real Being. But a sincere and scrupulous self-observation begins to shew us that we are *nobody*—nothing—just a confusion of things, inwardly, however our façade may suggest to others that we are something definite—and even suggest to us that we are something definite. But since Real 'I' exists in us, we can touch it under very exceptional conditions. Then we know what it would be like to have Real Being. As you have heard, sometimes under great and prolonged stress, under danger, under illness, under great fatigue and other things, a man touches Real 'I' in himself. Then everything is changed. Fear leaves him. Anxiety leaves him. Inner uneasiness leaves him. For the moment he has touched his goal. His whole feeling of 'I' is transformed. He is no longer himself as he was conscious of himself, but another person—an entirely new person. Everything false, unreal, invalid, vanishes. But we, as we are, have to work for long against everything false, unreal and invented, to reach this state permanently. That is, payment is demanded. Now one of the first payments in this sense is to realize that you are not one but many. This needs *work on oneself*. Do you, from this example, begin to see what payment means in the Work?

COMMENTARY ON HABITS

WORK-IDEA.

The Work says we must think in a new way to begin to change ourselves. The Work teaches that after a certain age we are nothing but a mass of acquired habits in every centre—habits in Thinking Centre, habits in Emotional Centre, habits in Sex Centre, habits in Moving Centre and habits in Instinctive Centre. All these habits keep us asleep because the centres cannot work and so we pass our existences not as we like, but as these habits dictate, and wonder why our lives are not what we expected. We do not even realize that they are habits. We *are* these habits, without seeing or knowing that this is the case. At the same time everyone is quite sure that they could easily change, if they wish to. This form of imagination assists, like all other forms of imagination, in keeping us asleep. Now if our centres were not overlaid by these habits, we would hear what they say to us about every occasion. But, as we are, centres do *not* speak to us.

COMMENTARY

The above was said originally in connection with the necessity of studying the construction of ourselves. We have to learn something about our machinery—in this case our habits. But, of course, we do not believe we have a machinery. People usually think that habits only refer to minor bodily habits. They do not understand that their Intellectual Centre—what they think by—is full of mechanical habits, and that their feelings, emotions, which belong to Emotional Centre, are also mechanical habits of feeling, habits of emotion. In other words, the Intellectual Centre and Emotional Centre are not awake, but overspread by habits.

Let us take the Intellectual Centre. Most people do not think but have opinions they have heard. These opinions can become habitual —that is, habits of the mind. Now if a man, a woman, begins to awaken a little and sees the necessity of *thinking* for themselves, they will find that there are so many acquired and borrowed opinions and traditions filling their Thinking Centre that they have absolutely no idea how to begin to think. And, of course, for the purposes of Nature, which Man asleep serves the world over, it is contrary to Nature's interest that anyone should really *think*. I suppose that if an animal began to think —say, a horse—a lot of trouble would start, quite apart from the trouble I have always had in connection with horses. But just consider if animals could really think. And also conceive if we all could really think for ourselves instead of following opinions, slogans, prejudices, traditions, catch-phrases, and even the last thing we read. Why, if we all could really think for ourselves, purely, we could live in a new world. But, as we are, we think from acquired opinions, borrowed ideas, from what we have been taught is right, and so on, according to our upbringing, our class, our education, our inner hatreds, jealousies and revenges. Now, as Gurdjieff said once: "Such a man does not think. *It* thinks—not he himself. And so he lives and dies without ever having thought." In another connection he said: "We must try to awaken the Intellectual Centre first of all. That is, it is necessary to begin to think for oneself. This Work is to make a man, a woman, *think*—and think in a quite new way." And on many occasions, Ouspensky said, in so many words: "Why ask me always what, say, is exactly the difference between self-observation and Self-Remembering? It is not for me to explain. You must see for yourselves. Try to observe— try to remember yourselves. You must begin to *think for yourselves.* This Work is to make *you* think—think what you are, think what you want, think indeed why you exist at all. Only by beginning to *think* can you change your life. Do you want your life to repeat itself just as it is? If so, do not above all even try to think. Just go on with your opinions. But then everything will recur just as it has happened already and you will have to repeat your life exactly as before."

Now this interested me very much. I had up to then believed that to change anything in oneself it was necessary to give up this or that physical habit such as smoking and so on. I had never realized that in order to change anything in oneself one has to begin to *think* in a new way and that unless there were some change in *thinking*, nothing else could be changed in oneself. That is, one had to start *at the top*—in the mind—before anything else could alter. So to-night I am going to try to shew you what this means. It is so very important an idea in this Work and also in fact in all esoteric teaching, as in the Gospels. Understand, then, that one cannot change oneself unless the mind changes. As long as you have the same *mental attitudes*, prejudices, opinions, and so on, you cannot begin to change—try as you like—and you will remain the same, unless your whole point of view, your whole way of thinking, changes first. "To change", Ouspensky said, "you must change your attitudes first."

Now let us speak first of what is said about the key to self-change in that extraordinary production called the Gospels. Notice how the whole idea of self-change, inner self-evolution, begins with one magical word. This word in the Greek is μετάνοια. Many have heard me speak of this word in connection with the Work and I do not think that what was said can be repeated enough. The introductory word to the Gospels and all their inner psychological teaching is this word μετάνοια which is wrongly translated as "*Repent*" and which really means "change your mind". In other words, it means "Think in a new way". μετα = beyond: and νοῦς = mind. So the word μετάνοια means "think beyond your mind" and that is equivalent to what this Work, which is Esoteric

Christianity, indicates when it teaches that in order to change we must think in a new way. That strange figure, John the Baptist, clad in skins, of whom Christ said that the least in the Kingdom of Heaven is greater than he—but that of men born of women he was the greatest—this strange figure taught two things in conjunction—"Repent—for the Kingdom of Heaven is at hand", which truly should be "Change your ways of thinking"—yes, but why? "Because the Kingdom of Heaven is at hand". What does that signify? It signifies the same as what the Work teaches. Can you find the parallel? Of course you can. What does the Work teach about *Man*? It says Man is not the same. Many different kinds and degrees of Man exist, No. 1, No. 2, No. 3—that is, Moving-Instinctive Man, Emotional Man, Intellectual Man. These, the Work says, are mechanical men who will never understand each other and so form the Circle of Confusion of Tongues, or Babel. It then speaks of higher categories of Man—No. 4 Man—that is, a man in whom all centres work so that he is not a one-sided man as, say, is a Moving Centre Man. Then it speaks of the Circle of Conscious Humanity—No. 5 Man, No. 6 Man and No. 7 Man. These form the "Kingdom of Heaven". From this example you will see that the Work-teaching about different categories of Man *makes you think in a new way*—that is, if you understand the teaching. And if you have patience to follow me, you will see that the message of John the Baptist, the herald of the teaching of Christ, is the same message as this Work gives: namely, "Think in a new way" and "The Circle of Conscious Humanity exists" —that is, the Kingdom of Heaven. Nowadays people wish to make Heaven on Earth. One must look around and consider what is happening. "For mankind to change, for a better state of things, each man, each woman, must begin to work on themselves and try to awaken from sleep." In such words did Gurdjieff many times indicate the *conditions* necessary for things to become better on this deep-down and unimportant planet. As it is, everything happens in the only way it can happen. It looks as if Man were *doing*. But only a Conscious Man can do. So everything happens in the only way it can happen. In this case, the theory of Determinism is right. But since a man can change and become a balanced man or even a Conscious Man, then, through his individual work, through his changing himself, others can change —and then things will not happen in the only way they can happen. One man, by work on himself, can change others—and others change others, and so on. But if all people are asleep, if no one understands what to do to change *themselves*, then all things will go on in the only way they can do—deterministically.

Now to return to the Thinking Centre or Intellectual Centre, and to the question of thinking in a new way. When we hear that there are *higher men*, we reflect. When we hear that Man was *created*—and created as an experiment in self-evolution—we reflect. When we hear that life on this planet is not in our interests unless we try to awaken, we reflect. When we hear that we are mechanical people and belong to the Circle of Babel we reflect. When we hear that unless we change ourselves, everything will remain the same, we reflect. When we hear that our level of Being attracts our life, we reflect. When we hear that if we remain as we are, everything will repeat itself just as it did before, we reflect. Do you, for instance, want to live the same life over and over again? The Work says if you change nothing in yourself, your life will endlessly repeat. When you hear that on having any mental contact with the Work and trying to make out for yourself what it is about, and so altering your previous so-called thinking, you may begin to alter your position in the totality of things—you reflect. To reflect means to bend your thinking back to yourself. Consider your life, do you want things different or do you want the recurrence of the same things? Everything repeats—as winter and summer. If you remain the same, you will experience the same. Surely you can see this from day to day. But the Work says it refers also to life after life— because everything is as a circle, and everything repeats. Now when you begin to reflect in this way, you begin to think for yourself—and this is the starting-point of self-change. You begin to become responsible for what you are. You begin to see that if you make no effort to change something of yourself everything will repeat—day by day—and life by life. Have you ever seen a propaganda child? You cannot change it. It has fixed ideas. If one reflects on this one begins to think in a new way—that is, one begins to think for oneself. Unless you yourself work on yourself you will have the same, over and over again. Do you wish this? I would say, in my case, No. Then what can possibly aid me? If I still internally consider, if I still submit myself to negative states without any struggle, if I identify with everything, with every thought and mood, then I certainly do not understand my life and its meaning on this Earth. So I add, reflect on what this Work teaches because only by reflecting privately will it enter your mind and alter your mind and *that*—this thinking in a new way—opens to each of you the possibility of changing your Being. Retain the same mental attitudes, the same prejudices, the same unchallenged viewpoints, the same fixed ideas and opinions, *and you cannot change anything in yourself*. The *mind* must first change. Hence it is said μετάνοια is the starting-point. That is, change of mind must come before you can become a different man, a different woman.

Now all this talk is about Intellectual Centre and changing it, for the Work teaches that unless you begin to *think in a new way* you can alter nothing and everything will go as before. This Work, intellectually, gives you the right thoughts and ideas that can connect you with Higher Centres—that is, make you receptive of another permanent ancient order of truth. But do not for a moment think that *that* is all. You must begin to have not only right thinking, right knowledge, but right Being. What is right Being? Being is different from truth. Being is just like this: Good = good will. Will belongs to Being. What is charity? Charity in the Greek = grace—graciousness. In the Gospel of John

it is said of Christ: "And we beheld him full of grace and truth."
Notice grace comes first. Just take your fanatical truth-people and
reflect.

Great Amwell House, February 21, 1948

COMMENTARY ON TIME

Work-Ideas.

(1) Centres work at different speeds.
(2) On one occasion Ouspensky asked Gurdjieff: "What is Time?"
Gurdjieff replied: "Time is Breath".

Commentary

Part I.—This Commentary is on some of the ideas about Time in the
Work. We will begin with the question of speed in different centres.
The centres in Man do not work at the same speed. What can be
understood by the term "speed of centres"? Take this example: If you
were to *think* how to move while running downstairs, you would
probably fall. Why? Because your thinking would be slower than your
movement. Again, if you have to think how to drive your car, you will
probably have an accident. Why? Because when you *know* how to
drive your car you scarcely think how to drive it. What, then, takes
charge of you when you run downstairs or drive a car? The Moving
Centre. Its mind is working. The speed of this centre outstrips the
speed of our ordinary thinking and by this I mean our Formatory Centre
which is one part of the Intellectual Centre—the slowest part. I am
not speaking of Emotional Thinking, for example, which is far quicker,
and is comparable to what people call intuition.

Now we understand that a slow person takes in things slowly and
a quick person quickly. The slow person takes things in one at a time:
the quicker person takes in two things together. The latter can see
connections between things that the slower person does not see. Some
people like to say: "One thing at a time" and think it is a good, sound
maxim. They like to get one thing finished first before they go on to
the next. Having, say, deployed their troops laboriously on the right
flank, they are astonished to find that the enemy has been massing his
guns opposite them all the while. They cannot think in terms of second
or opposing force, but only in terms of what they wish to do.

Now what is quicker means what is more comprehensive. We all
perhaps have had flashes of another consciousness in which we saw
many things altogether. We can be sure that this is due to the working

1127

of some part of a centre that has a higher rate of speed and sees "all together". Now when a centre is working whose speed is great, we experience the paradox of everything going very slowly and also of everything going in a flash. Sometimes our lives appear in this double way and I would say they always do. When, for example, we are in a car accident, we may become conscious in Moving Centre. This centre works 30,000 times more quickly than does the ordinary part of Intellectual Centre that we use. We then see everything as if in slow motion. Why? Because we are taking in far more impressions. The rate of perception, when we are momentarily conscious in Moving Centre, is enormously increased in the ratio of 1 to 30,000, ideally speaking, or at least something similar. You know if you take a cinema film of a jumping horse-race and expose, say, only six pictures a second, on the screen, the horses will go like lightning and violently. The normal rate is, say, 24. Now if you expose, say, 40 pictures a second, on the screen, the horses seem to sail slowly over jumps without effort, without violence—in fact, you will get the impression that they are not doing anything, but that the medium they are in is doing it, as if it formed vacuums and pressures that drew them up or pushed them down. Now when we become momentarily conscious in a centre, or part of one, that works at a higher rate of speed, we see things in slow motion. We take more photographs per second. It may seem endless time before our car hits the other car. And yet it may seem all over in a flash. Yes—to our ordinary centres it all took half a second. But to a centre working at a higher speed, that half-second became expanded enormously and so it seemed a long time before the crash came. This double experience of "time" has always interested me.

Let us now take the Emotional Centre. This centre can see many things together if it is really working and can draw so much together and connect it into a whole that it seems like clairvoyance. But since the Emotional Centre is drenched with negative emotions and personal self-emotions it rarely can perform its proper task and usually only makes us ill. If you can grasp that a higher speed of working of a centre means *expanded* time and a lower speed of working means *contracted* time it may help you to realize that our experience of "time" is relative to our state. You can, for instance, imagine a vast musical composition contracted down for small, poor orchestras—and then expanded to its fulness, when all its inner octaves and variations and subtleties are heard. So are our lives in small parts of centres. There are many recorded experiences, going far back in literature, of people experiencing a *change of time*, in the sense of expanded time. For example, they have believed they have been in some place, some other level of life for days, or years, and yet, falling down into the ordinary time-rate, have found it only a few seconds. Each second of *our* time contains many other scales of time. The Higher Centres in Man work at enormous rates compared with the Formatory Centre, which works most slowly of all centres and parts of centres in Man. Seen from Higher Centres the whole of one's life can be a moment. Yes—but also, paradoxically, each moment of your life can become a life.

In dreams time obviously varies. Dreams are of many kinds and come from different centres. Some long dreams take only a few seconds of clock-time. So one begins to see that psychic or inner time is different from solar or clock-time—or, to speak clumsily, physical, or outer time. The visible or outer surface of our bodies is in physical time which does not vary and goes at the same rate for all, although I have wondered if it does, because there seems so much "time" on one day and so little on another. Still, if some kind of time did not go in the same way for all, it would be awkward, as we might keep suddenly appearing or disappearing. So our bodies remain in one time. Our mental life, thoughts, feelings, in short, our inner psychic life, can experience many rates of time. Now each centre is a mind of a special kind, related to one aspect of life, and each centre has its speed—and again each part of a centre is a sub-mind and has its speed. You have heard that each centre works with its own energy or "petrol". These different energy-matters in the Work are called Hydrogens. Formatory Part of Intellectual Centre, in which our Consciousness usually dwells, works with *Hydrogen 48*, and this is a very slow centre and a heavy petrol. Emotional Centre should work with "petrol" or energy of half the density—namely, *Hydrogen 24*. If it does, it can theoretically work 30,000 times more quickly than Formatory Centre at its fullest extent. But usually it works with a denser petrol. Even so, you can observe the quickness of Emotional Centre in negative states, in jealousy, suspicion, etc. Sex Centre should work with *Hydrogen 12* but rarely does, usually using *48*. Moving Centre should work with *24* and may do in moments of danger —or, reversely, stops working, so to speak, in the paralysis of fear. Practice can make it use its proper Hydrogen—as in the long training of jugglers, where movements are quicker than the mind behind your eye can follow. The two Higher Centres work with *Hydrogens 12* and *6*. If we were conscious in either of them—if one or the other were behind the eye—the movements of a juggler would appear extremely slow, speaking from one angle. The denser the energy-material, the slower the working. In the Absolute—at the summit of the Ray of Creation—the finest energy, which might be called *Hydrogen 1*, penetrates and comprehends everything simultaneously. Its speed of work is beyond all human comprehension. The speed of light, 130,000 odd miles a second, is very, very slow motion by comparison.

Part II.—In answer to Ouspensky's question: "What is Time?" Gurdjieff replied: "Time is Breath". What can this possibly mean? We can however with some reflection realize that living things do not breathe at the same rate. We cannot, for instance, imagine that a minute organism, such as an amoeba, a minute living cell, takes three seconds to inspire and express air. Now the time of Man's breathing is about three seconds. He breathes in and out—that is, his complete cycle of breathing is roughly about twenty to the minute. In pneumonia, when the intake of oxygen is impaired by the affected consolidated parts of the lungs, he has to breathe more rapidly, when more oxygen is required. Yet he has an average "time of breath" of three seconds.

Mr. Ouspensky made out, at Gurdjieff's suggestion, a "Table of Time" in regard to this idea—namely, that Time is Breath. But first we must understand that when Gurdjieff said: "Time is Breath", he shewed that by the *sort* of Time Man lives in he means his relation to Time. We have already seen that Time is different in different centres. Mahomet saw a jar of water falling off the table. He went into a trance and was in Paradise for a long time. When he fell asleep again—that is, when he emerged into ordinary Time—the water had not yet reached the floor. So he was in a different order of Time. Now the Earth is a living thing from the Work standpoint and its Time is different from our Time. Understand again that Time is different not only for different centres, but for different classes of beings. The Time, say, of a cell, is different from our Time. A cell lives from our view for a very short time. Yet *for itself* it lives as long as we do.

Let us see briefly how the "Table of Time" deals with this difficult idea. In this Table we have first of all the idea that Man can only take in an *impression* that lasts for a certain time—in this case, for, roughly, a ten-thousandth of a second. An electric spark, a flash of light, lasting for one ten-thousandth of a second can just make an effect on his eye —that is, on his retina. Something far quicker will make no impression. It will not affect the machinery of the eye, being too quick for it. It is the same with the ear, which only can take in vibrations of sound up to a certain point. The next idea is *Time is Breath*. In the case of Man, Breath, as was said, is roughly three seconds. Now comes in a curious idea—called "Time of Waking and Sleeping". All organisms, minute or great, have a time of sleep, a time of waking, and they are quite different for different classes of Beings. Finally comes the "Time of Life"—taken in the case of Man as roughly 80 years. Understand that these figures are approximate. Now, if you will notice, the relation between each degree is roughly 30,000. That is, 30,000 times one ten-thousandth of a second—the "time of quickest reception of impressions" in Man—is three seconds, which is Man's time of breath. 30,000 times three seconds is roughly his time of waking and sleeping —namely, 24 hours—or, day and night. And 30,000 times day and night is roughly 80 years—the time of his life.

Now to-night we will scarcely go further, save to say that the world below Man—the world or cosmos of cells—of which Man is built up— has a different "time" and the world or cosmos that Man lives in —namely, Organic Life—has another "time" in comparison to Man. Man is composed of cells—myriads of them. Man lives in Organic Life on Earth. A cell compared to Man is as zero to infinity. A man in regard to all the living Organic Life on Earth—plants, fishes, birds, animals, etc.—is again a mere dot—and so as zero to infinity. Later on, more will be said of this. Notice that to Organic Life a man is unimportant and that to a man a single cell in his body is unimportant.

Now you may ask: "What is the use of all this—it only complicates everything?" Our trouble is that we suffer from a wrong feeling of 'I'. Now this Work is all about reaching a different feeling of 'I'. One way of doing this is to realize generally, from your inner understanding and not from your False Personality pretending to be modest, that we are very small in the Totality of things. This emotional perception purifies the Emotional Centre. Why? Ah, well, think—reflect—for yourselves. The Work says: "We must realize our nothingness." Yes, not artificially, but in a real sense. This drains the Emotional Centre of self-emotions and so opens it to another order of influences—namely, Higher Centres —which are fully formed and work in us continually—only we cannot hear what they say—being what we are. These big cosmic diagrams can help us to realize our position on this Earth and our state of Being.

The Table of Time in the Different Cosmoses

	Cells	Man	Organic Life	The Earth	The Sun
Time of quickest impression	$\frac{1}{300,000,000}$	$\frac{1}{10,000}$	3 seconds	24 hours	80 years
Time of Breath	$\frac{1}{10,000}$	3 seconds	24 hours	80 years	2,400,000 years
Time of Sleeping & Waking	3 seconds	24 hours	30 years	2,400,000 years	72,000 million years
Time of Life	24 hours	80 years	2,400,000 years	72,000 million years	2,160,000,000 million years

1131

COMMENTARY ON IMAGINARY 'I'
AND FALSE PERSONALITY

WORK-IDEA.

The Work says that if you want things different you must change yourself. Man is in Imaginary 'I' and False Personality. As long as he is in this inner situation he cannot develop internally and so everything will remain as before. He will attract the same life. Man has a wrong relation to himself. He lives in the basement of himself and so cannot reach his right life.

COMMENTARY

At a recent meeting here I spoke about Imaginary 'I' and False Personality from the point of view that unless this inner situation begins to alter, nothing can alter. This means that you will always attract the same life, the same experiences, the same disappointments, the same sense of frustration, the same boredom, the same internally unsatisfactory existences and so on. The Work says: "Change yourself and your life will change. Remain the same in yourself and everything in your life will remain the same and repeat itself". It is always worth while for a person to remind herself or himself of this central idea of the Work. Remain the same, as regards your Being, and you can only attract the same things that hitherto you have attracted. Understand that if you remain the same in your Being, in the kind of person you are, you cannot possibly have anything different. Change your Being—and your life will change. Do nothing to change yourself, and your life will—and *inevitably must* remain the same. Suppose some prominent feature in you centres in being lazy in regard to what you could be good at and you make any efforts but the right one. Remain lazy and your life will be the same. Suppose you are mean (to yourself or to others—as thinking meanly of others)—remain mean, and your life will be the same. You have no charity. Suppose you are a confirmed liar (to yourself and to others)—remain a liar and your life will remain the same. Begin to change yourself—and your life will instantly change. It is possible to understand that if one remains the person one is, nothing changes in one's life. You take everything in the same way. You may think by going somewhere you will change your life. After a time, everything will repeat itself as before. We look out, thinking that by changing outside things we can experience another life. But, if you reflect, how can this possibly be so? You can only experience yourself. You yourself, with your continual laziness, your particular meanness, your continual indignation or quarrelsomeness, your continual internal considering and pre-occupation with wretched yourself, that you exalt to heaven, your continual sense of self-pity and so on, will inevitably reproduce this tiresome opera called yourself wherever you go in space or in time. So you will experience the same difficulties and disappointments, East, West, North or South, wherever you go. Because you are always experiencing yourself you never see that the cause lies in yourself—in the kind of Being you have—in the kind of person you are. And let me say, each person is a formidable subject quite apart from the dazzling exterior. Now this Work is not about the dazzling exterior, but about the not-at-all dazzling interior. This Work does not direct the attention to the external side of things, seen *via* the exterior senses, but to the internal side, seen *via* the internal senses, which are more numerous than the external senses and far more interesting. So we come to what the Work says: "Man (or Woman) is in Imaginary 'I' and False Personality. As long as this is the case, nothing can change."

Nowadays, of course, it is very difficult in this extraverted world of people, where everyone thinks the solution of things lies in *outer* changes and political creeds and scientific discoveries—it is very difficult, I say, for anyone to have that reserve of force that makes it possible for a man or woman to hear even a single word of what this Work is teaching. Change, people think, can only be outside—not within. There is a continual outer noise or outer sensation or outer distraction going on —so much so that a person begins to think that unless he hears everything and sees everything, he does not properly live. This is the extraverted phase of life, which depends on the external senses being satisfied with external impressions. One can, however, get internal impressions from conscience—if we gain real conscience. As I said, the Work is internal, and is about change of oneself, not change in outer circumstances. I ask you, how can you have a better world if people are not better? But as people are losing all sense of understanding and do not wish to think at all, we can expect it will be more and more difficult to find people who wish to work on themselves. Everything is inevitably going *mass*—that is, no one thinks individually. Gurdjieff said once: "Nothing can stop the present movement of the pendulum. It will soon be either ants or bees." But he added that now, since people are throwing away the small amount of consciousness they are given, it is possible for some people to collect this unwanted and unused consciousness and begin to awaken. In the Gospels it says: "To him that hath shall be given, and from him that hath not shall be taken away even that which he hath." He said that there is only so much force of consciousness at any particular time. "It is like a gold bath," he said, in so many words. "If you dip too many spoons in it each will only get a spot of gold and become useless. The spoons will be neither one thing nor another. People do not understand that intelligence, for example, is weighed and measured like everything else on this planet. To be really intelligent" (and he emphasized the word) "is not possible for *everyone*. The reason is that intelligence is a measured thing, a force,

1133

in fact, a definite substance, of which there is a definite amount available at each period of time. If it is concentrated, you will as a result get a certain number of intelligent people. If you scatter it, no one will be intelligent, and we will even lose the instinctive intelligence that we share with the animals." I asked him once when I was in France if there were not too many people on this Earth for it to support. But I did not understand his reply save that it was based on the idea that everything happens in the only way it can happen and no one can *do* anything.

Now you can only collect conscious force from those not wanting it by Self-Remembering. If you are asleep—that is, identified with everything taking place outside yourself in the visible world and every-thing taking place inside yourself in your invisible world—with every thought, mood, emotion, sensation—then you are *asleep* and so not remembering yourself. You are in the so-called Waking State—the Second State—which Western psychology takes as full Waking Con-sciousness—a tragic mistake. Being asleep you will feed the big pain-factory of the huge machine of Organic Life. But recall that there is a Side-Ladder shewn in the Ray of Creation up to that level indicated externally by the actual Sun which corresponds with Higher Centres in Man's three-storey-house. By remembering yourself you cut yourself off for the moment from the drain of force that is being taken from you every moment by identifying. "If," said Gurdjieff, "Man were properly conscious, he would not serve Nature. He was created to awaken—to develop. But he is gradually losing all sense of himself—losing indeed everything of value for himself."

Now if you are in Imaginary 'I' and False Personality you will be used to the full by the forces acting on this Earth in relation to producing enough pain to satisfy the demands of our position in the Ray of Creation. As you know, or should know, Organic Life—this vast, sensitive film covering the surface of the Earth—is a transmitter of force to the satellite below the Earth in scale—the Moon. Everything, remember, is growing. We do not live in a dying Universe but a growing one. Our little branch on the enormous Tree is very unimpor-tant in the Totality of things. But everything has been worked out in detail for it. We have been told for ages how to come under other influences and no longer serve Nature—Yes—but it is necessary to work on oneself in order to do this. It cannot be done for you by legislation. If we could always self-remember, we would not serve the pain-factory of Nature. "Man," said Gurdjieff, "was born in a state of Self-Remembering. Being born among sleeping people, he fell asleep. This Work is to wake us up."

Now, how do you *yourself* serve this pain-factory? By actual pain? Yes, of course. By any other kind of pain? Yes, by much subtler pain than animals can offer. Take all the psychological pain that arises from Imaginary 'I' and False Personality—by envies, jealousies and hatreds, by all the unhappinesses of not being properly recognized, of not receiving what you think you are owed, by depression at not being the success that you think you should be—and a thousand and one other forms of subtle, psychological pain. The Gospels speak of a peace passing all understanding. Have you got this inner peace? How can we have it, if our centre of gravity lies in imagination—in Imaginary 'I' and in False Personality, which are both composed of imagination? Someone compliments you—your dress looks nice—you did so-and-so very well—you gave an excellent impression and so on. This satisfies Imaginary 'I' at any rate. It gives you a sense of peace. You love everyone. Yet I fancy this is not the peace passing all understanding. It merely satisfies your False Personality—your Imaginary 'I'—your picture of yourself. Wait a moment. Another person comes along and says your dress is the wrong colour and obviously dates, you weren't your best and didn't look it and you did not give a very good impression. And lo, where is this peace that comes merely from False Personality, from satisfied vanity? Can vanity ever be satisfied? Yes—a clever trick is vanity, in regard to the pain-factory, is it not? Your satisfaction has vanished. Now you are full of negative feelings. You hate everyone. That is, you are now a very satisfactory worker in the pain-factory— a star-worker—and draining away a good amount of force per second, which is used for other purposes than your own health or well-being. And yet, no doubt, you still are thinking that if you had another house, husband, wife, car—you would be really happy.

Now what is the cure the Work suggests in regard to Imaginary 'I'? The Work says: "Imaginary 'I' must go." The Work suggests that if you begin to use the first inner sense that can be developed called the power of self-observation, or Observing 'I', you will find that you have many different 'I's, all contradictory, and that you have no Real 'I' and so this Imaginary 'I' is not you at all. This is the first real step in the Work—to break up the imagination that you have one real, permanent 'I'. This illusion the Work calls Imaginary 'I'. To do this may take years—and I notice in some cases after many years, indeed, this illusion still holds its sway, with the result that nothing in Being can change very much. Now you cannot begin to work, in my view, *on False Personality*, until you begin to weaken the strength of that form of imagination called Imaginary 'I'. "How dare you, Sir, speak to me like that? Do you not know, Sir, who I am? I am Dr. Nicoll." Once you can bear to broaden your consciousness to that extent whereby you lose this self-important 'I'—often, oh, so modest—and see *with inner sight* that this pseudo-master you have followed hitherto is a form of imagination and is non-existent and that you can take everything in quite a new and different and easier way by shifting your feeling of 'I', and need not continue to be the unparallelled idiot you have been that has been the cause of your unhappiness—whether man or woman —then you can begin to see into your False Personality, in the midst of which lives Imaginary 'I' as in a fortress. This is a good thing to do. So start by what the Work teaches you to start with—observe how you

1135

are not one but many. See, for a fact, by self-observation, that you are not one 'I' but many. Notice how, speaking to your darling on the telephone so sweetly, if you cannot hear her, how soon another 'I' begins to speak to her—notice how you are *not* one and the same all the time—notice, in short, that Imaginary 'I' is imagination—get rid of this clever, psychological illusion, and then you will begin to see False Personality. This is the first step in awakening from the state of sleep that governs the world.

Great Amwell House, March 6, 1948

FURTHER COMMENTARY ON SELF-REMEMBERING

WORK-IDEA.

Man is not properly conscious. To become so, he must begin by remembering himself. But first he must through observing himself for a long period realize that he is asleep.

COMMENTARY

The Work speaks of Self-Remembering from several different angles. The first is that Man, capable of 4 States of Consciousness, knows only two states, the so-called waking state, which he takes as full consciousness, and sleep. However, *both* of these states are called sleep by the Work. For this reason it speaks of Humanity asleep, of the evils of life being incurable as long as Man is asleep, and so on. It says that Man should, normally, be in the 3rd State of Consciousness which it calls the State of Self-Remembering, Self-Awareness and Self-Consciousness, and was born to be in this state. But Man fell asleep, through hypnotism. This part of the teaching we are studying is of such importance that it must be repeated often. In observing other people, in observing the world, in observing ourselves, we gradually realize that the reason why things are as they are *is because Man is in hypnotic sleep*. This is the real explanation. And this idea has been taught for thousands of years. But so powerful is the hypnotism playing on mankind on Earth that it is not realized. Man is hypnotized into believing he is awake, fully conscious, that he has Real Being, Real Will, Real 'I', and that he knows himself and can do. He cannot see that he is a machine and that everything he does the machine is doing and that he ascribes to himself a thousand and one things that he does not possess. "For", as Gurdjieff said once, "this sleep of Man, of which I am speaking, is not ordinary sleep, but hypnotic sleep."

Now let us speak of Self-Remembering from another angle. The question might be asked: "If, as you say, the Work teaches that the normal state of consciousness in a man should be that of Self-Remembering, could you express in some way the difference between a man who remembers himself and a man who does not remember himself and lives in the so-called waking state of consciousness?" The answer that the Work gives to such a question is: "Yes—the difference can be expressed in a very clear way. The act of Self-Remembering creates new energies which are not formed in a man asleep." Now to begin with, to understand what is meant, it is necessary to study the 3 foods of Man and the transformations of these 3 foods that take place in the human machine. I will begin, in this commentary, by asking you if you believe that a man by Self-Remembering could keep himself alive for a longer time than another man who did not self-remember, supposing they were experiencing the same difficulties such as inadequate food, exposure, etc. From the Work point of view the answer is—Yes. Why? Because the man who self-remembers actually creates energies by the transformation of the food of impressions. · The Work teaches that Man lives on 3 foods—not one food. The most important food is called "Impressions"; the next important is "Air"; the least important is "Food"—ordinary food. Without impressions a man cannot live for a moment. Without air he cannot live for a minute. Without food he can live for a month or more. Now ordinary food on entering the body undergoes successive transformations into finer and finer substances. Everything in nature works by transformations. The egg is transformed, stage by stage, into a bird or snake, the seed into a tree. It is strange how many people look on this word *transformation* with suspicion, not seeing that their very existence was brought about by a series of transformations in the womb, of which they know nothing, and that the fact that they are alive is due to transformations going on at every moment in their bodies. They take themselves for granted and see no mystery anywhere. This is the trouble. Man, taking everything for granted, cannot grow, cannot develop. The sense of the miraculous is stifled. The wonder of his own existence simply does not enter his limited consciousness.

Let us speak further about transformation. The fire on your hearth is burning by transformation. The grass is growing through transformation. The grub turning into a butterfly is transformation. The thought in your mind is transformed into speech. Everything, seen psychologically, spiritually, is transformation. Yes—everything is transformation save, in regard to Man, at one place. That place is where impressions are received. We do not transform what our eyes see and our ears hear. Food received from the mouth is transformed first by the stomach. Air is transformed by the lungs. But impressions entering the brain are *not* transformed. This is the point that the Work lays such emphasis upon. Here (at the point where the entry of impressions is marked), you will notice that they do not pass on to anything finer. They remain as *48*. The Work teaches that if a man remembers himself *48* will pass on to *24* and *12*. At this place the First Conscious Shock is given and is called the Shock of Self-Remembering. From what has been said you will see that this shock must lead to *transformation*. As ordinary food is transformed for us without aid—so the food of impressions must be transformed in some similar way. But as we are it is not transformed. Beef steaks, as it were, remain beef steaks. Well, if that were the case as regards ordinary food we would die. Now you receive your life-problems, your life-situations, your life-conundrums, as *impressions*. This aspect of life enters not as physical beef steaks, but in another form. We are exposed to the food of literal beef steaks occasionally and we have the apparatus given us to digest—that is, transform them. But we do not—and, I notice, cannot—take in the corresponding idea that we are exposed to situations, problems, and so on psychically, spiritually. Can you see that a situation arriving suddenly as: "How awful, X has quarrelled with his wife," or "I have lost a packet on the Gold Cup", etc., etc., are all "beef steaks", as it were, coming in *via* impressions—that is, mainly through the eyes and ears—those other mouths in our faces distinct from nose and mouth? Each aperture takes in different material. And, as was said, we have for nose and air a transforming thing called the lungs, and for mouth and food a transforming thing called the stomach. But, to repeat, we have no transforming thing for impressions—*and we have to create it ourselves*. This is why the Work is called psycho-transformism. We have to learn how to transform *impressions*, which are psychological. Otherwise life will remain undigested, untransformed, in which case there will be no inner development. Remember that Man was, according to the Work, made a self-developing organism.

Now to transform life it is necessary to receive impressions in a new way and this is called the First Conscious Shock—given the name of *Self-Remembering*. Now a man asleep identifies with every situation—that is, with every impression coming in *via* eyes or ears. If he had no eyes or ears the situations that he suffers from all day long would not exist for him. So do you see that your psychological life, your problems, your worries, and so on, are all due to impressions entering the eyes and ears—and, let me emphasize—how you *react* to these impressions? Once you begin to grasp this, once you see what is meant, you begin to enter this Work in a real sense. When a man remembers himself at a difficult moment when he might easily identify with everything, he is beginning to give himself the First Conscious Shock.

In answer to the question: "Could you express the difference between a man asleep and a man self-remembering in some way?" the difference is expressed in the two diagrams that follow:—

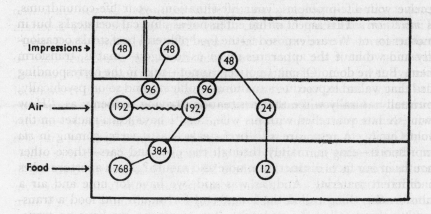

Diagram of Mechanical Man

Impressions →

Air →

Food →

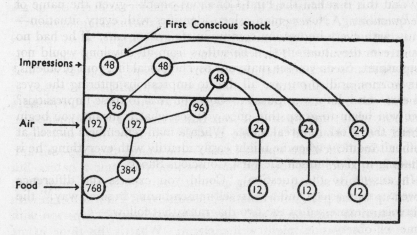

Diagram of a man remembering himself

First Conscious Shock

Impressions →

Air →

Food →

INTERNAL CONSIDERING

When you feel that someone has not behaved rightly to you, you feel that you have not been estimated at your proper value. For example, to feel insulted is to feel that you are not estimated at your proper value. So people often say, when insulted: "Do you know who I am?" or something like that. They mean that they have a certain valuation of themselves, so they say: "Do you know who I am?" meaning that if the other person did know, he would not dare to behave as he does. Of course, if you have little or no picture of yourself as being valuable, you will not be so easily upset. A high estimate of yourself naturally will make it more easy for you to feel that others do not estimate you at your proper value. So you will internally consider more easily. A person may even be so preoccupied with the question of others treating him rightly and with suspicions about whether others are laughing at him that his whole life may be said to be involved in internal considering. Or again, some persons may value themselves above others because of their sufferings. People cling to their own suffering and come to regard themselves as worthy of special evaluation because they have had all kinds of hardships, miseries and sufferings. They are offended if another person begins to talk of his own suffering. They feel that the other person does not consider them enough and that he is selfish. It is difficult for them to realize that other people also have sufferings. Nor do they realize that to see selfishness in others is to see the reflection of one's own selfishness, for the more requirements you demand from others, the more selfish will others appear to you.

What is it that causes us to begin to internally consider? Let us ask the question: "At what point or where do you start making accounts?" You start when you feel you are not estimated aright, when you feel you are undervalued. The waiter does not come when called. The shop-assistant serves another person first. Perhaps people do not look at you enough in the street, or, let us say, pay sufficient attention in general. Or one person seems persistently to ignore you. Or perhaps you hear what someone said of you: that is nearly always unpleasant. There are a thousand and one possible examples, less, and more, serious. Small incidents upset us easily—the waiter, the shop-assistant. These form short accounts and may eventually become a habit. But we have all sorts of long-standing accounts against others, some of them stored up in the past, unfortunately for ourselves. They all begin with this mysterious question of *one's own valuation of oneself*. A person with some self-observation might well exclaim: "What is this thing in me that is offended at this moment and has already begun to make accounts? Look, I can observe it at work in me collecting materials and beginning to remember unpleasant things and to find words and phrases to use against the other person so as to make him feel that he is under-estimated by me—in fact, to make him realize he is so much dirt. Is it a picture of myself? Is it Imaginary 'I'? Is it False Personality? Or what is it that is at the bottom of it all?" The answer is that what is at the bottom of it all is *where you identify with yourself*. All forms of internal considering, of which making accounts against another person is one form, belong to *identifying*. The Work says that we must study identifying down to its very roots. A man is only offended *where he is identified with himself*. And the Work also says that the study of identifying must begin with a study of where you are *identified with yourself*. It is here that you can be upset, hurt, offended, insulted, and so on. The being identified with oneself comes first, being upset and offended comes second, making inner accounts comes third.

Great Amwell House, Easter, March 27, 1948

A NOTE ON EXTERNAL AND INTERNAL ATTENTION

WORK-IDEA.

Man has more inner senses than outer senses. The object of the Work is to develop the inner senses. This, in turn, develops the perception of the outer senses.

COMMENTARY

As regards the outer senses, we notice only a minute fraction of what we see. To *observe* what we see is different from seeing. You see, say, a house a thousand and one times. Have you any idea how many windows it has? You see the street you live in every day. Have you observed its houses, shops, their form, outline, colouring, etc.? How many steps lead up to your flat? What is the colour of so-and-so's eyes? Now painting or drawing teaches you to observe what you see. This is taking in new impressions. To take in more impressions is to increase consciousness. The Work says: "We are not yet properly conscious although we ascribe full consciousness to ourselves." Now if you cease to take in new impressions, you cannot learn anything new. You refuse to adapt yourself. In order to learn anything new, which the Work says is necessary up to the end of life, it is necessary to take in new impressions. To read a book about something you know nothing about is to take in new impressions. It gives you new impressions and so new force. If you refuse, then you are not very intelligent. The Work says the first sign of intelligence is the power of adaptation. When people refuse to adapt to new circumstances, they begin to die. They will not take in new impressions, so the food of impressions is not sufficient and they become dead. "The number of dead people," Gurdjieff said, "walking the street—if you really knew—is incredible." Yes—one can begin to believe it if one begins to know something about oneself. If you realize you always say the same things, always take up the same attitudes, always do the same things, always have the same opinions and the same prejudices, you will see that you are really a dead person. You are psychologically dead long before you are physically dead. And it is extraordinary how psychologically dead people seem often to live a long time. But this realization that you are a dead man or woman is only possible in the force and light of the Work, through self-observation. To observe oneself is different from observing a bus or a tree. In order to observe a bus or tree the external attention is necessary. Simply to see a bus or a tree requires zero attention. To observe them—their colour, shape, and so on—requires directed attention. You see hundreds of buses and trees every day but do not observe them. It is all a vague, confused picture. In the same way, your inner life is a vague, confused picture. You do not observe it, but you are in general aware of it, as you are of buses and trees. If we were not in some degree aware of our inner life we could not focus inner attention on it any more than if we are not in some degree aware of the external world we cannot focus attention on it.

Understand then that we are given a starting-point on either side —outer and inner. Otherwise we could not begin to increase consciousness in regard to outer objects or inner objects. The development of that inner organ of perception called Self-Observing 'I' leads to the development of other inner senses that eventually lead us to an increasing sensitiveness to Higher Centres and their continual messages to us. In such a case, we are no longer controlled, so to speak, *only* by outer life as revealed by our five senses but have a source of motive different from the changing scenes of events in outer life. That is, the kaleidoscope of life with its pendulum-swings, its ups and downs, its continual shiftings, is no longer our sole motive-power. We then begin to realize what it is to be worked from inside, instead of only from outside. We get impressions from both sides—outer impressions and inner impressions. The False Personality is only turned outwards. To begin to "hear"—in the Work-sense—this must be gradually made passive. Then we begin to "hear" internally. If there were nothing to hear internally, this Work would not exist, esotericism would not exist, religion would not exist, and all inner development would be merely an idle dream and pure nonsense. However the Works says that not only have we higher or better parts of ordinary centres, but that we have two fully developed centres, working on us always, called Higher Centres, which we cannot "hear". In this connection the curing of the *deaf* in the New Testament means this psychological deafness. The man solely of the external senses is "deaf" in this way. All that the Work teaches practically is designated for a definite goal. It is not designed to make us good—whatever that means—and, as is often said, "Good at what?"—but to render passive a mass of artificial interposing material (of which the first layer belongs to False Personality) so that we may begin to "hear". It would be quite useless to try to get in touch with Higher Centres as we are. A tremendous amount of filth must be cleared away, as in that myth of Hercules and the Augean Stables. The chief source of filth is ascribing to ourselves what we do not possess—such as Real 'I', Consciousness, Will, Power to Do, and so on. That is, the chief source of filth is lying to ourselves, which belongs to the False Personality.

Since we are in such a state internally, it is necessary to *observe ourselves*. We possess Self-Observing 'I' which is turned inwards to the world of ourselves and not outwards into the external world which is foreign to us. Have you not ever felt how strange and foreign the external world is—these clouds, these beetles, these trees, these mountains, these earthquakes, these enormous, monotonous seas, these giraffes, these sand-flies, these deserts, these plates of food, that Sun, that Moon, those Galaxies, and the rest? Is it congruous to you? You find in self-observation and the development of the inner senses another world to which you really belong if you begin to touch impressions from Higher Centres. I can assure you, you will find this inner possible world far more congruous, for it is through those two transmitters, Higher Mental and Higher Emotional Centres, that the Conscious Circle of Humanity speaks to you.

Now let me speak about the idea of self-observation more fully. It is not simply an end in itself: it is a means, not an end. What is it a means to? I said just now that outer attention increases our consciousness of outer objects and that inner attention increases our consciousness of inner objects. What is an inner object? A thought is an inner object. A feeling is an inner object. If you observe a thought or a feeling—and they are quite different and arise from different centres—you will realize that it is something in you, *but not you*. When you do not observe your inner life it is merged with you and you are merged with it and everything lies in darkness. In this darkness, one is much victimized and set upon. It is therefore a good thing to let a ray of light in. This is self-observation. We become more and more conscious of what is *not us*. If you take your thoughts and feelings as yourself—that is, as *I*—if you say 'I' to them—you are inwardly in the greatest confusion and darkness. It is a long journey, getting rid of what is not us—what is *not I*. At first you find it difficult to say to nearly all thoughts, feelings, sensations: "This is not I". On the contrary, you will say: "But this *is I*." No, it is not, and the fact that you can observe it proves it. But this journey leads nearer and nearer to Real 'I', which you cannot observe. This is the end to which self-observation is the means.

Understand then that the development of the inner sense, called self-observation, is not an end in itself but a *means* to an end—that is, separating from what is *not I*. Try to realize when you are negative:

1143

"This is not I". But if you put the feeling of 'I' into the negative state, then two things occur. (1) You take 'I' as the negative state and speak and act from it—that is, you identify yourself with it. (2) It then has power over you. For whatever you identify with, outer or inner, has power over you and makes you serve it. Man was not made and born to be a slave, but owing to the powerful and constant hypnotism of life he falls asleep and is then a slave to everything with which he identifies. In this way, by this clever trick, mankind is kept where it is and endless quite useless pain and suffering is produced. This is what the Work teaches.

Now what you can observe internally you cease to be identified with. This begins inner freedom. You then can at night go through the day and all its mechanical effects on you. By observation, both at the time and in retrospect, you separate from all these effects. This is a marvellous gift. And if you employ it, the results are marvellous. But you must keep awake in order to do this. Once you know and then understand this secret, you have something comparable to the *pearl* spoken of in the Gospels.

Great Amwell House, April 3, 1948

THE WORK CONCEPTION OF ENERGY

The Work says every psychic act takes energy. Each centre uses its own energy. Each centre has two small accumulators connected with it. If these become run down the centre has no further energy. If your centres all run down you can enjoy nothing. "You must understand," said Gurdjieff, "one feature of the organization of the human machine. A very important rôle is played by a certain kind of accumulator. There are two small accumulators near each centre filled with the particular substance necessary for the work of the given centre. In addition, there is in the organism a large accumulator which feeds the small ones. The small accumulators are connected together, and, further, each of them is connected with the centre next to which it stands as well as to the large accumulator. Accumulators work in the following way. Let us suppose a man is working or is reading a difficult book and trying to understand it, in which case several rolls revolve in the Thinking Centre or apparatus in his head, or, let us suppose that he is walking up a hill and is getting tired, in which case the rolls revolve in the Moving Centre. In the first instance the Intellectual Centre and in the second the Moving Centre draws the necessary energy for its work from one of the small accumulators. When an accumulator is nearly empty a man feels tired. He would like to stop, to sit down if he is walking, to think of something else if he is solving a difficult problem.

But quite unexpectedly he feels an inflowing of strength and he is once more able to walk or to work. This means that that centre has become connected with the second accumulator and is taking energy from it. Meanwhile the first accumulator is refilling with energy from the large accumulator. The work of the centres goes on. The man continues to walk or to work. Sometimes a short rest is necessary to ensure this connection, sometimes a shock, sometimes an effort. Anyway the work goes on. After a certain time the store of energy in the second accumulator also becomes exhausted. The man again feels tired. Again an external shock, or a short rest, or a cigarette or an effort, and he is connected with the first accumulator. But it may easily happen that the centre has drawn energy from the second accumulator so quickly that the first one has had no time to refill itself from the large accumulator, and has taken only half the energy it can hold—it is only half-full. Having become re-connected with the first accumulator the centre begins to draw energy from it, while the second accumulator becomes connected with and draws energy from the large accumulator. But this time the first accumulator is only half-full. The centre quickly exhausts its energy and in the meantime the second accumulator has succeeded in becoming only a quarter full. The centre becomes connected with it, swiftly exhausts all its energy and connects once more with the first accumulator, and so on. After a certain time the organism is brought to such a state that neither of the small accumulators has a drop of energy left. This time the man feels really tired. He almost falls down, he almost drops asleep, or else his organism becomes affected, he starts a headache, palpitations begin, or he feels sick.

"Then suddenly again a short rest, or an external shock, or an effort, brings back a new flow of energy and the man is once more able to think, to walk or to work. This means that the centre has become connected directly to the large accumulator. The large accumulator contains an enormous amount of energy. Connected with the large accumulator a man is literally able to perform miracles. But of course if the rolls continue to turn and energy which is made from *air, food,* and *impressions,* continues to pour out of the large accumulator faster than it pours in, then there comes a moment when the large accumulator is drained of all energy and the organism dies."

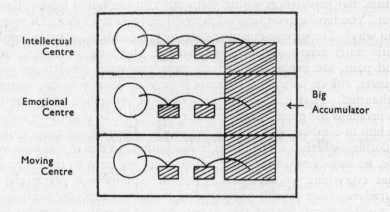

Intellectual Centre

Emotional Centre

Moving Centre

Big Accumulator

COMMENTARY

The point that I want to emphasize in this commentary is that every psychic act uses up energy. Faced with the external world of events, *via* the five senses, every reaction to what is seen, heard, touched, smelt, or tasted, takes energy. This specific energy is soon exhausted. If you go on smelling a rose, you cannot smell it any more. Why? The smelling of a rose exhausts a specific psychic energy. If you wish to enjoy parties, after a time you cannot bear them. Why? The specific energies for enjoying parties are exhausted. A long time ago—that is, to me, yesterday—I spent two years of training in rowing. I heard then, or overheard, my wise, immense and muscular pundits talking about how to train the Cambridge Boat. The idea was to row them all out every day until they were exhausted. That is, the specific energies of the centres required for rowing were each day exhausted. Later on, even in my time, another doctrine was brought forward—namely, to rest these particular energies and let other things in—that is, other interests—and then get down once more to the task in hand. The trouble, I understood, was that the crew became *stale*. Now what does *stale* mean? From the Work-teaching it means that certain accumulators connected with centres or parts of centres are exhausted. Yes, but it is possible to use other centres which are fresh. Everything you do, whether you row, or think, or enjoy parties, uses *psychic energy*. Is this very difficult to understand? It is difficult as long as you do not see that your contact with the external world of events is a psychic one. You think about something you see. This is psychic. Yes, but the seeing of a thing is psychic—that is, uses some energy that is psychic. Love is psychic—it employs an energy belonging to the Emotional Centre. All the centres use *psychic energy*—even Moving Centre. The psychic energies the centres use are *Hydrogen 48*, *Hydrogen 24* and *Hydrogen 12*. These energies are not things you can *see* with your outer senses, but experiences within yourself. You are full of beans. Excellent. You have a good time on shore. Then you feel awful. Of course. But why? The psychic energies whereby you combine, or make contact with, outer events, such as wine, women, and song, or danger, risk, and pain, are exhausted, and no more can wine, women, or song, danger, risk or pain get a response from you. Your response-power is exhausted. That is, your psychic power of combining with external impressions has gone. Gurdjieff once said: "A man must have sodium in him to combine with the chlorine of life. Then he can make sodium chloride—which is a salt. But if he has nothing in him to combine with life, he cannot make this salt." The point we have to understand is that everything we experience—and all experience is psychically in ourselves—takes psychic energy. And if we are temporarily exhausted of psychic energy we can take in nothing and so make no contact with outer life. A man, a woman, lying in bed almost dead with illness cannot take in anything from outer life. Why? There is no psychic energy left. It would be possible to talk a great deal about psychic energy, provided you understand what is meant. People do not see that their powers of combining with any outer event—a football-match, a party, a novel, a play, a book, a man, a woman, depend on the psychic energies one has. Imagine a complete depletion of all centres. Then you can go to theatres, go to parties, and so on, and feel nothing interesting. So do you see that your contact with life depends on psychic energies? If your Intellectual Centre has energy you can read study, and take in. If not, you cannot. If your Emotional Centre is exhausted, you can feel nothing. If your Sex Centre is depleted, you cannot feel sex. If Moving Centre is exhausted, you can hardly bother to pick up a thing you drop on the floor. And all this is not due to outer things but to inner things—that is, to the states of centres and parts of centres in regard to this psychic energy supplying them. Each centre and each part of a centre is like an engine which, having no petrol, cannot turn.

Now let us speak of different energies. The work says no amount of physical or mechanical energy will make vital energy ; no amount of vital energy will make psychic energy; and no amount of psychic energy will make conscious energy. So we can give Mr. Ouspensky's diagram about this point:

Conscious Energy
Psychic Energy
Vital Energy
Mechanical Energy
(Heat, Light, Electricity, etc.)

In speaking of this he said: "It is like this: a line is one-dimensional. No extension of this line will make a surface. Only by this line moving sideways will it make a surface. And no increasing of this surface will make a cube unless the surface moves up into another dimension."

Now we can understand at least from these illustrations that Mechanical Energy such as Heat will not make Vital Energy; no heat will make life—it may help life but it is not life-energy. And you may have a gorilla full of vital energy and expand him to a thousand times his size, but that will not make Psychic Energy—such as the energy of Intellectual Centre. But now comes the curious point: "No amount of Psychic Energy—say, intellectual energy—will make a man more *conscious*." The Work says that the energy belonging to *Consciousness* is not psychic energy. It says that for a man to evolve in himself he must become more *conscious*—and that that is only possible by a special effort, a special shock. The energy called *Consciousness* is on another plane to what the psychic energies working the centres are on. "Consciousness," said Gurdjieff, "does not evolve by itself. A man can, if he wishes and knows how, increase consciousness. But by thinking he cannot do so." And this remark of Gurdjieff reminds me of Christ's words: "A man by taking thought cannot add a cubit to his stature."

Now let us come to the practical side of this commentary. In the first place, if you are tired in one centre, use another one. If you are tired of thinking, then go and mow the lawn. Why? Because Moving Centre has energy and Intellectual Centre has not. In the second place, consider how negative emotions, negative thoughts, envies, malices, queer motives that are unpleasant, hatreds, resentments, drearinesses, and all the rest, take force from you. Why? Because they are psychic activities belonging to your psychology. When you review this idea from a certain level of consciousness (that is free to everyone to gain in this Work) you will have a further reason for not wasting your inner life, which depends on the existence of psychic forces in you, on useless practices. The psychic energies you waste in such activities—such as always pitying yourself or always envying, always saying you are no good at thinking or no good at anything you have never even tried to do, or in saying that you hate or dislike everyone (except your darling and infamous self)—and, in fact, everything the Work teaches you to avoid, to struggle with and not identify with—I say that these useless psychic activities, these useless expenditures of psychic energy, will strike you as being not merely a daily nuisance, but a sign of an inability to understand yourself more objectively and not identify with your typical reactions, which is the whole aim of the Work. Remember that all such useless psychic expenditure is not lost in this closed economical system called the Universe but is used for another purpose (and not to your advantage, by the way). But when you realize that if you waste your limited psychic energies all your life on such things as identifying, internal considering, making accounts against others, being negative with almost everyone you meet, self-justifying (Oh, yes, I am always right), hating, disliking everyone and everything as a habit, criticizing everyone but yourself, being superior (especially without knowing it), attributing to yourself things such as love, that have nothing to do with you and which you cannot command, and all the rest of what the Work is telling you every day to observe—then if you will waste the very soul and substance of yourself, that can lead you to your real self, in such useless and certainly widespread activities, you will not quite see what is being taught here and what *that Rope* means, in the Work-Parable, that you can catch hold of. For to begin to see the meaning of the quite gentle teaching of the Work, and so of that Rope, is, I have been told, the beginning of another understanding of life and of your own life.

Great Amwell House, April 10, 1948

THE FOOD OF IMPRESSIONS

WORK-IDEA

The Work teaches us that the human machine takes in three foods: (1) ordinary food, (2) air, and (3) impressions. From these three foods the machine produces the different energies for different centres to enable the machine to work. A man can therefore be ill from lack of any one of these three foods. Without ordinary food he can live for perhaps a few weeks. Without the food of air he can perhaps live a few minutes. And the Work says that without some food of impressions a man cannot live a moment.

COMMENTARY

We will speak only of the food of impressions. Both when waking and sleeping in the ordinary sense a man is getting *impressions*. When asleep in bed, for example, many impressions come from his body, from being hot or cold, from pain or comfort, from the muscles subserving breathing, from the heart beating, and so on. If all impressions could be cut off the man would die at once. Now let us take a man or woman in love who has not heard from the beloved. Suppose they begin to pine, waste away and get ill. Let us suppose they are taken to hospital. The doctors prescribe more nourishing food and drink, or they recommend a change of air, and so on. Yet the poor patients remain certainly ill, weak, wretched. Port wine every hour is no good. Then suddenly a telegram arrives: the beloved is still alive and is coming to-morrow. Do you not think that suddenly this woman, this man, becomes quite different? Of course. And what is the reason? What is this strange *food* that has made the change so rapidly? This strange food is the *food of impressions*. How was this food administered? By the telegram—by the wonderful news.

1149

Now long ago, when I and a few others were fighting for the recognition of the psychological factor in medicine, I sometimes used an illustration of the above kind—but it was met very heavily by the doctors of those days. I have little doubt that they would have liked to have the bit of paper on which the marvellous words were written, and weigh it and measure it and analyze its chemical components so as to find a physical cause for the transformation in the patient. I am sure that some of them, by sending similar telegrams to patients not in love, and getting no results, would say that it was obvious that telegrams were of no medical value. Well—that was the state of darkness in those first two decades of this century when the battle for the psychological factor in illness was being waged. And then came "shell-shock"—and actually eminent medical men searched in the blood for some unusual platelet, or some foreign body, to account for a man breaking down who had been in the trenches for months and months under heavy shelling, sniping, and mortar-bombs. Yes—this psychological factor was not recognized distinctly. Now if your food of impressions is nothing but daily horrors then *it will be very bad food* and will make you ill just as bad air or bad food without vitamins will make you ill—give you scurvy, and so on. I often think that the whole range of physical illnesses due to lack of vitamins, such as scurvy, etc., can be re-represented on the mental plane by a correspondence. A narrow, prejudiced, mean person, a jealous person, a negative person, for example, will take in negative impressions and so be ill on that level, whereas a person more generous and broad-minded will not. We pay for every wrong attitude, for everything we do not forgive, for everything we lie to ourselves about, for every negative state.

We will speak now about noticing—observing—the effect of impressions—about what the Work-term "food of impressions" means, practically. Take yourself. You hear that the horse you have backed has won. That is nice. Or you hear it has lost. That is not so good. Now the news that the horse has won or lost is one example of " food of impressions". Yet people occasionally say to me that they do not understand what "food of impressions" means. They understand ordinary food and drink. They are rather dubious when one speaks of *air* being a food. ("How can it be doctor? Why, you cannot even see it," as someone once said to me.) But they regard impressions being a *food* as sheer nonsense. Now suppose you are asked to dine with someone and feel hungry. The first course is, say, a real mixed grill, properly cooked. But the fashionable cellar you are dining in is warmed by an anthracite stove that leaks. So you get a headache. That is, the food of air is bad. Well, you struggle along. Then the person you are dining with says your dress does not suit you and you look awful in it. Now in such a case the actual food (*768*) is excellent; the food of air (*192*) is tainted with carbon monoxide and so poisonous; and finally the food of impressions—namely, "You look awful"—is not exactly very good. I fear you will not enjoy that evening. I think a badly cooked meal, in good air, and surrounded by charming companions, would be infinitely preferable. Yes—but we do not notice all this. We are blind to it. There is a proverb: "Better a dinner of herbs where love is, than a stall-fed ox and hatred therewith." What is the open secret? Better to eat a scanty meal with good food of impressions than a feast with negative emotions.

Now in taking in impressions it is necessary later on in the Work to realize that all impressions are in a sense internal even when we see another person outside us. Let us suppose a man sees his beloved, with her arms full of roses, advancing towards him across the sunlit lawn. He gains very strong impressions. His heart expands or contracts, or whatever it does. Consider for a moment. The sight of his beloved is an impression entering by rays of light into his eye as an image. This image, as in a camera, falls upside down on his sensitive camera-plate or retina. So his beloved is upside down. Then her upside-down image is received by about seven million light sensitive nerve-points which combine and send up through a million separate nerves this darling image to the brain. On the way this beloved image, first upside down, then split in a million separate nerve-impulses, is divided in such a way that one bit of the left brain at the back of the head receives one half of her and the right brain the other half, speaking very roughly, and each stimulates further millions of cells. When all the complex apparatus which relates us to the beloved and the roses is grasped a little, we realize that the external world of objects seen is the result of internal nerve-cell machinery. Yet it seems so close, so embraceable. But it is really very distant and therefore it is impossible to get into that immediate contact with it which we all desire and expect. But if you begin to *understand* your beloved and she you, through learning a common language such as the Work, you are far closer. We are far closer to one another psychologically than physically. Really, is it not laughable that the nice man, in the act of proposing, is proposing to the nice woman upside-down, and vice versa? A marvellous clever affair is all one can say—but it makes one reflect on the ancient idea that in some way this outer world is a sort of illusion.

* * *

At this present time, people are not necessarily only affected adversely by limited quantities of ordinary food, but also by lack of the right food of impressions. Dullness, drabness, monotony, mean lack of impressions. You must understand then that a person may be sick because of lack of that most important food of all—the food of impressions. Consider, then, the difference between a drab world of uniformity and a colourful world of differences. Which, do you think, will give you more food of impressions? Which world will be *psychologically* the right one? It will certainly not be the right one, if everything is reduced to a common level so that no differences exist. A man does not get rich impressions from *sameness*, but from *differences*.

This brings us to the question of the reception of impressions. How do we receive impressions from outside—or rather, on what do these impressions fall? They fall on *associations*. As a consequence, life tends to have the same effect day after day. The impressions, of course, are never just the same. It is our reception of them that is the same. Gurdjieff once said: "Try to see things without associations." Now if we could see things without associations we would be transported into a world of marvels. Impressions would fall on Essence. Gurdjieff was once asked: "What happens when impressions fall on Essence?" He replied: "Everything becomes more vivid." Now, as we are, impressions fall on a machinery of associations which distributes the impressions to different centres, mechanically. That is, impressions produce a mechanical habitual effect and do not gain the vividness they should. So we have to change our associations and this begins by realizing, briefly speaking, everything the Work teaches us to realize by means of self-observation and non-identifying. For example, the dawning realization that one is mechanical weakens associations based on the view that one is fully conscious. Seeing things from the Work point of view alters mechanical associations. This, in turn, increases the reception of the food of impressions. If we continue to think in the old way, we will not be able to loosen mechanical associations. You cannot reach a new feeling of yourself if you persist in your old thinking. So the Gospels teach that μετάνοια—that is, change of mind, or new thinking—is the starting-point for change of oneself. Associations are part of us. But we do not notice them. They act before we can see them acting. But with experience in self-observation we can notice both the incoming impression and the association it is about to set going, and eventually we can prevent it from doing so. This is a very good stage to reach in the Work, of inestimable value. Amongst other things, it enables one to see practically—and not to think theoretically—that the outer world only reaches us through, as it were, a mass of distorting lenses and that we do not really see one another but only our ideas of people or our associations with them with which we are identified. That is why, when people do not behave as we expect, we are upset. They do not correspond with the associations we have of them and ourselves. That is one reason why people put each other in prison. It is necessary to let go—to loosen these associations.

A UNIVERSAL LANGUAGE

WORK-IDEA

On one occasion it was said by Gurdjieff that in order to understand one another we must learn a common language. Ouspensky said that when people study this Work they begin to learn a common language and by so doing can begin to understand one another. It was also said by Gurdjieff that there is a *Universal Language*, by means of which all people in the world can converse with one another. In this connection Gurdjieff said that conscious art, as distinct from subjective art, is an example of *Universal Language*.

COMMENTARY

I will begin by saying that people imagine that if they speak the same word-language—say, English—they can understand one another by means of knowing the same words. But words mean many things. The use of a word like, say, *love*, seems quite a simple means of understanding one another. But each person has entirely different *ideas* connected with the word *love*—for example, "I love chocolate; I love money; I love my dog; I love my mink coat; I love a hot bath." One might indeed in a satirical mood add here a word: "also I love you." In using words in this way, merely as words, without any real *ideas* behind them, Babel arises—a confusion of mere words or of slogans or clichés belonging to associative thinking. It is like explaining a man by saying he is a Christian. Yes, but do you mean he has the Christianity of Man No. 1, or Man No. 2, or Man No. 3? Or again, of Men Nos. 4, 5, 6 or 7? In each case, the word "Christian" will mean something quite different. Why? Because of the ideas connected with the actual *word* "Christian". There are seven kinds of Christians, all with different ideas of Christianity. One can have richer or poorer *ideas* behind the words used, according to one's level of understanding. Now, if you come to think of it, all experience that leads to anywhere new is when you have an experience that is so far better than anything before that it makes what you thought good seem crude. The greater meaning absorbs the lesser: and this, by the way, is the solution of temptation and is the only thing that can heal and cure you—namely, contact with greater ideas, which make smaller meaning less hypnotic. Here I remind you where you are, in small Being. The Work is to build into us a whole series of new, inter-related ideas from another source, greater than ourselves, with which special words are connected, whereby to contact them magically. There is no word used in this system that does not refer to a distinct idea with tremendous power of meaning. When you have built into you the ideas of the Work as a receptive organism

—not in your external life-serving man, through outer superficial thought, but in your inner real, essential man, through seeing and feeling their truth privately, especially in your most lonely moments —then the ideas behind your words will be similar to the ideas behind the words of another person in the Work who understands the Work as you do. So you have a common language. And this shews you who is your neighbour in the esoteric sense. It is necessary to "love your neighbour"—not from mechanical but from conscious intercourse. And so you can begin to understand one another—a most extraordinary experience. Then everything becomes quite different in regard to relationship to others. You all have the means. What do you make of them—that is, apart from your *mechanical* impact with each other, which one must observe?

Now the density of meaning of a word depends on the quality and scale of ideas behind it. A word is nothing by itself. Its significance is due to the inflow of meaning it conducts. The commonest words used, such as "I" and "You"—what do they mean? The density of meaning of a word therefore depends on the ideas of thought behind it. When I reflect on this most dangerous word 'I' that has hitherto controlled my life in every situation, I begin to see what the Work means. Which 'I'? We are taught that there is a Universal Language: and we are taught that no one can understand another, unless they learn a common language. In regard to the latter this word 'I' is not valid. Note that a *common* language must lead up to a Universal Language—in which perhaps no such word as 'I' exists. Let us use here two Work Ideas: (1) the Meaning of Relative Thinking and (2) the Law of Octaves. As regards (1)—that is, relative thinking—the Work teaches that we must learn what relative thinking means and always think relatively. The word 'I', for example, is relative. To interpret briefly: a man takes himself as 'I'. Now I cannot understand the Earth, say, taken by itself. It is part of something else. Unless it becomes understandable that it is part of the Solar System no one will understand it rightly. Now in turn it must be realized that our Sun or Solar System is a very small part of the Galaxy that we see extended as a disc of light across the heavens. If I take the Earth *by itself* I am not thinking relatively. Nor can I take myself by itself. I am part of something. And further the Galaxy or Milky Way in which our Sun and Planets are a mere point is one of millions of other vast Galaxies or Star Islands with similar Suns and Planets, myriads after myriads. Now why cannot a person *understand* the Earth aright by taking it just by itself and not as a small part of a whole, which in turn is a small part of a bigger whole and so on? Consider this question later on in your discussion. If I take the Earth as a thing in itself, isolated from everything else and so independent, I will give to my study of the Earth a value that does not belong to it. If, especially, I believe that this minute Earth is the only important Planet in the immeasurable Universe of Suns and Galaxies—(and does not this Earth contain this wonderful thing called 'I'?)—then my thinking will be surcharged with my own truly blinding egotism. Something, somewhere, will be all wrong in my conclusions.

Now a scientific astronomer leads you out at night to see the stars through a telescope. Nothing happens. But sometimes, looking at the stars *when you do not mean to*, you get a strange emotion—a new food of impressions. One can describe such an emotion as beyond self-emotions. The emotion is a trace of real emotion and has nothing to do with the self-emotion of the False Personality. That strange emotion, I say, is a real emotion, and all *real* emotions are cognitive and dissolve away your little domestic emotions. Some emotions blind us, others open us. Real emotions always teach you something—not in *words*, but in *ideas*, emotionally apperceived. We do not receive knowledge only through the intellect. And notice that every centre catches rays of meaning from the realm of ideas in its own way, for every centre has an intellectual, emotional and moving side, and many important receptive sub-divisions. One can catch an *idea*, therefore, in many different ways, as a thinker, painter, poet, musician, carpenter, engineer, sculptor, dramatist, architect, juggler, business-man, fanatic, wife, mother, father, or simply as a man in a bowler hat.

Now we are fed by ideas on the side of food of impressions: but they have different origins. There are eternal ideas, which feed you always in time: and there are man-made ideas, which are fashions of time. The eternal ideas are called in the Work *C influences* and they come from the Conscious Circle of Humanity. The man-made ideas—the ideas or influences created by life—such as football-pools—are called *A influences*. Ideas act as influences upon us. An ideology, as it is called nowadays, is an idea people follow, such as the idea of freedom, equality, etc. Let us take the idea that one can be free, just like that. All can be free. How? The Work says we are under 48 orders of laws if we remain asleep. Since even Christ was not free but had to obey, one may wonder what the *quality* of this idea, this ideology, is that one can be free. Has it real ideas behind it? What is the level of it? Where does it originate in the Ray of Creation, which is the Scale of Being leading up to Absolute Being? We can understand a little what relative freedom means in the Work—that is, how we can come under higher influences by work on ourselves. Avoid negative emotions and you will come under new influences. That is clear. But then we in the Work use the word freedom in connection with an idea of great density of meaning which has the Ray behind it. It is *C* influences—descending from Greater Mind—from above our level. It is not a man-made idea of freedom—as if Man, who could not make a simple part of his brain or body, could be free in the common sense. This is sheer vulgarity. Can you be free when you do not understand in the least how you are made? Yet, as you know, the word *freedom* has escaped from the control of the real, esoteric ideas behind it and has, so to speak, lost its origin, its parentage, and wanders about in the world as a common danger. Yes, a danger. Because when a word breaks loose from its right connection of ideas it becomes a danger to every uneducated or unprincipled man. It is a word divorced from its real meaning, just like the word "love" of which we spoke. So we babble words, without meaning, and, in fact, make wars because of these words, escaped from their right connections with ideas. However, as we get older in stature in the Work, we begin to think of the meaning of the words we so easily, so mechanically, hurl at each other.

So, to think relatively, you must apperceive—that is, perceive consciously through seeing the truth of it—that we are all parts of a whole and, unless we know something of the whole, our ideas of ourselves are all wrong. I will give you this exercise in thinking. Begin by trying to think—and here I mean *think*, not running with the sweep and mill-race current of associative thinking that wastes you each day—begin to *think* first: "What is from myself, what is from others, and what is from something greater than myself that, say, is called ordinarily God?" Suppose you say something. Well, take the first two forces in the triad given here. Is what you say from yourself only? Of course not. And go on *thinking* like that—and finally come to your brain-machine. Did you create it and do you know the slightest thing about how it works? Such real thinking awakens *Emotional Centre*—that is, gives you real cognitive emotions, instead of, let us say, the "never-sent-to-the-laundry" emotions—the smell of self-domestic emotions in which one easily dwells without new ideas and their force. The Work is, in fact, a laundry. For what? Well, try to observe your habitual emotional state and thoughts. Do not you really want to wash them—and here, of course, comes in all the tremendous symbolism of the Gospels about *washing*—washing the whole body in water, washing the feet, and so on. May I say here that I am not saying that people should at once send their physical clothes to the physical laundry right away. We speak here of psychological clothes—that is, the ideas and attitudes you follow, because the first spiritual or psychological body, which we seek to make, is clothed in *what each of you takes as truth*. The mind is dressed in what you take as truth. We have to wash the mind and get better clothing. And so, again, comes in μετ νοια as the keynote of the Gospels, which means "change of mind". Well, that is like washing off the old to begin with. But is it not extraordinary that people, long in the Work, still possess the same ingrained attitudes, buffers, and so on? Why? Because they have not a wedding-garment—that is, they do not have any real desire for union with the truth of the Work. They merely talk about it—and often at enormous length—and then all go "back to their own houses", as the Gospels say—that is, to the old mental houses of themselves. That is, they do not wash themselves with the new truth of the Work but inwardly cling to their mechanical acquired implanted truth. So, hearing the Work, they go back "each to his own house."

Now I will give you another exercise in thinking relatively. You realize that relative thinking depends on seeing where a thing is in relation to what it is a part of and what is a part of it. I therefore put this before you for thought and discussion:

(1) Is religion the Part being interested in the Whole?

(2) Is the Whole being interested in the Part, charity, or conscious love?

(3) Is the Part being only interested in itself—selfishness?

(4) Is the Part being only interested in its parts—science?

Now we come briefly to octaves. All octaves refer to higher and lower by degrees. Let us try to start with Meaning and build a particular descending octave, entirely experimental. Remember this is a commentary.

Do	Eternal Meaning	("In the beginning is the Logos"—or Meaning)
Si	Eternal Meaning flowing into Eternal Ideas	(Here no thought exists)
La	Your Ideas of Thought which may be right or wrong	
Sol	Your Thoughts	
Fa	Your Desire for Speech	
Mi	Your Words literally uttered to express the ideas of your Thoughts	

Now, in regard to this teaching that there is a Universal Language, you will see that at the level *Mi* you will express the ideas behind your thoughts in your own particular native language—English, French, etc., so different people will not "understand"—as it is called—one another if they belong to different countries with a *word*-difference. But if you could speak to another person from, say, a higher level, you would be speaking, say, from ideas without words. Well, do you not see that there *must* be a Universal Language? Ideas are there before you even begin to speak from them. You learn a specific language of words and so cannot understand another who uses other words—and remember even if you use the same words you will *not* understand one another. But if you could by a gentle inner concentration convey an idea to another without the intervention of any word-language—that is, without opening your mouth—then do you see that the other person, if his mind is open, will hear you speaking to him *as if in his own word-language*? Now I will go on with this difficult subject later. But let me say that all clairvoyance, all communication at a distance, or anything that is connected with someone saying something apparently in you without language, apparently magically—all this has to do with *speaking from the level of ideas*. This is silent speech. Yet it is a form of speech, though not a descent to actual words. So you can even now understand how in learning a common language—that is, of ideas—the ideas of the Work—we may find curious results—apparently. If you grasp what has been said, it is not curious at all. On the contrary, it is to be expected. But I am speaking of people who have patiently taken the Work-ideas into their minds and arranged them and wish genuinely to marry with them internally by doing them. What is this secret marriage? It is to *work* on oneself in the way indicated by these ideas. If you do not *do* the new truth taught you, but merely talk of it endlessly, you are useless to the Work and you will get no results. The Work selects people in the long run. Yes, but remember this takes years and years to understand.

Mr. Ouspensky once said: "Don't listen to words: listen to the meaning behind the words."

Great Amwell House, April 24, 1948

LYING

Work-Idea

(1) Man ascribes to himself what he does not possess.
(2) Lying kills Essence.

Commentary

It is always difficult to make conscious to oneself that something is one's own fault. We may say it is, and some people have a kind of automatic way of saying it is. But we do not really accept it. In the Work we are taught that one of the things we have to observe and struggle against is self-justifying. In a commentary written some time back it was pointed out that if we justify ourselves we prevent things from coming home to us—we prevent ourselves from realizing what we actually did or said. In this way we avoid useful suffering. Useful suffering changes Being. Now self-justifying is one of many forms of lying continually going on in us. You must remember that we lie in one way or another most of the time—in fact, every time we say 'I' as if we had permanent 'I'. Lying saves us from useful suffering and replaces it often enough by useless suffering. This is one reason why the Work says that lying damages or even kills Essence. We can at least understand how it can prevent any development of Essence, because Essence can only grow through what is real, what is true. Essence cannot grow through lies. Only False Personality can. Essence is the most real part of us. False Personality is the most false part of us and if you observe it for long enough—if you can at all—you can watch how it lies all the time. In fact, it *is* a lie. It is a lie very difficult to separate from. Yet if it remains dominant, Essence cannot grow. That, in short, is why one works on oneself. The Work has a definite object. It is not about oneself being good, whatever that means. The Work is to make Personality passive and Essence active. Never forget this, and often reflect privately on it, because it is one of the great *ideas* behind the Work, and if the ideas of your thoughts are real ideas, your thinking will lead you somewhere. Also the inexhaustible power latent in the idea will help you. This *idea* about Personality and Essence, if you reflect on it at different times, will direct your thinking into the whole of the Work and shew you things that cannot be explained in words, without apparent contradiction.

Now lying makes wrong connections in you. Imagine an immense telephone exchange with millions of wires all rightly connected and then someone coming along and spending his life in joining the wires differently. Who is this evil someone? But the Work is not speaking here about ordinary lying, although that comes in as well, but of that category of lying that especially keeps Personality active and Essence passive. You have heard it said that in order to get in touch with Higher Centres, it is necessary to destroy all negative emotions and that all negative emotions shut the door, so to speak, to these Higher Centres. Now all negative emotions lie. They distort things. Truth destroys them, but they imitate Truth by leaving out things, by using half-truths, by adding, by connecting in the wrong way things that actually happened, and so on. When a person is negative he *always* lies. Notice it for yourselves. Two negative people can hurl the most fantastic lies at each other—that is, not hypothetical people that we can comfortably laugh at in a superior way—but *you* and *I*. Yes, exactly. If I am negative and you are, we can have a row at once and say all sorts of surprising things. In each of us is a big lie-factory—in the negative part of Emotional Centre. This, I say by way of commentary, is where hell is in you and there everyone hates everyone else and only violence and destruction mean anything. Let me again quote what Mr. Ouspensky once said: "This world is not controlled by sex or power but by negative emotions." And this, I would add, is the same as being controlled by hell. Certainly people make a grave mistake in thinking God controls this Earth. They either get everything in a muddle or become God-haters. But does not the Lord's Prayer start by saying: "*May* Thy Will be done on Earth"? If mankind were in touch with Higher Centres, it would be a different matter altogether.

Now we come to the category of lying to which the Work most deeply refers—namely, that we ascribe to ourselves what we do not possess. It is this, again in the deepest sense, that prevents contact with Higher Centres and the development of Real Being through the influx of entirely new meaning quite distinct from the meanings we have from external life—that is, *A* influences. We ascribe to ourselves the power of *doing*. We ascribe to ourselves the possession of one permanent, unvarying 'I'—that is, Real 'I'. We ascribe to ourselves the possession of Real Will—whereas, in fact, being made up of many different 'I's, we have at any moment only the will of one of these 'I's. We ascribe to ourselves the power of changing ourselves if we wish to—whereas we cannot change as we are and only justify ourselves when brought to the point—if ever we are. We ascribe to ourselves self-knowledge. We imagine, like that man in the parable who had collected stores in his barn, that we can calculate the future. All this ascription to ourselves of powers we do not possess is the real lying that the Work is ultimately concerned with. And this unconscious lying is what through self-observation we have to become gradually conscious of. Unless this begins in us, Personality—which of course thinks it can do—remains active and Essence passive. This becoming gradually conscious of the part that pride, vanity, buffers, and deep sleep play in our ordinary thinking and behaviour is called the first phase of the Work. What is this phase called? It is called *Awakening*. Gurdjieff said in so many words: "In the Gospels you find many esoteric ideas, but often in the wrong order, as if written by people who remembered what was said but did not understand sufficiently what was meant. In the Gospels we find the idea of dying to oneself. We find that there is the idea of re-birth and we find that there is the idea of awakening. But it is necessary to understand that a man cannot die to himself unless he has awakened to himself and understands what he has to die to. If he tries to die to himself without first awakening, he will not be re-born. But unless he spends a long time in awakening to himself, he cannot die and be re-born. For that reason a man must first observe himself practically and see what he is like. Only with this hardly-gained self-knowledge can he expect to get anything. One difficulty is that Man as he is thinks he knows himself and understands himself. No greater illusion could exist."

On one occasion in speaking of how people all ascribe powers and qualities to themselves that they must gradually realize they do not possess, Mr. Ouspensky said: "This is for a long time difficult to realize. Begin with one thing and observe it in yourself. Begin, say, with observing that you *pretend you know*. This is one of the worst forms of lying. Many people pretend they know what they do not know and keep up the picture all their lives. You must, in the Work, try to see that you follow, and are a slave to, life-long ideas. Only then can you begin to understand what inner sincerity means. Unless one has inner sincerity one cannot do this Work."

Now something has been said at times in these commentaries about the inner or psychological meaning of some of the Ten Commandments. For example: "Thou shalt do no murder," apart from its literal meaning, means that one must not murder anyone in one's thoughts. People are afraid to murder literally because of the fear of consequences in the world—such as police, and so on. In the Work this does not count. It is not *you* doing it, but fear doing it. If you murder in your thoughts you do spiritual murder. So we are taught: "Forgive one another." In connection with what we are speaking about, this commandment: "Thou shalt not steal", signifies psychologically: "You must not ascribe to yourself psychologically what you do not possess." For if you ascribe to yourself powers that do not belong to you, then are you not stealing? This is the psychological meaning of this particular commandment. The Work is to make us think in a new way and that means, for one thing, to think psychologically. What does it mean to think psychologically. Well, observe yourself and see what goes on inside you and what you consent to within but are frightened to express because of fear of loss of reputation, loss of money, loss of position, loss of being thought well of, and so on. Do you not understand that if you murder people easily in a psychological sense—that is, in your inner private world of thoughts and feelings—you are in spirit a murderer? Only one remedy exists: get to know yourself by long, sincere self-observation. Get rid speedily of the imaginary idea that you are a good man, a good woman. Real self-knowledge will stop you from murdering anyone, because you will find in yourself all that you hate in the other. And if you sincerely observe yourself in the light of the Work you will soon know what "stealing" means.

Great Amwell House, May 1, 1948

ON CONSCIOUSNESS

WORK-IDEA

The Work speaks of Four States of Consciousness. Man thinks he is fully conscious. The Work says that Man is not fully conscious and that actually he is asleep.

COMMENTARY

In this Work we begin with work on the Intellectual Centre and the Emotional Centre—that is, we begin with working on how we think and how we feel, through observing our mechanical thinking and feeling. We do not begin with physical habits, appetites, etc. This must be clearly understood by everyone who connects with the Work-teaching. For example, the Work, as originally taught, does not begin with work on Moving Centre. To begin with, say, Moving Centre, is Fakir Way. To begin with Moving Centre, when the habits of thinking and the habits of feeling remain unaltered, is to begin from the wrong end—that is, in the wrong order. A man may hold his arms out horizontally all his life until they are permanently fixed. But what will he himself gain? This Work—called the Fourth Way—does not begin at that end of a man, but starts from *how he thinks* and gives him new ideas to think from. So it begins with one's psychology, for how you think is part of your psychology quite distinct from your physical appearance, your physical body, your muscles, your complexion, your fatness, your thinness, your size, your weight, and all the rest that is observable by your external senses. No, the Work begins with another sense, directed not outwards but inwards into—yes, into what? Into how you think and how you feel. That is, self-observation is about your psychology—not your physique. A magnificent physique does not connote a magnificent psychology. Now how you think belongs to your psychology. You all think mechanically. And to think in a new way means that your mental psychology has to change. For if you wish to think in a new way and so change your mind and its ingrained habits of thinking, and at the same time wish to keep on thinking in the old familiar ways—then how can you change anything? To change, one must change. No one can change and also remain the same. To change one must leave, let go of, give up, what one was before. Yet we imagine we can take in new ideas and think in a new way and yet remain as we were formerly—a very strange view. "You cannot attach the Work on to yourself as you are," said Mr. Ouspensky. "You must let the ideas of the Work change your thinking. To think that all you have to do is to remain mentally as before and merely attach this Work on to your previous ways of thinking as something extra is simply not to understand what this Work is about."

Now there are two parables about this attaching the esoteric teaching of the Work on to the old basis of thought. Remember this Work is called Esoteric Christianity. The parables are as follows:

"No man rendeth a piece from a new garment and putteth it upon an old garment; else he will rend the new and also the piece from the new will not agree with the old. And no man putteth new wine into old wine-skins; else the new wine will burst the skins, and itself will be spilled, and the skins will perish. But new wine must be put into fresh wine-skins. And no man having drunk old wine desireth new: for he saith, The old is good." (*Luke V* 36-39)

Notice the apparent contradiction. This "new wine" is really old wine—that is, the ancient teaching. Do you see what is meant? Do you understand that these two parables are not about actual cloth or bottles? Do you see that they mean you cannot tack on, cannot merely attach, the ideas of esoteric teaching on to your previous ways of thinking? It is sufficient that in each of the three Gospels in which they occur, these two parables are related immediately after a passage describing how the disciples of John the Baptist and the disciples of the Pharisees came to Jesus and asked why his disciples did not fast. As if literal fasting, the keeping of rituals, could change the mind! But I leave you to ponder this for yourselves, save to add that it is a very wonderful thing to fast from your own thoughts sometimes, and think instead from the ideas of the Work.

Now let us take the Work-Idea that Four States of Consciousness are possible to Man, but he customarily knows only two. In this connection the Work says that in Western psychology a great mistake is made by taking Man's Consciousness as full Consciousness. In many ancient Eastern teachings, Man is not taken as properly conscious. As you know, the Work describes the state of consciousness in which people go about, talk, write, plan, make love, and so on, as being a state of hypnotic sleep. In this state of sleep, everything happens in the only way it can happen. Wars start and no one can stop them and people kill each other without wishing to, but because they have to. And a thousand and one other things happen which no one wishes but which inevitably happen just because everyone is asleep. People do not guess that this is the real explanation of why life on this Earth is as it is. That is, they do not possess this esoteric idea that Man is asleep and do not think from it, but think instead from the idea that Man is awake and fully conscious. They think wars take place because of certain people in the background and cannot understand that they take place because everyone is in a state of hypnotic sleep which cannot be thrown off save by direct help from those who have awakened and left behind them ideas to think from and instructions to follow.

Now you see it is no good tacking on this Work-Idea of Man being in a state of hypnotic sleep to our ordinary ways of thinking. It will not fit. It will be like old and new cloth, or new wine in old skins. It is an utterly different idea from any of the ordinary ideas we have about life. To think from it is to think in an utterly new way. Have you begun to think from this *idea*—both as regards life, other people and especially as regards your own self? Do you yourself comprehend, through self-observation, that you yourself are also asleep?

*   *   *

What do we seek? We seek to become more conscious—of ourselves and of others. We seek to be more aware of ourselves and at the same time of others. That is, we seek to increase consciousness. We seek to become more conscious of ourselves, of the kind of thoughts we have and the kind of feelings we have habitually—that is, mechanically. A mechanical, a fixed way of thinking or of feeling, will keep us where we are. And we seek to become more conscious of others. What is the most precious, the most mysterious, and the most indefinable possession we have been given? The answer is—*Consciousness*. We are given a little of this indescribable and unfathomable mystery. But, as we are, in a state of hypnotic sleep, we do not use this gift, but, as it were, surrender it to every pleasing mood, every passing thought. Now on one occasion, speaking to a person who was a singer and who had said: "Ought we not to place our consciousness as a singer places his or her voice in a room?" Mr. Ouspensky said: "This is a very good illustration. As we are, we place our consciousness, such as we have, on the wrong things. One must learn to control consciousness by placing it." Yes—and is it not true that you can *place* your consciousness so easily on the most unpleasant things in your life? And is it not true that you need not place your consciousness—such as it is—on such unpleasant things? Notice that consciousness activates—brings into consciousness—all sorts of deadly things. Consciousness is like light. What are you going to cast this light on? A man, a woman, are in one sense *where* they place their consciousness. Begin with developing Will in the sense of not placing your consciousness on unhappy, unpleasant things. I call this: "not going with these unpleasant 'I's". But where your consciousness is, there *you* are. Have you ever thought what consciousness is? Well, it is comparable, as just said, to light. You have a small electric torch. You always shine it on so much filth—and that, in the Work, means negative emotions, first of all. So the idea that one can *place* one's consciousness is valuable. You may think you know this already. Perhaps, but do you *do* it? One knows and also can learn many truths. But in this Work it is necessary to *do* the truths that we are taught. Now one form of self-observation is to notice on what you are placing your consciousness. You must become conscious of your consciousness. This leads to a definite increase of consciousness. If you are placing your consciousness on unpleasant things, you must become conscious of where your consciousness is fixed. After a time, this consciousness of consciousness grows. That is, you have a new consciousness of that former consciousness with which you were identified. This means you open up a consciousness on a higher level than the consciousness you formerly believed was full consciousness. All this, and similar work on yourself, leads you gradually to the Third State of Consciousness, Self-Remembering, or Self-Awareness, or Self-Consciousness. At this new level of consciousness, you begin to see your life in a new way—that is, to become newly conscious of it. Also at this level, you get, quite beyond question, help—new influences. That is, since you are beginning to awaken from the hypnotic sleep of life you begin to touch the first traces of another consciousness which is not that belonging to hypnotic sleep. The Work teaches that you can get help —but only in the Third State of Consciousness. If you remain fastened to yourself, you cannot get help because it cannot reach you. You are not *fine* enough internally.

Great Amwell House, May 8, 1948

BRIEF NOTE ON SELF-CHANGE

WORK-IDEA

Only the man himself can change himself.

COMMENTARY

It is impossible to change another by compulsion. No outer rules, regulations, laws, etc., can change the man himself. He may, through fear, or for reasons of self-interest, obey the regulations, etc., but this does not change the man himself. To change himself, the man must be in freedom. Compulsion will never do it. The man must see for himself the truth, before the truth will alter him. If Man could be changed in himself by the application of outer compulsion he could long ago have changed. But Man was created a self-developing organism, capable of a definite inner change, and no outer forces can bring about this *self*-development. Notice it is *self*-development of which the Work speaks. Self-development can only be in freedom—from oneself. A man is in freedom as regards inner development. Only he himself can will to change. If he understands enough, he will begin to change in the freedom of his understanding, for his understanding is his own and no one can take it away, or force it. If from understanding he wills to change himself, then it is possible for him to change. But first he must *understand*. Understanding, this Work teaches, is the most powerful thing a man can create. Without understanding a man can do nothing right, outwardly or inwardly. For example, people do not see the other side of themselves. They therefore blame each other for what is really in themselves. They see in others their own failings which they refuse to accept. When they begin to *understand* better, they cease to lead this one-sided life.

Now everyone knows that it is very difficult to accept anything adverse said about oneself. We are furious, contemptuous, and so on. Or if you point out another person's shortcomings, he will be furious also or contemptuous, and so on. I well know as a medical psychologist the awkward point where I had to say to the patient: "Yes—I can see you have been badly treated, never appreciated, never properly understood. You have told me all that very clearly. But do you think that it is possible that you are not quite the ideal person that you seem to imagine yourself to be, and that there may be some quite serious faults in yourself?" Now you can all imagine the haughty look, the frozen smile, the magnificent rising from the chair—and the slamming of the door—without, of course, the fee being paid. Yes—but what has happened? We were recently talking of this. What has been touched? What would you call it? Whatever you call it, it is this factor that prevents self-change.

1165

I was reading recently a volume describing a British Envoy's visit to Persia to see the Shah, somewhere early in the last century. The Envoy landed at Basra with squadrons of Huzzars, Horse-Gunners, magnificent tents, trappings, and all the rest. They advanced in a leisurely way to the capital because any hurry would have meant "loss of face". If the Shah sent a message, they replied a few days later. If the Envoy sent a message, the Shah replied a week or two later. If one side suggested a definite date, the other side expressed profound sorrow, but they were occupied on that particular date. Now all this ceremony was to enable the Envoy and the Shah to meet on equal terms—that is, without any "loss of face" on either side. Again, I ask you: what do you call this factor which exists in all, apart from Envoys or Shahs? Have you noticed it in yourself? All this careful adjusting of the external situation by the British Envoy and the Shah was to adapt it to this formidable factor for which we must try to find a name. It seems to lie very deep—deeper than False Personality.

Now let us glance briefly at the Work—this system of psychology that we are studying. The Work speaks constantly about the necessity of self-development. "Man", it says, "is an unfinished house." What is its starting-point? Its starting-point is *self-observation*. A man, a woman, must begin to increase their range of consciousness by observing themselves through this interior sense that we possess and which animals do not possess. Animals were not made for self-development: Man was. Animals cannot observe themselves: Man can. Now, if a person begins to observe himself in the light of the Work, he gradually, after years of work on himself, begins to see what no doubt others have pointed out or have been longing to point out. If he sees *for himself* something of this factor in him, which is so formidable and the source of so much violence, then it is not aroused antagonistically. He sees himself: he begins to accept what he would never have accepted from another. It is in this way that the Work deals with this otherwise intractable factor in Man. Now to all appearances you may have practised this Work for years and never really done a stroke of Work. Why? Because this formidable factor has remained untouched in you, as in a fortress, and has not yielded an inch.

Great Amwell House, 15 *May*, 1948

SELF-CHANGE

(CHANGE OF ATTITUDE)

WORK-IDEA

To change, a man must change his attitudes.

COMMENTARY

Last time we spoke of this intractable factor, common to all and lying in our depth, that causes us to react finally by violence. We spoke about "loss of face" and so on. To-day we speak about attitudes and their connection with this deep factor. Attitudes are acquired from the outer influences of life, such as education, country, religion, social position, and its prejudices, and so on. Very soon, a man, a woman, *become* their acquired attitudes through identifying. They, indeed, *are* their attitudes without knowing it. The basic idea of propaganda is to instil certain attitudes at an early age. If this is done with success, a person, quite unconscious of his attitudes, becomes them. This means that if you talk to such a person about anything that strikes against an attitude, he cannot hear what you say. I fancy this explains many apparently inexplicable things about others and about oneself.

Now attitudes begin to be formed in the Intellectual Centre from what one is told and then act on the Emotional Centre. That is, an attitude does not begin in the Emotional Centre: it begins with things you were told and accepted. These acquired attitudes, laid down in the mind, cause everyone to think from them. We think, in so far as we ever do, from these undetected attitudes. As long as these attitudes govern the mind, a man's thinking is not free, but is controlled by them. Yes—but the person is unaware that this is the case. He believes he thinks in freedom, from himself. Certainly he thinks "from himself", but he does not see that what he takes as "himself" is not really himself but a number of fixed attitudes that are continually acting on him without his knowledge. The Work is about tearing oneself away from this acquired side, so that centres can work naturally. If centres were not overlaid by attitudes and associations they would give us a quite different and richer life. Somewhere it is said in Scripture that God made Man upright, but that he has sought out many inventions. One invention is the invention of what he calls "himself". But it takes a long time to see that one is really an invention and that something very deep knows this quite well. Gurdjieff once said that people came to him and said they would give up everything to follow him. But when it came to giving up their ingrained attitudes they were offended and left. In the same connection Mr. Ouspensky said that when people had reached a certain stage of inner development they came to the point where they had to give up their particular beliefs—whether they were Mahometans, Anglicans, Catholics, Quakers, Presbyterians, Baptists, or whatever it might be. I remember his words: "This", he said, "is the most difficult thing to do and at this stage—I am speaking of schools—many leave. They go so far, but cannot give themselves up." He was speaking of acquired attitudes and how difficult it is to free oneself from them. Now what I want to point out, by way of commentary, is that our attitudes seem to rest upon this intractable difficult and violent thing in us that must eventually yield, so that we can become passive to ourselves and hear what Higher Centres are saying to us all the time. As I said last time, only the practical experience that there is something far above us can make this intractable thing bow down and submit. No outer compulsion, no outer rules or discipline, can do this. Only a long series of inner experiences, that for a long time one only half-believes in, can make it possible. The, so to speak, intractable, violent, prehistoric man or prehistoric woman has to become transformed into an accepting of all that you would at present never think of accepting. As I said, *amour propre* has to give way to *amor Dei*, and in this connection reflection upon the significance of the Ray of Creation can at least begin to alter our thinking because it gives an idea of our own smallness and insignificance.

To-day I want those who heard the last paper to consider the question as to whether they can agree that their acquired and unchallenged attitudes receive their secret force from this intractable and violent basis of what orthodox religion calls "unregenerate Man" —that is, Man not yet re-born in himself. I believe, from my own observation, that this is the case. Now when a man observes himself, he observes a lot of things that have their own importance, but he does not observe his attitudes. To speak with exaggeration, I may believe myself God—as so many lunatics do, which shews you how close this idea is to people. Since I believe myself God, I will never think of observing this in myself. Why? Because I take this attitude for granted. To believe oneself God is an attitude. So of course I will never think of observing *that*. Well, it is just the same with all attitudes. One simply accepts them—or, rather, one simply does not know that one has them, so one does not think of observing them. In fact, one simply cannot observe them and cannot *hear* anyone who is such a fool as to try to call attention to them. You cannot observe anything you take yourself as. A man, says the Work, before he can shift from where he is internally, must divide himself into two—an observing side and an observed side. That is, he must make his subjectivity objective. He must take *himself* as the object to observe. But if he remains entirely unconscious of his attitudes, how can he observe them? The most of what self-observation we can do is made useless by subsequent self-justifying. "A man", said Mr. Ouspensky, "who always justifies what he observes in himself cannot become objective to himself." That is understandable, if you reflect. But how can one observe something that is, so to speak, un-observable? One's attitudes are oneself. One takes them as oneself. No—one does not know anything about them. One does not say: "These attitudes I have acquired are me." On the contrary, one does not say anything. They are what you take for granted as *you*. If one *could* say: "These attitudes are me"—then it would mean that one has begun to become a little aware of them. That is, these attitudes would begin to be *objective* to you—to things in yourself that Observing 'I' can observe. But if you remain in inner darkness, how can you proceed? Well, I will end this short commentary by saying that although it is impossible to observe ingrained and fixed attitudes directly, one can begin after some time to notice the results of them. For example, you may begin to wonder why you always grunt like that when someone asks you to do something useless. You may say to yourself after a time-"I wonder why I always think that thing useless." The answer is: "Probably because of some fixed attitude that you are entirely unaware of." In this way one is led down to the fact of the existence of these attitudes in oneself. If such a merciful thing has happened to you—that is, if the Work has given you internal help—you will realize that behind this attitude, that you begin at last to become conscious of, dwells secretly this intractable factor common to us all. Remember that you cannot work on yourself unless you begin to wonder why you say what you say and do what you do and behave as you behave and feel what you feel and think what you think. To take yourself for granted, to imagine you are always right, to ascribe to yourself all that you do ascribe to yourself—all that form of sheer imagination will prevent you from seeing what esotericism means, what the Gospels mean, and what you mean.

Great Amwell House, May 22, 1948

NOTE ON OBSERVATION OF INTELLECTUAL CENTRE AND USELESS THINKING AND WRONG THINKING

WORK-IDEA

We must think in a new way. Mechanical Man thinks chiefly from attitudes. To change, attitudes must change.

COMMENTARY

Last time we spoke of attitudes and how, unless attitudes change, a man cannot change. Let us remind ourselves that the Work is about *self-change*. To do this Work without seeking change of oneself is like trying to lift an elephant. Or, put better, it is like standing on a plank and trying to lift it. It was also said that attitudes begin in the Mental Centre—in the mind. To change therefore, as Christ taught, and this Work teaches, it is necessary to change the mind, so as to think in a new way. Now a person with many fixed attitudes, acquired from upbringing, laid down in the mind, cannot think in a new way. He or she will continue to think in the old way. They will think from their ingrained fixed attitudes. As a minor example, a person has an attitude that Dickens is the only real novelist. Offer him Dumas, and he will no doubt reject it, and offer him anything modern and he will become cross. You can see how attitudes limit the mind in such a case. Now we have attitudes about life, about society, about religion, about people, about politics, about sex, about art, and so on, which prevent us from experiencing anything new. It is necessary to free the mind from these acquired attitudes, for they prevent a person from thinking for himself. And unless you begin to think for yourself about this Work you will never understand it, and in turn it will be unable to help you, for the Work can only help you and give you force through your understanding of it. For that reason understanding is said in the Work to be the strongest force you can make. A person with strong, mechanical attitudes belongs to those called "the blind" in esoteric teaching. One thing more must be added here: when you think or speak from a fixed attitude you are certain you are right. I advise some of you to reflect on this and observe when you are so sure you are right. You cannot observe attitudes directly, but you can observe the results of them. One result is this being certain you are right. If you can face examining the background of this feeling you are so right, you will find nothing but a bit of lath and plaster, nothing but a sentence or two that you read, a phrase or two you heard early in life at an impressionable age. I tell you seriously that a man, a woman, who has many attitudes in the mind is like a landowner with hundreds of acres fenced in and walled in every direction, not cultivated and so sterile. In this Work the mind must *first* awaken to the ideas taught and so begin to think in a new way and then, years later, the Emotional Centre begins to stir and awaken and give you a new feeling of yourself—a most blessed experience. You cannot awaken the Emotional Centre—which is the object of this Work —unless the mind awakens. But if your mind is fenced in by sterile attitudes and if you refuse to change them—or rather, if it never occurs to you that you have them and so you never suspect their existence— then you will bring into the Work all the latent violence that lies behind attitudes, which appears so suddenly when they are hit and belongs to this intractable factor in us all of which we spoke recently.

Mr. Ouspensky once said that among many things we defend so uselessly and lose force over is our ignorance. He said, in so many words: "What we do not know in comparison with what we think we know is incommensurable. Attitudes, which are first formed in the mind, make us think we know. We continually speak from attitudes as if we really knew, when we are ignorant. It is quite easy to see in others when they are speaking from attitudes. Everyone yawns or goes to sleep. A man who can only speak from attitudes is the greatest bore. But we do not see attitudes in ourselves." I asked him: "If I am speaking and begin to yawn myself, is that a sign I am speaking from attitudes?" It so happened that he yawned and I yawned after him and so we both laughed. But later I remember him asking me: "Have you ever observed that one can yawn at one's own thoughts? It is a useful thing to observe what mechanical trains of thought cause this. It is a sign that they are useless, that one should avoid them."

Now you know that self-observation begins with observing the centres. You must reach that stage where you can, by self-observation, distinguish the working of the Intellectual or Mental Centre from that of the Emotional Centre or that of the Moving Centre or that of the Instinctive Centre. A thought is different from a feeling. A feeling is different from a sensation. A sensation is different from a movement. Thought, feeling, sensation and movement are all different. Now if you observe your thoughts over a period you will see that they repeat themselves day by day. So you begin to glimpse your mechanicalness in the Intellectual Centre. Now people think they can change their thoughts at any time. All think they can receive and accept new ideas at any time. But it is the rarest thing in the world for this to be possible. The mind soon gets choked with fixed attitudes and habits of thinking taking the place of real thinking, and repeating and repeating themselves all your life. When you are listening to a new idea you are not listening, for before the speaker has got to the end of what he is saying, you have already marshalled all your arguments against it. One has only to observe oneself. Yet one is sure one has an open mind. Who would care to shout on the house-tops that he or she has a shut mind? In this darkness, this ignorance of ourselves, we live, ascribing to ourselves what we do not possess.

Now it is from attitudes that we argue. To argue is not to understand: to understand is not to argue. No one was ever changed by arguing. But we must try to make attitudes conscious and not argue. To make an attitude conscious is to deprive it of its power over you. Whatever comes into the light of consciousness is deprived of its power. If you insist on saying you have no attitudes you are insisting on keeping yourself where you are in the Scale of Being. Are you going to say that you have no great prejudices, no typical opinions, no bias, no hard places, no rigidities, in your mind? Surely, you cannot say such a thing seriously. But if a magician told you all the fixed attitudes and the resulting prejudices, opinions, etc., that characterize you, would you for a moment accept what he said? You would feel insulted.

In trying to accept the teaching of this Work with its ideas we do not notice that it will inevitably come up against our unconscious and mechanical attitudes. Everyone who is at the level of Good Householder has some power of thinking apart from attitude. But a fixed attitude can make you not believe what your own thinking does believe. Your attitude can say "No" automatically, whereas your own thinking says "Yes". That is, attitudes eat belief. That is why, in some cases, a person cannot hold on to what he or she saw for a moment, and falls back again. Attitude eats the force given to the mind by the Work. That is why it is so important to struggle to see attitudes in oneself. The new thinking is eaten up by the old thinking. The momentary feeling of mental freedom is replaced by the old mind based on attitudes.

Now try to see an attitude in yourself. I mean, *really try*. Realize that you have *not got* an open mind. I want—as always—examples based on your own self-observation. I do not want questions such as: "Is an 'I' the same as an attitude?" Do *you yourself* know that you yourself have fixed attitudes and that you practically know nothing of them? Have you noticed when you are speaking from attitudes? Do you understand from this talk why the mind cannot change as long as it is full of attitudes? Do you understand that you cannot undergo "change of mind" or what Christ called μετάνοια as long as your mind is fixed and walled into attitudes, into compartments, in which nothing can grow? And let me say frankly—do you understand that your whole life may be spoiled by the existence of these attitudes lying under the surface of your mind and unrecognized by you? Recollect: a man cannot change himself unless he changes his attitudes. Try therefore to see the results of attitudes. Notice when you feel shocked, for example. Notice when you feel intolerant, contemptuous, etc. Notice when you tut-tut at things. Notice when you judge, and if you can, notice when you are speaking from attitude. Notice your intonation and your expression and notice how bored others become. I suppose a person could speak all day from attitude without saying a single interesting thing. He cannot say anything interesting because he cannot use his mind. His mind is used by attitudes. So his mind cannot awaken. If this is the case, the whole of his inner development is arrested. He lives and dies a machine.

NOTES ON THE MEANING OF THIS WORK

WORK-IDEA

This Work is called Psycho-Transformism. The First Conscious
Shock is given at the place of reception of impressions falling on the
mind—that is, the Intellectual Centre. If the Work does not intervene between the incoming impressions from life and the way they
mechanically fall on the centre, everything will remain as before. One
remains a machine. A man can only begin to change when he changes
his mechanical attitudes in the Intellectual Centre that cause him to
react as he does. All attitudes *begin* in this centre. Later they affect
other centres. When impressions fall on fixed mental attitudes, the
reaction will remain as before. That is, there will be no psycho-transformism. Nothing will be transformed. This Work is about thinking
in a new way—that is, apart from fixed attitudes.

COMMENTARY

If you accept without demur, without challenge, your mental
attitudes, fixed opinions, and prejudices, your mind will not be able to
think for itself. If that is the case—you cannot change. To change it
is necessary to think in a new way. Most of one's thinking is simply the
recurrent expression of fixed attitudes that infest the Intellectual Centre
in a similar way to the infestation of the Emotional Centre by typical
recurrent negative emotions. So no psycho-transformism is possible.
The mind, with its fixed attitudes, its rigid lies and blind spots, will
cause every centre to react to life—that is, to impressions—in exactly
the same way as before. *The mind must change first.* I repeat once more
that in the fragments of esoteric teaching contained in the Gospels the
Greek word μετάνοια was taught from the start. Translated as *"Repent—
for the Kingdom of Heaven is at hand"*, it does not convey the inner
sense. To repent is emotional. To think in a new way is intellectual.
I again repeat: "μετα = beyond, and voῦs = mind". One has to get
beyond the ordinary mind in order to change and then the Emotional
Centre can awaken. And the ordinary mind we so poorly work with,
this poor, unsatisfactory ghost of a mind that has no real ideas furnishing
it with rich, daily meaning, but nothing but a lot of blind attitudes,
fixed opinions and prejudices—I say, this ordinary mind, as long as it
reigns in us, will make any change of oneself, any change in knowledge
and emotional being, quite impossible. So I do not understand why
some still ask: "Why is it necessary, for a man to change, for him to
change attitudes?" The answer is that attitudes block the mind and so
nothing can change. Yes—these terrible, proud, ingrained attitudes.

Now the greatest effort you can make is to *understand* what the Work is about. Understanding is the most powerful thing a man, a woman, can make—and the Work says we are born to *understand*—that is, it says we are born as self-developing organisms—a strange and extraordinary experiment on this tiny unimportant planet and one that may easily prove a failure, in which case we will be swept aside and another organism made. It is this self-development possible to us that psycho-transformism is about. Now I am going to bore you again by saying that some of you do not yet understand how mental attitudes will make it impossible to develop. The mind must change first, before anything else in you can change in the direction of this mystery of self-development. So it is necessary for us to struggle to make some of these attitudes conscious to ourselves. *Remember, a thing in you cannot change if it remains unconscious to you.* So the Work begins with self-observation. If you cannot observe a thing in yourself you cannot change it. Always remember this. Only the light can cure you—and the light means the light of consciousness. So try to become aware of attitudes in yourself. A man, a woman, may think they love someone. But if their early-acquired attitudes do not really accept this person, then, when a critical moment comes, it is obvious that this love merely floats on a far deeper antagonism. And yet, this antagonism is nothing but a bit of flint in the mind with nothing behind it. But like a bit of shrapnel in the brain it is difficult to draw it out without some kind of general collapse.

Now to change a mental attitude is to make room for the Work to change you. Stuffed full of attitudes, often of the most absurd kind, and, shall I add, out-of-date attitudes, you move about in life as a kind of stuffed idiot—yes, in saying this I am thinking of myself also. Look at a typical attitude entering the drawing-room and shaking hands with a similar typical attitude. Then notice it in face of a contrary attitude. Yes—it is amusing to notice these things but still more to notice them in yourself. The unconscious attitude—the unchallenged attitude—belong to our ignorance of ourselves and only long, calm, not negative, uncritical observation of ourselves—without any self-justifying—can make us conscious of our absurd frozen attitudes. This leads to self-knowledge. There is a divine ignorance which is one form of innocence as in babies, but there is another innocence arising from wisdom which is utterly different. For example, if after many years you realise you *cannot do* and therefore do not always blame others because you see they cannot do but realize it is always your fault for being negative, then you become innocent through wisdom—and innocence means, exactly, becoming harmless as a baby—not through ignorance but through knowledge—through understanding. Why do we blame another? Simply because we think this other person can do—that is, can be different. How about yourself? When we begin to work on ourselves we realize that we ourselves cannot do. So why have a grievance against others—as every one of you has? People make internal accounts all day long against each other—and this makes a curious unpleasant thick mass round people for which Gurdjieff has a strange Eastern word that

I cannot recall at the moment. People living together make this thick dense atmosphere—unless they work on themselves. Why? Because people fundamentally love themselves and no one else.

Now I am going, later on, to speak to you all from this angle of how the ideas in the Work can transform you. I have mentioned one— merely, that it is my fault if I am negative, not the other person's. This *reverses* you. Actually, every idea of the Work, if taken inwards, will transform you—that is, if the mind can accept it. But no one's mind will accept the ideas of this Work, even if heard for sixty years, unless they free the blocked mind so as to let living *ideas* take the place of dead attitudes.

*　　*　　*

Now reflect: the ideas of this Work are consciously designated to transform us. Take the brief example given above. The Work-Idea given above is that *if you are negative it is always your fault and not the other person's*. Does this transform you? Does this make you think in a new way? To think in a new way is to begin to transform yourself. Yes, but to *realize* you are to blame if you become negative, and not the other person, is to *reverse* yourself. You will understand later that all transformation of oneself has to do with a *reversal* in yourself—a seeing of everything the other way round. This is what transforms us.

Great Amwell House, June 5, 1948

THE TRANSFORMATION OF IMPRESSIONS

Work-Teaching

Gurdjieff once said: "About 70 per cent of people are ill from psychological reasons—for example, from wrong impressions."

Commentary

It can be said that there are, to begin with, three definite sources of illness, according to the Work-teaching. The human machine takes in *three quite distinct foods*—all necessary for it. We all realize vaguely that lack of the right food, in the ordinary sense of food, can lead to a thousand and one sorts of illness. Lack of citrous food, for example, causes scurvy and all its minor manifestations. Lack of fresh milk, butter or cod-liver oil, etc., causes rickets in the young and other things in the older people. Lack of certain necessary parts of wheat or rice damages the nervous system in different ways. Too much or too little fat or meat or cereals causes illness of endless varieties. I say that we

1175

realize that wrong food, in the ordinary meaning of the word, can be the source of many illnesses. But what we do not realize is that the human machine, for its right working, does not depend *only* upon this one kind of food. It depends on two other kinds of food, not as yet in ordinary medicine as clearly recognized as is the dependence of the body on food in the ordinary sense, although sunlight, which belongs to impressions, is recognized as a food in a way. These two other "foods" are formulated in the Work as "Air" and "Impressions". People do not think "air" is a *food*. Still less do they think that "Impressions" are a *food*. So I will remind you again of the diagram of the Three Foods entering the human machine, and make some further comments.

(*See Diagram on page* 1105)

You will notice that in the diagram Man is represented as a three-storey building or house. Into each floor or storey a different kind of food enters. The figures *768, 192* and *48* indicate the relative finenesses or quality of the food. Ordinary food for Man, *768*, is, so to speak, coarse food and requires many transformations in the human machine —that is, successive digestions—to be serviceable. *Air* is less coarse, less dense, and undergoes finer digestions or transformations in the body. And again, impressions are still less dense—that is, far finer. Now the finer a substance is, in this sense of successive transformations, the more powerful its effects. It is difficult to find analogies. We connect the word "powerful" with physical force, physical violence. But this is not what is meant. A finely bred race-horse is more powerful, in the Work-sense, than a cart-horse. Why? It is much cleverer. Also, as you have heard, Gurdjieff said a cooked potato is cleverer than a raw one. So one has to think—for oneself—what, in the Work, means *finer* quality. All substances that are of a finer quality are termed "cleverer". A cooked potato can be eaten by Man, a raw one by animals. And remember, as some of you can, that we ourselves can be and are eaten —for we are foods. Yes—just imagine—*we*, strutting about and eating everything on the Earth as by right—we are also in turn eaten by Beings we do not know, in the Scale of Being represented by the Ray of Creation. If we are cleverer we will be absorbed mentally into Beings of a higher level and participate in things quite marvellous that coarser beings cannot participate in. Enough of that side of the Work for the moment except to say that a person stuffed with attitudes, pride, self-merit, False Personality and the rest of it, is not acceptable food to Beings of a higher level of Intelligence.

The substance, or energy, rendered as *768*—ordinary food—is not such a clever substance as *192*, or, in turn, as *48*. Let us speak once more about this energy-substance that enters the top compartment of the three-storey factory that is called *impressions* and numbered *48*. Impressions can undergo *three* transformations: *48* into *24*, *24* into *12*, and *12* into *6*. Now as Gurdjieff said in so many words: "A man can

1176

be ill from wrong food of impressions". He added that most illnesses originate here—that is, most ill people are ill at first *psychologically*. If you ask me: "What is a psychological illness?" I will answer: "It has to do with this top compartment, whose food is impressions—what impressions you take in and identify with and so how you receive them and how you transform—digest—them." I suppose you all know, by self-observation, that if you become suspicious you tend only to take in impressions of others, of the outer visible scene, that amplify your suspicions. It is so easy to suspect—and so difficult to become passive to what others do and say. A simple trick comes in here by the forces whose object it is to keep us asleep and use us. Just a little hint—and if you have only fixed attitudes and no inner individual thought, it is just as if you descend into hell and remain there. Why? Because you gave way to the worst of all negative emotions that infest the Emotional Centre. Is it not the easiest thing in the world to suspect? Everything seems to fit together. And is it not the most difficult thing in the world to suspect yourself of being suspicious? Suspicion is always due to identifying—and remember, *identifying* is not love, and leads to hate so very quickly. Now this is an example of how the food of impressions can make us ill and it applies to all of us. Now let us take what is called nostalgia or home-sickness. I have seen, in the first war, when abroad, so many cases of, as it were, physical collapse, the source of which lay in the sphere of *impressions*. There were no longer the accustomed impressions coming in from the dear home, the dear country, from darling Mummy, and so on. So the person becomes ill, not through lack of ordinary food or air, but through lack of impressions. Can you catch what is meant here? Such people are not yet adult. In the case of a man—he is not yet adult. His head is turned backwards. His spirit goes backwards. So wherever he goes, even round the Earth, he really takes in no new impressions, because he is longing for what by now should not be his goal. I certainly am not going to speak of how it is with woman in this matter. Now a man, a woman, can look backwards, psychologically speaking, or look forwards. Here in the Work a great struggle is delineated, about which I will only say that if you believe in all this Work teaches you will be able to look forwards. And I am not speaking of new success in business or women or appointments or honour. No—I mean that something *internal* reverses its direction and you then realize that one must never look back. Christ said: "No man, having put his hand to the plough, and looking back, is fit for the Kingdom of God." (*Luke* IX, 62.)

Now if you habitually receive impressions negatively you will inevitably look back and so become ill. Not only that, if you are in the Work you will not be able to get on in it because whatever force you may make by Work-efforts will always be eaten by these habitual negative emotions which will cause you to lose all sense of direction. That is why the Work lays such great emphasis to begin with upon the necessity to make conscious to yourself your negative emotions by self-observation and become aware of them, for only in this way can you begin to work on them and not identify with them. If most of one's incoming impressions mechanically nourish negative thoughts and emotions, how great is one's inner darkness and how far one is from the Work.

Now impressions coming in as energy *48* can undergo, as was said, three transformations—that is, to a finer, cleverer, more intelligent energy numbered *24*, then to *12*, and finally to *6*, which is the highest, cleverest energy that Man can produce. But this does not happen in nature. It does not take place in Man asleep, in mechanical Man. Only when you begin to work on impressions and how you receive them in the light of a set of ideas that are not derived from life as it appears can this transformation of impressions begin. What, I ask you, have you transformed to-day in this respect? Your human machine has already transformed considerable quantities of energy *768* into finer and finer matters. Yes—but that is done for you. The transformation of the food called impressions is not done for you. And this is where a mechanical man can begin to cease to be a mechanical man.

Transformation of impressions is called in the Work "giving oneself the First Conscious Shock." Yes—you have heard this before, no doubt, but have you ever tried to give yourself this Conscious Shock? Have you ever tried to take in incoming impressions from the world in quite *a new way*? Certainly you will be unable to do so if you have not yet begun to *think in a new way*. And remember, the Work with all its teaching and its ideas is to make us think in a new way. That is, unless you have *for yourself* begun to see any truth in the Work-teaching, you will never be able to give yourself the First Conscious Shock—that is, you will never be able to take in impressions in a new way—which is the same as saying that you will never be able to *transform* impressions. Remember that another person is *impressions*—and all external life is *impressions* that you can receive and react to in one way or in another way. A person is impressions and their effect on you. Can you see what is meant?

SELF-TRANSFORMATION

WORK-IDEA

This Work teaches that Man is born incomplete, unfinished. But he is born as a self-developing organism. That is, he can complete himself. The Work is about how a man can complete himself. Man can transform himself and so complete himself.

COMMENTARY

What is this Work about? As children we play with toys—say, baby dolls and lead soldiers. Then as we grow up we are given a new set of toys. We play with having real babies, being real soldiers, and with many other things offered us to play with—such as money, position, business, politics—and, in the case of scientists, with the transformation of elements or molecules, making synthetic foods or atom-bombs, machines, and so on. We play at being patriots, leaders, virtuous, self-sacrificing people. We play at being husbands and wives. We play noble parts. We play at being religious. We play with all the adult toys given us in order to keep us fast asleep. Yes—a clever idea lies here. Is it not true, from this aspect, that all the world's a stage? Now the scientists occupy themselves with transformation—the transformation of one element into another in atomic chemistry, or the transformation of one substance into another in molecular chemistry. The mediaeval alchemist spoke much about the transformation of the element lead into the element gold. I believe that this is possible in atomic chemistry to-day. But of course what the real alchemists meant was the transformation of mechanical Man, symbolized by *lead*, into Conscious Man, symbolized by *gold*.

Now having played with our first set of toys and then with our second set of toys, a man, a woman, coming as it were to the end of meaning, may wish for something that is not playing with childish or adult toys. But, let me add, unless you have been through playing with some adult toys and learning the game, you cannot proceed further. We have all to go through the stage of adult toys—that is, having real babies, or being real soldiers, etc., or taking up a career, and, in short, doing your job in life. This stage corresponds to what the Work calls "level of Good Householder". And you will remember that this Work is not for those who have done nothing. It is not for tramps or lunatics. It is for those who have been responsible, who have done some job or other in life, and who have gained some wisdom from contact with life—that is, who realize that in life you cannot have your own way and that life is a second force or force of resistance to what in your phantasy you wish to attain to without any effort. Gurdjieff said: "If a man knows how to make coffee, to such a man I can speak." Many remarks of Gurdjieff's, like this one, sound trivial; but, knowing how he spoke, I realized that what he meant was a man who could plant coffee, grow it, look after it, and finally make coffee in a cup for you. That is, he meant a man who thoroughly knew his job. "To such a man," Gurdjieff said, "I can speak." Yes—but why did he say this? Because such a man has been up against the second force of life—the difficulties of labour, the diseases of the coffee-berry, the gathering of the berries, the storing of them, the transport of them, the marketing of them, the export of them, and all the hundred and one things that belong to such a business. In saying, with apparent simplicity, that he could speak to a man who could make coffee, Gurdjieff meant something far deeper than at first sight. He did not mean a man who buys tinned coffee and makes a cup for himself. He meant a man who knows all about coffee from beginning to end. Now such a man in the Work is called a Good Householder. It means a man, a woman, who has made something, become something, in life, by hard work—by effort—and so a person who has combatted with life as a force of resistance and won something—whether it be one thing or the other—say, a profession, a job, a valid position of some sort, or a family with its responsibilities and so on. Unless we do this we are ghosts—or rather, tramps. We are not real. Now the Work says unless the "level of Good Householder" is attained the Work cannot act on us aright. We have no life-wisdom. We expect miracles where none can happen. We have nothing laid down in centres of any value to us. Nor do we know what effort means in its most ordinary sense. Everything disappoints us— but it does not occur to us that we have to make an effort so that everything does *not* disappoint us. Remember we are all, on this planet, under forty-eight orders of laws. That is, all people, high or low, are under the same laws.

I will pass now from the idea of Good Householder to the further definition used in the Work concerning the Good Householder who no longer believes in life. This refers to a man, a woman, who have been through all that they have, as it were, taken on their shoulders—for remember, in Organic Life every living thing has to make effort—and have begun to think something like this : "Is there anything beyond this life? Is there anything I can find beyond what, as Good Householder, I feel it my duty to follow?"

We spoke just now of scientists transforming the atom and so on. But what can that lead to? I can well imagine a scientist saying: "I am sick of making atom-bombs", or a financier saying: "I am sick of money", or a politician saying: "I am sick of politics", or a soldier saying: "I am sick of being a soldier". Yes, one can begin to come to the end of life-meanings. Then what? What else is there? Now this Work is not about transforming outer life, or about transforming the atom, or one's financial or political or social position. It is about transforming *oneself*. It is about completing this incomplete thing called oneself—this thing born as a self-developing organism. Understand that this is only fully possible when one has played with the second set of toys seriously and properly. You will get nowhere in the Work, which is not about playing with toys, unless you have gained the level spoken of—that of a reasonably good life-man or Good Householder. Why? Because your centres will not have laid down in them enough rolls, enough experience, and you will not know how to make ordinary effort. You will have no life-wisdom. In short, you will still be perhaps playing with the first set of toys—dolls, lead soldiers, and so on—without knowing it. You will no doubt phantasy many lovely things—Queen of the May, etc.—but when it comes to doing something you will not be there or will feel ill or actually get ill. Understand life is the same for all of us. We are all under the same laws. It is equally difficult for all of us. A man, if he has plus, has also an equivalent minus. If you do not understand this you will waste so much force in saying: "if only". Think no one better placed than you, for everyone is placed just where they should be placed, for their own development.

Now, as was said, the Work is about self-transformation and is based on the definite idea that Man, created experimentally as a self-developing organism, has a definite *way* or *path* to follow in order to reach this further state of himself, once he has dealt enough with life and reached thereby a certain level of Being—which is first necessary. Let us take, in this connection, the Work-idea that a man, a woman, must work on being *identified*, and try to see how, by observing and working upon the state of being identified, one can begin to transform oneself. Take a man who is totally identified with his career. Everything he does is a source of worry to him. He is eaten on every side through identifying. To identify, in a literal sense, means to make oneself the same as—that is, to make yourself identical with something. Take a man who makes himself identical with his bank account. He loses his money and commits suicide—a common thing. Why does he do this? He does it because his money and his feeling of himself are identical. So when he loses his money, he feels he no longer exists. He feels he is annihilated. He is identified with something not really *him* at all. Now, as regards this man identified with his career—he wants, say, to become Prime Minister. He pulls wires, he intrigues, he sees all sorts of people whom otherwise he would not; he runs to and fro; he is in a continual state of anxiety, always keyed up, sleepless, and so on. This is quite all right for life—for the adult toys. But if all this leads him nowhere else in the long run, he retires and no doubt wonders what on earth it was all about. Consider how a star, a famous person, by the turn of the wheel of time becomes suddenly nobody. Remember life is a mill-race, a torrent, which we have to be in for a time, but which we have gradually to swim out of. Yes—we have to be in this mill-race to be men and women. The point is to get out of it later on. If you never plunged in you are no good. You thought no doubt to save your soul. But one must lose one's soul to find it again. Now these pictures of people totally identified are not to be sneered at for a moment. Each one of us pours force into the state of being identified over the most trivial things. Where is the centre of gravity of being identified? Every emotional part of a centre can identify. But the Emotional Centre itself is the centre of gravity of being identified. Mr. Ouspensky said once that the object of the Work is to awaken the Emotional Centre. He said, in so many words, that we have no real emotions, we only know the emotion of being identified. This, he said, prevents the Emotional Centre from doing its proper work. He said the Emotional Centre, if it were purified from negative emotions and identifying, would give us, for example, clairvoyance—the power of a cognitive knowledge quite different from the knowledge of the Intellectual Centre—such as a sense of danger, a sense of the future, and many things which belong to us by creation but which we have lost, having been brought up amongst sleeping people and being infected by negative emotions and states of identifying. Now if we work against identifying—if we observe it in ourselves—for, remember, you can change nothing in yourself if you have not yet observed it, become conscious of it—then by the mere fact of being aware of it, which is equivalent to confession of it—you will begin very gradually to dislike the emotional state of being identified. So here, briefly, is an example of how this Work can begin to transform you.

I will add one thing. All connection is through meaning. Unless a thing means something to you, you cannot connect with it. If you cannot see any meaning in this Work for yourself, you will not be able to connect with it. This Work teaches that Greater Mind exists and that unless a person can realize this, he will not be able to work on himself. Unless you realize the miracle of nature and the miracle of your own created existence, you cannot work; you will never, for instance, be able to separate yourself from the state of being continually identified with yourself, because you imagine *you* are the biggest person and that there can be nothing bigger than you. And here, I would like to draw your attention to the Ray of Creation and ask you to reflect upon where *you* come in on it. One must begin to realize that one is not exactly what one imagines.

NOTE ON SELF-REMEMBERING AND
SELF-ACKNOWLEDGEMENT

WORK-TEACHING

It is necessary to realize that we do not remember ourselves. Only by sincere self-observation over a time can we begin to acknowledge that we do not remember ourselves. This is the starting-point of being able to remember oneself. And this, in turn, is the starting-point of being *able to do*.

COMMENTARY

"Self-Remembering", said Mr. Ouspensky on one occasion, "means having an element of will-control. It is an act of *doing*. It is not dreaming of doing, but an action. At first it takes force because it is using something we are not accustomed to use. But later on it gives force." He added: "Self-Remembering is action because it is not only self-awareness, but is the capacity to do what you want to do—at first on a small scale, as, for example, to control yourself in a fit of temper or to behave differently on some occasion when, mechanically, you would have behaved as you always do." Now, in connection with these remarks of O., it is of course necessary for a man to begin to observe how he behaves first of all. If you have no idea how you behave, if you cannot see yourself at all, but are completely identified with yourself, then indeed all work on yourself is useless. You will have no idea what the Work is about or where its point of application lies—namely, in yourself. Remember, we are heavily guarded by buffers, attitudes, and pictures of ourselves, etc., in regard to attacks by others. To tell another his faults leads nowhere, except to bad feeling or violence. We cannot change one another, although we can make room for others to change. But this Work tells *you yourself* to *observe yourself* in the light of what the Work teaches, so that you can change yourself. That is, it starts inside you, like a spy, inside your heavily guarded fortifications. Yes, Observing 'I' is a spy. Therefore the whole matter depends on sincerity with oneself. If you refuse to acknowledge to yourself what you observe, you will get into a lifeless, negative inner tangle. If, on the other hand, you privately acknowledge it, then even if you find yourself unable to change anything, you find gradually that you are being helped—not in the way you expected—just because you acknowledge. So very much depends on this inner sincerity which is self-acknowledgement. It is the opposite of self-justifying. It opens things. Self-justifying shuts things. Let me add, however, that people may suppose they acknowledge while beneath lies self-justification and so their self-acknowledgement is spurious and opens nothing—in fact, closes inner things more than ever. In that case, the reception of forces from Higher

Centres—that is, help—is more blocked than ever by this lying to yourself. Now an act of self-acknowledgement is very brief just as is a moment of Self-Remembering. It has nothing to do with bewailing or lamentation or being negative. It is simply a sudden insight, a momentary surrender of the intractable self-will, a stepping-off of False Personality, and so a brief action of that Will that is not the self-will but comes from Real 'I'—for Real 'I' has no self-love and so no self-will, but Real Will. The result is that things can begin to be re-arranged in right order in oneself, for this is what Higher Centres are trying to do every moment. As we know, almost everything in us is wrongly connected up and we try to lead life with a machinery that not only is clogged with dirt and rust—such as fixed attitudes—but also connected up in a way that it was not designed for.

Now in the approach to the continual study of what Self-Remembering means, let me remind you that one of the first things said is that we must see that we do not remember ourselves but on the contrary are continually identified with everything that happens within and without. This realization can only come about gradually. To pretend it, is worse than useless. From this gradual realization we can become aware that we are mechanical, that we feel, think and act mechanically. We also imagine we can change anything in our behaviour: we begin to realize that we cannot. Now the realization of one's mechanicalness is called one form of Self-Remembering. New realization signifies new consciousness. This new consciousness shews us that what before we imagined was consciousness and conscious behaviour is not consciousness but mechanicalness. And it is this new consciousness that lifts us above our previous level of consciousness. It belongs to the Third State of Consciousness—namely, the State of Self-Remembering that everyone must seek in the Work. The next thing, in this first approach to the continual study of Self-Remembering, is to make some temporary aim and when you try to remember yourself to remember your aim at the same time. This has to do with what was said earlier, in connection with Self-Remembering being more than Self-Awareness because it contains an element of will-control—as controlling oneself in a fit of temper. To remember oneself in connection with a Work-aim gives force because it draws force out, say, of the fit of temper into itself. That is, it can do so. But do not think that every time you remember yourself and an aim of this kind together, you will be successful. If you are not, then acknowledge you are not and do not get negative—otherwise you will get wrong associations connected up with all your Work-efforts. Whatever happens, however you fail—never get negative over it. You will simply "feed the Moon"—that is, the negative part of the Emotional Centre. This part leads down to that sphere under twice the number of laws that govern the prison we are in on this Earth and is designated by the term "Moon". Understand there is a worse state beneath us. If you do not believe it, look around and consider what can take place in this present world. Now all negative states, whether religious or otherwise, will never get us anywhere and it is well worth coming to understand this thoroughly for here lies a great trap. Nothing can grow in the negative part of the Emotional Centre except more negative emotions. To imagine we can get anywhere by being continually negative, fearful, morose, sad, and so on, is a clever trap that seems to swallow millions of people easily.

Now we are taught that we have a *right* not to be negative. One must, of course, reflect *all* one's life on the meaning of this. Someone has apparently given us this right. But Gurdjieff also said: "We have a right to remember ourselves. Man, in fact, is born into this right— but he falls asleep." Now finally, reflect on the fact that help is there, but cannot reach us in the Second State of Consciousness, where we are identified with everything, but only when we are in the Third State of Consciousness. It is possible to say, in this connection, that, taking the Work only on the level of the Second State of Consciousness, charac- terized by identifying and by multiplicity of 'I's, all conflicting and wishing to go in different directions, people make a problem of every- thing, including the Work. And instead of relaxing and practising the Work, they worry about everything connected with it, not seeing that these worrying 'I's are just what they must not identify with.

Great Amwell House, June 26, 1948

WRONG WORK OF CENTRES

WORK-IDEA

The Work speaks of wrong use of centres.

COMMENTARY

On one occasion Ouspensky said to Gurdjieff in so many words: "People are turning into machines. People no longer think. They become almost perfect machines in some very small way, as in a factory full of machinery, and they are content to be so. In fact, if they began to think, they would cease to be such perfect small machines." In reply to this observation of Ouspensky, Gurdjieff said, in so many words: "Yes, that is quite true. But you must remember that Man has more than one mind. Actually he has, to begin with, five minds, correspond- ing to the five centres, which work in quite different ways. It all depends first of all on *which* mind, which centre, they use for the particular work they are engaged upon. If they use the proper mind, they will be able to think even better in the midst of all work with machines. But only if they use the proper mind for the purpose." He said: "You will understand later."

Now this conversation leads directly to the question of the right centre to use for any particular work. A man can use the wrong centre for a particular job. This is wrong use of centres. A man, doing a purely automatic hand-movement job, which cannot vary, may use Emotional and Intellectual Centre, as well as Moving Centre, in an unnecessary way. Say he has merely to tap something every second, but he concentrates on this small, minute, automatic task, with the result that he wastes force. He thinks and feels when it is only necessary to tap. This is wrong use of centres: it is like using three horses for a job when a donkey is enough. On one occasion Ouspensky said to me: "You take things too seriously. Try to understand what I mean." I replied later that to attach too much importance to something of no great importance is to take things too seriously—that is, to waste force. To attach great importance to small things may cause one to attach little importance to greater things. When I was in the carpenter's shop in France I remember watching a man who came in with a rough piece of box in order to cut two laths. He measured again and again, made pencil marks, frowned, protruded his tongue—as we do—and finally sawed the wood in half. Then he spent a long time in planing the two strips so as to make them exactly equal and tied them together carefully, and went off with them. He returned to get some nails and left the laths. Of course, such exact measurements were unnecessary and to plane a lath prevents the plaster sticking to it. It is an example of poring over something small unnecessarily.

Ouspensky once said: "Try to make important things important, and unimportant things unimportant." I am sure this is good advice. Try to do it. Try to observe what it is that is taking all your force. Is it important? On another occasion Ouspensky said: "A trained athlete is a man who knows how to eliminate unnecessary movements. Training is, so to speak, to learn how not to do things—not to do what is unnecessary. Then one does only what is necessary." On another occasion Gurdjieff said to someone who was looking at a bed of flowers: "You think. I only look." I fancy he meant that this person was thinking what variety of peony was growing. Of course, in that case you are trying to see beauty through formatory centre. Emotional beauty is quite different. Or say you go to a picture-gallery with another person who insists on giving you the history of the artist. Or you begin to argue. You will be unable to see the picture—that is, you are using the wrong centre for the job in hand. One must learn simply "to look" as Gurdjieff said. That is why you should, if possible, go alone to see pictures before you take another person. "Oh, Dr. Nicoll, do you not think that the rhythm running through that picture is wonderful? And look at the counterpoint represented in the colours. After all, painting is really two-dimensional music, is it not?" One mutters to oneself: "I do not know—but I know that I cannot see that picture in the presence of a person like you and probably never will be able to now because I will always associate your silly remarks with the picture." It is really extraordinary how many people think that beauty can only be seen through theories. Theories are intellectual. Beauty is emotional and also instinctive.

Now let us, in this brief paper on using the right centre, speak of waste of force in connection with Moving Centre. Some walk in agitation, others in stiffness. One can make all sorts of complex movements by habit—one might almost say, ceremonial movements, as a dog does, before settling down. But it is more in connection with muscle-tension that it is important to modify movements as far as is possible—and the limit is soon reached. I told you the story about how a man in France, when the pigs got into the tomatoes, walked very slowly, to avoid identifying and muscle-tension, and told Gurdjieff. I fear that Gurdjieff roared at him and leapt, so to speak, about 400 yards to those pigs. This is a good example of wrong use of centres—as if, when the house is on fire, you observe your Moving Centre and carefully try to make every movement consciously, with full deliberation. You must understand that people like that have no sense of scale, no sense of what, under the circumstances, is important or unimportant. This is really being stupid. Lack of seeing relative importance is a sign of being stupid. All intelligence, in the Work-sense, is being able to think *relatively*. Third Force—that is, the force that connects you with the *event*—is certainly in such cases not *Hydrogen 12*, a very high force of intelligence, but probably of the density of a piece of wood—say, *Hydrogen 1536*. I suppose the term "wooden-head" may be derived from some esoteric school in this respect. One notices such hints or sarcasms in fairy stories most of which come from esoteric schools of the past and contain great depth of psychological meaning. Now a man who is identified and at the same time wishes to study for an examination will not be using the right centre. He will waste force. It seems to me that one can study nothing without inner relaxation. Some people race through a book as if they were afraid of missing something. Of course, they miss everything. On the other hand, some sit down and stare at the book, groaning and sighing or even tying wet towels round their heads. Of course they are not using Intellectual Centre but almost their very bodies and muscles to take in the subject. I knew a man at Cambridge who used to stop smoking and drinking in order to read up for his examinations, but never grasped that if he really thought about what he was reading he would not have to deny himself in this way. He failed—but always, I fancy, felt that he had made real effort. It is like jumping into the Tigris to save a brute of a mule, when your wife and family are dependent on your Army pay. Wrong effort—and especially effort to avoid effort, which is rather different—leads to enormous expenditure of force without result. But the Work teaches that we live in an intelligent Universe and have to find out what efforts give results.

Now this paper is about something that requires examples. It is for all of you to try to give examples of wrong use of centres from your personal observation.

Great Amwell House, July 3, 1948

THE UNMANIFEST EARTH AND
THE MANIFEST EARTH

WORK-IDEA

Gurdjieff speaks of the Unmanifested Earth and the Earth—that is, the Manifest Earth.

COMMENTARY

Notice, first, that the Manifest comes from the Unmanifest. Now, what can be understood when it is said that this Earth is both unmanifest and manifest? Let us speak of this question to-day, because later it will be necessary to explain some of the meanings in the fuller delineations of the Table of Hydrogens or Cosmic Scale of Being given by Gurdjieff. More than 2,000 years ago at the beginning of the impulse that gave rise to Western civilization, Plato spoke of the Universe in two ways. He divided it into the Intelligible Universe (which can only be apprehended by the Mind and so is not manifested) and the Sensory Universe (which can only be apprehended by the external senses and is manifested). *Manifest* means what we can see. I can see you *via* my senses. But I cannot see your unmanifested side—your thoughts, sensations or emotions. All these are not manifest and so are invisible to me, save perhaps indirectly through your visible expression or gestures or movements. For this reason I have often emphasized that a man, a woman, is really invisible—although one can see their visible bodies. A person, then, is both manifest and unmanifest. Actually, I have used this phrase: "We must realize that we are all invisible people living in visible bodies and we can only signal to one another distantly"—a thought well worth-while reflecting on often, if we wish to practise external considering. Also you have heard of the term I have used—namely, "psychological country". It was said that we not only live in a visible sense-given country—such as your visible room, house, town, country, etc.—but in an invisible country, which is the same for all and is far larger and is touched only interiorly. For example, if you are in a negative state you are living in a particular and bad place in your internal psychological country, although you are still in your room or house in your physical or sense-given country. Do you imagine that two people living in the same visible part of space, the same room, are

1188

necessarily in the same place in their psychological countries? How rare is this. On the manifest side they are together, on the unmanifest side they are far apart.

Everyone is at this moment in a certain place in the unmanifested Earth to begin with. He is there because of his psychological state, not because of his physical body which remains at a particular place in the manifested Earth. The politician planning a political revenge, the murderer planning a murder, the artist planning a picture, the banker planning an investment, the doctor planning an operation, may all be in the same room together, yet psychologically they are all in different places in the unmanifest Earth—that is, in the psychological world in which we all really dwell. And, mark you, it is where we are in this unmanifested world that makes or breaks our happiness. It is not a question of whether we are at the Ritz or in a low pub. Does not this take a long time for people to realize who take all reality only in terms of the senses, in terms of the seen world and one's position in it? No— it all depends on where you are in this unmanifested world and if you are in the swamps of bitterness, self-pity and negativeness, then you are in a very bad place inwardly, although surrounded by every reasonable comfort or even luxury visibly. But if you begin to understand and practise this Work you will begin to understand better about this inner unmanifest and truly enormous psychological country in which all exist and in which we have to learn how to walk carefully and what to avoid. Gurdjieff said that to Conscious Humanity we are just like silly monkeys who never understand but only imitate. And notice here that nearly all this Work is concerned with where one is inside, not outside. One may make a fuss about the price of a hat, but not at all about sitting in a psychological bath of the worst mechanical negative emotions. So notice that Evil Karma comes *below* Mechanical Action and Good Karma above it.

Now to continue about the idea of manifest and unmanifest. Notice that the Conscious Circle of Humanity is above the "Earth", the manifest Earth, and, in fact, above the unmanifest Earth. Let me give you a parallel illustration. Understand that we have in us receptive faculties that can touch far higher levels than the external senses and the Manifest Earth. The brain, sheltered by the head-bones and protected by a water-cushion, is the most marvellous radio-reception machine created, far beyond Man's imitation of it. A radio contains only a few valves. The brain contains 14,000,000,000 valves in the form of separate nerve-cells, each with some 100 connections with each other. The living population of the Earth is about 2,000,000,000 people. The brain contains living intelligent nerve-cells that roughly amount to more than seven times the population of the Earth. They are "immortal" as regards the life of the body. That is, they do not die until the man dies. The other cells, composing the body—skin, liver, muscles, etc.—number 100,000,000,000,000—that is, one hundred thousand thousand million. These cells live and die many thousands of times.

But the brain is immortal relatively. What does all this mean? Does it represent another order of things? We see that in the body taken in terms of living cells, living brick-work, there are two types— short-lived body-cells and long-lived brain-cells, not only with quite different functions but with utterly different time-bodies—that is, lengths of life. They are comparable to the Mechanical Circle of Humanity, for Man is a cell in a greater, unmanifested body. Everything is made on the same plan, small and great. In the Hermetic Writings we read: "As above, so below." If we take the Circle of Conscious Humanity as being at the level of the "Sun", in the Ray of Creation, and we ourselves at the level of the "Earth", knowing nothing about the higher level, we must also consider how the Mechanical Circle of Cells in the body knows absolutely nothing about the brain-cells, which are the Conscious Circle of Cells that controls it. They think they act from themselves, as we think we do, and imagine they can do, as we imagine we can do. To them, as to us, this level is not manifested. We, for example, can see the manifest world, but can only touch the unmanifested Circle of Conscious Humanity by special means. We can touch it only internally by inner experience, not through the exteriorized senses—through touch, sight, etc. You have heard we have far more *inner* senses than the so-called five outer senses. Yet few can believe anything as true unless their five external senses, looking outwardly at the manifest world, corroborate it. But *belief* is not sense. It is something beyond sense—in fact, *non*-sense. To believe in what you can see or touch is not belief.

Some people stay very much in the same places all their lives, in their vast, inner, unmanifested, psychological country. It is as if one lived internally in a small village and always took the same walk. Every day the same thoughts and feelings repeat themselves, every day the same attitudes are at work, the same mechanical prejudices, the same buffers, the same automatic sentences. People live and die, just the same, not seeing their task, by creation—namely, to work against their daily mechanicalness and awaken from themselves. Man was not born to be mechanical, but to become conscious. Of such a man one might say. "He could not wander far from himself, for then he felt lonely, nostalgic, and so returned to the cares and emotions of his usual self, as quickly as possible. For this reason he could never have new experiences. He often complained but never said why." Understand by this that in regard to his inner world, he was not, to say the least, an adventurer. He wished for no change of mind. He preferred to live in the smallest parts of himself and wasted his life in complaints and negative emotions.

A FURTHER NOTE ON THE TABLE OF HYDROGENS

We spoke last time about further interpretations of the Table of Hydrogens as recently given by Gurdjieff. As you have heard before, the Universe, in the teaching of the Work, is divided into different orders of intelligences. The Universe is not all on the same level but is like a ladder. These different intelligences at different levels are designated by numbers and these numbers refer to intelligent energies on different scales, termed "Hydrogens". You already know that the centres work with different energies or hydrogens. We do not work with one energy, as, say, a machine does working with paraffin, but with many different energies coarser or finer. For example, the Moving Centre works—or can work—with a Hydrogen or energy that is far "quicker" than the formatory part of Intellectual Centre. In a moment of danger, provided one is not paralysed with fear, the Moving Centre can do things far more quickly than ordinary thought—that is, the quality of thought belonging to the mechanical or formatory part of Intellectual Centre. We do not work with one energy, because we are, to begin with, several different centres each of which works best with its appropriate hydrogen or energy. Owing to the fact that one centre can hypnotize another centre, the right working of centres—that is, each centre using its appropriate energy—is interfered with. The slowest, thickest, psychic hydrogen is taken, first of all, as *Hydrogen 48*. This energy works the formatory part of Intellectual Centre and is very slow and heavy, so to speak.

The Emotional Centre works, or should work, with *Hydrogen 24*— that is, with a fine petrol as contrasted with paraffin, let us say. The Emotional Centre, for this reason, can grasp a situation far more quickly than can the plodding formatory mind, that has to have everything explained slowly to it and advances logically step by step—an exceedingly boring process when it takes place in ourselves, and extraordinarily liable to make one yawn, and yet necessary. One centre can yawn at another. Remember that each centre and part of a centre has its proper use. As long as one begins to understand that man has different centres and that these centres work with different energies and that these different energies come from higher and lower levels of the created Universe—the finer from the higher levels and the coarser from the lower levels—then one can begin to make some sense of the Table of Hydrogens as a guiding idea. Understand that things are not on one level, but on many different levels, yet each level is valuable and important. Understand also that what is on a lower level is of necessity under more laws and what is on a higher level under fewer laws. Try to reflect on this Table in terms of a ladder of ascent and descent, each rung of which is important and necessary. Try to make it stand up *vertically* in your mind. Understand, also, that False Personality, Negative Emotions, and all the rest are very low down in this scale—this scale or ladder (ladder in Latin is *scala* and so, scale)—and lead to Bad Karma which is shewn as lying *under* Mechanicalness, and close to the level of the Moon, where we find *Absolute Nothingness*. Let us conceive that one idea of Absolute Nothingness is total meaninglessness. If everything becomes meaningless that is hell.

Now I must again ask you: do you yet see that things are on higher and lower levels? I ask you to think of these following remarks and reflect on them, for otherwise you will not get any connecting idea with this strange vertical Table of Hydrogens or values. So I ask you: "Are some states of yourself better than other states?" If you say "Yes", I agree. Understand then that the better states of yourself are higher in this Table than the lower states and more intelligent, more intriguing, with more depth of meaning. The more you make lovely things cheap, the less meaning they have. This is why you must make some things sacred or holy. Again, are some books greater than other books? Or is some music greater than other music? Or again, is some wine better than other wine? Or again, is some craftmanship finer than other craftmanship, or is some art greater than other art? And so on. If you agree in general you will understand better that this Table of Hydrogens, this scale of excellences, is just, what in a sense, you know already, however dimly, only it is put in different terms. We seek in this Work better states of ourselves. If you think nothing is worthwhile, I recommend you to reflect on the worthwhileness of realising this point and trying to learn how it can be gradually attained by the discarding, the non-identifying with, useless states of oneself through a growing insight. This is the Work in action.

From what has been said, you can see that the centres of Man open on to different levels of the Universe. In this sense Man is in himself a scale or ladder, a little Universe. He has higher and lower centres to begin with. Notice that Man is created with two higher centres, not necessary for adaptation to life concerns and successful careers, but yet fully developed. These two higher centres work with *Hydrogen 6* and *Hydrogen 12*. Notice also that the Sex Centre works with *Hydrogen 12* —that is, it should do so, but it cannot if connected with self-emotions and their resulting Negative Emotions, or with Formatory Centre, which invents theories about everything. For instance, people have formatory theories about what to eat, and in this case their theories interfere with the proper work of Instinctive Centre, which knows infinitely more about the inner working of the human organism—that is, your body and all its marvellous chemistry—than any intellectual or scientific theory does. Now notice that *Hydrogen 6*, as shewn in the Scale of Hydrogens accessible to and present in Man, comes from a level above the Sun. So Man has in him possible experiences far above his ordinary earth self—and here I would say that most of us are dimly aware of this and have perhaps had momentarily such experiences.

As I indicated in the last paper we must approach this difficult Table of Hydrogens, first of all, from the standpoint of the general ideas shewn in it without going into details. Man, therefore, is stretched out, upright, on a part of this total scale of living intelligences, and his head reaches to *Hydrogen 6* in the third scale. He can, however, descend as far as the Moon and even to that other side of the Moon never seen visibly—because as you know, the Moon always shows us the same face and no one has seen the other side—called in some ancient esoteric systems "Outer Darkness", and in this Work "Absolute Nothingness". You remember that Christ said somewhere, about people who will not forgive one another, that it is best to make peace while it is possible otherwise you will be delivered to the prison house and never get out until you have paid the uttermost farthing. And you must understand that this is impossible, as what we owe is beyond computation. So you can see that this Absolute Nothingness is where the mercy of God does not reach and so Gurdjieff said about that place that there is no Holy Spirit there. In the Hermetic System this place is called Abraxas or Infinity: above all it is necessary not to fall down so far as that. Understand that *something* is finite and *nothing* is infinite, and also understand that infinite means "unfinite"—that is, you come to nothing, you meet nothing but nothingness. And so it is, as it were, opposite to creation, which is something. Notice the whole Table, which is, of course, based on the great diagram of the Ray of Creation, is similar to a machinery of things going up or down—of ascending and descending—as Jacob saw in his vision of the Ladder with God at the top. That interesting, strange, teacher called Mani, who taught a little later than Christ, quite close to where I was in Irak between the rivers Tigris and Euphrates and called, therefore, Mesopotamia—between the rivers— compared the created Universe to a vast distillery—to separate the finer from the coarser. And that is why so many of the mediaeval esoteric teachers, concealing their teaching in terms of alchemy, spoke of *distillation*, and drew retorts, furnaces, and so on in their strange diagrams. To separate this coarse from the fine is our daily task in this Work. For example, can you see a negative feeling is coarse in comparison with a pleasant, good-natured feeling? Or again, is self-love a coarser feeling than adoration? From what has been said then, we realize that from the teaching of the Work we open on to different levels of the Universe. We have to unite the higher and the lower. We realize also from the Ray of Creation that the lower we sink through bad-will, considering, self-pity, laziness, and all the rest, the more we put ourselves in prison—that is, under more and more laws. So we have to make effort of some kind and accept this, not as a task imposed by other people, who never understand us and so on, but as a fundamental factor in our creation, and appearance, in this extraordinary Universe of Scale in which anyone can either rise or fall according to his inner integrity and level of understanding.

(1) This Table makes us see how *Greater Mind* or *Intelligence* exists —on successive levels. The Work says: "Unless a man believes in Greater Mind he cannot change". I add here that even scientists now admit there is a principle of *Order* working on matter—as the development of the germinal cell into a man. Otherwise all would be chaos.

(2) The Table shews that the lower in scale is subordinate to the higher level—or rather should be—otherwise the man is upside down.

(3) Man being stretched out vertically must unite into a harmony all the levels he does and can touch. This marriage of Heaven and Hell, this uniting of higher and lower, and vice versa, is what Man was created for, and it is an individual task.

(4) Bear in mind that the Work says that one cannot remember oneself unless there is an element of acknowledgement of the existence of Greater Mind during the act. Also remember that the most important thing in the Work is remembering oneself especially when things are difficult. This makes it possible for help to reach us because help only comes down as far as the third state of consciousness—namely, the state of Self-Remembering.

Great Amwell House, July 17, 1948

THE UNMANIFEST AS CAUSE OF THE MANIFEST

Control of Unmanifest Thought

Work-Idea

The Ray of Creation and the derivative Table of Hydrogens are diagrams referring to the Scale of Being. The Universe, understood aright, is a Scale of Being, higher and lower. For example, the Being and Intelligence of the level represented by the physical Sun is at a far higher level than the Being of the Earth. Similarly, the Being and Intelligence of *Hydrogen 12* is far greater, wider, more understanding and comprehensive, than that of *Hydrogen 48*. From this it follows that anything—let us say, a work of art—into which *Hydrogen 12* enters it at a higher level than one into which only *Hydrogen 48* enters and therefore more deathless. Notice how the Gospels still conduct meaning.

Commentary

To-day we will try to consider how, in the Scale of Being, that which is at a higher level is the cause of that which is at a lower level. We have to realize that the lower cannot act on the higher but the higher can act on the lower. If it were otherwise, the whole principle of the Ray of Creation would be violated and in place of a descending order in scale there would be chaos.

Now the higher is not manifest to the lower, but the lower is manifest to the higher. Nothing takes place *in* a man without a cause from the unmanifest world, but we do not notice this. The unmanifest thought, for example, is the cause of the manifest action. The idea in the architect's mind is the cause of the house that becomes manifest. And, as the Table of Hydrogens shews, the Unmanifest Earth precedes in scale the Earth itself. Now what precedes in scale is higher than what comes after. It follows therefore that the cause of a thing is at a higher level than the thing itself. In the Ray of Creation, which is a Ladder of Being, the Absolute is the Highest and so the Supreme Cause. In the Table of Hydrogens, the Unmanifest Earth is higher in scale than the Manifest Earth. So, similarly, the *idea* of a house in the mind of the architect is at a higher level than the house that becomes manifested eventually in Time and Space. The idea becomes manifest, but in reverse order to its conception. With the complete idea of the house in his mind, the architect must start with one brick, so to speak. He must start from the smallest manifest part to reach the whole. This fact, so little grasped, causes many people to give up too easily. They have a good idea but do not calculate the second force involved in getting this idea into manifestation, which involves, as it were, a reverse process and experiment and patience. Consider the patience involved in the creation of Manifest Man—the immense cycles of experiments on animals and plant-life, etc., before Man's manifest brain and body could be fashioned. Understand that Unmanifest Man preceded Manifest Man, just as the Unmanifest Earth preceded the Manifest Earth. Remember the Essence of Man comes from the stars.

Now one can go with what is lower or higher in centres, and so all this leads us practically to the observation of centres and we will speak of Thinking Centre. All centres can work on a low level. We are told that we must observe the work of our centres and learn to distinguish between them. Now if we do not observe our thoughts they may, and do, work out into all sorts of unpleasant manifestations that we could avoid if we were more awake. A thought is unmanifest, but it leads to an action. I am using the term as signifying not visible, not tangible, not evident to the five exterior senses. An action is manifest: the cause of an action may lie in a thought that is accepted as true. I said nothing takes place in a man without a cause in the unmanifest. If a thought enters the mind—and this it does from a still higher Unmanifest—and if you identify with it, it will become the cause of some action, or pain, or illness. If you identify with a thought you accept it. If you accept it, then it has power to work out in action. That is, you sign the cheque —or, to change the analogy, you post the letter—a familiar theme in dreams. It is just like writing an actual letter and hesitating before you post it. Once you have done this, you have to pay for the consequences which are now beyond your control. Anyone can have a negative thought. But if you consent to it, and express it—that is, post it—you are under its power and all its consequences. This is worth while reflecting upon. A negative thought can enter the mind. One can, if awake, watch it—but not shake hands with it—not consent to it—but, in fact, get tired of it. Once it knows it cannot entice you, cannot put you to sleep, cannot hypnotize you—with its poor little make-up—then, no doubt it will not come into the theatre of your mind again.

Now thoughts visit, like birds, the cage of your mind. Some are wonderful. All sorts of thoughts enter your mind—on different scales—with different Being—coming from different levels in the Scale of Being. To understand all this, to be able to observe it, one must have worked hard at observing the Thinking Centre and the kinds of thoughts that enter it. Most of the thoughts that enter freely are utterly useless—mere riff-raff. Until you can see something about the quality of the thoughts that enter you will remain asleep in the Intellectual Centre. You will be the victim of everyone, of anyone. We at least have to learn to distinguish in outer life between criminals, gangsters, evil people, tramps, lunatics, and people of good-will. Yes. But internally people do not do so. Why? Because they have no idea that we are as open to violence within as we are without. We have no system of thoughts, no teaching, nothing, in fact, to know how to act inwardly. We do not know what to work on inwardly—apart from the fact that we have no idea we have an inner life that it is our task to get into order. So we have to hear, think of, and see the truth of, another kind of teaching referring to what is within. For the state of yourself inwardly makes you either in heaven or hell. So the Work says: "The mind must change first. You have to begin to think in a new way. This Work is to make you begin to think in a new way." And you will all remember that in the Gospels the same thing is taught under the word μετάνοια—that is, thinking *beyond* how you think at present—that is, change of mind. The mind cannot change without new ideas from which to think. I cannot explain to you the change of mind that comes from beholding and gradually understanding that the Universe is a Scale of Being and that the Unmanifest is the cause of the Manifest. So I advise you to notice continually your thoughts and separate from every thought that can make you negative. If you think evil, if you think negatively, it will all work out into action or illness. One can do a lot of work on the control of thought and the distinguishing between negative thought and useful thought. Every event can be taken negatively through some thought about it. Events are being offered you every moment. If your thought is unobserved, if you cannot see your thought, you will probably take every event negatively. Remember that the thought can be observed and not allowed to infect the Emotional Centre. But if it is identified with, it will rouse the negative part of Emotional Centre with all its endless miseries.

1196

ESSENCE AND PERSONALITY

WORK-IDEA

The Work teaches that there are two Neutralizing Forces or Third Forces. One is life as seen: this Third Force, this Neutralizing Force of life, keeps Personality active and Essence passive. The other force is the Work, Esoteric Teaching, which comes from a source that is not life as seen: only this Third Force can bring about the miracle of making Personality passive and Essence active.

COMMENTARY

You will understand by now that as long as the Personality, formed in us by our contact with manifest life, is active, then the inborn, real part of us, called Essence, cannot grow. A man, a woman, living only by the acquired side in themselves, the Personality, the social or business or professional side, cannot possibly have peace of mind, internal happiness, or a real centre of gravity. Why? Because the acquired Personality, which controls them because it is active, is not really themselves, but outside themselves, and depends on how others behave to them in life. For this reason they must seek endless outer changes, excitements, varieties, and praise, congratulations, and so on, to keep up this fiction of themselves that they can take as themselves and that depends on outer life. Fictional Personality, for instance, marries fictional Personality, and nothing is real, but all is a kind of pretence concealing so much tiredness. Now if you are for a moment conscious in Essence, everything is, as Gurdjieff said, richer, more vivid, more real. But no one can get back to Essence artificially. People try to do so by drugs, excitement, and so on, but this is not real. One has to pay beforehand to reach Essence aright. *Relatively* speaking, everything belonging to Essence is real and everything belonging to Personality is unreal. I say, on purpose, *relatively* real and unreal. We understand that Personality *must* be formed in us before Essence can grow beyond the stage it reaches through its own power of growth. And Essence can then only grow at the expense of Personality—that is, in my case at the expense of Dr. Nicoll or in your case at the expense of this fine man, this superior woman, called—well, called by your Christian name and surname. I would like you all to say internally your life-names. Now your name—say, Mrs. Evangeline Blessington Smith —is not you—nor is Mr. Sidmouth Clarendon Barrington—you. In fact, they are your greatest enemies and do all they can to prevent Essence from growing. And what a job it is to see this for oneself and what a job it is to try to liberate oneself from this fiction to which one is an unhappy slave all one's life. Can you not envisage Mrs. Blessington

Smith sweeping into the room now and saying: "I so much enjoyed the little paper we had last week" or Mr. Clarendon Barrington entering in a bored way and saying: "I would like to know exactly what Personality is, in a few words, as I have to go to the Palace at 9.30." Well—that is just what things are like. And all this is to illustrate what life as a Third or Neutralizing Force means and how it will inevitably keep Personality active and Essence passive. As was said many times before, the first education for us on Earth is to form a good rich Personality. The second education is to make it passive and to transmit everything valuable in it to Essence so that Essence can grow —this little boy, this little girl, in you all. There are valuable things in a good Personality but they belong, so to speak, to the attitude "I can do". It is not these good things you have learned that have to be sacrificed. It is their framework, the feeling, the identification with them, that has to be surrendered. As long as a man, a woman, ascribe to themselves all their excellent qualities, Essence cannot grow. Consider this idea and reflect on it. One has to begin to see that, in the larger scale and meaning of things, one does not really know how one thinks or moves or feels. Now the Personality, which is governed by the False Personality, will have none of that nonsense. It says: "*I* did it", "*I* thought it", "*I* conceived it", and so on. And so everyone is jealous and hates others and rushes into print, and is all day offended, and spends a life-time of grievances in explaining how one was overlooked and so on. Yes—notice where you are offended and try to observe why.

Now if anything grows in the soil of Essence instead of in the soil of Personality everything is quite different. Growth in the soil of Essence is real. A man only quarrels owing to a sense of unrealness, his inner lostness. What is real in oneself never quarrels or argues about anything. And since Personality is tinctured with what is acquired from life and so not quite real, not your own, people quarrel. But who has what is of Essence does not wish to quarrel with anyone because it is real—and so *is so*. The source of the so-called inferiority complex is the Personality and especially its controlling power, the False Personality. If Essence develops there can be no sense of inferiority. How could there be? We are all inferior to ourselves because we are in Personality and not in Essence when something is not quite real—say, in what you say, or pretend to be. And what can any of us say is real? The more you blow yourself out, like that toad in the fairy-story, the more unreal and unhappy you will feel and the more touchy and dramatic you will be, and so on. Why? Because it is all pretence, artificial, not real. A touchy person is necessarily a person who feels unreal. Do you agree? Well, consider this in yourself through self-observation. Notice *where* you are touchy—then observe what it is you are so touchy about. Yes —this belongs to real self-observation.

Now Essence cannot grow from what is unreal. What is essential, what is real, cannot be touchy. If you really understand something, you are not touchy—but I admit this is a difficult matter to unravel. People who *think* they know, like doctors, or scientists, are very touchy. Still, you must admit that you are not touchy about—well, what? What can you say you are not touchy about? An interesting line of self-observation. I wonder if any of us are not, under certain circumstances, touchy about almost everything. I would only say that the difference between your picture of yourself and your actual capability makes you touchy—makes everyone extremely touchy.

As I said, we are touchy about what we are not, but pretend we are, and this makes violence. But you must understand this Work is directed unto ourselves and that as long as violence, jealousy, hatred and all the rest reign in us, we cannot awaken—unless we become conscious of it —and we are no use in regard to the Conscious Circle of Humanity to which no man or woman can get either by bullets, knives, guns, or muscles, or by violent hatreds, by fanatical fury, or by any mediaeval device of that kind. We must remember that the Work speaks of *Consciousness* as its supreme object all the time—of becoming more conscious of oneself—that is, the kind of person one really is apart from the dressed-up person—it speaks of the idea that we have to become far more conscious of the other person—in fact, see the other person in oneself. When you kill, you and the killed are the same. When you vilify, you and the vilified are the same. In the Esoteric Dance that Christ taught his disciples, the phrases are:

"I would be saved, and I would save.
I would be loosed, and I would loose.
I would be wounded, and I would wound.
I would be born, and I would bear.
I would eat, and I would be eaten.
I would hear, and I would be heard.
I would be thought, being wholly thought.
I would be washed, and I would wash."

(*The Apocryphal Acts of John*)

Certainly, a strange dance, and also certainly far deeper than we think. But at least we can see it is becoming conscious in two forces—in opposites—in yourself and in the other person. The Work teaches that we must first become conscious in one force—that is, we must observe what we are and wish for—then in two forces, and finally in three forces.

Now Essence, since it comes from the stars, is at a higher level than Personality which is formed in us by life on the manifest Earth. Essence, being therefore a higher thing, is a much more real thing. Yet it is undeveloped—a child that has to be taught, at the expense of Personality. You will say: "How can the lower teach the higher—the higher by origin in scale?" I will answer you and say that the Personality— the lower—cannot teach Essence, the higher, unless the Work enters Personality. Then the Work, coming from outside, from what you hear and learn, will speak to Essence from Personality. It may have been that once Essence could be taught the Work directly from within, from Higher Centres. Nowadays, in the world of sleepers, the Work must come from outside, from schools in the world, and so enter first the Personality. This is why one task of Esoteric Humanity was to raise culture to a degree in which people could hear and understand enough to take in the Work. The Personality had to be built up, by education, by all the arts, sciences, literature and so on, to make it possible for mankind to grow and keep open a connection between "Sun" and "Earth"— or, if you use the language of the Gospels—between Heaven and Earth. For once Man falls totally asleep, he will be no longer of any use and will be swept aside or made to destroy himself by wars. Man comes at a critical point in our Ray of Creation—at the shock *Fa-Mi*—and he is so complex just because he was designed to keep a connection between higher and lower, to be a Nitrogen or Third Force between the upper and lower parts of the Ray. This idea helps a person to remember himself—that is, to pass from an animal into a MAN.

Great Amwell House, July 31, 1948

FURTHER NOTE ON WORK-EFFORT

It seems possible to say that we have, in general, many wrong ideas about making Work-effort. We think of effort as something difficult, comparable to always climbing steep, rocky mountain-sides, choosing the worst, eating dry crusts, standing when you can sit, wearing, so to speak, sack-cloth and ashes, and so on. I do believe that Work-effort is intelligent and is based on what one has observed in oneself, in the light of the Work-teaching. Right effort is not like the clown in a circus making useless effort to assist. We laugh at him. But is not the clown, indeed, a picture of us? No, right effort comes from the understanding, from seeing what it is necessary at any particular time to work upon in oneself, and so, often, it is something quite simple and quite easy. It is like finding the right switch or using the right key. Do you realize that years of wrong effort are useless and worse and that such effort is incommensurable with a single moment of right insight and right effort? I sometimes think that one of the tragical things about some religious people is that they have made wrong effort all their lives and so distorted and harrowed their whole character that they have become crystallized in negative sides of themselves.

Now, in this connection, one example of intelligent effort is to cease to believe in a fixed opinion, and let other viewpoints come in. This is right effort on oneself and will make some growth of Being possible. You must understand that a person full of fixed attitudes, acquired buffers, and mechanical prejudices is in prison. He incarcerates himself in the prison of his own mechanical psychology. He lives and dies in this prison, unless rescued by psychological truth. We are, of course, all in prison, and the Work is to shew us how to *begin* to get out. I say, *begin* to get out. But if a person does not try to begin to get out, if he remains a mechanical man, he will not be helped, and by himself he cannot get out.

Now, to speak briefly of effort, To *remember oneself* is the rightest effort a person can make. This effort has nothing to do with groans and sighs and sour faces, nor has it anything to do with labouring up mountain-sides, as it were, or patiently suffering in loud silence in a corner, or anything like that. No, the effort of Self-Remembering is just like fitting something to what fits it. It is like making a connection and holding it. It is not forgetting but remembering to make this connection a few times a day or even once. And, as I have often said, begin by trying to stop everything—movement, thought, tension, feeling, strain—let everything go—and maybe you will catch a glimpse of Self-Remembering. You know you cannot remember yourself if you are glued to life. In trying to *stop* everything, you are stopping all that glues you to life. This exercise can totally change you in a flash. It makes connection with what seeks to help you—to lead you out of prison. You cannot reflect on this possible miracle enough. But constantly *thinking* about your cares and problems and what to do is exactly wrong effort and will make you identify more. You are then like a person who wishes, so to speak, to drag a ship up to the top of a mountain. Of what use is such an effort? Do you think you can sail in the snow on a mountain-top?

Now intelligence is first defined in the Work as the power of *adaptation*. To try to bring things to what *you* want or *think* right, instead of getting off your perch and seeing how to deal with things, is useless effort. How many people I have noticed during my long years in the Work who have a similar expression—that is, the hard determined look of making things conform to what they think right. Such people do not yet understand this Work—that is, they do not make effort from their understanding of the Work, but from what they, by acquired values, buffers, attitudes, and all the rest, understand is right. The Work is to shew you another kind of what is right. Why, they are like people who think the sun goes round the Earth and start from the Ptolemaic idea. And, standing on the Earth of themselves—that is, what they think right—they wish to make, not only the whole Cosmos, but everything in their daily life, including the Work itself, to swing round and obey them. It is a good thing to begin to see what it means to obey the Work. Otherwise so much effort will be quite stupid, quite useless, and even ridiculous—like hauling ships on to tops of mountains and so on. And here comes in the recognition of one's own nothingness and the idea that Man cannot do. We have therefore to think in a practical sense, about right Work-effort.

While writing this short paper, for instance, I found myself crossed inside—as if there were cobwebs. By going back in my mind, I found I had not answered a letter which I should have answered and that the reason I had not was because of a slight negative emotion. So I answered it. This is a very small example of right Work-effort at the right time. You may all say that this is too easy. Well, is it so easy to observe? Some will say they have no time for that kind of triviality. Well, it is just on those so-called trivial things that your well-being and inner states depend and I can assure you that this is so. It is like so many things said in that Esoteric Work called the Gospels. How many times are you told there to make peace, to forgive, while you are in the way, to cancel things, before you proceed to anything further? All this is about right effort. You know how laying up every day rather unpleasant things belongs to that tremendously important thing called in the Work "your inner accounts". It is just like anything else. You are travelling in a ship and only have to give in signed chits. They seem small. But when presented they often stagger you. You had no idea you owed so much. Now, if we could learn to make effort in this kind of thing, our efforts would be more intelligent. So you can glimpse the idea that right effort is not climbing mountains or hauling ships on to the top, or sitting in sackcloth and ashes or anything of that kind.

Now a last note on this question. Do you recollect that you are told in the Gospels that when you make effort you must not shew it?

You must not make it painfully—and how painfully—obvious to everyone that, say, you are not speaking to-day, or not eating bread, or not going to the usual lavatory, or not wearing your best dress, and so on. Now in the Gospels many things are said about not "shewing off". Why? Because it all goes into the False Personality. So when you make effort, do it in secret, and shew nothing outside. On reflecting on this, I have often thought that effort that shews *outside*—such as sackcloth, crusts, never sitting down, etc.—must inevitably be *wrong effort*. And I have already said how wrong effort—and I speak also of the Work— may lead a man, a woman, into a worse situation than life would have led them into. Effort is in secret. Effort is to do with *you* and the extent of revelation of the Work in you. Effort is in secret between you and your understanding of the Work. Effort is not making things do what you think is right. It is not hauling ships on to mountain-tops. It is not altering others to suit your idea of what they should be. It is not standing high in yourself and making the Sun turn round you. Effort is realizing that you need a great deal to make you less unhappy. Effort is observing calmly what attitudes and cruelties in your outlook make you all wrong with your life. And right effort begins with self-observa- tion and continues into Self-Remembering. Pray that you can under- stand and make *these* efforts instead of thinking that effort means something totally useless.

BUFFERS, PICTURES AND WORK-SHOCK

WORK-IDEA

We are born awake and without inner contradictions. It is all very tiny. We grow up among sleeping people who have ceased to see their own contradictions because they have formed buffers. So, instead of having Real Conscience, we form buffers too and also fall asleep—in fact, very early. If all people had no buffers, they would have Real Conscience, and no war, violence, lying and so on, would exist.

COMMENTARY

No one can observe a buffer without self-observation and the special memory that comes from self-observation. A man, a woman, must begin to become conscious of certain kinds of contradictions in themselves. Buffers are artificial things, that prevent the shocks of contradictions from coming home. They prevent us from seeing what we imagine from False Personality we are and did and said, and what we actually are and did and said. Now, without observation, a man cannot change. Always clearly see this. Always meditate on this. If you do not observe yourself you cannot be different. A man must *suffer* from his observation of himself, but never become negative. A complacent man, heavily buffered, with pictures of himself, will tend to think the Work is good for other people, but that it is not connected with himself in any serious way. Owing to the action of buffers, whereby he does not see contradictions in himself, and the continual activity of self-justifying that goes on in connection with buffers, and the hypnotic effect of pictures of himself, a man, a woman, may pass years, even all their years, in the Work, without yet seeing how it applies to them *here* and *now*. That is, they remain asleep even though the Work is trying to waken them at every moment. "To shift from where you are", Gurdjieff said, "it is necessary to divide yourself into an observed and an observing side."

Now for everyone without exception it will take a very long time to see what one is, apart from imagination. This is merciful. As Gurdjieff said: "If a man's buffers were suddenly destroyed, then he would see all the contradictions in himself. He would then go mad." You must try to see that some people (naturally I am not speaking to any of you) attribute to themselves, say, great kindness. They live on one side of a buffer. This is a picture. They can easily hate, but excuse themselves. They attribute to themselves great efficiency, the capacity to deal with every situation—and actually are stupid. Or it may be they attribute to themselves steadiness, calmness, and so on. Now it would take a long time to enumerate all the virtues that people (naturally, of course,

I am not speaking of ourselves) attribute to themselves. On the flimsiest grounds people attribute good qualities—that is, what they esteem as virtues—to themselves. So they rest in themselves, on pictures, which prevent them from seeing the other side of the buffer. Such people are not yet tested. What is real in oneself can never become a cause of being upset or become a picture. We had a paper on this point recently, where it was recommended that one should notice where one became touchy. It was said that one is always touchy about something that is not real in oneself—some pretence—that is, some picture. A picture is a form of imagination about oneself—that does not correspond with the reality of oneself. It does not take in the opposite side —that is, the side on the other side of the buffer. A buffer stands like a wall between two sides that contradict each other. "No one," said O., "can grow if they are nothing but a mass of buffers." He added that once a buffer is destroyed, it can never form itself again. He also said that Gurdjieff taught that as long as we live by means of buffers that prevent us from seeing contradictions, Real Conscience can never open to us. Acquired Conscience is quite different. Real Conscience is the same for all people.

Now to-day I am speaking of pictures in connection with buffers. One can see the agreeable, even wonderful, side of oneself, being so good, tactful and kind, and all the rest. Let us observe ourselves a little deeper than that sort of surface psychology. I say, for all the heavens' sake, let us go deeper—even so far as seeing *the other side of the picture* that we cling to—that is, the other side of the buffer—this intervening wall that lies between our imagination, what we imagine, and what we are, and keeps us comfortable and prevents Real Conscience from touching us. This *dark* side—that is, not acknowledged, not conscious, side—must be mixed with the other side. Yes—very disturbing it is to be touched by Real Conscience. It is indeed merciful that we have plenty of buffers and pictures to stifle it—especially as it has little or nothing to do with our ideas of what it is to be good, kind, patient, right, calm, tolerant, and all the rest of the things that the False Personality prides itself on possessing and ascribes to itself. Only the realization of one's own nothingness, in its first rather terrible visitation, can make you understand what I mean here—when you begin to realize there is practically *nothing* in you that is worth anything under the incandescent light of Real Conscience. So it seems that the object of the Work is—how shall I put it?—well, say, to shake us up a little bit—to shift us a little bit —to make us think in a new way a little bit—to make us see ourselves a little more differently. Yes—that is putting it very nicely. It is such a long process, is it not? It is certainly what the Work is about— namely, it is about *you* and about *you* changing even a little bit. But how we resent being given even a little shake—a small shock. How pictures, buffers, self-justifying, and the giants of pride and vanity, and all the hosts of False Personality gather their forces together and hiss and spit and are outraged, offended, at the very suggestion

that one is not the most perfect example of manhood and woman-
hood on this Earth. Just notice for yourself, say, when you are given
a little shock.

Great Amwell House, August 21, 1948

ON BEING UNDER DIFFERENT LAWS

Work-Idea

It is necessary to work against mechanicalness. Try to observe
your mechanicalness—otherwise you will remain under the Law of
Accident.

Commentary

A mechanical man cannot mechanically become a Conscious Man.
The consciousness of a Conscious Man does not happen mechanically.
A mechanical man remains a mechanical man all his life unless he
begins to work on himself and give himself the necessary shocks to
awaken. A man may be mechanically a good or a bad man. But in
either case he is a mechanical man—a machine. Now the Work says
that as such he is not under the Law of his Fate, but under the Law of
Accident. There are different orders of laws that Man can be under.
Lowest is the Law of Accident. This includes all mechanical people,
good or bad in the ordinary sense. Of this teaching, as originally given,
Gurdjieff said: "A man may be under the Law of Accident: or he may
be under the Law of his Fate: or he may be under the Law of Will."
He added: "A man—that is, a real Man, a conscious Man—is under
the Law of Will." On another occasion, when he said that Humanity
in general is under the Law of Accident, he was asked about psychology.
He said: "A mechanical man has no psychology. He is a machine.
He reacts always in the same way to any external stimulus. A machine
has no psychology. How could a machine have a psychology? Only
a man who begins to know himself and work on himself can be said
to begin to have a psychology. And if a man has Real 'I', and so Real
Will, then indeed has he a psychology." Gurdjieff was asked how a
man could pass from the Law of Accident to the Law of Fate. He said,
in so many words: "Only by a growth of Essence, which is what belongs
to him. A machine-man, a mechanical man, reacts from Personality,
which does not belong to him. Personality is under more laws than
Essence. To speak briefly," Gurdjieff went on, "Personality is under
48 orders of laws and False Personality under 96, Essence is under
24 orders of laws, and a right development and growth of Essence can
lead even further, say, to a man being under only 12 orders of laws

1205

—that is, under the laws of the Sun. Then," added Gurdjieff, "he is under the Law of Will."

Now, on hearing this, I have thought many and many times this: What puts us *obviously* under the Law of Accident? From what Gurdjieff said in regard to Essence and Personality, it is clear that a man has two things in him: what is his and what he thinks is his. Ouspensky said: "It is a question of what is real and what is unreal. Essence is the real part in comparison with which Personality is unreal. There is always what belongs to a man and what does not belong to a man. A growth of what belongs to a man means a development of Essence. A growth of what does not really belong to a man means a growth of Personality." Now if I ask this question of myself: "What puts me obviously under the Law of Accident?" I might answer it theoretically on the basis of what has been said above, by saying that it must be everything in me that does not really belong to me. Why? Because what really belongs to me has to do with my Essence, and Essence, we are told, is under the Law of Fate and not under Accident. Let me make this clearer. Essence is what belongs to you. Personality is what you have acquired from contact with external life. Only from what belongs to you can there be a growth of Essence. For example, if I have to learn a subject I am not intended to, in order to pass an examination, the result will not be a growth of Essence—that is, of what belongs to me—but a growth of Personality. Notice here the strange idea—strange, at least, at first sight—that by straining yourself in a direction that does not belong to you, you will pass more and more under the Law of Accident. You may then find yourself in a part of your inner vast psychological country that is really foreign to you or even hostile.

Now in these Commentaries of mine, I will now say that a growth of what belongs to one—that is, a growth of one's Essence—signifies a growth of one's understanding, for understanding belongs to you, and that a growth of understanding signifies a growth of consciousness. It is wrong to petrify the mind with the image of consciousness as simply a thing in itself—a thing termed "consciousness". The term "consciousness" has no meaning unless it is a consciousness of something, and in saying this I am aware of a certain state of consciousness, which seems to have no content, which, however, I have noticed has a content comparable to the feeling of 'I' freed from external bonds—that is, freed from identifying.

Now a development of consciousness is a development of meaning. It is, as Ouspensky said, in speaking of inner octaves, seeing a thousand things where one only saw one thing. It is seeing a thousand connections where one formerly saw only one connection. It is seeing a thousand distinct meanings where one only perceived one meaning. It is this growth of inner richness that denotes an increase of consciousness. Consciousness is light. An increase of consciousness illuminates more and more. Instead of seeing only the table you see the whole room in which it stands and then you see the house in which the room is and so on. So, therefore, an increase of consciousness is that which makes you think more and more *relatively*. Relative thinking, as O. defined it, is seeing the part in relation to the whole and not seeing the part only, as isolated. A narrow soul, with a few acquired and fixed judgments, will pass an unhappy life always judging from some very small part, some detail, acquired by Personality. This will very much hinder the action of the Work. The entry of the Work into us—that is, the influences of Higher Centres—can only be perfect when we realise our own total nothingness—when, that is, we perceive through long, uncritical and sincere observation that we really do not know anything and really are nothing like what we imagine, and all the rest, of which we so often speak in these conversations here. But this realization cannot be reached by oneself—otherwise it is an affair of self-pity and negative emotion. It is given—in flashes. It is, in fact, close to a positive emotion which, as you know, is only given us as a reward and which is something none of us can create in ourselves. No, a positive emotion is a reward. What we call a "positive" emotion is harnessed to negative emotion so that in mechanical life love and hate are nearly indistinguishable. But a positive emotion has no opposite and can never become evil hate. In Higher Centres there are no opposites. And let me say here the more difficult and despising you are the more opposites will be in you —a remark, I fancy, good for us all, especially those who imagine by a picture of themselves that they are full of loving-kindness, and who, if hit a little shrewdly, become devils of hatred, contempt, revenge and all the rest. In this connection, on one occasion, some twenty years ago, I said to Ouspensky: "Why don't you begin to work on X? He would be quite valuable." He said: "Yes—but I will not do so. He would cost too much blood. At first I would satisfy his ambition. Then he would hate me and I would have endless trouble." Then Ouspensky cocked an eye at me and said: "I have had enough trouble with you." Now you must admit that this was like that eating of a little book, I think, in Revelation, which was sweet in one place and bitter in another.

Now, to return to the question of growth of Essence, we can see that all growth of understanding signifies a growth of Essence and a growth of consciousness. If you work over many, many years, and keep hold on the rope of the Work, very gradually you will notice that your understanding of the ideas of the Work is becoming wider and wider. And, looking back, you will see that what you thought was self-observation was not. You realize that you were, without knowing it, playing with flat, two-dimensional things, which gradually turn into three- and then finally into four-dimensional things. You will then perhaps, to take a single example, see what it means that your Being has a mass of buffers, pride, vanity, fixed attitudes, pictures, lies, acquired false values, and so on, that you actually took as final truth —and that you knew nothing and so could not be talked to, because if you had been, everything would have been caught in the wrong way by your tiny understanding. The single example I mentioned is this. You have all heard that unless buffers are destroyed you cannot hear Higher Centres or have Real Conscience. Yes. Now you may *know* both sides of a buffer but you cannot carry your *consciousness* from one side to the other. So the buffer remains. To know and to be conscious are not the same. At some other time we may speak of this further.

Now we turn to easier examples of what puts you under the Law of Accident. I will add only one thing: if you think by now you know all about the Work, give this self-complacent spot up completely. Pack your bag and begin to move to another place in your inner psychology. It is said there are so many dangers in the Work. I have listened to these dangers. By way of commentary I will add the terrific, the terrible danger of thinking that you already know all about the Work and sitting flat and probably going bad.

Now the Work is to live it and just as you have to live ordinary life so you have to go on living this life of the Work, which never ends.

Great Amwell House, August 28, 1948

ON IDENTIFYING WITH YOUR PART IN LIFE

WORK-IDEA

The Work teaches that whatever we do consciously belongs to us and whatever we do mechanically is lost to us.

COMMENTARY

One can live one's life consciously or mechanically. To do anything consciously means that one is not identified: to do the same thing mechanically means that one *is* identified, in which case it is rather that the thing does you than that you do the thing. In order to understand the Work and re-understand it and again re-understand it and so on, over and over again, until the Works stands upright in one's Being like a tree and brings everything into right order and relation and so into harmony—in order to understand the Work, it is useful to remind oneself frequently of the illustrations given by way of commentary. Take the illustration that we are all down here on this planet, each with a part to play, but we have all fallen asleep and instead of playing our part as an actor does, we have taken the part as ourselves. That is, we have identified with our part and so become it—for to identify means to make yourself the same as, which is much the same as saying to become something that is not you.

1208

Imagine an actor who, dressed as a king on the stage, suddenly thinks he is actually a king, and walks out in his robes and crown into the street. It is something like what has happened to Humanity. Once awake, it fell asleep. And in teaching that Humanity is asleep the Work adds that as long as Humanity remains asleep nothing can be done to make things better on this Earth. Man must awaken from sleep. But although Humanity as a whole remains asleep and cannot awaken, individual people can try to awaken from sleep and may succeed. Now to begin to take your life consciously is one way of beginning to awaken. For example, if you do not go with your negative emotions at a particular moment, there will be a loss on one side and a gain on the other. The mechanical side will lose force and there will be a gain on the conscious side. This struggle is always going on in a person who begins to understand the Work practically. Whenever you do not go with your mechanical reaction to life and people, there is a gain of force on the conscious side. You are then taking your life consciously instead of mechanically as everyone else does. As the Work-Idea quoted at the beginning of this paper says: "Whatever we do consciously is ours, but what we do mechanically is lost." You will see, in the light of this remark, that in the case of two men leading much the same lives outwardly, one ends up with nothing and the other with much. Why? Because the first man lets his part play him, while the second man plays his part consciously. The first man was not conscious of what he was doing, the second was conscious, even though both of them were doing the same thing. Now you do not have to go into a monastery or ascend a physical mountain to live your life more consciously. This Work, this method of awakening, is for those *in life*, and life furnishes the material to work on. But here comes in a difficulty that may take years to see and that some hardly ever see. It is not exactly that external life furnishes the material to work on, although this is true. It is rather that the way you take external life is the material to work on. Life is a changing kaleidoscope of events, always turning. The difficulty is that people take life and their reactions to life as the same thing. They find it difficult to realize that the same incident in outer life, such as a thunderstorm, is not the same as their mechanical reaction to it, and does not affect everyone in the same way as it affects them. That is, the storm, which is part of outer life at the moment, and is a neutral, impersonal thing, and their mechanical reactions to it, which are personal, say, alarm, seem identical to them. Can you grasp what is meant? Some people enjoy storms. A storm —that is, an event in life—can produce different reactions in different people. Well, it is upon these mechanical reactions in oneself that one must begin to work by practising non-identifying and all the Work teaches. So you will see that it is not exactly identifying with external life and its continual procession of different troubles and complexities called events that one has to work upon but upon how one takes these events and incidents and troubles. That is, upon how one mechanically reacts to them. But, as was said, few people reach this idea save after long years.

Now people who have heard all this before say: "What is our part in life? How do we know what it is?" The answer is this: at first everything that happens to you is your part and you have to do it consciously, deal with it consciously, as if it were something told you to act on the stage. Later you will see what belongs to the Law of Accident and what to the Law of Fate. But at present begin by taking everything that comes to you as *work*—that is, not identifying (if you can), remembering yourself, not thinking that it is someone's fault, and so hating, etc. A little well-formed ship, riding up and down the waves of life, is a good illustration of what has to be done eventually to understand why we are on Earth—that is, not to identify with all the troubles that come. Some people think that life should be wonderful. But life cannot be so, because there is always Second Force—force of opposition to what you want. If you are wise, you begin to see it is no one's fault, say, as husband and wife, etc., that things do not go as you think they should. I often think that badly life-trained people think they are entitled to happiness without understanding that it has to be earned by hard work on oneself. People are becoming even more asleep than used to be the case.

Great Amwell House, September 4, 1948

FURTHER NOTES ON SELF-OBSERVATION

OBSERVATION OF DEPRESSION IN CENTRES

WORK-IDEA

Man is not one but a multiplicity. He has not one mind but several minds. He has not one 'I' but very many 'I's.

COMMENTARY

In order to get to know themselves, a man, a woman, *must observe* themselves. Without self-observation there can be no self-knowledge. People, of course, imagine they know themselves and live in this illusion. It is precisely this illusion that prevents them from realizing that they do not know themselves and that in place of self-knowledge they have imaginary pictures of themselves which do not resemble themselves as they really are and which only complicate their lives with pretences and lead them in a hundred and one wrong directions. Nursing these pictures of themselves, as it were, like precious dolls, they rarely catch even a glimpse of themselves, and, if they do, they hug their dolls more closely. In saying all this, I am not exaggerating. This is what Gurdjieff taught and after many years in the Work I know its truth. We live with the most ridiculous ideas of ourselves and as a result we cannot change, cannot grow, and so cannot understand anything new. Everyone stands before a mirror most of the day. Have you noticed this? But it is not a mirror really. A real mirror distorts nothing and reflects without criticism exactly what is before it. It is this mirror that we need—a real, objective mirror and not an imaginary one. But how many could survive having their imaginary mirror, whether self-flattering, or self-pitying, or self-debasing, taken away and replaced by a true one? Would we not all go mad when we saw everything in us exactly as it is? A man must needs penetrate very far into himself before he could bear such an experience. His consciousness of what is in him would have to be vastly enlarged. His self-knowledge would have to be deep and genuine, based on long, uncritical self-observation—and then, of course, if this were the case, his whole idea and sense and feeling of himself would have changed, so much so that he might already be in sight of Real 'I' which is our own true goal, and he might even catch a glimpse of the Master behind Real 'I'. Let us clearly grasp that there can be no approach to Real 'I' if one is stuffed with illusions, lies and pretences about oneself.

Now, as regards self-observation, people do not follow what the Work teaches. Take, for instance, depression. People in the Work say, just as people in life say: "I feel depressed", and think they have observed themselves. Well, they have not. They have not begun to observe themselves. If you wish to observe what you may unthinkingly call depression, you have to observe from where it arises. From what part of the machine is it coming? From which centre? For instance, it may be coming from the Intellectual Centre. You will say: "How can depression originate in the Intellectual Centre? Surely depression must always arise from the Emotional Centre". Well, if you say that, you certainly have not observed yourself. The Emotional Centre may be quite cheerful and yet you are aware of depression existing somewhere in you. Now, if you cannot get used to the idea that you are not one single, unvarying person, but a multiplicity of 'I's and so of contradictions, you will never understand. One part of oneself may be cheerful and another part depressed. "How," you will say, "can such a thing happen? *I* am either cheerful *or* depressed." In that case you think of 'I' as one thing and so all along your career in the Work you will make the most elementary blunders both in understanding yourself and in understanding the Work, because you cannot see or acknowledge that you are not one but many. A loss of prestige is certainly involved here. "Noble fellow"—yes, but I fear that this "noble fellow" is a picture. "Perfect honesty and virtue"—yes, but I fear that this "perfect honesty and virtue" is a picture. "Utter integrity"—yes, but

I fear the same thing again. So, seeing through your own bluff, as it were, you cease stalking about full of nobleness, honesty, virtue and integrity. Actually, we are quite different from our pictures—and indeed, far more interesting. Yes, we do steal jam still. Yes, we do lie, and so on. Yet—and is it not strange?—you can watch people becoming old and dried up because they still nurse their dead dolls, still cling to what is not themselves, and so lose all possible contact with the essential springs of their real existence. In such a case, the Personality has conquered—particularly with the aid of the False Personality. You can see a great many people in this situation every day if your mental eyes are opened to the inner state and level of others. It is especially interesting to watch when a person stops and pitches camp for good in this long, strange, psychological journey called the Work. They meet a small difficulty and halt and settle down. There are some interesting parables about this. And it is all because of these false pictures of themselves that they worship and cling to.

Now one source of depression is obviously these pictures. So in observing the origin of depression you must observe whether it comes from a picture that has been injured by some chance remark. Of course, you will not be able to observe the picture directly, because it is imaginary. But you will be able to observe the remark, and from that, after perhaps many years, gradually deduce the picture that dominates you and prevents you from escaping from its narrow jealous power. I remind you here of what was said recently about touchiness and noticing what makes you touchy—a very useful and practical form of self-observation.

Now, to return to observing depression—as was said, it can originate from different centres. It may, for example, be due to Instinctive Centre borrowing force owing to a slight infection. It may arise from the Intellectual Centre—and certainly often does in the case of women perhaps more than with men, but I do not know. Intellectual depression is a very well-marked form of depression and is not primarily due to the Emotional Centre. The worst depression possible originates in the Emotional Centre itself, only here again are many forms involving different parts of the Emotional Centre. Depression centred in the moving part of Emotional Centre is common enough and is merely a kind of boredom. Depression arising from the emotional part of the Emotional Centre tends to violence. Depression arising from the intellectual part of Emotional Centre is dangerous because it is connected with a loss of faith in God, taking God here as the source that gives us our daily bread—i.e., our daily supply of meaning for our existences. Then there is the depression that comes from people giving up some of their usual interests and sources of meaning, from some wrong aim. To give up a source of meaning without having another to take its place is to tamper ignorantly with the balance of the machine. Remember, we are taught in the Work that the First Conscious Shock can be given safely—it does not tamper with the machine. Reflect here on all that the First Conscious Shock means. Then again there is the depression that comes from allowing old stereotyped 'I's to criticize Work-'I's—the old criticizing the young in oneself—which is an ancient theme in myths—as Kronos or Time eating his children.

All that has been said is to shew how wide self-observation must become and how silly it is to say, for instance: "I am depressed", and leave it like that. One at least can begin by asking oneself: "What 'I' is depressed?" But in this paper, which is more about centres, I cannot go into this aspect of self-observation dealing with 'I's. Suffice to say that 'I's live in every part and sub-division of the different minds or centres in our machines. But I will add that we may be haunted by an evil 'I' that seeks to drag everything down into despair and meaninglessessness. Well, watch and observe this evil 'I' continually.

Great Amwell House, September 11, 1948

A NOTE ON VIOLENCE

Work-Idea

A man cannot "do" unless he overcomes violence. Violence always breeds violence. "Doing" by means of violence is not "doing". All history, which is a history of crime, shews how violence cannot "do" in the Work sense. War follows war.

Commentary

On one occasion Ouspensky shewed us clearly that from the esoteric point of view everything had to be done through the realization of *how* to do things and this enabled one not to act violently. He said this does not mean acting from the sentimental reason of not forcing people but from the standpoint of understanding how useless it was. In this connection he said how the virtuous behaviour of people is mechanical or sentimental because it is done merely for the sake of the behaviour itself, and not with the knowledge of why such behaviour might be necessary. On many occasions he spoke of mechanical behaviour as distinct from conscious behaviour. A man, say, is trained to behave in a certain way. In the case of mechanical behaviour, this man behaves therefore as he *must* do, as he cannot help doing. It is mechanical, whether it is good or bad behaviour. He may imagine he could behave otherwise, but when the situation arises he behaves as he always does. Conscious behaviour is only possible when a person has observed and separated from mechanical behaviour which lies in Personality. A conscious man behaves from his understanding of what is necessary. Possessing Will, he can *will* his behaviour. But a mechanical man is governed from outside—that is, by external circumstances—and so cannot *will* his behaviour in any particular situation from an independent source within. Now as long as a man is governed from outside he will not be able to overcome violence. Ouspensky said: "Violence is an emotional state in all people—doing things with violence, trying to impose upon others, coerce them, and so on."

Now notice that Ouspensky said that violence is the emotional state of all people and reflect on what that means. People do not think they rest ultimately on violence. Yet regard what happens in life *now*, and historically. Who is the man or the woman who can say that their basis does not rest on violence? You may have charming pictures of being charming. Well, I advise you to look more deeply. And here I would add this: How can we conceive a person not ultimately based on violence—a man, a woman, that nothing would make violent? And so for a moment let us reflect on an early conversation of Ouspensky's about what a *Conscious* Man might be as apart from a highly developed *Mechanical* Man in life. In thinking of a Great Man, a Conscious Man, we tend to think of a larger Life-Man. He would be a larger man simply—a larger Mechanical Man—a giant, so to speak. But this is a quite wrong idea of what a Conscious Man would be, because a Conscious Man is a *different* man from a Mechanical Man. He is not larger, stronger, more wealthy, and so on. He is an *utterly different* kind of man. He is a man not based on violence. That is, he is a man of another kind, who is not interested in or affected by what interests or affects a Mechanical Man. In fact, he might appear a very ordinary man. Yet ruffle even his hair and he does not mind, because he is passive to violence. Violence does not govern him—and so there is nothing in him to catch hold of—no jealousy, no envy, no hatred, and so on. Why? Because he is a *different* man from us and his centre of gravity is not outside him. Is he then imperturbable? Why, if the house is falling down in an earthquake, he would probably run out of it first. Yet he is not *based* on violence. We can therefore, at our small level of understanding the Work and what the difference is between a Mechanical Man and a Conscious Man, realize that a Conscious Man never acts from violence, and so, in this exercise of self-study, observe the part that violence plays in us and from this deduce whether we are near the Conscious Circle of Humanity or not.

Now, as Ouspensky taught, violence, from the esoteric standpoint, is useless. What does the esoteric standpoint mean? It means that from the standpoint of the Conscious Circle of Humanity, from which comes all esoteric or inner teaching, violence is the sign of a Mechanical Man—and a Mechanical Man, however many rituals and creeds he follows, is incapable of reaching a high level of Being unless he has worked, and again worked, on his violence. Understand, there are no results through violence. Violence breeds violence with all its hatreds, revenges, jealousies, envies, and so on. Is this not a formidable factor to face in one's work on oneself? I would say so from my own experience with myself—and I hope you understand that we have experiences in life and experiences with ourselves, and they are different, and the Work is mainly about one's experiences with oneself. I would say that we have to deal with this lunatic and tramp called oneself. Yes, an interesting study. I once said to myself, reviewing how I had behaved violently on a particular occasion: "It is obvious I am a tiny bit a mad person to behave as I have done." You will understand that through the power of the Work I actually could see myself in the wrong. But I assure you that if you are only in the power of life you will never see that you are really wrong, and so will continue to act from open or latent violence.

Great Amwell House, September 18, 1948

FURTHER NOTE ON VIOLENCE

Work-Idea

A man cannot "do" unless he overcomes violence. Violence always breeds violence. "Doing" by means of violence is not "doing". All history, which is a history of crime, shews how violence cannot "do" in the Work sense. War follows war.

Commentary

We spoke last time of how Conscious Man acts without violence. Since the Work teaches that we are based on violence, we must not imagine that just hearing from time to time that this is so is going to change anything in us. The study of violence in oneself is a life-long study. Mechanical Man is rooted in violence and one meaning of re-birth is to be born beyond violence—to become conscious in thinking and feeling on a level beyond violence. On the level of violence, in the plain, so to speak, we have many enemies. That is, at our ordinary mechanical level we have many dangerous violent 'I's that are our enemies and seek to destroy our understanding. For nothing destroys understanding more than violence. But if we rise above this plain, if, so to speak, we ascend the mountain a little way, we are no longer subject to violent 'I's. Our difficulty then is to keep our thought strong enough to remain at that level. So we fall down in our thinking very soon—at least for many years—partly because we have not yet understood the secret—namely, that to get to a different level, we must give up certain habitual ways of thinking and feeling, to begin with. We do not see that psychological movement is as real as physical movement

1215

and that both demand effort. To ascend the mountain in oneself requires effort and to maintain the position reached requires effort. We must realize from the Ray of Creation that there are different levels in ourselves. So one must not only remember oneself in many different ways, but intimately associate oneself with the ideas of the Work, so that they enter the mind and effect small transformations of mechanical states at all times. This continual inner intercourse with the Work, which especially demands the presence in oneself of a good Work-memory and the possession of a book of good photographs of oneself, taken over many years by means of self-observation, gradually brings about, or rather, makes possible, many changes, some quite unexpected. One begins to feel the existence of another will apart from one's self-will, and with this inner perception one becomes aware of many meanings, hitherto hidden, in some of the most familiar Work-sayings that one hitherto thought one understood well enough already. Let us all realize that Understanding, the most powerful force we can create in ourselves, always lies in seeing more and more deeply what we thought we understood. That is, *Understanding*, if this continual intercourse with the Work is kept going, is the development of inner octaves. Where we saw previously only one thing, we now see ten, a hundred, a thousand things. Do you see what is meant here? As O. said—and I will give what he said from what I remember, but not verbatim—he said: "The Gospels are a test for your development of understanding. You may imagine you know and understand them. But, as you begin to change, as your level of understanding grows, you will see more and more things in what you thought you understood." And he added: "The Gospels are esoteric books. They will accompany you all through your work. Their meaning is such that they develop as you internally develop."

Now, from this, let us pass to the difficult sentence in the Gospels about the Kingdom of Heaven, which is, for me, to begin with, the Conscious Circle of Humanity. In the Work, which comes from Conscious Man, we wake eventually, after years of dullness, quibbling and misunderstanding, to realize that another will must be born in us by beginning to obey what the Work says, not by compulsion, but through the increasing light of the understanding of *why* the Work exists and what we mean and what it means to us. In looking round at a world of violence, we simply see violence breeding violence. War, which is based on violence, threatens Man always, because Man is based on violence. From this, possibly, we realize that our individual work is to observe violence in ourselves. Well, what does this strange phrase in the Gospels mean? Christ is speaking of John the Baptist, who had literal but not psychological understanding, and so was clad in animal skins. Christ says:

"Verily I say unto you, Among them that are born of women there hath not arisen a greater than John the Baptist: yet he that is but little in the kingdom of heaven is greater than he. And from the days of John the Baptist until now the kingdom of heaven suffereth violence and men of violence take it by force."

(Matt. XI, 11, 12)

In speaking of this strange thing, I will recapitulate first of all what Ouspensky said about violence. He said: "Violence is an emotional state in all people—doing things with violence, trying to impose upon, and coerce, to insist. From the esoteric point of view this is useless —nothing can be *done* in this way. A violent man cannot *do*. Even although a man has *knowledge*, if he has not overcome violence in himself, his work will go wrong." Then he added: "The meaning of 'the kingdom of heaven suffereth violence and men of violence take it by force' is this. It means violence on oneself. Not to act with violence is violence on oneself. A man, in observing himself and finally realizing where he is violent—in which centre, in what forms of behaviour, and so on—must do violence to himself to overcome his violence." Speaking as I am in terms of commentary on what the Work teaches, I would say that violence on oneself, on one's violence, requires the highest possible insight into what one is. Because if one works consciously on oneself in regard to one's violence, one then can see that one can only get to a higher level, only go up this mountain that we spoke of, through *force*—and all force is gained only by working against a feature in oneself. So the higher level of oneself, represented relatively by a psychological state at a better level than one's mechanical state, is only gained by violence on certain 'I's, certain habits of thought, feeling, attitudes, pictures, and so on. This gives *force*. Also Ouspensky said once: "You will gain most force by working on your Chief Feature." To work on anything in oneself that is a habit and so mechanical gives some force. Notice that the Kingdom of Heaven is taken by *force* and understand that *force* is made through not going with your mechanical self. If I do violence to Dr. Nicoll, I will get force. Where I put this force belongs to another conversation, but I will only say here: "Unless you have an aim, to make force by working against some mechanical or habitual side of yourself is not enough. One must work on oneself, deny oneself, so that the force goes into one's aim."

CRISIS

WORK-IDEA

Two ultimate and irreducible laws govern the Universe. One is the Law of Three Forces—that is, that for any manifestation to take place three forces are necessary to produce it. The other law is the Law of the Octave, or the Law of Seven, which states that there is a slowing down of vibrations at two points—namely, between *Mi* and *Fa*, and *Si* and *Do*. The Law is called the *Order of Manifestation.*

COMMENTARY

We speak to-day of the Law of Seven or the Law of Octaves, represented as the Scale *Do, Re, Mi, Fa*, etc. Octaves are of two kinds —ascending, *Do, Re, Mi*, etc.—or descending, *Do, Si, La*, etc. As the term "slowing down of vibrations" is not easy to grasp at first, let us understand that, say, in an ascending octave, *Do, Re, Mi, Fa*, etc., there is a difficult place to pass between *Mi* and *Fa* where a shock is necessary to enable the development of the Octave to proceed. In the development of anything, say, an ovum into a baby, a critical point is reached between the stage *Mi* and the next stage *Fa* and, in fact, a new blood circulation must be effected about the third month. Or, to change the illustration, in learning anything whatsoever, a similar point will inevitably be reached, where, unless a shock is given, the development of learning (say, a foreign language) will stop unless an exceptional effort is made. The result is that you have *Do, Re, Mi* people and, by contrast, *Fa* people. Most education is scarcely *Do, Re, Mi*. So one might speak of a *Re* man, a *Mi* man, a *Fa* man—but I say this by way of commentary. I have not heard this delineation of differences in people given by Ouspensky. But we can understand that a master of a musical instrument is not a *Re* man or a *Mi* man. He is certainly a *Fa* man, or even a *Sol* man in his octave of development. I hope you will see what I mean in quite a simple way. Octaves, like everything else in the Work, gives the sense of scale—of lower and higher—of the possibility of growth and development in anything you take up from yourself. But this means effort and few people make effort from themselves, but prefer to do as little as possible. I will call now this curious *Mi-Fa* in everything *crisis*. First I want to speak of this *Mi-Fa crisis* in nature. Take those hardworking birds, with their constant air-lift to feed their fledgelings. Some birds have to migrate. Owing to the wonderful "radio" in their Instinctive Centre, some birds, having finished the hard work of bringing up one or two or even three lots of fledgelings, collect mysteriously together, when this is over, and set off on an immense journey—some by Hungary on to Africa. During this journey thousands, hundreds of thousands, perhaps, die. They are too weak. Those who were fledglings only a few months back have to face this ordeal—this ordeal by crisis—which I am relating to the passage between *Mi-Fa*. Some pass—some fail.

Let us look at the diagram of this difficult passage between *Mi-Fa* on the Board.

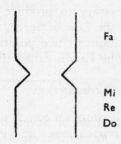

It is like a tube, narrower between *Mi* and *Fa*. It means that everything has to face—at this crisis-point *Mi-Fa*—something difficult that requires a shock—an unusual effort. This describes diagrammatically a narrowing difficult passage—in short, as I said, a *crisis*. In nature we seem to see this "narrow place" acting everywhere, if we look for it. And this indeed connects with the idea of natural selection, in its original formulation—namely, the unfit die and the fit survive, and this is called "the survival of the fittest", a phrase which I believe first was introduced by Darwin, or maybe later. Throw a number of puppy-dogs into a pond—some swim, some sink. Here the selection test is swimming and of course only the fittest for swimming survive. It is a crisis for them in regard to that Second Force. That is, *all* cannot survive. In the case of migrating birds only those capable of long flight survive; the rest die—even in millions. So here we see a selective Law of Nature—a point of *Mi-Fa*.

Now we can see, by way of commentary, that here is a crisis—I mean some passage between a *Mi-Fa* situation—between one state and another in effectiveness. Here recollect that Christ said: "Many are called, but few are chosen." Understand that I speak in commentary. This *Mi-Fa* situation, this crisis even in nature, occurs on every scale. There are, for example, stages in this Work, where, in keeping your aim, you meet this crisis *Mi-Fa* at long intervals. But also there is every day a small-scale crisis *Mi-Fa* in which (just when you are going to really tell someone what you think of them) you remember yourself. That is, you give yourself a shock. And I may add, this remembering yourself at different times, in relation not only to larger events but down to the smallest trivial things—the domestic scene—is what constitutes the "Sly Man's Pill". "The Sly Man's Pill", said Ouspensky on one occasion, "is Self-Remembering in different ways at different times, according to the situation ".

Now what is the dictionary meaning of the word *crisis* that I am introducing by way of commentary? It comes from a Greek word meaning *a separation, a choice, a decision*. A moment of crisis is thus a moment in which a choice must be made. And, as I said, each day you have small-scale crises in which it is quite possible to make a separation, a choice, a decision. If you do this, if you watch yourself, observe yourself, you can notice this small *Mi-Fa*, and by adding the Work to your mind and how it is thinking, you may transform the whole day as a result of this shock at the right moment, before things have got far too difficult to transform and you are plunged into a mess of identifying and negative emotion. It is like turning the front wheel of a bicycle the right way before you fall off it into the mud.

We have to grasp firmly with our minds that this place of narrowness, *Mi-Fa*, this difficult moment, must inevitably come in everything —in all we attempt as well as in every relation that we make. I said recently in this commentary that in regard to what we attempt we do not try long enough and also that we do not like one another enough. To alter things in any way shocks are necessary. To revolve in the circle of one's laziness is simply death. When we realize that this crisis, *Mi-Fa*, is in the nature of the Universe and is not some person's fault, we begin to grow up. We even climb on the box and take the reins in our hands, realizing that it is *oneself* that has to learn how to live. Through studying the Work and its teaching, in relation to the study of oneself, we learn not only where we want energy and what efforts we have to make, but also what is inevitable in the very nature of things—namely, the existence of Second Force or force of resistance in regard to everything we want, and also this narrow place of crisis called *Mi-Fa* where, unless a shock is given, everything dies away and nothing is achieved.

Now what are the general characteristics of the ascending octave? If we take the Ray of Creation as an ascending octave—that is, starting from the bottom and going up—we see that each rising note includes more and more until, at the summit, all is included in the Absolute. For instance, the note *Sol*—our Solar System—is included in all Suns—that is, our Galaxy composed of millions of Solar Systems, and so on. From this point of view, the note *Re* contains more than *Do*, the note *Mi* more than *Re* and so on. *Do*, for instance, might represent one individual, *Re* a number of individuals regarded as one small whole, *Mi* a number of these small wholes united into a larger whole, and so on.

Now let us look at the crisis in the world to-day and see how we can relate it to this narrow place *Mi-Fa*. The difficulty appears to be to make a federation of Western nations. Let us represent the octave thus:

Fa   a union of European nations

—

Mi   one European nation

Re   a group, class, profession, etc.

Do   an individual.

From this *suggestion* of an octave we see the difficulty lies at the place of *Mi-Fa* and consists in the inability to sound the note *Fa*. To sound it would mean, of course, an expansion of consciousness in every individual and so a shock. At present the individual can easily sound the note *Mi*—that is, can feel his nation, his patriotism, and so on—but would perhaps feel a severe loss in becoming non-national. And yet, from the teaching of octaves in the Work, every note must sound and there would be no loss—for a man must sound all the notes, especially the note *Do*—the individual. One note *must not* annihilate another. *All must sound* in a harmony. This is the Work solution, as I understand it.

Great Amwell House, October 9, 1948

NOTES ON WORK ON ONESELF

WORK-IDEA

There are Three Lines of Work—Work on oneself, Work in connection with others and oneself, and Work in connection with the Work itself and oneself in relation to it.

COMMENTARY

We speak mainly about the First Line of Work to-night—namely, *Work on oneself*. Unless a person works on himself or herself, the Second Line of Work remains theoretical and imaginary. Work on oneself brings in all that the Work teaches practically and is the necessary starting-point. For example, if you are always internally considering, you will not be able to work in connection with others—which demands external considering—i.e. putting yourself into their situation. Work on oneself helps us to learn how to live more consciously in every day affairs. Usually we identify so much that we end up the day on the debit side. Everything has "got you" and you have been in a bad temper all day. That is, life has all day conquered you and eventually drained you of any such conscious force you may have had. It has taken from you and given you nothing. You will, most of you, understand by now that we must find something that will prevent this being drained by the daily events of our existence through identifying and considering.

We have to grasp the teaching of the Work more and more clearly in this respect. The Work says that, as we are mechanically, force is drained from us. Yes—continually, by worrying, by anxiety, by getting negative, and, in fact, by every variety of identifying. So the Work teaches at the start: "A man must remember himself." Why? Because if anyone remembers himself, it stops this terrible draining of force that takes place through continual identifying—yes—even identifying with having lost a halfpenny, and crawling under beds, lifting carpets, in order to find this halfpenny and worrying about it all day and night. Do you regard this as an exaggeration? I assure you that all of us are just like this. We make, through this customary identifying and so lack of Self-Remembering—we make, I say, the most trivial and silly things of enormous importance and therefore suffer most patently from this great illness, this disease of sleeping mankind, which the Work diagnoses as *Identifying*. Mr. Gurdjieff called it the most terrible illness on this planet. And, as you know, the Work system explains that when a man or woman is thoroughly identified they are asleep and then are in a condition of hypnosis and so are *used* by the two sheep-farmers controlling the Earth-Moon terminal for their own purposes—namely, for meat and wool. So wars, revolutions, epidemics, go on—a good opportunity for plenty of meat and wool. Now this "good news", as Gurdjieff called the Work which he brought to the West, has as one of its main ideas that it is possible for a man to awaken from the Earth-Moon hypnotism and separate himself. How? By an inner act called Self-Remembering. This gives a shock—the First Conscious Shock. But all that the Work teaches is also necessary—about self-observation, not considering, not identifying, not self-justifying, not self-pitying, not falling into negative emotions without any struggle, not believing the thoughts that come while in negative states, not allowing yourself to lie to yourself, not living in pictures of yourself, and a hundred and one other things that we have been studying in this system during these years. But the supreme thing is Self-Remembering. If we leave out Self-Remembering we leave out the real psychic act, performed internally, that constitutes the First Conscious Shock. It is by means of this First Conscious Shock that we are separated from the strange hypnotic sleep of mankind on this Earth.

This is the heart and substance of the "good news" brought by Gurdjieff to the West—and Gurdjieff called it "esoteric Christianity". Bear these words always in your mind. Exoteric religion is one thing: esoteric teaching is another. And once you have begun to realize, for your own private selves, the message of this teaching, you will be able to read the Gospels in a new way and see for yourselves that Christ was not teaching Christianity as we are taught it—if you can bear this paradox. I will add here that it is more than interesting to read again the scattered fragments of Christ's teaching present in the Four Gospels and pick out what was really meant, in the light of the Work. Nothing is more releasing for the fast-bound religious mind that holds many in prison—yes—now—at this moment.

Now let us turn to this supreme factor that Gurdjieff and Ouspensky taught—namely, the giving to oneself the First Conscious Shock called Self-Remembering. It is given at the place of incoming impressions.

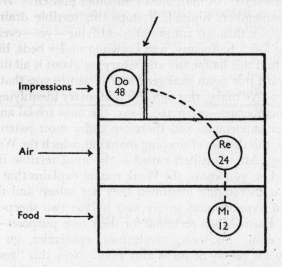

Gurdjieff taught that a man, a woman, does not digest the food of impressions. Air as food has a stomach for digestion called the lungs. Food has the ordinary stomach—and just imagine if all the food you have eaten to-day were to lie in masses and layers inside without any digestion. But we have to create a stomach in the top storey to digest impressions. How can you "digest" the sight of a person you dislike? And do you realize that everyone you know is impressions coming in? The Work teaches that the human machine is *given* a mechanical shock called breathing. It then teaches that it is possible to give this human machine in which we live, fed by the three foods, first ordinary food, second the food of air, and third the food of impressions, a certain shock which is not given mechanically. This shock is only given consciously. So it is called the First *Conscious* Shock. And, as I said, it is the giving of this First Conscious Shock that distinguishes between a man immersed in life, under all the hypnotic influences of life, and a man who is beginning to separate himself from hypnotic sleep and moving in the direction of Conscious Humanity, which Christ calls the Kingdom of Heaven. So we might say by way of commentary that there are those who live mechanically, aided by the mechanical shock of air alone, and those who begin to give themselves the First Conscious Shock. Can you see that the latter are different from the former? The human machine can work quite well *without* the First *Conscious* Shock being given. It then serves Nature and the purposes of the Earth-Moon terminal. But Man was created a *self-developing organism*. He was created not only to serve Nature, but to serve another order of laws, spoken of in every page of the Gospels. He was created with the possibility of *remembering himself*—that is, of giving himself the First Conscious Shock. But you will see that it is only *he himself, she herself*, who can do this. I will speak perhaps next time further about this. But if you want to see, formulate, understand and vision in your mind what this Work is about, all that is said above may assist you when you forget everything and fall asleep. The mind then can help—but only if you have registered the strength, the outline, and indeed the very bones of the Work in your minds. If the Work is still something on the blackboard and not in your most intimate thoughts, then nothing will help you. You will still be running around trying to find a bigger blackboard.

Great Amwell House, October 16, 1948

EVALUATION

Work-Idea

The Work says very many things about evaluation. For example, it says that the octave of inner development, and so change of level of one's Being, begins with the Note *Do*, which is termed "Evaluation of the Work". The Note *Re* is application of the ideas to oneself. The Note *Mi* is realization of personal difficulties. The Work also says that its ultimate aim is to awaken the Emotional Centre.

Commentary

We can understand without great difficulty that *evaluation* is, at its root, emotional. To evaluate is to *feel* that something is important, valuable. To think a thing is valuable is quite different from feeling a thing is valuable. Theoretically, many things may be valuable, but they are not valuable to you unless you feel their value. To find this Work, to sit and hear it, even to know a little about it, does not mean that you value it. In that case, the Work cannot act on you. You do not swallow it. So it is not in you. There are many parables in the Gospels which refer to evaluation. For instance:

"The kingdom of heaven is like unto a treasure hidden in a field; which a man found and hid; and in his joy he goeth and selleth all that he hath and buyeth that field." (*Matt.* XIII 44)

Gurdjieff used to say: "What do you want?" This is almost like saying: "What do you evaluate?" One man may say: "Riches";

1224

another may say: "Health", and so on. Solomon, when asked the question by God, answered: "Understanding". Now, as material for self-observation, ask yourself: "What do I evaluate?" It is very interesting to observe oneself from this angle. If you are sincere with yourself, the answer will possibly amaze you. But this kind of self-observation is very difficult and requires very great inner sincerity and need—that is, evaluation. One must, in short, really want to know oneself more. Most people do not evaluate self-knowledge, not understanding that when you know something fully in yourself you are separated from it. Why? Because it becomes objective to you as something seen internally and so cannot work unconsciously in you, as when you identify with it so that it makes you ill, moody, and so on, in repeating cycles, without your seeing why. Self-observation is to make things in yourself more and more conscious to you, so that you can say: "This is not 'I' ". Otherwise you are glued to them and under their power—that is, identified with what is not you. They then act on you unconsciously—often in terrible and morbid ways. But you remain unconscious of them, taking it all as 'I'. So you are not conscious of them. But, without evaluation, you cannot observe yourself. You do not think it worth while. Yes, self-observation can become tedious—unless you see why you have to observe yourself in order to change your Being.

Now whatever you do observe uncritically, and accept inwardly, makes room for some more hidden factor, good or bad, to begin to emerge into the light. The light is consciousness. Ouspensky once said we work in the dark at first and self-observation is to let a ray of light in. He said that all the internal machinery of our centres is comparable to a vast factory lit by one or two candles. That is, we do not see mechanical associations and connections or how one thing depends on something else, such as wrong attitudes, or what is wrongly linked up or where leaks of energy occur and so on. If we observe, if we work, he said, after a time we get a few more candles lit and begin to see where some things are obviously wrong. That is called: "Seeing wrong work of centres", such as, for example, that we begin to notice, to observe, that we always use the wrong machine—say, the Emotional Centre—for certain problems in life which demand the use of the machine called Intellectual Centre. But, as I said, if people have no evaluation of self-observation, if they do not see that it is of any value to them, they will continue to blunder through life, making the same mistakes and getting into the same difficulties. How long a time does it not take to realize that one's level of Being attracts one's life and its incidents. People try this and try that outward thing, believing everything will now be different. But the same situation will develop —maybe with different people or in another country, but just the same as before. Why? Because they do not evaluate the idea of self-change and do not realize that the trouble lies in themselves. Self-observation is to bring about self-change. It is a method of change of Being, because it begins to make you *conscious* where you were not conscious, and consciousness, which is light, frees you. In the words of Paul:

"All things when they are admitted are made manifest by the light: for everything that is made manifest is light. Wherefore he saith, Awake, thou that sleepest, and arise from the dead and Christ shall shine upon thee." (*Eph.* V, 13, 14)

Your Being cannot change if you do not become more conscious of it. How could it? Your level of Being and your level of consciousness are closely connected. If through self-observation you become more conscious of your Being and what is in it, then your Being will alter even a little—and you will no longer attract just the same situations and difficulties, failures, etc., which, hitherto, your Being has always attracted. But you must evaluate this, evaluate these ideas of the teaching—and make them more valuable than at least some other things that at present you evaluate most, probably without noticing it. There is only a certain amount of room in us. Things are weighed and measured. You cannot evaluate everything equally. We have to select what is valuable. This is a very strange process, this selection. The most real, the inner part of you, may have already selected. But the external, artificial part does not agree yet. And so you may have to lead a double life for a long period—not unconsciously, but consciously, being aware of this inner contradiction. In connection with this, one can certainly see that the evaluations dear to False Personality, which belongs to the external side of us, are not likely to be the same as those of the more genuine and real inner side. I speak to those who have begun to notice the effect of False Personality on their inner side.